ARKANSAS: A NARRATIVE HISTORY

ARKANSAS

A NARRATIVE HISTORY

SECOND EDITION

JEANNIE M. WHAYNE
THOMAS A. DEBLACK
GEORGE SABO III
MORRIS S. ARNOLD

With a Foreword to the First Edition by Willard B. Gatewood
and a Foreword to the Second Edition by Ben F. Johnson III

The University of Arkansas Press
Fayetteville
2013

First Edition 2002. Second Edition 2013.

Manufactured in the United States of America

ISBN-10: 1-55728-993-X
ISBN-13: 978-1-55728-993-3

17 16 15 5 4 3 2

Designed by Liz Lester

♾ The paper used in this publication meets the minimum requirements of the American National Standard for Permanence of Paper for Printed Library Materials Z39.48–1984.

LIBRARY OF CONGRESS CATALOGING-IN-PUBLICATION DATA

Whayne, Jeannie M.
Arkansas : a narrative history / Jeannie M. Whayne, Thomas A. DeBlack, George Sabo III, Morris S. Arnold ; with a foreword to the first edition by Willard B. Gatewood, and a foreword to the second edition by Ben F. Johnson III. — Second edition.
pages cm
Includes bibliographical references and index.
ISBN 978-1-55728-993-3 (cloth : alk. paper)
1. Arkansas—History. I. DeBlack, Thomas A., 1951– II. Sabo, George. III. Arnold, Morris S. IV. Title.
F411.A772 2013
976.7—dc23
2012044181

Map Sources and Boundary Files: Minnesota Population Center. National Historical Geographic Information System: Version 2.0. Minneapolis: University of Minnesota, 2011, http://www.nhgis.org. *Historical Atlas of Arkansas* (1989), University of Oklahoma Press. Arkansas Gazetteer Online—Cities, Features, Maps & Data, www.hometownlocator.com. *Arkansas and the Land* (1992), University of Arkansas Press. *Battlefields of Arkansas Post* (2003), Arkansas Post National Memorial. *Arkansas: A Narrative History* (2002), University of Arkansas Press. 2006 Statewide CIR County Mosaic, Arkansas Geographic Information Office, www.geostor.arkansas.gov. The *Encyclopedia of Arkansas History & Culture,* http://encyclopediaofarkansas.net. Cultural, Society and Demography Database, Arkansas Geographic Information Office, www.geostor.arkansas.gov. The Delta Cultural Center—Helena, AR, http://www.delta culturalcenter.com. National Hydrography Dataset, Flowline and Waterbody Feature Class, Arkansas Geographic Information Office, www.geostor.arkansas.gov. Pea Ridge National Military Park, Garfield, AR, *The Campaign for Pea Ridge* (2001), The Civil War Series: Eastern National Publishing. Center for Advanced Spatial Technologies: University of Arkansas, http://pg.cast.uark.edu/maps.php. *National Atlas of the United States* (Reston, VA), www.nationalatlas.gov. Arkansas Oil and Gas Commission—Little Rock, AR. United States Geological Survey, http://gisdata.usgs.gov. *Cultural Encounters in the Early South: Indians and Europeans in Arkansas* (1995), University of Arkansas Press. *The Expedition of Hernando de Soto West of the Mississippi, 1541–1543* (1993), University of Arkansas Press. *Delta Empire: Lee Wilson and the Transformation of Agriculture in the New South* (2011), Louisiana State University Press. *The 18th Annual Report of the Bureau of American Ethnology—1896–'97,* Smithsonian Institution, Government Printing Office. *Indian Affairs Laws and Treaties* (1904), Washington: Government Printing Office. Seismicity of the United States, U.S. Geological Survey Professional Paper 1527, United States Government Printing Office. U.S. Geological Survey: Earthquakes Hazards Program. 2010. National Atlas of the United States, 2005–06, Territorial Acquisitions of the United States: National Atlas of the United States, Reston, VA, www.nationalatlas.gov.

To Willard B. Gatewood

CONTENTS

FOREWORD TO THE SECOND EDITION

Willard Gatewood in his foreword hailed the first edition of *Arkansas: A Narrative History* as a notable milestone confirming the unmistakable advancement in the scholarship and writing of the state's history over the past quarter of a century. This trenchant, graceful portrait of the state, as Gatewood noted, came from four authors who themselves had contributed significantly to the blossoming of Arkansas studies.

These same accomplished scholars in this welcomed revised edition of *Arkansas: A Narrative History* have incorporated new scholarship that explores and reveals the state's experience within broader historical contexts. The writers have brought to bear their diverse areas of expertise to render adroitly the complexity of developments while maintaining narrative coherence. Readers will not become lost; rather, they will discover much in this rich volume about a state too often veiled by stereotype and misunderstanding.

Arkansas was indeed a small parcel with an extended frontier phase before the catastrophe of the Civil War obliterated the stirrings of prosperity. A long recovery once again fueled cautious hope until nascent industrialization fell victim to the collapse of the American economy in the Great Depression. Yet, out of the crisis of global war, the state leapt into an era of economic modernization marked by political reform and persistent struggles for greater equality and rights. If Arkansas by the twenty-first century still ranked in the lower echelons of various measures for social and economic well-being, its comparative acceleration from rural periphery toward the national mainstream was nothing short of remarkable.

Going beyond mapping large-scale historic shifts, the authors reveal that under the seemingly calm surface of tradition roiled clashing interests, evolving community networks, and intrusive outside forces. Arkansans in no era, at no time stood still. The first peoples lived in a web of intricate social relations stressed and broken by the settlement of Europeans. A mélange of geographic and ecological zones belied the easy characterization of antebellum upland yeoman and lowland cotton nabobs. A divided state marched into the war that divided the nation. The chasm between Arkansas and the nation as a whole appeared to widen with the rise of northern industrial urban centers attracting waves of immigrants. Yet, Arkansas towns orbited the smoky metropolises through the gravitational pull of new consumer products and business interests. On the other hand the state's rural majority remained a people apart, leading to new fault lines that both old guard political leaders and earnest reformers attempted to seal.

Those hoisting the banners of reform into the twentieth century concentrated upon the necessity of good roads and good schools to secure a prosperous future based upon sound business principles. Nevertheless, even those advocating change worked at cross purposes depending upon the particular crusade, and consensus became even more a lost cause as industrialization picked up steam following World War II. The civil rights movement was decisive in wrenching Arkansas politics off a well-worn path. Even the incomplete victories for equality and democracy transformed state government from an exchange market of personal favor to making policy through debate and process. Similar reconfigurations became readily apparent in other areas of life. The success of international but homegrown companies in the northwest rim spurred a new metropolitan hub that rivaled Little Rock, the only city the state had ever known. The continuing growth of urban areas nurtured organizations and institutions in the arts and culture. The last chapter in the volume makes clear, however, that the distinctive sound of Arkansas music grew from lonely and empty places away from city lights, echoing worlds lost and others dreamed about.

The authors have retained the strengths of the original volume while altering the organization of several chapters to ensure clarity and to blend new research unobtrusively into the elegant narrative. They have consistently met the challenge of offering a comprehensive history that reflects current interpretations without letting matters slip into sinkholes of academic preoccupation. The final section is not only a judicious account of events since the publication of the first edition but a penetrating discussion of the interaction of race, suburban expansion, educational opportunity, and shifting voter loyalties.

No less than the first edition, this revision of *Arkansas: A Narrative History* is a compelling introduction for those who know little about the state and an insightful survey for others who wish to enrich their acquaintance with the Arkansas past. The book reflects the authors' craft and commitment to tell the story fully and honestly.

—BEN F. JOHNSON III

FOREWORD TO THE FIRST EDITION

Anyone attempting to compile a bibliography of scholarly studies on Arkansas history as late as the mid-1970s would surely have been impressed by how few such studies existed except for the high-quality articles appearing in the *Arkansas Historical Quarterly* since its founding in 1941. At that time book-length scholarly studies concerned with the historical experience of Arkansas and its people would scarcely have filled a single shelf in a small bookcase. The dearth of such books had far-reaching consequences. For one thing, it led to the virtual omission of any consideration of Arkansas in works that purported to deal with the South, even though the state has been a part of the region since admission to statehood in 1836. Another result was that much of what was known about Arkansas, both inside and outside the state, was gleaned from impressionistic, highly subjective treatments, often written by individuals guided more by a determination to confirm preconceived notions than by a concern for balance and objectivity.

As the history of Arkansas related in the following pages clearly demonstrates, there is no longer a need to rely upon such works. In the last two decades, the quantity of books based on careful research and dedicated to the pursuit of objectivity has so dramatically increased that they now would completely fill all shelves of a much larger bookcase. A variety of developments, including the activities of dedicated individuals, account for the proliferation of such works, but the role of the University of Arkansas Press, established in 1980, has been of critical importance. Beginning with its first book released the following year, the press has published a succession of scholarly works that explore various aspects of Arkansas's past—economic, political, social, cultural, and environmental—from prehistoric times to the end of the twentieth century. The talented authors of this volume, three historians and an anthropologist, have been active participants in the recent flourishing of Arkansas history; each has contributed significantly to the rapid expansion of historical scholarship devoted to the state. Drawing upon this greatly expanded scholarship, the authors have produced a work that includes ethnic and racial groups, women, and others often ignored in previous studies. It is altogether appropriate, therefore, that the University of Arkansas Press should begin its third decade by publishing *Arkansas: A Narrative History,* a model work that belongs alongside the best state histories.

Informed in its scholarship, rationally organized, and written in clear, graceful prose, this volume is extraordinarily comprehensive in its treatment of Arkansas's past, from prehistoric times when it was inhabited by various Indian tribes through its colonial era under French and Spanish rule, early statehood, and the Civil War and its aftermath to the present. Throughout, it exhibits a sense of balance, maintains a view that places Arkansas in the larger perspective of the region and the nation, and effectively combines descriptive narrative and interpretative analysis. Careful to emphasize the role of geography in the historical development of the state, the authors also, quite appropriately, devote especial attention to its rural character, reliance upon agriculture, and efforts to industrialize. In the process they provide a wealth of information that illuminates similarities and differences that existed between the course traveled by Arkansas and those traveled by other southern states. While the authors focus on changes that have occurred over time, they are no less forthright in underscoring the continuities, some of which have persisted since the early years of statehood.

By any manner of reckoning this is an extraordinarily valuable addition to historical literature, one that provides a highly readable and comprehensive account of an often-neglected corner of the Trans-Mississippi South.

—WILLARD B. GATEWOOD

PREFACE

Arkansas: A Narrative History originated in 1997 when University of Arkansas Distinguished Professor Willard B. Gatewood brought the coauthors together and launched a project to create a concise, one-volume history of the state. Determined to produce a volume that was affordable, that would be of use in the college classroom, and that would also appeal to the general public, we quickly realized that formidable challenges awaited our efforts. The needs of teachers and the interests of the general public demanded treatment of the full sweep of Arkansas history from prehistoric times to the present. Our own sentiments further stipulated a balanced treatment of different time periods, groups of people, and cultural institutions. To achieve these goals within a volume of modest size, we chose to emphasize events that transcended the particular times and places with which they were associated to reflect major trends and trajectories that brought our state to its present moment in history.

This second edition of *Arkansas: Narrative History* begins with a new chapter focusing on Arkansas geography, cowritten by George Sabo and Thomas DeBlack. It includes a number of maps highlighting various features of Arkansas's natural landscape and seeks to ground the reader in this place called Arkansas.

George Sabo follows with an examination of Native American prehistory that emphasizes cultural developments in the context of changing environmental and social conditions. The goal is to reconstruct, as accurately as present evidence allows, the world created by native peoples in the mid-South. This world suffered cataclysmic shock when adverse climatic changes coincided with the arrival of European explorers and colonists. These circumstances truly did create a new world, out of which Native American cultures of the historic era emerged. Sabo discusses how these newly emergent groups carried forward the legacy of their ancestors in maintaining economic and social institutions that proved crucial to the survival of early colonial endeavors. Quapaws, Caddos, and Tunicas cleared and worked the agricultural lands that provided crops to European immigrants, and Quapaw and Osage hunters produced meat and other products, including hides, tallow, and bear oil, that became important commodities in colonial exchange economies. The transfer of goods between indigenous and immigrant groups was facilitated by native social institutions that permitted incorporation of Europeans into existing economic and political networks.

Morris S. Arnold continues this theme with a detailed examination of the face-to-face accommodations that French and Spanish colonists worked out with neighboring Indian communities. In forging this analysis, Arnold concentrates on regional events and circumstances instead of rehashing the larger colonial objectives of European nations. Rather than focusing on the intrigues of France, England, and Spain, intrigues which led to wars for empire that did, indeed, have an impact on native populations, Arnold examines the patterns of intermarriage, of diplomacy and political alliance, of economic interaction, and other cultural accommodation through which these groups created functioning communities that withstood the local manifestation of international contests.

Another unique aspect of Arnold's treatment of the colonial era is his incorporation of the roles that a number of minority groups, including women, African Americans, and Jews, played in establishing the institutions that continued into the territorial era. Arnold examines the contributions made by those groups to the development of legal, governmental, and religious institutions, the production of goods, and the organization of market economies.

Jeannie M. Whayne's examination of the territorial era demonstrates how these multicultural relationships unfolded during the subsequent era of American settlement. The observations recorded by William Dunbar and George Hunter, explorers dispatched by Pres. Thomas Jefferson into the new territory, revealed the persistence of interethnic social and economic accommodations existing along the Ouachita River region. Whayne revised the chapter for the second edition, careful to include reference to new work on Arkansas's native peoples, work that challenges the "middle ground" thesis and posits a "native ground" approach.

Some Native Americans came to believe that the New Madrid earthquakes of 1811–1812 were a sign that they were wrong to forsake their own traditions in favor of European customs. These fears were realized when the Americans abandoned the accommodation of Quapaw interests with their different vision of how frontier Arkansas should evolve. The era of mutual relationships came to an end when white settlers transplanted plantation agriculture and slavery to lands previously occupied by the Quapaws and other indigenous groups. The removal of Native Americans from Arkansas occurred in the 1820s and 1830s against a backdrop of political intrigue involving competing groups of whites. The differences were manifestly economic and pitted the southeastern section against the northwestern area. Businessmen and politicians in the central section—where the capital city came to be located—established crucial ties to the southeastern planters and played a critical role in tilting the balance of power in that direction. Given the Southeast's ties to plantation agriculture and slavery, planters there influenced the drive for statehood in the 1830s, a drive that was influenced in part by the growing division over slavery within the nation.

Thomas A. DeBlack next illustrates how the decision to move to plantation agriculture and slavery thrust the state into the Civil War and how that momentous decision shaped Arkansas history in the postwar period. Arkansas was poorly positioned, in any case, to assume the burden of financing a war, given its precarious financial condition. The failed experiments with a real estate and state bank early in the state's history left Arkansas financially vulnerable. DeBlack's treatment deals nicely with the major events leading up to, during, and following the Civil War, revealing how those national events affected people in different parts of the state and how they produced the conditions that gave rise to late nineteenth- and early twentieth-century events and institutions. His Civil

War chapter incorporated a number of new color maps especially commissioned from Joseph Swain, maps that provide a better sense of the battles fought in Arkansas.

Whayne's 1880 to 2012 chapters show how the state fared in the New South era and became preoccupied with economic issues arising out of the bankruptcy caused by the failed banks and the decision to leave the Union and join the Confederacy. While attempting to do justice to the political history of the state and major events taking place during the twentieth century, Whayne focuses on crucial themes that remain important as we enter the twenty-first century. One major theme is the evolution of the state's transportation system, from one relying first on steamboats, then on railroads and roads upon which motorized vehicles could travel, and finally on a modern intermodal transportation network connecting the state to the rest of the nation. The means to finance this system proved to be a problem that plagued governors and legislators throughout this period. Similarly, the impulse to improve schools and educational programs faced hard economic realities as well as some cultural resistance to the intrusion of the state into the affairs of the family. Planters in eastern Arkansas, moreover, were reluctant to educate a workforce that might find opportunity elsewhere. Whayne also suggests tensions resulted from promotion of industrial development in the context of a rural agricultural economy. Arkansas's industrial boosters faced insurmountable problems not simply because leading agriculturalists were reluctant to support industrialization but also because of a lack of concentrated populations needed to provide an industrial workforce. Early in the century, much of the population was unschooled in the ways of industrial society. Despite the emergence of urban centers in central and northwest Arkansas, by the end of the century much of the state's population remains unprepared for the new economy and its emphasis on advanced technology.

Arkansas failed to emerge as a Sunbelt South state late in the century, but in the early twenty-first century began to lay the foundation for educating its workforce sufficiently to take advantage of the new knowledge-based industries. Arkansas was forced to confront the inadequacies of its educational system by small school districts that brought suit against the state for violating constitutional guarantees of an adequate and equitable education. The new edition of the text includes substantive treatment of the continuing integration embroglio confronting central Arkansas, a problem that became notorious in the 1950s but which remains largely unresolved. The racial overtones that were manifested within the resistance to educating a plantation workforce have not dissipated and remain a major challenge to the state. The Civil Rights Acts of 1964 and 1965 ushered in a new era for the state's African Americans and transformed political and social landscapes, but vestiges of the old attitudes and prejudices remain in place.

The challenges confronting Arkansas as we enter a new century include finding ways to fund transportation and educational improvements, developing solutions to persisting social problems, and promoting the kind of economic development that will enable the state's citizens to participate in the modern global economy.

ACKNOWLEDGMENTS

The authors are greatly indebted to the many scholars who have done pathbreaking work in the study of Arkansas history. They established a solid foundation of fact and analysis, without which this textbook would have been greatly diminished in value. We wish especially to thank the individuals at the various agencies and archives who provided assistance: The University of Arkansas Special Collections Division; the Arkansas History Commission; the Archives of the University of Arkansas, Little Rock; Southwest Arkansas Regional Archives; the archives at Ouachita Baptist University; the Butler Center at the Central Arkansas Library System; the Old State House Museum; the Historic Arkansas Museum; and the Mosaic Templars Cultural Center. The many years of journal articles published by the *Arkansas Historical Quarterly* were particularly useful on several crucial issues. We are especially indebted to the good folks at the Southern Tenant Farmers Museum in Tyronza and Lakeport Plantation House in Lake Village, both entities run by the Heritage Studies Program at Arkansas State University. We would like to take this opportunity to acknowledge a relative newcomer to the historical community, the *Encyclopedia of Arkansas History & Culture*, an online encyclopedia that functions as part of the Central Arkansas Library System and provides an invaluable service to the public and scholars alike. Jeannie M. Whayne would like to thank her coauthors for their forbearance and acknowledge the many students who have enrolled in her classes in Arkansas and southern history. Their questions and comments provided insights into what had been either omitted or treated too briefly in the first edition. She thanks her colleagues Patrick Williams and Michael Pierce for their thoughtful observations. Thomas DeBlack also thanks his coauthors and joins Whayne in recognizing the contributions of the many county and local historical societies across the state, particularly for the yeomen work they have done in publishing county and local histories. George Sabo acknowledges his coauthors and also the many students in his classes for helping him refine his ideas about Arkansas Indians, and the Caddos, Cherokees, Osages, Quapaws, and Tunicas, who over many years have generously taught him much. Morris S. Arnold joins in the above acknowledgments and thanks his coauthors for their indulgence. All four of us would like to thank our excellent geographer, Joseph Swain of Arkansas Tech University. Thanks to his expertise the book is complimented by new versions of maps that appeared in the first edition and many additional images and maps, some of which are now in color. We would all like to thank our spouses and families for their many kindnesses as we each took time away from them for this work. Finally, we would like especially to acknowledge Willard B. Gatewood, who, over a decade ago, urged us to come together and write this book. The first edition was the result of his encouragement. This second edition, sadly, comes to press without his good offices as we lost him late last year. We take this opportunity to dedicate this book to his memory.

ACKNOWLEDGMENTS

ARKANSAS: A NARRATIVE HISTORY

CHAPTER ONE

A Land "Inferior to None"

Happen! happened in Arkansaw: where else could it have happened, but in the creation State, the finishing-up country—a state where the sile runs down to the center of the 'arth, and the government gives you title to every inch of it? Then its airs—just breathe them, and they will make you snort like a horse. It's a State without fault, it is.

—THOMAS BANGS THORPE, "The Big Bear of Arkansas"

The soil of the Arkansas bottoms is inferior to none in the world.

—ALBERT PIKE, letter to the *New England Magazine,* 1835

Millions of years before the first human being set foot there, dynamic forces were shaping the land that would become the state of Arkansas, making it one of the most varied and beautiful in the American nation. Some 500 million years ago, all of present-day Arkansas was covered by the waters of what we now know as the Gulf of Mexico. Shallow waters teeming with marine life covered the northern part of the state, and as sea creatures died their shells became incorporated in bottom sediments that later formed into limestone. The tiny fossils that can be found today in that limestone provide a record of this era in the state's geological history. Over time, the land began to emerge from the water, as ancient continents collided to form a supercontinent called Pangea. The first to emerge was the land in the northern and western regions, where the collision of continents gradually thrust the land upward. The land in the southern and eastern parts of Arkansas remained underwater for a much longer period. When the waters finally receded from this region, they left a flat and rolling landscape that resembled the ocean floor it had been for so long. See plate 1 following page 126.

Pangea: A supercontinent formed by the collision of the other continents about 300 million years ago. This supercontinent persisted throughout Paleozoic and Mesozoic eras until it began to break up some 200 million years ago.

At the conclusion of this lengthy period of dynamic change (roughly one million years ago), Arkansas assumed the general geologic pattern that exists today. A diagonal line running northeast to southwest divides the state approximately in half, with the areas north and west of the line being characterized by mountainous uplands, while the southern and eastern parts are flat or rolling lowlands. This geologic division would have profound implications for social, economic, and political development in Arkansas. But for all its significance, this division of Arkansas into highlands and lowlands greatly oversimplifies the complex nature of the state's geology. Today geologists recognize six major natural divisions in Arkansas. Three—the Ozark Mountains, the Ouachita Mountains, and the Arkansas River Valley—make up the highland region, and three others—the West Gulf Coastal Plain, the Mississippi Alluvial Plain (the Arkansas Delta), and Crowley's Ridge—constitute the lowlands. See plate 2 following page 126.

The Ozark Mountains

Perhaps the most well known of these natural divisions is the Ozark Mountains. Occupying the northwest corner of the state, the Ozarks reach elevations over two thousand feet higher than in the lowlands. See plate 3 following page 126. Technically, these mountains are actually what geologists call an elevated plateau. After the continental collision forced this land upward, a long process of erosion began that gradually lowered the surface of the land until it reached layers that were resistant to erosion. The result was the creation of a relatively flat, level plateau. Over long periods of time, rivers dissected the Ozark Plateau creating three smaller, discontinuous plateaus separated by valleys and erosional remnants in the shapes of hills and mountains. These plateaus are called the Springfield Plateau, the Salem Plateau, and the Boston Plateau.

Plateau: An area of fairly level high ground.

The Springfield Plateau extends westward from St. Louis, Missouri, to southwest Missouri, northeast Oklahoma, and northwest Arkansas. It is composed largely of highly soluble limestone and a flint-like rock called chert that was an important resource for stone tool-making American Indians during the prehistoric era. Much of this plateau is forested, but sizable areas of prairie with level land and tillable soil drew early settlers from southern Missouri to the area. Today the cities of Fayetteville and Springdale (Washington County), Rogers (Benton County), and Harrison (Boone County) are located in the Springfield Plateau.

Prairie: A large open area of grassland.

North and east of the Springfield Plateau lies the Salem Plateau. The vast majority of this plateau lies in Missouri, but the southernmost part crosses the border into north-central Arkansas. The soil here is much thinner and poorer than in the Springfield Plateau. Some nineteenth-century accounts described large parts of the region as "barrens." Today, Eureka Springs lies on an escarpment between the Springfield and Salem Plateaus, and the towns of Mammoth Springs (Fulton County), Mountain Home (Baxter County), Calico Rock (Izard County), Cherokee Village (Sharp and Fulton Counties), and Yellville (Marion County) are located on the Salem Plateau.

Escarpment: A long, steep slope at the edge of a plateau.

The third plateau, the Boston Plateau (commonly called the Boston Mountains), lies south of the Springfield Plateau. Reaching elevations of up to 2,600 feet above sea level, this plateau is the highest in the Ozarks. The region is characterized by magnificent mountain vistas, but its rugged nature limited transportation and agricultural development, which led to the creation of an isolated, hill-country culture that gave the Ozarks its "hillbilly" image. The Boston Plateau was traditionally the poorest section of a region that was for much of Arkansas history the poorest in the state.

Hardwood forests of oak and hickory dominate the Ozark landscape, and clear, spring-fed rivers like the King, the Spring, the Buffalo, and numerous other streams cut deep valleys through parts of the Ozarks. The best known of these Ozark rivers is the Buffalo. Originating in the Boston Plateau, the Buffalo follows a generally east-to-west course for over 150 miles through present-day Newton, Searcy, and Marion counties before entering the White River in Baxter County. The beautiful bluffs, rapids, and waterfalls created by this river, in addition to the clear water and the abundance of fish, birds, and other wildlife make the Buffalo one of the most scenic rivers in the nation.

The Ozarks are also home to another of the state's most unique features. Water seeping through cracks in the region's limestone base causes the underlying rock to dissolve, creating large caves. The most spectacular of these may be Blanchard Springs Cavern near Mountain View. This massive underground cave contains an underground river, stalactites (formations descending from the cave's ceiling), stalagmites (formations rising from the cavern floor), columns (where stalactites and stalagmites meet), and extensive areas of flowstone (sheet-like calcite deposits formed where water flows down a wall or along the floor). Bats, snails, spiders, and the rare Ozark blind salamander (the first cave-dwelling amphibian found in the United States) find a home in the cavern. Another geological feature—rock shelters eroded into the faces of vertical limestone and sandstone bluffs—was used extensively by prehistoric American Indians for short-term occupation. The dry environments of many rock shelters made them suitable for the storage of nuts and grains.

Travelers to the Ozarks have long been impressed by the region's great natural beauty. The geologist Henry Rowe Schoolcraft left an account of his visit to the Missouri and Arkansas Ozarks in 1819–1820. He wrote, "It is a mixture of forest and plain, of hills and long sloping valleys, where the tall oak forms a striking contrast with the rich foliage of the evergreen cane, or the waving field of prairie-grass. It is an assemblage of beautiful groves, and level prairies, of river alluvion, and high-land precipice, diversified by the devious course of the river, and the distant promontory, forming a scene so novel, yet so harmonious, as to strike the beholder with admiration; and the effect must be greatly heightened, when viewed under the influence of a mild clear atmosphere, and an invigorating sun, such as is said to characterize the region during the spring and summer."

The Ouachita Mountains

The Ouachita Mountains make up the second part of the Arkansas highlands. Lying south of the Ozarks, the Ouachitas extend from eastern Oklahoma to the western edge of

Ozark rock shelter. Photo by George Sabo III. *Courtesy of the Arkansas Archeological Survey.*

present-day Little Rock in central Arkansas. Like the Ozarks, the Ouachitas were created by the collision of continents, but here uplift was only a minimal factor. Rather the collision folded layers of rock over other layers. Riverine erosion accentuated the folds, shaping them into a series of east-west running ridges. Sandstone and shale compose much of the Ouachitas, but the region also has deposits of quartz crystals and novaculite, a hard, dense stone prized for use as a whetstone during historic times and by ancient American Indians as a material for stone tool-making long before that. Pine forests predominate on the warmer south-facing slopes of the Ouachita's ridges, while the cooler north-facing ridges tend to favor hardwood forests. The valleys between the ridges are mixtures of pine and hardwood. Streams in the region tend to follow the east-west fold patterns, and rainwater that follows the folds below ground emerges at various points in the region as hot springs, most noticeably at today's Hot Springs National Park.

On his expedition up the Ouachita River with fellow Scottish immigrant George Hunter in 1804–1805, William Dunbar described the land along the Ouachita River just below the hot springs:

> From the river camp for about two miles, the lands are level and of second rate quality, the timber chiefly oak intermixed with others common to the climate and a few

Ouachita Mountains. Photo by Mary Beth Trubitt. *Courtesy of the Arkansas Archeological Survey.*

scattering pine-trees; further on, the lands on either hand arose into gently swelling hills, clothed chiefly with handsome pine-woods; the road passed along a valley frequently wet, by numerous rills [small brooks] and springs of excellent water which broke from the foot of the hills: as we approached the hot-springs the hills became more elevated and of steep ascent & generally rocky.

The Arkansas River Valley

In 1819 the English-born naturalist Thomas Nuttall traveled up the Arkansas River from Arkansas Post on the river's lower reaches to Fort Smith. As he passed the point where Little Rock would soon be established, he remarked on the changing nature of the lands that bordered the great river. "After emerging as it were from so vast a tract of alluvial lands, as that through which I had now been traveling for more than three months," he wrote, "it is almost impossible to describe the pleasure which these romantic prospects afford me. Who can be insensible to the beauty of the verdant hill and valley, to the sublimity of the clouded mountain, the fearful precipice, or the torrent of the cataract." This region, where the river passes between the Ozarks and the Ouachitas, is known as the Arkansas River Valley. The same geologic forces that caused the Ozarks and Ouachitas to be uplifted forced the area between them downward into a trough that was carved and sculpted by the Arkansas River. Up to forty miles in width and extending from the Oklahoma border to the Mississippi River, the River Valley contains characteristics of both the Ozarks and the Ouachitas, with both uplifted plateaus and folded ridges, and pine and hardwood forests. Other features are unique to the region. The wide bottomlands provide fertile farmland and also feature bottomland forests and swamps. Pockets of coal and natural gas are also found in the region. See plate 4 following page 126.

Trough: A long hollow in the earth's surface.

Three unique features of the River Valley are Mount Magazine (Logan County), Mount Nebo (Yell County), and Petit Jean Mountain (Conway County). All are mesas—isolated hills with steep sides and flat tops. Mount Magazine is the highest point in Arkansas, reaching an elevation of 2,753 feet above sea level. The mountain is also famous for its diverse butterfly population. Ninety-four of the 134 species of butterflies in Arkansas can be found there, including the rare Diana fritillary. Petit Jean Mountain contains the greatest concentration of prehistoric American Indian pictographs (rock paintings) in the state. Mount Nebo was an important landmark for navigation along the Arkansas River during the early historic era. The three mountains provide magnificent views of the bottomlands and rolling uplands that characterize most of the River Valley.

Mesas: Isolated hills with steep sides and flat tops.

Thomas Nuttall reported that he was "amused by the gentle murmurs of a rill and pellucid water, which broke from rock to rock. The acclivity, through a scanty thicket, rather than the usual sombre forest, was already adorned with violets, and occasional clusters of the parti-colored Collinsia. The groves and thickets were whitened with the blossoms of the dogwood (Cornus florida). The lugubrious vocifications of the whip-poor-will, the croaking frogs, chirping crickets, and whoops and halloos of the Indians, broke not disagreeably the silence of a calm and fine evening."

The river itself and its adjacent lowlands have long served as a transportation corridor for both animals and people. Long before highways or railroads, the river was a major artery of commerce for early Arkansans, and some of the state's earliest settlements grew up along its banks. Today Fort Smith, Ozark, Clarksville, Russellville, Morrilton, Conway, and several smaller communities are located in the River Valley.

The West Gulf Coastal Plain

Even after most of the water that originally covered Arkansas had receded, much of the southwestern region remained covered by a wide, shallow lagoon that was home to a variety of living things ranging from microorganisms to shellfish to dinosaurs. Near present-day Nashville (Howard County), paleontologists found the tracks of a number of huge dinosaurs that had traversed the area between 150 and 200 million years ago, when the climate was hotter and much more humid than today. Recent investigations led by University of Arkansas geosciences professor Steve Boss have identified numerous species, including *Acrocanthosaurus atokensis*, one of the largest predators ever to roam the earth's surface, as well as gigantic long-necked, plant-eating sauropods. The remains of the shellfish eventually formed a soft version of limestone known as chalk. See plate 5 following page 126.

Paleontologists: Scientists who study the life of past geological periods through fossil remains.

Because various parts of the Coastal Plain formed at different times, the soil in this natural division varies widely. It ranges from the fertile farmland and bottomland forest of the Red River and the Blackland Prairies in the west to the later (and poorer) sandy pine-covered regions in the east. The varying soils gave rise to varying ways of life. In the western portion of the region, farming and livestock raising predominate, while in the east, timber harvesting is a major economic activity.

Several varieties of minerals are found in the Coastal Plain. Bauxite (used in making aluminum) is found in Saline County, and the discovery of oil and gas near present-day El Dorado and Smackover created a boomtown economy in the early twentieth

Nashville dinosaur tracks.
© 2011 *University Relations, Photo Russell Cothren.*

century. A unique mineral found in the Coastal Plain comes from near present-day Murfreesboro (Pike County). Thousands of diamonds have been found at the site of an ancient volcano that exploded millions of years ago.

The Mississippi Alluvial Plain (the Delta)

The last part of Arkansas to take shape was the southeastern region. As the climate cooled dramatically some 110,000 years ago, thick glacial ice scoured northern parts of the continent. When the last vestiges of the ice sheets began to melt some 11,500 years ago, rivers filled with outwash spread deep sedimentary deposits across the more southerly regions. The Mississippi Alluvial Plain and a remnant elevated area in eastern Arkansas called Crowley's Ridge were created during this period. The Mississippi Alluvial Plain, better known as the Delta, occupies roughly the eastern third of the state. The most obvious feature of the Delta landscape is its flat, level surface. Maj. Amos Stoddard, a U.S. Army officer who came to the region in 1804, noted that the land "presents an almost perfect level, and . . . is much more elevated on the river than in the rear of it. This vast tract affords a thick growth of large and tall trees, mostly cotton wood and cypress, with extensive cane breaks . . . from fifteen to twenty feet in height. . . . All these lands are of an alluvial nature, and extremely fertile." Tupelo trees are also common. For the earliest white settlers, these dense forests, impenetrable canebrakes, and large swamps made travel through the region difficult or impossible. See plate 6 following page 126.

Alluvial: Deposits of clay, silt, and sand left by flowing floodwater in a river valley or delta.

Ecologist Tom Foti has written that the Delta is "a land of rivers, built by rivers, and defined by rivers." The foremost of these is the Mississippi River, which has carved and sculpted the Delta landscape for millions of years, as it followed an ever-changing path southward to the Gulf of Mexico. Its frequent floods have been a bane to travel and settlement in the region, but those same floods have deposited tons of incredibly fertile soil over the area, making the Mississippi Alluvial Plain one of the richest agricultural regions in the world.

The Arkansas River has also played a major role in creating the Delta. From its headwaters in Colorado, the Arkansas flows east-southeast across Kansas and Oklahoma before entering western Arkansas near Fort Smith (Sebastian County) and continuing southeastwardly through the Arkansas River Valley before entering the Mississippi Alluvial Plain near Little Rock. The river continues its southeasterly path through the Delta and enters the Mississippi River in eastern Desha County. At almost fifteen hundred miles in length, the Arkansas is the nation's sixth longest river.

Other major streams have also shaped the Delta landscape. The White River begins its 722-mile journey in northwest Arkansas, flowing north into Missouri before crossing back into Arkansas near Bull Shoals in Marion County. The river continues on a southeasterly course, entering the Mississippi Alluvial Plain near Batesville and proceeding 295 miles through the Delta before entering the Mississippi in Desha County just north of the mouth of the Arkansas. The Black and the Cache rivers flow southward from northeast Arkansas into the White. To the east the L'Anguille and St. Francis rivers flow southward along opposite sides of Crowley's Ridge. The smaller L'Anguille joins the St. Francis in eastern Lee County, not far from where the St. Francis enters the Mississippi just north of present-day Helena.

In parts of the region, American Indian communities living in the area between A.D. 900–1600 built large, fortified towns that were supported by an agriculture based on the production of corn, beans, and squash. The first white settlers subsisted on the abundant game and fish, but later settlers accumulated great wealth by exploiting the fertile land. In the sandy soils along the rivers, cotton became the primary crop, and by the mid-nineteenth century the region was tied to plantation-style agriculture and to the institution of slavery.

Within this region there exists a subregion consisting of a broad terrace covered by wind-blown dust (loess) underlain by a substratum of clay. Originally covered by tall prairie grass, today the region is largely covered by croplands. The clay base in the region's soil causes it to hold water, making the Grand Prairie an excellent region for growing rice. This Grand Prairie extends over half a million acres and covers all or part of four counties—White, Lonoke, Prairie, and Arkansas. The entire Alluvial Plain is a major bird migration corridor in the fall and spring, and the numerous flooded rice fields in the Grand Prairie annually attract tens of thousands of migrating ducks, making the area one of the nation's best duck-hunting regions. Other smaller terraces are common north of the Arkansas River.

Loess:
A loosely compacted deposit of wind-blown sediment.

For untold centuries, the region's rivers changed course with almost every flood, wreaking havoc on settlers and creating a nightmare for anyone attempting to plot out permanent county or state boundary lines. Improved flood-control measures that were put in place after the disastrous Mississippi River flood of 1927 have greatly decreased the danger of flooding and stabilized the course of the Arkansas and Mississippi rivers.

Crowley's Ridge

Running from north to south through the northern half of the Mississippi Alluvial Plain is an elevated strip of ground that varies in width from a half mile to twenty miles and rises up to two hundred feet above the flat Delta land. This ridge takes its name from Benjamin Crowley, one of the first white settlers in the region (c. 1820). Crowley's Ridge runs for over 150 miles from extreme northeast Arkansas to Helena on the Mississippi River in Phillips County, disappearing briefly just north of present-day Marianna (Lee County). The ridge, which has its origins near Cape Girardeau, Missouri, is the sixth and smallest natural division in Arkansas. As elsewhere in the Delta, the receding waters of the Gulf of Mexico left deposits of sand and marine organisms here. But unlike in the Delta the rivers did not remove all of this material. Instead they left a narrow ridge that was gradually overlain by riverine deposits of sand and gravel. Originally much lower than it is today, the ridge was built up to its present height by loess that has accumulated in some places to a depth of fifty feet. This loess is severely prone to erosion, making landslides a threat. See plate 7 following page 126.

Thousands of years ago, the Mississippi River actually flowed west of the ridge and the Ohio River flowed to its east, near the path of the modern Mississippi River. Over time, the Ohio retreated north and the Mississippi changed course to flow west of the ridge. Today hardwood forests of oak and hickory trees are found here, as are some of the most valuable gravel deposits in the state.

The heights of Crowley's Ridge provide a spectacular view of the surrounding Delta. The German traveler and sportsman Friedrich Gerstacker, who lived in Arkansas from 1837 to 1843 including for a time on the ridge, described one such vista looking east from the eastern edge of the ridge on a foggy morning. "The thick white fog, through which not a tree was visible, north, south, or east, looked like the sea, and I was prompted to look out for a sail; the glowing red ball of the sun as he worked his way through it, cast a roseate hue over all. As the sun rose higher the fog began to disperse, and the tips of the highest trees appeared. As the fog vanished, it gave place to a boundless extent of green, unbroken by any rise, save that on which we stood. I remained for a long time in silent admiration of the fascinating sight."

Climate

The other major environmental feature that has impacted the development of Arkansas is the climate, which is defined as the general weather conditions that prevail in an area over a long period of time. Climatic changes have a profound impact on the type of vegetation that can exist in a particular region. In Arkansas, the climate, like the land itself, has gone through a dynamic series of changes over time. At the end of the last Ice Age the mid-continental climate was colder than it is today but seasonal variations in temperature and precipitation were much less pronounced. Spruce and jack pine forests extended across the upland parts of Arkansas and much of the Gulf Coastal Plain. Spruce boreal forests covered much of the Mississippi Alluvial Plain, though mixed deciduous woodlands grew along the river bottomlands. Animal life was very different as well: though several familiar species including deer and elk were present, now-extinct species of large mammals roamed the land, including mammoths and mastodons, giant sloths and llamas, peccaries, and large bison.

Warming temperatures between 14,000 and 10,000 years ago, temperatures caused glaciers to retreat and vegetation to expand into newly emerging habitats. Oak and hickory woodlands dominated the northern part of the state, while the south was characterized by oak and hickory mixed with southern pine.

Boreal: Of, relating to, or comprising the northern biotic area, characterized especially by the dominance of coniferous forests.

Deciduous: Falling off or shed seasonally at a certain stage of the development of the life cycle.

Cypress and tupelo trees and a few hardwoods characterized the Mississippi Alluvial Plain. As we have seen, grassland prairies remained in parts of Arkansas, remnants of a drier period in Arkansas's ancient past.

A period of pronounced global warming developed between 8,000 and 5,000 years ago. Climate patterns interacting with topography, soil, and hydrography produced different patterns of vegetation and wildlife in each of Arkansas's major physiographic regions. These changes had important consequences for American Indian communities across the mid-South.

Modern landforms and habitats developed with a return to more temperate and moist conditions after 5,000 years ago. A "blip" in this environmental trajectory occurred between circa A.D. 1400–1850, the result of another global climate change called the Little Ice Age when cooler conditions prevailed. Protracted episodes of drought were experienced in many parts of Arkansas, with dramatic consequences for animals and plants as well as human settlement patterns and economic activities.

Today Arkansas has what scientists refer to as a humid subtropical climate, defined as a region with a hot summer and no specific dry season. Summers are generally hot and humid with high temperatures in the center of the state averaging around 90 degrees in the summer and 50 degrees during generally mild, drier winter months. When warm, moist Gulf air clashes with cool, dry air moving east from the Rocky Mountains, strong thunderstorms are produced. Arkansas has approximately sixty days of thunderstorms. Tornadoes are also common in the state. On average Arkansas experiences 26 tornadoes a year, but 107 tornadoes were recorded in the state during 1999. Thunderstorms and tornadoes are most common in the spring, but they can also occur in the fall and winter. Three of the state's deadliest tornadoes occurred in the months of November, January, and February.

Rainfall averages between forty-five and fifty-five inches per year, but snowfall averages only five inches per year. With fertile soil, adequate rainfall, and over two hundred frost-free days a year, the southeastern part of the state is ideal for plantation-style agriculture.

Arkansas experiences all four seasons of the year, and the state has long been known for its changeable, unpredictable weather. Longtime residents are fond of telling newcomers, "If you don't like the weather in Arkansas, just wait a few minutes and it will change." Change has, in fact, been the operative word in describing the geology and climate of Arkansas. These geologic and climatic factors set the stage upon which human activity in Arkansas would take place, and it continues to influence activity in Arkansas today.

CHAPTER TWO

Native American Prehistory

Arkansas history began a very long time ago, when ancestors of modern American Indians began migrating out of central Asia at the end of the last Ice Age. Before this event, no humans lived in the Western Hemisphere. We can compare the remarkable achievement of these people in colonizing new and previously unseen lands to our own attempts to explore and—perhaps someday—inhabit the moon or other distant planets. Who were these people, whom modern archeologists call Paleoindians? When did they enter North America? When and how did they reach Arkansas, and what did they do once they arrived?

We know from DNA studies, skeletal and linguistic evidence, and archeological studies that Paleoindians descended from Ice Age hunters who learned to survive frigid environments of Europe and western Asia late in the Pleistocene epoch, some time after 28,000 B.C. Between 17,000–12,000 B.C., slightly warmer conditions made it possible for some of those people to reach North America on foot by following migrating herds of animals across Beringia—a thousand-mile-wide land mass connecting Siberia and Alaska. Beringia was created by lower sea levels when much of the world's water supply was frozen in continental ice sheets more than a mile thick. At first, ice sheets covering much of northern North America prevented land-based hunters from migrating beyond western Alaska, though it was possible, after about 14,500 B.C., for maritime groups to reach the Americas by sailing from island to island in hide-covered boats across the north Pacific rim. North American ice sheets began to recede about 11,500 B.C., opening new land routes into the continental interior. Modern archeologists believe that Paleoindians probably crossed into North America via both land and maritime routes. The land route across Beringia closed around 10,000 B.C., when rising sea levels again separated Siberia and Alaska. Entering a new world containing no major biological competitors, Paleoindians migrated rapidly and within only a few hundred years their descendants had colonized extensive areas in North, Middle, and South America. Their ability to adapt to diverse environments in newly settled lands demonstrates a remarkable level of skill and ingenuity.

Pleistocene Epoch: The geological era that includes the last series of Ice Ages, from 2,588,000 to 11,700 years before the present (B.P.). The Pleistocene and (current) Holocene epochs represent the Quaternary Period.

Beringia: A Pleistocene age land bridge (now inundated by the Bering Strait) that connected eastern Siberia and western Alaska.

Arkansas's First People: Entering a New Land

Paleoindians were a migratory people, moving across the land in pursuit of animals they hunted, never settling permanently in one place. When Paleoindians reached southeastern North America around 10,500 B.C., they discovered a land much different from today. Mammoths and mastodons, along with giant bison and paleollamas (a larger version of the modern llama) roamed expansive grasslands following their own migratory patterns. Modern zoologists refer to these large animals as Ice Age or Pleistocene megafauna. There were smaller animals, too. Caribou grazed in scattered tundra zones, and elk and smaller game lived in forest and forest-edge habitats along larger rivers and streams. Today these habitats are found at different latitudes, but during the Ice Age they existed side by side, creating an environmental mosaic unlike anything we find in today's world. There were few edible plant foods then, and most streams and rivers were too cold to support fish, shellfish, or other edible species. Animals—most exhibiting great mobility—served as the main source of food and other materials. A special set of skills, supported by an equally specialized technology, helped Paleoindians cope with challenging conditions.

Migratory: A pattern in which a group or population (of people or animals) undertakes large-scale movements across the land, never settling permanently in one location.

Megafauna: Ice Age species of animals (now extinct) that were much larger than modern counterparts, including mammoths, mastodons, giant bison, tapirs, sloths, camels, paleollamas, etc.

Paleoindians manufactured elegant spear points using a stone-working technology developed by Upper Paleolithic ancestors in Europe and Asia. Called Clovis points by modern archeologists, these long, sharp, willow leaf-shaped points have a distinctive "flute" or channel extending from the base toward the tip. The flute made it possible to socket the point within a bone or ivory foreshaft that in turn could be fitted to the end of a longer shaft. This weapon could be thrust into an animal from close quarters or hurled from a distance. A throwing stick, or atlatl, was used to increase the force with which it could be thrown. Outfitted with this weaponry, Paleoindians hunted even the largest animals and secured abundant amounts of meat, hides, and other materials including bone, antler, and ivory.

Finely crafted stone cutting blades and blunt-end scrapers provided a handy means for butchering animal carcasses and cleaning and softening hides. Paleoindians used finely made antler or ivory needles and sinew thread to make warm and well-fitting hide clothing. Such clothing by itself provided adequate protection against cold and wet conditions.

With a mobile lifestyle tied to the habits of migrating herds of mammoth and mastodon, Paleoindians had no need for permanent houses. Temporary dwellings including lean-tos and pole-frame tents covered with hides provided adequate protection from the elements, especially when warmed by glowing campfires. Paleoindians erected these shelters at temporary campsites located in areas providing natural protection from adverse weather conditions, access to fresh water and raw materials for tool manufacture, and—perhaps most important—a favorable vantage for observing the movements of game animals. Paleoindians used domesticated dogs for transporting tent poles, hide coverings, and other items as they moved across the land.

Kill sites are among the most common types of Paleoindian sites found by modern archeologists. At the Domebo site in southern Oklahoma, archeologist Frank C. Leonhardy of the Museum of the Great Plains excavated Clovis points and butchering tools along with the remains of a Columbia mammoth radiocarbon dated to around 9,000 B.C. At the Kimmswick site in Missouri, paleontologist Russell W. Graham and colleagues from the Illinois State Museum found Clovis points and other Paleoindian artifacts dating to approximately the same period associated with remains of mastodons and a variety of other animal species, including deer, rabbit, squirrel, and gopher. The discovery of all these species together at Kimmswick tells us that Paleoindians in this part of the country occupied a complex environment where they made effective use of a wide range of habitats containing diverse food resources.

Radiocarbon date: A measurement, based on analysis of radioactive carbon isotopes, that indicates the age of organic material (such as charcoal or bone) preserved in archeological or geological contexts.

No Paleoindian hunting or camping sites have yet been found in Arkansas, though artifacts from this time period have been collected across the state. Since Clovis materials are relatively scarce in Arkansas, there must have been only a few Paleoindians at first, perhaps no more than one hundred to one hundred and fifty people across the entire state, living in scattered groups each consisting of perhaps two dozen or so members. The largest concentration of finds occurs in the eastern part of the state. This suggests that the first groups migrated down the Mississippi River from the northern plains, where earlier Paleoindian remains have been found. As migrating groups entered the mid-South, some began to settle down, adopting more localized patterns of movement based on seasonal distributions of game animals and other food sources and availability of stone for tool making.

After several generations in the mid-South, sometime around 8,500 B.C. at the beginning of the Holocene epoch, Paleoindians faced another significant challenge when large Ice Age animals became extinct. Archeologists and paleontologists debate whether this extinction was caused by climate change, by hunting, by disease, or by some combination of factors. Earlier episodes of climate change did not cause extinction, and Paleoindian hunters represent the only new ecological variable introduced at this time, suggesting they did indeed play some role. However it occurred, the extinction of large Ice Age animals forced descendants of Paleoindians to change their way of life. Deer, elk, and modern bison (smaller than the Ice Age bison species)—already present when Paleoindians entered the mid-South—became the

Holocene Epoch: The current geological period that began after the end of the last Ice Age about 11,700 years ago.

primary animals sought for food and other materials. In contrast to Ice Age megafauna, which followed predictable migration routes and thus could be hunted at places favoring the safety and success of Paleoindians, deer are solitary wanderers while elk and bison follow different annual migration patterns, requiring new encounter strategies and hunting techniques. To what extent changing hunting patterns affected other aspects of life is a question many archeologists are now attempting to answer.

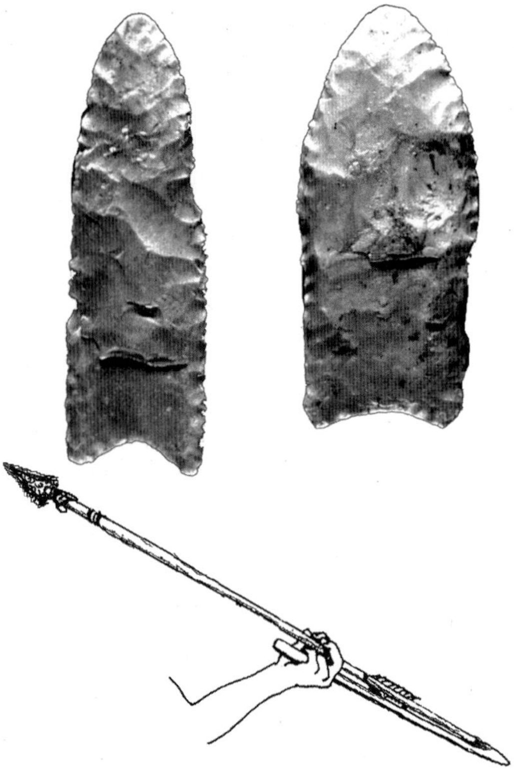

Paleo-Indian points (*top*) with artist's reconstruction of a throwing stick and dart assemblage (*bottom*). *Courtesy of the University Museum Collection, University of Arkansas.*

Did Paleoindians possess any distinctive social practices or religious beliefs? This question is difficult to answer, because such intangible aspects of culture are not directly reflected by artifacts preserved in the ground. But some material remains do provide interesting clues about ancient social practices and religious beliefs.

One common feature of stone artifacts found at Paleoindian sites across North America is that many are made of nonlocal raw material. Paleoindians typically made Clovis points and some other stone tools from raw materials gathered from distant sources, even when that exotic material is no better than locally available stone. This phenomenon may reflect a survival strategy used even today by hunting and gathering groups who provision themselves from mobile and widely dispersed natural resources. Such groups depend on accurate information about the ever-changing distribution and abundance of animals, plants, and other materials across extensive territories, and they must be aware of circumstances (like climate-induced changes in the environment) that can affect the availability of those resources. At the same time, groups must space themselves at sufficient distances from one another to avoid competing for the same resources.

Maintenance of periodic contact among widely scattered groups provides one very effective way to keep groups appropriately spaced across the landscape while simultaneously providing a means for communication. Periodic visits made possible by journeys to obtain exotic raw materials can ensure a regular flow of information between widely scattered groups, enabling them to keep tabs on changes in the distribution of people, animals, and other resources across very large territories. Neighboring groups can call upon one another for assistance in times of need, or invite one another to share in windfall harvests, such as mammoth or mastodon kills. Social relations among such groups also provide access to mates for marriageable men and women, thereby strengthening ties between distant groups with added layers of kinship. In sum, maintenance of long-distance social contacts based on a contrived "need" for exotic goods—like stone for tool manufacture—can provide a safe and effective way to ensure a high level of information exchange among widely dispersed groups. Perhaps this is why we consistently observe the use of exotic raw material in Paleoindian stone tool assemblages across Arkansas and the mid-South.

Modern hunters and gatherers around the world also typically think about their ties to nature and tasks such as food-getting in religious terms, and they organize such activities in relation to kinship concepts. Community welfare is often seen as dependent upon ritual maintenance of kindred ties of mutual obligation with unseen forces of the spirit world, including guardian spirits of various animal and plant communities on which people rely for food and other goods. This way of thinking produces views that are very different from our own. Hunting, for example, is not just an activity performed to put meat on the fire; it is considered a social contract with the spirit world involving rituals that convey respect for the soul of the animal in exchange for meat and other materials given up for the benefit of the hunter and his family. This idea is a common feature of hunter-gatherer religious views the world over.

Evidence for such sentiments among Paleoindians comes from the Cooper Site in northwest Oklahoma, where Lee Bement of the Oklahoma Archeological Survey found ancient artifacts mixed with extensive deposits of bison bone representing repeated hunting and butchering episodes. One bison skull found among remains of the first hunting episode provides intriguing evidence of ritual activity. On that skull a red zigzag line was painted on the frontal bone. The pigment appears to be hematite (or red ochre, as it is often called), a substance widely used by Paleoindians and other ancient hunters for ritual purposes. This evidence suggests that Paleoindians living in the mid-South also attached religious principles to their quests to obtain food.

Archeologists recognize the emergence of a new way of life around 8,500 B.C. in response to animal extinctions and other environmental changes associated with the end of the Ice Age, including an increase in the availability of plant foods. This new cultural pattern is named after a distinctive artifact, called a Dalton point. Similarities in the manufacture of these and earlier Clovis points suggest that Dalton people descended from earlier Paleoindians. Dalton culture represents the first adaptations to emerging Holocene environments.

There are many more Dalton sites in Arkansas than earlier Paleoindian sites. The distribution of Dalton sites is also more widespread, indicating that these people made wider use of newly developing habitats and resources. Increase in site numbers indicates a corresponding increase in population, to perhaps five hundred or more for the entire state.

Dalton preform, spear point, and reworked points (*top*); adze blade and reconstructed adze (*bottom*). *Courtesy of the University Museum Collection, University of Arkansas.*

Dalton people developed a more sedentary way of life; they occupied multi-season base camps for extended periods—perhaps several years at a time—from which they traveled to other nearby localities to hunt, fish, collect nuts and other plant foods, and gather stone for manufacture of tools, weapons, and other implements. Dalton people also invented new kinds of woodworking tools, such as stone-bladed adzes and celts, reflecting an increase in the use of wood for making a variety of items including more substantial dwellings.

Sedentary: A pattern in which groups or populations occupy a specific location for an extended time.

The most fascinating Dalton site examined by archeologists is the Sloan site, located on the summit of a low sand dune in the Cache River Valley in eastern Arkansas. Excavations led by Dan Morse of the Arkansas Archeological Survey revealed that the site contained numerous clusters of artifacts, including used and unused Dalton points and other tools such as drills and perforators, adzes, scrapers, knives, engravers, abraders, hammerstones, and raw materials for stone tool production. Dalton points were by far the most numerous artifacts, many of unusually large size. The distribution of these artifacts was also intriguing: several clusters formed two-meter-long alignments, consistently oriented in a northeast to southwest direction parallel to the dune's long axis. Careful sifting of excavated sediments produced dozens of small, badly eroded bone fragments, many subsequently identified by University of Arkansas bioarcheologists Keith Condon and Jerome Rose as human. On the basis of this evidence, the Sloan site has been identified as a Dalton cemetery in which grave offerings were placed with the dead, presumably for use in the afterlife. Dated at 8,500 B.C., the Sloan site is considered the oldest cemetery in the Western Hemisphere. Its use signals development of a new and special relationship between the living community and the land containing the buried remains of its ancestors. This relationship would remain an important feature in the cultures of all subsequent American Indian communities living in and around Arkansas.

The Archaic Era: Creating New Environments

The Archaic era, extending from 8,500 to 600 B.C., was a time of extraordinary development, partly in response to climate changes but partly also the result of Indian efforts to modify natural surroundings to better suit their needs. The most far-reaching change involved domestication of several native plant species. Over the past quarter century, archeologists and botanists have discovered new evidence (much of it coming from collections preserved at the University of Arkansas Museum) identifying Arkansas and the mid-South as one of the world's great centers of agricultural origins. And plant domestication was but one of several activities through which local Indian communities began to reshape southern landscapes.

Artifacts from this period illustrate how Archaic Indians developed tools and technologies capable of effecting such changes. Large chipped and ground stone adzes and axes attest to the importance of tree felling and woodworking for construction of permanent dwellings and manufacture of dugout canoes. Other ground stone implements, including milling basins and grinding stones, provided a means to produce meal from nuts, seeds, and other plant foods that became increasingly available as climates warmed and deciduous forests expanded. In fact, the abundance of carbonized nut shells in Archaic period trash pits, coupled with preference for hardwood fuels from nut-bearing tree species, suggests that Indians of the Archaic period began to manage hardwood stands by thinning out smaller trees to increase the crown breadth—and thus improve nut production—of well-established, larger trees.

Some archeological sites dated to this period, particularly dry Ozark rock shelters, yield artifacts made of organic materials. These provide more insight into the rich material culture developed by Archaic Indians. Bone fish hooks and harpoon heads (along with notched pebbles interpreted as net weights) attest to development of a fishing technology as rivers and streams began to slow down and warm up, providing habitats suitable for fish, shellfish, turtles, and other aquatic species. Bone and antler needles and awls provide evidence for continued manufacture of tailored clothing. Examples of clothing made of skins sewn with deer sinew thread have been found in addition to clothing made from woven plant fibers. Bracelets and necklaces made of various kinds of marine shell, obtained via long-distance trade, added ornamentation to body and dress. Woven fiber nets and baskets have also been found, illustrating an important nonfood use for native plant materials.

Plant and animal remains preserved at many archeological sites increase our understanding of how Archaic Indians expanded their food-producing economies. Deer provided meat and marrow for dietary needs plus antler, bone, hides, hooves, and sinew for manufacture of clothing and other items. Turkey, opossum, squirrel, rabbit, and waterfowl were also taken, along with fish, shellfish, and turtle. Plant foods, especially nuts and acorns, became increasingly important dietary staples. Hickory nuts have a high fat content, which made them an important food for Archaic Indians whose vigorous lifestyle required a higher intake of fat than lean animal flesh could provide. A broad spectrum food-getting economy based on hunting forest animals and birds, fishing and collecting other aquatic species, and collecting a variety of plant foods including nuts and acorns, wild seeds, fruits, and roots was in place by 6,000 B.C. Variations on this economy took hold in many regions in relation to locally available resources and group preferences. For example, Mary Beth Trubitt's excavations at the Jones Mill site demonstrate that Middle Archaic (6,000–4,300 B.C.) populations living along the Ouachita River in southwest Arkansas relied heavily on seasonal harvest of hickory nuts, supplemented by hunting and fishing. The large number of notched pebble weights found at the site suggests extensive reliance on net fishing.

Most Archaic communities across the mid-South organized their living arrangements around permanent base camps occupied year-round, surrounded by other sites used for specialized activities such as hunting, nut harvesting, stone quarrying, and cutting wood. Base camps consisted of several dwellings along with outdoor activity areas for food preparation, manufacturing, and other tasks. Dwellings had circular floor plans with bark-covered, pole-frame walls and grass-thatched or bark-covered roofs. Central hearths provided heat and light, surrounded by benches for sitting, sleeping, and storage.

Long-term success of Archaic Indian economies supported continuous population growth, as indicated by substantial increases in archeological site numbers from Early to Late Archaic times. Archeologists estimate that several thousands of Indians occupied Arkansas by the end of the Archaic period.

Population growth gave rise to corresponding increases in the numbers of communities occupying an ever-changing landscape. An interesting social phenomenon developed during this era, in which settled communities began to use material objects to signal their identities. This is seen in the emergence of regionally distinctive styles of dart points and a few other categories of high-visibility artifacts. At first, only a few archeologically recognizable style zones existed. By Late Archaic times (3,000–600 B.C.), stylistic differences in artifacts mark a much larger number of individual territories. Archeologists believe that use of material items to signal community identities arose in response to a variety of needs, including needs to regulate spacing, organize trade relations, and promote fluid social interactions among growing numbers of groups now living in closer proximity to each other. It is likely that clothing and other elements of body presentation, including tattooing and hairstyles, also played roles in the expression of social identities, but such evidence is unfortunately not preserved in the archeological record.

Artifact styles: Differences in the ways materials are made and decorated that reflect individual and social group identities and aesthetic preferences.

Many Late Archaic communities made regular use of cemeteries to bury their dead. Some of these cemeteries were used for many generations, further cementing sacred ties between living communities and lands inherited from their ancestors. Only a few Archaic burial sites have been excavated—not enough to identify social or religious meanings reflected in different burial customs. Some burials possessed very elaborate grave offerings, including artifacts made of exotic or unusually attractive materials,

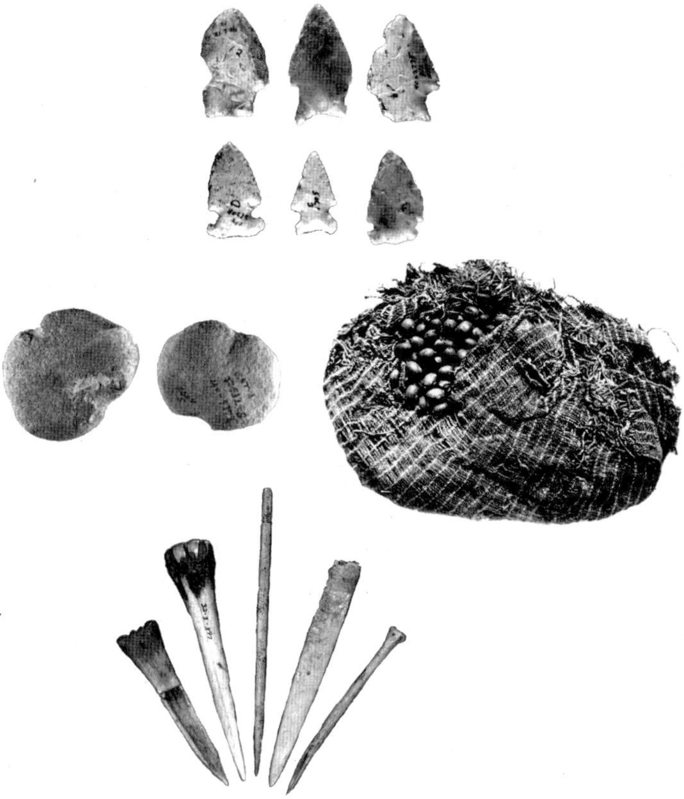

Archaic dart points (*top*), notched pebbles used as net weights (*middle left*), woven bag containing acorns (*middle right*), and bone awls and needles (*bottom*). *Courtesy of the University Museum Collection, University of Arkansas.*

suggesting the beginnings of status differences among members of some Archaic Indian communities.

As Archaic communities increased in size and became more sedentary, exchanges between groups took on added importance. This is illustrated by increases in varieties of nonlocal materials found on archeological sites. Contacts developed to provide for the information needs of earlier populations were now used to move increased amounts of material goods. Trade in commodities developed as an important strategy to offset occasional fluctuations in local supplies of food and other items.

A second response to the need to provision growing populations involved an increase in use of plant foods that led gradually to domestication of several native species. Clearing vegetation around base camps, building houses, disposing refuse, and foot traffic and other outdoor activities all contributed to disturbance of soil habitats around active settlements. As a result, several grass and "weed" species that prefer cleared and disturbed areas invaded these sites, including chenopodium (lambs quarters), knotweed, marsh elder (sumpweed), maygrass, and little barley. All these plants produce highly nutritious seeds. Studies of plant remains preserved at archeological sites across the mid-South by paleoethnobotanists like Gayle Fritz of Washington University in St. Louis and Bruce Smith of the Smithsonian Institution provide evidence of how Archaic Indians learned to manipulate the annual reproduction cycles of these plants—and a few others, such as sunflower and several species of wild gourds and squashes—by weeding out smaller plants and sowing the stored seeds of larger and more prolific plants. These practices introduced selective pressures that favored development of varieties possessing characteristics desired by Archaic Indians. In time, this selection led to the evolution of cultigens, or domesticated plant species, that produced more food but now at the cost of manual planting and tending by humans. The overall result, achieved between 2,500–1,500 B.C., was significant expansion in production of nutritious, storable plant foods, along with the advent of gardening as a new food-producing strategy. This increase in food sources in turn supported growing populations. The resulting environmental relationship was one in which more numerous and larger communities began to impact and reshape regional landscapes to a much greater extent than before.

Cultigen: A domesticated plant species that possesses characteristics maintained by human intervention in reproduction and growth cycles.

One social consequence of these developments is seen in the first examples of ceremonial mound and earthwork construction across the Southeast, beginning around 5,000 B.C. Studies by Marvin Jeter of the Arkansas Archeological Survey demonstrate that the earliest mound building in southeastern Arkansas dates to about 1,200 B.C. Placement of mounds on prominent landforms near local population centers suggests use for community rituals and for marking sacred places. The most spectacular example of Late Archaic mound building is attributed to the so-called Poverty Point culture, which began about 2,000 B.C. At the famous Poverty Point site near Epps, Louisiana, Archaic Indians built numerous earthworks including several artificial mounds, the largest of which is in the shape of a huge bird. Six sets of concentric earthen embankments, each about six feet high and eighty feet across, formed an immense semicircle some four thousand feet in diameter. The Poverty Point site was by far the largest Archaic ceremonial center constructed in the Southeast.

A trade network emanating from the Poverty Point site drew the participation of dozens of communities throughout the central and lower Mississippi Valley and Gulf Coastal Plain, including some in southeastern Arkansas. This resulted in a widespread distribution of distinctive artifacts, including carved stone beads and figurines of naturalistic and stylized humans, insects, animals, and birds. These objects, in company with the large bird effigy mound, represent an expansion in use of artistic media to symbolize relationships between human and other communities, including spiritual forces, that made up the world as it was understood by ancient Southeastern Indians.

The trade network supporting such widespread distribution of Poverty Point art objects suggests a high level of coordination and cooperation among Indian communities across a large part of the Southeast. The impressive earthworks at the Poverty Point site are likewise the product of a well-organized labor effort. Both phenomena point to the emergence of new forms of leadership that transcended local communities. As novel and effective as these institutions might have been in mobilizing geographically separated communities and their leaders around shared principles and goals, the

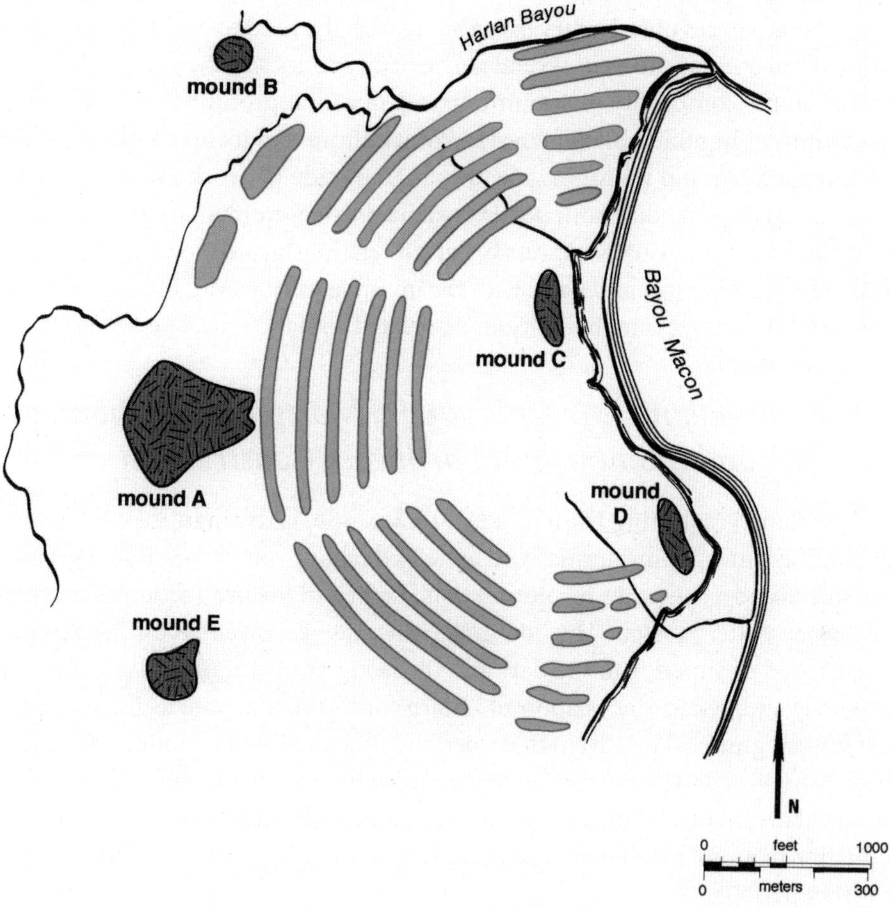

Map of the Poverty Point site, Louisiana. Drawing by M. Jane Kellett. *Courtesy of the Arkansas Archeological Survey.*

Poverty Point network could not be sustained over the long run. The trade network contracted, the Poverty Point site itself was abandoned around 1,000 B.C., and mound building declined throughout the Southeast. The latest archeological evidence compiled by Tristram R. Kidder of Washington University in St. Louis suggests that global climate changes undermined the riverine-oriented subsistence economies of many Late Archaic communities in the lower Mississippi Valley. The rise and fall of the Poverty Point culture thus represents an early but transitory experiment in cultural elaboration that included the participation of at least some groups in southeastern Arkansas.

In sum, the Archaic period was a time marked by several cultural achievements. New strategies for harvesting an increasingly wide range of natural resources supported substantial population growth and permitted many communities to become increasingly sedentary. Stylistic differences in the manufacture of material items emerged as a mechanism permitting groups to project distinctive social identities. The environmental consequences of sedentary living along with the need to expand local food production led to domestication of several native plant species and the advent of gardening. Increases in the complexity of community organization prompted a variety of social experiments, exemplified by the Poverty Point culture and its innovations for organizing human labor and managing a wide-ranging trade network. Artistic representations in a variety of media, from portable artifacts to monumental earthworks, reflect continuing efforts to visually express beliefs in relationships connecting humans with animal and plant communities and with the invisible spirit world. Elaboration of these trends produced cultural manifestations associated with the subsequent Woodland era.

The Woodland Era: Cultivation, Mortuary Ceremonies, and Monumental Earthwork Construction

The Woodland era, lasting from 600 B.C. to A.D. 900, is distinguished by continued growth of sedentary communities and increased reliance on domesticated grains. The latter stimulated a container revolution that resulted in the production of many kinds of fired-clay pottery vessels. The bow and arrow was also invented during this period, which proved so superior to the dart and throwing-stick complex that it was quickly and widely adopted as the weapon of choice for hunting as well as for conflict with other human groups. The advent of gardening—the small-scale production of domesticated plants—led to proliferation of new soil working tools, including digging sticks and hoe blades made of chipped stone, bone, and shell. Finally, this period witnessed production of a wider variety of nonutilitarian or ornamental objects than was the case for earlier periods.

Rock art in the form of petroglyphs (carved or engraved images) and pictographs (painted images) occurs at many archeological sites where bedrock outcrops or large boulders are present. Some motifs—representing humans, animals, birds, and insects in addition to geometric and abstract forms—correspond to Woodland and subsequent Mississippi era designs incorporated on portable artifacts such as pottery. (It is likely that rock art was also produced by Archaic and perhaps even Paleoindian groups, but as yet we have no confirmed examples from those earlier periods.) Some rock art is believed to be the result of individual (e.g., vision quest) and group (e.g., thanksgiving and renewal) rituals performed to sustain relationships between humans and the spirit world. Other examples mark routes or boundaries, or illustrate important social or religious concepts. Artistic designs on a variety of media, including rock art, pottery, woven fabrics and basketry, and carved stone smoking pipes and figurines, also played increasingly important roles in signaling social identities through local variations in style and design application. Artworks produced in all of these forms provide fascinating glimpses into the thought worlds of pre-Columbian Indians in Arkansas and the mid-South.

Rock art: Artistic images applied by means of painting or engraving onto natural rock surfaces.

Woodland arrow points (*top*), chipped-stone hoe blade (*bottom left*), and decorated ceramic jar (*bottom right*). *Courtesy of the University Museum Collection, University of Arkansas.*

Woodland Indians maintained the diversified subsistence economy inherited from their Archaic predecessors. Hunting and trapping, fishing, gathering wild plant foods, and gardening all contributed to the food base, though nut gathering and gardening activities expanded rather significantly at the expense of efforts devoted to hunting and fishing. Sometime during the first millennium A.D., corn, which had been domesticated in Central America beginning around 8,000 years ago, made its way into the mid-South where it was gradually incorporated into Woodland food-producing economies. Increased reliance on plant foods gave rise to more elaborate food storage technologies, providing an additional mechanism for offsetting periodic shortages in local harvests.

The growing importance of plant food production also affected settlement and land-use strategies. The distribution of fertile soils, and access to areas containing those soils, became an important consideration influencing decisions about village location. Local communities began to pay special attention to locating their villages where productive garden plots could be established.

A good example of this practice was documented in excavations conducted by Randall Guendling and George Sabo of the Arkansas Archeological Survey at the Dirst site along the Buffalo River in north-central Arkansas. The site was occupied intermittently during the Dalton, Late Archaic, and Early Woodland periods by successive groups of partially sedentary, seasonally mobile hunters and gatherers. The site was then occupied between A.D. 600–900 by a sedentary Late Woodland community that supported itself by deer and elk hunting, fishing, nut and wild fruit gathering, and garden cultivation of chenopodium, little barley, maygrass, knotweed, squash, and corn. Remains of corn were found in amounts small enough to suggest that it was but a minor food resource at that time. More important among garden crops were chenopodium, little barley, and squash. Analysis of the environmental context of the site location, however, revealed that the Dirst settlement was strategically located to assure access—even under periodic flood conditions—to several dispersed and generally small stretches of bottomland habitats containing the only soils in the region capable of supporting garden cultivation.

The Late Woodland occupants of the Dirst site also began to use shell-tempered pottery vessels that could withstand the thermal shock of direct exposure to fire. This change from an earlier use of grit-tempered pottery may have been a technological response to increased use of dried grains in the diet, which require prolonged boiling for which earlier grit-tempered vessels are poorly suited. In any case, this new innovation gave rise to a proliferation of pottery forms during the Late Woodland and subsequent Mississippian periods.

Finally, excavations produced information on changes in dwelling architecture. During Early Woodland times, the Dirst site occupants constructed light, circular pole-frame dwellings much like those made throughout the Archaic period. The Late Woodland component featured more substantial square dwellings with internal hearths and food storage pits, suitable for more permanent occupation.

By Woodland times, trade networks for exotic raw materials and finished ceremonial artifacts stretched across eastern North America. During the Middle Woodland period, these networks were coupled with a widespread ceremonial cult represented by what archeologists refer to as the Hopewell culture, which originated in the Ohio River Valley around 200 B.C. The most remarkable feature of this culture was the practice of burying high-status community leaders beneath conical earthen mounds. Some of these mounds are quite large, standing as conspicuous markers of local ceremonial landscapes. These burials are usually accompanied by hordes of artifacts, many of nonlocal materials fashioned into elaborately decorated artworks. Hopewell ceremonialism spread to many areas, leading to the construction of thousands of burial mounds and other earthworks across eastern North America. In some localities, extensive mound and earthwork complexes were built to serve as local and perhaps regional ceremonial centers.

The influence of Hopewell ceremonialism in pre-Columbian Arkansas is seen at the Helena Mound site, which formerly existed near the confluence of the Mississippi and St. Francis rivers. Here, excavations conducted in 1960 by James A. Ford of the American Museum of Natural History revealed that several individuals were buried in massive log tombs covered by conical-shaped earthen mounds. Of the many people buried in these mounds, one was an adolescent female whose grave goods included a copper- and silver-covered panpipe, copper ear spools, a drilled wolf canine and shell bead belt, and pearl and conch shell bead armbands, bracelets, and necklaces. An adolescent buried in such a conspicuous location and with such elaborate goods, dying before reaching an age sufficient to have achieved high status based on accomplishment, was likely born into a high-ranking family whose members were uniformly accorded special considerations in all of life's events. The elaborate burial treatments associated with the Hopewell culture thus reflect use of specially crafted material items to identify newly emerging differences in

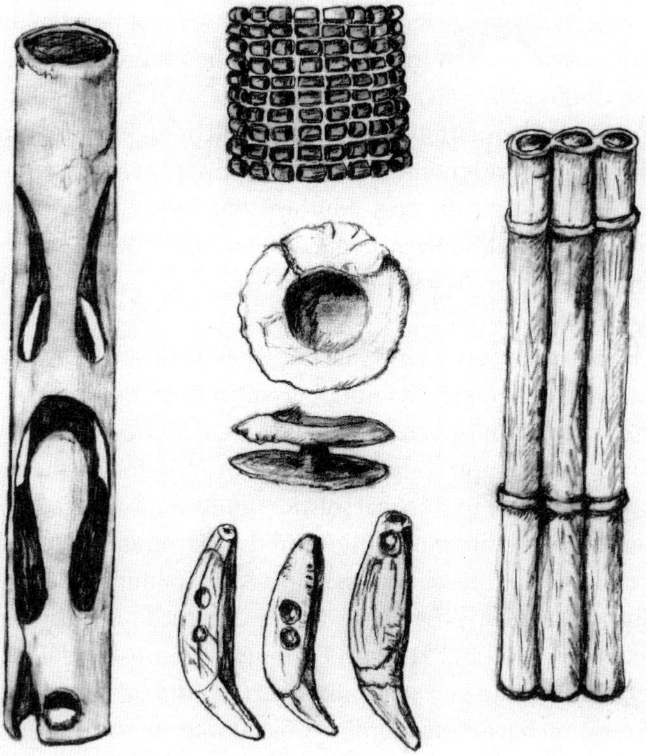

Decorated native copper ferrule *(left)*: carved-shell bead wristband, copper ear ornament, and drilled wolf-teeth ornaments *(center)*; copper-jacketed reed panpipe *(right)*. Artifacts from the Helena Mound site. Drawing by M. Jane Kellett. *Courtesy of the Arkansas Archeological Survey.*

status and rank within communities now larger and more complexly organized than ever before.

Status and rank: Status refers to the prestige or power an individual or group holds in a particular society, while rank refers to a specific position (for example, chief or warrior) within a hierarchically organized society.

As increasing numbers of communities reorganized themselves according to hierarchical principles, ways in which people interacted with one another became increasingly influenced by differences in prestige and power, illustrating the emergence of new patterns of social complexity. The advent of hierarchies in human communities also stimulated new thinking about the organization of the spirit world, now regarded as comprising a ranked hierarchy of beings and forces.

The best evidence for this new way of thinking is represented at the Toltec site located near Scott, Arkansas. This site actually has nothing at all to do with Toltec Indians of Mexico, but a nineteenth-century landowner believed (incorrectly) that the impressive earthworks at the site were built by ancient Mexican mound builders and so the site came to be called "Toltec Mounds." Here, people of the archeologically defined Plum Bayou culture constructed at least eighteen earthen mounds across a large, flat area surrounded on three sides by a mile-long earthen embankment and ditch complex and on the fourth side by Mound Pond, a relict segment of an earlier channel of the

Arkansas River. Some of these mounds were of a new type—huge and pyramidal shaped with a flat upper surface—intended not to cover burials but instead to support buildings. Natchez Indians, who continued to use platform mounds into the historic period, typically built temples, mortuary houses, or other shrines on the elevated surfaces of these mounds, to serve as focal points for community rituals conducted by high-status leaders. During the Late Woodland era, platform mounds became important symbols of newly developing social hierarchies now part of most Southeastern Indian communities. (Platform mounds also occur at some Middle Woodland ceremonial centers, but so far no evidence of buildings constructed on the surfaces of these mounds has been found.) See plate 8 following page 126.

A long-term research effort supervised by Martha Rolingson of the Arkansas Archeological Survey confirmed the presence of buildings on at least some of the platform mounds at the Toltec site. But of greater interest is the discovery that several mounds are aligned to form an astronomical observatory for monitoring the rising and setting positions of the sun relative to seasonal solstices and equinoxes. As intriguing as this phenomenon is, the Toltec site is not unique in this astronomical function, which in fact became quite widespread across eastern North America during Woodland and Mississippi times. What was the purpose of this widely observed practice?

One explanation is that communities like Plum Bayou gained considerable social prestige by successfully executing strategies that linked earthly affairs—like periodic rituals—with the cyclical movements of astronomical objects like the sun, moon, and certain stars or constellations. In Southeastern Indian religious belief, astronomical objects are associated with powerful spirit beings; the sun, for example, is regarded by most Southeastern Indians as the highest deity, the Supreme Being. Sites like Toltec make a powerful statement about the organizational clout of their builders, who demonstrate an ability to link ritual calendars, for example, to heavenly objects representing the transcendental powers of the universe. This capability had an important precedent, as we have seen, in the Poverty Point culture of the Late Archaic period. What makes the Toltec site (and other astronomically aligned Woodland mound centers) different from Poverty Point is the durability of its social and ceremonial practices. Woodland mound building did not come to an end. Even as sites like Toltec were eclipsed by later centers, their astronomically aligned mound-building traditions evolved directly into the platform mound traditions of the subsequent Mississippi period. What the leaders of societies like Plum Bayou may have figured out is that they could link secular authority claims to emerging concepts of hierarchical powers associated with the spirit realm. Thus, individuals who could demonstrate an ability to command public works projects connecting their communities to powerful spiritual forces acquired the wherewithal to command the respect and allegiance of other members of their communities. By the same measure, any community demonstrating the ability to construct those works gained a claim to priority over their neighbors.

This astronomically organized mound-building tradition gave rise to a Late Woodland cultural landscape comprised of power centers like Toltec, surrounded by lower-ranking support communities. Power centers became focal points of religious activities celebrating connections between human communities, led by high-ranking elites, and spirit communities similarly comprised of hierarchically ranked beings and forces. Through time, growth of these Late Woodland communities—with their agrarian economies, social hierarchies, power centers, and elaborate ritual organizations—developed unprecedented levels of social and cultural complexity, giving rise to subsequent Mississippian cultures.

The Mississippi Era: Agricultural Ecosystems and the Growth of Territorial Competition, Surplus Production, and Elaborate Ceremonies

Archeologists use the term "Mississippian" to refer to cultural developments in the mid-South between A.D. 900 and 1541. The latter date is when members of Hernando de Soto's expedition arrived and produced the first written descriptions of the land and its inhabitants. Population growth, the advent of large-scale agriculture, and the emergence of large, compact communities—some with populations numbering in the thousands—are hallmarks of this era. Throughout this era, Arkansas was populated by tens of thousands of Indians living in communities spread across the state.

Mississippian Indians made a number of technological advances. These include manufacture of larger and more specialized tilling implements, including large hoe blades manufactured of stone, mussel shells, and bison scapulas. Many stone blades were made from a special kaolin chert mined from quarries in southwestern Illinois and from there traded widely across eastern North America. Finely made woodworking tools, including numerous axe and celt forms, are found in great numbers on many village sites, suggesting regular clearing of forested areas to obtain wood for fuel and construction purposes and to clear larger tracts of land for community agricultural use. Certain areas—like the Mississippi Valley—contained sufficiently rich soil resources to support intensive field agriculture. By the sixteenth century, some larger Mississippian communities had agricultural fields extending, as one of Soto's chroniclers put it, from one town to the next. Pottery technology also developed into a specialized craft, in which artisans produced exquisitely decorated vessels in a wide range of forms, some produced specifically for trade and others for use in ceremonial contexts. A proliferation of artworks on other media, including stone, shell, bone, and copper, also developed during this period. The intricacy of artistic designs displayed on some materials makes it possible to discern the handiwork of specific individuals. Regional stylistic variations continued to reflect social group identities and statuses. The motifs represented on many of these objects also provide fascinating glimpses of symbolism associated with Southeastern Indian religions.

Native communities in many parts of the Southeast turned from mixed economies to a stronger reliance on agriculture. From A.D. 1250 on, intensive production of corn, beans, and squash supported large populations in many areas. Corn, which can yield

Mississippian chipped-stone hoe (*top left*) and ground-stone celt (*top right*), decorated ceramic vessels (*middle*), and wood and antler mask (*bottom*). *Courtesy of the University Museum Collection, University of Arkansas.*

abundant harvests even with simple, hand-held agricultural technologies, is deficient in lysine, an amino acid that humans require. Meat and fish contain lysine, and so do beans. The Southeastern Indians' "Three Sisters"—corn, beans, and squash—together provide a nearly complete complex of nutrients. Mississippian Indians often used corn, beans, and squash in stews prepared with bits of deer or turkey meat or fish.

In some parts of the Mississippi Valley, reliance on field agriculture produced competition over control of fertile lands. This led to violent conflicts between competing groups. In regions where such hostilities were common, local communities concentrated their settlements within or adjacent to large, fortified towns, which offered refuge when violence raged.

While most people pursued basic agricultural activities, occupational specialization also developed. This specialization was aimed at the production of surplus goods that could be traded to neighboring communities who for whatever reasons were unable to produce those goods for themselves. For example, salt making became an important activity in southwestern Arkansas, where artesian springs bring briny water to the surface from salt deposits deep below the ground. Arkansas Archeological Survey archeologist Ann Early excavated a Mississippi period Caddo Indian site near modern Arkadelphia where salt making was an important industrial activity. Briny water was boiled in broad, shallow pans placed on rocks over large hearths. The residue was then packaged in skins or pottery vessels for trade to communities in areas lacking access to natural salt sources. Salt is a necessary additive in agriculturally based diets. Other groups specialized in the production of different commodities, such as hides, grain, meat, or utilitarian or ceremonial objects, some crafted from rare and exotic raw materials.

Profits acquired through such commerce were controlled by leaders who managed the associated trade networks and, to some extent at least, controlled the distribution of wealth objects within their communities. Wealth was represented by consumer goods (food and utilitarian objects, for example) along with prestige items—nonutilitarian objects, such as finely crafted maces or ceremonial celts, whose possession reflected a specific rank or office. Some communities succeeded better than others in managing their wealth, and in some places powerful leaders emerged who could extend their influence over neighboring communities and their leaders. This created a settlement landscape comprised of both large and small towns along with a hierarchy of temple mound sites; the latter functioning much like medieval European church and castle towns, where the most powerful community leaders resided and where officials conducted important ceremonies and festivals on behalf of community members scattered across the surrounding countryside.

Large, fortified agricultural towns of the Nodena and Parkin communities in northeast Arkansas, studied by Arkansas Archeological Survey archeologists Dan and Phyllis Morse, Jeffrey Mitchem, and Robert Mainfort, represent examples of the societies that thrived in the fertile Mississippi Valley. The main towns of those communities contained platform mounds that supported the residences of some leaders, shrines dedicated to the memory of ancestors, and temples housing sacred fires that served as focal points for religious activities. Open plazas in the town centers played host to a series of regularly scheduled ceremonies performed to honor peoples' accomplishments, renew and solidify social and political institutions, and celebrate life-sustaining relationships connecting earthly communities with invisible forces of the spirit world. Hundreds of houses sheltered the resident population, which numbered in the thousands. These houses were square, typically measuring about ten meters on a side. They had clay-plastered floors, walls constructed of stout posts driven into the ground or set into excavated wall trenches and covered with woven mats or sheets of bark, and grass-thatched roofs with clay-plastered, central smoke holes. Wood and clay walls and excavated moats surrounded the main towns. Large grain storage facilities are found at some Mississippian villages, suggesting that agricultural produce was stored in centralized facilities and redistributed by community leaders. Studies of mortuary practices at cemeteries associated with these communities, however, have not produced strong evidence for pronounced social ranking, raising intriguing questions about the nature and deployment of power and authority in these societies. See plate 9 following page 126.

A second type of community is represented among the late prehistoric Caddo Indians in the Red River Valley in southwest Arkansas and adjacent parts of Louisiana, Oklahoma, and Texas. Extensive studies of sites in this region document settlements consisting of individual temple mound sites surrounded by dispersed family farmsteads. There is no evidence of fortification or of community field agriculture. Instead, communities consisted of scattered family farmsteads, each with their own dwellings, special-purpose structures, crop fields, and woodlots. Houses were entirely grass thatched and circular in shape, built on frameworks of tall upright posts drawn together at the top, with smaller cross members woven in between. European eyewitnesses observed that the construction of these houses continued into the seventeenth century, and they described them as resembling tall, grass-covered beehives. Special-purpose structures included covered work platforms and household grain storage silos set on top of upright posts. The religious and ceremonial centers of these communities can be identified by the presence of one or more platform mounds supporting temples and mortuary structures, with nearby plazas. Like their contemporaries in the Mississippi Valley, some Caddo leaders extended authority over the leaders of neighboring communities, producing hierarchically organized, multivillage societies. Unlike their Mississippian counterparts, Caddo leaders did not control the economic resources of their communities. Individual families controlled production of essential goods and contributed to the material support of their leaders. During historic times, Caddo social organization consisted in part of a very high status class of warriors, perhaps accounting at least in part for the lack of village fortifications. See plate 10 following page 126.

Recent studies suggest that funerary rites in both areas served to reorganize relations among the living in addition to memorializing the dead. A spectacular example is represented at the Spiro site, just a few miles west of Fort Smith. Though damaged extensively by looting in 1935, subsequent studies permit a partial reconstruction of events. During the thirteenth century, the Spiroans erected a small platform mound into which they excavated a basin for deposit of the intermingled remains of the dead along with their funerary objects. This communal treatment was terminated at the beginning of the fifteenth century, when a new facility was erected over the decommissioned ossuary. The remains of a single individual (accompanied by two retainers) were placed on a newly created, circular floor space along with an unparalleled number of sacred objects including countless marine-shell beads, embossed copper plates, conch-shell cups and pendants engraved with elaborate mythic imagery, carved stone and wood figurines depicting both humans and mythic beings, functional as well as ceremonial weaponry, piles of woven fabrics and tapestries, and woven basketry containers filled with ceremonial regalia. Archeologist James A. Brown of Northwestern University interprets the arrangement of all of these items as a cosmogram, or sacred image symbolizing the sacred powers of the universe. Following the deliberate, ceremonial arrangement of these items, the assemblage was entombed within a hollow chamber that was then buried within the primary lobe of a large earthen mound, creating a monument symbolizing the enduring relationships between ancestral legacies and the affairs of the living community.

Many funerary items from the Spiro site are decorated with motifs representing a religious and ceremonial movement—the so-called Southeastern Ceremonial Complex—that originated during the tenth and eleventh centuries A.D. at the great metropolis of Cahokia (near modern St. Louis) and subsequently attracted participation of communities extending from the Atlantic and Gulf coasts as far inland as the edge of the Great Plains on the west and the western Great Lakes on the north. The level of artistry exhibited by these materials is extraordinary, and compositions illustrated on many items are highly detailed, throwing extraordinary light onto the religious beliefs and ceremonial practices of Mississippian societies. Some prominent motifs represent amphibians, snakes, and spiders, which among historic Southeastern Indians are symbolically associated with a watery Below World representing disorder and destruction along with the promise of a hopeful future. Numerous bird motifs and other avian symbolism represent the Above World beyond the vault of the sky, symbolizing order and creative power along with ancestral legacies. A variety of combination motifs, the most common of which is a winged serpent often shown with the head of a deer or a panther, represents the possibility of conjoining the antithetical powers of Above and Below Worlds for the benefit of communities inhabiting the earth's surface. Engraved images showing dancers dressed in elaborate regalia further suggest that the potentially dangerous prospect of conjoining sacred forces could be accomplished through appropriate ritual activity performed by specially trained practitioners. In sum, these and other artistic motifs illustrate that many religious beliefs and ceremonial practices of historic Southeastern Indians trace back at least to Mississippian times. Many archeologists consider the Southeastern Ceremonial Complex, and its fascinating corpus of art objects, the preeminent cultural achievement of Mississippian societies in eastern North America.

Many parts of Arkansas and the mid-South lacked the environmental resources needed to support intensive field agriculture. This was true across much of the Ozark and Ouachita Mountain regions and in parts of the lower Mississippi Valley, where hunting, gathering, and gardening communities persisted throughout the Mississippian era. Different subsistence orientations did not prevent those groups from maintaining economic, social, and ceremonial ties with agricultural neighbors in adjacent regions. In the western Ozark Highlands, for example, many communities constructed local mound centers. Excavations at these mounds by Marvin Kay and George Sabo of the University of Arkansas reveal use for mortuary ceremonies celebrating relationships between the living community and the spirits of ancestors. The manner in which mounds were constructed and evidence of mortuary ceremonialism preserved at these sites point to close affiliations with Spiroan communities in the Arkansas River Valley. The presence of various nonlocal raw materials at many Ozark mound centers further suggests that they served as nodes in long-distance trade networks that supplied exotic materials for manufacture of special ceremonial objects. These connections made it possible for many

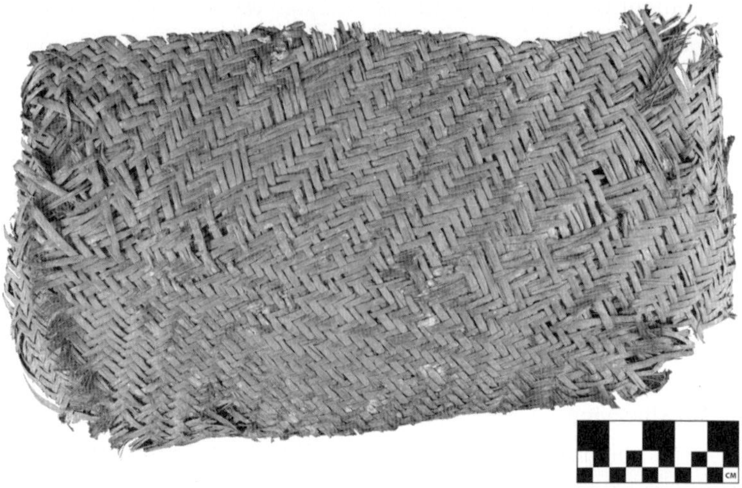

Ceremonial basketry from Spiro site. Photograph by Leslie C. Walker. *Courtesy of the University Museum Collection, University of Arkansas.*

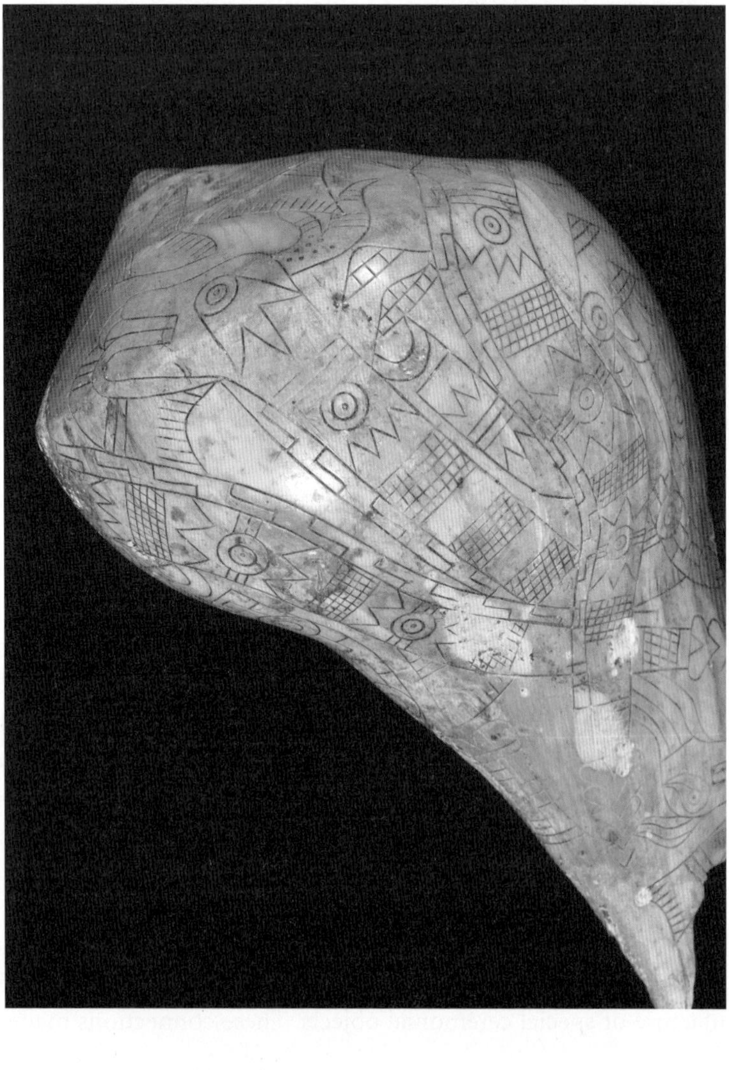

Ceremonial shell cup from Spiro site. Photograph by George Sabo III. *Courtesy of the University Museum Collection, University of Arkansas.*

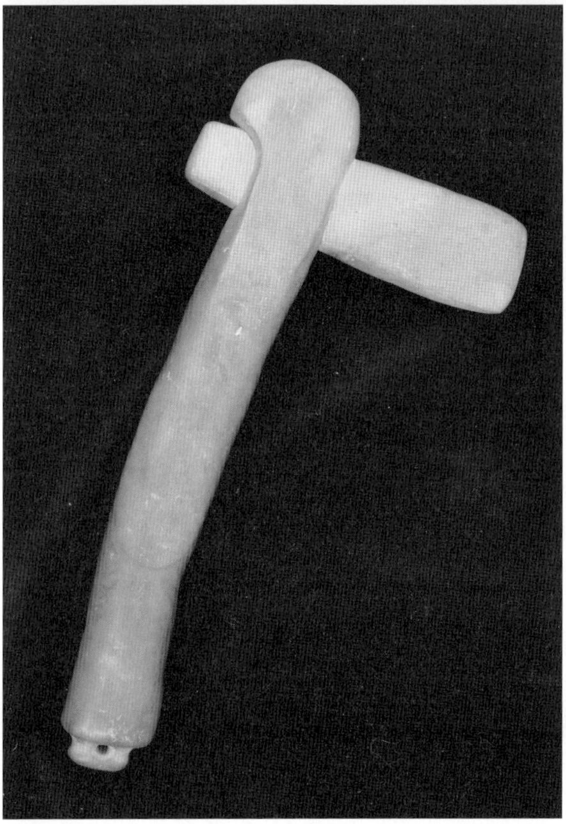

Ceremonial shell pendant from Spiro site. Photograph by George Sabo III. *Courtesy of the University Museum Collection, University of Arkansas.*

Ceremonial stone axe from Spiro site. Photograph by George Sabo III. *Courtesy of the University Museum Collection, University of Arkansas.*

late prehistoric communities, regardless of their size and location, to participate in the Southeastern Ceremonial Complex and other widespread traditions of Mississippian culture. Few if any communities remained isolated during this period; instead, most participated regularly in extra-regional economic, social, and ceremonial alliances.

Ceremonial carved stone pipe from Spiro site. Photograph by Mary McGimsey. *Courtesy of the University Museum Collection, University of Arkansas.*

A few hierarchically organized societies in the Southeast persisted into historic times. Most well known of these are the Natchez and Caddo societies encountered by Spanish and French explorers in the early eighteenth century. Many archeologists consider the historic Caddo and Natchez communities as models of the kinds of societies that persisted throughout much of the Mississippi period. By the eighteenth century, however, most Southeastern societies had become far less complexly organized than their pre-Columbian ancestors. In some cases, this "devolution" can be traced to environmental consequences of population concentration and overuse of soil resources. Tree-ring data collected from across the Southeast by University of Arkansas geographer David Stahle and associates identify the onset of extensive drought conditions, beginning in the late fifteenth century, which undoubtedly added to the stresses affecting local agricultural economies. Transmission of Old World diseases in advance of direct contact with Europeans may also have contributed to declines in some areas. Through the combined effects of these circumstances, Southeastern Indian societies contacted by European explorers during the sixteenth century and thereafter generally were smaller and less complexly organized than their Mississippian predecessors.

Despite the impacts of these unfortunate events, the long trajectory of Southeastern Indian cultural development created a legacy in the land that played an important role in the history of European exploration and settlement. Opportunities and constraints that seventeenth- and eighteenth-century European explorers and settlers found in Arkansas and the mid-South relate in large part to the distribution of Southeastern Indian communities. In the next chapter we examine how this Indian presence influenced the earliest Spanish and French explorations of Arkansas.

CHAPTER THREE

Spanish and French Explorations in the Mississippi Valley

The Spanish Entrada of Hernando de Soto, 1539–1543

The single event most profoundly affecting sixteenth-century American Indians in Arkansas and the mid-South was the 1539–1543 exploration of the region by the Spanish conquistador Hernando de Soto. His army of more than six hundred soldiers, accompanied by horses, armored war dogs, and an emergency food larder in the form of droves of live hogs, had a devastating impact on Indian communities across the Southeast. Soto's forces introduced new diseases, enslaved thousands of Indians, pillaged and destroyed villages and agricultural fields, escalated warfare, and disrupted social and economic systems throughout the region.

The consequences of Soto's expedition have long been acknowledged. Southeastern Indians had difficulty repelling the Spaniards' use of wholly unfamiliar warfare technologies and strategies. Spanish swords, lances, and crossbows were brutally effective at close quarters. Armored horses and mastiffs added to the terror of Spanish attacks. European military strategy was also designed for killing on a scale unimagined by Southeastern Indians. So when Soto demanded food and hostages from communities he visited, Indians generally had two options: comply, or resist and suffer even worse consequences. A third option, available only with foreknowledge of the Spaniards' arrival, was to abandon the homeland and seek refuge elsewhere until it was safe to return.

To these circumstances we may add one more that has emerged as a result of recent studies of climate change. The fifteenth century witnessed the onset of what climate scientists call the Little Ice Age, a global event bringing generally cooler and wetter conditions that persisted into the nineteenth century. More important than general patterns were highly variable local impacts. In the mid-sixteenth-century Southeast, drought conditions of protracted length and of a severity unequaled during the past five hundred years affected the region, imposing great stress on Indian agricultural economies. Therefore, in attempting to measure the impacts of Soto's expedition on native peoples of the Mississippi Valley, it is necessary to factor in ecological effects of devastating climate changes.

Little Ice Age: A period of global climate change that brought cooler conditions and drought to many parts of the mid-South coinciding with the arrival of European explorers.

Soto's army reached the Mississippi River in the spring of 1541, after two long years in search of wealthy native civilizations like the Aztec and Incan empires defeated by Spanish conquistadores in the first decades of the sixteenth century. Soto, in fact, had taken part in the overthrow of Atahualpa's Inca empire at Cajamarca, Peru, a decade earlier, in 1532. In the Southeast, Soto led his forces into numerous Indian villages, confiscating food and capturing thousands of Indians to serve his army's needs, but finding no valuables comparable to those taken in Mexico and South America. Soto destroyed numerous villages, towns, and crop fields in his battles with native groups, but he also lost many men and horses and much equipment. Disenchantment soured the mood of his soldiers, and in the coming months Soto found it ever more difficult to sustain hopes for a great reward. See plate 11 following page 126.

On May 8, 1541 (in the Old Style or Julian calendar), Soto's army entered the Indian province of Quizquiz, which modern scholars led by ethnohistorian Charles Hudson of the University of Georgia put on the eastern side of the Mississippi River in present-day Mississippi and Tennessee. While encamped there the Spaniards received a visit from Aquixo, the leader of a populous community on the opposite side of the river. Aquixo claimed that his province, along with Quizquiz, was subject to an even more powerful leader named Pacaha, who lived farther north on the west side of the Mississippi. Imagining that a wealthy Indian province was finally within reach, the Spaniards began preparations to cross the great river. They felled many trees for logs to build four large rafts, and early on the morning of June 18 the crossing took place. Where the crossing took place has not been determined with certainty, but it may have been south of modern-day Memphis.

Julian Calendar: The calendar adopted in 45 B.C. by Julius Caesar, containing 365 days divided into twelve months with a February leap day added every fourth year. It was replaced by the modern Gregorian calendar, introduced in 1582 by Pope Gregory XIII, which added adjustments to synchronize with the solar year.

Ethnohistorian: A scholar who uses information in primary historical records to reconstruct and study native communities and their interactions with Europeans.

On reaching the opposite bank, the Spaniards passed through the now-abandoned province of Aquixo and turned north. They entered the province of Casqui after two days of very difficult travel through swampy lands. One chronicler described the higher ground more hopefully as being "well peopled with large towns, two or three of which could be seen from one town." Fields of corn and groves of nut and fruit trees filled the open spaces between Indian settlements. The main town of Casqui was reached on June 24, which modern scholars believe is the Parkin site (now Parkin Archeological State Park) in Cross County. Recent archeological investigations conducted there by Jeffrey Mitchem have produced several European artifacts, including sixteenth-century coins, brass harness bells, and faceted glass beads.

The leader of Casqui met the Spaniards on the road leading into the main town. He brought along gifts of food and hides and offered to lodge Soto's men in the village. According to the accounts, severe drought had parched the Indians' crop fields, and

Hernando de Soto, by Gary Simmons. *Courtesy of the artist.*

Soto, who proclaimed that he was the "son of the sun," was asked if he could help bring rain. Soto ordered his men to erect a cross on the summit of a large earthen mound in the center of the village, and on the next day Spanish priests performed a ceremony of adoration. It rained on the following day, convincing the Indians—so say the accounts—that Soto truly was a man possessing extraordinary powers.

From Casqui the Spaniards pushed on to Pacaha, where Soto was led to believe that he might find gold. The village was ransacked but produced no gold. The "sacred metal" revered by the Indians was copper; though highly prized by Southeastern Indians (who considered it a gift from the heavens), it was only a low-value commodity in the eyes of sixteenth-century Spaniards. Even so, the Spaniards were impressed by other things they saw. Rodrigo Ranjel, Soto's secretary, described the town as "a very good one, thoroughly well stockaded; walls were furnished with towers and a ditch round about, for the most part full of water which flows in by a canal from the river." The fortifications at Pacaha must have been viewed by the conquistadores as wood and packed-earth versions of the stone battlements surrounding their own towns in Spain and Portugal.

The Spaniards remained at Pacaha for more than a month. Detachments of soldiers explored the surrounding countryside, but found only encampments of mobile Indians on late summer hunting and fishing excursions. Prospects for the discovery of great wealth began again to grow dim.

From Pacaha the Spaniards returned briefly to Casqui, and then continued southward along the St. Francis River to another province called Quiguate. The Spaniards described Quiguate as the largest town they visited in all of La Florida. While there, Soto learned about another province named Coligua located in mountainous lands to the northwest. Since the Spaniards knew that gold and silver most often came from mountainous regions, they spent a week slogging through very swampy, uninhabited terrain to reach the "River of Coligua" (the White River) along the eastern edge of the Ozark Mountains, probably near present-day Batesville. The Spaniards' appearance took the Indians by surprise, indicating that no communication had been received from Quiguate, Casqui, or Pacaha. Soto found many buffalo hides at Coligua, but no gold or silver. With food supplies short and reckoning that prospects would be unfavorable if they continued traveling north, Soto turned his path to the southwest.

At Calpista along the White River, the Spaniards found "an excellent salt spring." Palisema, along the Little Red River, contained a few scattered houses and only a little corn. At Tutilcoya, probably near Conway, Soto heard about a large province located farther up the "River of Cayas," which modern scholars believe to be the Arkansas River.

The Spaniards arrived at the settlement of Tanico in the province of Cayas on September 16. Here, perhaps somewhere in the vicinity of modern Russellville, they found a well-populated region with plentiful fields of corn. But here Indians lived in scattered settlements unlike the compact, fortified towns found along the Mississippi and St. Francis rivers. The Spaniards remained in Cayas for three weeks, observing Indians making salt at brackish ponds by straining the brine through baskets and then boiling it. The Indians of Cayas evidently carried some of this salt to distant provinces where it was traded for other goods.

From Tanico, the Spaniards crossed over to lands south of the Arkansas River, and traveled upstream to another mountainous area where they entered the province of Tula. Tula Indians spoke a language that guides from Tanico could not understand. Ann Early suggests this was a Caddoan-speaking group located in the northern Ouachita Mountains south of modern Fort Smith. Expedition accounts describe the Tula Indians as expert buffalo hunters who were not intimidated, as other Indians had been, by the Spanish cavalry. Using long buffalo hunting lances, Tula warriors killed many Spanish horses and riders.

Finding no gold and little food at Tula, the Spaniards turned back toward the central Mississippi Valley, passing through the provinces of Quipana and Quitamaya. Continuing east, they returned to the Arkansas River about midway between Little Rock and Pine Bluff, where they spent the winter of 1541–1542 at the main town of the province of Autiamque. Fearing Indian attacks, the Spaniards erected a stockade around part of the town. Winter brought extremely cold weather, so the Spaniards ventured only occasionally out of their compound to gather firewood. For an entire month they were snowbound. Juan Ortiz, a survivor from the Narvaez expedition (an earlier Spanish expedition that set ashore in Florida in 1528) whom Soto had rescued and who thereafter had served as a translator, died that winter. Thereafter, the Spaniards had considerable difficulty communicating with the Indians.

In the spring of 1542, Soto led his dwindling army farther down the Arkansas River through the province of Ayays to Anilco, located at or near the southern tip of Little Prairie north of the Arkansas River in what today is southern Arkansas County. Here the Spaniards found another densely populated agricultural region and hope swelled again as they described the village landscape as the richest they had so far observed. According to one account, the Indians had already abandoned the main town and set it to fire prior to the arrival of the Spaniards. Finding the food stores intact, the Spaniards occupied an undamaged part of the town, only to discover Indians returning at night to retrieve as much corn as they could carry.

The Spaniards moved on to Guachoya, another nearby town located on the south side of the Arkansas River just upstream from its confluence with the Mississippi. There, Soto intended to seize more food and build boats to send to Cuba for much-needed supplies. Accordingly, he sent out a cavalry detachment to determine the distance and shortest route to the coast. The detachment returned eight days later, having accomplished nothing other than wandering, lost, through boggy and desolate terrain.

Disheartened by this news, alarmed by increasing boldness of the Indians, and growing evermore doubtful about his prospects for success, Soto sent a final message to another Indian named Quigualtam, a powerful leader whose province was said to be located at a distance of several days' travel down the Mississippi River. As was his practice, Soto claimed that he was the "son of the sun" and demanded that "in token of love and obedience [Quigualtam] should bring him something of what was most esteemed in [his] land." Soto's fervent hope was the return of a gift of gold from a humbled Indian chief. Instead, Quigualtam replied, a few days later, that it was not his custom to visit anyone; rather, others served and obeyed him. In reply to Soto's claim of being the son of the sun he said, "Let him dry up the great river and he [Quigualtam] would believe him."

Quigualtam's reply enraged Soto, now ill with fever. Fearing that attack was imminent, he ordered his own soldiers to attack the previously visited town of Anilco. The Spaniards fought with such cruelty that even their own accounts of the battle reflect shame and remorse. They gained nothing from the assault, and on May 21, 1542, Soto died.

Luis Moscoso de Alvarado was elected to take command of the expedition. Soto was quietly buried at Guachoya, but when the Indians found the grave the Spaniards exhumed the corpse, wrapped it in blankets weighted with sand, and sunk it late at night in the Mississippi River. When the leader of Guachoya asked about Soto, Moscoso replied that he had gone to the sky, as he had often done before.

Moscoso and the remaining soldiers, now numbering about three hundred, decided to head toward Spanish settlements in Mexico. Two routes lay before them: down the

Mississippi and along the Gulf Coast, or over land. The latter route was chosen with the hope of finding food at Indian villages along the way. On June 5, the Spaniards departed Guachoya and headed west.

Traveling up the Arkansas River perhaps as far as Pine Bluff, the army turned to the southwest and followed the southern edge of the Ouachita Mountains. Passing through the province of Chuguate, the Spaniards reached the Ouachita River between present-day Malvern and Arkadelphia. Continuing southward to the Red River Valley, they entered the province of Naguatex where the Indians launched a well-organized attack that divided Spanish forces and nearly succeeded in overwhelming them. An Indian captured by the Spaniards revealed the attack had been a joint effort planned by the leaders of Naguatex, Amaye, and Hacanac. This Indian's further statement that the cacique (leader) of Naguatex was the "captain and head of all" indicates the existence of a large and well-organized network of communities—much like Pacaha's—subject to a single, powerful leader.

Cacique: A term used by sixteenth-century Spanish explorers (based on a Nahuatl term) to refer to the leaders of Indian communities.

At Naguatex, where the Spaniards camped for a month, Moscoso sent out a message inviting the esteemed leader to visit him. Two days later messengers returned bearing news that the leader was on his way. The venerable old man soon arrived, "well attended by his men." According to one account, the Indians approached the Spaniards "one ahead of the other in double file, leaving a lane in the middle through which the cacique came." Moscoso treated the cacique well because he knew he would need this leader's help to continue the journey.

After their stay in Naguatex ended, the Spaniards entered into present-day Texas, where they had trouble finding enough food for themselves and their horses in villages they visited. The Spaniards had become used to plundering Mississippian villages where produce from the surrounding countryside was stored in community granaries. Caddo Indians of eastern Texas had a different economic organization. Each family stored its own crops at scattered farmsteads. To make matters worse for the Spaniards, these Indians, too, began to hide their corn.

Eventually the expedition reached the province of Guasco, still in Caddo country, where the Indians possessed turquoise and cloth obtained in trade from tribes located farther west. Here the Spaniards found a little corn and learned of a "River of Daycoa" located ten days travel toward the west, where a different group of Indians lived. Moscoso sent a detachment of men to investigate. The soldiers found a desolate area occupied only by small groups of hunters and gatherers who spoke a language that the Guasco Indians could not understand.

This was the end of the trail for the Spaniards. They decided to return to the Mississippi River and spend the approaching winter building boats in which to descend to the gulf. The return trip was very difficult. Passing back through lands they had plundered, the Spaniards found very little food and Indians hostile to their return.

Finally reaching Anilco, the Spaniards found the Indians destitute, having neglected to plant their fields after Soto had destroyed their town. The Spaniards spent the winter at a nearby province named Aminoya. There, they melted down most of their remaining armaments to make spikes for use in construction of seven boats. In one of the few strokes of good luck the Spaniards experienced in Arkansas, the Mississippi River flooded in June 1543, its waters rising just to where the newly constructed boats lay. The Spaniards eased the boats into the water on July 2 and began their long voyage down the river. Additional losses were suffered when Indian attackers, including some from Quigualtam, came after them in large war canoes. When the beleaguered flotilla finally reached the mouth of the Mississippi River, a lone Indian standing on the bank called out: "If we possessed such large canoes as yours, we would follow you to your own land and conquer it, for we too are men like yourselves."

Who were the Indians the Spaniards encountered in Arkansas? We cannot answer this question with certainty, because accounts of Soto's expedition provide only sketchy information about native populations and even sketchier information about routes traveled and places visited. Names attributed to the Indians the Spaniards met, or sometimes only heard about, may be names used by the people themselves or names they were called by other people, such as native guides or interpreters who spoke other languages. It is often impossible to decide which is the case. Spanish chroniclers undoubtedly also introduced many phonetic errors as they translated Indian words into their own languages (archaic dialects of Spanish and Portuguese). These circumstances all complicate our efforts to use exploration accounts to determine the cultural identity of sixteenth-century native communities.

The most frustrating problem, however, lies in the fact that French explorers Marquette and Jolliet, who were the next Europeans to visit Arkansas, used completely different names to identify Indians they met in 1673. It is also clear that the cultural landscape French explorers observed in the Mississippi Valley was much different from the one described by earlier Spanish writers. For example, Marquette and Jolliet mention only a single Mitchigamea (an Illinoian Indian group) village in northeast Arkansas, a region Soto's chroniclers described as one of the most populous in all of the Southeast. Whether any of the groups identified in seventeenth-century French accounts were descended from groups mentioned in the earlier Spanish accounts is another question for which there is no satisfactory answer.

Some information provided in Soto expedition accounts permits speculation concerning possible cultural identities of native populations in sixteenth-century Arkansas. First, language barriers can be identified that separated Cayas and Tula, and Anilco and Guachoya. There likely were others, but even this information can be used to outline major linguistic boundaries. Southeastern North America is a region where extensive linguistic diversity existed among native tribes, and anthropologists have found it useful to identify groups in relation to their membership in broad families of closely related languages. The five major language families represented in the Southeast are Algonkian, Muskogean, Iroquoian, Siouan, and Caddoan, and native words recorded in the accounts can sometimes be used to infer membership in one of these families.

Second, reports of instances in which Indians were surprised at the arrival of Spaniards suggest the existence of cultural boundaries. Such boundaries evidently separated Casqui and Pacaha in northeastern Arkansas, and the province of Coligua along the eastern fringes of the Ozarks from all of the groups in the central Mississippi Valley. Luis Hernández de Biedma's statement that Spaniards arrived at Tula "before the inhabitants had any notice of us" also corresponds with the above-mentioned linguistic boundary separating that group from inhabitants of the Arkansas River Valley.

A third category of information consists of differences in settlement patterns, that likely also reflect cultural boundaries. Compact, fortified towns located along the Mississippi, St. Francis, and lower Arkansas rivers can be contrasted with dispersed farmsteads observed in the province of Cayas farther up the Arkansas River and in the Red River region of southwest Arkansas and eastern Texas.

It is possible to infer from this information the existence of five regions. First is the central Mississippi Valley from Pacaha on the north to Anilco on the south, and extending up the Arkansas River as far as Autiamque. Next is the lower Mississippi Valley extending from Guachoya to the south for an undetermined distance but probably at least as far as Quigualtam. Third is the lower White River Valley beginning at Coligua and extending for an undetermined distance up that valley toward the Ozarks. Fourth is a Ouachita Mountain region minimally including Tula, whom we assume were Caddoan speakers. Last is a Red River Valley region of more Caddoan speakers. It is possible, of course, that other cultural regions existed.

It is difficult, if not impossible, to attribute modern tribal names to the groups occupying these five regions. Least contentious is the Caddo cultural identity attributed to sixteenth-century inhabitants of the Red River Valley. Many scholars have suggested that the Tula were a northern offshoot of the Caddo tribes living farther to the south, and some believe that they were antecedents of the Cahinnio Indians encountered in the Ouachita Mountain region by French explorers in the seventeenth century. Others argue that Tula Indians were an ancestral group of Wichitas, another Caddoan-speaking group who in later historic times lived on the Southern Plains.

The cultural identities of the remaining groups are harder to determine, and attempts to make such identifications have stimulated considerable debate. Marvin Jeter has suggested a Tunican affiliation for groups along the Arkansas River in the province of Cayas and especially in the town of Tanico. A 1673 map drawn by Father Marquette suggests that Tunicans lived along the Arkansas River then, if not earlier. The southeastern Arkansas province of Guachoya has also been considered Tunican. A number of archeological sites in that region have produced sixteenth-century Indian ceramics that resemble slightly later ceramics from Tunica sites in western Mississippi. Late-seventeenth-century French accounts also mention Tunican groups along the lower Ouachita River in Arkansas as well as near Bayou Bartholomew in extreme southeast Arkansas near the Louisiana state line.

Much debate, however, concerns the cultural identity of sixteenth-century groups inhabiting the lower Arkansas River Valley and adjacent portions of northeastern

Arkansas. Dan Morse suggests that Pacahans (and perhaps the rival Casquins as well) were ancestors of later Quapaw Indians. Quapaws are Siouan speakers and they lived in four villages around the confluence of the Arkansas and Mississippi when French explorers descended the Mississippi River in the late seventeenth century. However, the square houses found on sixteenth-century sites in northeastern Arkansas and along the lower Arkansas River differ significantly from the bark-covered longhouses described by seventeenth-century Frenchmen visiting Quapaw villages. An alternative hypothesis, offered by Michael Hoffman, is that the Quapaws migrated into the lower Arkansas River Valley after the 1543 departure of the Spaniards but prior to French explorations. This hypothesis is based on a Quapaw tradition that describes their ancestors coming to Arkansas from homelands in the lower Ohio River Valley, whereupon they drove away other groups of Tunican and Illinoian Indians. In a more recent essay Marvin Jeter suggests that protohistoric tribal movements were possibly even more complicated, and that a northern offshoot of the Natchez Indian nation might have occupied at least part of the lower Arkansas River Valley. Clearly, much additional research is required to resolve these issues.

Protohistoric: A term used by archeologists and historians to refer to the A.D. 1500–1700 period in the Southeast when the first contacts between Europeans and Indians began to occur but few historic documents were being produced.

Encounters with Spanish explorers had tragic consequences for native peoples of the Southeast, whatever their cultural identities may have been. Impacts of battles and of enslavement took a horrific toll upon native populations. Introduction of Old World diseases against which the Indians had no immunity—smallpox, tuberculosis, plague, typhus, influenza, yellow fever, measles, and possibly malaria and mumps—also affected many groups. These impacts were compounded by the effects of environmental changes documented by recent tree-ring studies by David Stahle and associates that have identified evidence of severe droughts at the time the Spanish invasion took place. The combined pressures of population reduction and environmental stresses must have resulted in tremendous cultural losses. Deaths in disproportionate numbers of elderly people responsible for passing on important cultural traditions, and of the young who would inherit those traditions, dealt fatal blows both to the heritage of the past and hopes for the future.

Many larger and more complex Southeastern Indian communities collapsed in response to these circumstances, leaving intact only smaller communities organized on the basis of local kinship rules and interpersonal relationships. Some of these communities, particularly those who had only minor or indirect engagements with the Spaniards, were able to mend wounded bodies, villages, and lands and resume their lives, though now with what must have been a vastly altered perspective on the world. Other groups could only collect the shattered fragments of their former existence in the hope of developing new cultural ways (often in new locations) that maintained some ties with the past but looked toward a new and significantly different future. These were the societies encountered by the next wave of explorers: Frenchmen who voyaged down the Mississippi River from Canada and Illinois.

French Expeditions down the Mississippi, 1673–1686

Eager to expand the economic fortunes of New France, King Louis XIV's colonial minister Jean-Baptiste Colbert and Quebec governor general Louis de Buade, Compte de Frontenac encouraged several explorations of the North American interior. One of the most important of these began in June 1673, when the Jesuit missionary Jacques Marquette departed from Green Bay, Wisconsin, with his fur-trader companion Louis Jolliet on an expedition to explore the Mississippi River in search of an outlet to the "Southern Sea"—as the Caribbean Ocean was then called. Traveling in two canoes with several Indian guides, they arrived the following month at a village of Akamsea Indians located along the Mississippi a few miles north of where the White River enters (the name Akamsea and variations thereof—e.g., Akansas, Arkansas—comes from a term used in reference to Quapaws by Algonquian-speaking Illinois Indians, who guided early French explorers down the Mississippi). Quapaws, who probably had already received information about the pending arrival of explorers from their Illinoian neighbors to the north, welcomed Marquette and Jolliet with a calumet ceremony and then regaled them with a feast. The calumet used in the ceremony (a decorated wooden shaft with a carved stone tobacco pipe attached to one end) was presented to Marquette as a symbol of peace and friendship and to ensure safe travel through the territories of Quapaw allies. With access to English traders blocked by enemy Chickasaws who controlled the opposite side of the Mississippi River, Quapaws were quick in urging Marquette to stay and instruct them in the mysteries of the Catholic faith, undoubtedly perceiving his presence as the most sure way to open trade relations with the French. Perhaps in order to discourage their visitors from moving on, Quapaws advised the explorers that the lower reaches of the Mississippi were heavily populated with many enemy tribes. Gaining from this information a confirmation that the Mississippi River did indeed flow south to the sea, Marquette and Jolliet decided at this point to return north, assuring Quapaws that their desire for a priest would be satisfied.

Calumet: A decorated wooden shaft, attached to a carved stone pipe, that seventeenth-century Indians in the Mississippi Valley used in greeting ceremonies to welcome visitors into their villages.

Nine years later the Quapaws were visited by a larger group of French explorers led by René-Robert Cavelier, Sieur de La Salle. Born in Rouen, France, in 1643 and emigrating to Canada in 1667, La Salle played a crucial role in opening up the Mississippi Valley for French exploration and settlement. A successful fur trader and tireless explorer of the Great Lakes region, La Salle turned his attention to the Mississippi River after it was rediscovered in 1673 by Marquette and Jolliet. La Salle won the support of King Louis XIV in 1678 to build a series of forts along the Mississippi as part of a search for the great river's mouth. The first of these forts, named Crèvecœur, or "heartbreak," was constructed along the Illinois River during the winter of 1679–1680 when La Salle's party suffered many hardships. Forced to return north the following summer for additional provisions, La Salle delayed his exploration until late in 1681. He finally reached

La Salle at the mouth of the Mississippi. *From Josiah H. Shinn,* History of the American People *(New York: 1893), 59.*

the Mississippi, the destination he had sought with great difficulty for four long years, in February 1682.

Traveling down the Mississippi in a dense fog on March 12, La Salle and his party of Frenchmen and Illinois Indian guides, numbering about forty people in all, struck for the eastern bank of the river and began felling trees to construct a protective barricade when they heard what they believed to be war cries coming from the noisy Quapaw village of Kappa, located on the western side of the river, where a celebration was in progress. When the Quapaws noticed the Frenchmen's activities, they sent out a canoe with observers, one of whom fired an arrow toward the strangers. Henri de Tonty, La Salle's aide and a trader with considerable experience among Indians of the Illinois country, understood this as a sign, and by not returning fire assured the Quapaws that he and his companions had come in peace. La Salle sent a calumet obtained from Illinois Indians to the Quapaws, and soon six village leaders came forth bearing their own calumet.

As they had done earlier with Marquette and Jolliet, the Quapaws put on a grand celebration to welcome their guests. Displaying on wood pole racks an assortment of gifts intended for the Frenchmen, the Quapaws brought out two elaborately decorated calumets. The leaders and warriors arranged themselves in the middle of the open ceremonial grounds and struck up a song accompanied by the chime of gourd rattles and the beat of drums made by stretching damp hides over fired-clay pottery vessels. A second song was performed while warriors proceeded one at a time to a post set in the center of the grounds which they struck with war axes while relating gallant achievements, after which they presented gifts to La Salle. While this was going on, leaders smoked the calumet and passed it around for everyone else to partake. La Salle, recipient of several dozen dressed buffalo hides, directed his men to follow suit in striking the post and distributing gifts in return from supplies he provided.

The next day, March 14, La Salle took possession of the region in the name of the king—calling the territory La Louisiane—with great and elaborate ceremony. The Frenchmen set up a column adorned with a plaque emblazoned with the royal coat of arms and an inscription, then recited a proclamation in which the Quapaw-French alliance was announced. They processed around the column at the lead of chanting priests, and fired volleys from guns while shouting, "Vive le roi!" We can only guess what Quapaws made of this spectacle, but surely they attempted to understand the performance in terms of counterpart elements of their own ceremonies. In an act reminiscent of Soto's visit to the region more than a century earlier, La Salle also had a large cross erected on the surface of an artificial platform mound, which Quapaws regarded with considerable interest according to the expedition's missionary, Father Zénobe Membré.

La Salle's entourage visited three other Quapaw villages, all located along the lower Arkansas River, at each of which additional feasts and gift exchanges took place. On March 18, La Salle continued his voyage down the Mississippi with Quapaw guides leading the way as far as the villages of their allies, the Taensas Indians. Upon reaching the Gulf Coast, La Salle performed another ceremony of possession, similar to the one performed at Kappa, before returning upriver. When the explorers returned to the Quapaw villages several weeks later, the Indians were amazed by the fact that not one Frenchman had been lost. Accordingly, they put on feasts of special honor and exchanged additional gifts with the Frenchmen. Father Membré noticed that the cross planted earlier at Kappa was now surrounded by a circle of cane stalks.

Upon his return to Montreal, La Salle sailed to France where he gained audience with Louis XIV to request support for a naval expedition to the mouth of the Mississippi, where a small colony would be established to secure France's claim to Louisiana against English encroachments from the east and Spanish advances from the west. The king approved La Salle's plan, which contained misleading information concerning the distance between the Mississippi River and Spanish territories to the west. La Salle was granted two vessels, the *Joly* and the *Belle,* along with supplies for the contingent, which included about one hundred and thirty men, women, and children who would comprise the colony's founding population. La Salle chartered two additional ships, a large cargo vessel called the *Aimable* and a smaller vessel named the *St. François.*

The flotilla departed France on August 1, 1684. On the voyage across the Atlantic, La Salle had a falling out with Captain Beaujeu of the *Joly*. The *St. François,* loaded with valuable supplies, was captured by Spanish pirates. Then the expedition sailed past the Mississippi Delta, landing in Matagorda Bay near present-day Victoria, Texas, on February 20, 1685. The *Aimable* was wrecked during the landing, the crew able to rescue only a few of its supplies. As soon as the colonists and the remaining supplies were offloaded, Beaujeu and the *Joly* returned to France, leaving La Salle with one remaining supply ship, the *Belle.*

La Salle's settlement, named Fort St. Louis, experienced difficulty from the start. The *Belle* was lost in an accident in the fall of 1686, leaving the colonists desperately short on supplies. Illness and disease followed; these and other hardships brought growing discord among the dwindling number of colonists. La Salle undertook three overland expeditions in search of "his river," intent on reaching supply posts in the Illinois country. The first expedition ventured unsuccessfully to the west. The second expedition followed a better route toward the northeast, but La Salle succumbed to a fever from which he spent a month in recovery at a Caddo village in eastern Texas. On the third expedition, which departed in January 1687, La Salle was murdered by a small group of disgruntled companions who briefly commandeered the expedition before committing additional murders among themselves.

At this point some expedition members disappeared into Caddo villages, but Henri Joutel and five others, including La Salle's brother Jean Cavelier, continued their northeastward trek. Traveling from village to village with the assistance of Caddo guides, the small group of refugees made its way back to the Arkansas country where they were led to the Quapaw village of Osotuoy on the lower Arkansas River. There they discovered, to their amazement and relief, a small trading house built in the French style and operated by Jean Couture and another Frenchmen named Delaunay. This post, the first Arkansas Post, had been constructed the previous year by Henri de Tonty, who had revisited the Quapaw villages en route down the Mississippi during an unsuccessful search for La Salle's settlement. See plate 12 following page 126.

Hoping to improve relations with their new French allies, the Quapaws eagerly questioned the travelers for news of La Salle, whom they fondly remembered. Fearing the consequences of revealing the unfortunate truth about the Fort St. Louis disaster, Joutel reported only that they had just come from La Salle's new settlement on the coast where they hoped soon to return with a load of supplies; secretly, he confided the facts to Couture. Joutel and his companions agreed only to an abbreviated version of the ceremonies the Quapaws offered to perform in their honor before continuing on their way. Upon departing Arkansas Post, Joutel and his companions left a young boy from Paris, named Barthélemy, as a pledge to demonstrate their intent to return. Meanwhile, nearly all Fort St. Louis colonists perished, many from disease and starvation and the rest from an attack by Karankawa Indians. Two young boys, Pierre and Jean Talon, survived the attack and were adopted by an Indian family. They were later repatriated when a French warship captured a Spanish vessel on which they were being held; their story revealed finally and in some detail the tiny colony's fatal end.

La Salle's adventures along the Gulf Coast played an important role in fueling international rivalries, especially between France and Spain, for control of the vast borderlands region west of the Mississippi and north of Mexico. France's attempt to colonize the lower Mississippi Valley might have ended in Matagorda Bay had Henri de Tonty not established his small trading post along the banks of the Arkansas River. The existence of the 1687 Arkansas Post permitted Joutel and his companions to continue their journey to Montreal, where information they transmitted stimulated continuing interest in the region. The native groups occupying the lower Mississippi Valley provided a network of social, economic, and political relationships into which Tonty and subsequent European colonists became incorporated. Before we continue our exploration of the colonial era, let us consider first the native communities living in Arkansas when French colonial endeavors began.

CHAPTER FOUR

New Traditions for a New World: Seventeenth- and Eighteenth-Century Native Americans in Arkansas

French and Spanish explorers who visited Arkansas during the seventeenth and eighteenth centuries left valuable accounts of native people they met. Groups identified in these accounts include Quapaws living around the Mississippi and Arkansas River confluence, Caddos living in the Red and Ouachita river valleys, and Tunicas and closely related Koroas living in the Mississippi Valley region of central and southeastern Arkansas. Osage Indians, who controlled a vast territory that included much of northern Arkansas, established their main villages along major tributaries of the Missouri River.

As descendants of pre-Columbian communities described in the second chapter of this book, Quapaws, Caddos, Tunicas, Koroas, and Osages carried into the historic era legacies of their more ancient ancestors. Those legacies are reflected in cultural practices around which descendant communities organized their affairs. This chapter summarizes the most characteristic traditions and practices each of these groups carried into the historic era, as events in colonial Louisiana began to shape the destiny of the American South.

Quapaws

Quapaws belong to the Dhegiha subdivision of the Siouan language family and are closely related to Osage, Omaha, Kansa (Kaw), and Ponca tribes, all of whom speak similar dialects. From the time of their first encounters with early French explorers, Quapaws maintained steadfast alliances with European and American neighbors. Their strategic location astride the Mississippi River midway between St. Louis and New Orleans gave Quapaws an important role in the development of the Louisiana colony.

Wakondah: The creative, universal life force in Osage and Quapaw religious thought.

Quapaws believed that a supernatural force called Wakondah created the world before people emerged from the womb of the earth to live upon its surface. They attributed supernatural qualities to the sun, moon, and thunder, and they believed that plants and animals also possessed spiritual gifts that could assist human endeavors. Quapaws shared a widely held belief among Southeastern Indians in human responsibility to maintain, through periodic ritual performances, a favorable balance of relationships among various communities—plant, animal, and human—sharing the earth's surface and the spiritual forces influencing affairs of the world.

Quapaw villages exhibited a distinctive layout and architecture that provided the setting for an equally distinctive pattern of community life. Four villages existed at the end of the seventeenth century, named Kappa, Osotuoy, Tourima, and Tongigua. Each consisted of elongated dwellings, often referred to as longhouses, arranged around a central, open plaza. The council house stood closest to the plaza, where there was also a partially enclosed, elevated platform on which village leaders and other important people sat during outdoor ceremonies. Longhouses occupied by several families related through the male (or father's) line were constructed by driving poles into the ground in parallel rows, then bending and tying the tops of the poles to create an arched framework that could be interwoven with horizontal laths. The framework was covered with sheets of bark. Platforms for sitting and sleeping were constructed along inner walls and at the ends of structures. Hearths set along the midline provided each family with heat, light, and a place to cook their meals. Each village also had a sacred temple for important religious ceremonies. These were built in the same way as houses but with a square floor plan. Seventeenth-century French accounts indicate that some temples stood on ancient platform mounds.

Quapaw society was organized in terms of inherited statuses and relationships acquired through marriage. Each individual belonged to a descent group traced through his or her father's line. Identification with a particular generation or even with a particular family was less important than membership in a descent group. Adult brothers and male cousins, along with their wives, lived together in the longhouses described above, each family occupying part of the house surrounding their hearth.

Descent groups were organized into clans, of which nineteenth-century anthropologists counted more than twenty. Each clan had a guardian spirit—usually an animal or some element of nature, such as lightning—considered to be relatives who conferred on clan members the right to perform sacred rituals. Although names of only a few Quapaw clans have been preserved in the historical record, clans were divided into two groups, called Sky People and Earth People. Clans representing the Earth People performed rituals that helped sustain community physical and material well-being while clans representing the Sky People performed rituals devoted to maintenance of spiritual affairs. Sky People and Earth People divisions also regulated marriage, since a person could only marry someone belonging to certain clans in the opposite division.

Clan: A kinship-based social unit in Southeastern Indian communities with various ceremonial responsibilities, with membership determined by line of descent.

Each village had an overall leader whose office was inherited through the male line. Although community members accorded these leaders considerable esteem, their authority rested mainly on powers of persuasion. A council of male elders and clan leaders assisted the leader at village councils, at war councils, and during various other ceremonies. Village councils met in large council houses, where participants were seated by rank. The leader and council of elders occupied positions of highest honor, followed by warriors and then other community members. Each village made decisions concerning only its own affairs. Representatives attending inter-village councils discussed issues affecting the tribe as a whole.

Public ceremonies marked important events in the life of Quapaw communities. Planting ceremonies held in spring honored the efforts of women who sowed and tended crops and offered thanks to creative forces associated with sunshine, rain, and the earth's fertility. A Green Corn ceremony performed later during summer celebrated and gave thanks for successful crop production, and provided an opportunity to renew family ties. Gifts and prayers offered throughout the year helped maintain this cycle of life.

Many rituals involved complicated practices associated with esoteric knowledge. Accordingly, some Quapaws underwent special training to acquire skills that permitted them to serve their communities as medical specialists, genealogists, and leaders of ceremonies performed to celebrate the passage of individuals through crucial stages of life, such as naming ceremonies for infants, marriage ceremonies, and funeral rites.

Quapaws centered their food production on agriculture. They grew corn, beans, squash, gourds, melons, and tobacco in large fields scattered around villages. Quapaws also cultivated fruit trees introduced by European colonists. They collected wild plant foods, including fruits, nuts, seeds, and roots. Deer, bear, and buffalo provided meat, hides, tallow, and oil. Small mammals, turkeys, fish and other aquatic species, and waterfowl were also taken. Quapaws kept dogs and European-introduced chickens and horses as domestic animals.

Quapaw women managed crop production, and they also butchered animals captured in the chase and prepared hides. They gathered wood and wild foods, cooked food, cared for children, and managed household affairs. The agricultural cycle was marked by a series of rituals that recognized their contribution to the maintenance of the community. Quapaw participation in the colonial era frontier exchange economy, though limited in comparison to many other tribes, created additional work for women in preparing hides and other commodities intended for trade.

Men hunted, fished, waged war, and managed community and political affairs. Men held most political and religious leadership positions. Village council deliberations required that participants first undergo ritual acts of purification, which often included taking sweat baths or "washing" the body with smoke from a special fire, since these were regarded as sacred proceedings. As with women, trading demands of the frontier exchange economy also affected men's activities.

Quapaw women wore deerskin skirts that reached from the waist to the knees. Clothing and bodily ornamentation continued to serve the age-old tradition of signaling social identities based on tribal and clan membership, gender, and age grade. Married women wore their hair loose, while unmarried women wove their hair in braids rolled into coils secured behind the ears and decorated with ornaments. Men wore only loincloths during warm seasons, later adding leggings, moccasins, and cloth shirts as these became popular during the colonial era. They decorated themselves with tattoos and strings of beads in their ears and noses. Everybody wore buffalo robes to ward off the cold of winter. For ceremonial occasions, Quapaws painted themselves red and black and wore headdresses, masks, and other ornaments decorated with paint, feathers, buffalo horns, and animal furs. See plate 13 following page 126.

Other items of material culture—many of which were stylized to reflect Quapaw identity—include woven cane and animal skin mats used to cover sitting and sleeping platforms. Quapaw women made woven baskets, pottery vessels, and wooden platters used for household as well as for ceremonial purposes. Quapaw men earned high regard for their skill in manufacturing dugout canoes, a trade item sought by many other groups. They hunted with bows and arrows and used spears to catch fish. Gourd rattles and drums added a musical component to public ceremonies.

Relations with other tribes consisted of warfare with enemies or alliances created with friends for purposes of trade or to wage war against a common enemy. War preparations involved elaborate rituals to purify participants and ensure the blessings of spirit beings. Warriors who agreed to participate received a small token to secure their commitment and to guarantee a subsequent reward if the attack succeeded. A war club painted red, the color symbolizing war and bloodshed and also the color associated with poisonous insects and snakes, was placed at the edge of enemy territory or, alternatively, an arrow insignia would be carved into a tree. Quapaws sometimes enlisted allies from other tribes. Prior to battle, warriors in paint and full regalia acted out the anticipated battle. The war leader, after fasting and undergoing additional purification rites, made a final speech to inspire his followers before the group commenced their journey into hostile territory.

Trade relations, especially with Europeans, grew steadily during the colonial era. Quapaw involvement in the frontier exchange economy, in which crops, meat, hides, and other indigenous products were traded for European goods, had a profound effect on the economic roles of men and women, as increasing time and effort became directed toward production of the goods sought after by European merchants. In return, Quapaws and their neighbors gained access to new kinds of food, clothing, tools and utensils, and firearms, on which they became increasingly dependent and through which many changes were introduced to day-to-day activities and appearances.

> **Frontier exchange economy:** An economic system in colonial Louisiana in which Indian goods (food, hides, other animal products) were exchanged with traders, via face-to-face bartering, for European goods (firearms, cloth, ornaments, tools, etc.).

The calumet ceremony was an important rite for securing alliances with other groups, Indian or European. The calumet, or "peace pipe," was a two-piece object consisting of a decorated wooden stick, about two feet long, attached to a bowl carved of red pipestone, or catlinite. The calumet ceremony was an elaborate affair involving feasting, dancing, gift exchanges, and, of course, passing the calumet for all of the participants to smoke. The ceremony created kinship-like relations between participants so that allies would be bound by the same kinds of mutual obligations that clan or family members shared. Sometimes, the calumet ceremony was used to adopt outsiders into social positions vacated by important or well-remembered people who recently had died.

The calumet ceremony served as the primary means by which Quapaws interacted with Europeans and Americans during much of the historic era. Consequently, obligations and expectations shared by clan members in Quapaw society extended to relations with Europeans and Americans. Throughout much of the colonial era, relations between Quapaws and their French and Spanish neighbors were so close that Europeans often established their settlements alongside Quapaw villages. Intermarriages (the extent of which is uncertain) created ties that conferred a multiethnic character on both Quapaw and neighboring European villages.

Osages

Like Quapaws, Osages also belong to the Dhegiha subdivision of the Siouan language family. Their eighteenth-century villages were located on the Missouri and Osage rivers in southwestern Missouri, but seasonal hunting and trading forays brought them annually into northern Arkansas.

Osages called themselves "Children of the Middle Waters." In the beginning, Wakondah separated air, earth, and water from the original middle waters to create a place for people to live. Major components of the universe are sky and earth, and night and day, representing everlasting cycles through which all living things pass. Osages trace their origin to a time long ago when the Sky People descended from the heavens and met the Isolated Earth People whom they joined to create the Osage tribe.

Osage villages were organized with reference to cosmological principles defining the major dimensions of the universe. Houses stood on either side of a main road running east to west, which symbolized the earth's surface between the sky above and the underworld below. Two village leaders lived on opposite sides of the main road in the center of the village. Sky People occupied clan neighborhoods on the same side of the road as their leader, while Earth People arranged their houses on the opposite side, with their leader.

Osages lived in oval or rectangular dwellings, built in much the same way as Quapaw longhouses and covered with buffalo hides, bark sheets, or woven mats. These houses had smoke vents in the roofs and doors opening to the east (village leaders' houses had two doors, one at either end). Some houses occupied by several related families measured as much as one hundred feet long. Smaller, circular huts were constructed for use as single-family dwellings or as sweat lodges. In permanent villages, special lodges provided space for council meetings and rituals.

Sweat lodge: A small hut where the internal temperature could be raised for performance of purification rituals.

Osages divided their overall population into five major groups, called bands, each of which had its own village. Village life was patterned by customs maintained by a group of religious leaders called Little Old Men. This group of male elders was responsible for establishing standards for appropriate conduct, advising village leaders, making important decisions affecting tribal affairs in times of peace and war, and maintaining sacred knowledge and traditions. To attain the ranks of Little Old Men, serious-minded individuals underwent lengthy instruction, which began during youth. Individuals could pass through as many as seven degrees of learning, at each degree acquiring familiarity with, and authority to use, a particular body of sacred lore. One might compare such intensive training with advanced degree programs offered at modern universities.

Little Old Men: Osage religious leaders who undertake a lifelong commitment to mastering sacred lore.

Osages trace their ancestry through the father's line. Like Quapaws, individuals belong to clans, each representing one of two divisions—Sky People and Earth People. Every clan was responsible for rituals and other activities performed on behalf of the entire tribe. An interesting feature of split ritual responsibilities is that members of Earth People clans were required to assist Sky People clans, and vice versa. In this way, division of ritual responsibilities among the clans produced a set of activities that created an overall solidarity of purpose. Each clan also appointed representatives to village and tribal councils. Osage villages thus had two overall leaders: the leader of the Sky People was in charge of matters related to peace, while the leader of the Earth People was responsible for matters concerning war.

Families, rather than individuals, planned for marriages of children. Men and women had to marry outside of their clan division and usually outside of their village. A young man's family typically sent gifts to a prospective bride's family. These were kept if the marriage proposal was accepted and returned if not. Sometimes a man took his first wife's sisters in marriage, and, since inheritance passed through the male line, a man often married his deceased brother's widow so that he could provide for his brother's children.

Hunting, gathering, and gardening produced most of the food and raw materials consumed in Osage communities. Men and women cleared fields along river bottoms adjacent to each village during spring. Women from each family tended their own plots of corn, beans, squashes, pumpkins, and tobacco until the plants were established. Residents of several villages then gathered together in large camps and traveled west during summer, to Kansas and Nebraska, to hunt buffalo. During the hunt, the tribal camping circle reflected the village arrangement of clans and divisions. The bow and arrow was the primary hunting weapon until it was replaced by firearms in the colonial era. Men, women, and children all participated in the hunt, each group playing specific roles that were coordinated in strict military order. Hunting groups returned to the villages in autumn to harvest ripened crops, and to gather nuts, fruits, and other wild plant foods. People from several villages gathered again in fall to hunt buffalo, deer, elk, and other animals in favorite areas. Northern Arkansas was one area used extensively by Osage groups during early historic times. During winter people moved back to their Missouri villages, surviving on stored garden produce and animals taken locally. A late winter or early spring hunt for beaver and bear took families away from their villages once again, until it was time to return for spring planting.

Osage men hunted and waged war, defended their villages against enemies, and managed most community economic and political affairs. Men shaved their heads, leaving only a scalp lock or roach extending from the forehead to the back of the neck. Different scalp lock designs identified a man's clan membership. Men wore deerskin loincloths, leggings, and moccasins, with bearskin or buffalo robes added during cold weather. They wore ornaments in their ears and on their arms, and warriors tattooed their upper bodies. Body paint was worn for ceremonial occasions.

Women performed a wide variety of activities in addition to planting and tending crops and preparing meals. Women built houses, along with most of the interior furnishings and utensils. They also worked hides and made clothing, and wove sashes, belts, neckbands, and cords from buffalo hair and nettle weed fibers. Special decorations were added to items used in religious and social ceremonies. Following a widespread practice among Southeastern Indians, many items were made in ways designed to reflect Osage identities and social statuses.

Women kept their hair long and loose. They wore deerskin dresses cinched at the waist with woven belts, along with leggings and moccasins. Jewelry consisted of earrings, pendants, and bracelets, and many women decorated their bodies with elaborate tattoos. They donned ceremonial garments decorated with bits of ermine and puma fur for special occasions, perfumed with chewed columbine seed. Osage women wore scented powder and perfume made from flowers and enhanced their complexions by rubbing the dried pulp of pumpkins into their skin.

Family, clan, and village all shared in the responsibilities of raising children. Fathers instructed sons in skills of hunting and warfare, while mothers taught daughters how to tend crops and manage domestic affairs. Elders taught values and important social and religious beliefs. Each child was carefully nurtured so Osage culture would persist through succeeding generations.

Major changes in the Osage way of life came through their involvement in trade with Europeans. Occupying the prairie ecotone connecting woodland environments on the east and plains environments to the west, the Osages found themselves in a geographical position well suited for managing trade relations connecting tribes scattered across a wide area with merchants in St. Louis, the major regional trading center. Consequently, involvement in the frontier exchange economy did much more than affect the economic roles of men and women in Osage communities; it had a profound impact on larger political and military alliances, as other Indian groups challenged Osage control of trade across the prairie-plains borderlands.

Caddos

Several communities dispersed around the Great Bend of the Red River in southwest Arkansas and eastern Texas comprised the Kadohadacho alliance of Caddoan speakers. The Natchitoches Indians lived in several villages in what is now present-day Louisiana.

Osage traders, by Charles Banks Wilson. *Courtesy of the artist and Nancy Pillsbury Shirley.*

Hasinai villages were located farther west along the upper Angelina and Neches rivers in east Texas. The Cahinnios, allies of the Kadohadachos in the seventeenth century, lived in the Ouachita River drainage in western Arkansas.

The Kadohadacho, Natchitoches, and Hasinai alliances each consisted of several autonomous communities connected through diplomatic ties. These groups, plus the Cahinnios (whose population distribution is less certain), represent the southern core of Caddoan-speaking people. Distantly related to Plains Caddoan speakers including the Wichitas, Pawnees, Arikaras, and Kitsais, the southern groups occupied a vast area between the northern borderlands of New Spain and the Mississippi Valley. Consequently, southern Caddos played a pivotal role in the contests for empire between France and Spain.

Creation stories tell how the Caddo world came to exist. One Kadohadacho version traces origins to a cave in a hill named Chakanina (or "place of crying") out of which came an old man from the underworld bringing fire, a pipe, and a drum. The old man's wife accompanied him, bringing corn and pumpkin seeds. Others followed, both people and animals, but before they could all make their escape Wolf closed the cave's entrance, trapping forever those who remained below. The people on the surface wept bitterly for those left behind, before they dispersed across the land to create their new homes.

Caddo settlements consisted of several family farmsteads dispersed at intervals along major rivers and streams. Some of these settlements stretched for miles. Extended (multigenerational) families or groups of closely related families occupied an area of sufficient size to build dwellings and clear crop fields. A typical farmstead consisted of one or two grass-thatched, circular dwellings plus elevated corncribs, work platforms, and log mortars for pounding corn into meal. Family garden plots and woodlots surrounded the farmsteads. The compound of the village leader, or *caddi*, usually occupied a central place in the dispersed community of farmsteads. The sacred fire temple, managed by a set of priests who conducted sacred rituals, was also located in close proximity to the farmsteads.

Caddi: Caddo village leader.

Since several families might occupy a single house, these structures sometimes measured as much as sixty feet in diameter. A hearth fed by four large logs oriented to the cardinal directions occupied the center of each house, lit from an ember brought from the fire in the village's sacred temple. The sense of community that nearby families shared derived in part from common use of the sacred fire to light family hearths, thereby linking each household to the same temple. At the rear and along either side of the interior were family quarters containing sleeping platforms elevated three or four feet above the floor, made of woven cane mats supported by a pole framework. Buffalo robes covered the mats, and additional mats—some decorated with brightly colored designs—were arched over the platforms to create alcoves. Other platforms and lofts provided storage space for food supplies and utensils. Although each family maintained its own supplies, the central fire was shared by all. A head woman prepared meals from contributions made by each family, and supervised most other domestic activities.

The building blocks of Caddo communities consisted of clans. Every person belonged to a clan. Clan affiliation was inherited either from the mother or the father, depending on which parent's clan was regarded as the strongest. An individual from one community could always identify members of his or her clan when visiting other communities and therefore could rely upon those individuals for shelter and assistance. People chose as spouses members of other clans.

Political organization was based on a hierarchy of offices. Leadership at the community level was vested in the office of the caddi, who held authority in numerous civic and religious affairs. Upon the death of this leader, the office would pass to the eldest son or closest male heir. Many other officials assisted the caddi in directing community affairs, including house construction and preparation of fields. Other specialists performed specific rituals including blessing food and treating illnesses. A head priest known as the *xinesi* possessed authority in both civil and religious affairs that extended across several allied communities. The xinesi was a full-time managerial specialist, supported by contributions from the families of associated communities.

The Caddo world was populated by many spirit beings. The Supreme Being, Ayo-Caddi-Aymay, was regarded as the most powerful spirit. His power was represented by the sun in the daytime sky and the sacred fire burning on the community temple mound. This deity had authority over other beings and forces that affected daily events in the world. Rituals performed throughout the year served to maintain positive relations among the observable and unseen components of the Caddo world. The most important ceremonies regulated the agricultural cycle. A forecasting ceremony was held in spring, at which priests contacted spirit beings to obtain information with which to make an almanac for the coming year. A planting ceremony served to honor women as they began the sacred task of crop production. A first fruits ceremony was performed later in the summer to bless the crops as they began to ripen. A harvest ceremony held in the fall was the largest celebration of the year, during which the people gave thanks for the year's crops and performed other rites that reinforced community solidarity. Other important activities, including house construction, warfare, trade fairs, births, marriages, and deaths, required the performance of additional rituals.

Xinesi: The head priest who presided over sacred fire temples in Caddo villages.

Ayo-Caddi-Aymay: The Supreme Being in seventeenth-century Caddo belief.

House construction and the clearing and planting of fields were communal activities that reveal much about the nature and organization of Caddo villages. When a new house had to be constructed, the caddi set a date for the event and dispatched his assistants to notify community members and assign each person's responsibilities. On the morning of the appointed day, the caddi arrived at the building site and took his seat in a place of honor from which he could observe the work. At the call of the individual in charge of the work detail, others arrived bringing wall posts, laths, bundles of grass thatch, or other materials they had been assigned to supply. Everyone pitched in to build the house using these materials. Upon completion, a priest performed a blessing ceremony and the participants shared a feast provided by the new owners of the house.

Caddo women planted fields of corn, beans, pumpkins, squashes, watermelons, sunflowers, and tobacco. Family fields were cleared adjacent to the farmsteads. As with house building, the preparation of fields in spring was a community undertaking. When the time came for the crops to be planted, the residents of a community, including the caddi (who again served in the capacity of overseer), gathered at one farmstead to clear the ground with picks and hoes and prepare the soil for sowing. These preparations generally took only part of the day to complete. As the work was in progress, the family whose fields were being cleared prepared a feast to be shared, followed by games and socializing. Community members prepared each farmstead's fields in turn, until all of the village planting was finished.

Additional food sources included buffalo, bear, deer, smaller mammals and birds, fish and shellfish, and nuts, berries, seeds, and edible roots. The bow, typically made of the strong and resilient wood of the Osage orange or bois d'arc tree (*Maclura pomifera*), was the main hunting weapon. Hunters also made cane arrows, with a sharpened fire-hardened tip or a stone point at the end. Hunters sometimes disguised themselves to resemble the animals they were hunting, occasionally also using decoys.

Osage Orange (or, bois d'arc): A highly prized type of wood used for making Indian bows and other implements.

Caddo women roasted green corn ears and also parched corn, seeds, nuts, and roots on hot coals before grinding them into flour or meal. Sometimes the flour was mixed with water or bear oil and eaten cold. Meal was boiled to make gruel, flavored with squash,

Caddo woman, by Gary Simmons. *Courtesy of the artist.*

beans, or pieces of meat. Flour was also mixed with water and formed into loaves that were baked on hot stone slabs. Meat was eaten after roasting or cooking in a broth.

Caddos living near salt marshes, or salines, made salt by boiling the briny water in large, shallow clay pans. The salt remaining in the pans after the water evaporated was stored for later use or for trade. In addition to salt, the Caddos traded other materials, including bear oil or grease and the wood of the Osage orange tree, prized across the Southeast for the manufacture of bows.

Caddo women also excelled at making pottery, baskets, woven mats, and dressed skins. They decorated pottery vessels with intricate designs, especially those intended for use in rituals. Vessels were created in many shapes, including platters, bowls, jars, and bottles, and these served a variety of food storage, preparation, and consumption needs. Trade items, such as salt and bear oil, were also transported in pottery vessels.

Women crafted finely made and often highly decorated baskets and mats woven from cane splints. Woven baskets served domestic as well as ritual needs. Sacred objects stored in temples were kept in special lidded baskets. Woven mats, often elaborately decorated, were used as floor and bench coverings in houses and in temples. Priests offered specially woven mats to the sacred fire in preparation for the annual planting ceremony.

Men wore breechcloths and moccasins, adding wraps made of deerskins or buffalo hides during cold weather. Women wore skirts made of deerskins or woven cloth. In warm weather they went topless. Women and men wore special deerskin garments with brightly colored decorations for ceremonies. One such garment worn by women consisted of deerskins that were dyed to a deep black color, then decorated with hundreds of shiny white shell beads.

Caddo men kept their hair trimmed short, except for a long lock that was braided or decorated with feathers or shell ornaments. Caddo women wore their long hair braided and tied close to the head. Both men and women had tattoos, although women evidently were more enthusiastic about this than the men, frequently decorating their faces, arms, and torsos with elaborate designs. Both sexes painted designs on their faces and bodies for religious ceremonies. Dress and bodily decoration served as symbolic representations of social group membership, status, and even personal identity.

Warfare was an important means by which southern Caddos maintained the integrity of their territory against pressures from the Apaches to the west and Osages and other Plains tribes to the north. War expeditions were undertaken to seek revenge for deaths or for other insults inflicted by neighboring tribes. When the leaders of a Caddo community wished to organize a war party, they sent ambassadors bearing requests for support to allied communities. Elaborate rituals were performed in preparation for battle, along with offerings made to spirit beings to gain their sanction and support. Other ceremonies and various contests served to sharpen the physical capabilities of the warriors and whip up their fervor. Warriors were separated from the rest of the community throughout these proceedings, and funeral ceremonies might be performed prior to departure, so their souls would travel unimpeded to the afterworld should they be killed in battle.

Funeral ceremonies consisted of a series of rituals intended to facilitate the travel of the dead person's soul to the afterworld. First, the body was washed and dressed in fine clothes. Two priests then chanted and placed offerings of tobacco and bows and arrows upon an empty wooden coffin. While the grave was being dug, the body was placed in the coffin along with articles required in the afterlife. Then a third priest gave the eulogy, and the coffin was carried to the grave while arrows were shot into the air to warn the keeper of the House of Death that the dead person's soul was on its way. Offerings of food placed on the grave were replenished over the next several days, until the family was certain the soul had completed its journey to the afterworld.

The hierarchical organization of Caddo society provided a framework for interaction with Europeans during much of the historic period. When European travelers approached Caddo villages, a contingent sent out from the village met them along the path leading into the village. Members of these welcoming parties singled out the European leaders and escorted them to the dwelling of the caddi, or to a specially erected ceremonial structure. There, the visitors were seated in a place of honor. The calumet served to create a bond of friendship between the leaders that extended to other members of their respective groups.

The finely honed diplomatic skills of Caddo village leaders came into play throughout the colonial era. Caddo leaders often played important roles, at the request of European and American officials, in negotiating alliances and political arrangements among groups inhabiting the contested borderlands separating northern New Spain on the west and the Louisiana Territory on the east.

Tunicas and Koroas

The Tunica language is distinctive among Southeastern Indian languages but is most closely related to the Muskogean family. In the sixteenth century, Tunica Indians occupied an area extending along both sides of the Mississippi River in Tennessee, Mississippi, and eastern Arkansas. In the late seventeenth century, French explorers and missionaries reported Tunica Indians and closely related Koroa Indians (who probably also spoke a Tunica dialect) living along the Arkansas and Ouachita rivers and along the Mississippi River south of the Arkansas. By 1699, most Tunicas had relocated their villages along the lower stretch of the Yazoo River in present-day Mississippi. Within a few more years the Koroas were severely reduced and remnants of that tribe also moved to the lower Yazoo. In the aftermath of the Natchez Rebellion of 1729, the few remaining Koroas along with the Natchez moved in with Chickasaws, while the Tunicas relocated farther down the Mississippi River.

The Tunicas recognized supernatural powers in many aspects of nature, although they attributed a female identity to the sun—considered male by most other groups—and they recognized fire as a deity in its own right, and not, as many Southeastern Indians believed, that it was merely a symbol on earth of the sun's power. Each village contained a sacred fire temple in which religious specialists performed community rites. One Frenchman saw small statues of a woman and a frog in one of these temples.

The woman may have symbolized the sun or upper world, while the frog probably symbolized the watery underworld, as it generally did among Southeastern Indians.

Tunicas built circular houses by setting upright posts in the ground and weaving cane laths through them. Walls were plastered with clay, and grass thatch covered dome-shaped roofs. Small doorways provided the only source of natural light, and the only exit for smoke from small fires that provided additional light and warmth. A member of La Salle's 1682 expedition reported that Koroas decorated their houses with "great round plates of shining copper, made like pot covers." Outdoor cooking fires and above-ground granaries were also constructed near each house. Dwellings were arranged around an open central plaza with a temple at one end. Tunica temples stood on platform mounds in at least some of the villages.

The social life of Tunica communities is known only in fragments. Leaders apparently inherited their offices. In the eighteenth century some villages had two groups of leaders with separate responsibilities for civil affairs and warfare. Warriors achieved distinction for valorous exploits, which entitled them to wear special tattoos. Some men, probably leaders and successful warriors, had several wives, a practice that was not uncommon among Southeastern tribes. Upon death, the deceased were ceremoniously buried with possessions required for life in the afterworld. One French visitor to a Koroa village wrote that games, dances, and feasts took place in the settlement's open plaza.

Like many other Southeastern Indians, Tunicas grew corn and squash, collected wild plant foods including persimmons and other fruits, berries, nuts, seeds, roots, and herbs and hunted deer, bear, and occasionally buffalo. Unlike many Southeastern Indians, Tunica men, rather than women, tended the crop fields. Tunicas also produced salt at seeps and other natural deposits, some of which they traded to other groups.

Tunica men wore deerskin loincloths during the warm seasons, and like other Southeastern Indians decorated themselves with tattoos, beads, and pendants. Women wore short, fringed skirts of cloth woven from the inner bark of mulberry trees. They also tattooed themselves and further enhanced their appearance with beads, pendants, and earrings. Women kept their hair in a single, long braid that hung down the back or was wrapped about the crown. In cold weather, men and women wore mantles of mulberry cloth, turkey feathers, or muskrat skins.

Pressures felt by the Tunicas stemming from the expanding influence of English traders and their native allies on the eastern side of the Mississippi led them to abandon their settlements along the lower Yazoo in 1706. Moving farther down the Mississippi, the Tunicas established new villages—still arranged according to traditional patterns—at a location across from the mouth of the Red River known as Portage de la Croix. This location put the Tunicas closer to the settlements of their French allies. Veteran traders, the Tunicas sustained themselves through a combination of farming, hunting, and commercial activity and by adopting members of less fortunate tribes. This saved the Tunicas from extinction—the fate of so many other small tribes in the Mississippi Valley during the colonial era.

CHAPTER FIVE

Indians and Colonists in the Arkansas Country, 1686–1803

In the summer of 1686, almost eighty years before there was a St. Louis, more than thirty years before New Orleans was laid out, and thirteen years before the French founded the colony of Louisiana, French Canadians established a post on the Arkansas River about twenty miles by water from its confluence with the Mississippi. This *Poste aux Arkansas* (Post at the Arkansas), as the Canadians called their little settlement, served, except for a short hiatus in the early eighteenth century, as a trading and military post until the Americans bought the colony in 1803. Arkansas Post survived as a small village well into the twentieth century, and in fact did not completely disappear until the 1970s when it gave way to the memorial established by the National Park Service.

It is nevertheless safe to say that Arkansas Post is not particularly well known today, even in Arkansas, partly because it is, as it was in 1686, out in the middle of nowhere. Many residents of the state will probably not even realize that there was a colonial Arkansas (the phrase has an odd ring), that their last king was Carlos IV of Spain not George III of England (England never held sway over the Arkansas region), and that, for three weeks, the Emperor Napoleon claimed sovereignty here.

One of the reasons that Arkansas's colonial past is not well known is that not even the slightest physical trace of a colonial occupation has survived above the ground. In the neighboring states of Missouri, Louisiana, Mississippi, and Texas (in fact, in parts of each of them barely one hundred miles from Arkansas's border), eighteenth-century buildings and cemeteries serve to stir the imagination and keep alive the memory of a time when France, Spain, and England all vigorously competed for hegemony in the heart of America. In Arkansas, however, all that bears witness to that early struggle are a few French names for places, rivers, and mountains, many now mangled beyond the possibility of easy recognition. Who would guess, for instance, that buried deep in the name of Smackover, a small town in Union County, is the French phrase *chemin couvert,* which means covered way, a term of art usually associated with military fortifications? And Tchemanihaut Creek (pronounced Shamanahaw) in Ashley County, though the name has an Indian look and sound to it, is actually a corruption of *chemin à haut,* French for high road.

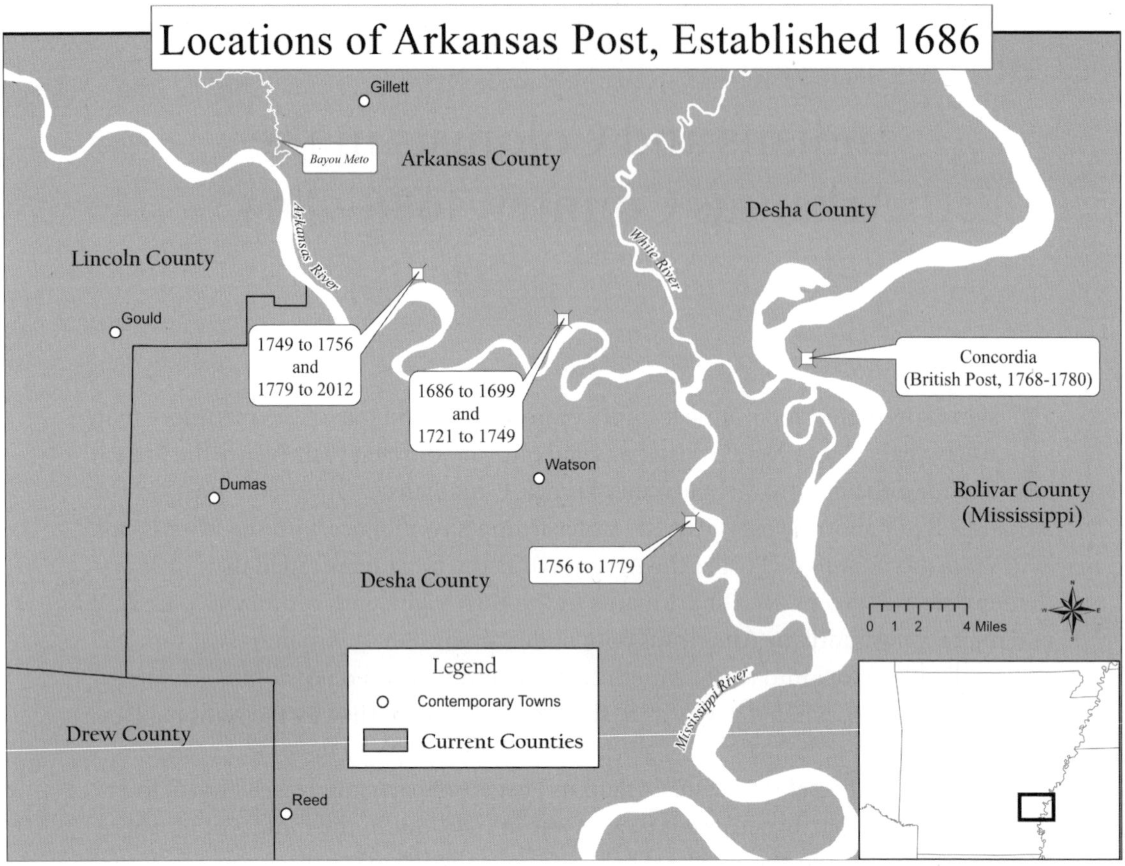

Locations of Arkansas Post, Established 1686. *Courtesy of Joseph Swain.* (Sources: Arkansas Geographic Information Office, Arkansas Post National Memorial, *Encyclopedia of Arkansas History & Culture,* National Atlas of the United States.)

A Peripatetic Settlement

French Canadian traders situated their outpost on the first relatively high ground that they encountered after entering the mouth of the Arkansas River. This place, called then and now Little Prairie, in Arkansas County near where the little community named Nady is located today, had been occupied for centuries by various Indian groups. When the traders came, the Quapaws were living there. The French called them the Arkansas because that was what the Illinois Indians, allies of the French, had called them. Native Americans had chosen to settle on this little detached part of Grand Prairie because it was near the great Mississippi highway, was out of the floodplain for the most part, had abundant fresh water available from the nearby stream later named Menard Bayou (the Arkansas River was brackish but its water was drinkable in a pinch), and the woods close by provided fuel for fires and material for houses. The French chose the spot because the Quapaws were there, and the French wanted to trade with them and engage them in a military alliance against the English of Carolina and their Indian allies, principally the Chickasaws. The environment and the Indians would continue to play important roles in the choices that the Europeans made, but their imperial ambitions also provided significant motives for their activities in the Arkansas region. See plate 14 following page 126.

The first "owner" (in the minds, that is, of Europeans) of the lower Arkansas River was one Henri de Tonty, an associate of Robert Cavelier de La Salle. King Louis XIV of France had commissioned La Salle to explore the Mississippi and establish alliances with all of the Indian tribes that he encountered. Tonty settled six of his men at the Post, one of whom was a ship's carpenter from Rouen named Jean Couture, who presumably supervised the construction of the single house that we can certainly say was erected at this first Post. Frenchmen who visited Tonty's settlement only about a year after it was founded reported that its mission was to monopolize the Quapaw trade, serve as a way station for travelers between the Illinois country and the Gulf of Mexico, and establish a presence in the middle of the continent to thwart the western advance of the English colonies. This was, to say the least, an ambitious undertaking for six people, but imperial ambitions in those days were large—in fact, grandiose—and the mission of the Post never really deviated from its original one during the entire colonial epoch.

For reasons that are not entirely clear, this first Arkansas Post seems to have been abandoned by 1699, when Jean-Baptiste Le Moyne de Bienville finally established the colony of Louisiana on the Gulf Coast, though the rivers of the region, and especially the Arkansas River, continued to be visited more or less regularly by the *coureurs de bois* (forest rangers) and *voyageurs* (boatmen) who hunted and traded with the Indians of Louisiana and Canada. The English, moreover, moved quickly to fill the void: A Carolina trader named Thomas Welch had sent goods to the Quapaws in 1698, and an Englishman had by 1700 married into the tribe. The French then established a missionary among the Quapaws named Father Nicholas Foucault. He was Louisiana's first martyr: His Koroa Indian guides murdered him in 1702 after he abandoned his efforts because of a lack of success and some unspecified disagreements with the Quapaws. In 1700, an Englishman had boasted that he would kill the first French priest whom he encountered in the Arkansas region, so it is not impossible that the English had had a hand, directly or indirectly, in the disagreements between Father Foucault and the Quapaws and perhaps even in the missionary's death itself.

Voyageurs: "Boatmen"; hunters and traders who traveled the rivers of colonial Louisiana, carrying trade goods and supplies.

Coureurs de bois: Literally "woods runners" or "forest rangers"; a term used in reference to mobile fur trappers and traders.

Though the English traders seem to have departed from the Arkansas in the early eighteenth century, Welch evidently maintained some influence among the Quapaws even as late as 1708, for in that year a Quapaw delegation attended a council at the Yazoo River, during a colonial conflict called Queen Anne's War, where Welch tried to engage them in the English effort to destroy the French Louisiana capital at Mobile. Governor

Bienville of Louisiana reported, however, that Welch's blandishments fell on deaf ears, and Bienville was probably correct, since he was an extraordinarily canny Indian negotiator, and he monitored the moods of the various tribes of Louisiana with an uncanny accuracy.

In 1720, John Law, a banker from Scotland who was the most famous financier in eighteenth-century France, and whose private company had taken over the Louisiana colony, decided to revive the settlement at the Arkansas. He took a personal interest in the place, made sure that his company granted him a huge tract of land on the lower Arkansas River, and set about recruiting colonists to settle there. A few thousand people did migrate to Louisiana under his auspices, many of them German peasants from the Alsace region of France, some of whom were destined for the Arkansas; but large numbers of these colonists perished *en route* and on the Gulf Coast after arrival, and none of the Germans made it to Law's projected settlement on the Arkansas River. A few French indentured servants (*engagés*) of the company, and some workmen, did arrive at the old site of Tonty's Post in 1721, to prepare the way for the colonists. But when John Law's bankruptcy and disgrace intervened, the Germans assigned to his Arkansas concession settled instead in the lower part of the colony, principally at a place called then and now the German Coast, where these peasant farmers soon became the main suppliers of vegetables and other foodstuffs to the growing population of New Orleans. Back at the Arkansas, Law's *engagés* were released from their contracts, and a few stayed behind to become hunters, traders, and small-time farmers. In 1727, the Jesuit Father Du Poisson, missionary to the Quapaws, reported that only about thirty Frenchmen had remained to make a home in the wilderness.

Engagés: "Employees"; employees who usually worked for a trader or merchant.

A military garrison was first assigned to the Arkansas in 1721, to provide security for Law's colonists, but it was recalled a few years later. Once it was reestablished in 1731 or 1732, there was a military presence on the Arkansas throughout the colonial period. The number of soldiers there, however, was never large, varying from as few as six to perhaps as many as a hundred, depending on the exigencies in which the region found itself.

One of the circumstances on which the government of Louisiana kept a wary eye was the mood of the Chickasaw nation, ancient foes of the Quapaws and much attached to the English, who lived to the east in what is now the state of Mississippi. During the 1730s and 1740s, the Quapaws joined in various French military efforts to destroy the Chickasaws, and they frequently raided the Chickasaw villages, bringing back scalps and prisoners to be burned alive or adopted. A truly splendid scene that a Quapaw artist painted on a buffalo hide in about 1750, which survives in a Paris museum, probably records one of these raids. See plate 15 following page 126. During the 1740s, the colony of Louisiana got drawn into a general conflict between the French and the English known as King George's War, and in 1749 the Chickasaws (with perhaps a few Choctaws and Creeks) launched a full-scale attack on the Post. Their scout, according to one report, was a drummer who had deserted from the French garrison. Though the French repulsed the attack, it was not without a considerable loss: A number of men were killed, and several women and children were captured and taken as prisoners to the Chickasaw towns.

This English and Chickasaw success greatly alarmed the French government in New Orleans, and it ordered the Post moved and rebuilt about six miles upriver by land (perhaps fifteen by water) to a place in what is now Arkansas County that the French called *Écores Rouges* (Red Bluffs), where the Arkansas Post National Memorial is now located. The Quapaws had moved there shortly before the attack because of devastating floods, and their absence was probably a main reason that the Chickasaw siege had enjoyed so much success. The French, not surprisingly, had resolved to rejoin their Quapaw allies for defensive purposes. Environment and geography had again forced a choice on the French and the Quapaws. A rather large investment was made in a new fort and settlement at the new site, but in 1756, only seven years after its relocation, the outpost moved yet again, this time downriver, to a site in what is now Desha County about ten miles by river from the Mississippi River. It is likely that the need to be close to that main artery during the Seven Years' War, so the Post could be of service to the French convoys that plied the great river, provided the impetus for this change of location.

Geography had again influenced the activities of the French, and environment would dictate what kind of settlement, if any, was going to gather around the little isolated military outpost that was created at the new location. This third Arkansas Post was across from Big Island, in the middle of a vast alluvial plain, where annual floodwaters made agriculture virtually impossible, the soil was sandy, and the insects frequently devoured what few crops managed somehow to survive. Every spring, the inhabitants braced themselves for the Mississippi floods that would overwhelm the waters of the White River, roar through a cutoff between it and the Arkansas, rush down the chute on the western edge of Big Island, and overrun the little French *Poste aux Arkansas.*

The Frenchmen built their houses on a small rise behind the fort, and on six-foot stilts to boot, but still almost every year there were two feet of water in the fort and sometimes even in the most elevated dwellings. The levees that the farmers struggled to raise were not effective against the inundations, and the Post's denizens could not afford to build bigger ones as their neighbors to the south had done above and below New Orleans. The topography in the environs of the Post thus made it impossible to attract farmers to the place in any numbers. If there was going to be a settlement there at all, and even that was not obviously so, it would have to be a trading and hunting community. But it proved impossible to attract many people to settle at the Post, and by 1777, almost a century after its founding, there were only fifty-one civilians, white and black, at this most remote of Louisiana's outposts of empire.

The few traders and merchants at the Post were drawn to this sink not so much to trade with the Quapaws as to outfit the numerous hunters who had been attracted to the Arkansas region to exploit the abundant wildlife that flourished there because the region was virtually empty of people. The Quapaws, who numbered about ten thousand when Marquette and Jolliet first visited them in 1673, had been decimated by smallpox in the 1690s. By 1700, their population was probably no more than a thousand, and

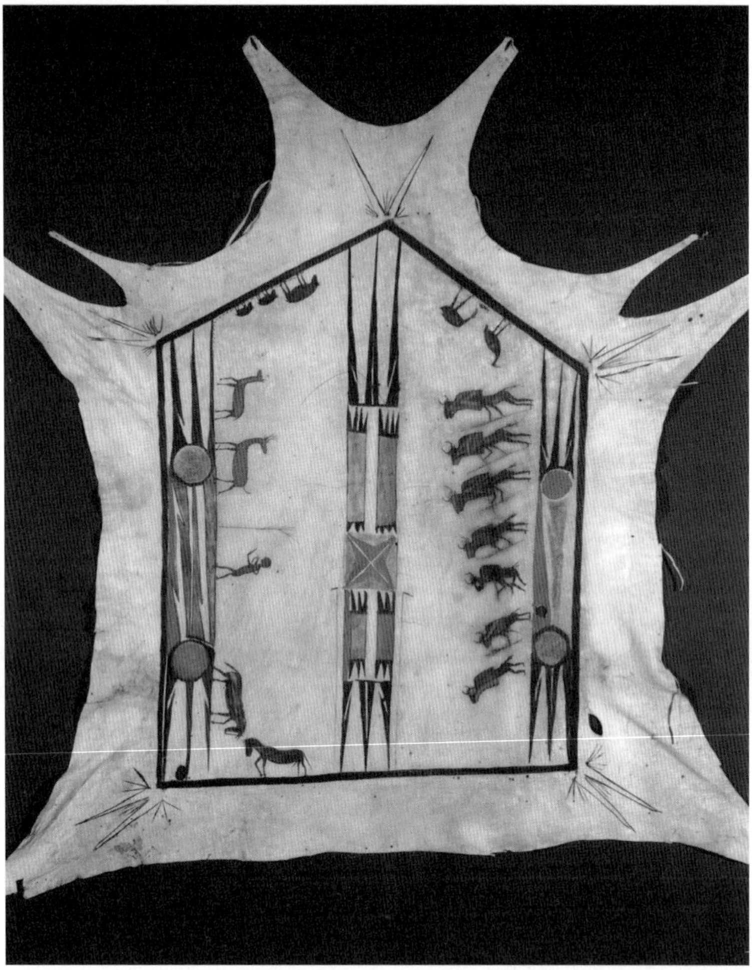

Robe of the Buffalo Hunters, Quapaw painted buffalo hide, circa 1750. *Courtesy Musée du quai Branly, Paris.*

later epidemic episodes had reduced them to around seven hundred souls by 1770. The only substantial group of Indians that regularly ventured into the Arkansas region during the period to exploit the animal life were the Osages, who claimed much of the northern and western part of the state as their hunting territory. There were small groups of other tribes, mostly little bands or remnants, who occasionally migrated into the area in search of game. Chief among these were some Illinois (Miamis and Kaskaskias), many of whom were taken in by the Quapaws, and a group of Abenakis (or Loups). Very late in the colonial period a significant number of Cherokees, and roving bands of Choctaws and Chickasaws, were driven across the Mississippi to hunt by the expanding frontier of American settlement.

In 1779, Capt. Balthazar de Villiers, a very able commandant who served six years at Arkansas Post, finally succeeded in getting the governor's permission to move his town and fort out of the floodplain, this time for the last time, back upriver to the high land at *Écores Rouges*. Here his prospects for creating an ordered, agrarian community were a good deal brighter, and conditions at the Post improved measurably in its new

Bequette-Ribault house, early nineteenth century, Ste. Genevieve, Missouri. Houses like these were built in Arkansas Post during its colonial period and afterward. *Photo by Gail K. Arnold.*

location. By 1790, a gristmill or two had appeared there (they would have been horse powered), a sawmill was erected around 1802, and soon after the Louisiana Purchase a cotton gin was built. By the late 1790s, the population had steadily grown to almost four hundred people, white and black, a parish had finally been created, and priests were at least sporadically instructing the young in elementary matters.

The Post also achieved a kind of architectural maturity in its waning years as a colonial outpost. By the middle of the 1790s, many of the houses there were constructed in the distinctive creole style typical of the other settlements of Louisiana. These houses were built of upright logs and had double-pitch hipped roofs, wide galleries all around (onto which the interior rooms opened), casement windows with shutters, French doors, and frequently a double fireplace in the center. These dwellings were, to be sure, small enough: They usually had just two rooms and contained only about four hundred square feet; the largest on record was around one thousand square feet. But the covered galleries could effectively double the amount of living space available to occupants and were frequently used as sleeping porches. Then, too, the kitchen was usually in a separate building. The larger house lots were surrounded by tall stockade fences that sometimes enclosed orchards, outdoor ovens, kitchens, smokehouses, barns, and even blacksmith shops. The stockades provided a defense against unwanted human intruders and animals alike.

Despite the significant improvements that were wrought, the colonial Post did not achieve the agrarian respectability that Villiers and his successors had hoped for. There were never more than a few true farmers there, eight or ten at the most, though some late-coming Germans and Frenchmen set an example by growing large amounts of wheat. Most of the farmers supplemented their income by trading and hunting, and the Post was not self-sufficient: To the very end of the colonial period, the Spanish garrison sometimes had to depend on flour from the Illinois country, or from Ohio, to sustain itself. Roving Indian bands (mostly Choctaws and Chickasaws) sometimes stole the horses that the farmers used for plowing and occasionally stole even the very crops themselves.

Arkansas Post was the only real settlement ever established during the colonial period in what would become the state of Arkansas. It is true that events during the American Revolution spurred the Spanish to establish a command on the Ouachita River in 1782, at first at a place called Écore à Fabri (modern-day Camden, Arkansas), where Capt. Jean Filhiol attempted to coax the dispersed hunters of the region into a militia unit and sedentary life. They were living in lean-tos and tents made of poles and skins, as the Indians of Arkansas had done for millennia. But an utter lack of success at Écore à Fabri soon required Filhiol to abandon the post there and refocus his efforts farther down the river, where he founded Ouachita Post, present-day Monroe, Louisiana. In 1797, a little fort was built on the Mississippi River across from Memphis at what the Spanish called Campo del Esperanza (the Field of Hope); it sheltered a tiny garrison of eight soldiers and provided a base for three or four sailors who patrolled the great river in armed pirogues (dugouts) in search of invading Americans. But no real town sprang up there until the American period was well under way (it was called Hopefield), and the river had claimed the fort itself by 1810. A number of hunters occupied the White River and Black River regions sporadically from the middle of the eighteenth century, and some others used the future site of Little Rock, which they called *Petit Rocher*, as a rendezvous place; but almost all the settlements made there were temporary camps and corresponded only to the hunters' peripatetic style of life.

In 1719, Jean-Baptiste Bénard de La Harpe established an outpost at a Caddo village on the Red River, not many miles northwest of Texarkana, just outside the present boundaries of the state of Arkansas. The Caddos, a sedentary agricultural people, were looking for protection from Osage and Chickasaw raids that had greatly reduced their population and virtually destroyed some of their villages. The official moniker of La Harpe's post was St. Louis des Caddodoches, which makes it sound rather grand, but its population never exceeded seventy or eighty. Like Arkansas Post, it attracted a small number of traders and farmers, and a tiny garrison of perhaps six soldiers sometimes occupied the fort there. The resident farmers did occasionally manage to produce a wheat crop, and they even built a flour mill, but Osage attacks finally led to the settlement's abandonment in 1778.

Economy, Government, and Religion

The Arkansas region fairly teemed with game animals, and products of the hunt formed the chief exports of the Arkansas country. There were some deerskins, otter pelts, beaver pelts, bearskins, and bobcat skins shipped from the Post, but the skin and fur trade was

Painting by Alexander de Batz of Indians trading in Orleans in 1735. The goods shown in the left foreground are buffalo ribs, buffalo tallow, and bear's oil, the same products that Arkansas exported in the colonial period. *Courtesy of Peabody Museum, Harvard University. Photograph by Hillel Burger.*

not a very significant part of the economic activity there until the very late eighteenth and early nineteenth century. The exports that were the most important for most of the colonial period were salted buffalo meat, buffalo tallow, and bear's oil.

While the general reader will associate the buffalo with the Great Plains of the Midwest, the fact is that buffalo inhabited the Arkansas region in great numbers in the seventeenth and eighteenth centuries. Huge canebrakes in the river bottoms and in extensive lowlands provided buffalo with a congenial forage, as did Little Prairie, the Grand Prairie, and the smaller prairies with which Arkansas was dotted at the time. Vache Grasse (fat cow) Prairie near Fort Smith was no doubt so named because it was an excellent place to shoot buffalo cows, the ribs (*plats cotés*) of which were the choicest and most succulent cut of the animal. The residents of New Orleans consumed large quantities of Arkansas buffalo meat, as did soldiers garrisoned throughout Louisiana. An Arkansas commandant who wanted to ingratiate himself with his governor in New Orleans would send him a couple of dozen salted buffalo tongues, along with pecans from the St. Francis River region, as a present. These delicacies found their way even to the tables of noblemen in Madrid, where they were greatly appreciated and much sought after.

Plats cotés: Buffalo ribs, typically preserved by smoking; an important trade commodity supplied by French traders.

Tallow, the rendered fat of the buffalo, was used for a number of purposes, such as burning in lamps and making candles. In the 1770s, François Ménard, a Post merchant who became in time the richest man in colonial Arkansas, contracted with the Spanish government to furnish ten thousand pounds of buffalo tallow to the Havana shipyards for caulking boats. But bear's oil was the most versatile of Arkansas's eighteenth-century products. One principal use was for illumination: The government bought great amounts of it for lamps in its buildings and, late in the colonial period, for use in the New Orleans streetlight system. It was also used as a base for face paint by the Indians, as a mosquito repellant, as a drink, as cooking oil, and even as salad dressing. Some colonial Louisianans claimed that it was as good as the best olive oil in Europe. In the winter, the oil solidified into a white lard and was spread on bread like butter. Because it was commonly stored and shipped in a sewed-up deerskin, Louisiana records often refer to "a deer of oil." The town of Oil Trough in Independence County owes its name to the hunters' practice of filling pirogues with bear's oil (thus making a trough of oil), covering them, and floating them down the Mississippi for markets in New Orleans and elsewhere.

Since money was scarce in colonial Arkansas, most products were traded for goods. The kinds of goods that the Indians and French hunters of the Arkansas country took in exchange for their products provide us with a revealing record of an important part of the material culture of many of the people of the time. For hunting and war, traders offered guns, wadpullers, flints, powder, and balls; for clothing, they provided blankets of various quality, trade shirts, shoes, Limbourg (a lightweight woolen cloth, often of red or blue), twilled woolen serge, beads, and wool ribbon; and some trade inventories even mention white and blue paint that Indians used for decorating their faces and bodies. In 1758, the king's warehouse at the Post contained breechclouts, awls, strike-a-lights, folding knives, and butcher knives. One could even buy candles, flour, biscuit (hardtack), and four kinds of nails at this government store, along with rum and brandy.

Governing the Arkansas in the colonial period proved more than a little difficult, because of its remoteness and the nature of its population, and because neither the French nor the Spanish (who took over Louisiana in 1766) ever made much of an investment in government there. Lt. Gov. Athanase de Mézières, who lived in Natchitoches, once described some of the denizens of the Arkansas River as "the most wicked men, without doubt, in all of the Indies," and this was not an isolated opinion. It was the lot of the commandant at the Post to bring such order as he could to the affairs of his district. See plates 16 and 17 following page 126.

Commandant: The military officer who was the head of the government at Arkansas Post.

The commandant was always a military officer, usually a lieutenant or a captain, who was posted to Arkansas for a few years and would then be sent to a command elsewhere in the colony. He was a marine during the French period, and while the Spanish were in possession of the country he was an army officer in the Fixed Regiment of Louisiana. Besides being commander-in-chief of the forces stationed at the Post, the commandant was also the sole civil and military judge for the entire region and ambassador to the Indian nations. He carried out the judgments of the New Orleans courts, and acted as the Post's notary, a nonforensic lawyer, drafting, executing, and recording contracts, deeds, manumissions, marriage contracts, bills, notes, and the like. (Forensic lawyers, that is, lawyers who appeared in court, were never tolerated in Louisiana, for, as an early ordinance excluding them from the colony had explained, such pettifoggers stirred up and maintained unnecessary quarrels.)

The commandant, in other words, was the government. He was, of course, expected to exercise his authority according to law, and French and Spanish law, each in its turn, was put in place and enforced to a degree at the Post. As early as 1712, for instance, the Custom of Paris, a legal code that governed certain civil relations, including marital property, was adopted as the law of Louisiana, and the gentry of the Post followed this code in their marriage contracts. There was some legislation passed on the continent that applied only to the French or Spanish colonies, or to Louisiana alone, and Louisiana institutions also passed laws to govern the affairs of their colony. Early in the Spanish period, the Leyes de las Indias (Laws of the Indies) were made applicable to Louisiana. Though there was, therefore, a lot of law that nominally bound him, the commandant possessed a great deal of residual authority at remote forest settlements like Arkansas Post, and he regularly laid down local police regulations and even drafted rules that fixed the rights of the merchant creditors of the Arkansas hunters.

Since there was only one person with real power and authority in the Arkansas country, the costs of governing the region were, to say the least, minimal. But providing government there was even less expensive than at first might appear, for officers' salaries were very low. The expectation was that the commandant would be a trader and a merchant during his sojourn at the Post; indeed, the great bulk of his income was typically derived from his private enterprises, not his public emolument. This could sometimes involve the commandant in a conflict of interest. One commandant, for instance, was reprimanded when he offloaded a boat containing supplies intended for his garrison and substituted his private merchandise in their stead, and several commandants were called upon to judge cases involving their business competitors, many of whom they cordially despised.

While a functioning, even-handed government had a difficult time gaining a purchase in the Arkansas country, at least there was always someone there who was nominally in charge of it. The church, however, struggled even to maintain a presence. The church was a full partner in the state's imperial ambitions, and traders, soldiers, and priests were the vanguard of the European expansionist effort. The church's main objects were to convert the native peoples and minister to the French residents, but its priests understood and quietly accepted their political role as the government's eyes and ears in the Indian villages, where the native people often called them "Black chiefs" because of the robes they wore. (A missionary also frequently carried medicines to his station, and helped residents draft legal documents, so he operated literally as a doctor, lawyer, and Indian chief.) The English across the Mississippi understood the political role that the church played in the French colonial effort, which provided one reason for the deep and abiding enmity that developed early on between English traders and French missionary priests. One New Englander wrote in 1720 that "he ought to be a *cunning* man that treats with the *Indians,* and therefore the French leave that business to the Jesuits."

In fact, only a year or two after he founded Arkansas Post, Henri de Tonty set his mind to developing what he called his French quarter at his new settlement and asked the Jesuits to establish a priest there. In 1689, he granted two parcels of land at the Arkansas to the Jesuits, and promised to build two chapels and two houses for a missionary: one site, presumably, was to be used to minister to the French in residence, the other to Indian neophytes. These large plans came to naught, however, for the Jesuits never sent a missionary to Tonty's Post. And while the Seminarians of Canada aspired to settle among the Quapaws in the waning years of the seventeenth century, it was not until 1701 that Nicholas Foucault was able to establish himself there, and, as we saw, he became Louisiana's first martyr only a little more than a year later. Unfortunately, the priest destined for Law's colony in 1721 died on his way upriver. The Jesuit Father Du Poisson established himself at the Arkansas six years later, and was enjoying some success in his effort to learn the Quapaw tongue; but in 1729 the Natchez Indians killed him while, according to one report, he was standing at the altar celebrating mass in the church at Natchez. There were priests for a time at the Post during the 1740s, but the exact nature of their activities there is more than a little obscure.

The only priest who sojourned long enough in the Arkansas region during the French period to have had much influence was Louis Carette, a Jesuit who came to the Post in 1750 or 1751 and followed it in its peregrinations up and down the Arkansas River. He did his best to bring order to the place, but in 1758 he resigned in dismay because of the sacrilegious character of his flock, and no priest took up residence at the Post again until the 1790s. In the meantime, the settlement had to make do with the services of priests who were traveling through on the way elsewhere.

It was not until 1796, fully one hundred and ten years after the Post was founded, that the first canonical parish was created there. In that year, Father Pierre Janin, who had fled the French Revolution and landed in Philadelphia in 1794, had made the mistake of telling the Bishop of Louisiana and the Floridas that he did not like big cities; so the bishop had indulged Father Janin's preferences and named him the first parish priest at Arkansas Post. When he was called away three years later to minister to the more important congregation in St. Louis, the little parish at Arkansas failed and was never revived.

One upshot of all this was that whatever influence the church could have brought to bear as a partner of the civil government at the Post was very much attenuated. The church had found itself unable to sustain a presence in the region because the Post was so tiny and remote. The episodic attempts to establish a mission among the Quapaws were too short-lived to have had a significant effect on the native belief system, and the efforts of the priests who ministered to the Post's French populace had usually proved no more rewarding than had the work among the Indians.

The church did enjoy some initial success in protecting its religious monopoly in the province. Protestants were at first excluded altogether, but late in the colonial period the Spanish were forced to let them immigrate to the colony without adopting the Roman Catholic religion. They were not, however, allowed to worship publicly. Some sturdy Lutheran farmers from the United States settled at the Post in the late 1790s; we do not know whether they practiced their religion privately, though it would seem highly probable that they did.

Jews, too, were excluded from Louisiana early on but Jewish merchants began to settle in New Orleans around 1757, and by 1759, according to one Louisiana official, there were six of them "engaging in wholesale and retail commerce with the same liberty as French businessmen." Why these Jewish merchants were allowed to remain in the colony is not altogether clear: Some critics of the governor unkindly suggested that he had been bribed. Although Gov. Alexander O'Reilly expelled most Jews from Louisiana in 1769, a number of them returned in rather short order, and they do not seem to have been officially molested thereafter.

It appears that there were no Jews living in Arkansas during the colonial period. Arkansas colonial residents did, however, have dealings with Jews. For instance, Etienne Layssard, who was the king's storekeeper at the Post in the 1750s, was at an earlier time evidently the New Orleans correspondent for the Jewish businessman, Josue Henriques Jr., who was a resident of Curaçao. In 1748, Henriques, in the very first recorded association of Jews with trade in Louisiana, shipped a cargo of goods to New Orleans, where the man who received them sold them and absconded. Layssard sued to have the faithless consignee's property seized on Henriques's behalf.

The famous Jewish merchant Isaac Monsanto, who lived in New Orleans, had business dealings with all the Mississippi towns, and there is evidence that François Ménard of Arkansas Post was one of his customers. We know more certainly that Monsanto sold goods on credit to a "Mr. Devidiers" (probably Balthazar de Villiers) who lived at Arkansas Post, and when Monsanto died, the governor instructed the Arkansas commandant to help Monsanto's executor collect debts that the denizens of Arkansas owed the estate. It is possible, perhaps even likely, that Monsanto sojourned at the Post on at least one occasion, since he sometimes traveled from New Orleans to the Illinois country for business purposes.

What kind of reception Monsanto and his coreligionists might have been accorded at the Post and elsewhere in Louisiana is a question that does not have an obvious answer. Monsanto's expulsion from the colony in 1769, along with other Jewish residents of Louisiana, was perhaps not attributable so much to his religion as to his business success. (A number of English merchants were turned out of the colony at the same time.) Jean-Bernard Bossu, a French officer who claimed to have visited Arkansas Post three times, maintained that the French merchants of New Orleans were "enemies of the Jews on account of competition."

But these French merchants may have been ready to use religious prejudice to achieve their business objectives. Bossu recites a story about a Christian Indian in New Orleans who, he says, became enraged at the Jewish merchant David Dias Arias because some French competitors had identified him as "a descendant of those who had committed a heinous crime in the Old World by making Our Savior, Son of the Master of Life, die shamefully like a thief on the cross." According to Bossu, the Indian would have killed Dias Arias if a French officer had not intervened: The officer, Bossu would have us believe, convinced the Indian that because "the Son of the Great Spirit had pardoned them for his death, the Indians should do likewise." Even if Bossu's story is not true (many of his stories are not), it furnishes evidence of the kind of racial and religious intolerance that some of his readers would have found credible.

Society and Social Life

Though the Post was remote and the life there was rugged (one disgruntled commandant dubbed it "the most disagreeable hole in the universe"), there was an active social life there. There were numerous *cabarets* (bars) and a billiard parlor or two at which liquor, coffee, sugar, tobacco, and other luxury items were available. Card playing was a favorite pastime, and frequent balls, some lasting all night, provided needed diversion. In fact, Sunday afternoon following mass (if any) was a favorite time for dances; and, after the Louisiana Purchase, Protestant preachers at the Post were scandalized when French ladies appeared dressed in their ball gowns in the back of the church, listened curiously to the sermon for a few minutes, and then unceremoniously stole away to attend the afternoon's festivities.

One difficult but important question about life at the Post is the extent to which the French and the Quapaws socialized together. When mixed-blood marriage ceremonies took place in the Quapaw villages, there were surely attendant celebrations in which both Indians and whites participated. Festivities after church marriages between whites and Indians, and after baptisms, must also have included both races. Quapaw chiefs often dined with the Post commandant at his table in his house, especially on the day when the government delivered the annual present to the Quapaws. Such occasions were sometimes the scene of general celebrations in which hundreds of Indians and whites took part, consuming great amounts of meat, corn, and liquor.

Sometimes, medals were presented to the Quapaw chiefs at these events in the presence of a large assembly of Quapaws, Frenchmen, and Spanish soldiers, and the commandant personally placed the medals around the necks of the honorees while the garrison's drum rolled and the fort's cannons thundered. A Spanish commandant in the 1770s once purposely timed a volley from his cannons to coincide with the moment that the Quapaw chiefs sat down at his table to dine: The resulting reverberation knocked the dishes from the walls of the commandant's *salle* (dining room), and this, so the commandant reported at least, greatly impressed the assembled Indian dignitaries with the might of the Spanish king. Post residents also regularly attended annual fairs at one of the Quapaw villages, probably at a time that coincided with the Indians' green corn festival in early June.

The letters of commandants and the reports of European visitors to Arkansas are full of detailed descriptions of society at the Post; and even when one discounts them properly for the inevitable class bias of the people who wrote them, it is plain that the class structure at the Post was skewed toward the lower orders and that among them lawlessness and poverty was a not uncommon feature. The dangers and difficulties of the hunting life, particularly the risks posed by the Osages who very jealously guarded what they regarded as their exclusive animal reserves, made it more or less inevitable that the white *voyageurs* and hunters drawn to the region would be among the most economically desperate men of the colony. The commandants at the Post despised most of them, calling them vagabonds, debauchees, bankrupts, riffraff, and professional drunks who valued lead more than silver or gold, owned nothing but their guns, and knew nothing except how to shoot them. Many of these hunters, in their turn, were deeply unhappy with the treatment that the merchants, including the commandants, afforded them. At least one disgruntled hunter, and probably more, joined in the English effort to take the Post during the Revolutionary War because of trade disputes with the commandant. Because the hunters were penniless for the most part, the merchant class was forced to outfit them on credit and wring whatever payment they could from them after they had completed their hunt. All this helps us understand why an Englishman, describing his voyage down the Mississippi in 1766, had sniffed that "the few banditti of the Arkansas Post" barely deserved notice.

While numerous *voyageurs* and hunters congregated at and around the Post, and constituted the largest part of its population, there were, nevertheless, representatives there of almost all the classes of which colonial Louisiana could boast. Though no titled nobleman ever made his home in Arkansas, the Post did give shelter to a few gentry with high-sounding names containing the particle "de," a highly reliable indication of gentle birth. Jean-François Tisserant de Montcharvaux, Marie Françoise Petit de Coulange, and her son, Charles Melchior de Vilemont, provide excellent examples of these. Almost all the ladies and gentlemen of the Post were associated with the military.

Just below these on the social scale were the substantial merchants, like François Ménard, who was one of the few early civilian residents of Arkansas who was literate. He may even have had a university education, for he first appears in the Arkansas in 1770 as a surgeon attached to the Spanish garrison. He was a highly successful merchant whose main business was supplying hunters for their annual campaign, trading with Indians, and exporting peltries, buffalo meat, tallow, and bear's oil to New Orleans and elsewhere. He may also have employed hunters, because one commandant complained about a large contingent of people whom he maintained at his house. In addition, Ménard was a *habitant,* that is, a farmer, as some other merchants were. The number of serious farmers at the Post was very small, though, perhaps no more than ten or twelve at any one time, even by the end of the eighteenth century. As we saw, it appears that the Post was not reliably self-sufficient, since the garrison imported flour throughout the colonial period.

The lives of the women at the Arkansas Post are, in some respects, even less visible in the surviving records than the activities of the free and enslaved Africans there. That is partly because women married early, and during the time of their "coverture," as their marital condition was called, they suffered from certain civil disabilities: They could not bring lawsuits in their own name, and their husbands had the power to manage and control the community property. Although a wife could retain the property that she brought to a marriage, and could inherit other property that would not become part of the community, she could not deal with this separate estate without her husband's participation.

It is true, though, that a married woman in Louisiana could sue her husband for wasting (mismanaging) the community assets, an advantage not given to Englishwomen, and she enjoyed some other legal advantages over her English sisters. A French married woman, for instance, could become a *marchande* (merchant) and contract and own the property associated with her business the same as if she were single. It would be a mistake, moreover, to think that the civil disabilities visited on married women rendered them dependent and powerless. For instance, Madame Villiers, wife of Post commandant Balthazar de Villiers, was very active in her husband's mercantile affairs, and traveled constantly between the Post and New Orleans, transacting his business and dealing with New Orleans merchants and with the governor on commercial matters, acting essentially as her husband's partner.

There is reason to think that women were prime movers in the various efforts to establish a church at the Post, and actively sought the services of a priest to minister to the people and instruct the young. Women encouraged religious observance at the Post in other ways as well. For instance, in 1770, Madame DeClouet, wife of Post commandant Alexandre Chevalier DeClouet, left certain undescribed ornaments as a gift for the little chapel at the Post when she and her husband departed for New Orleans upon the expiration of his tour of duty at the Arkansas. Traditional female activities of a nurturing character also earned the women of the Post respect and gratitude. For instance, in 1769 our same Madame DeClouet set the example for the other women at the Arkansas by nursing the victims of an epidemic that had struck the Post.

Widows, it is important to note, could be powerful people, and since many women outlived their husbands, there were frequent opportunities for them to enjoy full civil emancipation. Colonial Arkansas produced a number of these enfranchised widows. Marie Françoise Petit de Coulange, for instance, who was born at Arkansas Post in 1732, had survived three husbands, all of them quite well-to-do, by the time she was thirty-nine. She did not thereafter remarry, and she became one of the richest people in the entire colony. (Her son, Charles de Vilemont, served as commandant of the Post from 1794 to 1802, and a town in Chicot County once bore his name.) François Ménard's relict was probably the richest person in the 1793 census of Arkansas Post: She owned nine slaves and on François's death she had succeeded to his very considerable mercantile business. Wealthy widows could afford to act in a very independent way, and they did. For example, in 1796, when the governor asked Post slave owners to contribute to a fund to compensate Pointe Coupée *habitants* for slaves executed and exiled in

Habitants:
"Planters"; colonial settlers comprising the class of farmers settled around places like Arkansas Post.

Marie Françoise Petit de Coulange de Vilemont, born at Arkansas Post in 1732. *Courtesy of Mrs. Elmire Villere Dracken, New Orleans.*

Capt. Charles Melchior de Vilemont, commandant of Arkansas Post from 1794 to 1802. *Historic Arkansas Museum, Little Rock.*

the wake of an abortive slave revolt, all of them agreed to do so except Madame Vallière, the widow of Capt. Joseph Vallière, former Post commandant. She had simply refused, and if she gave a reason to Captain Vilemont, the local commandant, he did not bother to report it to the governor.

Women nevertheless frequently appear in the records in highly distressed circumstances. For instance, Indian slaves were common throughout colonial Louisiana and most of them were women. Many of these enslaved women toiled as concubines and laborers for hunters and trappers in the Arkansas country, and, as we would expect, some were subject to shocking abuse. A Spanish priest, for example, reported that in 1770 a Frenchman at La Harpe's post on the Red River was keeping five captive Indian women of various nations at his house "for the infamous traffic of the flesh." In other words, these women were forced into prostitution. The priest made unsuccessful attempts to rescue them. The lieutenant governor of Louisiana, in whose company the priest was traveling, witnessed the situation but did not lift a finger to ameliorate it.

Throughout the eighteenth century, Comanches abducted numerous Spanish and mixed-blood women from communities in northern New Mexico. Most of these women were physically and sexually abused by their captors and a number of them were sold as slaves to the Wichitas (the French called this tribe the *Panis*), who lived high up the Arkansas River in Oklahoma and on the Red River in Oklahoma. The Wichitas were tattooed all over their bodies and practiced ceremonial cannibalism. In the 1780s, the Arkansas commandant reported that there were a number of captive white women for sale in the Wichita village, and some of them were redeemed by French hunters who claimed them as their slaves.

In 1780, María Banancia, one of these enslaved women, wrote a pitiable letter from *Écores Rouges* to Governor Gálvez, begging him to free her from the clutches of a brutal, drunken hunter with the suggestively truculent nickname of La Bombard ("The Mortar"). She said that La Bombard frequently beat her, claimed that she was his property because she had cost him good money, and threatened to resell her "into the forests" where she would never be heard of again if she complained of his ill treatment. In a later legal proceeding against La Bombard, he freely confessed to beating her, but, in a revealing admission, said that he did so because she had stolen something from the Wichitas when she was in their village. It appears that La Bombard believed that he had a perfect right to punish her physically for this transgression. One of his companions accused him of raping María, a charge that he denied.

Althanase de Mézières, the lieutenant governor stationed at Natchitoches on the Red River, who had reasonably frequent contact with and news from the Wichita tribe, believed that captive white women among the tribe often suffered sexual abuse from their captors. But, in a classic case of blaming the victim, he said the women would never be accepted if they were released because of the "well-merited shame which they would suffer among Christians for their infamous inchastity." At least three of these former Indian captives, however, did find husbands at Arkansas Post in the eighteenth century. María Benancia was one of these. She married her countryman Martin Serrano, a soldier at the Post.

White women were sometimes captured and abducted by Indian raiders even at the Post itself. In 1749, a number of French women and children were taken during the attack by the Chickasaws. Most of them, if not all, were later ransomed at Charleston and Mobile, but not before undergoing a harrowing ordeal. An Englishman who had lived for years among the Southeastern Indians reported seeing one of them with her Chickasaw masters: She was constantly praying in a distracted way and clutching at her rosary. But enemies located on the plains or across the Mississippi were not the only ones who could inspire terror in the women of Arkansas. In the early 1770s, when the Quapaws were being held in only the most tenuous way to the Spanish alliance, a large party of them caused such an alarm at the Post that all the women and children had crowded into the commandant's bedroom, where they had huddled together, holding one another and crying. It is small wonder that commandants at Arkansas Post sometimes wished that they could afford to send their wives to New Orleans, where they could live without fear.

The black population of the Arkansas region, including the Post, was never large: Even as late as 1798 the Post census listed only about sixty slaves, all black or mulatto, in a total population of almost four hundred. They spoke a French dialect sometimes called Afro/creole and perhaps an African language or two as well. A number of these slaves would have been engaged in agricultural work: Most of the French farmers in late-eighteenth-century Arkansas had a few slaves to help them in their fields, but no one, so far as the record goes, ever owned more than the eleven whom Joseph Bougy claimed in 1794. The German Lutherans at the Post, though excellent agriculturalists, owned no slaves at all, a fact that raises an inference (perhaps a strong one) that they were conscientiously opposed to slavery.

Although some of the slaves of the Arkansas worked at agriculture, captive Africans engaged in a wide variety of activities there in the colonial period. In 1789, for instance, Capt. Joseph Vallière's household servants served dinner to an American visitor, and it is probable that his servants were black slaves. Four years later, when Capt. Pierre Rousseau put in at the Post to have the rudder of his Spanish war vessel inspected, Captain Vallière supplied him with an old black artisan who soon had him on his way with newly manufactured parts for his ships. Since Rousseau paid the artisan directly with a draft on the treasury in New Orleans, it is possible that the old man was a free person of color, acting on his own account, but slaves often served as the trusted agents of their masters and conducted business for them without direct supervision. For instance, in the 1770s a merchant at Concordia left his trading post in the hands of his black clerks when he embarked on a brief trip. Most interestingly, at least one of these slaves was literate, for when they found it necessary to abandon the store they left behind a note in English explaining why they had done so. Many Africans in the Arkansas region showed other signs of assimilation into the white culture. For example, in 1793 some of François Ménard's slaves requested Father Gibault, the local priest, to say four masses for Ménard when he died. They paid for the church services with tobacco, grown on plots given over to them for their own use and profit, as was the custom throughout Louisiana.

Blacks also worked as laborers for merchants, dressing and packing hides, preparing other exports for shipment, and loading carts and boats. In 1793, for example, the widow Ménard had nine slaves at Arkansas Post, but she produced no crop, and the census lists her as a merchant, not a farmer. There were also a few, a very few, identifiable free black men at the Arkansas, some of whom engaged in farming on a small scale; and the 1790 census reveals the presence of two free mulatto women, both of whom occupied themselves as seamstresses. Although there is no evidence of free blacks serving in the Arkansas militia, as they did with distinction in the lower reaches of the colony, there were five blacks in the party that James Colbert had led in the attack on Arkansas Post during the American Revolution.

Cruel penalties were inflicted on slaves convicted of committing crimes against whites. In 1742 a runaway slave of the Sango nation (from the Congo region), who belonged to Madame Lepine of Arkansas Post, attacked and seriously injured a French soldier bent on returning him to his mistress. He was originally sentenced to death, but, probably because he was too valuable to execute, his sentence was commuted. He was flogged for a number of days running at the crossroads of New Orleans, his right ear was cut off, and he was condemned to wear a six-pound weight on his foot for the rest of his life. Despite the dreadful punishment that often awaited recaptured fugitive slaves (*marons*), bondsmen ran away with some frequency. Three or four slaves belonging to Post merchant François Ménard found sanctuary among the Choctaws in the late eighteenth century, and it seems likely that they were never recovered. Others were not so lucky: One of the many police duties of commandants on the Arkansas River was the capture of runaway slaves, and commandants' letters often included requests that masters reimburse them for costs incurred in effecting these arrests. Those expenses sometimes included rewards given to Quapaws who had captured *marons* and had brought them to the commandant.

Marons: Runaway slaves.

In 1781, the French-Quapaw *métis* named Chalmet, while hunting on the Bayou Bartholomew between Arkansas Post and Ouachita Post, encountered and captured a young black runaway whom he had found sitting with a gun near a little campfire. Chalmet had resolved to keep the slave, but Captain Villiers intended to make him give the young man up and return him to his master. This is the only indication that the Quapaws possessed any black slaves in the colonial period, though it would not be surprising if they owned a few.

Métis: Descendants of mixed French/ Indian alliances or marriages.

Fugitive slaves who were captured were imprisoned until the commandant could determine who their masters were. In 1783, for instance, *engagés* of François Ménard seized a black slave on an island in the Mississippi. The Arkansas commandant believed that the runaway belonged to one James Sullivan of Louisville, but he nevertheless drafted a notice that he sent to New Orleans, evidently for circulation to the other towns and posts of Louisiana, and perhaps also to some of the constituent republics of that new country called the United States. The notice read:

> Notice of a Black Runaway Held in the Fort of Carlos III of Arkansas.
> Cezar, a creole [i.e., native] of Virginia, age twenty years more or less, with large eyes, well-shaped nostrils, long chin, and no beard, five feet and six inches tall, lean body, and suffering greatly from back [or kidney] pain. Arkansas, 1 August 1783.

That same year, Captain DuBreuil reported that on his arrival at Arkansas Post he had found a *maron* in the Post jail who had fled from Natchez where his New Orleans master had sent him to work. No one had wanted to take charge of the runaway, so DuBreuil, feeling an obligation to shelter him from the cold, had taken him in. The slave had begged DuBreuil to ask his master for mercy, and DuBreuil had written the governor requesting him to use his good offices to intercede.

The white residents of colonial Louisiana, who were greatly outnumbered by their slaves in the lower part of the colony, were always alert to the possibility of a slave uprising; and when the slave conspiracy was uncovered in 1795 in Pointe Coupée, the government executed twenty-three slaves implicated in the plot and exiled thirty-one others to hard labor outside the province. Eighteenth-century revolutionary ideas about equality and the rights of man had penetrated even so remote a colony as Louisiana.

Though there is no evidence of slave conspiracies at the Arkansas, in 1778 Captain Villiers complained that "vagabonds" and fugitive slaves were leading forays against the French hunters of the Arkansas River, pillaging and even killing them. Perhaps there was at least the beginnings of a *maron* community on the Arkansas River, in which some whites cooperated, though the fugitive slaves to whom Villiers had made reference may well have been Indians, or mainly so.

However that may be, it appears that the few farmers and gentry who owned slaves at Arkansas Post felt themselves attached by class and economic interest to the distant planters of lower Louisiana. Proof of this comes from a revealing event that occurred in the wake of the abortive Pointe Coupée rebellion. Governor Carondelet wrote to Captain Vilemont asking him to prevail on the Post slave owners to contribute voluntarily to a fund to compensate the owners of the slaves who had been executed or exiled for their part in the conspiracy. The aim was to raise $15,000 from the province as a whole, and the slaveholders of the Post, save one lonely holdout, answered the call by donating the requested six *reales* (seventy-five cents) for each slave that they owned. The effort raised a grand total of $34.75 from the denizens of Arkansas Post.

French and Quapaw Relations

Probably the most interesting aspect of life in colonial Arkansas, perhaps even the Post's real and most important story, has to do with the ways in which Quapaws and the Europeans who lived there found to coexist.

After the Americans took over Arkansas Post in 1804, what especially struck visitors there was the symbiosis that the natives and the French had achieved in the five or six generations that they had lived together on and near the Arkansas River. A number of these visitors maintained that intermarriage between the Quapaws and their French neighbors had been common, but the matter is somewhat controversial. An important cultural datum, though, that can serve as a useful starting point for considering this question, is that the Quapaws sometimes used marriage as a way to establish ties between their tribe and its trade allies. So, as early as 1700, when English traders were attempting to gain a foothold in the Arkansas country, one of them married a daughter (maybe two) of an important Quapaw headman. A similar alliance occurred about seventy years later when the English took possession of the east bank of the Mississippi River following the end of the Seven Years' War: An English trade mission boldly intruded up the Arkansas River and established itself in a Quapaw village, and one of its number promptly married a chief's daughter.

It would be odd if the Quapaws did not forge these kinds of bonds with the colonial French as well, given the closeness of the relationship between them for upwards of 120 years. It is true that the colonial sacramental records reveal only one or two such unions. But these records are sporadic and incomplete, and in any case largely irrelevant, because diplomatic trade marriages would have taken place in the Quapaw villages according to Indian custom. These connections quite obviously would not have left a trace in any church records. In addition, there are numerous contemporaneous histories and reports, some of them evidently independent of each other, that assert that the French residents of Arkansas intermarried with the Quapaws from very early times and in some numbers. We also occasionally learn of French-Quapaw *métis* in letters from the Post. Of course, these *métis* may have been the offspring of informal connubial connections not fully sanctioned by either the church or by Quapaw custom; or they might even have been the product of casual interaction. And sometimes European observers mistakenly assumed that the *métis* whom they saw in and around the Post had Quapaw origins, when instead they owed their lineage to marriages between French hunters and their Indian slaves from other tribes. Church records do report these unions in some numbers. The extent to which Frenchmen and Quapaws entered into marital arrangements is probably not determinable to any very certain degree on the basis of this equivocal record.

While conjugal relationships, whether formal or not, serve as examples of the closeness that the two very disparate peoples inhabiting the Arkansas region achieved, in other ways the native Americans remained quite distinct from the European colonists. For example, the French and Spanish had scant success in applying their laws to the Quapaws because the Quapaws insisted on maintaining their sovereignty and refused to cede jurisdiction over members of their tribe to foreign nations. Father Vitry, a military chaplain who visited the Quapaws in 1739, explained that the Indians valued their freedom greatly, and the records reveal that Quapaws exhibited their independence and individuality both internally within the tribe and collectively in their external dealings with their European allies. Father Vitry cautioned his readers, for example, that the Quapaws reserved the right to abandon a military venture at any time without the permission of its French commander: They retained control of their own warriors and never considered themselves auxiliaries. He also remarked on another highly important feature of Quapaw society, namely, that chiefs did not have the power to order their warriors into battle. That was a matter for persuasion and consensus.

Events that occurred when the Spanish took formal possession of Arkansas in October of 1769 reveal rather clearly how the Quapaws had conceptualized their political relationship with the French and how they intended to continue to view it with their new European ally. In that year, the Quapaw great chief Cossenonpoint put his mark to a document that he and Captain DeClouet, who commanded at the Post for Spain, had prepared together. The instrument said that Cossenonpoint, as chief of the great medal and great chief of all the Quapaw warriors, promised to recognize the new Spanish governor, Alexander O'Reilly, as his father and to listen to everything that DeClouet told him on O'Reilly's behalf. It is important to note, first of all, that the recognition of the governor as a "father" did not, in the Indian culture and idiom, come outfitted with the same patriarchal freight that such an undertaking would carry in European societies. Quapaw fathers were generous providers as much as disciplinarians, and in Quapaw society the primary duty of protection and care fell to them. Quapaw fathers were entitled to be presumptively regarded as wise men, but a reflexive obedience was certainly not owed them; and so the assumption of the father role by the French and Spanish governments placed heavy duties

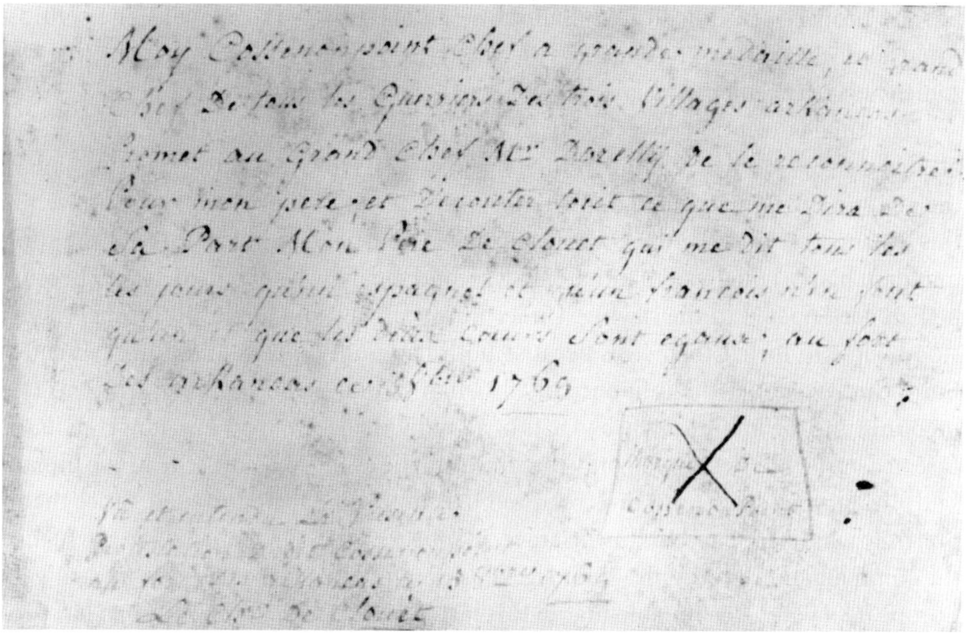
Moy Cossenonpoint chef a grande medaille, et grand chef de tous les Quapaws des trois Villages arkansas promet au Grand Chef Mr Oreilly de le reconnoitre pour mon pere et d'ecouter tout ce que me dira de sa part Mon Pere De Clouet qui me dit tous les jours que les Espagnols et les François ne font qu'un que les deux Couronnes sont egaux; au fort des arkansas ce 15 8bre 1769

Instrument executed by the Quapaw great chief Cossenonpoint on October 15, 1769, at Arkansas Post. *Courtesy of Louisiana State Museum, New Orleans; on loan to the Louisiana State Museum from the Louisiana Historical Society.*

of support on the Europeans, but did not give them significantly extensive rights over the Indians and their behavior.

The Quapaws' retention of the essential aspects of their sovereignty is even more evident in Cossenonpoint's undertaking to "listen to" what DeClouet told him. In this highly important phrase, the parties adopted a familiar Indian idiom that was used to describe a well-respected and influential chief: The Spanish commandants at the Post not infrequently evaluated the various Indian leaders in their bailiwick for the governor, and those whom they believed to be particularly useful and dependable they described as "much listened to." So what Cossenonpoint was saying to the Spanish was that he would regard the Spanish governor as a "chief," that is, as an important leader, worthy of being listened to; but, as we have already seen, this was, in Quapaw society, a long way from accepting the governor as a European-style commander-in-chief. The governor, in other words, had to be content with being Indianized, just as the lower orders were to a very large degree.

A comparison of Cossenonpoint's promise with the oath of allegiance that the French of the Arkansas took the same day to the Spanish monarchy makes the Quapaws' reservation of sovereignty, and the delicacy and tenuousness of their ties to the general Spanish interest, even more evident. The Frenchmen at the Post pledged fidelity to the Catholic Spanish king, swore that from that moment on they recognized him "as master of [their] life and property," and dedicated themselves "to his supreme royal will." The contrast could hardly be greater: The Quapaws promised to listen respectfully, an activity that falls somewhere between hearing and heeding; the French swore abjectly to obey.

The single exception of record to the Quapaws' refusal to submit to European law occurred in 1778, when Captain Vallière cajoled the Quapaws into executing one of their number who had killed an American hunter without provocation. But even in this instance it seems that the Quapaws achieved a partial cultural victory, for the commandant had originally demanded that a second Quapaw be executed as well because he had participated in the slaying. Under European law, of course, both perpetrators stood liable to forfeit their lives because both had guilty minds and both had acted: European law, under the influence of Christian thinking and teaching, concentrated on punishing the intentionally bad acts of all individuals. Quapaw law, however, in the case of a homicide, demanded only that the death be avenged ("covered," as the Indians said) by another death, and thus required that only one life be forfeited. Since that is precisely what happened in this instance, it appears that the Quapaws had persuaded the commandant to recognize their legal customs and not to exact the more stringent European penalty. It is notable that in this instance the application of Indian law produced a more merciful result than European law would have.

On many other occasions, Europeans were simply unable to apply their law to Indians at all. For instance, when a Quapaw chief struck at a Spanish commandant with a hatchet during a drunken confrontation, the officer was powerless to do anything about it, despite the condign punishment that would have awaited a white person who had dared to offer such an insult to the representative of His Most Catholic Majesty. Sometimes the Quapaws were influential enough even to have their own legal customs applied to Frenchmen when those customs were directly contrary to European law. An example occurred in 1754, when the Quapaws succeeded in prying pardons from the Louisiana governor for six soldiers who had deserted from the Post garrison and were subject to the death penalty under military law for doing so. Guedelonguay, a Quapaw chief, argued vigorously and successfully that the soldiers were entitled to clemency because they had sought refuge in the Quapaws' *cabanne de valeur* (house of valor) where religious rites were practiced, and under Quapaw sanctuary law this provided them with protection from punishment. The Quapaws were such important allies that the governor felt obliged to grant their request.

Cabanne de valeur:
A French term used in reference to Indian (specifically, Quapaw) sacred temples.

The French and Spanish authorities worked hard to nurture and maintain the Quapaws' allegiance, and they forged some significant institutional connections with them that were designed to carry out their undertaking to be the Quapaws' "father." To uphold their end of the bargain, for instance, the Spanish provided the Quapaws with a gunsmith to keep their weapons in good repair and with an interpreter (who was sometimes a *métis*), who acted as a kind of Indian agent for the Europeans. The centerpiece of the European effort, however, was the annual present to the tribe, which included, in addition to the trade goods already mentioned, kettles, hoes, pipes, bells, and even silver-braided longcoats and trousers. This gift-giving had probably grown out of an Indian custom that called for a reciprocal exchange of gifts between allies on important occasions, but the aspect of mutuality had soon dropped out of the arrangement in Louisiana and it had evolved into an annuity, perhaps a form of tribute even, from the European "father."

During the Spanish period, the principal impediment to European expansion in the Arkansas region was the mighty Osage nation, which, while it lived most of the year in villages in what is now Missouri, claimed northern and western Arkansas as its hunting territory, and thus often interfered with French hunters operating on the Arkansas River west of Little Rock. It appears that Arkansas hunters preferred to work the upper reaches of this river between Little Rock and Fort Smith, and they even ventured well into Oklahoma. Bears were probably more common or fatter in the mountainous region, and buffalo significantly larger and more numerous on the plains of Oklahoma, and thus the richness of the game in these places proved an attraction, often a fatal one, to the denizens of the Post. However that may be, between 1770 and 1800 alone, the Osages killed more than fifty hunters on the Arkansas River, some under extremely gruesome circumstances.

The Quapaws occasionally retaliated against these Osage depredations, but the usual Spanish policy was to try to negotiate with the Osages and bring them to terms. There was, in any case, little practical hope of ever subduing the mighty Osage nation, since the meager Spanish forces, even taking the militia into account, were simply not up to anything like a successful campaign against them. The sad truth was, as well, that Spanish officials in New Orleans regarded the deaths on the Arkansas as unfortunate but not sufficiently important to avenge, because that might inconvenience the merchant class of St. Louis, who had an oligopoly on trade with the Osages and depended heavily on the tribe for their living. This attitude on the part of the New Orleans and St. Louis grandees enraged Commandant Villiers at the Arkansas, and he demanded to know whether commerce was to be cemented with the blood of innocents. In the 1790s, the Spanish finally undertook some half-hearted sorties against the Osages, but they met with no success, and the government soon turned its military attentions to the more pressing threat of an American invasion. The Osages continued to harry the hunters of the Arkansas until the end of the colonial epoch.

The Quapaws were more than a little amazed by the nonchalance of the Spanish government's reaction to the killing of its own people in such substantial numbers, and they were inclined to regard the Spanish government as pusillanimous. Spanish equivocation and impotence may, in part, have accounted for the attitude of the Quapaws toward the American Revolution. The Quapaws had, from about 1768, frequented an English trading village called Concordia that was established after the Seven Years' War across the Mississippi from the mouth of the White River. The English there were always spreading sedition among the tribe, ridiculing the Spanish army, its ordnance, and its fort at the Arkansas, and they predicted that Spain would soon be swept from Louisiana for good. Much of what the English said, especially about the ludicrously dilapidated condition of the Spanish fort and the weakness of the garrison at the Post, corresponded with what the Quapaws already knew from their own observation and experience.

So when the Spanish joined the American cause against the British during the American Revolution, it is not surprising that the Quapaws were less than enthusiastic about committing themselves to the enterprise. When the English attacked the Post with a Chickasaw force in 1783, in one of two Revolutionary War engagements fought west of the Mississippi River, the Quapaw tribe remained aloof and refrained from helping the Spanish. As one village chief put it, only the great chief Angaska had the authority to commit the tribe to a white man's war, and he had not given the word. There is evidence that Angaska had gotten wind of the attack before it came and had failed to warn the garrison, and some Spaniards even fumed that Angaska had actively connived in the British effort to destroy the Post. It is true that four members of the tribe joined with some Spanish soldiers in a daring sally from the fort that routed the invaders and turned the day in the Spaniards' favor. But these Quapaws were acting as individuals who happened to have been in the fort when the attack had come in the wee hours of the morning. One of them was a French-Quapaw *métis* named Saracen, whose rescue of an officer's children from the Chickasaws after the battle was later commemorated in a church window in Pine Bluff.

Trade with the Quapaws, as we saw, was not especially remunerative, but one aspect of it, the provision of liquor (brandy and rum) to the Indians, was of concern throughout the colonial era. French and Spanish authorities, depending on the perceived needs of the moment, blew hot and cold on prohibiting the liquor trade with the Quapaws. On the one hand, liquor caused considerable havoc: Inebriated white hunters and Indians alike made for forgetful debtors and unreliable warriors. On the other hand, liquor was very much in demand, frequently in preference to any other good. In the 1760s, for instance, Comdt. Alexandre DeClouet allowed that the Quapaw alliance simply could not be held together without liquor, and the English across the Mississippi at Concordia constantly importuned the Quapaws with it in an effort to undermine their attachment to the Spanish. The French residents of the Arkansas, moreover, were occasionally in such dire straits that they were forced to trade liquor with the Quapaws for corn.

DeClouet, despite his misgivings, eventually prohibited the liquor trade with the Quapaws, but later commandants resorted merely to licensing liquor traders in an attempt to control the flow of spirits into the Indian nation. This kind of restriction did not at first sit well with the tribe: Quapaw leaders complained that every other kind of trade was free and open, and argued that the regulation of the liquor trade with them constituted an irritating and insulting discrimination. When Captain Villiers, a vocal devotee of the free market, resolved to open this trade to anyone, some of the *habitants* and merchants of the Post became alarmed and petitioned the governor to prevent it: "A wiser decision," they believed, would be to establish "a single place . . . where drink would be distributed to [the Indians] in an orderly and proper manner." Villiers's original decision with respect to trading liquor at the Post, he explained to the governor, had been to license only one *cabaret* for selling liquor by the glass (*en detail*), "to prevent the disorders that a free distribution might generate" on account of "the Indians by whom we are surrounded." He had, however, allowed any merchant to sell liquor, even *en detail,* for consumption off premises.

The Quapaws' attachment to the virtues of free enterprise was not long lived. In 1786, three Quapaw chiefs asked the governor to prohibit the liquor trade with their tribe altogether because of widespread alcohol dependence in their nation. The governor temporized, and, during a three-month period alone, five Quapaws died in alcohol-related brawls. Finally, in 1787, after a minor Quapaw chief was killed during yet another drunken altercation, and his mutilated body was thrown into the Arkansas River, the governor forbade the sale of liquor to the tribe entirely. "All traffic of drink with the Indians" must cease, the governor ordered, "because of the consequences" that had flowed from that trade. Violators of the ban, the order warned, would have their goods confiscated and would be imprisoned for an indefinite term.

This prohibitionist effort, as we would have expected, was not successful, or at least not entirely so, for late in the colonial period Captain Vilemont complained to the governor about "the great influx of Indians [no doubt Choctaws and Chickasaws] who are difficult to contain when they drink." Since the small population of the Post would be unable to protect itself from the disasters that Vilemont predicted, he asked the governor to forbid the importation of rum to the Post completely except for the use of the *voyageurs* and sailors who worked the rivers. A short time later, a petition from some leading citizens at the Arkansas seconded Vilemont's request, and they pointedly noted not only that liquor had had a pernicious effect on the behavior of the Indians, but also that the French hunters' immoderate use of it had made debt collection more difficult.

Despite these and other occasional conflicts, conditions in the colonial Arkansas country had virtually conspired to optimize prospects for peaceful coexistence and cooperation between the Quapaws and the Europeans who lived there. Around 1700, the Caddos who had lived in Arkansas retreated south, some to join the Caddodoches on the great bend of the Red River in east Texas, others to positions lower down the river in Louisiana. This left the Quapaws as the only tribe permanently residing in the region. So even a very generous estimate of the number of people occupying Arkansas in the late eighteenth century yields a population density there of only about one person (Indian, white, and black) to every five square miles. (Present-day Western Sahara has a population density ten times as great.) There was therefore no real competition between the Europeans and the Quapaws for either land or animal resources in the territory that the tribe claimed. Because there was plenty to go around, a frequent source of friction between colonists and native people was eliminated.

In addition, the European population consisted for the most part of highly individualistic hunters, who proved unreliable militiamen, and the French and Spanish garrisons were small and its soldiers often unseasoned and undisciplined; all of this added greatly to the military usefulness of the Quapaws. This helps explain why the French and the Quapaws joined together in the 1770s to build a road connecting their settlements, the first road construction project of record in the state. Connubial arrangements of some sort between whites and Indians would seem to have been more or less inevitable because few French women wished to venture up to the Arkansas to share the lives of white men there, and, besides, the practical skills of the Indian women made them ideal partners for the white hunters, traders, and merchants of Arkansas Post.

It is also significant that the French, and then the Spanish in imitation of them, never attempted to cajole, coax, or force the Quapaws into becoming mission farmers; indeed, the Spanish did not proselytize the Indians at all. This was in complete contrast to the old-fashioned imperialist plan that the Spanish doggedly pursued in California beginning about 1770 by creating a line of presidios and missions along the Pacific Coast. Nor did the European powers that claimed to hold sway over the Arkansas country try to incorporate the Indians into their legal systems in any significant way. It is well known that proselytizing was a significant cause of strife between whites and Indians, but it needs saying that the same would be true of attempts at legal assimilation. Like religion, law is an expression of the highest ethical and moral aspirations of a people, and their attachment to it can prove to be tenacious. The respect that colonial Louisiana officials showed to indigenous legal and religious traditions no doubt did a great deal to ingratiate them with the Quapaws' political and religious leaders.

Whatever may have been the case elsewhere in North America, therefore, it would seem right to characterize the small number of Europeans who came to Arkansas during its colonial epoch as more like immigrants than invaders. It is true that immigrants do not typically claim sovereignty, build forts, and establish garrisons. But French and Spanish claims to sovereignty over Arkansas were basically hollow: The Indians did not consider themselves subjects, and the Europeans did not even pretend that they were. This was hegemony writ small.

End of an Era

In 1800, Spain, under a secret treaty, retroceded the colony of Louisiana to France, but France did not move to retake possession of the province until late in 1803. By then, France had already found it necessary to sell Louisiana to the United States, and the French interregnum lasted only twenty days, after which, on December 20, 1803, the American government took possession of the colony.

An American lieutenant named James Many did not venture up the Arkansas River until March of 1804 to receive the Post of Arkansas on behalf of his nation. There he found Capt. Caso y Luengo commanding a Spanish force already reduced to three soldiers. The settlement that Many entered comprised about four hundred souls; and the dilapidated fort that he occupied for the United States was worth, so its appraisers reckoned, only 631 dollars, a small enough sum for one hundred and twenty years of imperial effort.

Civil government was slow in coming to the Post. For a few years, Lieutenant Many and his successors imitated, no doubt to the great relief of Post residents, the military government of the previous French and Spanish regimes, judging and settling disputes and recording documents themselves. It would not be long, however, before a new republican machinery was put in place, and the old colonial residents of Arkansas soon found their mores and themselves rudely shoved aside. New arrivals from the United States were not slow to criticize the French creoles whom they encountered, damning them wholesale as a lazy and superstitious lot, excluding them from government offices and from jury service, ridiculing their religious practices and even the way that they built their houses. The French language languished, too: The only item that the *Arkansas Gazette*, a weekly newspaper established at the Post in 1819, ever published in French was a small, four-line notice for a local political candidate who was evidently plumping for the creole vote.

The Post itself soon received an official snub. It served as the Arkansas territorial capital from 1819 to 1821, but with the creation of Little Rock in the latter year the seat of government was moved there. About a decade later, Washington Irving used the two towns to contrast the idle creoles of Louisiana with the bustling American immigrants, hard after the main chance, who were soon to engulf them for good. In one of his stories, he pictured the Post as the paradigmatic creaky creole village, inhabited by an amiable collection of indolent Frenchmen; Little Rock he filled with lawyers, banks, newspapers, and electioneering candidates, all engaged in a furious competition. For this tale, Irving invented the phrase "the almighty dollar" to describe what the enterprising newcomers were out after. Irving was deliberately caricaturing both the French and the Americans to a degree, but he was certainly right about the complete substitution of cultures that had rapidly occurred in the Arkansas country.

With the removal of the capital to Little Rock, the Post found itself an almost instant backwater. The old French houses that survived, with their tall chimneys and their distinctive galleries all around, succumbed to the drubbing that Union gunboats gave the town in 1863. Though a small settlement managed to survive, and the United States Government stoutly maintained a post office called Arkansas Post until 1941, today there is nothing left of the first European settlement in what became Jefferson's Louisiana. The federal government, however, some decades ago established the Arkansas Post National Memorial at the old town site, with a fine visitors' center that features exhibits and a film outlining Arkansas's colonial history. And a considerable amount of archeology has been undertaken at two of the former locations of the village: There have been important discoveries, including the probable site of Tonty's first outpost. Perhaps these finds augur a future for the Post as distinguished and fascinating as its past.

CHAPTER SIX

The Turbulent Path to Statehood: Arkansas Territory, 1803–1836

The period between 1803 and 1836 marked an important formative era in American history and the territory of Arkansas. The young United States fought for and established its territorial integrity, devised and began to carry out a draconian Indian policy, and reinvented its political party system after the Federalists and Democratic Republicans dissolved. All of these developments would have their parallels in Arkansas. This place, called "remote and restless" by historian S. Charles Bolton, began its integration into the national political economy almost immediately after the Louisiana Purchase of 1803. Within fifteen years it became a staging ground for the removal of Indian groups east of the Mississippi River, and it began the process of dispossessing its own American Native population. It developed a political party system divided between Whigs and Democrats, and, like other frontier territories, it revealed a decided preference for the Democratic Party. Finally, by the 1830s its agricultural economy began to mimic that of the southern states dedicated to slavery, with a plantation elite coming to dominance even as they constituted a distinct numerical minority of the white population. Cotton plantations became concentrated in the southeastern section of the state where the descendants of planters from places like Virginia and Kentucky settled. Meanwhile, hill people from the Appalachia Mountains, largely, settled in northern and northwest Arkansas, and though some of them owned slaves, few held more than a couple of slaves or practiced large-scale agricultural production. The drive for statehood in the mid-1830s exposed this geographical divide, a divide which would only grow more pronounced after Arkansas became the twenty-fifth state of the Union in June 1836. See plate 19 following page 270.

The Louisiana Purchase

The Arkansas region came into the possession of the United States by virtue of the Louisiana Purchase of 1803, an altogether unexpected and monumental real estate transaction. When James Monroe departed for Paris in January, he had orders only to assist the American minister to France, Robert R. Livingston, in negotiating the purchase of the city of New Orleans. Pres. Thomas Jefferson dispatched Monroe on this important mission largely to secure the loyalty of American settlers west of the

Appalachians who relied on the Ohio and Mississippi rivers to get their goods to market. Although Jefferson and others might have entertained dreams of extending the contours of the new nation beyond the Mississippi River, the isolated and virtually unknown outpost called Arkansas Post hardly excited anyone's interest. New Orleans, located near the mouth of the Mississippi, constituted the gateway to the Gulf of Mexico and the world beyond. The matter was urgent; the concern for the interests of American producers was real. They had received a lesson in the city's importance in October 1802 when Spain, just a month before handing over New Orleans to the French, had effectively halted American trade there. Americans had become suspicious about French goals in the area when it became known that the French and Spanish had entered a secret treaty ceding the vast area known as "Louisiana" to the French in 1800. When the French took possession of the city of New Orleans in 1802, the Americans felt sure that they would continue the unpopular Spanish policy concerning American trade. In fact, some believed that the French were behind the closing of the city to American trade while it was still under Spanish rule and that Napoleon Bonaparte had sinister goals in doing so. After all, Bonaparte's expansionist dreams in Europe had embroiled that continent in war, and for a while he entertained notions of a New France in the Americas. Two factors diverted his attention, however: the ongoing revolution in the French colony of Saint-Domingue (now Haiti), and his plans for war with England in Europe.

Unaware that Napoleon's goals in America had changed because of the events in Saint-Domingue and in Europe, Jefferson and others determined to do something about securing a commercial outlet for the citizens on the western fringe of the United States. The loyalty and well-being of nearly one million settlers between the Appalachians and the Mississippi River was at stake, and even though purchase of New Orleans alone would leave the French in possession of Louisiana, the acquisition of the city would alleviate the most pressing obstacle to trade. When James Monroe arrived in Paris on April 11, he discovered that on the previous day, the French offered to sell not only New Orleans but all of Louisiana, approximately 828,000 square miles. Surprised at the proposal but recognizing the implications, Monroe and Livingston pursued the offer, and on April 30, 1803, they completed a treaty making the United States the purchaser of the Louisiana Territory for the asking price of $15 million.

While the extraordinary purchase more than doubled the size of the United States, it also enhanced the young country's potential as a world power. However, the purchase brought with it some troubling concerns. It necessitated the extension of military and governmental authority over a territory about which little was known. The boundaries themselves were not clear, and no one knew how many individuals lived in the area. Although New Orleans and St. Louis were better known, some intelligence existed about Arkansas Post where a trading post operated to conduct diplomacy with Native Americans in the vicinity and to service the hunters and trappers engaged in the fur trade. The Quapaw Indians, located in three villages near the Post, had established treaties with the previous European powers exercising authority in the region, the French and the Spanish. These treaties worked to the benefit of both the Europeans and the Quapaw, and these Native Americans hoped that they could continue such alliances with the New Americans. The realization of certain Anglo-American goals for the region, however, dictated a different posture toward the Quapaw, one that had devastating consequences for them.

Jefferson's plans for the territory were initially unformed, but his ideas evolved over the next few years, even as he eagerly studied available maps and books on the unexplored area west of the Mississippi and pondered how the territory fit into his vision for the country. He recognized the implications for his Indian policy and considered resettling the troublesome Indians east of the Mississippi River to a location somewhere in Louisiana. He supposed that whites should be discouraged from settling there until available land east of the river had been fully occupied, and he even thought it might be wise to offer whites already in the territory land on the eastern side of the river in order to preserve the territory for Indians. However, these ruminations were not the immediate concern. Both Congress and the president, though not always in concert, wrestled with how to integrate the territory into the nation. Congress eventually concluded that the Land Ordinance of 1785, which provided for the rectangular survey of land, would extend to the new territory, making it possible for the orderly sale and settlement of land there. They also determined that the Northwest Ordinance of 1787, which outlined the steps necessary for moving from territorial status to statehood, would apply, making it clear how the territory was to be integrated into the political system. The Louisiana Territory was eventually divided, new territories formed, and new states ultimately emerged. Arkansas became the third state organized out of the territory in 1836.

Land Ordinance of 1785: Established the Township/Range/Section system for sectioning off land to expedite sale of federal lands.

Northwest Ordinance of 1787: Established the procedures by which territories of the United States would become states and banned slavery in the northwest territories.

The division of the Louisiana Territory began almost immediately. In 1804 Congress established Orleans Territory, encompassing the present state of Louisiana. In 1806 Congress formed the District of Arkansas—named for the Indians known as the "Arkansa." Its name originated, apparently, with an Illinois Indian guide who accompanied Father Jacques Marquette and Louis Jolliet in 1673 in their exploration of the Mississippi River. The guide characterized the Quapaw, then living in villages just up the Arkansas River, as the "Arkansa." The district remained a part of the larger Louisiana Territory, with its northern boundary at thirty-six degrees, thirty minutes, established in 1808. It remained underappreciated and remote, in part because its administration was the province of New Madrid, in present-day Missouri, a ten-day trip from Arkansas Post. The residents there thus enjoyed—or suffered under—little government, and according to one historian, given its remote location, Arkansas likely remained under military authority longer than any other place in Louisiana. In 1812, when Orleans Territory became the state of Louisiana, the Arkansas District became a part of Missouri Territory. It continued to be ignored by authorities in Missouri, and thus local forces, largely those around Arkansas Post, shaped developments there. When Missouri officials began to consider applying for statehood in 1818, they understood that they would need to narrow its boundaries if they had any hope of success with their petition to Congress. In addition to abandoning areas west and north of present-day Missouri, they excluded the District of Arkansas and a part of Lawrence County that was contiguous to it. In 1819 this area consolidated and achieved separate territorial status, becoming the Territory of Arkansas. In that same year, the Adams-Onis Treaty relinquished a piece of the territory on Arkansas's southwestern corner to Spain, ending a long struggle over the international border. Arkansas lost a segment lying below the Red River, but still its western border extended well into present-day Oklahoma. That would change in 1828 when a new boundary was drawn in order to establish "Indian" territory. The only other modification to its boundaries occurred when Missouri became a state in 1820. Certain citizens with greater ties to the proposed new state petitioned to have the area, now known as the boot hill, affixed to Missouri.

Adams-Onis Treaty: Negotiated in 1819 between the United States and Spain, it gave the United States Florida but, more important for Arkansas, it established the southwestern border of the Territory of Arkansas.

Exploring the Territory

The first American "emissaries" to the Arkansas region arrived in the winter of 1804–1805, but their exploration was cursory and unenthusiastically pursued. Although they identified the trees, plants, and animals they encountered, they provided few details and made no drawings. Aside from some experiments at the "hot springs," they were more interested in providing intelligence about how to explore the region generally than they were about their findings on Arkansas. In fact, a trip up the Ouachita was a consolation prize after certain safety and diplomatic concerns diverted them from their original plan. They had intended a more important expedition up the Red River as part of Jefferson's goal of establishing the precise boundaries of the purchase. The Mississippi River clearly marked the eastern boundary, and Jefferson assumed, accurately as it happens, that the great Stony Mountains (the Rocky Mountains) marked the western limit, but considerable ambiguity attended the southern and northern boundaries. Jefferson dispatched Meriwether Lewis and William Clark to discover the northern boundary in the spring of 1804, and he planned another expedition up the Red River in late 1804 to establish the southern limit. Because of Spanish hostility to an expedition that would skirt Spanish territory and because Congress exhibited reluctance to fund another expensive expedition, Jefferson altered the course of the proposed expedition up the Red River and settled for a less ambitious and less expensive exploration of the Ouachita River and the famous "hot springs" in present-day central Arkansas.

The constraints operating on Jefferson also forced him to select two immigrant Scotsmen who were acceptable, if not entirely suitable or qualified, for the Ouachita

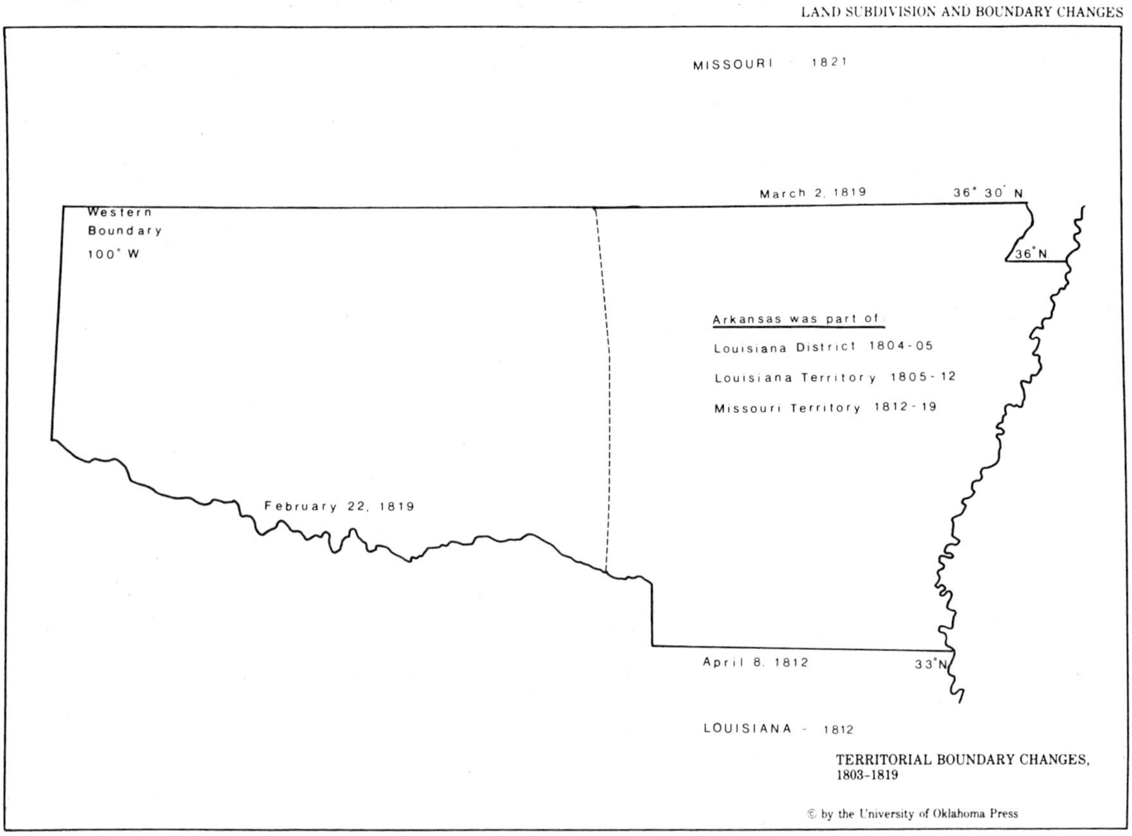

Arkansas territorial land subdivision and boundary changes. *From Gerald T. Hanson and Carl M. Moneyhon,* Historical Atlas of Arkansas *(Norman: University of Oklahoma Press, 1989).*

River expedition. William Dunbar, a noted scientist and wealthy Mississippi planter, was in poor health and reluctant to accept the commission. Dr. George Hunter, an apothecary and qualified physician, who established himself in Philadelphia as a chemist and entrepreneur, was known to be an overly ambitious man. Although the Lewis and Clark expedition is far better known today, the excursion up the Ouachita River made Dunbar and Hunter famous in their own day, for they returned and reported their findings long before their more celebrated counterparts. While their reports provided some practical information about how to explore the territory and thus influenced later expeditions, it also furnished the first evidence that a complex sociopolitical system already existed in the territory. Although it was clearly sparsely populated, many white and Indian hunters frequented the area, and some of them called the place home.

The Dunbar-Hunter expedition actually began where St. Catherine's Creek meets the Mississippi, about fifteen miles below Natchez, on October 16, 1804. It constituted the nearest landing to Dunbar's plantation, "The Forest," where he was known as a

William Dunbar. *Courtesy Mississippi Department of Archives and History.*

"little nabob." Dunbar, probably accompanied by two servants and a slave, boarded the fifty-foot, flat-bottomed Chinese scow, which George Hunter had designed specifically for the expedition. On board was Hunter, his teenage son, twelve soldiers, and a sergeant. They descended the Mississippi, passed Fort Adams the next day, and camped at the mouth of the Red River. On October 18 they began the ascension of the Red, detoured up the Ouachita River when they reached it five days later, and arrived at the Post of Ouachita on November 6. At the post, which was also known as Fort Miro and would later became the city of Monroe, Louisiana, Dunbar and Hunter rented a flat-bottomed barge in place of the inadequate scow, which hung too low in the water, and hired a pilot-guide who was familiar with conditions upriver. They resumed their journey on November 11 and four days later crossed thirty-three degrees north latitude, which had been established by Congress that year as the dividing line between the territory of Orleans and that of Louisiana. It would eventually become the state line between Louisiana and Arkansas. While the trip thus far had been difficult, it was to become even more so as the weather worsened, and the rapids grew more fierce. The barge they secured at the post, however, was much better at negotiating the shoals and rapids than Hunter's scow, a fact not lost on Dunbar who carefully recorded his observations about the kind of craft necessary for exploring the rivers in the newly acquired territory. Discounting the five days they spent at the post, it took them almost twenty-four days of travel to reach the Arkansas line, a distance of roughly 240 miles. It took

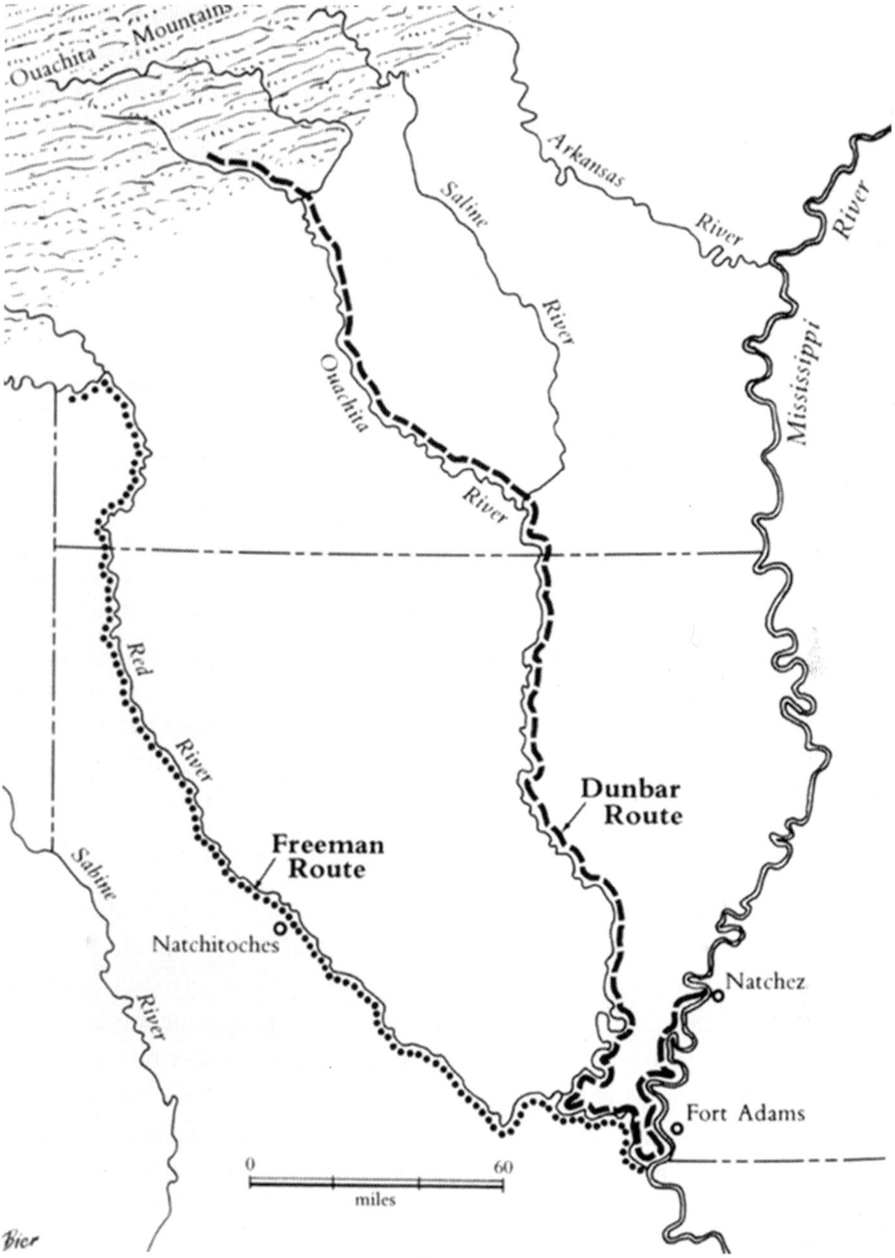

Ouachita and Red River expeditions (routes outlined). *From Donald Jackson,* Thomas Jefferson and the Stony Mountains: Exploring the West from Monticello *(Chicago: University of Illinois Press, 1981).*

another twenty-two days for them to travel the nearly 248 miles to the hot springs, which, considering the rougher rapids upriver, was a significant improvement.

On December 6 the party reached Ellis camp, which the pilot identified as the ideal place to disembark for the eight-mile hike to the hot springs. If ever there was a moment when Dunbar and Hunter should have recognized the fact that this was not an isolated wilderness, it was at the hot springs. The soldiers were put to the task of transporting supplies, and even though this task was met with the customary grumbling, they did not have to bear the tents, for a cabin and several rough huts for use by convalescents would house the men during their sojourn there. The structures were meant for use during the summer, however, and Dunbar directed them to build a chimney at one end of the twelve-foot-long cabin to protect against the cold. Believing that the springs had curative powers, whites bathed in and drank from them. In fact, Ellis Camp was named after a Major Ellis from Natchez who, along with two companions, was purportedly cured of his ailments there. The pilot reported that he himself had been restored to health after bathing in the springs the previous year. The experiments Dunbar and Hunter conducted on the waters there, looking for any evidence of its medicinal properties, suggest why they selected the hot springs as their destination. Although Hunter apparently preferred exploring the region around the springs, presumably looking for ore or salt deposits, he joined Dunbar in chemical analysis of the springs. On Christmas day the two men amused themselves with such experiments while the soldiers, who had hoarded their liquor rations for the occasion, celebrated loudly. In the end, Dunbar and Hunter found no evidence that the waters possessed any unusual ingredients. Neither did Hunter find any evidence of substantial salt deposits or valuable minerals that might excite his, or anyone else's, interest.

Their reports, filed separately and widely published, were the first to provide a glimpse into the new territory after the purchase, and Dunbar and Hunter revealed more in their diaries and reports than they realized. They were entering what everyone considered an isolated wilderness but, in fact, they almost daily encountered white or Indian hunters or evidence of their recent passage. Rivers in this period were highways, and the Ouachita was apparently a well-traveled one. The whites they encountered were not only of French extraction, but some of them were part Indian. This speaks to a complicated and fluid geopolitical situation that had several components. Although it is possible to talk about white politics separately from Indian and Indian politics separately from white, the fact is they were intertwined, sometimes in subtle ways and sometimes in not-so-subtle ways.

The period immediately after Louisiana Purchase marked a tumultuous and formative one in Arkansas's history in which thousands of whites and Indians moved into the territory, particularly along the rivers, and the nature of the relationship between these two groups altered dramatically. The period before and immediately after the purchase represented what historian Richard White has termed the "middle ground," where whites and Indians borrowed from each other culturally and collaborated in their economic activity. White was referring to interactions in the Great Lakes region, primarily in the seventeenth and eighteenth centuries, and one might question its application to early nineteenth-century Arkansas. Certainly historian Kathleen DuVal argues in *The Native Ground* that Indians in Arkansas held their own, retaining their cultural identity. However, the middle-ground hypothesis provides a useful way to understand the accommodation of whites and Indians to each other in the period before the onslaught of white settlement after the Louisiana Purchase. This accommodation continued into the territorial era but eroded rapidly as new white settlers, desiring to acquire land to grow cash crops for an expanding market, began to demand the removal of the Indians. As the number of whites increased, they no longer "needed" the Native Americans and thus no longer accommodated to them. Arkansas was in the process of being incorporated into the market economy of the United States, and, specifically, into the sociopolitical structure that was peculiar to the American South. Slave owners and cotton producers, even though they were in a numerical minority (just as they were in other southern states), would come to dominate Arkansas politically, economically, and socially. Although the American government officially removed the eastern Cherokee to the territory in 1818 and provided the Choctaw with a reservation there in 1820, Jefferson's vision of settling eastern Indians in the region collapsed in the face of white settlement.

Middle ground: The collaboration and cultural exchange between Native Americans and Europeans who encountered each other in the frontier.

Native ground: A phrase coined by Kathleen Duval that posits an alternative to the middle-ground collaboration and highlights the persistence of Native ways in the face of European incursions.

Even before the Louisiana Territory, the integrity of native tribes like the Quapaw had experienced some challenges as Indians east of the river moved into the region. Motivated largely by the encroachment of white settlements east of the Mississippi, bands of Illinois, Delaware, Shawnee, Chickasaw, Choctaw, and Cherokee entered Arkansas to hunt in increasing numbers, and by the late eighteenth century, they established villages. But they typically hunted deer rather than buffalo, and their hunting strategies disturbed buffalo habitats and greatly troubled the Quapaw. Meanwhile, some of the Cherokee were refugees from the Indian wars in east Tennessee, which caused serious divisions within the tribe. Because they feared the American push westward, the Spanish tolerated the migration, and some Spanish officials secretly encouraged these disaffected Indians to wage guerrilla war against the Americans. Although apprehensive about Choctaw and Chickasaw immigration because of their longstanding alliance with the English, the Spanish accepted them because they served as a buffer between the Osage and the Spanish-allied Caddo in western Arkansas. The Caddo, who had once occupied a corner of southwestern Arkansas, had been pushed out by the Osage in the eighteenth century, and had settled in Caddo villages in what would later become north Texas. The Osage, who had permanent settlements in southwestern Missouri, still claimed hunting rights in northwestern and north-central Arkansas, and put up a determined struggle against white and Indian incursions. They represented the greatest native threat to President Jefferson's plan to encourage eastern Indians to move into the territory after the purchase.

French hunters had long been in the area, but their numbers increased and other Europeans began to move west of the Mississippi River in the late eighteenth century. The migration west was spurred in part because the United States was securing its authority in its territories east of the river, and some settlers in Illinois Territory, for example, resented it. The U.S. military presence was irksome, specifically because it was accompanied by demands for provisions and necessitated the quartering of troops in private residences, but the Northwest Ordinance of 1787 acted as an additional impetus for migration. The ordinance required the release of slaves and stimulated an exodus from Illinois Territory into what was then Spanish Louisiana. While most of the settlements founded as a result were located above what would become the Missouri-Arkansas state line, some newcomers secured Spanish land grants, and small settlements were established below that line on the Black, White, and St. Francis rivers. For example, Antoine Janis, who was probably from the well-known Janis family of Kaskaskia, a river town in Illinois Territory, entered Arkansas in the late eighteenth century as a fur trader and secured a grant of land on the White River. Others also secured grants along the White, Black, and St. Francis rivers, and although few of their thinly populated settlements survived much beyond the territorial period, they represented the first white outposts in northeastern Arkansas.

Perhaps the greatest contribution that Dunbar and Hunter rendered in making their expedition up the Ouachita was the information they recorded on the Indians and hunters they encountered. Again, while they did not themselves recognize the implications of their remarks, they painted a picture of a complex and changing sociopolitical structure. Dunbar, who had carried on a lengthy correspondence with Jefferson, and Hunter, who was later referred to as "that renown man of Jefferson," were aware of the president's plans for the Arkansas region, and they had harsh words for the Osage. Yet they were relatively generous in their remarks about the other Indians they encountered or referred to. In fact, they often portrayed Indians in a far more complimentary light than they did the whites they met. But Dunbar acknowledged the integrity of both white and Indian hunters when he remarked about their custom of depositing their skins over two forked posts in sight of the river. According to custom, such deposits were sacrosanct, and no hunter would violate them. Rather than being an uncivilized wilderness without rules, the territory had its unwritten laws that men typically abided by. But a few days after Dunbar remarked about the custom, an incident occurred that suggested that this practice was eroding in the face of the incursion of newcomers into the region.

One of the most important revelations concerning Indians and white hunters appears in Hunter's account of events occurring on November 21, 1804. On that date the expedition noticed a pictograph on a tree near their breakfast encampment. The pictographer had removed some bark from the tree and painted a scene depicting a man on horseback with one hand pointing toward the river and the other toward the woods. Two other figures, one of them wearing a round hat, a typical Indian symbol for a European, were apparently shaking hands. This seems to represent an expression of friendship. When Hunter took a party into the woods in the direction the horseman was pointing, they found a hunter's camp and fourteen deerskins tied in a bundle on a pole. Just as they arrived at the camp, however, another white man, by the name of Campbell, appeared. Campbell, a carpenter who was taking a consumptive man to the hot springs, had encamped near the expedition the evening before and had apparently left his boat to hunt in the woods. He claimed that he had placed the skins there a year before for an Indian chief by the name of Habitant, but Hunter doubted his story, concluded that the skins belonged to a Choctaw Indian, and took possession of them, determined to locate the rightful owner or deposit them at the post on the way back downriver for safekeeping. Hunter believed that if he left the skins in place, Campbell would take them, and the expedition might be blamed. Perhaps he feared retaliation for violating the custom and thought that if he had possession of the skins he could surrender them in exchange for safe passage.

Whether Campbell had made an agreement with an Indian by the name of Habitant or not, the assertion that he had done so suggests the cooperation that existed between white hunters and Indians. Hunter's disbelief did not necessarily represent an ignorance of this kind of cooperation, but rather his distrust of Campbell. It may well have been that Campbell was truly a scoundrel violating a long-held custom. But neither Dunbar nor Hunter was predisposed to trust a man of Campbell's social standing. Just as they routinely denigrated the soldiers, they also dismissed their own pilot as a man who was "not remarkable either for his judgment or veracity." They seemed to place white hunters, however, in a separate category. From hunters they could secure essential information about the terrain and about conditions upriver. For example, from an "old Dutch hunter" named Paltz, they received intelligence about hostilities between the Osage and the Chickasaws, Choctaw, and certain other "Indian nations." They encountered Paltz and his three sons encamped on November 29. Having lived for forty years on the Ouachita and before having traversed the White, the St. Francis, and the Arkansas rivers, Paltz provided them with valuable information about the interior of Arkansas. His information about the Arkansas River was of particular interest to Dunbar and Hunter, for they were anticipating an important expedition up that river. That expedition never occurred, and the one that did take place was led by Lt. James Wilkinson, who, unfortunately, devoted only a few pages in his diary to Arkansas. The Dunbar-Hunter accounts would serve as the only substantive information by expeditioners in the early territorial period. Fortunately, Dunbar and Hunter wrote copiously and revealed much about the area.

Accommodation, Resistance, and Removal

The Dunbar-Hunter accounts were widely circulated and captivated readers in both Europe and the Americas. They reveal a great deal more than Dunbar and Hunter might have imagined, for the explorers betrayed their own biases and preconceptions concerning white hunters and Indians, biases they shared with the vast majority of the white population. Aside from the useful information that hunters could supply, they were destined to receive a greater portion of respect simply because they had supposedly imbibed the virtues of the wilderness by having spent time in it. This was the period in American history when hunters were becoming romanticized, in part because they were penetrating the frontier and the frontier was becoming a crucial component of the American nation. It represented the possibility of seemingly endless expansion and opportunity and became inextricably bound up in the American psyche. No longer were they viewed as having become more savage because of exposure to the wilderness; rather they were regarded as more virtuous. This altered view coincided with a new appreciation for Indians. From the beginning, colonists had held contradictory views of the Indians they encountered. On the one hand, they were viewed as murderous savages who engaged in cannibalism and incest. On the other hand, they were innocent creatures of the wilderness, and as the wilderness itself began to define America, it was endowed with the finest of virtues. Both views of Indians remained a part of the American consciousness at the time of the Louisiana Purchase, except that the "innocent" Indian was becoming the "noble savage," and the white hunter had benefited by exposure to him and through his association with the wilderness itself.

At the same time that hunters were being ennobled by this experience, they were also carrying the seeds of destruction. It was through them that Indians were introduced to what one anthropologist has termed the frontier exchange economy and were becoming inextricably bound up within it. This process began early in the previous century, as Indians established relations with French hunters. Another Dunbar and Hunter encounter exemplifies the economic links existing between the French and the Indians. On January 10, 1805, they met a Mr. Le Fevre, who was an Illinois Territory immigrant to Arkansas. He had amassed a substantial number of skins with the help of several Delaware and other Indians and apparently had an arrangement with the Indians to supply them in return for peltry. While Le Fevre's arrangement highlights the way that whites and Indians worked together, it also suggests one mechanism through which the blending of white and Indian cultures occurred. A Delaware Indian whom Dunbar and Hunter encountered on November 28 suggests how the acculturation process could be personified. The Delaware Indian introduced himself as Captain Jacobs, and although he had an English name, he had painted vermilion around his eyes. While Hunter failed to describe him in more detail, and Dunbar did not mention him at all, Jacobs clearly inhabited two worlds, the Indian and the white.

John B. Treat's letters from Arkansas Post further illustrate the way that Indians were engaged in exchange relationships with whites. Treat, an agent dispatched by the U.S. Government to open a trading "factory" with the Indians, arrived at Arkansas Post on September 4, 1805. One month later he observed that merchants competed with one another to advance supplies to "honest and active" persons who then assembled a party of hunters, which could be as small as ten hunters but was occasionally much larger.

This could well have been the kind of arrangement Le Fevre was working under. Chickasaw, Choctaw, and Quapaw had been fitted out, Treat wrote, and their hunting parties restricted to an area between the Arkansas and St. Francis rivers and as far northwest as the Osage would allow. In fact, Treat reported that the Arkansas Post merchants were apprehensive about the safety of their investment, for the newly appointed governor of the Louisiana Territory, Gen. James Wilkinson, had prohibited trade up the Arkansas, White, and St. Francis rivers. He had apparently been moved to do so after a deputation of Osage approached the Post and requested recognition of friendship. Restrictions on trade had plagued merchants operating out of Arkansas Post for nearly a century, and they were not the only impediment to business. A hunting party could be attacked by hostile Indians, as likely as not the Osage, or a merchant might advance funds to an unscrupulous or careless hunter. In any event, through the system of advances that tied them to trade with Europeans, Indians became indebted and found it difficult to disassociate themselves once becoming involved.

The process of cultural blending, which had been encouraged by the economic ties to the French and Spanish, had serious consequences for the Quapaw. The growing economic dependence upon European goods—steel axes, brass kettles, and so on—and the goods the Quapaw hunted and exchanged with the Europeans—particularly buffalo meat—forced an adaption that fundamentally altered the social organization of work. Quapaw men began to hunt buffalo with much greater frequency, and Quapaw women began to spend far more time processing buffalo products, all in order to accommodate their role in the frontier exchange economy. As these changes became more ingrained within Quapaw social structure, the Quapaw became intrinsically more dependent upon the exchange.

A similar process took place wherever Indians came into contact with Europeans, but as historian Morris S. Arnold points out, the Quapaw had fewer goods to exchange than Indians elsewhere. Perhaps even more potentially devastating to Quapaw culture, therefore, was the annuity system that bound them to the French and then the Spanish. To the Quapaw the annuities represented an alliance that inherently recognized their independence and their importance. To the French and Spanish the annuities were a means to an end. Because these Europeans failed to populate the Louisiana Territory in sufficient numbers, they needed alliances with the Quapaw in order to maintain the integrity of their geopolitical claims to the area. So in order to achieve their rather limited goals in the Arkansas region, the French and Spanish needed Quapaw cooperation, and the annuities helped secure that. The alliances that the annuities sealed, however, led to Indian involvement in disputes between whites several times in the eighteenth century, and the events at Arkansas Post late in the Revolutionary War period are a case in point. The attack on the Post by the English and their Chickasaw allies also demonstrates how longstanding animosities between Indians often coincided with those of the white nationalities to which they were obligated. The Quapaw, bound by annuities to the Spanish at Arkansas Post, and the Chickasaws, tied to the British in similar ways, were ancient enemies. Thus these complicated alliances reflected more than the manipulation of Indians by whites in wars for empire in the New World. Clearly they had immediate and often violent ramifications, but the system of annuities that were but a part of these alliances had a more insidious component with long-term consequences. Gradually, as the Quapaw, for example, became essential to the functioning of Arkansas Post in the eighteenth century, they became more enmeshed in the system of annuities and more dependent upon them, both psychologically and materially.

Nothing that occurred in the eighteenth century, however, prepared the Quapaw for the coming of the Americans after the Louisiana Purchase. The Americans themselves were curiously conflicted and contradictory in their goals for the region. Thomas Jefferson and others saw it as a solution to the Indian problem in the east and hoped to transplant eastern Indians to the Louisiana Territory. However, this plan reflected a lack of appreciation for the Indians already living within the area, and, in any case, was soon to be thwarted by the actions of white settlers and politicians who accompanied territorial expansion. While the French and Spanish had been unable or unwilling to people Arkansas with their own, the American government at first could not, and finally, would not, contain the white settlers who flooded into the region. These Americans had little need for the Quapaw, and the American government's failure to regularly extend the accustomed annuities reflected their indifference. The Quapaw likely understood the significance of the difference between the French or Spanish and the Americans, but because of cultural accommodation within Quapaw society and because of the sheer power of the Americans, there was little they could do beyond temporarily forestalling the inevitable.

The Quapaw, who eagerly allied with the Americans, discovered that their loyalty gained them nothing but dispossession. The Osage, who more aggressively pursued their own interests, found themselves overwhelmed by the power and determination of the Americans. They were actually forced into reservations before the Quapaw. Resistance to the Americans was futile, and even those Indians who successfully adapted to the white marketplace would find accommodation to be no refuge from the onslaught of the white appetite for land. While Quapaw attempted to live peaceably in their traditional villages in happy alliance with the Americans and while the Osage attempted to resist American encroachment violently, Cherokee emigrants to Arkansas in the early nineteenth century, who had had two hundred years of interaction with Americans east of the Mississippi River, chose yet another path. Their alternative was similar to that of the Quapaw, but they went much further along the road to adaptation to white culture. They adopted log-cabin architecture, white agricultural implements, and American clothing. To all appearances they looked very much like their white neighbors, so much so that Thomas Nuttall, a botanist who traveled the Arkansas Territory in 1819, remarked favorably upon their "civilized" ways. He was impressed by the extent to which they had adopted white culture, but anthropologists suggest that a closer examination of the spatial organization of their communities and their social units reveals that much remained of traditional Cherokee culture. While they had incorporated white ways into their own cultural milieu, they were not actually identical to their white neighbors, but neither were they like their Cherokee ancestors. In Arkansas they built homes and established prosperous farms along the St. Francis River (and later along the Arkansas River), but they would find that their status as Indians would secure them only a temporary place in Arkansas.

Of course, acculturation was not enthusiastically applauded by all Cherokee. The Cherokee prophet Skaquaw (the Swan) delivered a speech in June 1812 telling Cherokee to abandon their villages along the St. Francis and move west. He was suggesting isolation from the whites rather than a futile attempt at annihilation, although, in the end, isolation was no more viable. Skaquaw's prophecy had been inspired after the New Madrid earthquakes of 1811–1812 led to the calling of a series of intertribal assemblies. The earthquakes seemed a sign that Indians had chosen the wrong path in accepting white influences, and many heeded his call for a return to tradition and a rejection of white acculturation. Meanwhile, many whites were eager to take over Indian lands. In some respects, the New Madrid earthquakes serve as a metaphor for a sea change in the nature of the relationship between whites and Indians in the Mississippi Valley. As accommodation gave way to removal, the middle ground gave way to the "breaking ground."

Breaking ground: The dissolution of the middle-ground collaboration between Native Americans and Europeans, particularly after the Louisiana Purchase and the New Madrid earthquakes.

Three earthquakes occurred between December 16, 1811, and February 7, 1812. Rated as among the twenty greatest earthquakes to occur anywhere in the world and the worst to hit North America, the first of three earthquakes began with a severe shock at approximately 2:00 A.M. on December 16, 1811. The quake was centered in northeastern Arkansas but named for the town of New Madrid in southeastern Missouri, which, with 103 villagers, was one of the most densely populated places in the stricken area. The first shock was followed five hours later by an even more powerful one that destroyed the few brick buildings in New Madrid and knocked down log and frame houses throughout the earthquake zone. Two additional severe shocks occurred on January 23 and on February 7, 1812, but hundreds of aftershocks punctuated the larger ones and the tremors and shocks lasted for at least one year. One chronicler counted 1,874 shocks between December 16 and March 8, and he classified eighteen of them as either violent or very severe. While the largest shocks could be felt in an area covering approximately one million square miles, their force brought devastation to parts of southeastern Missouri and northeastern Arkansas. New lakes were created and old ones went dry. Sinks, sand blows, and sunk lands replaced forests and farmlands. Travelers on the river reported the disappearance of whole islands, and some people foolish enough to place structures close to the river watched them disappear or disappeared with them as the riverbank collapsed, sometimes burying flatboats carrying cargo, crew, and passengers unlucky enough to have tied to the shore there. White settlers and Indians along the St. Francis River took the brunt of the earthquake in Arkansas, and many of them, Indian and white alike, abandoned their homes, never to return. See plate 20 following page 270.

New Madrid Earthquake. *From James Lal Penick Jr.,* The New Madrid Earthquakes, *rev. ed. (Columbia: University of Missouri Press, 1981).* Caption reads, "The Great Earthquake at New Madrid, Henry Howe, The Great West (Cincinnati, 1850), p. 237, in the State Historical Society of Missouri, Columbia, Mo."

New Madrid Act: An act of Congress that provided land certificates in Arkansas to those settlers in Missouri whose land was damaged by the New Madrid earthquakes of 1811 and 1812.

The quakes created the Arkansas "sunk lands," an area that became swampy and subject to complete inundation every spring. The existence of the sunk lands retarded settlement in northeastern Arkansas for another century, but the earthquakes also resulted in an Act of Congress in 1815 that encouraged white settlement elsewhere in Arkansas. On February 17, 1815, Congress passed the New Madrid Act providing certificates, which came to be known as New Madrid certificates, to individuals who had owned or had claims to land destroyed or made relatively worthless by the earthquakes. Between 1810 and 1820, the number of non-Indian settlers in Arkansas increased from 1,062 to 14,273. At the same time, the American government was instituting a removal policy that brought thousands of Indians to parts of Arkansas, but the arrival of the new white settlers marked the end of the "middle-ground" period in Arkansas history. No longer would cultural borrowing and peaceful cohabitation characterize the white-Indian relationship in Arkansas. Interested in producing a cash crop for the market, white settlers resented the presence of Indians on valuable land and were determined to displace them. Within his own lifetime, Jefferson would witness the futility of his plan of placing Indians on the unsettled Arkansas lands.

The assault on Quapaw habitation of Arkansas began because of their occupation of valuable lands along the Mississippi and Arkansas rivers, land that was clearly suited for plantation agriculture. The Quapaw represented the first and greatest obstacle to the development of the plantation system in Arkansas. Initially the American government protected the rights of the Quapaw to their lands, but not because of any great desire to champion the interests of a valued ally. When, in 1816, Gov. William Clark of the Missouri Territory sent representatives to Arkansas County to warn white settlers to relinquish claims to Quapaw lands, he did so because those white settlements threatened to create disputes with the Indians and among the Indians and thereby undermine the Jeffersonian plan to resettle eastern Indians in the region. The government had only loosely continued the annuity system that had flourished under the Spanish and French, and the Quapaw were sufficiently unimpressed with the Americans to ally with the Cherokee in their war with the Osage in 1817, solely for the purpose of destabilizing the region and undermining American relocation plans.

The government would find, however, that it could not effectively prohibit white settlement on Indian lands. By 1818 certain white settlers, territorial politicians, and newspapermen in Arkansas dedicated themselves to appropriating Quapaw land. The era of "inclusion," which one historian has deemed the period when Indians and whites accommodated each other, was about to give way to an era of exclusion, when the federal government was to join battle with white settlers to remove Indians from the disintegrating middle ground in Arkansas. It is perhaps no coincidence that this would occur just when John C. Calhoun, an avid expansionist and no friend to the Indian, would become secretary of war in the first year of James Monroe's presidency. Calhoun believed that America's defense depended on the existence of white settlements on the perimeter, and thus he had no qualms about removing any Indians who inhibited the settlement of whites in the territory. He instructed the governor of the territory to secure a land cession from the Quapaw. The Quapaw agreed to an alliance with the Americans and considered the treaty they signed on August 24, 1818, as an opportunity to secure their interests. The generous annuities promised at the meeting seemed to both seal the alliance and end years of uncertainty with regard to the receipt of annuities. The terms demanded by the Americans, moreover, appeared entirely reasonable. The Americans recognized Quapaw ownership of two million acres and required only that they forfeit ownership of approximately thirty million acres of land in south and southeastern Arkansas that the Quapaw used only for hunting. Since the Americans granted them perpetual hunting rights in those lands, the Quapaw believed they were striking a good bargain and securing valued allies in the Americans. The American government, however, had no need of alliance with the Quapaw and instead would demand further cessions and finally the removal of not only the Quapaw but every other Indian group in Arkansas.

While the Quapaw represented the greatest obstacle to plantation agriculture in southeastern Arkansas, the Osage presented a direct threat to the relocation of eastern

Indians to central Arkansas. During the last decades of the eighteenth century, they had expanded their "territory" in western Arkansas, driving the Caddo in southwestern Arkansas into present-day Texas. They viewed with alarm the voluntary settlement of eastern Indians in Arkansas, but agreed by treaty in 1808 to give up all their claims to hunting rights in northern Arkansas except for an area in extreme northwestern Arkansas. In a subsequent treaty negotiated by William Lovely and then renegotiated two years later, the Osage gave up additional land within Arkansas. Finally, in 1825, the Osage gave up the rest of their Arkansas lands and relocated to Oklahoma. A conditioning factor to the treaties negotiated between 1808 and 1825 was the existence of much friction between the Osage and whites and, particularly, between the Osage and the Cherokee Indians who were flooding into Arkansas.

In 1805, it was estimated that about one thousand Cherokee were living along the St. Francis and the White rivers, but beginning in 1812, the Cherokee moved to the north side of the Arkansas River, locating themselves between the present cities of Morrilton and Fort Smith. This placed them in direct contact with the Osage and created tensions that erupted into violence between the two groups on a number of occasions. A treaty negotiated in 1817 called for some Cherokee east of the Mississippi River to exchange their lands there for lands near those already settled along the Arkansas River. This was the catalyst for no fewer than five wars that broke out between the Cherokee and the Osage. The first of these occurred in 1817 and was partly responsible for the creation of Fort Smith, which was intended to ameliorate hostilities between the Cherokee and Osage.

The superintendent of Indian affairs in the territory, William Clark, picked up on efforts initiated by William Lovely in 1816, and in negotiations with the Osage conducted in St. Louis in 1818, purchased a tract of land north of the Arkansas River. That triangular tract, which came to be known as Lovely's Purchase, was intended to serve as a buffer zone between the Osage and Cherokee. The effort to establish peace between the two groups failed, however. A Cherokee hunting party was attacked by a band of Osage in early 1820, and three Cherokee were killed. The Cherokee demanded that three Osage warriors (a number equal to the Cherokee who lost their lives) be surrendered to them. The Osage refused and a series of violent incidents followed. S. Charles Bolton suggests that "the Osage suffered more from these hostilities than the Cherokee, and they had fewer resources with which to sustain themselves." A treaty was signed in 1822 but soon war broke out a final time and lasted until 1825 when a final treaty was negotiated which called for the removal of the Osage to Oklahoma.

Lovely's Purchase: Negotiated in 1818, this purchase of a triangular tract of land north of the Arkansas River was intended to provide a buffer between the Osage and Cherokee, then engaged in an intense struggle.

Even as the Osage were being removed from Arkansas, another of their enemies of longstanding, the Choctaw, were experiencing the same fate. The Choctaw had begun to move into Arkansas in the late eighteenth century and had established at least one village on the Arkansas River by 1819. On more than one occasion they had warred against the Osage, and when in 1820 a treaty was signed providing for the removal of Choctaw from

Mississippi and Alabama to a reservation in Arkansas contiguous to the Osage, war threatened once more. But the Osage were not the least of the problems confronting the Choctaw. Three thousand white settlers, who lived in the area ceded to the Choctaw, threatened to make war against them and circulated petitions in protest. The Arkansas General Assembly sided with the settlers, in part because many legislators regarded plans to resettle eastern Indians in Arkansas as a direct threat to their own interests. The general assembly petitioned Congress to reconsider the decision to relocate the Choctaw to Arkansas, and by 1825 a new settlement was reached which witnessed the removal of all Choctaw to southern Oklahoma. See plate 21 following page 270.

Cherokee removal to Oklahoma was soon to follow. Although the Cherokee were clearly the most assimilated Indians in Arkansas, they too represented an obstacle to white settlement. After the 1817 removal of the eastern Cherokee to Arkansas, those located in Arkansas, which represented about one-third of all Cherokee, became known as the Cherokee Nation West, and in 1818 they invited a Protestant mission board to send missionaries to attend them. Cephas Washburn and Alfred Finney subsequently established Dwight Mission in 1820 near the present city of Russellville. The mission founded the first school in Arkansas and flourished until the Cherokee removal to Oklahoma in 1828. The missionaries followed the Cherokee to Oklahoma, and Dwight Mission was abandoned. In late 1828 and early 1829, a boundary was established between the Cherokee nation and Arkansas which became the western boundary of Arkansas (except for the southwestern corner which was surveyed after Texas won its independence from Mexico in 1836).

The Quapaw, meanwhile, were also facing removal from Arkansas. The secretary of the territory, Robert Crittenden, who frequently acted as superintendent of Indian affairs in the absence of territorial governor James Miller, was not only opposed to the policy of removing eastern Indians to Arkansas, he was also determined to rid the territory of the Quapaw. He was not alone in this position. Prominent white men who had recently located in Arkansas regarded the placement of eastern Indians on Arkansas lands as a threat to the development of the territory and thus a threat to their own political and economic advancement. Many ordinary white settlers simply wanted Indian lands, and both groups began to urge the relocation of the Quapaw so that their valuable acreage in southeastern Arkansas could be opened for white settlement.

The departure of Governor Miller in 1824 and the arrival of the new territorial governor, George Izard, did not work to the advantage of the Quapaw. Although Izard would not be content to allow Crittenden to run the affairs of the territory as had Miller, he would prove to be no friend to the Quapaw. By the time Izard had arrived, Crittenden and others had engaged in a public campaign to discredit the Quapaw, referring to them as indolent and worthless savages, and had convinced the secretary of war (who had charge of Indian affairs in that era), John C. Calhoun, that the Quapaw actually desired removal to the Caddo reservation along the Red River in Louisiana. Although this was patently false, a treaty was forced on the Quapaw on November 15, 1824, which required not only their removal but their amalgamation with the Caddo. In return, they were promised a small allotment and were allowed to remain in Arkansas through

Dwight Mission. *Courtesy of the Arkansas History Commission.*

the winter of 1824–1825. Chief Heckaton appealed to the new territorial governor in June 1825 to postpone the removal further, but Izard merely suggested that the chief send representatives to Louisiana to examine the site, and he agreed to allow Antoine Barraque, a Frenchman who traded with the Quapaw and who had their confidence, to accompany the delegation.

What Barraque and the delegation of Quapaw found in Louisiana was most unpromising. The Caddo and their Indian agent, George Gray, were unenthusiastic if not hostile to the newcomers. Nevertheless, with Barraque in charge, the Quapaw began their march to the Red River in early January 1826. They were settled on land adjacent to the Red River and planted their crops, only to have them flooded and ruined twice in the spring. That summer, sixty of them died as destitution set in, and some, under the leadership of Saracen, a Quapaw with French blood, returned to Arkansas. Others drifted back as well and took up residence in remote, swampy areas, which they believed white settlers were least likely to desire. The federal government allowed them to remain, allocated one-fourth of the tribe's annuity to those in Arkansas, and urged them to amalgamate with the Cherokee.

The next few years saw further deterioration of the Quapaw position in Louisiana and a worsening of their treatment in Arkansas, where white settlers began to roughly remove them from the shacks they occupied. But the situation in Louisiana was worse than that in Arkansas, and by November 1830 all of them had returned to Arkansas. Although this heralded the reunification of the tribe, something that Chief Heckaton, who had been practically the last Quapaw to leave Louisiana, was committed to, their troubles were far from over. The lion's share of their annuities were still going to Louisiana, and their ability to provide for themselves was seriously undermined by both their residence in the swamp and their tenuous hold on even those inadequate lands. They were now more than ever dependent upon annuities, but bureaucratic delays prevented their dispersal even after the federal government permitted them to be distributed in Arkansas. Even when they were finally resumed, they were not regularly allocated and were periodically suspended.

The appointment of John Pope in March 1829 after Izard's death in late 1828 resulted in the arrival of a man more sympathetic to the plight facing the Quapaw. Although a Jackson appointee, he deviated from the callous Jacksonian attitude toward Indians. Meanwhile, even some citizens in Arkansas began to temper their strong language and call for more humane treatment of the Quapaw. In December 1830, Chief Heckaton accompanied Ambrose H. Sevier, Arkansas's territorial delegate, to Washington, D.C., to seek an audience with President Jackson. Although it is unlikely that Heckaton was successful in his effort to see the president, he did begin correspondence with Jackson's secretary of war, John Eaton, concerning the assignment of tribal lands in the vicinity of Arkansas Post. More significantly, perhaps, was his plea to Eaton to allow the Quapaw to live as American citizens and to permit the apportionment of some of their annuity for the education of young Quapaw at the Choctaw Academy in Kentucky. In other words, Heckaton, who had for so long attempted to keep the tribe together and retain its cultural identity, was now himself suggesting assimilation.

Secretary Eaton apportioned almost half the tribal annuity for educational purposes, but he refused to sanction the purchase of land in Arkansas for the Quapaw. Thus they remained in a vulnerable situation. The annuities earmarked for dispersal to the Quapaw were only sporadically available, and a decision to suspend all annuities, issued by a new commissioner of Indian affairs, Elbert Herring, in January 1832, put the Quapaw in an impossible position. Their situation became so desperate that Governor Pope gave official sanction to Heckaton's earlier plea for the purchase of Arkansas land for the Quapaw by making the recommendation himself. His unusual recommendation prompted a reassessment of their situation and a hearing before the Stokes Commission, a commission appointed to reexamine the government's Indian removal policy with regard to eastern Indians. Meanwhile, leading politicians and newspapers renewed their attack on the Quapaw, once again referring to them as worthless savages, but a new subagent, Richard Hannon, began to press for their relief. On May 13, 1833, the Quapaw reluctantly agreed to their final removal from Arkansas, this time to Indian Territory. Although they were to be assigned their own reservation, many Quapaw were no longer willing to trust the federal government and failed to accompany the trek that began in September 1834. Some returned to the Red River, some went to Texas, and some even joined the Choctaw, temporarily at least, in southern Oklahoma. Saracen and a few others remained in Arkansas. Government policy had finally achieved what Heckaton had so long sought to prevent: the partial dissolution of the tribe.

Political and Economic Development

The removal of the Quapaw and other Indians from Arkansas replicated the same process occurring elsewhere in the nation in the antebellum period. It was clearly connected to the territory's economic and political development in the 1820s, which itself mirrored that of the young nation. In the 1820s, political factions emerged in concert with the advent of the second party system; and agricultural enterprises similar to those arising in southern states appeared. In northern and northwestern Arkansas, small farming and animal husbandry began to emerge and in southeastern and southern Arkansas, cotton plantation agriculture developed. While slavery was widespread across the territory it began to become more concentrated wherever the plantation system dominated.

Antebellum: occurring or existing before a war, especially the American Civil War.

Pres. James Monroe signed the act creating Arkansas Territory on March 2, 1819. The next day he appointed two men to the top positions in the new territory who would come to represent two squabbling factions that would eventually solidify around the election of 1824 and emerge as representative of the Democratic Party in the 1820s and Whig Party in the 1830s. Monroe appointed Brig. Gen. James Miller of New Hampshire as territorial governor and Robert Crittenden of Kentucky as territorial secretary. Because Governor Miller did not arrive in Arkansas until December 1819, the ambitious young secretary found himself in a position to assume authority. Miller might have been expected to exert his seniority, once he finally arrived, given that he was an experienced military man and the hero of Lundy's Lane, an important War of 1812 battle. Skill on the battlefield did not in this case, however, translate into effective leadership in administering the new territory's affairs. The principle problem with Miller's administration of his duties was not incompetence but lack of interest. He was absent from the territory more often than he was within it, and thus Secretary Crittenden carried on the appropriate duties.

Twenty-two-year-old Robert Crittenden, a Kentucky native from a distinguished family, recognized the opportunity open to him, and even before Miller arrived in Arkansas, he began to take the initiative. The act creating the territory provided that it commence operations on July 4, 1819, but in Miller's absence, Crittenden, by law, became the acting governor as of that date. He waited for Miller until July 28 and then he called the newly appointed three judges—Robert P. Letcher, Charles Jouett, and Andrew W. Scott—together in Arkansas's first legislative body. In addition to declaring in force all the laws applicable to the Territory of Missouri, they provided for the judicial and financial mechanisms under which Arkansas could be governed. They divided Arkansas into two judicial districts, each to have its own circuit judge, and they established the offices of auditor and treasurer. Finally, they passed an act to raise public funds to pay for the territory's administrative expenses. On August 3 they disbanded, and the three justices left the territory to Crittenden's care. Although Judge Scott would later return with his family, Jouett and Letcher abandoned their appointments and were later replaced.

The first of many controversies involving Crittenden began with his actions in October, however. With Miller still absent from the territory, Crittenden called for an election. On November 20, 1819, voters selected James Woodson Bates as a delegate to Congress. They also elected a five-member legislative council representing the five counties, and a nine-member house of representatives. Acting under the assumption that an 1816 act of Congress applied to Arkansas Territory, Crittenden believed that Arkansas was entitled to elect a legislative council, but questions arose as to whether the 1816 law applied or whether Arkansas was required to adhere to an 1812 act that stipulated that the legislative council was to be appointed. If the latter applied, the new territory's house of representatives was to send eighteen names to the president, and the president was to appoint the council members. When Miller arrived on December 26, 1819, he took the position that the 1812 law applied, that Arkansas was not entitled to elect a legislative council, and that the election had been illegal. Arkansas was a territory of the "first grade" and only a territory of the second grade could elect its own council. The governor called a special session of the general assembly, and on February 7, 1820, a debate ensued over how to resolve the problem with the allegedly illegal election. Two factions, one allying with the governor and one allying with Crittenden, emerged. In an address that was measured and carefully worded, the governor urged those assembled to share responsibility for the error and pass a resolution requesting Congress to validate the election. Crittenden was opposed to the governor's solution, however, because it implicitly placed much of the blame on himself. The general assembly was first inclined to support Crittenden, but the legislators were ultimately convinced by the governor. At the next regular session of the legislature, held in October 1820, the governor announced that Congress had affirmed the election.

In early 1820 Crittenden became a key player in another early controversy, yet again pitting the young secretary against the territorial governor. No one seriously disputed that the ill-placed Arkansas Post was an inappropriate location for the capital of the new territory. The question was where to relocate, and there were several contenders. One likely choice was the "little rock," located in the middle of the new territory along the Arkansas River. Bernard de la Harpe, on an expedition to explore the Arkansas River, had discovered it in 1722 and recommended the placement of a trading post there. No such trading post was established by the French or later by the Spanish during their occupation of the territory. Sometime during the second decade of the nineteenth century, a white hunter and trapper, William Lewis, lived there with his family in a rude shack that they occupied only briefly during every year. After securing a preemption certificate that gave him title to the land and shack in 1814, he sold it in the fall of that year and then disappeared from the historical record. The title changed hands several times before being acquired by William Russell, a St. Louis land speculator. See plate 22 following page 270.

Determined to make the most of his investment in Little Rock and other tracts in Arkansas, Russell played a role in circulating the petition to Congress for the establishment of Arkansas Territory. He secured several hundred acres at the Little Rock site, in addition to the original Lewis claim, and he was present at Arkansas Post when the territorial legislature convened in February 1820. He made a compact with Townsend Dickinson, an attorney from New York whom he met at Arkansas Post, to help lobby the territorial delegates to relocate the capital to Little Rock. But the legislators were unable to decide between that location and Cadron, a small settlement located nearby, and postponed the matter to the October session. Between the February and October sessions, a number of legislators and influential men purchased "lots" at the Little Rock site, including Robert Crittenden, William Trimble, Robert C. Oden, and Judge Andrew Scott. Dickinson acted as agent in the transactions while Russell lobbied the legislators directly to support the Little Rock site. During the October session itself, Joseph Hardin, the speaker of the territorial house, secured several Little Rock lots, and on October 10, 1820, the bill to remove the capital to Little Rock passed by a majority of three. Governor Miller, who owned lots at Little Rock but who was building a home at Crystal Hill near Cadron, was opposed to the relocation of the capital to Little Rock and thus the decision was a disappointment to him. While other territorial officials moved to the new capitol, Miller refused to do so, moving instead to nearby Crystal Hill. Robert Crittenden opened a law partnership in Little Rock in connection with Chester Ashley. That partnership marked the birth of one of two major factions in Arkansas during the territorial era. It would eventually align with the Whig Party when it emerged latter. The other faction, which revolved around Governor Miller, would ultimately coalesce around the newly emerging Democratic Party after the 1824 election. But this would happen without Miller. In late 1824, Miller was named collector for the post of Salem, Massachusetts, and left Arkansas.

When Miller left his post in Arkansas, Pres. James Monroe, who was then finishing out his second term in office in 1824, appointed Arkansas's second territorial governor. This time he nominated George Izard, scion of a successful diplomat, politician, and planter from South Carolina. Izard had been educated in military schools in England and France and had taken his university degree in Edinburgh. He achieved the rank of major general during the War of 1812, and had to be persuaded by Monroe to accept the governorship of Arkansas Territory. His appointment was confirmed by the Senate on March 3, 1825. Although he was Monroe's choice, Pres. John Quincy Adams sanctioned the appointment after his inauguration in March 1825. Izard, unlike his predecessor, was unwilling to allow Crittenden to run the territory. He called Crittenden back from Washington, where he had the territorial papers in his possession—a common practice in that period—and began to administer affairs. Aside from temporarily forestalling the first attempt to remove the Quapaw, he regularized certain functions of government, including reorganizing the territorial militia. He died in November 1828, just in time to give Andrew Jackson, the newly elected president, the opportunity to replace him.

Jackson appointed John Pope, who had campaigned for him. Pope, a native of Virginia, had moved to Kentucky with his family where he attended school and studied law. He served in the Kentucky legislature and as a United States senator before he ran afoul of public support for the War of 1812. His opposition cost him his political career. He left the Senate after his term expired and practiced law until his support for Jackson in 1828 put him back in the limelight. He was appointed governor in 1829 upon Izard's death, but he became embattled with Arkansas's Democrats, and then he broke irrevocably with the president over the latter's bank policy in 1833. In 1835 he was replaced by the secretary of the territory, William Fulton, who had been intriguing against Pope almost since arriving in Arkansas.

William Fulton had gained his position as secretary of the territory in 1829, displacing Robert Crittenden as part of President Jackson's determination to put his own men in place. The fate of Robert Crittenden, however, had been determined as much by local opposition as by the election of Jackson. A duel with Henry Conway in 1827 had not only resulted in Conway's demise, it had also witnessed the deepening of a bitter rivalry between the Crittenden faction, which would later become linked with the national Whig Party, and the Conway faction, which was wedded to the Jacksonian Democrats. Henry Conway was survived by two brothers, James, who would become the first governor of Arkansas in 1836, and the much younger Elias, who would become governor in 1852. These brothers, together with several cousins and in-laws (including Ambrose Sevier and Benjamin Johnson), formed a political "Dynasty," also known as the "Family," which ruled Arkansas virtually unchallenged until the Civil War.

The election of Jackson in 1828 to the presidency did not stimulate the creation of the Arkansas Dynasty, nor did it mark the beginning of the rivalry between the Family and Crittenden. The disputes that emerged at the time of the formation of Arkansas Territory in 1819 were followed by a series of disagreements, and over the course of the next decade, the two major factions emerged, one consisting of Crittenden and his followers and the other, the Conway-Johnson-Sevier Family. As the two factions began to coalesce in the 1820s, the *Arkansas Gazette*, founded by William Woodruff, allied with the Family. Woodruff is credited with bringing the first printing press to Arkansas Post soon after the creation of the territory and moved to Little Rock when the capital relocated. In his early years as editor and publisher, he maintained political neutrality but ultimately allied with the Family during the election of 1827, which pitted Henry Conway against Robert Oden, a Crittenden follower. Conway and Crittenden had actually been allies for a brief period in the early 1820s. Conway, who was appointed to the post of receiver of public monies for the territory in 1820, secured Crittenden's support in 1823 when he successfully sought to become territorial delegate. The two men would find themselves in opposite camps the next year over the 1824 presidential contest between Henry Clay and Andrew Jackson. While neither of their candidates was elected to the presidency, the hostilities between the two men intensified and spilled over into the election for territorial delegate in 1827. Henry Conway was running against Robert Oden, who was supported by Crittenden, who supplied Oden with information about alleged indiscretions committed by Conway. The charge was that Conway had used six hundred dollars allocated for the Quapaw for his own personal use. Conway responded that the secretary had given him permission to use the funds for expenses and that he had reimbursed the money. Personal invective characterized the campaign, and soon Conway and Crittenden were trading other insults and accusations against each other. Conway decisively won the election, but the overheated language continued until October 27, 1827, when the two men found themselves facing each other with dueling pistols in hand. Because of a fatal duel in 1820 between Superior Court judge William O. Allen and none other than candidate Robert Oden, dueling was illegal in the territory, so Conway and Crittenden met on the east side of the Mississippi River on October 29, 1827. Conway died twelve days later from a bullet wound suffered as a result.

Crittenden survived the duel, but his political fortunes began to slide. Deprived of the territorial secretary's position in 1829, he continued to maneuver politically, and his supporters even gained control of the legislature in 1831. But then another controversy followed which did irreparable damage to his career: the "ten sections." controversy. When the United States government transferred ten sections of land to finance the construction of a building to house the territorial legislature, Crittenden offered to exchange a brick building that he had recently constructed in Little Rock for the ten sections. His faction in the legislature secured the votes to approve the transaction, but Governor Pope believed that the building was worth far less than the ten sections and vetoed the bill. When the ten sections were later sold for far more than the building was worth, it became clear that Crittenden had misrepresented its value and his reputation suffered. He ran for territorial delegate in 1832, but lost the election to Ambrose Sevier, a cousin of Henry Conway's who had been appointed to stand in Conway's stead as territorial delegate upon his death in 1827. Crittenden himself died suddenly in 1833 at the age of thirty-seven, apparently of a heart attack, leaving the infant Whig Party in the hands of others.

Ten Sections controversy: Originated when Robert Crittenden offered to exchange a building he owned for ten sections of land Congress had awarded the territory in order to build a statehouse.

Throughout the early territorial period, Arkansas's economy had been developing apace, and the emergence of cotton agriculture in the south and southeast became one of its paramount features. Agriculture was not new to the territory, of course. At the time of the Louisiana Purchase, the Quapaw and the Caddo had been engaged in growing crops for at least two centuries, but John Treat, writing in 1805, reported that agriculture in the Arkansas Post region was in its infancy. Treat's assessment of its possibilities, however, read like an advertisement. The fertile soil and the mild climate had allowed whites, who had been growing crops in the area for only a few decades, to achieve some impressive yields of wheat, hemp, and flax on what Treat regarded as some of the best arable land in the country. Livestock, particularly cattle and sheep, were thriving on a prairie not far from the Post. His only negative comments referred to the depredations of blackbirds and crows on the corn crop and the lack of ginning facilities to make cotton production viable. The latter problem, however, was even then being remedied, for Treat reported that a gin was under construction.

No precise figures are available for the acres under cultivation by whites in Arkansas at the time of the Louisiana Purchase or for the number of white persons in the area, but Treat indicated that most of them came from the states of Pennsylvania, Maryland, and Virginia and that of the sixty or seventy families at the Post, half a dozen of them were engaged in farming near the Post or just up the Arkansas River. The 1810 census, which enumerated persons at the settlement of Hopefield, at the mouth of the St. Francis, and on the Arkansas River, counted 1,062 persons. Since it ignored those who settled up the St. Francis and on the White and the Black rivers, the census is generally regarded as inaccurate. In 1814 a census for the purpose of apportioning seats for the legislature in Missouri Territory was completed, and it counted 827 adult white males. This represented a 50 percent increase over the number of adult white males appearing on the 1810 census. One historian has postulated that this probably represents an overall population of about 1,588 persons. In the six years that followed, the population of the district increased dramatically. The 1820 census recorded a population of 14,273, and significantly, while John Treat and other observers indicated that only a small minority of the households in the first decade of the nineteenth century were farming, a much larger percentage was so engaged in 1820. In that year 3,613 persons (25.3 percent of the total population) were farming.

Based on the number of slaves in the population, the growth of plantation agriculture was not keeping pace with the general growth in population in the second decade of the nineteenth century. Although the slave population between 1810 and 1820 had increased from 136 to 1,613, this represented a percentage decline of from 12.8 to 11.3 percent. The next decade would see a dramatic reversal of this trend, when the number of slaves in the population would rise to 15.1 percent, but before this could occur, the impediments to plantation agriculture would have to be removed.

Despite this dramatic increase in population and the greater reliance on farming, certain impediments to growth existed. First, claims to possession of Spanish land grants, necessitating the creation of a Land Commission, left the title to tens of thousands of acres of Arkansas lands in question. Second, the issuance of New Madrid certificates, designed to resettle persons displaced by the great earthquake of 1811 and 1812, created numerous disputes in Arkansas over title to land claimed by those holding preemption certificates and those holding the New Madrid certificates. Preemption certificates were secured by those who had squatted on land and subsequently made a claim of ownership.

In addition to the problems associated with identifying legitimate land claims, before plantation agriculture could expand in the Arkansas District, certain political handicaps had to be overcome. Arkansas was without much jurisprudence throughout its early territorial period. At times it fell within the jurisdiction of the New Madrid judicial district, and at times it was allowed to administer its own affairs. The difficulty of making a ten-day trip to attend court discouraged many from regularizing their holdings, and, in any case, aside from the difficulty of settling land claims, the absence of courts encouraged certain lawless individuals to abide in the region. In the end, to fully secure its population, the district required separate territorial status.

The District of Arkansas became a part of Missouri Territory in 1812, but when citizens in what would become the state of Missouri in 1820 began to petition Congress for statehood in 1817, they excluded the area located below thirty-six degrees and thirty minutes. That included the southern portion of Lawrence County and four other counties that had been created out of the old District of Arkansas in the period between 1812 and 1818—Clark, Hempstead, Pulaski, and Arkansas. Missouri's petition opened the way for the creation of Arkansas Territory and a solution to the problems of governance there.

Petitions to admit the new state of Missouri and to create Arkansas Territory, however, stimulated a congressional debate centering on the issue of slavery. The resolution of this debate would have profound implications for both the new state and the new territory. Not only would their fates be linked to those of the South in the national political arena, their agricultural economies would become heavily dominated by cotton plantations, and local political divisions would result from the power of the planter class. Although the debate over the admission of Missouri as a slave state is much better known, a similar debate arose over the Arkansas Territory bill, that is whether to allow slavery to continue in the proposed Territory of Arkansas. It involved many of the same issues, and the manipulation of the Arkansas question played an important role in the formulation of the Missouri Compromise. Residents of the future Territory of Arkansas began to petition for its creation in March 1818, and the House of Representatives actually began considering the question on December 16 of that same year. Ironically, it would be two more months before Congress witnessed the introduction of the Missouri Enabling Act. But Congress was fully aware of the pending Missouri Act and apparently made a decision to decide that question first. The Arkansas bill was referred to a committee that was to consider what to do about the territory south of thirty-six degrees, thirty minutes and recognizing, in any case, that the area was without effective government because of its isolation from Missouri's territorial capital and that it possibly required separate territorial status whatever the outcome of the Missouri petition for statehood. The latter, however, would become center stage for a grand drama that would lead Thomas Jefferson, at home in retirement in Monticello, to remark "this momentous question, like a fire bell in the night, awakened and filled me with terror. I considered it at once as the knell of the Union."

The seeds for the first great debate the young country faced over slavery arose when the Missouri Enabling Act was introduced on February 13, 1819. The bill's sponsors were shocked by the introduction of two amendments designed to abolish slavery in the new state. New York representative James Tallmadge's amendments proposed to bar the further introduction of slaves to Missouri and free all slaves over the age of twenty-five. On February 15, the House of Representatives approved the Tallmadge amendments and sent them both to the Senate where they were to meet a different fate. Meanwhile, on February 16 the House began consideration of the Arkansas Territory bill. This time, it was another representative from New York, John Taylor, who had seconded Tallmadge's amendments to the Missouri bill, who introduced amendments identical to those which, as far as the House version of the bill was concerned, effectively abolished slavery in the new state of Missouri. The supporters of slavery, however, having been alerted by the Missouri amendments, had marshaled their forces and presented a powerful challenge to the Arkansas bill's sponsors. On February 18, they defeated the first of the amendments, that barring the further admission of slaves into the territory, by a vote of seventy-one to seventy, but they were initially unable to defeat the second amendment, that which freed slaves over the age of twenty-five. That one passed by a vote of seventy-five to seventy-three in its second reading, but the proslavery strategists continued to work behind the scenes to defeat the amendment, and when it came up for its third reading on February 19, they secured a vote of eighty-eight to eighty-eight. Henry Clay was the Speaker of the House and entitled to cast the deciding vote in the event of a tie. As an arch opponent of the amendment, he was able to break the tie in favor of the southern position. Representative Taylor subsequently offered three other amendments designed to restrict slavery in the territory, but they were also defeated. In his third and final effort, he introduced a motion proposing that a southern dividing line be identified at thirty-six degrees thirty minutes whereby slavery would be excluded from all territory north of that line. Although Taylor was defeated in this, his final attempt to impose prohibitions on slavery in the proposed territory of Arkansas, the thirty-six degrees, thirty minutes dividing line would become a crucial factor in the famous Missouri Compromise, which allowed Missouri to enter the Union as an exception to this general rule. Slavery remained intact in Missouri, but it was understood that no other territory above that line could enter the Union as a slave state.

The resolution of the Arkansas Territory bill virtually guaranteed the expansion of plantation slavery in the new territory. As the plantation system grew in the 1820s and 1830s, black slavery became a major demographic feature in southeastern Arkansas. Northeastern Arkansas, heavily damaged by the New Madrid earthquakes, remained too swampy for easy access and for agricultural development. While there were slaveholders in northwestern Arkansas, they were fewer in number and held far fewer slaves. Some northwestern Arkansas slave owners held a sufficient number of slaves to work them in gangs and produce a cash crop, but the soil was not fertile enough to devote much acreage to cotton, so they grew wheat and corn. Transportation was inadequate but sufficient enough to move their crops to markets—south to Fort Smith and north to Missouri. Rivers were important but, aside from the White River, which flowed north into Missouri before reentering northeastern Arkansas, they were inadequate to the task of transportation, so roads, which were little more than improved Indian trails, were relied upon. The Carrollton Road was the most "improved" road running out of northwest Arkansas in the territorial era, and it ran east, linking up with the Southwest Trail in northeast Arkansas. The vast majority of the white population in northwest Arkansas did not own slaves—or owned only one or two—and occupied themselves in small farming enterprises, mainly of the subsistence variety. Most settlers came from mountainous areas in Kentucky, Tennessee, North Carolina, and Virginia (later West Virginia), and they replicated the economic system with which they were familiar. They grew some corn, but they were principally occupied in raising livestock, and they depended upon the open range. Just as they imported an economic system they knew and understood, they brought with them certain egalitarian ideas and had a special attachment to social, economic, and political independence. While they were not opposed to the institution of slavery, they were suspicious of the wealthy planters of southeastern Arkansas.

Many of the planters of southeastern Arkansas were the sons and nephews of planters in the lowlands of Kentucky, North Carolina, and Virginia. They were part of the vanguard of southerners who led the expansion of the plantation system westward. They were few in number during the territorial period, but they grew wealthy as cotton production increased. They relied heavily on rivers—the Arkansas and especially the Mississippi—to get their crops to market in Memphis and St. Louis to the north and, particularly, to New Orleans to the south. Consequently, most settlement was along the rivers, but as roads were improved, settlement away from the rivers increased. The old Southwest Trail was too far to the west of the southeastern delta to be of much use to planters there, but it passed through Washington, Arkansas, in the southwest and stimulated settlement in that region. Gradually other roads, which had been little more than Indian trails, were improved, linking the southeastern Arkansas planters to Little Rock and to points in Louisiana.

The linkage to Little Rock would prove to be of great significance, not only economically but also politically. Little Rock was fortunately positioned in that the Southwest Trail, designated a military road under Andrew Jackson, linked it with Missouri to the northeast and Texas to the southwest. It entered northeastern Arkansas (west of the area damaged by the earthquakes) from Missouri and stretched southwesterly and intersected with Little Rock before passing through southwest Arkansas into Texas. It was the first road in Arkansas to be improved after the Louisiana Purchase. Other, smaller roads led into Little Rock, but because of the influence of Henry Conway, delegate to Congress in 1824, the first "military road" constructed in Arkansas linked Little Rock to Memphis. It was completed in 1828 and was often impassable. That road was later extended west toward Fort Smith. In addition to its fortunate geographic location, Little Rock's status as the capital city made it the hub of the territory's political universe and many of the most prominent politicians had interests in southeastern Arkansas. The importance of these connections would be brought into sharp relief when delegates gathered to create a state constitution in early 1836. Indeed, the differences between the northwest and southeast would become a major feature of the debate over the creation of that document.

The statehood question first arose in the early 1830s, and while the northwest and southeast did not appear to be divided over the issue, Arkansas's two political factions were not initially in agreement over the question. Charles Bolton's *Arkansas: Remote and Restless, 1800–1860* provides a cogent summary of the agitation for statehood and an analysis of the argument outlined by the editor of the *Arkansas Advocate*, which represented the Crittenden faction. In 1830, editor Charles Bertrand argued that "the Census of 1830 would show that the territory had grown substantially and was ready to end what he called its 'territorial vassalage.'" A subsequent letter to the editor from "Aristides" suggested that statehood "would lead to a dramatic increase in population" and thus statehood would result in greater economic development. That writer also

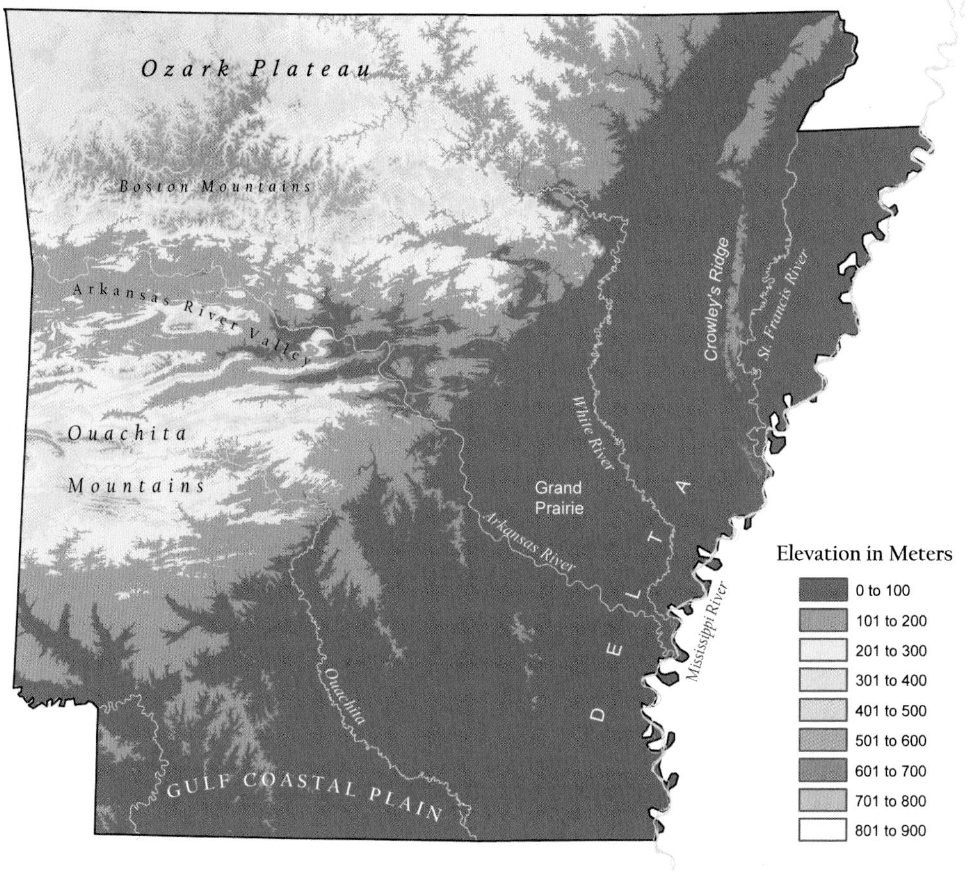

PLATE 1. Arkansas Elevation. *Courtesy of Joseph Swain.* (Sources: U.S. Geological Survey, National Elevation Dataset ned.usgs.gov.)

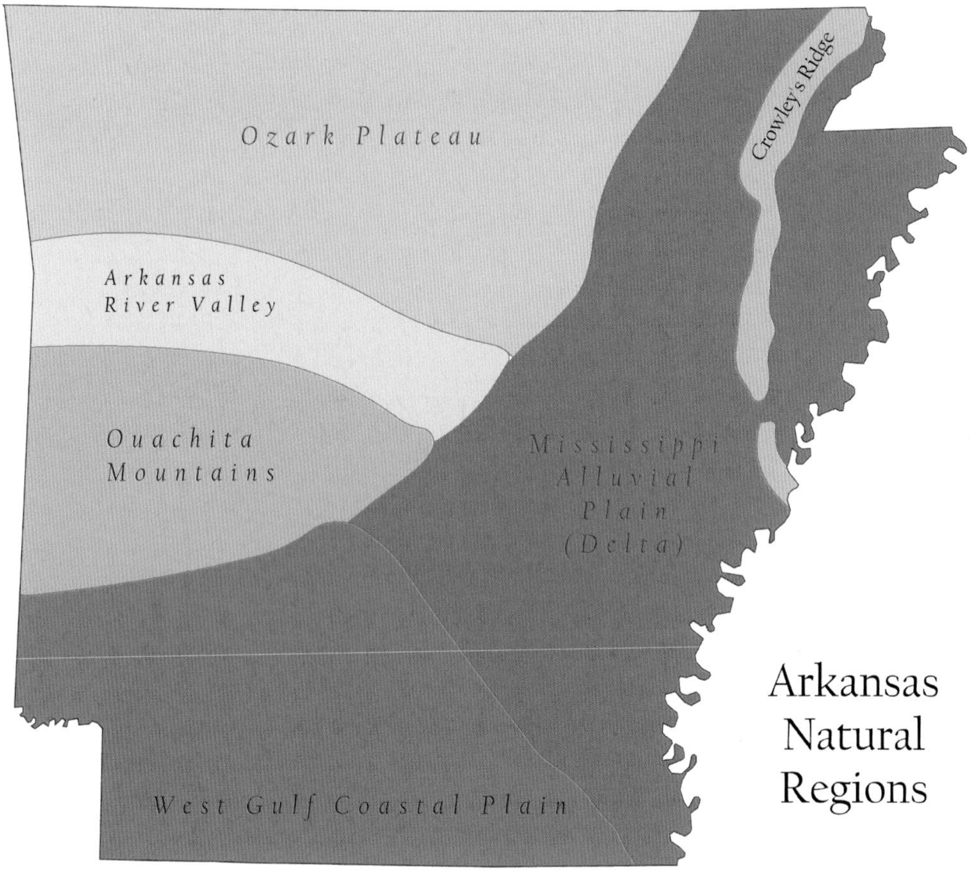

PLATE 2. Arkansas Natural Regions. *Courtesy of Joseph Swain.* (Sources: Arkansas Geographic Information Office, *Encyclopedia of Arkansas History & Culture,* U.S. Geological Survey.)

PLATE 3. Ozark Mountains. Photo by George Sabo III. *Courtesy of the Arkansas Archeological Survey.*

PLATE 4. Arkansas River Valley. Photo by George Sabo III. *Courtesy of the Arkansas Archeological Survey.*

PLATE 5. West Gulf Coastal Plain. Photo by Carl Carlson-Drexler. *Courtesy of the Arkansas Archeological Survey.*

PLATE 6. Mississippi Alluvial Valley. Photo by John H. House. *Courtesy of the Arkansas Archeological Survey.*

PLATE 7. Photograph of Crowley's Ridge. Photo by Julie MacDonald. *Courtesy of the Arkansas State University Museum, 2012.*

PLATE 8. Artist's reconstruction of Woodland period solstice observations at the Toltec Mounds site. *Courtesy of Arkansas State Parks.*

PLATE 9. Artist's reconstruction of the fortified Mississippian town at the Parkin site. *Courtesy of Arkansas State Parks.*

PLATE 10. Artist's reconstruction of a dispersed Caddo village. Painting by Ed Martin. *Courtesy of the Arkansas Archeological Survey.*

The Hernando De Soto Expedition Route in Arkansas

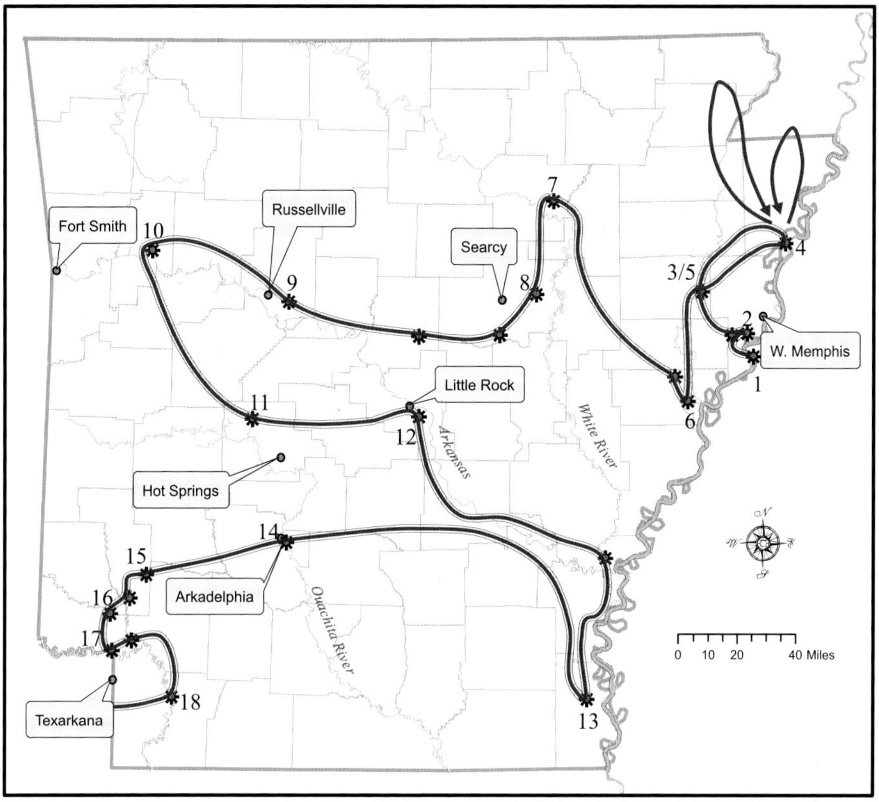

1. Initial Crossing (Norfolk Landing), June 18, 1541
2. Pouncey, Aquixo Province, June 19, 1541
3. Casqui Capital (Parkin Archeological Site), June 25, 1541
4. Pacaha chiefdom, June 28, 1541
5. Casqui Capital (Parkin Archeological Site), July 30, 1541
6. Quiguate, August 4, 1541
7. Coligua, September 4, 1541
8. Calpista, September 7, 1541
9. Tanico, Cayas Province, Late September, 1541
10. Tula, Late September 1541
11. Quipana, Late September 1541
12. Autiamque, November 2nd (Wintered)
13. Guachoya, (Lake Village), De Soto Died, March 21, 1542
14. Chaguate, Summer 1542
15. Aguacay, July 4, 1542
16. Pato, July 17, 1542
17. Amaye, July 17-18, 1542
18. Naguatex, July 21 (23), 1542

PLATE 11. Hernando de Soto Route through Arkansas. *Courtesy of Joseph Swain.* (Sources: Arkansas Archeological Survey, Arkansas Geographic Information Office, National Atlas of the United States, Proceedings of the De Soto Symposia.)

PLATE 12. Arkansas Post, by Annie Hatley. *Courtesy of the Arkansas History Commission.*

PLATE 13. Quapaw man, circa 1700, by Charles Banks Wilson. *Courtesy of the artist.*

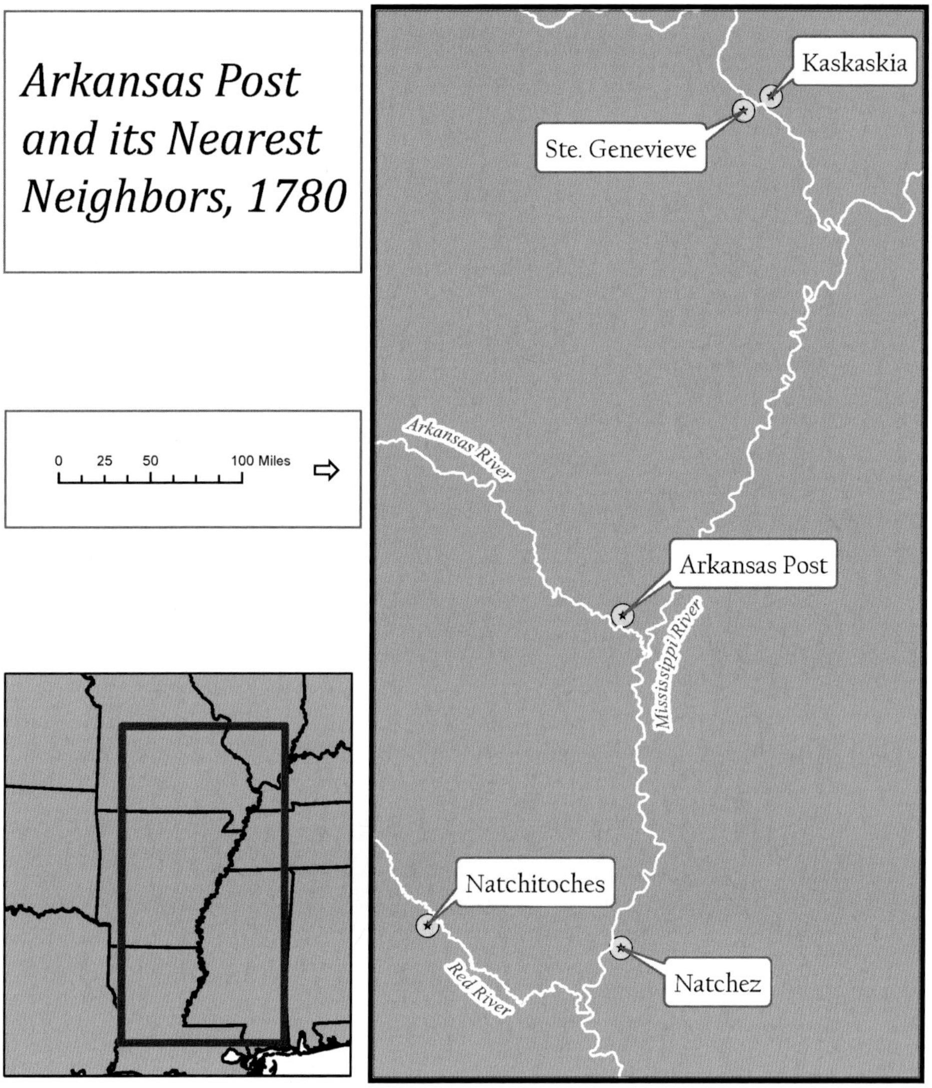

PLATE 14. Arkansas Post and its Nearest Neighbors, 1780. *Courtesy of Morris S. Arnold and Joseph Swain.*

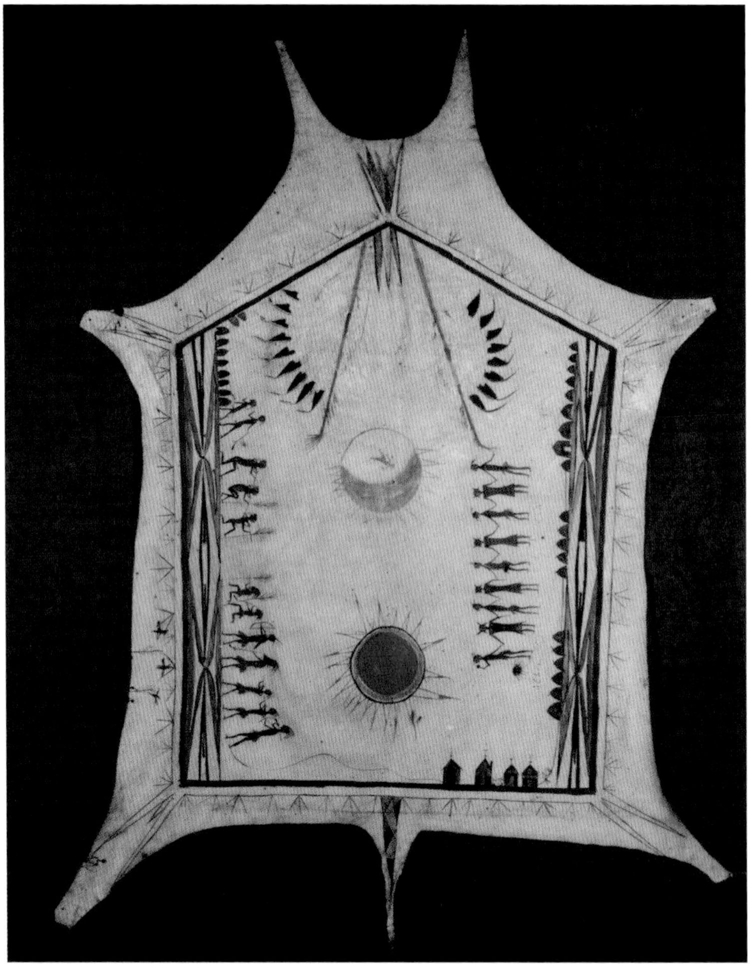

PLATE 15. Robe of the Three Villages, Quapaw painted buffalo hide, circa 1750, showing the Quapaw villages, Arkansas Post, and a battle between the Quapaws and the Chickasaws. *Courtesy Musée du quai Branly, Paris.*

PLATE 16. Joseph Bernard D'Hauterive de Vallière, 1742–1797. Commandant of Arkansas Post from 1790 to 1794. *Historic Arkansas Museum, Little Rock.*

PLATE 17. Captain Alexandre Chevalier DeClouet, 1726–1789. Commandant of Arkansas Post from 1768 to 1770. *Dupré Library, Univerity of Louisiana at Lafayette.*

PLATE 18. Marie Félicité de Vallière Vaugine, 1770–1806. Daughter of Joseph Vallière. *Historic Arkansas Museum, Little Rock.*

expressed concern about the federal government's alleged plans to relocate the Chickasaw Indians to Arkansas and seemed to believe that achieving statehood would give Arkansas greater leverage in deciding that question. The *Arkansas Gazette*, which continued to represent the Family position, published a letter from "Henry," who focused attention on the financial burden that would accompany statehood. The federal government paid for much of the cost of territorial administration, and in the absence of those funds, taxes would have to be imposed on the citizens of Arkansas. As Charles Bolton notes, "Henry" also suggested "that the Chickasaws could not legally be located in an existing territory and that it was foolish to talk about statehood until Arkansas had the necessary population."

Ambrose Sevier, territorial delegate and Family member, adopted the *Gazette*'s position when he ran for reelection in 1831, but certain developments were taking shape that would cause him, the Family, and the *Gazette* to reconsider. Sevier was motivated by at least three factors. First, as Jack B. Scroggs has noted in his thorough analysis of the statehood question published in the *Arkansas Historical Quarterly*, Family considerations were a significant factor. Richard M. Johnson of Kentucky, who was brother to Benjamin Johnson, was preparing for a possible run for the vice presidency in 1836, and his Arkansas relatives hoped to be in a position to assist him. Benjamin Johnson was a territorial Superior Court judge but, more important, he was father-in-law to Ambrose Sevier and one of the most prominent members of the Family. A second factor motivating Sevier and the Family was the desire to support Andrew Jackson in his battle with the ever-strengthening Whig Party. The territories held some of Jackson's strongest supporters, and many territorial officials were Jackson appointees. A third factor, however, proved to be the one that led most directly to action on the statehood question. When it became clear that the free territory of Michigan was intending to apply for statehood, Sevier and others with slaveholding interests became alarmed about the possibility of disturbing the balance of power within the Senate, a balance between slaveholding and non-slaveholding states. The question of slavery in the Arkansas Territory had been decided at the time the territory was created in 1819, and the Missouri Compromise had confirmed that when it permitted slavery in the territories below the thirty-six degrees, thirty minutes dividing line. The principle of pairing a slave territory and a free territory motivated Sevier to take action abruptly during the 1834 session of Congress. Sevier had no opportunity to prepare his constituents for his change in position on the issue of statehood, for the Michigan petition was circulating and the delegate from Florida, the only other southern territory that might apply for statehood, was absent from Congress. Sevier saw his opportunity and did not hesitate to grasp it. On December 17, 1834, he presented a resolution to Congress asking that the Committee on Territories consider the question of statehood for Arkansas Territory. Sevier's constituents back in Arkansas were caught by surprise, but the *Arkansas Gazette* supported his new position. Aside from criticizing the fact that Sevier acted without consulting his constituents, the *Advocate* also supported his actions. Only the *Arkansas Times*, a third Little Rock newspaper, objected. Their objections echoed in one respect those first advanced by the *Gazette* in 1831. They expressed concern about the financial burden of statehood. But the *Times* also suggested that the drive for statehood was one led by planters and for planters and that it would create a greater financial burden for non-slaveholders, a burden not worth bearing.

Despite the qualms expressed in the *Times*, momentum for statehood continued to grow in Arkansas, but Whigs in Congress were acting to block the effort. They recognized that both territories would support their archenemy, Andrew Jackson, and they hoped to stall the drive for statehood, at least until after the election of 1836. Ultimately, Arkansas and Michigan were each required to hold a special census to ascertain whether they had the required population but neither was authorized to draft state constitutions. When Michigan's lawmakers began to draft a constitution without authorization, planning to present the finished document to Congress as a fait accompli, Arkansas determined to do the same. William Fulton, who by that time had replaced Pope as territorial governor, was initially opposed to this maneuver and did not lend his support to the effort until he was certain it had President Jackson's backing.

The drive for statehood was given an additional boost when the special census conducted in Arkansas revealed that the territory had actually surpassed the 40,000 population required for admission as a state. A total of 52,240 individuals resided in Arkansas. With the census behind them, the territorial legislature began to debate the calling of a constitutional convention. Such a convention required the election of delegates, and difficulties arose almost immediately. Those representing the interests of southeastern planters hoped to establish a formula whereby they would be able to send more delegates to the convention than their free white population might otherwise allow. As S. Charles Bolton points out, "the lowland south and east in this division had only three-fourths as many white people as did the highland north and west, but it had twice as many slaves." The southeastern delegates hoped to adopt the three-fifths rule—a method of counting slaves familiar to most because it was the formula used in the United States Constitution—in order to gain greater representation for their area. David Walker, a Whig from Fayetteville, led the northwest Arkansas faction in the battle to adhere to a count of the free white population only. Unsuccessful in securing the three-fifths formula, the planters successfully maneuvered for apportionment by districts rather than by population, with each geographic district electing an equal number of delegates: twenty-six for the northwest and twenty-six for the southeast.

The battle over apportionment resumed when the elected delegates met in Little Rock in January 1836. Under an admonition to act quickly in order to present the proposed state constitution to Congress in time for it to be considered along with Michigan's constitution and petition, the delegates nevertheless engaged in heated debate over representation. In the end, they agreed to the district representation scheme but identified three rather than two districts: the southeast, the northwest, and a middle district made up of Pulaski, Saline, and White counties. Pulaski, within which Little Rock was located, was by far the largest of the three counties, and everyone understood that the capital city's ties to the southeast would have significant political ramifications.

Under this scheme, eight delegates each were apportioned to the southeast and northwest and one delegate was apportioned for the middle district. Despite the concerted opposition of David Walker and twenty-one other delegates from the northwest, it passed by six votes.

The thorny issue of representation notwithstanding, the new constitution was, by the standards of the day, a democratic document. Voting was limited to free white adult males, but there were no property requirements either for voting or for holding office and poll taxes were prohibited except as a device to raise funds for counties. The governor, the state legislators, and almost all local officials were to be popularly elected. The governor would have a four-year term but was limited to serving only eight years in any twelve. State representatives had terms of two years, state senators four, and there was no limit on the number of terms either could serve. The legislature was clearly the dominant branch of state government. It not only chose the state's U.S. senators but also all Supreme Court and circuit judges, the secretary of state, the state auditor, the state treasurer, and the circuit attorneys. It could also override the governor's veto by a simple majority vote.

The Arkansas convention completed its deliberations and finalized the constitution on January 30, 1836. Although a courier, delegate Charles F. M. Noland, was dispatched to convey the document to Washington, he took a circuitous route as a precaution against winter storms, and by the time he arrived in the capital on March 8, the U.S. mail had already delivered a copy of a special edition of the *Arkansas Gazette* containing a complete draft of the Arkansas constitution. The ultimate success of the effort to secure statehood for Arkansas was not assured, however, and the forces for and against admission prepared to engage each other in debate in Congress. The Whigs understood that both Arkansas and Michigan would be supportive of the Jacksonian Democrats and thus, just as they had the year before, sought to delay consideration of statehood for the two territories until after the 1836 elections. Meanwhile, some northern congressmen opposed statehood for Arkansas on the basis of its status as a slave state. As Jack Scroggs notes, "A continuous stormy session of twenty-five hours duration marked the final effort of the Whigs to delay the bills, with administration forces facing the recurrent problem of maintaining a quorum. Acrimonious debate characterized the struggle, with several members being called to order for caustic comments." Ultimately, however, the Democrats prevailed and both bills passed on June 13, 1836. The president signed the bill creating the state of Arkansas on June 15, 1836.

In less than three decades, from the time of the Louisiana Purchase until Arkansas became the twenty-fifth state of the Union, the "remote and restless" territory passed through a monumental transformation. It moved from a small European outpost of little real importance and even less economic and political activity, to full membership in a new and potentially powerful nation. Native Americans struggled, vainly, to maintain a place on the territory's stage, for the interests of white settlers and citizens prevailed over Indian hopes and dreams—and over bargains they made with U.S. officials. By the 1820s removal was in full swing, orchestrated by a group of self-interested politicians who made the territory their home, their place to realize the opportunity for economic and political gain. The expansion of the slave plantation system into the territory became a defining element and positioned Arkansas to play a small role in the great Missouri Compromise, the first time the nation faced the implications of slavery.

The young men who occupied positions of political power in Arkansas were not all of one accord, however, and by the early 1830s had divided as Democrats and Whigs, and sometimes went beyond mere invective in settling their disputes. They largely united, however uneasily, in the drive for statehood, seizing the opportunity to assume a more purposeful and important role in the nation's political economy.

CHAPTER SEVEN

"The Rights and Rank to Which We Are Entitled": Arkansas in the Early Statehood Period, 1836–1850

After a lengthy and often-tedious struggle, Arkansas was admitted to the Union as the twenty-fifth state in June 1836. Six years previously the editor of the Little Rock–based *Arkansas Advocate* had proclaimed that statehood would give Arkansas "the rights and rank to which we are entitled," and most Arkansans probably agreed that the action validated Arkansas's position in the Union. But events of the early statehood period confirmed many of the worst fears of those who had thought the move premature. The new state's meager resources proved inadequate to fill the void created by the loss of federal revenues, and the first attempt to address those financial problems ended disastrously, saddling the state with chronic financial instability. Those who hoped that statehood would improve Arkansas's image as a violent and lawless frontier found instead that subsequent events confirmed rather than refuted that image. In the years between 1836 and 1850, statehood would prove to be a very mixed blessing.

Government in the Early Statehood Era

The first state elections in Arkansas were held in August 1836, and they demonstrated conclusively the dominance of the Democratic Party in the state and the power of the political alliance known as "the Family." Arkansas voters elected James S. Conway the state's first governor; the new state legislature chose Ambrose Sevier and former territorial governor William Fulton to be the state's first two U.S. senators; and Benjamin Johnson was appointed to be the first federal district judge for Arkansas. The Family's influence extended to the national level where Johnson's brother, Senator Richard M. Johnson of Kentucky, was the Democratic candidate for vice president on a ticket with Martin Van Buren.

Archibald Yell was elected to be the new state's lone congressman. Yell had come to Arkansas in 1834 and had quickly become a leading proponent of statehood. Like the Conways

"The Family": "The Family" was a powerful alliance that dominated the Arkansas Democratic Party and state politics in the years between statehood and the Civil War. Many of its members were related by blood or by marriage. Principal members included Ambrose Sevier, James Conway, Benjamin Johnson, and Chester Ashley. Also known as "the Dynasty."

James Sevier Conway, first governor of the state of Arkansas. *Courtesy of the Arkansas History Commission.*

and Sevier, Yell came from Tennessee, and he shared their devotion to Jacksonian politics. But though he enjoyed Family support in his race for Congress in 1836 and in his successful race for governor in 1840, Yell pursued an independent course. A personal friend of President Jackson with a strong base of personal support in northwest Arkansas, Yell was less dependent on the Family than many Arkansas office seekers. In addition, he was a gifted politician who, contemporaries observed, could out-talk, out-drink, out-shoot, and out-pray any opponent.

In the years following the death of longtime territorial secretary and Family opponent Robert Crittenden, the political faction he had led would align itself with the national Whig Party. The Whigs' chief unifying principle was opposition to Andrew Jackson, but the party also supported an economic program that called for protective tariffs, federally funded internal improvements, and a second Bank of the United States. Led on the national level by Henry Clay of Kentucky, the party had great appeal to those business interests involved in the emerging market economy and drew to its ranks men of wealth and privilege, including many large planters.

Whig Party: The Whig Party was a national political party whose chief organizing principle was opposition to Andrew Jackson. They also favored an economic program that included protective tariffs, federally funded internal improvements, and a second Bank of the United States.

Under the leadership of Crittenden's handpicked successor, Albert Pike, the Whig Party in Arkansas provided the state with a number of capable men, and Pike himself was the intellectual and oratorical equal of anyone in the state. Little Rock would be a Whig stronghold in Arkansas throughout the state's early years, but the Whigs never exerted enough popular appeal in the state to wrest control of the reins of government from the Family. They remained a minority party in Arkansas until the slavery controversy destroyed the national party in the 1850s. Throughout the first quarter century of the state's existence, the Democrats controlled all the major state offices and a majority of the seats in the state legislature.

The first state legislature that assembled in September 1836 in the unfinished statehouse faced major problems. The financial concerns that had made many Arkansans reluctant to pursue statehood proved to be well founded. With low tax rates on real estate (the principal source of tax revenue), few assets to sell, and fewer government services for which to charge licenses and fees, the money the state took in was barely sufficient to maintain the most basic governmental operations.

The absence of banking institutions in Arkansas meant that those funds the state government did derive went to banks outside the state. It also meant that there were no lending institutions capable of stimulating economic development. To address this deficiency the state constitution specifically empowered the legislature to charter two banks, and the first state assembly wasted little time in doing so. It created the Bank of Arkansas (also known as the State Bank), a state agency whose directors were appointed by the legislature. Headquartered in Little Rock, the bank had branches in Fayetteville, Batesville, Arkansas Post, and Washington. The State Bank was to serve as the repository of all state funds, and it could issue bank notes (paper money) that could be used to pay debts owed to the state. Additionally, it was allowed to sell bonds backed by the state government and to use the proceeds for operating funds. The bank would then lend money to attract and promote business, using the interest from those loans to repay the state, which would in turn pay the bondholders. Similar plans were in operation in other states.

Albert Pike, between 1850 and 1854. Portrait by Edward Payson Washbourne. *Special Collections Division, University of Arkansas Libraries, Fayetteville.*

State Bank of Arkansas: The State Bank of Arkansas was chartered by the first state legislature. It was designed to serve as a repository for all state funds and to promote business activity throughout the state. Through corruption, mismanagement, and a national economic downturn, the bank was declared insolvent in 1843.

While the State Bank was at least nominally a state agency and was designed to promote business activity throughout the state, the Real Estate Bank of Arkansas was a creation of, by, and for the state's planter interests.

Real Estate Bank: The Real Estate Bank was chartered by the first state legislature. It was designed to promote the interests of the state's planters. The bank issued loans on inflated land valuations, and by 1841 it was insolvent.

State representative Anthony H. Davies, a Chicot County planter, wrote the bill creating the bank, and another twenty-eight Chicot County planters purchased 6,286 of the banks 22,500 shares. The bank's headquarters were in Little Rock, but three of its four branches were in the southern and eastern lowlands—Columbia in Chicot County, Helena in Phillips County, and Washington in Hempstead County. Only the Van Buren branch in northwest Arkansas was outside of the cotton-growing area of the state.

Like the State Bank, the Real Estate Bank's operating capital came from the sale of state bonds, but unlike the State Bank, the Real Estate Bank also sold stock, which could be purchased with land or crops. Shareholders were permitted to borrow up to one-half the value of their shares. Also unlike the State Bank, the governor appointed only two of the nine directors of each branch bank with the stockholders choosing the other seven. The directors of each branch then chose two of their members (one of whom was required to be a gubernatorial appointee) to be members of a central board. The state thus pledged itself to back the financial transactions of an entity over which it had little actual control.

Though fraught with the potential for abuse, with favorable economic conditions and careful management, the banks might have succeeded. Absent either, they were doomed to failure. Both banks opened in December 1838 and initially redeemed their notes in specie (gold and silver). But like many unregulated banks throughout the country, the banks issued paper money far in excess of their specie reserves. To compound the problem, both made questionable loans without adequate securities. The Real Estate Bank, in particular, made loans based on inflated land valuations. Rumors of unfair appraisals and complaints of favoritism in the dispensing of its stock dogged the bank almost from its inception. Many of the state's political elite of both parties were deeply involved. Ambrose Sevier, for example, secured a $15,000 loan on 1,084 acres of land with an appraised value of $32,000 but an assessed value of only $13,975. The bill's author, Anthony H. Davies, mortgaged 1,926 acres appraised at $37,212 to cover a $30,000 loan, although only 185 of the acres were in cultivation.

The State Bank also suffered from corruption. The books of the Fayetteville branch bank were stolen, and when they were recovered, several pages of cash transactions had been ripped out. The bank's cashier soon fled to Texas. The banks also suffered from poor timing. They went into operation one year after the beginning of the Panic of 1837, a severe national economic downturn brought on by a host of factors including a depression in England, falling cotton prices, and the failure of the domestic wheat crop.

The situation was exacerbated by the shortsighted policies of the Jackson administration. Jackson's destruction of the Second Bank of the United States in the early 1830s removed the last vestige of federal regulation of state banks, resulting in the kind of financial irresponsibility demonstrated by the two Arkansas banks and dozens of others across the nation. In 1836 Jackson attempted to halt the wild speculation by issuing the Specie Circular, which required land payments to be made in specie. The act destroyed public confidence in paper money and brought ruin to many financial institutions across the country.

The effects were first felt in the East, but by 1839 the shockwaves reached the Southwest (now known as the Old Southwest after the country expanded to the Pacific coast) where land speculation and easy money had run rampant. Land and crop prices plummeted. By 1839 both Arkansas banks were in trouble. The Real Estate Bank ceased operations in July 1841. Acting under the bank's charter, the directors appointed themselves as receivers and refused to turn over the books to the legislature. Receiver Albert Pike built a magnificent Greek Revival mansion in Little Rock, but the receivers did nothing to repay the money owed the state. Two years later, the State Bank was declared insolvent.

The banking fiasco left the state with a debt of over three million dollars. It brought financial ruin to many Arkansans, resulted in hundreds of lawsuits, left the state's credit in shambles, and fostered a distrust of banking. The fact that both Democrats and Whigs were deeply involved prevented either of the major parties from using the issue for partisan purposes, but certain individuals were tarred by their involvement with the banks. In 1842 Sevier came under especially harsh criticism for his role in both banking ventures. A committee of the state house of representatives cleared him of any wrongdoing in his actions involving the State Bank, but a separate committee report on his conduct involving the Real Estate Bank concluded that he had "seriously damaged the interests of the bank and of the state." A third of the Democratic house members joined with the Whigs in voting to formally censure Sevier for his actions. Though a subsequent legislature rescinded the censure, the action left a black mark on Sevier's record and severely damaged his reputation.

In 1844 the legislature overreacted and adopted the first amendment to the state constitution, which stated that "No bank or banking institution shall be hereafter incorporated, or established in the state." It was a classic example of throwing the baby out with the bath water. Arkansas had needed a sound banking system in 1836, and it still needed such a system in 1844. Now, economic progress, if it came, would have to do so without the aid of state government.

The banking debacle also led to the most infamous event in the history of the Arkansas legislature. In a special session in the fall of 1837 (the first session in the new state capitol), house speaker and Real Estate Bank president John Wilson got into a verbal sparring match on the house floor with state representative Joseph J. Anthony, one of the bank's staunchest critics. When Anthony refused Wilson's order to take his seat, Wilson charged down from the speaker's chair and physically assaulted Anthony on the house floor. In the struggle that followed both men drew knives, and Wilson fatally stabbed Anthony. See plate 23 following page 270.

Wilson was subsequently tried and acquitted of murder but was expelled from the legislature. His actions did not, however, appreciably diminish his appeal to his constituents. He was reelected to the state legislature in 1840. In the legislative session of that year, Wilson had to be restrained from another knife-wielding attack on another Real Estate Bank critic. He subsequently defaulted on his Real Estate Bank loan and disappeared into the wilds of Texas.

Wilson's actions highlighted another of the young state's persistent problems—its image. The Arkansas Territory had developed a reputation as a refuge for the fringe elements of society. The English traveler George William Featherstonhaugh, who passed through the territory in 1834, noted:

> This territory of Arkansas was on the confines of the United States and Mexico, and, as I had long known, was the occasional residence of many timid and nervous persons, against whom the laws of these respective countries had a grudge. *Gentlemen*, who had taken the liberty to imitate the signatures of other persons; *bankrupts*, who were not disposed to be plundered by their creditors; *homicides*, *horse-stealers*, and *gamblers*, all admired Arkansas on account of the very gentle and tolerant state of public opinion which prevailed there in regard to such fundamental points as religion, morals, and property.

In a less eloquent moment, this same traveler referred to the "criminals, gamblers, speculators, and men of broken fortunes, with no law to restrain them, no obligation to conceal their vices, no motive to induce them to appear devout or to act with sobriety." An early Arkansas political figure (who lived to regret the remark) was more blunt, "[E]very man left his honesty and every woman her chastity on the other side of the Mississippi, on moving to Arkansas."

As the Wilson-Anthony affair clearly demonstrated, however, the violence that characterized early Arkansas was not limited to outlaws and the fringe elements common to every frontier. In the territorial period, Superior Court judge Andrew Scott shot and killed fellow judge Joseph Selden in a duel that originated over a card game. In the same year that territorial secretary Robert Crittenden mortally wounded territorial delegate Henry Conway, Ambrose Sevier fought a bloodless duel with future Whig congressman Thomas Newton. The Anthony-Wilson affair quickly quashed any hopes that statehood would bring an end to such violence.

In 1844 Democratic newspaper editor Solon Borland pummeled Whig editor Benjamin Borden in a fistfight on a Little Rock street. Borden then challenged Borland to a duel. The two parties met in the Indian Territory west of Fort Smith, and Borland shot the martially challenged Borden in the chest. (The wound was not fatal, and both men returned to their Little Rock newspapers.) Borland continued his assault on the state's reputation after his election to the U.S. Senate. In 1850 he attacked Senator Henry Foote of Mississippi on a Washington street, and two years later bloodied the nose of the superintendent of the census on the Senate floor. Another Arkansas congressman struck a fellow representative during a debate on the House floor. Such incidents seemed to confirm Arkansas's reputation for violence.

That reputation was compounded by a lingering image of Arkansas as the home of the poor and shiftless. One of the most enduring examples of that image is "The Arkansas Traveler." Originally the "Traveler" was the story of the passing of the frontier, when squatters were beginning to fade from the scene. Based on an incident that occurred during an 1840 campaign trip through a remote region of the state, the image and accompanying dialogue provide a humorous glance at a squatter whose humble lifestyle and recalcitrant ways contrast nicely with Sandford Faulkner, a sophisticated Arkansas plantation owner and politician trying to find his way back to civilization.

Faulkner told the story to many an appreciative audience. However, later appropriators of the image and dialogue made the character of the traveler an outsider, leaving the squatter and his family to represent Arkansas. With this change, Arkansas became the butt of the joke, a fact that left many in the state unhappy with the *Traveler* and the damage it caused the state's reputation. See plate 24 following page 270.

"The Arkansas Traveler": "The Arkansas Traveler" was the name of a story and a song based on an incident in the 1840 campaign in which a sophisticated Arkansas planter had a humorous encounter with an unlettered but clever squatter. Later appropriators of the image and dialogue made the traveler an outsider, leaving the squatter and his family to represent Arkansas and making Arkansas the butt of the joke.

Arkansas Society, 1836–1850

But if many Americans viewed Arkansas as a place of violence, lawlessness, and poverty, others saw it in a different light. Massachusetts native Thomas Bangs Thorpe spent much of his life in Louisiana, but his fictional humor often used Arkansas as a setting. One of Thorpe's best-known stories was his 1841 piece entitled "The Big Bear of Arkansas." The story's principal character is a loud, good-humored braggart named Jim Doggett, who regales his fellow steamboat passengers with stories of the state's natural grandeur. When a listener comments that mosquitoes are large in Arkansas, Doggett replies, "If they are large, Arkansas is large, her varmints ar large, her trees ar large, her rivers ar large, and a small mosquitoe would be of no more use in Arkansaw than preaching in a cane-brake." Thorpe's tales of hunting the state's abundant bear population contributed to early Arkansas's reputation as "the Bear State."

A different approach to the same theme is found in the writings of Charles Fenton Mercer Noland. The Virginia-born Noland moved to Arkansas, settling at Batesville where he studied law and became a Whig politician, but he is most remembered for his regional humor stories set along the Devil's Fork of the Little Red River in Arkansas. Noland began his writing in the 1830s, and his stories continued to appear in various publications for the next two decades.

Writing under the pen name Pete Whetstone, Noland described the bear hunting, horse racing, fighting, politics, and other events that characterized life on the Arkansas frontier. Noland's characters are often boisterous and given to some of the same braggadocio as Thorpe's Jim Doggett, but they are portrayed more realistically than Thorpe's character and more sympathetically than the Arkansans described by Featherstonhaugh and other early observers. As historian S. Charles Bolton notes, "His [Noland's] characters are backwoodsmen, but they are also southern yeomen and Jacksonian Americans, imbued with the democratic values that Jackson found so useful and Tocqueville found so interesting."

Another writer who helped shape the image of Arkansas in the early antebellum period was Albert Pike. A native of Massachusetts, Pike traveled widely as a young man and wrote accounts of his travels as well as poetry and some satirical pieces. But it was perhaps his descriptions of the richness and promise of Arkansas's land that most affected the region's image. Arriving in the territory in 1833, Pike settled in Pope County where he taught school. In 1835 he proclaimed himself "a citizen of Arkansas for life," and began to write glowing accounts of the region to skeptical and often-condescending friends back East. In 1835 he wrote to the *New England Magazine*:

> The soil of the Arkansas bottoms is inferior to none in the world; and the facilities offered a man for making a living and a fortune there, are nowhere equaled. A poor man comes here, whose necessities have driven him from the States. He has not a cent in the world—nothing but his axe and his rifle. He goes into the Arkansas bottom, cuts a few logs, and his neighbors help him raise a hut, with a wooden chimney, daubed with mud. . . . In four or five years that man will raise twenty bales of cotton and a thousand bushels of corn, and be steadily enlarging his crop and increasing his income.

Numerous others echoed Pike's sentiments. John Meek moved to Union County from South Carolina in the early 1840s. In an 1842 letter to a friend back home, he wrote:

> We are all in health at present (thank God) & have enjoyed fine health this year but if you saw the Christal Springs we have to drink from, & the pure clean undulating Country with tall forests shading it and waving under a delightful breeze from the Rocky Mountains you would not wonder at our health being good, & we have the most fertile soil I ever saw. . . . The poorest land in our country would beat in Corn, Cotton, Wheat, oats or potatoes, any land in Laurens or New'y, S[outh] C[arolina].

He closed with an appeal for the friend to join him in Arkansas and admonished him, "Do not think we are out of the world, 20 days by land would bring a horseback traveler from your place here and it is a good road and good accommodations and no Indians on the road, but well settled with civil settlers."

In the early statehood period, thousands of settlers came to Arkansas to share in the opportunities that Pike and Meek described. Many of these emigrants sought lands that were similar to the ones that they were leaving. Accordingly, those from the highlands of the upper South tended to prefer the mountainous regions of Arkansas, while those from the Deep South favored the lowlands. They often came in groups composed of extended families, following other family members who had come previously. In her book *Communities of Kinship: Antebellum Families and the Settlement of the Cotton Frontier*, historian Carolyn Billingsley chronicled the migration of one such family. In 1837 fifty-nine-year-old Thomas Keesee Sr. organized a wagon train to take his extended family and slaves from Alabama to Saline County, Arkansas, where some of his kinsmen had settled the previous year. This cotton-growing family was attracted to fertile bottomland along the Saline River with its close proximity to Little Rock, the Southwest Trail, and the Arkansas River, the state's major commercial lifeline. By 1840 Keesee and his relatives made up 131 of Saline County's 1,162 white citizens (about 8 percent), and they owned 140 of the county's 399 slaves (35 percent). Such instances were not unique. Across the state and the region, certain families came to dominate the political, social, economic, and religious life of their new communities.

Both the state and the federal government encouraged the immigration of families by generous grants of land. Under the terms of the "Donation Law" of 1840, settlers could obtain tax-forfeited lands by agreeing to pay the future taxes. In 1850 the law was amended to permit a family to obtain a 160-acre plot for every member of the immediate family regardless of age or gender. In 1841 the federal government turned over 500,000 acres to the state, which then offered it to the public at $1.25 an acre, with the proceeds going to finance internal improvements. Two years later the state received the right to sell the sixteenth section of each township to fund schools, making over 900,000 additional acres available. In 1850 the national government began turning over to the state over seven and a half million acres of "swamp and overflow" land, and by 1859 the state had disposed of over three and a half million of these acres. Despite these opportunities to buy land, many immigrants to Arkansas in the antebellum period simply "squatted" on unsurveyed tracts of federal land, a policy that the federal government encouraged through "preemption laws," which gave the squatters the right to purchase 160 acres where they had settled for the minimum price.

By 1840 the state's population stood at 97,574, a threefold increase over 1830 and almost twice the figure at the time of statehood only four years earlier. But despite these gains, Arkansas in 1840 remained very much a frontier state with an average of fewer than two people per square mile. Its population was six times smaller than Alabama, and almost four times smaller than the neighboring states of Mississippi and Louisiana.

In *Arkansas, 1800–1860: Remote and Restless*, Charles Bolton provides a good portrait of Arkansas settlers of this period. Almost all Arkansans were farmers, approximately one-third of whom owned their own land while the rest "squatted" on government land which they hoped one day to purchase. Livestock were ubiquitous. There were twice as many cattle and four times as many hogs in the state as there were people, and a typical Arkansan ate about four times as much pork as beef. Corn was grown statewide and was the basis of the subsistence agriculture that characterized much of the state.

The log cabin remained the dominant style of housing. The simplest was the so-called single-pen variety, a one-room structure, sixteen to eighteen foot square, made from oak logs. The more elaborate "dogtrot house" or "double pen" consisted of two cabins built side by side under a common roof with an open area in between. Since the average Arkansas family contained six people, privacy was at a minimum, and eating, sleeping, and cooking all occurred in one or two rooms. Travelers to the region noted little difference between the houses of the poor and those of the more well-to-do. See plate 25 following page 270.

Early Arkansas had few amenities of civilization and was a particularly hard place for a woman to live. Consequently in 1840 men outnumbered women in Arkansas by three to two, and women of childbearing age made up only about 17 percent of the white population, the lowest in the nation. Those women who did come to Arkansas proved to be extremely prolific, however. The birth rate for Arkansas women was the highest in the nation, 43 percent higher than the national average. Women married early and began bearing children almost immediately. Bolton notes, "Women in their twenties lived with an average of three children, most of them under ten. Women in their thirties lived with five or six youngsters, three or four of them under ten." Large families were seen as a distinct economic advantage on the frontier where land was plentiful but labor was in short supply. The hardships involved in bearing and raising such large numbers of children, however, were staggering.

In addition to her responsibilities as a mother, an Arkansas woman had to slaughter animals for food, cook the meals, tend to the house, care for the sick, assist her husband in the fields at planting and harvest time, and, when requested, offer advice on economic matters. Yet despite the contributions women made to the care and maintenance of the family, Arkansas society remained highly patriarchal. Women had no political rights, and educational and occupational opportunities outside the home were almost nonexistent.

Adding to these hardships was the lack of social opportunities. In a sparsely populated state where homesteads were often far from the nearest neighbor, Arkansas women frequently suffered from intense loneliness. Mary Ann Owens and her family came to Arkansas from Tennessee in the fall of 1838 when she was only eight years old, taking up residence in south-central Arkansas in what would become Dallas County. She found Arkansas to be "a perfect wildriness at the time inhabited by wild beast and Indians with hear and there a whight settler." Shortly after their arrival, she noted, "an old woman came in saying she had walked five miles to see Mother for she had not seen a white woman before for four years." In 1847 Mary Ann married Dr. John Sims, and the union produced three children before the doctor died in 1855.

The couple's life was generally happy, but the doctor was often away from home, and Mary Ann sometimes stayed with her mother, who lived about six miles away. After one stay of seven weeks, she returned to her own house, and noted, "I remember how lonely I felt when I arrived at home. There was not a white person on the place save me and my two little children. The first thing I did was to sit down and take a hearty cry, but I concluded that was too childish so I got my baby to sleep and went to work to arrange my household matters which occupied all my time and at night I felt quite fatigued."

Mary Ann found solace in evangelical religion. In her journal she recorded that "in the summer of 49 I joined the Misseonary Baptist church" and later noted, "I attended worship at Mount Pleasant—what a sweet repast it is for the soul to meet with kindred spirets around [the] table of the Lord." Many other women shared her experience, finding in evangelical Christianity not only religious nurturing but also the chance for interaction with and mutual support from other women.

Arkansas would later come to be considered a part of the so-called Bible Belt, but in the early antebellum period it was largely an irreligious place, and travelers to the region commented on the appalling conditions they found there. One early missionary who passed through the Arkansas Delta noted, "It is painful to witness the deplorable state of morals in this place. The Sabbath is awfully profaned; idleness, drinking, swearing, and gambling almost universally prevail."

By the second decade of the nineteenth century, a hardy group of Protestant preachers, fired by the religious revivalism known as the Second Great Awakening, attempted to transform the situation. A Baptist preacher, George Gill, delivered a sermon at the Mount Olive community along the White River in northeast Arkansas on Christmas Day in 1814, and four years later the first Baptist church in what would become the Arkansas Territory was founded on the Fourche-a-Thomas River in northeast Arkansas. By 1840 there were thirty-seven Baptist churches in the state.

The Baptist contribution was significant, but as historian Charles Bolton has noted, "It was the Methodists who brought southern evangelicalism into Arkansas." As early as 1814 the Methodist preacher William Stevenson had conducted religious services for isolated settlers along the Southwest Trail. In the tradition of early American Methodism, Stevenson sought to create a "circuit," a regularly traveled route served by an itinerant preacher on horseback. The primitive conditions of travel in frontier Arkansas made such efforts a daunting task. An early preacher described the conditions in his journal:

> [O]ur road disappeared under water [in] the Black River Swamp. . . . [My horse] went down till he was nearly buried alive in quicksand and water. . . . My heavy saddle-bags were left behind in the mud. . . . We entered a dismal swamp, thirty-two miles wide, and . . . unusually full of water . . . varying in depth from six inches to three feet. . . . Had I been offered one thousand dollars to retrace my steps, it would have been no temptation.

These hardships notwithstanding, Methodist circuit riders became a regular feature of life on the Arkansas frontier. "If you hear something lumberin' through the canebrake," went one common saying, "it's either a bear or a Methodist preacher, and either one's bound to be hungry!" These early ministers utilized any available structure to conduct services, and those services were sometimes rowdy affairs. One preacher remembered:

> One warm day I was preaching in a school-house in the woods. Some of the congregation had stacked their rifles against a tree, and hung up their powder horns on the limbs. Their hounds had laid down together, and for some cause while the service was going on the dogs got into a general fight. Every fellow went for his own unmannerly dog, some pulling them apart by their legs, others pelting them with clap boards, and of course, I had to wait until the war was over. The women took advantage of the interval to light their cob pipes. When the men at last subdued the dogs, they returned to the congregation, the women put their pipes in their pockets, I resumed my discourse where I had left off, and the meeting closed in an orderly manner.

The Methodists also organized "camp meetings," outdoor religious gatherings that lasted for several days. Camp meetings drew people of all denominations or no denomination at all from the surrounding countryside to a central location for preaching and singing and served a social as well as a religious function.

Presbyterians (regular and Cumberland), Disciples of Christ, Episcopalians, and other denominations entered the state's religious scene in the years before the Civil

War, but Methodist and Baptist churches far outnumbered the combined total of all other Christian denominations. After a slow start, the number of churches increased dramatically in the 1840s and 1850s. By 1850 there were 168 Methodist and 114 Baptist churches in the state, and by 1860 those numbers increased to 505 and 281, respectively. While many Arkansans attended religious services, church membership in the antebellum period remained relatively small. Baptists generally required some evidence of a salvation experience before admitting a person to the church rolls and dismissed members for immoral behavior. Methodists imposed a probationary period on prospective members. Probably fewer than one in five Arkansans was formally affiliated with a church in 1860.

If organized religion made inroads into antebellum Arkansas, public education largely did not. From its inception, the state lagged behind much of the rest of the nation in the education of its citizens. While there was no public taxation to support the creation and operation of schools, the federal government subsidized education in the state by setting aside the sixteenth section of every township for the support of local schools and two townships for the creation and support of a university. But the revenue generated from leasing these lands proved insufficient to support a public school system, and the problem was compounded by a haphazard system of organization and administration.

The effort to establish a viable school system was further hampered by what one state official described as "the indifference that pervades the public mind on the subject of education." As a result, no viable system of public education was established, and no public university was founded in the state before the Civil War. Many wealthy Arkansans employed private tutors for their children and opposed the use of tax money for public education. Many poorer Arkansans had neither the time, the money, nor the inclination to pay for their children's education, through taxes or otherwise. Thus, for the majority of the state's citizens, the education system remained a hodge-podge of public schools and private academies manned by underpaid and often incompetent teachers.

A comparison with Michigan, Arkansas's sister state, is revealing. The two states entered the Union within a year of one another (June 1836 and January 1837) and had at the time approximately the same populations. Yet by 1850 Michigan had 2,714 public schools to Arkansas's 353 and 110,445 pupils in public schools compared to Arkansas's 8,493. Michigan derived $88,879 for public schools from taxes, while Arkansas collected $250. Michigan reported 7,912 adult white illiterates, Arkansas 16,819. In addition Michigan had 280 public libraries containing 65,116 volumes, while Arkansas had one public library with 250 volumes.

Even by Southern standards, Arkansas lagged behind. As late as 1860, when North Carolina enrolled more than two-thirds of its white school population for an average term of four months, about half of Arkansas's school-age children did not attend any school at all. Most of the rest attended only sporadically.

In spite of these handicaps, several Arkansas communities developed reputations as centers of learning. Private academies flourished in northwest Arkansas at Fayetteville and nearby Cane Hill, in central Arkansas at Little Rock, in southwest Arkansas at Springhill and Washington, and in south-central Arkansas at Tulip and Princeton. These academies or "subscription schools," taught by an itinerant schoolmaster who charged a set price per pupil, were almost always segregated by gender and usually operated for two to three months a year. As these communities grew, the length of the term increased, and teachers became more permanent.

Higher education was rare indeed, but northwest Arkansas had two institutions of higher learning in operation by 1852—Cane Hill College (supported by the Cumberland Presbyterian Church) and Arkansas College at Fayetteville. St. John's Masonic College opened its doors in Little Rock in 1859. Despite the efforts of these early institutions, however, formal education remained beyond the reach of most Arkansans. Perhaps as many as one in four adult Arkansans could neither read nor write and thus remained largely ignorant of events outside their own locality. The lack of a system of public education deepened Arkansas's isolation from the rest of the nation.

That isolation was further compounded by the abysmal state of transportation. In the 1820s Congress provided funds for the construction of a "Military Road" from Memphis to the Indian Territory via Little Rock and Fort Smith. The road, intended to facilitate defense of the frontier and constructed, in part, by U.S. Army engineers, reached Little Rock in 1827 and Fort Smith the following year. A second military road stretched from southern Missouri through Little Rock to Fulton on the Red River. Federal specifications called for the roads to be "opened 16 feet wide and entirely cleared; all brush and saplings 6 inches in diameter to be cut even with the ground; all trees between 6 and 12 inches in diameter, within 4 inches of the ground; and all trees over 12 inches within 8 inches of the ground; the stumps to be well trimmed."

In the late territorial period the federal government contributed over a quarter of a million dollars to improve the condition of the road from Memphis to Little Rock, but parts of the route that passed through the lowlands of eastern Arkansas were often underwater, and other portions were covered with rocks and fallen trees. Federal funds to complete the project dried up after Arkansas achieved statehood in 1836, and little progress was made in road building throughout the remainder of the antebellum era.

Regular stagecoach service began on a crude road between Little Rock and Hot Springs in the late territorial period, and by the early statehood era coaches made a tri-weekly run between Little Rock and Washington, Arkansas. But even on "good" roads, overland travel was slow and uncomfortable at best, dangerous at worst. On other roads, actually little more than trails, it was often impossible. The trip from Little Rock to Hot Springs (a distance of fifty-four miles) took nineteen and a half hours, while the journey from Little Rock to Washington (slightly over a hundred miles) took fifty hours.

An army officer who traveled by stagecoach from Little Rock to Fort Smith in 1850 recalled, "The greatest inconvenience of traveling over this route is, that one is three days without any sleep. In fact, they hurry us on day and night, over one of the roughest roads any poor mortal ever journeyed—not even allowing sufficient time for meals." The following year a Fort Smith editor lamented, "We have no roads of any kind except a few that are merely cut out and not fit to travel over." Prior to 1850 there was not one mile of railroad track in the state, and no bridges crossed any of the state's major rivers. River travel remained the safest and most efficient form of transportation throughout the antebellum period.

The Mexican War, the Gold Rush, and Westward Migration

In this remote frontier region, the rare appearance of a celebrated figure created quite a stir. Former Tennessee congressman David Crockett, whose exploits were already legendary, passed through Little Rock on his way to Texas in November 1835. Crockett and his party had intended to stay only one night and had taken rooms at Charles Jeffries's City Hotel. But celebrities of his caliber were rare in the capital city, and the town fathers determined to make the most of it. They hastened to the hotel and found the famous Tennessean behind the establishment skinning a deer he had shot on the two-day ride from Memphis. Crockett was persuaded to attend an impromptu dinner in his honor where, in his inimitable style, he regaled his largely Whig audience with attacks on the Jackson administration and stories of his recent defeat for reelection to Congress. (Crockett delighted in telling his listeners that, on learning of his defeat for reelection to Congress in 1835, he told his constituents, "You can all go to hell, I'm going to Texas.") The following morning when Crockett and his party departed down the Southwest Trail for Texas, a few impressionable young Arkansans may have joined him.

Many Arkansans shared Crockett's fascination with Texas. Events there were followed closely by the Arkansas press, and several of the major figures of the Texas Revolution of 1836 had ties to Arkansas. Stephen F. Austin had speculated in Arkansas land and served for a time as a territorial judge. James Bowie and his brothers had claims to thousands of acres of land in Arkansas, almost all of them fraudulent. Sam Houston spent time at both Little Rock and Washington and was instrumental in helping the Cherokees settle in the territory. At least two Arkansans died with Crockett and Bowie at the Alamo in March 1836.

Then, as now, many Arkansans were ambivalent about their large neighbor to the southwest. As early as the 1820s Arkansans had worried that the lure of cheap land in Texas robbed Arkansas of immigrants and lowered land values in the territory, and that fear continued after Texas won its independence from Mexico in 1836. Yet Ambrose Sevier and other prominent Arkansas political figures supported the notion of westward expansion and "Manifest Destiny" and felt that Texas annexation would not only increase the size of the country but would add to the power of the slave South. That reasoning was not lost on Northern "free-soilers," and Texas soon became caught up in the growing controversy over slavery. Fears of exacerbating that dispute precluded any attempt by the United States to annex Texas for almost a decade.

The Texas question was a pivotal issue in the presidential election of 1844. The Democratic candidate, James K. Polk of Tennessee, came out strongly for annexation of Texas. The Whig candidate, Henry Clay of Kentucky, had originally opposed annexation. But under pressure from the Southern wing of his party, Clay changed his position and endorsed annexation. The flip-flop hurt him in the North, and in New York the abolitionist Liberty Party won enough votes to give that state and the election to Polk. The 1844 election was also significant in Arkansas. Historian Michael Dougan has called it "the highwater mark of the two-party system" in the state. Both presidential candidates had strong followings in Arkansas, and both parties fielded strong state tickets. In the end, Arkansas gave its electoral votes to Polk, and elected Thomas Drew, the Family-backed Democratic candidate, governor.

Chester Ashley. *Courtesy of the Arkansas History Commission.*

The death of Senator Fulton in August of 1844 provided an added incentive for aspiring politicians. Archibald Yell eyed the vacant seat with great interest as did the prominent Little Rock attorney Chester Ashley. Ashley had amassed a small fortune through a series of lucrative, if sometimes questionable, land transactions. He had been active in the movement to relocate the capital to Little Rock (where he owned a considerable amount of land) and later built one of the city's first great houses there, a Greek Revival mansion located on Markham Street between Cumberland and Scott. Ashley had at one time been a law partner of Robert Crittenden but had dissolved the partnership and become, along with Ambrose Sevier and William Woodruff, a leader of the opposing political faction. By the mid-1840s, however, Ashley's influence in the Family-dominated Democratic Party had waned, and he was often at odds with his former allies. Still he was a man of acknowledged talent and considerable influence, and the legislature chose him to fill out the remaining two years of Fulton's term. Ashley took his seat in the Senate in March 1845 and shortly thereafter made a powerful speech in support of the annexation of Texas.

When the United States did annex Texas in March 1845 it brought tensions with Mexico to the boiling point. Mexico had never recognized the independence of its former province and viewed the American action as a virtual declaration of war. After Texas was formally admitted to the Union in December 1845, an American army under Gen. Zachary Taylor was dispatched to the Rio Grande, the traditional boundary of the American claim. Mexico insisted that the boundary was a hundred miles farther to the north and thus viewed the American presence on the Rio Grande as an invasion of Mexican territory. In late April 1846, Mexican forces crossed the river and attacked the

The Chester Ashley mansion in Little Rock. *Historic Arkansas Museum, Little Rock.*

American positions. Shortly thereafter, claiming that Mexico had invaded American territory and "shed American blood on American soil," the president asked for a declaration of war, and Congress responded in early May, authorizing Polk to call up fifty thousand volunteers.

The secretary of war requested that Governor Drew organize one regiment of cavalry and one battalion of infantry. The cavalry regiment was to assemble at Washington in southwest Arkansas, while the infantry was to report to Fort Smith to serve as replacements for the regular army troops there who had been ordered to the Rio Grande. While there was little interest in frontier duty on the state's western border, there was great enthusiasm for service in Mexico. Young men eager for glory and adventure and aspiring politicians eager to pad their resumes rushed to enlist. By July, 44 officers and 749 men organized into ten companies had assembled at Washington.

The officers of the companies were allowed to choose the regimental officers, including the top position of regimental colonel. The only prominent Arkansan with any significant military experience was former governor Archibald Yell. At age seventeen Yell had volunteered to fight with Andrew Jackson in the Creek War (1813–1814) and later saw action in Jackson's capture of Pensacola in November 1814. He then moved on with "Old Hickory" to New Orleans where he participated in the epic American victory against the British in January 1815. Yell later served as a lieutenant in the First Seminole War (1818). One historian has noted that, including his service in the Mexican War, Yell had "fought the Indians, the Spanish, the British, and the Mexicans in all the wars that occurred during those four decades when the young and lusty United States was expanding from one coast to the other."

Yell was serving in Congress and was considering a run for the U.S. Senate seat then occupied by Chester Ashley when the war broke out. Without resigning his seat in Congress, he rushed back to Arkansas to enlist as a private. In addition to his military experience and the support of President Polk, Yell was a skilled and beloved politician and possessed great personal courage. It was little wonder that he was elected to lead the Arkansas regiment as its colonel.

The only other prominent Arkansan with military experience was Albert Pike. Pike had been involved in military affairs almost since the time of his arrival in Arkansas in 1832. He commanded the First Company of Arkansas Artillery, which had formed in the fall of 1836 to protect the citizens of Little Rock against possible attacks from Indian tribes passing through Arkansas on their way to the Indian Territory. Such attacks were highly unlikely given the peaceful nature and scarce resources of these tribes, and "Pike's Artillery," as the company was soon known, saw action mainly in parades and other ceremonial occasions. Nonetheless, Pike drilled his men in infantry and artillery tactics and developed a reputation as a competent officer and a strong disciplinarian.

Archibald Yell, second governor of Arkansas. Yell was killed at the Battle of Buena Vista in the Mexican War. *Courtesy of J. N. Heiskell Collection/UALR Archives and Special Collections.*

If Pike's military credentials recommended him for a high position, however, his Whig political affiliation weighed against him. The majority of the company's officers, like the majority of Arkansas officeholders, were Democrats, and their political loyalties carried over into their military service. They chose Solon Borland, the volatile doctor, politician, and editor of the state's major Democratic Party newspaper, as major, and John Seldon Roane, an ambitious young attorney and Democratic politician, as lieutenant colonel. Pike had to content himself with the role of company commander.

The Arkansas regiment left Washington in mid-July 1846 and proceeded to Shreveport and then on to San Antonio, arriving in late August. The regiment was soon at war not with the Mexicans but with Gen. John Wool, the overall commander of the American forces at San Antonio. On his first inspection of the regiment shortly after its arrival, Wool found the Arkansas encampment poorly organized, unsanitary, and generally undisciplined. He soon took to referring to them as "Yell's Mounted Devils."

The criticism was largely justified. Of the ten company commanders, only Pike had bothered to drill his troops on the long journey from Washington. Few of the ambitious politicians who led them or the independent frontiersmen in the ranks were accustomed to taking orders from strangers, and they chafed at any attempts at discipline. When Wool found one Arkansas volunteer peering into his tent and threatened to shoot him if he didn't leave, the soldier responded by threatening to shoot the general. When Yell refused to move his camp to a site he deemed undesirable, Wool had him arrested.

Only Pike, who shared Wool's respect for discipline and training as well as his Whig politics, seems to have met with the general's approval. Wool often detached Pike's company from the rest of the regiment and allowed it to act independently.

Wool's command moved out in September, leaving four Arkansas companies behind to escort additional supplies. The advance elements crossed the Rio Grande in late October. Unfortunately, events of 1847 seemed to confirm the regiment's poor reputation. In January Borland and thirty-four other Arkansans were sent on a reconnaissance mission to the town of La Encarnacion. Failing to post guards while they spent the night in the town, they were surrounded and captured by Mexican cavalry and taken to Mexico City. Borland later escaped and took part in Gen. Winfield Scott's successful campaign to capture the Mexican capital.

The following month when an Arkansas soldier was killed by a Mexican civilian, a group of enlisted men rode into a nearby town and killed or wounded several civilians they suspected of the murder. General Taylor, who was trying to avoid such depredations against Mexican civilians, demanded that the "cowardly assassins of unarmed men" be found and punished, and he threatened to send two companies of Arkansas troops back to the Rio Grande. But a numerically superior Mexican force was moving north to engage him, and Taylor needed every available man. The perpetrators went unpunished, but the incident was widely reported and roundly condemned in the American press, and it further tarnished Arkansas's image in the rest of the nation.

Later that same month, Taylor moved his army to Agua Nueva in north-central Mexico. Three days later, he was joined by Wool's force, bringing the total American strength to about five thousand. On February 21, Maj. Ben McCulloch and his company of Texas Rangers reported to Taylor that a Mexican army of twenty thousand men was moving in his direction. Taylor decided to withdraw nine miles to a more defensible position seven miles south of the village of Saltillo near the sprawling Buena Vista ranch. Colonel Yell's regiment covered the American withdrawal. When they joined the main body of the army at Buena Vista, the Arkansans were assigned to a position on the extreme left and left center of the American line.

Scattered fighting began on the afternoon of February 22, but it was inconclusive. Taylor had gone to Saltillo, where Pike's command was stationed, to inspect the defenses there. When he returned to Buena Vista on the morning of the twenty-third, he brought Pike and his men with him. By the time Taylor reached the field, the battle was already underway. The main Mexican attack concentrated on the American left where the Arkansans were positioned. Accounts of this part of the battle vary greatly. Some contended that the Arkansans fought stubbornly before retreating in the face of an enemy who outnumbered them three or four to one. Others contended that they ran at the first sound of gunfire.

Pike believed that Yell had ordered his men to fall back to a more defensible position, but the undisciplined troops ran toward the rear in confusion and panic. Yell attempted to reform his men but could not compel them to stand. What happened next remains a matter of conjecture. According to some accounts Yell deliberately charged headlong into the oncoming Mexican lancers in a desperate act of valor. Other versions reported that he simply lost control of his horse, and the panicked animal carried him into the oncoming Mexicans. Whatever Yell's intent, the result was fatal. He was cut to pieces, with one lance shattering his skull. A strong counterattack halted the Mexican advance, and American artillery and rifle fire sent them scurrying in retreat. That night the Mexicans withdrew, leaving the victorious Americans in control of the field. Taylor's outnumbered forces had pulled off one of the greatest feats of arms in American history.

In his report Taylor praised Yell, Roane, Pike, and "a portion of the Arkansas regiment." But other sources leveled harsh criticisms at the Arkansans. Not the least of these critics was Pike himself. Having previously referred to Yell as "totally incompetent" and "the laughing stock of the men," Pike tempered his criticism after Yell's death, even remarking that Yell had "behaved most gallantly" at Buena Vista. But he could not restrain himself from criticizing the regimental officers' leadership. "It is a sad thing that brave men . . . should be . . . destroyed for want of discipline. . . . The Colonel [Yell] and the Lieutenant Colonel [Roane] had never drilled them since they left San Antonio."

All such criticisms were doubtless tinged with partisan politics, and the Democrats were soon responding in kind. Roane wrote a letter to a Little Rock newspaper in which he declared that Pike and his men had taken no part in the battle at Buena Vista. Infuriated by this falsehood, Pike challenged Roane to a duel. In late July 1847 the two men confronted each other with pistols on a sandbar in the Arkansas River opposite Fort Smith. Fortunately for both, their marksmanship did not match their political invective. The two men fired twice without result before the surgeons intervened to prevent another exchange. They then shook hands, agreed never to discuss the matter again, and dined together before returning to their homes.

The record of Arkansas's participation in the Mexican War was decidedly mixed, but the significance of the American victory, finalized by the signing of the Treaty of Guadalupe Hidalgo in February 1848, was overwhelming. The Mexican Cession gave the United States over 500,000 square miles of new territory (more than a million square miles counting Texas), and the newly acquired territory was not long in paying dividends. In late January 1848, gold was discovered at Sutter's Mill in California (near present-day Sacramento). Reports of easy wealth to be found in the West reached Arkansas in the late summer and early fall of that year, and many Arkansans, like thousands of other Americans, quickly fell victim to "gold fever." Citizens of Fort Smith and Van Buren, on opposite banks of the Arkansas River near the border with the Indian Territory, quickly began to promote their towns as ideal jumping-off points for the journey to the gold fields. In March 1849 a Fort Smith reporter noted, "The streets are literally crowded with California wagons and teams."

Numerous Arkansas companies began organizing for the trip to the gold fields, and they were joined by others from twenty-five states and at least four foreign countries. One estimate placed the number of "forty-niners" who chose the Arkansas route at three thousand. The five miles of riverbank between Fort Smith and Van Buren were crammed with people, and the economies of the two towns boomed as the demand for supplies exploded. The population of Fort Smith doubled, and a Van Buren resident estimated that local merchants took in at least sixty thousand dollars. Mules, horses, oxen, corn, and a host of other supplies were at a premium. Downriver, Little Rock also experienced a boom as emigrants passed through the city on their way to the jumping-off points.

The principal Arkansas route passed through the Indian Territory and the Texas Panhandle, then on to the halfway point at Santa Fe or Albuquerque in the New Mexico Territory. Here the trail turned south and crossed southern Arizona Territory to San Diego on the southern California coast before turning north toward San Francisco and the gold fields, a total distance of about twenty-three hundred miles.

Companies were composed largely of males (often as much as 90 percent) and were organized along military lines with specific instructions regarding the nature of supplies to be taken and the maximum weight allowed. The requirements of one company, the Little Rock and California Association, were typical. They stipulated, "Every member of the association binds himself to provide the following articles and be with them at Fort Smith, on the last day of March, 1849, to wit: 100 lbs. bacon, 125 lbs. flour, 25 lbs. coffee, salt, pepper, etc., in proportion. . . . He shall also provide 5 lbs. of powder and 12 lbs. shot; one rifle or shot gun; pistols and knife." In addition, every member was to provide "a good substantial wagon with four good mules; and this wagon shall not carry over 2,000 lbs."

Most companies tried to depart in late March or early April in order to ensure that their livestock would find an adequate supply of grass on the prairies. One company, organized by citizens of Fort Smith, departed the town on April 11, 1849, with 479 people. The company's seventy-five wagons, pulled by five hundred oxen and a like number of horses and mules, stretched three miles in length, making it one of the largest groups to take the trail. It quickly became apparent that it was entirely too large, and the expedition split into numerous smaller units.

Wagon trains hoped to make fifteen to twenty miles a day, allowing them to complete the journey in under six months. For most travelers, that proved to be an overly optimistic projection. The spring of 1849 was unusually wet, and the combination of inexperienced travelers, overloaded wagons, and roads rendered nearly impassable by rains slowed travel and dampened spirits.

A Helena native wrote to his hometown newspaper in mid-April 1849, "We have had bad roads and worse weather all the time. On the thirteenth, after a hard day's travel through drenching rains and deep mud, we encamped three miles east of the Little river. On the fourteenth cold rain and north winds prevailed until about four o'clock in the afternoon, when it commenced snowing, and continued to snow during the evening and night, and covered the ground to a depth of three inches." Faced with such hardships, more than a few travelers reported that they "had seen the elephant" (had seen what they set out to see) and returned home.

Others persevered. Those who made it as far as Santa Fe found the frontier town to be a den of drinking, gambling, and prostitution. The town was violent, even by

Arkansas standards. "I think it was a little of the hardest place I was ever in," one Arkansan noted. "Men shoot one another for past time. Not a day without the enactment of a bloody tragedy." Prices were astronomical. A bushel of corn that cost 35–40 cents in Fort Smith costs $2.50 in Santa Fe or Albuquerque. Still some found the cultural dissonance intriguing and wrote home glowingly of the Mexican *fandangoes* and the beautiful Hispanic women they encountered.

On the next part of the journey, the problem was not too much water but too little. Across the arid southwest, grass grew scarce and tempers short. Internal dissension threatened many companies, and it was not uncommon to see larger groups split into smaller units either to avoid further strife or to better facilitate grazing their animals. In this climate, animals faltered, and wagons had to be abandoned. Rivers were a welcome sight for weary travelers, but crossing the swift Rio Grande and the Colorado River held hazards all their own.

Rather than the predicted six months, most trips took seven or eight. A few of those hardy souls who made the journey found the fabled wealth they had sought. Most did not. What they did find were harsh conditions in the mining camps, disease, homesickness, and, again, exorbitant prices. Bacon, which sold for 4–6 cents a pound in Fort Smith, cost $1.25; flour which went for 3 cents a pound in Arkansas sold for 56 cents a pound. Perhaps most galling to some Arkansans, whiskey, which could be had back home for 35 cents a *gallon*, sold in the gold fields for 25 cents a *glass.*

Some Arkansans found wealth in California not by prospecting for the elusive golden nuggets but by providing services and supplies to those who did. Teamsters could make from $300 to $400 a month hauling supplies to the camps and mines, and enterprising Arkansans soon found other ways to profit from the rush. Kirkbride Potts left a wife and eight children at his home at the foot of Crow Mountain on Galla Creek (near present-day Russellville) to seek his fortune in the gold fields. Like so many others, he failed to find it. He did, however, find a tremendous demand for beef, and in 1851 he returned to California where, his daughter reported, he was "merchandising in Sacramento City." She does not mention what he was "merchandising," but five years later he was back in California herding over three hundred head of cattle.

The boom continued in 1850 leading some to fear that the gold rush fever was depopulating the state and depressing land values. Such fears proved to be unfounded. Unfavorable reports from the gold fields soon helped stem the tide. A letter to the *Fort Smith Herald* from one disillusioned emigrant, written in late January 1851, noted, "Not a single Arkansas man who came to this country either last year or this year, has made 1/10 part of his anticipation," and closed by advising the readers to "stay home & not come to California." Many heeded his advice, and traffic along the overland trails fell off dramatically in 1851.

It swelled again the following year, but the new emigrants were predominantly settlers seeking land and a permanent home in the West. Women and children now joined with their husbands in making the journey. More clearly marked routes and lighter wagons enabled them to complete the journey in shorter time, but like the forty-niners who preceded them, this second wave of emigrants faced innumerable hardships, disappointments, and misfortunes in their search for a better life. One such group became involved in one of the greatest tragedies of the entire westward movement.

In mid-April 1857 a party composed largely of prosperous farmers from northwest Arkansas set out from near present-day Harrison bound for a new life in California's central valley. Of the approximately 135 members of the company, at least fifteen were women (mostly young mothers), and sixty were dependent children. A large herd of cattle estimated at anywhere between three hundred and a thousand head accompanied the party on its way west.

The caravan of thirty to forty wagons was led by fifty-two-year-old George Baker and forty-five-year-old Alexander Fancher, both veterans of earlier trips to California in the gold rush days. The route Baker and Fancher chose was the Cherokee Trail, which had been opened in 1849 by members of the Cherokee Nation and a group of whites from northwest Arkansas (possibly including Baker). Because it was less traveled than some other western trails, the route offered ample grazing for cattle.

The trail led through Kansas into Colorado Territory where it turned north into southern Wyoming. Proceeding west again it linked up with the Oregon-California-Mormon Trail at Fort Bridger. From there it turned south along the Mormon Trail into the Salt Lake Valley in northern Utah. By August 3, the party reached Salt Lake City. Countless others had followed this trail in the preceding eight years to reach California, and the Baker-Fancher party anticipated no major problems. They were tragically mistaken. As one recent historian notes, the party "had come to the wrong place at the wrong time."

The Utah Territory was home and sanctuary to a religious sect that called itself the Church of Jesus Christ of Latter-day Saints but was more commonly known as the Mormons. Founded by Joseph Smith in New York in 1830, the movement grew rapidly, but Mormon religious beliefs and their attempts to institute a form of government based on those beliefs had brought them into repeated conflict with their non-Mormon neighbors. Driven successively from New York, Ohio, and Missouri, they moved in 1839 to Illinois where they established a settlement called Nauvoo on the banks of the Mississippi River. Once again they fell into serious disputes with non-Mormons, and in 1844 a mob killed Smith and his brother. Faced with extermination if they remained in Illinois, the Mormons, under the leadership of Brigham Young, decided to relocate to the Far West where they would be outside the jurisdiction of the United States and isolated from hostile neighbors.

In the summer of 1847 they established themselves in the barren valley of the Great Salt Lake, and Mormon settlements soon spread throughout the territory. But their dreams of an isolated kingdom soon disappeared. The United States acquired the territory from Mexico in 1848, and the gold rush of the following year sent thousands of Americans streaming through Mormon territory on their way to California. Relations between the United States and the territorial government had been strained from the beginning, with non-Mormon territorial officials complaining of constant interference and harassment by Mormon officials loyal to Brigham Young, who was now the territorial governor.

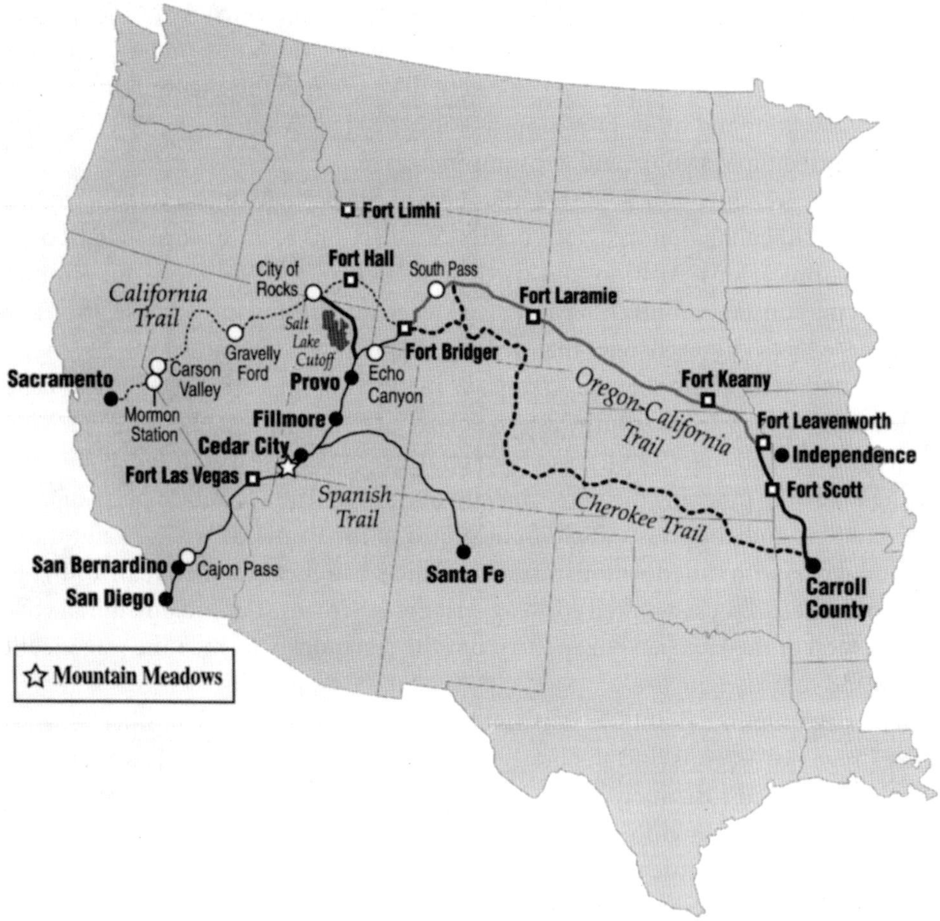

Route of the Fancher-Baker party to Mountain Meadows. *Courtesy of Will Bagley.*

The situation deteriorated to the point that Pres. James Buchanan ordered the U.S. Army to the region in the spring of 1857. When news of the president's order reached the Mormons, they determined to resist. Mormon preachers harangued crowds to prepare themselves for an invasion, and suspicion and hostility toward outsiders grew.

It was into this tense environment that the Fancher-Baker party entered in the summer of 1857. Their situation was compounded by another, unrelated event. In May of that year a popular Mormon elder named Parley Pratt had been brutally stabbed to death near Fort Smith by the angry husband of woman whom Pratt had taken as his tenth wife. The fact that the Fancher-Baker party was from the same region of the state as Pratt's murderer only served to increase the enmity that the Mormons felt for the company.

The Arkansans were probably unaware of the events surrounding Pratt's murder, but the party had encountered elements of the U.S. Army on its way to Utah and were likely to have been informed of the unrest there. Fancher and Baker apparently felt that these events posed no threat to them for they chose the southern route across Utah rather than a northern route that would have taken them more quickly out of the territory. As they moved south from Salt Lake City, however, evidence of Mormon hostility soon became apparent. At settlements along the way Mormons, under strict orders from Brigham Young not to provide "one kernal" of grain to the enemy, refused to sell the party the flour and other provisions it badly needed. When the party's large herd of cattle grazed on Mormon land, tensions increased.

Mormon accounts indicated that members of the party further antagonized local residents by ridiculing their religious beliefs. Such actions seem strange in light of the company's precarious position and its dependence on the Mormons for supplies, although the constant rebuffs the party faced when attempting to purchase provisions may have led to sharp exchanges that degenerated into personal attacks.

On Sunday, September 6, the Arkansans made camp in a spring-fed valley called Mountain Meadows in the southwestern corner of the territory. The valley provided abundant grass and water, but it was a poor choice for a defense if attacked. Before sunrise the following morning the party was surrounded and attacked by a party of about three hundred Indians, most of whom belonged to the Paiute tribe. The Paiutes were on good terms with the Mormons, and their chiefs had met with Brigham Young the previous week to discuss a united effort against the U.S. Army. The Indians' initial volley killed several of the Fancher-Baker party, but the rest quickly formed the wagons into a circle and returned the fire.

The siege continued until Friday morning, when John Lee and another Mormon leader drove two wagons into the besieged camp under flag of truce. It was apparent that the party had lost many animals and was running low on ammunition. The Mormon emissaries convinced the Arkansans that their only hope was to give up their arms, turn over their cattle and supplies to the Indians, and put themselves under the protection of the Mormon militia.

The Arkansans, who had few alternatives, agreed. The members of the company were placed in separate groups according to age and gender. The first wagon that left the encampment carried children under six years old. Lee walked behind this wagon, and behind him followed a second wagon containing two or three wounded men and one woman. At some distance behind the second wagon, the women and older children followed on foot. About a quarter of a mile farther to the rear marched the remaining men of the party, each escorted by an armed Mormon guard.

When the women and children reached a narrow passage between surrounding hills, a mounted Mormon officer ordered a halt and commanded his men to "Do your duty." The command was a signal for each of the Mormons guarding the Arkansas men to shoot his prisoner. Most did. That firing was the predetermined signal for the Indians and some of their Mormon allies who swarmed out of the brush and butchered the women and older children with hatchets and knives.

Accurate casualty figures for what came to be called the Mountain Meadows Massacre are impossible to determine. One recent historian places the number at 120, including about fifty men, twenty women, and approximately fifty children between the ages of seven and eighteen. "Measured in lives lost," historian David Bigler notes, "the massacre at Mountain Meadows was the second worst tragedy during America's westward migration during the nineteenth century."

Seventeen children under six years of age were spared and placed in Mormon homes. In 1859 all seventeen were reclaimed and returned to family members in Arkansas. The Mormons billed the U.S. Government several thousand dollars for boarding and sheltering the children in the interval. At least fifty Mormons took part in the massacre, and many more attempted to cover up the outrage by placing the blame solely on the Indians. The degree of Brigham Young's involvement in the massacre is still debated, though he clearly participated in the cover-up and took no action to punish the perpetrators.

The killing was too massive and involved too many people for the truth to stay hidden for long, however. In 1859 the U.S. Army, at the urging of the victims' Arkansas relatives, launched an investigation of the massacre. Their report placed the blame squarely on the Mormons. As the truth of the story leaked out, pressure for punishment of the responsible parties grew within the Mormon community as well. In the end, John Lee was chosen to bear the guilt for all involved. He was excommunicated by the church in 1870 and twice tried for murder. The second trial resulted in a guilty verdict, and, in March 1877, Lee was taken back to Mountain Meadows and shot by a firing squad.

Mountain Meadows Massacre: Incident that occurred in 1857 when a party of 135 Arkansans headed for California was attacked in southern Utah by a combination of Paiute Indians and Mormons. After surrendering to the Mormons under a promise of protection, over a hundred members of the party, including men, women, and children, were massacred.

In many ways, Mountain Meadows marked a tragic end to the brief and colorful episode in Arkansas history that began with the gold rush of 1849. Historian Priscilla McArthur eloquently summarized what she called the "California experience," noting, "The legacies . . . were good, bad, ambiguous, and individual. . . . Some understood their moment in history; others had a more limited vision. . . . Some were embittered by their experience, others were broadened and enobled by theirs. . . . That most failed . . . did not make them fools in their dream or in their search. For most, seeing the elephant had been a sadder but wiser experience."

In the years that followed, Texas, not California, continued to be the destination of choice for many Arkansans, and Arkansas never became the major jumping-off point for the westward movement that some of the state's leaders had hoped. But the turbulent years of the Mexican War and the gold rush did witness dramatic and far-reaching changes in the economic, social, and political course of the state's history.

CHAPTER EIGHT

Prosperity and Peril: Arkansas in the Late Antebellum Period, 1850–1861

The first decade and a half following statehood gave little indication that Arkansas was prepared to shed its reputation as a poor, frontier society. In the 1840s frontier conditions still prevailed, and many Arkansans, particularly those living in the highland regions, remained tied to subsistence agriculture. But by the 1850s significant changes were underway that would transform the state's economy and positively impact the lives of many of its citizens. Growing numbers of Arkansans were becoming involved in the emerging market economy, and a cotton-based plantation-style agriculture had taken firm root in the fertile lands of southern and eastern Arkansas. By the late antebellum period Arkansas stood on the verge of a prosperity unknown in its history. But at the core of that prosperity lay the seeds of its dissolution.

The Arkansas Economy in the Late Antebellum Period

In his analysis of the U.S. Census records for Pope County in west-central Arkansas in 1850, historian Ted Worley provides a revealing portrait of an Arkansas county that, in many ways, resembled the state as a whole. Pope County was a geographically diverse region, containing both the highlands of the Ozark Plateau to the north and lowlands along the Arkansas River in the south. The county's white population stood at 695 families with an average family size of 6.1. It was a young society with 62 percent of its white population under fifteen years of age and only eighty-eight people over sixty.

The citizens of the county had come from twenty-four states and four foreign countries, but 95 percent had been born in a slave state. A hundred families owned slaves, but only nine owned ten or more, and only three of these owned enough (twenty) to be considered a planter. There were no free blacks in the county. The county had eleven one-teacher schools enrolling a total of 326 pupils and operating on an income of $3,892 ($12/student) per year, none of it from taxes.

More than 80 percent of the population made a living by farming and raising cattle. The remainder were carpenters, blacksmiths, lumbermen, tanners, and wagon makers with a few of what would today be called professional people—lawyers, doctors, teachers, and preachers. The average family owned fifteen head of cattle, thirty-three hogs, and four milk cows. Despite these rather meager holdings, Pope County residents were largely self-sufficient. Farmers grew enough corn to feed both people and animals, and enough cotton, when combined with wool from the county's abundant sheep herds, to provide adequate material for clothing. But this was not merely a "hog and hominy" existence. Pope County farmers also grew oats, wheat, sweet potatoes, Irish potatoes, peas, beans, flax, hops, and tobacco.

Equally important, Pope County residents possessed a wide variety of skills necessary to self-sufficiency. Worley notes:

> The average farmer could build a house, make his fences of rails, construct an ash-hopper, gather tannin from bark and tan hides, mould bullets, make plows, churns, and shoes, including the pegs that held them together. He could find a bee-tree, hit a squirrel's head with a rifle, or make a gig for taking fish. His wife could spin, weave, make clothing, quilts, soap, candles, and even medicine. She knew how to render lard, what greens were good to eat; she could cook on an open fireplace, do the washing in the creek, and in a pinch could help worm tobacco, tie up fodder, or grit new corn for bread.

In these early communities, family and kinship networks played a large role, often determining the economic, social, and political viability of an individual or group. But what the individual or family could not do alone, they did with the help of the community at large. "It cannot be emphasized too strongly," Worley writes, "that the self-sufficiency of the pioneer was only in part due to individual effort; the welfare of every family was the concern of the neighborhood."

Despite the fact that both the county and the state as a whole remained largely societies of self-sufficient farmers, signs of an economic transformation were apparent. In Pope County there were thirteen sawmills (two of which were steam powered), two tanneries, and one cotton factory. One county resident operated a tar kiln (which extracted tar from pine knots) and sent the tar by flatboat to New Orleans.

In the county and throughout the state artisans practiced their trades. Gunsmiths, cabinetmakers, potters, and silversmiths made a living and produced a rich material legacy even while competing with eastern manufacturers. Some rejected the factory system with its strict division of labor for the freedom of running their own shops on the Arkansas frontier. Blacksmith James Black, who had apprenticed to a silverplater in Philadelphia, ended up in Washington, Arkansas, producing what is likely the earliest form of the bowie knife, a form copied by cutlers as far away as Sheffield, England. Gunsmith John Pearson had been the mechanic for Samuel Colt (the maker of the first revolver) before taking his trade to Fort Smith. Women in the antebellum period had fewer opportunities for creative expression, but many excelled in the textile arts. See plate 26 following page 270.

Artisan:
A skilled craftsman.

bowie knife: The bowie knife was a large knife specifically designed for use in personal combat. Named for Jim Bowie, a member of a pioneer family who settled in early Arkansas and Louisiana, the first knife was produced by blacksmith James Black at Washington, Arkansas, in the 1820s.

While these Arkansans practiced their crafts, commercial centers were springing up along the state's rivers. Little Rock, strategically located in the center of the state at the point where the Southwest Trail crossed the Arkansas River, was bustling with business activity, and, as the state capital, also exerted great political influence in the state. But as Charles Bolton has pointed out, the state's river system created a decentralized market that allowed other settlements to develop into regional commercial centers.

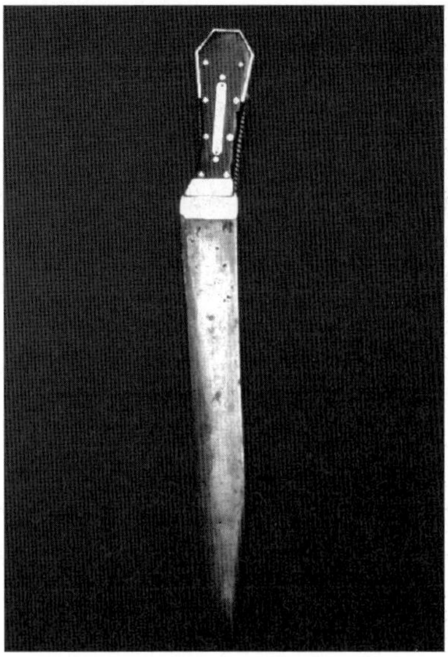

The thirteen-inch knife known as "Bowie No. 1" because of an engraving on the escutcheon plate, possibly the original bowie knife. *Historic Arkansas Museum, Little Rock.*

Along the Arkansas River in northwest Arkansas, Fort Smith flourished. In the 1850s the army guaranteed the fort's status as a permanent post by designating it a quartermaster depot, and local merchants carried on a brisk trade with Native Americans being resettled in the Indian Territory to the west and with troops stationed at the forts there. Roads led from the town to Texas and California, and in 1858 Fort Smith became a station on the Overland Mail Company route. Just downriver, Van Buren served the needs of the surrounding countryside. In extreme northwest Arkansas, Fayetteville became a leading center of commerce even without the benefit of a river, as large numbers of settlers moved into the region in the 1830s. Along the White River in north-central Arkansas, Batesville and later Jacksonport became centers of commercial activity. The same was true of Helena and Napoleon on the Mississippi River. The towns of Fulton, situated along the Red River, and Washington, located on the Southwest Trail near the Red River, served the needs of Arkansans in the southwestern part of the state, while Camden on the Ouachita River dominated commerce in south-central Arkansas.

If rivers were the highways of commerce, steamboats were its vehicles. While Robert Fulton is generally given credit for developing the steamboat, the boats that plied Arkansas waters and those of other western rivers were largely the creation of Henry M. Shreve, a famous riverboatman whose broad, shallow-draft vessels were well suited to shallow, fast-moving rivers like the Mississippi, the Arkansas, and other rivers in the state. (Between 1833 and 1838, Shreve also supervised the clearing of the famous Red River Raft, a logjam of snags, driftwood, and floating trees that began above Natchitoches, Louisiana, and extended upriver for over a hundred miles. The obstacle's removal made it possible for boats to operate again on the upper reaches of the Red, and it also lowered the water level, thereby opening more land to cultivation.)

Red River Raft: A massive logjam on the Red River stretching over a hundred miles upriver from near Natchitoches, Louisiana. The raft obstructed travel on the middle reaches of the Red until it was cleared by Henry M. Shreve in the years between 1833 and 1838.

The western steamboats were built, one boatman noted,

"of wood, tin, shingles, canvas and twine." The cylindrical boilers, located on the main deck, were the heart of the machine. These crude devices were capable of producing great power, but they were also the source of many explosions and fires.

The boats were of two main types. Side-wheelers, which had paddlewheels mounted on each side of the engine, were easier to maneuver, while stern-wheelers, which featured a single paddlewheel mounted at the back of the boat, could accommodate more freight on the main deck and could operate more easily on shallower rivers. Some passengers traveled and slept on the main deck with the cargo, while others found better accommodations in cabins on the second or "boiler" deck. Above the cabins on the third, or "hurricane deck" was located a pilot house. At the front, or bow, of the boat, one or two long gangplanks, hinged to the deck, were held aloft by booms until needed for embarking or disembarking freight and passengers.

These early western boats bore little resemblance to eastern steamboats or to the large floating palaces that would later grace western waters. "It was an unlovely structure," one historian has written, "slab-sided and crudely ornate." In March 1822 the *Eagle* became the first steamboat to reach Little Rock, and the *Robert Thompson* reached Fort Smith the following month. The *Eagle* displaced slightly over a hundred tons and took seventeen days to make the trip upriver from New Orleans to the capital. By the mid-1830s, however, larger steamboats like the *Arkansas* were operating on the Arkansas River. The *Arkansas* was over 150 feet long and displaced well over two hundred tons. It had a spacious, well-lighted cabin with fifteen staterooms for male passengers and another cabin for female passengers containing four staterooms. More important, by 1836 boats of this type could make the round-trip from New Orleans to Little Rock and back in sixteen days.

The steamboat *Waverly* reached Batesville on the White River in January 1831, and boats were soon in operation on all the state's major rivers. Wherever they went, steamboats caused great excitement. Not only were the boats mechanical wonders, but they also connected Arkansas to the wider world, bringing passengers from other parts of the country, eastern and regional newspapers, and merchandise from New Orleans, Cincinnati, St. Louis, and other cities.

Steamboat travel was, from its inception, a dangerous affair. "The hazards of western river travel were many," historian Carl Lane noted. "In most places the top of the river was extremely near the bottom." Even the most skilled pilots found it difficult to keep up with the ever-changing channel. "Shoals, built up overnight after an upcountry rain, and snags and sawyers and caved in banks lurked beneath the surface of the river," Lane wrote. "The snags were the most feared of the river's unseen dangers. To hit one, especially going downstream with the current adding to the speed, was almost always fatal, for the boat usually sank quickly into deep water."

The Arkansas River's swift currents, sandbars, and constantly changing depth soon gained it a reputation as "the graveyard of steamboats." The average lifespan of a boat was less than five years. Even if a boat did survive all the hazards of the river, low water could keep it from its intended destination. The upper reaches of the Arkansas were often unnavigable during the late summer and early fall. Still, for all their liabilities, steamboats

The steamboat *Eagle,* shown here in a drawing by present-day artist Richard DeSpain, stopped briefly at Little Rock in March 1822 on its way to Dwight Mission near present-day Russellville. *Courtesy of Region's Bank.*

were an invaluable economic asset, bringing merchandise to the growing commercial centers and transporting agricultural products to market. They were especially important in promoting the expansion of large-scale cotton production in the state.

Since Eli Whitney's invention of the cotton gin in 1793, the production of short-staple cotton had skyrocketed throughout the South, and in the early 1800s the center of that production had moved from the southeastern states to the fertile lands of the Southwest. In the river bottoms of Arkansas's southern and eastern lowlands, planters and farmers grew a variety of crops, including corn, peas, beans, and potatoes, but as early as the 1820s cotton had become the territory's leading staple crop. To a large extent, the cotton planter's entire year's schedule revolved around preparing the ground, planting, cultivating, and picking cotton.

Cotton was planted in April and May. Two or three weeks after planting, as the young cotton plants began to put on leaves, a cycle of chopping the weeds and plowing was repeated periodically until the end of July. By the middle of the summer, as the cotton blossoms began to give way to bolls, the crop was "laid by," and cultivation ceased. Picking began in late August or early September and might extend well into the new year, particularly if the fall season had been rainy. In an average year, a planter could expect to make one bale per acre. By the time the harvest ended, it was time to begin preparing for the next year's planting.

In spite of all this care and attention, cotton was a fickle crop. Planters complained that it "would promise more and do less and promise less and do more than any other green thing that grew." Too much or too little rain could prove fatal, and an early frost would cause a plant to stop producing. Diseases such as wilt, rust, dry rot, and insects such as cutworms, lice, caterpillars, bollworms (though interestingly, not boll weevils, a scourge which originated in the late nineteenth century and from which antebellum planters were exempt) could devastate a crop. Even good crops could fall victim to falling prices.

Despite these pitfalls and unpredictable fluctuations in price, cotton production nationwide steadily increased throughout the nineteenth century. Arkansas produced over 6 million pounds (approximately twelve thousand, 500-pound bales) of cotton in 1840, a trifling amount when compared to Louisiana's 152 million pounds or Mississippi's 193 million pounds. By 1850, however, Arkansas produced over 26 million pounds (roughly 52,000 bales), the majority of it in the Delta, and the expansion continued throughout the next decade.

The growth of slavery in Arkansas was inexorably linked to this expansion. The majority of white Arkansans owned no slaves, and Arkansas ranked near the bottom of all slave states (thirteenth of fourteen) in total number of slaves in both 1840 and 1850. But while the state's slave population lagged behind those of other slave states, the percentage of increase in slaves in Arkansas far exceeded that of any other state. Between 1830 and 1840, the number of slaves increased by 335 percent, and from 1840 to 1850 by 136 percent, greatly outdistancing second-place Mississippi, which experienced a 197 percent increase in the 1830s and a 58 percent increase in the 1840s. By 1860 Arkansas would be home to over 111,000 slaves and over eleven thousand slave owners.

In 1840 slavery existed in almost every county in the state, and the census conducted in that year reported that Washington County in extreme northwest Arkansas was still one of the top-ten counties in the state in terms of slave population. Historian Gary Battershell has pointed out that slavery remained an important fact of life for the residents of much of the Arkansas upcountry until the time of the Civil War. This was particularly true for counties like Pope and Johnson, which contained rich bottomland along the Arkansas River. Battershell notes that while the percentage of upcountry slaveholders in the total population declined from 1840 to 1850, the actual number of slaves and slaveholders both increased. Further, while slaveholdings were smaller in this region, slaveholders enjoyed great social and political prominence.

The small slaveholders of the highlands were more the norm than the exception among Arkansas slaveholders. Orville W. Taylor, the great historian of slavery in Arkansas, has noted that as late as 1860, 5,806 (51 percent) of Arkansas's 11,481 slave owners held no more than four slaves, 4,312 (37 percent) held between five and nineteen slaves, and only 1,363 (12 percent) owned twenty or more slaves, enough to be considered "planters."

Planter: Term generally applied to a slave owner who owned twenty or more slaves.

But this small group of wealthy slaveholders possessed a disproportionate share of the state's wealth. In dispelling the myth of economic equality on the frontier, Charles Bolton has pointed out that, between 1840 and 1860, the wealthiest 10 percent of taxpayers owned more than 70 percent of the taxable wealth in the state. "In terms of the distribution of wealth," he writes, "Arkansas was a very unequal society." And in an agricultural society that measured a man's status largely by the amount of land and slaves he owned, the planter class also exerted an influence in social and political affairs far out of proportion to their actual numbers.

By the 1830s, a slave-based, plantation-style agriculture was rapidly developing along the rivers of the state's southern and eastern lowlands—the Mississippi, the Arkansas, the Red, and the Ouachita. As cotton production soared in the Arkansas Delta in the late antebellum period, the slave population expanded rapidly. In 1830 Chicot County in the southeastern corner of the state had a total population of 1,165 of whom 888 (76 percent) were free white, 270 (23 percent) were black slaves, and seven (.6 percent) were free persons of color. Slave owners were a minority of the county's population, and almost all of those who did own slaves owned only a few. Only two men in the county owned twenty or more slaves.

By 1840, however, the white population of the county had increased by only 217 people to a total of 1,105, while the slave population had skyrocketed from a total of 270 in 1830 to 2,698, an increase of almost 900 percent. Whites now accounted for only 29 percent of the county's population, while black slaves accounted for 71 percent of the total. By 1850 whites made up barely 23 percent of the population, while the slave population rose to 77 percent. Chicot County exceeded any other county in the state in proportion of slaves to total population and was second only to Union County in total number of slaves. Sixty planters owned twenty or more slaves, thirty-three owned fifty or more, and eight owned one hundred or more. The largest slave owner in the county, Horace Walsworth, owned 230 slaves.

Clearly, by 1850 Chicot County more closely resembled Washington County, Mississippi, directly across the river, than it did Washington County, Arkansas, in the state's northwestern corner. One historian noted, "With its flat, fertile fields along the Mississippi and preponderance of large plantations and slaveholders, Chicot County was more nearly representative of the idealized Southern plantation country than any other Arkansas county."

Slavery in Arkansas

By 1860 there were 111,115 slaves in Arkansas, constituting 25.5 percent of the state's total population of 435,450. The southern and eastern lowlands contained at least three-quarters of the state's slave population, and the majority of slaves in Arkansas lived on larger holdings. Most of them were employed in the production of cotton. A large-scale cotton operation was a heavily labor-intensive enterprise that required a steady supply of cheap labor. Before the fertile land would produce cotton or any other crop, it had to be "cleared" of trees and underbrush, a difficult and time-consuming job. Even after the clearing was accomplished, it took years of additional "grubbing" away bushes, clearing stumps, and leveling to make a field smooth. Planting, cultivating, and picking also required a large labor force.

On large plantations, slaves generally worked in gangs under the direction of a white overseer or a black "driver" and were organized according to task. One historian noted, "A typical arrangement was to divide slaves into plow-hands, who usually consisted primarily of able-bodied men but sometimes included women, and hoe-hands, less fit for strenuous endeavor; on some plantations, lighter work still—for example, weeding and yard cleaning—was assigned to members of a 'trash gang' made up of children and others incapable of heavy labor."

During harvest times, slaves rose before dawn and often worked until after sundown. Picking cotton was a backbreaking task. Solomon Northrup, a free black kidnapped into slavery on a Red River plantation, remembered, "[E]ach slave is presented with a sack. A strap is fastened to it, which goes over the neck, holding the mouth of the sack breast high, while the bottom reaches nearly to the ground. Each one is presented with a large basket that will hold about two barrels. This is to put the cotton in when the sack is filled. The baskets are placed at the end of the long rows." A skilled picker could pick well over two hundred pounds of cotton a day.

In Arkansas and the other states of the Southwest, the abundance of cheap, fertile land maximized the potential for profit on well-run plantations and made slaves an extremely valuable commodity. By the late antebellum period the economy of this region was booming, and slave prices in Arkansas were among the highest in the South.

Laws regulating slavery in Arkansas in the early nineteenth century had been enacted by the legislature of the Louisiana Territory in October 1804. While whipping remained an acceptable form of punishment, the Louisiana code had eliminated some of the harsher features of previous slave codes such as branding and the cutting off of ears, reforms which nineteenth-century slave owners proudly pointed to as evidence of the increasingly humanitarian nature of the institution.

As Arkansas changed in status and jurisdiction over the course of the next three decades, additional laws were added, but the restrictions on slaves' activities generally were the same as they had been since the introduction of slavery by the French and Spanish. Slaves were forbidden to carry guns, to assemble in large groups, to leave the plantation without a pass, or to buy or sell any commodity. The various laws concerning slavery were incorporated in the first digest of Arkansas laws, compiled under the direction of territorial governor John Pope in 1835. But the actual treatment of slaves varied from one plantation or slave owner to another.

Aside from census and deed records, little evidence remains to shed light on the actual nature of the "peculiar institution" in Arkansas. Many of the few remnants that do exist are the result of interviews with former slaves conducted under the auspices of the Works Progress Administration's (WPA) Federal Writers' Project. In the years between 1936 and 1938, interviewers (predominantly white) talked to over 2,300 former slaves from across the South. The results were published years later as *The American Slave: A Composite Autobiography.*

The narratives have to be viewed with a skeptical eye for a variety of reasons, not the least of which is the fact that the former slaves were reluctant to be truly forthcoming when speaking to white interviewers. In *Bearing Witness*, his excellent edited collection of the narratives of former Arkansas slaves, folklorist and historian George Lankford has warned that "the enduring racism of the Jim Crow era, coupled with the poverty of the Great Depression, made it unlikely that the former slave would say anything which might be risky to his or her immediate circumstances." Historian John W. Blassingame noted, "Since many of the former slaves still resided in the same area as their masters' descendants and were dependent on whites to help them obtain old-age pensions, they were naturally guarded (and often misleading) in their responses to certain questions." Therefore, the former slaves often combined a generally benevolent judgment of their own masters with a harsh condemnation of neighboring slave owners and of the institution in general. These reservations notwithstanding, the slave narratives remain a valuable source in understanding the institution of American slavery. The portrait of Arkansas slavery that emerges indicates that slave society in Arkansas was much like that in the slaveholding states of the Deep South.

For many years, historians of the institution believed that the physical and psychological horrors of slavery, including the frequent separation of family members by sale, precluded the formation of a strong sense of community in slave society. Revisionist studies of the 1970s challenged this assumption, arguing that a true slave community, based on a foundation of slave Christianity and strong, relatively stable, two-parent families, did exist. Farsighted slave owners understood the importance of family in the slave community and were hesitant to break it up. Eugene Genovese, a leading historian of the institution of slavery, noted that good masters observed a certain code with regard to punishment and the breaking up of families. "With notable exceptions they [the slaves] did not rail against whipping as such, long enforced as a common method of punishment; they did rail against cruel, excessive, and especially arbitrary whipping," Genovese maintains. "A master who used his whip too often or with too much vigor risked their hatred. Masters who failed to respect family sensibilities or who separated husbands from wives could be sure of it."

Recent studies have indicated that the two-parent nuclear family was less common in Arkansas than in the older slave states. Historian Carl Moneyhon has noted a correlation between the size of a slaveholding and a slave family's stability. Because larger slaveholding operations provided a more stable economic environment and a greater opportunity for a slave to find a suitable mate, the two-parent nuclear family was more likely to exist and survive on a larger holding than on a smaller one.

Slaves on both large and small holdings had certain basic expectations of slave masters, including adequate food, housing, and clothes. But they also expected a certain degree of autonomy from whites and occasional time off from work to enjoy the company of friends and family within the slave community and to practice their religion.

Religion was a particularly important issue for slaves and a particularly difficult one for masters. As a result of the great evangelical crusades of the early nineteenth century, Christianity made vast inroads among American slaves and became a major factor in shaping the black community. Slave religious experiences varied greatly. Some masters permitted their slaves no religious services at all. A Union County slave recalled, "We didn't have no church no nothing. Worked from Monday morning till Saturday night. On Sunday we didn't do nothin' but set right down on that plantation." Some slaves worshiped in biracial services along with whites, others in segregated services with white preachers hired by the masters.

As might be expected, the sermons that flowed from these white preachers stressed themes acceptable to masters. "Sermons urging slaves to be obedient and docile," one historian remarked, "were repeated *ad nauseam.*" Lucretia Alexander, a slave on a Chicot County plantation, recalled,

> the preacher came in and preached to them [the slaves] in their quarters. He'd just say "Serve your master. Don't steal your master's turkey. Don't steal your master's chickens. Don't steal your master's hawgs. Don't steal your master's meat. Do whatsomever your master tells you to do." Same old thing all the time.

But there was another aspect to slave religion. "Regular Sunday worship in the local church was paralleled by illicit, or at least informal, prayer meetings on weeknights in the slave cabins," historian Albert Raboteau writes. "Preachers licensed by the church and hired by the master were supplemented by slave preachers licensed only by the spirit." In the so-called invisible institution of slave Christianity, meetings were often conducted in secret, and the theological themes were very different from those espoused by white preachers. A major theme was deliverance from oppression and the equality of all men before the Lord. Lucretia Alexander remembered,

> My father would have church in dwelling houses and they had to whisper. My mother was dead and I would go with him. Sometimes they would have church at his house. That would be when they would want a real meetin' with some real preachin'. It would have to be durin' the week nights. You couldn't tell the difference between Baptist and Methodist then. They was all Christians. . . . They used to sing their songs in a whisper and pray in a whisper. That was a prayer-meeting from house to house . . . once or twice a week.

With regard to the treatment of slaves, it is clear that conditions varied widely from one plantation to another. Fanny Johnson, who was born a slave on the Woodfork plantation near Grand Lake in southern Chicot County in the 1850s, recounted her own experience and those of her grandmother to a Federal Writers' Project interviewer in 1936. Her absentee master owned several plantations and maintained a residence in Nashville, Tennessee. Johnson recalled, "The Woodfork colored folks was always treated good. . . . We had plenty to wear and lots to eat and good cabins to live in. . . . During the week there was somebody to cook for us. On Sunday all of them [the slaves] cooked in their cabins and they had plenty. . . . The Woodfork people never had to go nowhere for food." But Johnson was quick to point out that the same was not true on all plantations. "The women on the next plantation, even when they were going to have babies didn't get enough to eat," Johnson recalled. "They used to slip off at night and come over to our place."

The situation was the same with regard to the breaking up of families. "He [Woodfork] didn't believe in separating families. He didn't believe in dividing mother from her baby." But Johnson remembered her grandmother telling her about plantations where "they did take them away from their babies. . . . The wagon would drive down into the field and pick up a woman. Then somebody would meet her at the gate and she would nurse her baby for the last time."

With the master absent, the slaves' daily dealings were with the plantation's overseer. Fanny Johnson recalled, "Most of the times the overseers was good to us." But here again, things were worse on other plantations: "On the next one they was mean. Why you could hear the sound of that strap for two blocks. . . . The 'niggah drivah' would stand and hit them with a wide strap. The overseer would stand off and split the blisters with a bull whip. Some they whipped so hard they had to carry them in."

Overseer: Person charged with the day-to-day management of the slave labor force on a plantation.

A Union County slave remembered that his master was "a right mean man" who "whipped his slaves a lot" and "would whip the women the same as he would the men." Some planters and overseers used the whip to prod slaves to pick a certain amount of cotton. A Chicot County slave remembered hearing her mother say that "lots of times she would pick cotton and give it to others that couldn't keep up so that they wouldn't be punished. She had a brother they used to whip all the time because he didn't keep up."

There were factors that mitigated against overuse of the whip. "Throughout the South," one historian commented, "publicists denounced as un-Christian masters who mistreated those placed under their authority, and stressed the need for 'moderate,' predictable punishment for offenses that were clearly spelled out." Fear of public disapproval or the master's own deeply held religious convictions also served to prevent harsh treatment. Many antebellum ministers placed great emphasis on the master's duty to treat his slaves fairly and humanely.

On a more practical level, planters realized that slaves scarred by the whip were worth less on the auction block, and experience taught them that extreme or arbitrary punishment was counterproductive. Consequently, many masters attempted to use rewards as well as the threat of punishment to maintain order and maximize output on the plantation.

But the slave narratives clearly indicate that use of the whip was commonplace in Arkansas and throughout the slave South, and even on those plantations where it was used infrequently, the whip was an omnipresent threat. It was, Arkansas writer Bob Lancaster noted, "the most obvious symbol of the degradation and indignity that slavery forced on these people, blighting their lives and those of their children—and thus many of their memories of slavery focused on the whip and on those who wielded it." For most slaves, another historian concluded, "the lash came to symbolize the essence of slavery."

Slaves had little recourse to such abuse. Whites often outnumbered blacks and were well armed, factors which severely limited opportunities for large-scale resistance.

Accordingly, American slaves attempted only a few such revolts, and those that did occur were quickly suppressed. Still, slaves did find ways to resist. They deliberately worked slowly and inefficiently, faked illness or injury, intentionally destroyed farm tools, and stole from the master. Others simply ran away. Perhaps a thousand a year managed to reach the North and freedom, but in a society where the color of one's skin was a badge of bondage, such successes were the exception rather than the rule. An advertisement in the *Arkansas Gazette* in October 1832 indicates the fate that befell many runaways. It reads, "Was committed to the jail of Chicot County, on the 3rd of September, 1832 . . . a Negro Boy, who calls himself HARRY. . . . He had on, when committed, a checked shirt and linen pantaloons."

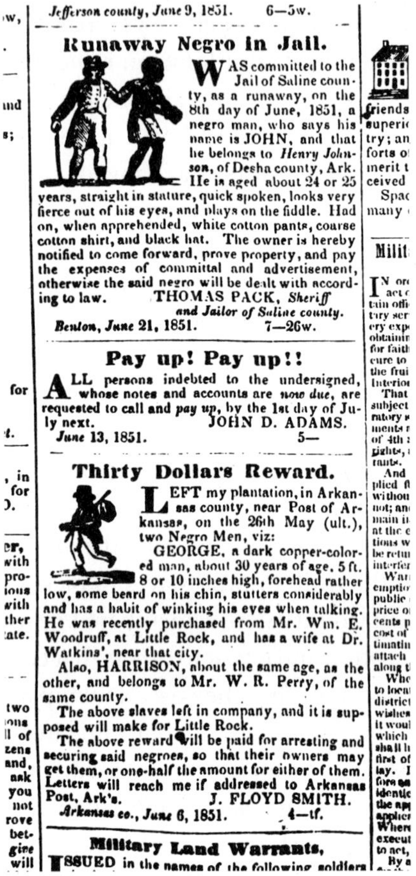

Jefferson county, June 9, 1851. 6—5w.

Runaway Negro in Jail.

WAS committed to the Jail of Saline county, as a runaway, on the 8th day of June, 1851, a negro man, who says his name is JOHN, and that he belongs to *Henry Johnson*, of Desha county, Ark. He is aged about 24 or 25 years, straight in stature, quick spoken, looks very fierce out of his eyes, and plays on the fiddle. Had on, when apprehended, white cotton pants, course cotton shirt, and black hat. The owner is hereby notified to come forward, prove property, and pay the expenses of committal and advertisement, otherwise the said negro will be dealt with according to law. THOMAS PACK, *Sheriff and Jailor of Saline county.*

Benton, June 21, 1851. 7—26w.

Pay up! Pay up!!

ALL persons indebted to the undersigned, whose notes and accounts are *now due*, are requested to call and *pay up*, by the 1st day of July next. JOHN D. ADAMS.

June 13, 1851. 5—

Thirty Dollars Reward.

LEFT my plantation, in Arkansas county, near Post of Arkansas, on the 26th May (ult.), two Negro Men, viz:

GEORGE, a dark copper-colored man, about 30 years of age, 5 ft. 8 or 10 inches high, forehead rather low, some beard on his chin, stutters considerably and has a habit of winking his eyes when talking. He was recently purchased from Mr. Wm. E. Woodruff, at Little Rock, and has a wife at Dr. Watkins', near that city.

Also, HARRISON, about the same age, as the other, and belongs to Mr. W. R. Perry, of the same county.

The above slaves left in company, and it is supposed will make for Little Rock.

The above reward will be paid for arresting and securing said negroes, so that their owners may get them, or one-half the amount for either of them. Letters will reach me if addressed to Arkansas Post, Ark's. J. FLOYD SMITH.

Arkansas co., June 6, 1851. 4—tf.

Military Land Warrants,

ISSUED in the names of the following soldiers

Ad for runaway slaves in the *Arkansas State Gazette and Democrat,* July 4, 1851.

Rather than trying to reach freedom in the North, most runaway slaves remained in the vicinity of their own plantations, often hiding in nearby woods before returning after a few days to face his master's ire. Slave owners seldom advertised or hired slave catchers for those runaways thought to be in the immediate area. Most owners came to accept these temporary absences as a part of the normal routine and generally punished such slaves mildly when they returned.

A few slaves resorted to physical force against masters or, more commonly, abusive overseers. Some of these attacks were premeditated, but the vast majority were spontaneous responses to mistreatment or abuse. In general, such attacks were too great a challenge to white supremacy and to the master's authority to be tolerated, and punishment was swift. A Delta overseer's journal entry for January 27, 1849, notes, "Saw where an overseer was buried that was killed by one of the Negroes in 1844. The Negro was taken from the jail in Columbia by a mob out back in the woods and hung."

In some cases, however, slaves facing punishment appealed over the head of an overseer directly to the master, and, not infrequently, the appeal met with success. Despite appeals to white unity across class lines, owners often sided with their slaves against their overseer. "Overseers came and went," one historian observed, "the slaves remained."

By any standard, the overseer's task was a difficult one. He was charged with the care of the slaves, land, livestock, and farm implements, and was responsible for the success or failure of the crop. Generally despised by the slaves, overseers were also held in low esteem by the masters who considered them at best a necessary evil and at worst as ignorant, dishonest brutes. Overseers understood the tenuous nature of their position. One remarked, "If there ever was . . . a calling in life as mean and contemptible as that of an overseer—I would be right down glad to know what it is."

Of all the overseer's responsibilities, the greatest was the care and welfare of the slaves. He was expected to exercise firm control to ensure that slaves worked at maximum efficiency but to avoid the excessive use of force that might injure the owner's property or destroy morale. He was constantly aware, noted one historian, that "[s]laveowners fired overseers who treated their slaves too leniently, and much more often those who treated them too harshly." A good overseer learned to walk the fine line between abuse and overindulgence and to work within the guidelines set by the owner.

Another important aspect of slave society is less frequently discussed in the literature of the period—sexual relationships between white masters and female slaves. Miscegenation, Genovese notes, generally "occurred with single girls under circumstances that varied from seduction to rape and typically fell between the two," and "manifested itself in acts of love in the best cases, sadistic violence in the worst, and ostensible seduction and imposed lust in the typical."

Elisha Worthington of Chicot County, whose 12,500 acres and 543 slaves made him, by 1860, the largest landowner and slaveholder in the state and one of the largest in the South, established a lasting relationship with a slave woman that produced two children. Worthington not only acknowledged the offspring—a boy and a girl—but raised them at his Sunnyside plantation and provided for their education at Oberlin College in Ohio. The son studied in France before returning to Sunnyside in 1860. He would play an important and controversial role in Chicot County in the postwar years.

Miscegenation was only the most extreme example of the complex series of relationships between white masters and black slaves. The fact that the vast majority of American slave masters were resident rather than absentee owners assured that they would not only be more actively involved in the management of the plantation but also more actively involved with the personal lives of their slaves.

An early white resident of the county no doubt overstated the case when she described an idyllic situation in which the slaves were "protected by their owners, whom they loved and obeyed. Free from care, no thought of food nor clothes; they knew they had comfortable homes and would be cared for in times of sickness or distress." But a recent historian of American slavery has concluded that, while former slaves remembered slavery as "a barbaric institution" and "had bitter memories of particular injustices they had endured," many "tempered their overall condemnation of slavery with fond recollections of particular experiences and sympathetic portrayals of particular owners, and testified to the pervasive nature of slave-owner paternalism."

The slave narratives abound with references to "our white folks." Whites in turn often spoke of their slaves as "our black family" and treated them as such. Louisa

Hartley, writing to her sister in Virginia in 1848 concerning her impending move with her husband, six children, and nine slaves from Mississippi to Arkansas, remarked that "the lands in this Country are very high [so] we think it would be to our interest to go where they are cheaper as our family is getting so large numbering 17 black and white." Miriam Hilliard, the wife of a wealthy planter in southern Chicot County, wrote in her diary of the "great relief and joy" her family experienced when one of their slaves who had been lost in the swamp returned safely, and she took the side of her house servant, Rob, when a visitor accused him of stealing, noting that Rob "would as soon have touched the plague" as the visitor's possessions.

Existing side by side with the slaveholders' genuine affection, was a strong sense that slavery was a mixed blessing, often more of an unpleasant duty than an asset. A month after she openly rejoiced at the safe return of a family slave and defended her trusted house servant, Miriam Hilliard wrote, "Negroes are nothing but a tax & annoyance to their owners. From fear or mistaken indulgence any degree of impertinence & idleness is tolerated . . . . I believe it to be my duty, as long as I own slaves, to keep them in proper subjection and well employed."

In Chicot County, where by 1850 blacks outnumbered whites by three to one, this sense of responsibility was tinged with a sense of unease. Chicot County overseer Horace Ford reflected in his journal for February 26, 1849, "Today I am the only white man on the place," and Miriam Hilliard noted, "Within the last few months . . . several . . . person's dwellings have been set on fire and burned to the ground." When her husband, Isaac, left his Grand Lake plantation for a business trip, she recorded in her diary, "Alone—Kept Bowie Knife under my head, and Rob plays sentinel, in adjoining chamber." Miriam's brother, John, sold his plantation and returned to Kentucky. "He is wearied with southern life & negro property," she wrote, "and is rejoiced to quit." It was an opinion she came to share. "When we change our residence," she wrote in June 1850, "I cast my vote for a free state."

But the Hilliards did not give up their plantation or their slaves. Like many other Arkansas slaveholders, they found slavery was simply too profitable to relinquish. By 1860, Arkansas produced 367,393 bales of cotton. Cotton prices remained relatively low throughout the first half of the 1850s. But in 1856, prices rose by over three cents to 12.4 cents per pound, the highest price since 1838. Throughout the remainder of the decade, the price only once dipped below eleven cents per pound. In May of 1857, a writer to the *Arkansas State Gazette and Democrat* remarked, "If cotton will only hold present prices for five years, Arkansas planters will be as rich as cream a foot thick." It seemed entirely possible that he was correct. The economic gains of the 1850s far surpassed anything in the young state's history. Agricultural production was up dramatically statewide. The cash value of farms in Arkansas increased almost sixfold between 1850 and 1860.

Signs of economic development were also beginning to appear in other areas. The troubled Cairo and Fulton Railroad, long supported by the Family, had begun to move south from St. Louis toward the Arkansas border, the Memphis and Little Rock line had actually laid thirty-eight miles of track in the state, and the Mississippi, Ouachita,

This photograph showing young Harriet Ashley, the granddaughter of Chester Ashley, being held by her slave nurse is illustrative of the complex relationships between slaves and masters in the antebellum period. *From the Collection of Mr. and Mrs. Sterling Cockrill.*

and Red River line had laid about twenty-seven. Arkansas in 1860 still had less railroad mileage than any state in the Union except Oregon, but despite these shortcomings, industry, particularly in the western and northwestern sections of the state, was growing. By 1860 manufactured items were valued at almost three million dollars. In terms of real estate and personal wealth per capita, Arkansas ranked sixteenth of the nation's thirty-three states, and the states of the Old Southwest constituted the fastest-growing economic region of the country. After a slow and clumsy beginning, Arkansas seemed to be on the verge of a promising economic future.

While the prosperity of the 1850s was a statewide phenomenon, the economic gains were particularly pronounced in the slaveholding regions of the state. Orville Taylor has observed that while the cash value of farms in six northwestern counties with few slaves increased fourfold between 1850 and 1860, in the six lowland counties with the highest concentration of slaves the cash value of farms increased more than sixfold. The growing concentration of slaves in the southern and eastern sections of the state, combined with immigration to the lowlands from Deep South states, forged closer economic and cultural bonds between those regions while it exacerbated the sectional differences within Arkansas. Thus as Arkansas's economy experienced unparalleled growth in the 1850s, the social, economic, and political dissonance between highland and lowlands increased.

Politics in the Late Antebellum Period

The last years of the 1840s also witnessed a dramatic shakeup in the state's political leadership. Archibald Yell's death at Buena Vista in early 1847 cut short a political career that included two stints in the U.S. Congress and one term as governor. In April 1848

U.S. senator Chester Ashley contracted a fever during the Senate session of that year and died within a week.

The previous month Pres. James Polk appointed the state's other U.S. senator, Ambrose Sevier, as minister to Mexico for the purpose of concluding peace negotiations. Forced to resign his Senate seat, Sevier hoped for the appointment of a political ally who would step aside and allow him to reclaim the seat in 1848. But Gov. Thomas Drew, a Democrat who had enjoyed Family backing but who also had support among independents, broke with the Family shortly after his renomination for a second term earlier in the year and appointed Solon Borland, a rising political star since his Mexican War exploits, to serve out the remainder of the term. In November the Democratic-controlled general assembly chose Borland to serve the full term. Disheartened and possibly weakened by an illness contracted in Mexico, Sevier died on December 31, 1848, at his plantation home near Little Rock.

Though he had been overwhelmingly reelected to the governorship in 1848, Drew was experiencing personal financial problems. In January 1849 when the state legislature failed to come through on what he considered a promise to raise his salary, he resigned. In October of that year, Judge Benjamin Johnson, one of the founding members of the Family, died at the age of sixty-five. James Conway, another Dynasty stalwart and the state's first governor, died in March of 1855.

The deaths of Yell, Ashley, Sevier, Johnson, and Conway marked the passing of the first generation of Arkansas's political leadership. Their demise prepared the way for the rise of a new generation of young politicians. Solon Borland was one such man. Another was John Seldon Roane, who had gained some notoriety, if not renown, for his service in Mexico and his subsequent duel with Albert Pike. Drew's resignation gave Roane the political opening he was waiting for. A compromise candidate of a divided Democratic caucus, Roane went on to narrowly defeat his Whig challenger in a March 1849 special election that was widely ignored by Arkansas voters. In an election in which only 6,518 people cast votes, Roane won by a margin of sixty-two votes.

The Dynasty was also experiencing significant changes. The deaths of several of its founding members, the lingering taint of the banking fiasco, and a growing dissension within the Democratic Party created the greatest challenge to Family dominance since statehood. Robert Ward Johnson soon emerged as the acknowledged leader of the second generation of Family politicians. The eldest son of Judge Benjamin Johnson, Robert had accompanied his parents to Arkansas, but returned to Kentucky for his formal education before moving on to Yale University where he studied law.

Even as a young man, Johnson evidenced a strong inclination to carry on two important Family traditions—politics and dueling. In 1833 he sought retribution against three men who had tried to bring impeachment charges against his father, attacking one with a walking stick on a Little Rock street, fighting a duel with another, and threatening to horsewhip the third. When he was not engaged in fighting duels or otherwise defending the family honor, Johnson won a reputation as a fearless prosecuting attorney in the district around Little Rock and later served as attorney general of the state before being elected to Congress in 1846. In Congress, Johnson quickly developed a reputation as a supporter of John C. Calhoun, an outspoken advocate of "southern rights," a term that encompassed a traditional southern aversion to the centralized power of the federal government (especially when that power was not used to the South's benefit) and a defense of the rights of the individual states to decide for themselves on such issues as economic development, moral reform, and especially the maintenance of slavery.

Robert Ward Johnson, leader of the second generation of "Family" politicians. *Courtesy of the Arkansas History Commission.*

The Missouri Compromise of 1820, which had laid the groundwork for Arkansas's admission to the Union as a slave state, kept the lid on the slavery controversy for a quarter of a century by balancing the admission of slave and free states, but events of the late 1840s again stirred the controversy over slavery. The rush to California following the discovery of gold swelled that territory's population far beyond that required for statehood, and in 1849 California requested admission to the Union as a free state. California's admission threatened to undo the carefully crafted balance between slave and free states in the U.S. Senate.

In January 1850, Senator Henry Clay of Kentucky brought forward a series of resolutions that he hoped would solve the problem. Clay proposed to admit California as a free state, organize the remainder of the Mexican Cession without restrictions as to slavery, abolish the slave trade (though not slavery itself) in the District of Columbia, and adopt a more effective fugitive slave law. Debate raged over the provisions for the next nine months, but Congressman Robert W. Johnson did not take long to make up his mind.

The same month that Clay introduced his compromise proposals, Johnson issued an "Address to the People of Arkansas" in which he proclaimed that "the Union of the Northern and Southern States, under a Common Government for a period beyond this Congress is a matter that may be seriously questioned." He urged Arkansans to support John C. Calhoun's call for a southern convention at Nashville, Tennessee, which he hoped would transcend traditional party politics and usher in a new era of southern unity. "The South," he proclaimed, "will present to the world one united brotherhood and will move in one column under a banner—EQUALITY OR INDEPENDENCE, OUR RIGHTS UNDER THE CONSTITUTION WITHIN OR WITHOUT THE UNION! ! !" When his strong stand failed to find a receptive audience, Johnson intensified his rhetoric, warning of the "fanaticism" of northern abolitionists and accusing his opponents within the state of "treason to their own land—hostility to the honor and interests of their own people."

Gov. John Seldon Roane was also a strong spokesman for southern rights, as were both of the state's U.S. senators, William Sebastian and Solon Borland. In March, the fiery Borland physically attacked moderate Mississippi senator Henry Foote on a Washington street because Foote had referred to him as a "servile follower of Calhoun." In their extreme zeal, however, Johnson and his fellow southern radicals had dramatically miscalculated the mood of their constituents. While the great majority in 1850 supported southern rights, most continued to hope for compromise within the Union. Even before the Nashville Convention had assembled, one of the state's most influential Democratic newspapers, William Woodruff's *Arkansas State Gazette and Democrat,* chided Johnson for his "peculiar views" and noted, "Our people do not believe that the time has yet come when they are to be called upon to assist in dismembering the Confederacy. It is the universal sentiment that the Union must be preserved; and the universal belief is that it cannot be dissolved." It also condemned Johnson's "wholesale denunciation of those of his constituents who do not choose to endorse his views."

A correspondent to the paper from Chicot County in the heart of the state's cotton-producing region proclaimed himself to be a strong supporter of slavery and southern rights but also "a Union man" and a friend of compromise. He condemned Robert Johnson's views as "offensive in terms and heretical in principle," and concluded that "[a]s long as the South deals in bombastic declamation in regard to Southern chivalry, disunion, secession, southern confederacy, and all such nonsense, the patriotic, honest men of the free states will not unite with them, and the question will remain unsettled." He added that a tour of the state satisfied him "that Arkansas is still American, altogether American, in hope, thought, and feeling." Whig leader Albert Pike declared that he was "for the Union, the whole Union, and nothing less than the Union."

Senator Borland returned to Little Rock in the summer of 1850 and quickly surmised that the majority of Arkansans did not share his extreme views. He began to soften his rhetoric (never an easy task for Borland), declaring in Little Rock in July his great love for the Union. He did not return to Washington in time to vote against the compromise he had so roundly condemned.

In September the various individual bills that collectively came to be called the Compromise of 1850 passed both houses of Congress after nine months of contentious debate. Robert Ward Johnson had strenuously opposed the compromise measures to the end, voting only for the bill that provided for the adoption of a stricter fugitive slave law. Governor Roane, himself a Jefferson County planter, condemned the Compromise as "unjust" and added, "I would dissolve the Union for there is no security in it." Many lowland Democrats shared Roane's sentiments, but a combination of Whigs and Unionist Democrats in the state legislature blocked any efforts to formally repudiate the Compromise. Most Arkansans, like most other Americans, were relieved that the crisis had passed.

Despite the best efforts of their political leaders, Arkansans failed to rally to the cause of southern rights in 1850. Why was this so? Historian James Woods has provided several answers to this question. To begin with, Arkansas had only been in the Union for fourteen years when the controversy over California came to the fore, and many Arkansans still needed federal protection and federal aid. Citizens of western Arkansas, bordered by the Indian Territory, wanted the protection and economic benefits that the presence of federal troops supplied. Delta residents were beginning to derive substantial profits from cotton and stood to benefit further from a federal swampland reclamation project begun in 1850. It is also important to remember that slaveholders and their families accounted for less than 20 percent of Arkansas's population in 1850. And, as previously noted, most Arkansans were too preoccupied with their own survival on this frontier society to worry too much about the threat to slavery.

But while the Dynasty failed to convince Arkansans of the immediacy of the southern rights cause, it did continue to dominate the state's politics. In September 1850 a disheartened Robert Ward Johnson, stung by harsh criticism from much of the state press and many of his constituents, announced that he would not be a candidate for reelection. But in April 1851 the state Democratic convention "drafted" Johnson as its candidate for Congress, citing his "fidelity to southern rights and public success." His "fidelity to southern rights" notwithstanding, Johnson had learned his lesson, and he tempered his fire-eating rhetoric. Campaigning in northwest Arkansas, he assured his audience that he was "the truest and best friend of Unionism" and did not propose secession as the remedy to the South's ills. He was reelected with over 57 percent of the vote.

A Chicot County planter who had disagreed with Johnson's strong stand for southern rights but voted for him anyway explained, "I did not approve of Mr. Johnson's opinions or his course. . . . I have not changed. But he is now the nominee of a democratic convention. I am a democrat. I shall vote, or not, just as I please; but I certainly . . . will not vote for the Whig candidate."

The Dynasty's fortunes received an additional boost when Elias Conway received the Democratic Party's nomination for governor. The youngest of Thomas and Ann Rector Conway's seven sons and the younger brother of former territorial delegate Henry Conway and former governor James Conway, Elias Conway had served as state auditor from 1836 to 1848 and had been active in Family politics.

In the election of 1852, Arkansans continued their Democratic tradition by voting for Franklin Pierce over Whig candidate Winfield Scott, a hero of the Mexican War. Even Whig leader Albert Pike thought Scott to be "soft on slavery." Elias Conway was elected governor. When Solon Borland resigned his Senate seat in 1853, Governor Conway appointed Robert Johnson to fill the position. The state legislature unanimously elected Johnson to a full term in 1854, further strengthening the Family's grip on the major state offices.

In the years following the election of 1852, the national Whig Party divided over the issue of slavery and ceased to be a major factor in Arkansas or national politics. The new political parties that sprang up to fill the void had little appeal in Arkansas. This was particularly true for the new Republican Party, which first fielded a candidate for president in the election of 1856. The Republican platform favored homesteads, protective tariffs, and internal improvements, but staunchly opposed the extension of slavery into the territories, a development that many southerners considered essential to the survival of the institution. Accordingly, the new party had almost no adherents in the slaveholding states.

The other new party to develop in the 1850s was the American Party. Originally organized in secret fraternal lodges, the party became commonly known as the Know-Nothings because its members answered, "I know nothing," to inquiries about the party's composition and goals. Its founding principle was opposition to foreign immigrants, particularly Roman Catholics. The Know-Nothings showed strength in New England, the Mid-Atlantic states, and parts of the South, but for obvious reasons its appeal in Arkansas was limited. The state simply had too few foreign immigrants and Catholics to arouse much enthusiasm, so in Arkansas the Know-Nothings served as a vehicle for all those who opposed the Dynasty. The party enjoyed its greatest strength in Little Rock where longtime Dynasty opponent Albert Pike penned an anti-Catholic pamphlet, and it captured the city's elections in 1856. But that same year Pike repudiated the national party because he thought it weak on the issue of slavery. In the presidential election of 1856, the Know-Nothings polled less than 40 percent of the popular vote in Arkansas, its poorest showing in any southern state.

Thus it appeared that by the middle of the 1850s the Dynasty was without serious challengers. Ironically, the greatest challenge to Family hegemony would come from within the Democratic Party and would be led by a man who shared the southern rights sentiments of its leaders. Thomas Carmichael Hindman was the diminutive (barely five feet tall), hot-tempered son of a prominent Mississippi planter who had served in the Mexican War and in the Mississippi legislature. In 1849 Hindman's older brother, Robert, was killed by Col. William C. Falkner (the great-grandfather of author William Faulkner who added the "u" to the family name) in what a Mississippi jury later determined was an act of self-defense. The verdict did not satisfy Thomas Hindman, and animosity between Hindman and Falkner continued, culminating in 1851 when Hindman challenged Falkner to a duel. A third party succeeded in preventing the duel from taking place, and Hindman and Falkner reconciled their differences. But the incident provided insight into young Hindman's character. One acquaintance opined that Hindman had "a wonderful talent for getting into fusses" and another thought that he gave the appearance of being "perpetually anxious to have a duel."

Hindman moved to Helena in 1854 and married the daughter of a wealthy land speculator. A lawyer by profession but a born politician, he soon immersed himself in the politics of his new state. Intelligent and a gifted orator, Hindman initially ingratiated himself to the Family by holding a three-day political rally at his Helena home in November 1855 at which he castigated the Know-Nothings and expressed his belief that "[t]he purpose of any real Southern party is to protect slavery." In the gubernatorial elections of the following year, Elias Conway easily defeated Know-Nothing candidate

James Yell (nephew of Archibald) with 65 percent of the vote, and the state gave its support to Democrat James Buchanan for president.

But if Hindman and the leaders of the Family were concerned with the protection of slavery, most Arkansans were not, and the growing national crisis kindled little interest in the state. By the mid-1850s cotton prices had increased to their highest level since 1838, and while Kansas was engulfed in civil war over slavery, a Camden newspaper urged its readers to "Forget about Kansas and rejoice in our glorious wealth, delightful showers, and abundant crops."

In 1858 the Family rewarded Hindman for his service by supporting him in a successful race for the congressional seat in the northern district. He was thirty years old and had been a resident of the state for only four years, yet in that brief time he had made a socially and economically successful marriage and had become a major player in state politics. For the average man, this meteoric rise would have been immensely satisfying. But Hindman was not the average man. As one chronicler noted, he was "a man who regarded Arkansas as an empire of which he should be emperor."

Dynasty leaders had thrown him a large bone which they felt would assuage his appetite, but for Thomas Hindman, it was not enough. He desperately wanted William Sebastian's U.S. Senate seat when the term expired in late 1858. When the Dynasty supported Sebastian for reelection, Hindman was furious. He turned against the Family and established his own newspaper, the *Old Line Democrat*, in Little Rock and by the following year was at war with his former allies.

In November 1859, Hindman threatened to publicly denounce the Family in Little Rock, prompting Robert Ward Johnson to travel fifty miles from his Jefferson County plantation to the capital to confront the Helena upstart. When Hindman failed to show, citing health problems, Family members denounced him as a coward. In January of the following year, only the intervention of congressional colleagues prevented a duel between Representative Hindman and Senator Johnson in the nation's capital.

His failure to appear in Little Rock and his fiery temperament alienated some Arkansans, but Hindman nonetheless proved to be the most potent challenger to the Dynasty in the state's history. Unmatched as a public speaker, he became a rallying point for dissident Democrats who had long chafed under the Dynasty's domination of the state's politics. As the individual county conventions met in early 1860 to choose delegates to the state Democratic convention, it became clear that the Hindman forces would mount a serious challenge to the Family's hegemony.

The Dynasty planned to secure the party's gubernatorial nomination for Robert Ward Johnson's younger brother, Richard H. Johnson, while ensuring that Johnson's U.S. Senate seat went to retiring governor Elias Conway the following November. The Hindman forces were strong enough to prevent Richard Johnson from obtaining the customary two-thirds majority necessary for nomination, but the Dynasty's control over the party machinery enabled it to suspend that requirement and make Johnson the nominee by a simple majority. The Family also managed to control the writing of the party platform and to secure the selection of six of its members to the eight-man delegation to the Democratic national convention to be held later that month in Charleston, South Carolina. The platform rejected popular sovereignty and insisted on the federal protection of slavery in the territories.

Arkansas delegates shared the hostility felt by most southern Democrats for Illinois senator Stephen Douglas, the favorite of the northern wing of the party. The "Little Giant" had enjoyed great southern support when his Kansas-Nebraska Act (1854) promised to open the remainder of the Louisiana Purchase to slavery under the doctrine of "popular sovereignty," but he had alienated them with his "Freeport Doctrine" of 1858, which suggested that territories could evade the terms of the *Dred Scott* decision simply by refusing to provide the police powers necessary to enforce slavery. (In the 1857 case of *Dred Scott v. Sandford* the Supreme Court ruled that Congress could not ban slavery from the territories.)

Events of late 1859 dramatically increased the tension nationwide. In October of that year, the fanatical abolitionist John Brown led nineteen men in a raid on the federal arsenal at Harper's Ferry, Virginia, for the purpose of arming the slaves he believed would rush to join him. The plot was far-fetched and enjoyed no hope of success. Brown and his men were overwhelmed by a detachment of U.S. Marines led by Lt. Col. Robert E. Lee. Before the month was out, a Virginia court convicted Brown of treason and conspiracy to incite insurrection, and on December 2 he and six co-conspirators were hanged.

The shock waves from Brown's raid swept across the South and helped to further polarize the nation. Throughout the winter of 1859–1860 rumors of slave insurrections abounded in the southern states, and southerners became more determined than ever to resist those who threatened the survival of their "peculiar institution." Many ceased to distinguish between the abolitionists who wished to destroy slavery and others, like the new Republican Party, who wished only to restrict its spread. John Brown was still very much on the minds and tongues of southern delegates as they prepared to assemble for the national convention in April 1860.

Northern delegates enjoyed a majority at the Democratic convention, and Douglas remained the leading contender for the party's nomination. Two things stood in his way. The first was the party rule that required a two-thirds majority for nomination. The second was the city the party had chosen to hold its convention. Charleston, South Carolina, was the center of southern rights extremism and the place least hospitable to the Douglas candidacy. When free state delegates refused to accede to southern demands for federal protection of slavery in the territories, delegates from seven southern states walked out of the convention. Six of the eight Arkansas delegates ignored the instructions of the state convention and joined the walkout.

With further progress impossible, the convention agreed to reassemble in Baltimore in mid-June and adjourned without nominating a candidate. The Baltimore convention, however, proved no more amenable to compromise than had the Charleston assembly. Once again Deep South delegates walked out, this time followed by delegates from the Upper South. The same six Arkansas delegates who had joined the Charleston walkout, joined this one as well. The southern delegates hastily assembled their own convention and nominated John C. Breckinridge of Kentucky, the sitting vice president of the United States, as their candidate for president on a platform pledging federal protection for slavery.

But while much of the country was riveted to the explosive events on the national political scene, Arkansans were preoccupied with events at home. In the interval between the demise of the Charleston convention and the convening of the Baltimore convention, another political bombshell exploded back in Arkansas. The high-handed means by which the Dynasty had dominated the state convention had only deepened the divisions in the state Democratic Party. Hindman secured his renomination for Congress from the northern congressional district, but it seemed that no serious rival would appear to challenge Richard Johnson for governor. Then in May, Henry Rector, a forty-four-year-old planter and attorney from Saline County who had served as a state representative, U.S. Marshal, and as a justice on the state supreme court, announced his candidacy for governor as an Independent Democrat. Rector was Gov. Elias Conway's first cousin and a longtime member of the Family, but his relationship with his kinsmen had been a rocky one.

The gubernatorial campaign of 1860 was, one historian noted, a "fratricidal war." The Dynasty had thrived for over a quarter century by portraying itself as the party of Andrew Jackson and the common man. Now, adopting the tactics successfully employed by the Whigs in the presidential election of 1840, the Hindman press set out to cast Rector as the true champion of the common man and the Dynasty as aristocratic and corrupt. Rector, a longtime political insider and, since 1854, a prominent Little Rock attorney, was portrayed as a "poor, honest farmer of Saline County, who toils at the plow handles to provide bread, meat, and raiment for his wife and children." Meanwhile from the stump, Hindman charged, "Of all the unholy alliances and corrupt political influences that ever crushed the energy of a free people, that of Johnsonianism was the most blighting, withering and corrupt."

The charges struck home. Not only did dissident Democrats and former Whigs flock to the Rector camp, many members of the lower echelons of the Dynasty itself joined the anti-Family crusade. They could identify with the frustrations felt by both Hindman and Rector at the overbearing dominance of Family leaders. As usual, issues were secondary in the campaign, and personalities were primary. Charges and counter-charges swirled from both camps in a steady stream. By most accounts, Rector was a fair public speaker while Johnson was a disaster on the stump. A Whig newspaper in Batesville suggested that Johnson quit making public addresses entirely, because "[h]e loses votes every time he speaks."

Rector's one substantive issue was a proposal to postpone payment on the state debt for twenty-five years and to use the money instead for internal improvement, particularly railroads. On the major issues of the day—southern rights and the expansion of slavery—the opposing factions were in complete agreement. Both strongly supported the expansion of slavery into the territories and held out the possibility of secession as a final remedy. Ironically, at a time when national politics was at its most sectionally polarized, sectional divisions in Arkansas were almost nonexistent. Both candidates campaigned in and drew support from all quarters of the state. Arkansas voters went to the polls on August 6, but it took two weeks to tabulate the final vote. The results marked the end of a political era. Rector received 31,948 votes to Johnson's 28,487. To compound the Family's fiasco, Hindman was reelected to Congress from the northern congressional district and a Hindman ally, Edward Gantt, was chosen to represent the southern district.

Historians have long debated the reasons for this turn of events. Rector may have benefited from the votes of the Old Line Whigs who saw in his candidacy a chance to vote against the Dynasty and for a member of the Little Rock elite who shared many of their views on economic matters. In an age when personal politics was triumphant, Johnson was no doubt hurt by his poor speaking style. While Rector was himself no Demosthenes, he had the accomplished Hindman to proclaim his cause. Other historians have contended that Rector benefited from the influx of newcomers to the state who had no ties to the old ruling oligarchy and were disappointed with the state's lack of progress.

James Woods has suggested that the greatest factor may well have been Hindman's organizational, oratorical, and political skills. Unlike previous challengers, Hindman was able to bypass the Dynasty-dominated Democratic Party machinery and appeal directly to the voters. Unlike the Whigs, he was able to disassociate the Dynasty from its image as the party of the common man and to portray it instead as a group of wealthy aristocrats. In Rector, the Family's opponents had a candidate who could appeal to many different groups. To the poor and disaffected, he was the rebel challenging the entrenched aristocratic governing class. To Delta slave owners, he was a staunch defender of slavery. To the former Whigs, he was a member of the Little Rock elite who shared many of their economic ideas.

Behind it all lay the political genius of Thomas Carmichael Hindman. While Richard Johnson had inherited the bloodlines of the Family, it was Thomas Hindman who embodied the political and oratorical skills that were the true legacy of Ambrose Sevier. The defeat of the Family was a landmark event in the state's history and seemed to presage the rise of a new political alignment in Arkansas. But the new political landscape was not as clearly defined as it might first have appeared. For one thing, though Rector owed his election in no small measure to Hindman, he was in no sense Hindman's puppet. Rather, the man Arkansans had chosen to guide the state during this critical period was an eccentric maverick determined to steer his own course.

In addition, despite the bitter personal animosity between them, on the major issue of the day, Hindman and the Family were largely in agreement. The Family had long been known as champions of slavery and southern rights, while Hindman had clearly established his own credentials as a fire-eater. If anything, the Helena politician was a greater zealot on the issue. While the Family tended to view disunion as a possible, if regrettable, solution to the problems confronting the region, Hindman saw it as an absolute necessity and a positive good. James Woods has written that, as the presidential election of 1860 approached, Hindman did all he could to "out-southern" the Dynasty on every major issue. Still, the tides of national politics were inexorably drawing the former antagonists closer together.

The Road to Secession

Four men sought the presidency in 1860, but only three found support in Arkansas. Abraham Lincoln of Illinois, the candidate of the Republican Party, ran on a platform favoring a protective tariff, free homesteads for farmers, and internal improvements. The party remained firm in its resistance to the extension of slavery. Its platform also denounced John Brown's raid and recognized the right of each state "to order and control its own domestic institutions." Lincoln had already struck a moderate tone, stating his view that slavery was "an evil, not to be extended, but to be tolerated and protected only because of and so far as its actual presence among us makes that toleration and protection a necessity."

Such distinctions had long since been lost on many southerners, however. The Little Rock *True Democrat* did print the party's platform on its front page, but noted, "We do not believe that Lincoln or any abolitionist can ever be President of the *United* States. The Fourth of March that sees him inaugurated will see two empires where there is now one Confederacy." Lincoln drew little support in Arkansas or the rest of the South.

Of the three remaining candidates, Stephen Douglas, the candidate of the northern wing of the now-sundered Democratic Party, enjoyed the least support in the state. Opposed by both the Family and the Hindman camp, Douglas forces had few newspapers to champion their cause and also lacked the financial resources to sponsor the rallies and barbecues so necessary to political campaigns in the mid-nineteenth century.

Those problems did not plague the supporters of the new Constitutional Union Party. Organized largely by former Whigs in the border states in early May, the party was intent on keeping the Union together. Its platform was "the Constitution of the Country, the Union of the States, and the Enforcement of the Laws," and its candidate was John Bell of Tennessee, a wealthy slave owner. In Arkansas, Bell found great support among former Whigs, including many of the wealthy planters of the southern and eastern parts of the state. Accordingly, there was plenty of money to conduct a full campaign with all the attendant rallies, parades, and barbecues. Press support was also abundant, including the powerful *Arkansas Gazette,* which tried diligently to portray John C. Breckinridge, the nominee of the southern wing of the Democratic Party, as the candidate of extremism, disunion, and treason.

These aspersions notwithstanding, Breckinridge remained the most formidable candidate in Arkansas. He enjoyed the support of the vast majority of the state's newspapers as well as the backing of both rival Democratic factions in the state. The presidential campaign forced the Dynasty and Hindman's followers into an uneasy alliance that was made more difficult by the fact that they were still warring vigorously over state politics.

In the end, each camp supported Breckinridge in its own way, and the Kentuckian drew support from across a wide ideological spectrum. As usual, Hindman's campaign was the most radical, heaping criticism on Douglas and generally adopting the position of the most extreme of the southern fire-eaters. The Dynasty's campaign, however, stressed adherence to the constitutional arguments adopted by the Supreme Court in the *Dred Scott* case.

Breckinridge also gained support from an unlikely source. Longtime Family opponent Albert Pike had foregone participation in national politics since withdrawing from the American (Know-Nothing) Party in 1856. But the political crisis of 1860 brought him once more into the fray. Pike produced a lengthy and reasoned letter that defended the "state rights" theory and the *Dred Scott* decision and challenged the doctrine of popular sovereignty. As Pike biographer Walter Brown has pointed out, Pike also believed in the right of secession, but unlike the Family or Hindman, he remained committed to the Union and warned that his future adherence to the southern Democratic Party was predicated on its remaining loyal to the Union.

The wide divergence of opinion among Breckinridge supporters seemed to bear out Stephen Douglas's oft-quoted opinion that not every Breckinridge man was a disunionist, but every disunionist was a Breckinridge man. Whatever their political persuasion, Arkansans realized the critical nature of the election to the future of their state and nation. On election day, November 6, 1860, Camden attorney John Brown wrote in his diary, "This is the most important day to the United States and, perhaps, to mankind since July 4, 1776." Almost 80 percent of the state's eligible voters went to the polls, the highest percentage turnout in the state's history. The final returns showed a clear, if modest, victory for Breckenridge. The Kentuckian received 28,783 votes (53 percent), to Bell's 20,094 (37 percent), and Douglas's 5,227 (9 percent).

An analysis of the vote reveals that Bell did best in those parts of the state where the Whigs had traditionally done well—among the wealthy planters of the Delta and in the business-oriented urban areas where voters feared a disruption of commerce. Breckinridge ran strongest in the traditionally Democratic northwest and among the farmers and small slave owners of south and southwest Arkansas who hoped to rise to planter status. It may seem strange that the candidate most identified with slavery and states' rights found such great support in an area where slavery was least important. But the northwest part of the state had always been staunchly Democratic, and the best explanation may be that these voters were influenced more by party loyalty than by the overheated rhetoric about slavery. John Brown, a Bell supporter and former Whig, opined that Breckinridge enjoyed his greatest support among "people who did not read," and there may be considerable truth to that assertion. Michael Dougan has pointed out that many people in the areas of Breckinridge's greatest support were either illiterate or in areas without newspapers. Clearly the election reflected not only a Whig-Democrat pattern but a rich-poor alignment as well.

In addition to Arkansas, Breckinridge carried all the Deep South and Gulf South states, garnering almost 850,000 popular votes and seventy-two electoral votes. Douglas received almost 1.4 million popular votes, but carried only one state (Missouri) and twelve electoral votes. Bell received almost 600,000 popular votes and carried the border states of Virginia, Kentucky, and Tennessee. None of this was enough to offset Lincoln's near sweep of the more populous free states. Final national returns gave the Republican candidate over 1.8 million popular votes and more important, 180 electoral votes. Though he received slightly less than 40 percent of the total popular vote, his electoral vote total easily surpassed the total of his three rivals.

In Arkansas, reaction to Lincoln's election was generally mild. On November 17 the *Gazette* editorialized, "Lincoln is elected in the manner prescribed by the law and by the majority prescribed by the Constitution. Let him be inaugurated, let not steps be taken against this administration until he has committed an overt act, which cannot be remedied by law." The editor hoped that the election might spur the growth of a new conservative opposition movement built around the nucleus of the Constitutional Union Party. Albert Pike also refused to accept Lincoln's election as a cause for breaking up the Union. He hoped rather that it might unify the South around a new sectional party. Even the Democratic press seemed to take the result in stride and urged caution and restraint. The Family-controlled Fayetteville *Arkansian* advised its readers to "wait until after his [Lincoln's] inaugural and see what course he will pursue." Only the Hindman press spoke of secession.

In mid-November, only days after the election, the Arkansas General Assembly convened for its biennial session. On November 15, Henry Rector was inaugurated as the state's sixth governor and the first from outside the ruling Dynasty. Rector had a reputation as something of a fire-eater, but he was also largely an unknown quantity. Legislators and common citizens eagerly awaited his inaugural address to see what position he would take on the major issue of the day. Acknowledging "the bare possibility that the North may still be induced to retrace her steps, and award to the southern states the rights guaranteed to them by the constitution," the governor stated that he could not "counsel precipitate or hasty action, having for its object a final separation of the States, and breaking up of the Union." But he also spoke of the "fanaticism of the North" and "the irrepressible conflict" between slave and free states and warned that "the states stand tremblingly upon the verge of dissolution." Near the conclusion of his remarks, he cut through the ambiguities of "states' rights" and "southern rights" and went directly to the heart of the matter. "The issue," he proclaimed, "is the Union without slavery, or slavery without the Union."

Key members of the state's congressional delegation pushed hard for secession. Both Hindman and Congressman-elect Edward Gantt gave inflammatory addresses to the General Assembly in late November. Senator Robert Johnson soon joined in, publishing an open letter to his constituents that reached the state in mid-December. He said that he regarded the secession of the southern states as a fact and that "Arkansas must go with them." Governor Rector added his voice to the growing clamor in a written address to the legislature on December 11, noting, "The Union of States may no longer be regarded as an existing fact" and warning Arkansans to "gird her loins for the conflict" he felt certain was to come.

These appeals notwithstanding, the legislature refused to be stampeded into a hasty action. It began the task of selecting a replacement for the retiring Senator Johnson, a clear sign that legislators did not feel that secession was imminent. On December 20 they chose Dr. Charles Mitchell of Washington, a Family member and a strong advocate of states' rights, who nonetheless refused to call for immediate secession. That same day, South Carolina voted an Ordinance of Secession dissolving its union with the other states. This action, coming only six weeks after Lincoln's election and over two months before his inauguration, caught many Arkansas Unionists and even some secessionists by surprise, and it hastened the demise of the old political alignments.

The following day Senator Johnson and Congressman Hindman, less than a year removed from their near-duel in Washington, collaborated on a joint statement calling for a state convention to consider secession. It was now clear that the same unlikely political alliance that had carried the state for Breckinridge was now united behind secession. The old political alignments dissolved as the issue of secession polarized the state along sectional lines. Unionist sentiment was strongest in the upland counties of northern and western Arkansas. Secession forces were greatest in the southern and eastern parts of the state where many former Whigs joined lowland Democrats to form a common front.

On December 22 the state house of representatives called for a state convention to consider the issue, although the more conservative state senate did not concur until January 15. By the terms of the measure, voters would go to the polls on February 18 to decide whether or not to call a convention and to elect delegates. Unionist candidates had the unenviable task of asking voters to reject the convention while at the same time soliciting their votes as a delegate to the convention.

The Unionist dilemma was compounded by events of early 1861. Between January 9 and February 1, six more Deep South and Gulf South states left the Union, including the neighboring states of Mississippi, Louisiana, and Texas. Local affairs also contributed to the secession frenzy. In November 1860 sixty-five soldiers of the Second U.S. Artillery Regiment had occupied the federal arsenal in Little Rock. In January a rumor that the garrison was to be reinforced spread by telegraph from Little Rock to Memphis and then downriver to the secessionist stronghold of Helena. Firebrands there demanded that the governor seize the arsenal.

Such a precipitate and illegal action was too much for Governor Rector. He replied that while Arkansas was still in the Union, the governor of the state had no right to seize federal property. But, as always, Rector was not content with a clear and unambiguous statement. He went on to say that any attempt to reinforce the arsenal would be an act of war. By the time his adjutant-general (who was also his brother-in-law) reworded and released the statement, it appeared that the governor was encouraging a spontaneous action on the part of the people to seize the arsenal. By the end of January over a thousand "volunteers" from the Delta had arrived in the capital. In Pine Bluff a group of secessionist fired on the *USS Tucker* as it was heading up the Arkansas River in the mistaken belief that the ship was carrying federal reinforcements to Little Rock.

In the capital city the governor tried to disavow any call to arms, but the hastily assembled volunteers were in no mood to listen. With the situation spiraling out of control, Rector took a gamble. On February 6 he called on the federal commander at the arsenal, Little Rock native James Totten, to peacefully surrender the post. Outnumbered and without any orders from Washington, Totten agreed to the governor's demands. The federal troops evacuated the arsenal on February 8 and marched through a jeering crowd to Fletcher's Landing just downstream from the city, where they made camp. As the soldiers waited there for a steamboat to take them out of the state, a group of Little Rock women presented Totten with a sword commending his gallantry. Totten and his small command waited at the landing until February 12 when they boarded the steamboat *Madora* and proceeded to St. Louis.

On the surface, the bloodless seizure of the arsenal seemed to be a great triumph for the governor. In fact, however, the opposite was true. Far from being a hero, Rector was seriously damaged by the affair. Arkansas Unionists denounced him for precipitating a crisis where none existed, and even secessionists sensed that the governor had lost control of the situation.

On February 18, 1861, in Montgomery, Alabama, Jefferson Davis of Mississippi took the oath of office as president of the new Confederate States of America. That same day Arkansans went to the polls to vote on whether to hold a convention to consider secession. The results reflected the ambivalence most Arkansans felt about the issue of secession. An overwhelming majority of Arkansas voters favored the convention (27,412 to 15,826), but the majority of the delegates elected to attend the convention opposed secession. Clearly while Arkansans were willing to consider the possibility of secession, many were in no hurry to secede.

On March 4, 1861, Abraham Lincoln assumed the office of President of the United States. In his inaugural address, Lincoln expressed his belief that the union of states was perpetual, and he pledged to enforce the laws and hold federal property. At the same time he insisted that he had no intention of interfering with slavery where it already existed. Addressing the South directly, he said, "In *your* hands, my dissatisfied fellow countrymen, and not in *mine*, is the momentous issue of civil war."

That same day, the Arkansas convention assembled to take up that question. The make-up of the delegates, like the vote itself, reflected the clear geographic division in the state. Unionists from the northern and western portions of the state enjoyed a narrow majority of the seventy-seven delegates. In a key early vote to select the president of the convention, Unionist and former Whig David Walker of Fayetteville narrowly defeated a secessionist candidate by a vote of forty to thirty-five. It was indicative of the course the convention would take. While the Arkansas Unionists majority never exceeded five votes, it was enough to decide all the major questions.

The secessionist press thundered for disunion, secessionist

Secession conventions: Arkansas held two conventions to consider whether or not to secede from the Union and join the Confederate States of America. The first, which met in March 1861, steadfastly refused, by a narrow majority, to take the state out of the Union. However, a second convention held in May 1861, after the attack on Fort Sumter and the president's call for troops to suppress the rebellion, overwhelmingly voted to secede.

delegates gave impassioned speeches, and delegates from the seceded states of South Carolina and Georgia addressed the convention. Confederate president Jefferson Davis sent his own representative, and both Governor Rector and Senator Johnson made personal appeals. The previous month Johnson had urged Arkansans to defend "our equality in the Union, our social system, our property, our liberties." Now with the convention in session and the whole issue of secession hanging in the balance, his argument went to the real heart of the matter—the threat to slavery. The ascension of Lincoln to the presidency, Johnson argued, would lead to "the extinction of four million dollars of southern property, and the freedom, and the equality with us of the four millions of negroes now in the South."

Still, the Unionist majority was unmoved. After two weeks of intense deliberation, the convention rebuffed every attempt to pass an ordinance of secession or even to allow a popular referendum on the issue. Finally, fearing that southern and eastern Arkansas might attempt to secede from the rest of the state or that Rector would attempt to bypass the assembly by taking the issue directly to the state legislature, the Unionists agreed to a referendum to be held on the first Monday of August in which Arkansans would vote either "for secession" or "for cooperation."

Arkansas secessionist pilloried the Unionist delegates, but the Crawford County town of Van Buren fired a thirty-nine-gun salute in honor of the thirty-nine delegates who had held firm against secession and the town's two returning delegates were greeted by a cheering crowd and a brass band. Both sides prepared for a four-month-long campaign leading up to the August referendum.

Despite the heated words and animosities that characterized the March convention, Unionists and secessionists were in agreement on several major issues. Both were committed to the protection of slavery, and both agreed that any attempt to coerce the seceded states back into the Union would be legitimate grounds for the state to secede. Such an action, the delegates had declared, would be "resisted by Arkansas to the last extremity." This was the Achilles' heel of the Unionist position and put them at the mercy of events over which they had no control. Events in South Carolina would soon alter the political balance in Arkansas and bring the state to a critical juncture.

Confederate authorities in South Carolina had demanded the surrender of Fort Sumter in Charleston harbor and made it clear that any attempt by the federal government to resupply the fort would be considered a hostile act. Lincoln had pledged in his inaugural address to "hold, occupy, and possess" federal property. On April 4, 1861, he decided, against the advice of a majority of his cabinet, to attempt to resupply the fort with provisions only. Two days later, he notified the governor of South Carolina of his intentions.

The "momentous issue of civil war" and the onus for starting that war now passed into the hands of Confederate president Jefferson Davis and his advisors. On April 9, the Confederate government decided to act. Davis ordered the Confederate commander in Charleston to prevent the fort from being resupplied. On April 11, Confederate authorities in Charleston demanded the federal garrison's surrender. The demand was refused. At 4:30 A.M., April 12, 1861, Confederate gunners opened fire on Fort Sumter. The fort sustained a continual bombardment for thirty hours without the loss of a single life, but further resistance was clearly futile. The federal garrison surrendered the fort on April 14.

The following day, President Lincoln called for a force of 75,000 men to suppress the rebellion, including 780 men from Arkansas. Governor Rector's response came one week later. "In answer to your requisition for troops from Arkansas to subjugate the Southern States, I have to say that none will be furnished. The demand is only adding insult to injury. The people of this state are freemen, not slaves, and will defend to the last extremity, their honor, lives and property against Northern mendacity and usurpation."

For secessionists, the attack on Fort Sumter and the president's response were political godsends, and even the cautious Unionists of March now felt compelled to move into the secessionists' camp. On April 20 John Brown, the Whig planter and Unionist from Camden, wrote in his diary, "The war feeling is aroused, the die is cast. The whole South will be aroused in two weeks." *Gazette* editor Christopher Danley, another longtime opponent of secession, added, "Now that the overt act has been committed we should I think draw the sword, and not sheath it until we can have a guarantee of all of our rights, or such standards as will be honorable in the South."

Governor Rector wasted no time in seizing the initiative. Though Arkansas had not formally left the Union, he ordered former senator Solon Borland to take command of the state militia and seize the federal outpost at Fort Smith. A thousand men boarded three steamboats for the trip up the Arkansas River. Crowds cheered the men at every town and landing along the way. The militia reached Fort Smith on April 23 only to find that the federal garrison had withdrawn into the Indian Territory with all its equipment and supplies. The militia's return trip downriver to Little Rock was a triumphal procession as crowds again lined the riverbank to cheer the great "victory" over federal forces.

In late April, chairman David Walker reluctantly called for the state convention to reassemble at Little Rock on May 6 to once again consider the question of secession. Walker, a staunch Unionist, had been under extreme pressure since the attack on Sumter, and he was now convinced that Missouri and the other border states would soon secede. The convention assembled at ten in the morning before packed galleries. A motion was quickly made to prepare an ordinance of secession. The document was ready by three o'clock, and the delegates reassembled to vote. The outcome was a foregone conclusion. A last desperate attempt by a few die-hard Unionists to submit the question to the people was overwhelmingly defeated, and the roll call proceeded in the tense and hushed chamber.

In stark contrast to the vote of two months earlier, only five of the seventy delegates voted to remain in the Union. In response to the chairman's appeal for a unanimous vote, four of these added their names to the ordinance of secession. Only Isaac Murphy of Madison County refused to join the secessionists' bandwagon. "I have cast my vote after mature reflection and have considered the consequences," Murphy stated, "and I cannot conscientiously change it." As Murphy concluded his remarks, Mrs. Frederick

Trapnall, the widow of a prominent Little Rock attorney and one of the leaders of the capital city's society, tossed a bouquet of flowers at his feet, but most in the packed galleries jeered in derision.

In the end, Murphy's principled stand made no difference. Shortly after four in the afternoon on May 6, 1861, Arkansas declared that it had severed its bonds with the Union that it had so eagerly joined only twenty-five years earlier. The state now faced the greatest crisis in its history.

CHAPTER NINE

"Between the Hawk & Buzzard": The Civil War in Arkansas, 1861–1865

The Civil War was the most divisive and destructive event in Arkansas history. The war exacerbated sectional and cultural divisions and engendered personal animosities that continued long after the fighting had ended. While slavery was the underlying cause of the conflict, Arkansans went to war for a variety of reason—to fight for what they saw as the "Southern way of life," to defend homes and families, to affirm their manhood, to seek excitement away from the often-dreary routine of farm or small-town life, or, in the case of black Arkansans, to fight for their freedom. Initially most went because they wanted to; because war was the great adventure for a young man in the nineteenth century. Most had never been in battle before, and many had never ventured more than a few miles from the place where they were born. They shared a romanticized view of war that would quickly be shattered by the boredom and disease of camp life and the horrors of the battlefield. What began with parades and stirring speeches in 1861 would end in injury and death for thousands of young Arkansas men and unimaginable hardships for those parents, sweethearts, wives, and children who remained at home. See plate 28 following page 270.

A Call to Arms: The War in 1861

The Arkansas secession convention remained in session through June 3, but the near unanimity that had characterized the secession vote soon disappeared. Many old-line Whigs, who had composed the Unionist element before Sumter, joined with their former enemies, the Family Democrats, to pass a series of measures including the legalization of banking, the preparation of a new state constitution, and the reapportionment of the state senate. They also reduced the governor's term from four years to two and placed the state militia under the control of a three-man board (of which the governor was a member) rather than under the direction of the governor alone. These last two measures were a direct slap at Governor Rector, whom many conservatives had long distrusted and whom Family Democrats had never forgiven for his "betrayal" in 1860.

But there was more at work here than personal animosity toward the governor. Both the conservative Whigs and the Dynasty Democrats were determined to ensure that radical secessionist elements did not take control of the convention. *Gazette* editor

Danley had written to a friend, "I think the conservative men of the convention should take charge of the affairs of the state and prevent the wild secessionists from taking us to the Devil." The five-man Arkansas delegation to the Confederate Congress was headed by Family stalwart Robert Ward Johnson, but the other four men had been Unionists before Sumter. The convention pointedly rejected Hindman's attempt to join the Confederate congress. As James Woods has noted, "The Whig-Dynasty leaders simply did not want change to get out of hand, so they took control of the new government. Thus the revolution against the Union would not become a revolution at home."

A more serious challenge to state unity arose in the mountainous regions in the north-central part of the state where opposition to secession remained strong. By late 1861 a group of citizens from Searcy, Izard, Carroll, Fulton, Marion, and Van Buren counties in north-central Arkansas formed what may have been the first organized resistance group in the Confederacy. The Arkansas Peace Society was a clandestine organization whose members pledged to resist the war effort. Local citizens or Confederate authorities quickly rounded up many members of the society. Seventy-eight were chained together in pairs and marched under guard to Little Rock where they were given the choice of enlisting in the Confederate army for the duration of the war or being tried for treason. Some of those arrested later were given a similar choice. Most chose the former, but opposition to Confederate authority continued in the region throughout the war. Other Arkansans chose to openly oppose the Confederacy by enlisting in the Union army at the first opportunity. Despite having the third-smallest white population of any Confederate state, Arkansas provided more troops for the Federal army than any other Confederate state except Tennessee.

Arkansas Peace Society: The Arkansas Peace Society was a clandestine organization in north-central Arkansas whose members were opposed to the Confederate government and the war. Many members of the group were arrested and given the choice of serving in the Confederate army or being tried for treason. Most chose the former but later deserted and fought for the Union.

Outside of the northern and western regions of the state, however, many Arkansans greeted secession with a burst of enthusiasm. A Little Rock volunteer artillery company fired a salute from the statehouse grounds, and thousands of young men from around the state rushed to enlist. Many came as a unit from local communities, armed only with old flintlocks, squirrel guns, or shotguns, and with a prominent local citizen in command. Some of the more affluent even brought along a slave to tend to their food and clothing. Their unit names were designed to reflect their hometowns or home counties as well as their courage and enthusiasm—the Camden Knights, Hempstead Hornets, Polk County Invincibles, Chicot Rebels. Historian James Willis has written that no other state had a larger proportion of military-age men fight for the Confederacy than Arkansas. Helena, whose 1860 white population numbered slightly over a thousand, contributed six generals to the Confederate cause including Patrick Cleburne, generally considered to be one of the best divisional commanders in the Confederate service.

Many of the new enlistees thought that if the war came at all it would be glorious, brief, and victorious. The events of February and April 1861 seemed to confirm those notions. Had not a hastily assembled band of volunteers compelled the surrender of the arsenal in Little Rock without firing a shot? And had not federal troops at Fort Smith abandoned their post and fled before the advance of the Arkansas militia? Adoring crowds cheered the young warriors as they marched, and local leaders made stirring orations. "We, who were to represent them in the war, received far more adulation than was good for us," noted young Henry Morton Stanley (who would find international fame a decade later in his search for the famed African explorer David Livingstone). "The popular praise turned our young heads giddy, and anyone who doubted that we were the sanest, bravest, and most gallant boys in the world, would have been in personal danger! Unlike the Spartans, there was no modesty in the estimate of our valour."

Unfortunately that valor was not matched by experience or knowledge of the military arts. An officer sent to the state to evaluate military preparedness and training reported to the Confederate secretary of war, "Arkansas has less the appearance of a military organization than any people I ever yet knew." The enthusiasm of enlistment soon gave way to the boredom of camp life and drill. "The idea of wearing out my strength and spirits in the monotonous routine of camp life is far from being agreeable," one soldier wrote. "If I could shoot a few Yankees, I would be perfectly content to go home." But camp life brought more than monotony and boredom. As the young men from isolated communities gathered in large numbers, disease ravaged their ranks. Hundreds died of measles, mumps, typhoid fever, pneumonia, or diarrhea long before they ever had a chance to fire a shot in anger.

Trans-Mississippi Theater: The area of Civil War operations west of the Mississippi River.

Strategically, Arkansas was critical to the Confederate war effort in the Trans-Mississippi Theater. Without Arkansas, the Confederacy could not hope to maintain its tenuous hold on the Indian Territory to the west or to control western Louisiana to the south. But even more important, without Arkansas as a base of operations, there was little hope of claiming the critical slave state of Missouri for the Confederacy. However, these factors seemed to be lost on the Confederate high command in Richmond, which viewed Arkansas primarily as a source of men and material for the fighting east of the Mississippi.

The majority of Arkansans who signed on to fight for the Confederacy in 1861 were quickly inducted into the regular Confederate army and shipped east of the Mississippi River. The First Arkansas Infantry under the command of former state legislator and Mexican War veteran James Fagan was present at the First Battle of Bull Run in July 1861, though the unit was not engaged in the actual fighting. Arkansas soldiers would take part in most of the war's major engagements including the battles of Shiloh, Vicksburg, Gettysburg, Chickamauga, Atlanta, and Franklin.

The first Arkansas troops to see action were those in northwest Arkansas who joined a force of Texas and Louisiana troops under former Texas Ranger Ben McCulloch in June 1861. McCulloch, the first general Confederate officer in Arkansas, had been commissioned a brigadier general in the Confederate army in May 1861 and given the task of keeping Federal forces out of Arkansas and the Indian Territory. That same month Federal forces had abandoned all their posts in the Indian Territory, but Confederate authorities were still concerned about the possibility of an invasion of the region from Kansas, either by regular Union troops or by marauding bands of Kansas jayhawkers, which would establish a strong Federal threat on the Confederacy's (and Arkansas's) back door. The cooperation of the various tribes in the Indian Territory, particularly the so-called Five Civilized Tribes (Cherokee, Choctaw, Chickasaw, Creek, and Seminole) would be critical to the defense of the region. Accordingly in May 1861 the Confederate government sent Albert Pike as special agent to the Indians west of Arkansas.

Five Civilized Tribes: Name given by whites to the Cherokees, Choctaws, Chickasaws, Creeks, and Seminoles. Their cooperation with the Confederacy was considered critical to the defense of the Indian Territory.

Pike's task was made easier by the fact that some members of all the tribes were slave owners and by the fact that few of the Indians had any affection for or real allegiance to the United States Government. By August 1, 1861, Pike had concluded treaties with the Choctaws, Chickasaws, Creeks, and Seminoles that cemented an alliance between the tribes and the Confederacy, provided for the raising of Indian troops for Confederate service, and guaranteed that all money due them under laws and treaties with the United States would be paid by the Confederate government. The treaties also specified that Indian troops would not be asked to serve outside the Indian Territory without their consent.

The only group that Pike had failed to win over also happened to be the most powerful of the five tribes—the Cherokees. Because of the tribe's importance and because of its location just across the Arkansas border north of Fort Smith, Arkansas authorities were most anxious to conclude a treaty with the Cherokees. But tribal politics made such negotiations difficult. In December 1835 a small group who advocated removal west of the Mississippi had signed the Treaty of New Echota with the federal government, surrendering claims to tribal land in the southeast. The majority of the tribe opposed removal, and the action created a serious division between them and the members of the so-called Treaty Party. Over ten years of bitterness and violence followed, but in 1846 the two factions had signed a treaty that recognized one government for the Cherokee Nation, with John Ross, the leading opponent of removal, as the tribe's principal chief.

Pike's first mission as special commissioner had been to the Cherokee capital at Tahlequah to visit with Ross, but the Cherokee leader had steadfastly resisted Pike's offers of an alliance with the Confederacy. While Ross clung to a policy of neutrality, another group of Cherokees led by Stand Watie signed on to fight for the Confederacy. In addition to Watie's Cherokees, by the fall of 1861 the Confederacy had a force of fourteen hundred mounted Indian warriors from the Choctaw, Chickasaw, Creek, and Seminole tribes in the field supported by five hundred white soldiers.

As summer drifted into fall, the pressure on Ross grew. He and his Cherokee followers were increasingly isolated in the Indian Territory, surrounded by Indian soldiers

Confederate general and former Missouri governor Sterling Price has been called by one historian "the central figure in the Civil War west of the Mississippi." *Courtesy of the Arkansas History Commission.*

from the other tribes who had sworn allegiance to the Confederacy. Events in Missouri would soon help convince him to change his mind.

When Ben McCulloch was appointed to command in Arkansas and the Indian Territory, his orders were to remain on Confederate soil and adopt a defensive stance. But in August 1861 McCulloch decided to move his command, including one regiment from Arkansas, into southwest Missouri to join a force of Missouri Confederates under the command of former Missouri governor Sterling Price. Price was being fiercely pursued by a Federal army under the command of Brig. Gen. Nathaniel Lyon. When McCulloch's reinforcements swelled Price's army to almost eleven thousand men, he turned to meet his pursuer.

The two armies met at Wilson's Creek, twelve miles below Springfield, on the morning of August 10. The resulting battle was one of the bloodiest small battles of the war. Federal forces suffered over twelve hundred casualties; the aggressive General Lyon, one of the early Union heroes of the war, was killed; and the Yankees were forced to retreat back toward their supply base at Rolla, Missouri. The battle had also been costly for the Confederates. Of the eleven thousand Rebels engaged, twelve hundred were killed, wounded, or missing. For many of the two thousand Arkansas soldiers involved, Wilson's Creek ended forever the notion of war as a romantic endeavor.

The victory at Wilson's Creek, combined with the news of the Rebel victory at Manassas, Virginia, in July and continued pressure from within the Indian Territory, persuaded Cherokee principal chief John Ross to enter into a treaty of alliance with the Confederacy. Despite the treaties, however, the allegiance of the members of the Five Civilized Tribes would remain divided throughout the war. Eventually over twelve thousand Native Americans would serve in the Confederate army, while another six thousand would fight with Federal forces. (John Ross was captured by Union forces in the summer of 1862 and spent the remainder of the war in Washington, D.C., and Philadelphia attempting to explain his short-lived alliance with the Confederacy to federal authorities. Three of his sons, three grandsons, and three nephews served with Union forces during the war.)

The victorious Confederate commanders at Wilson's Creek soon fell out over what strategy to pursue next. To Price's consternation, McCulloch withdrew his command into northwest Arkansas. Price pursued the retreating Yankees. He reoccupied Springfield and then set out for the Missouri River, forcing the surrender of the Federal garrison at Lexington just west of Kansas City and spreading panic among Missouri Unionists. But, as historian James McPherson has noted, Price soon "learned the difference between an invasion and a raid." More than half his army left him either to return home to harvest their crops or to act as bushwhackers. The popular uprising he had hoped for never materialized, and, short of men and supplies, Price began to retreat toward the southwest corner of the state.

When McCulloch's Arkansas troops returned to their camps in northwest Arkansas, they were met by Thomas Hindman, now a general in the Confederate army, who urged them to immediately transfer into the regular Confederate service. They understood that this meant leaving the state, and most refused. Whole companies disbanded and went home. The harsh realities of war quickly dampened much of the martial ardor of the previous spring. By the fall, volunteering fell off dramatically statewide.

The Confederate command structure in Arkansas was also changing. Confederate authorities in Richmond, Virginia, had reached the conclusion that relations between McCulloch and Price had deteriorated to the point where neither could effectively serve under the other. They sent Earl Van Dorn, a Mississippian and a longtime friend of Jefferson Davis, to take command over both in what was to be styled the Military District of the Trans-Mississippi. Van Dorn had West Point credentials, but he was reckless, and he lacked a real understanding of the situation in the Trans-Mississippi. He established his headquarters at Pocahontas in northeast Arkansas because he intended to launch an invasion of southeast Missouri in the spring of 1862. "I must have St. Louis," he boldly proclaimed in a letter to his wife, "then Huzza!" Events in northwest Arkansas soon forced Van Dorn to alter his plans.

From Pea Ridge to Prairie Grove: The War in 1862

In mid-January 1862, twelve thousand Federal troops under Brig. Gen. Samuel Curtis moved against Price, forcing him to abandon his base at Springfield, Missouri, and retreat down the Telegraph Road, the primary route between southwest Missouri and northwest Arkansas. Curtis was a fifty-six-year-old West Point graduate and Mexican War veteran who had worked as a civil engineer and railroad promoter in civilian life. He had helped found the Republican Party in Iowa and in 1856 was elected to Congress where he was a strong supporter of Abraham Lincoln and a staunch opponent of slavery and secession. Although Curtis had limited experience, he would become the most successful Union field commander west of the Mississippi River.

Despite freezing winter weather, Curtis relentlessly pursued the retreating Rebels, and advance elements of his army skirmished repeatedly with Price's rear guard. On February 16, 1862, one such skirmish spilled across Big Sugar Creek into Arkansas. This brief engagement near Pott's Hill was the first battle on Arkansas soil in the Civil War. The following morning the Union army invaded Arkansas, its band blaring patriotic music. It was barely nine months since the vote for secession. The Confederates fell back before the Federals' advance, ransacking and burning much of Fayetteville before finally halting in the Boston Mountains. Curtis, his supply lines dangerously extended, halted his pursuit and dispersed his forces into two large camps—one just west of Bentonville and the other at Cross Hollow (between the present-day towns of Springdale and Rogers).

Gen. Samuel R. Curtis led federal forces to victory at the Battle of Pea Ridge in March 1862. The battle helped secure Missouri for the Union. *Courtesy of J. N. Heiskell Collection/ UALR Archives and Special Collections.*

The Federal invasion disrupted any notion Van Dorn had for a spring invasion of southeast Missouri. Instead, he hastened to the Boston Mountains to take personal command of Confederate forces, reaching there on March 2. He wanted to regain the initiative as soon as possible and quickly planned a surprise attack on Curtis. He sent a message to Albert Pike in the Indian Territory ordering him to move with his Indian troops to a rendezvous point at Bentonville, and on March 4 Van Dorn's army, some sixteen thousand strong and supported by sixty-five cannon, moved out of the Boston Mountains and headed north. It was, historian William Shea notes, "the largest and best-equipped Confederate military force ever assembled in the Trans-Mississippi," enjoying a numerical advantage over Union forces in both men and guns. Van Dorn hoped to impose himself between Curtis's divided forces and defeat them in detail. If he could score a decisive victory, the road to Missouri would be wide open. But by the time his troops arrived at Bentonville on March 6, Curtis had been alerted to the Rebel advance and had concentrated his army in a strong defensive position on high ground overlooking Little Sugar Creek.

Van Dorn now faced a dilemma. The three-day march in freezing weather had exhausted his army, and a straight frontal assault against such a strongly defended position would be suicidal. But a retreat would cost him the initiative and render his proposed invasion of Missouri untenable. He decided on a bold plan. He would send his army on a night march around the Federals' right flank and behind a rocky hill called Big Mountain to reappear along the Telegraph Road in the Federal rear. Curtis would be cut off from his lines of supply and his strong position rendered useless. On paper the plan was a good one, but the harsh winter weather and the deplorable condition of his men squandered much of the tactical advantage that Van Dorn had sought. Hundreds of exhausted, hungry soldiers fell by the wayside during the night. By morning on March 7, Price's division had reached the Telegraph Road, but much of McCulloch's command was strung out all the way back to Little Sugar Creek, its progress slowed by barricades of trees that Curtis's troops had felled across the roadway.

Fearful that the remainder of his command would not reach Elkhorn Tavern in time, Van Dorn ordered McCulloch's division to take a shortcut around the front of Big Mountain. The two elements would unite around noon at a stagecoach stop named Elkhorn Tavern along a broad plateau called Pea Ridge. Unfortunately for the Rebels, Federal patrols detected the Confederate movement. Curtis launched separate attacks on the two converging wings of the Confederate force, one on each side of Big Mountain. Meanwhile he began the Herculean task of turning his army 180 degrees to face the threat from the rear.

Sharp engagements soon broke out along both ends of Big Mountain. To the southwest, McCulloch's men had the better of the early fighting, as his cavalry quickly overran the small force that Curtis had sent against him. Pike's Cherokees drove off two isolated companies of Federal cavalry, and a few of the Indians killed, scalped, and mutilated some of the Union soldiers before being driven off by Federal artillery. Though he was not responsible for the atrocities by his Indian troops, Pike received the blame, and the incident left a blemish on his reputation for the remainder of his life. See plate 29 following page 270.

Despite their early success, events soon took a disastrous turn for the Rebels. The disaster began when McCulloch was killed by a volley fired by a company of Federal infantry as he rode forward to survey the field during a brief lull in the fighting. Before the day was over, a second Confederate general was killed and a third captured. The leaderless Rebels drifted away from the battlefield. To the southeast of Big Mountain, Van Dorn and Price pressed the outnumbered Federals hard but were driven back by artillery and the fierce determination of Curtis's soldiers. See plate 30 following page 270. During the night of March 7–8, both sides consolidated their forces. A portion of McCulloch's command joined Price and Van Dorn near Elkhorn Tavern, while to the south, Curtis gathered his forces along Telegraph Road. On the morning of March 8, Curtis waited for Van Dorn to renew his attack of the previous evening. But it soon became obvious that the Rebels were not coming. Van Dorn was dangerously low on ammunition, and his supply train was still at Little Sugar Creek over ten miles away.

Curtis now seized the initiative. For two hours he pounded the Rebel lines with twenty-seven cannon. Then at ten o'clock he sent ten thousand troops toward Elkhorn Tavern. Van Dorn realized that he could not hold and ordered a general retreat. He led the retreat himself, fleeing to the east while large numbers of his soldiers were still engaged and most of his wounded still lay on the field. The victorious Federals converged on Elkhorn Tavern where their commander saluted them, waving his hat and shouting, "Victory! Victory!" Van Dorn had frittered away his splendid opportunity and suffered at least two thousand casualties in the process. Union losses numbered almost fourteen hundred killed, wounded, and missing. In the days following the battle, hundreds of starving Confederate soldiers drifted away from the army and went home. See plate 31 following page 270.

The Battle of Pea Ridge was one of the most significant battles in the entire Civil War, and it marked a dramatic turning point in the war in Arkansas. Missouri remained securely in Union hands, and the Confederacy in Arkansas suffered a defeat from which it would never fully recover. For Arkansas Confederates, the aftermath of the battle was even more disastrous than the battle itself. In response to a request from Gen. P. G. T. Beauregard, Van Dorn transferred the remainder of his army across the Mississippi River to Corinth, Mississippi, taking not only the bulk of able-bodied soldiers, but animals, equipment, arms, and ammunition. His actions left Arkansas virtually defenseless, and Union forces soon took advantage of the situation.

Curtis had fallen back to Missouri until it was clear that Van Dorn's destination was Mississippi and not Missouri. On April 29 he reentered Arkansas near Salem, reaching Batesville on May 2. On May 4, a separate Federal force occupied Jacksonport about twenty-five miles to the southeast. The two Federal forces combined and began to move toward Little Rock, one hundred miles to the south. The capital city's fall seemed certain. On June 2 the *New York Herald's* banner headline announced "Capture of the Capital of Arkansas," noting that Curtis's army was "in full possession of the city," and that "[t]he Arkansas State legislature has scattered, and the governor fled the State." The headline was premature, but the *Herald's* report of the governor's departure was correct.

An alarmed and outraged Governor Rector had, in fact, packed up the state archives and fled, although only to Hot Springs, not Mississippi as the *Herald* reported. From there he fired off an angry letter to President Davis, pleading for immediate assistance and threatening to secede from the Confederacy if help was not forthcoming. Unbeknown to Rector and other Arkansas Confederates, however, the steam was quickly going out of the Federal offensive. Curtis had been ordered to send ten regiments east of the Mississippi to join Federal forces in southern Tennessee, reducing his force to about twelve thousand men, and his supply line back to his base at Rolla, Missouri, was stretched dangerously thin. Though Curtis could not know it, Texas cavalry units were arriving in the Little Rock area. The Texans were on their way to duty east of the Mississippi, but they were quickly commandeered by Confederate authorities and sent north to oppose the Federal advance.

By mid-May Rebel units were attacking Federal foraging parties. The Federal commander realized that his situation was deteriorating. He withdrew to the north bank of the White River at Batesville and asked his superiors to send supplies from Memphis via the Mississippi, Arkansas, and White rivers to his beleaguered command. He soon decided to abandon his plans to seize Little Rock, however, and instead marched his army down the north bank of the White River to meet the relief flotilla halfway. When he failed to make contact with the supply ships at Clarendon, he turned his army eastward toward the Mississippi River town of Helena.

As the Federal army moved it altered the nature of the war in Arkansas, transforming it from a contest of army against army into a "total war" designed to destroy anything that might be of use to the Rebels and to weaken civilian morale. Completely cut off from its base of supply, the army was totally dependent on forage and provisions from the surrounding countryside. Federal soldiers plundered barns and private residences, seizing livestock, food, and anything else they needed or wanted. They burned public buildings and private homes, bringing the horrors of war home to the civilian population. "I am roaming the wilds of Arkansas, and desolating the country as we pass," one Yankee soldier wrote. "We make a clean thing of almost everything as we pass along, in the way of forage, both for man and beast." An Iowa soldier added, "Fields all burned out, houses, barns, cotton-gins, and fences burned. . . . No white men to be found. Women crying but makes little impression on us."

Total war: Strategy of warfare that was designed to consume or destroy anything that might be of use to the enemy and to weaken civilian morale by bringing the war home to noncombatants as well as the enemy army.

The Union army's march transformed the war in another way as well. As the blue-clad soldiers moved through the Delta, slaves fled from nearby plantations to follow them. The Emancipation Proclamation was still months away, but black Arkansans along the line of march were not inclined to wait for an official proclamation. The Union army was their ticket to freedom, and thousands rushed to embrace it. Unlike most Federal commanders in other theaters, Curtis made no effort to return them to their masters.

His Midwestern soldiers felt that they were fighting to preserve the Union rather than to end slavery, and some, if not most, had been sympathetic to slavery when the war began. For many, however, their first face-to-face encounter with the institution changed their thinking. An Illinois officer wrote home, "Now I have witnessed the unnaturalness of slavery with my own eyes and with disgust." Another noted, "I am not yet quite an Abolitionist, but am fast becoming one."

With the Federal threat to the capital at least temporarily removed, the governor returned to Little Rock in late May. Meanwhile, in an attempt to bolster its sagging fortunes in Arkansas, Confederate authorities sent Thomas Hindman back to the state as commander of the Military District of the Trans-Mississippi. Early in May Hindman had been promoted to major general, completing a meteoric rise from the rank of colonel in less than a year. His courage, organizational ability, and zeal were unquestioned, but all the talents he possessed would be tested in his new command. "I found here almost nothing," Hindman remarked on reaching Little Rock at the end of May. "Nearly everything of value was taken away by General Van Dorn."

What he lacked in men and material, however, Hindman made up in fanatical devotion to the cause. For many, the strident words of the previous spring were hollow rhetorical flourishes, but not for Hindman. "I have come to drive out the invaders," he announced, "or perish in the attempt." In the weeks that followed, Hindman assumed dictatorial powers, declaring martial law and strictly enforcing the conscription act. In an attempt to slow the advance of the Federal army, he ordered Arkansans along the Yankees' line of march to burn their cotton and other crops, drive off their livestock, and poison their wells. In addition he authorized the use of so-called partisan rangers, bands of guerrillas whose purpose was ostensibly to stage hit-and-run raids on detached Federal units and harass its lines of supply.

Hindman's order gave legal sanction to a brutal and merciless guerrilla conflict that historian Daniel Sutherland has called "the real war" in Arkansas. Some of the "Partisan

Rangers" were legitimate guerrilla fighters, strongly dedicated to defending the state against the northern invaders. Their actions seriously disrupted Federal operations in Arkansas, tied down large numbers of enemy troops, and compelled Union forces to employ harsh countermeasures. But many of the "partisans" were little more than armed bandits whose only causes were self-aggrandizement and the settling of personal grudges. They preyed not only on the Yankees but on civilians of all political persuasions and contributed greatly to the breakdown of law and order in the state.

Thomas Carmichael Hindman, Arkansas politician and military leader. *Walter J. Lemke Paper, Series 3, Box 3. Number 483. Special Collections Division, University of Arkansas Libraries, Fayetteville.*

Hindman's tactics failed to halt the progress of Curtis's army, but they did help keep Little Rock out of Federal hands for another year. The Federal army entered Helena without opposition on July 12, followed by thousands of former slaves (known to the Union soldiers as "contraband"), and the river town quickly became a Union supply base and a port for the Federal riverine fleet. Adding insult to injury, Curtis established his headquarters in Thomas Hindman's house and freed his slaves.

Guerrilla warfare: A type of irregular warfare in which small bands of combatants confront a larger force by using greater mobility and employing tactics such as ambushes and hit-and-run raids.

Hindman could take some solace from the fact that Curtis was not occupying his new residence in Little Rock. In his brief stint as overall commander of the Trans-Mississippi, Hindman's draconian actions had three major effects—they created a viable fighting force almost out of thin air; they prevented, at least for the time being, the capture of the capital; and they earned Hindman an enmity from many of his fellow Arkansans that they had previously reserved only for the Yankees. Camden's John Brown condemned Hindman's "tyrannical acts of military power" and "military despotism," and Albert Pike railed against Hindman's "substitution of despotism" for constitutional government. So great was the outcry against Hindman that Confederate president Jefferson Davis was forced to demote him and reorganize the department.

Contraband: Name given to former slaves who left their plantations and farms to follow the Union army to freedom as it marched through their region.

The political situation in the state was also about to change. After taking the state out of the Union, the secession convention had rewritten the state's constitution, including a provision reducing the governor's term from four years to two. Governor Rector realized that this action was little more than an attempt by his enemies in the Family to punish him. After attempting unsuccessfully to have the state supreme court set aside the provision, Rector announced as a candidate for reelection.

His chief opposition was Harris Flanagin, an attorney and a former Whig from Clark County. Flanagin had been a delegate to the February and May state secession conventions and had voted in favor of secession at both. After the ordinance of secession was passed, he left the convention to accept command of Company E of the Second Arkansas Mounted Rifles. In the reorganization that followed Pea Ridge, Flanagin was elected regimental colonel, and the Second Arkansas was transferred east of the Mississippi River where it became part of the Army of Tennessee. His candidacy for governor was backed by an unlikely coalition of prewar enemies including Thomas Hindman and the Family's Elias Conway.

Since Flanagin was serving in the army outside the state, it was impossible for him to campaign, and historians still debate whether or not he even wanted the position. But it also made it difficult for Governor Rector to attack him. In a campaign carried out largely in the press, the Rector camp could do little more than charge that Flanagin was actually a Yankee Irishman whose real name was O'Flanagin. The appeal did little to sway voters. In the October election, Flanagin received 18,187 votes to Rectors 7,419 and was inaugurated as Arkansas's seventh governor on November 14, 1862.

Though he tried to address some of the serious issues confronting the state, the absence of money precluded any significant action. The state had suspended tax collections and attempted to finance the war effort by issuing paper bonds. The plan had failed disastrously, leaving the state government with few funds to confront the crisis. Most of the major decisions in the state would devolve on the military authorities. Unfortunately for Arkansas, the military leaders sent to the state by the Richmond government were unequal to the task.

In the summer of 1862 Confederate president Davis sent his old friend Maj. Gen. Theophilus Holmes to take command in Arkansas. Holmes was a fifty-eight-year-old North Carolinian and West Point graduate who had compiled a distinguished record in the Mexican War. His Civil War service, however, was marred by controversy and failure. He had been so ineffective in the Eastern Theater that he was relieved of command, and he had requested to be dismissed from the service. But instead Davis put him in charge of one of the most difficult theaters of the war. Holmes lacked the manpower, animals, and supplies to effectively operate in such a far-reaching theater, Richmond was constantly requesting that he send additional troops east of the river to assist in the defense of Vicksburg, and, to compound his problems, he was now in charge of Hindman.

Perhaps nowhere in the entire war did two such disparate personalities attempt to forge a working relationship. Hindman was belligerent, impulsive, and decisive, and he believed that the best way to defend Arkansas was to take the war to the enemy. Holmes was timid, indecisive, and so plagued by poor health and premature old age that his troops soon gave him the unflattering nickname of "Granny." Remarkably, despite their differences and the adverse conditions, they soon had another viable fighting force in the field.

In late 1862, Holmes placed roughly half his troops at various locations along the Arkansas and White rivers to counter any Federal invasion coming from Helena or elsewhere along the Mississippi River. The remainder he placed in northwest Arkansas to deter any Federal invasion coming out of southwest Missouri. These latter troops were under Hindman's personal direction, and the fiery commander wasted little time in lobbying his new superior officer for permission to use them against the Federals.

In October 1862 three divisions of Federal troops invaded northwest Arkansas and briefly occupied Fayetteville and Bentonville. In early November, two of the three divisions returned to Springfield leaving only one division under Brig. Gen. James Blunt in northwest Arkansas. The aptly named Blunt was an aggressive, no-nonsense amateur soldier from Kansas whose zeal for the offensive matched that of Hindman. That very aggressiveness had left him deep in northwest Arkansas and dangerously isolated from the remainder of his army.

By early December, Blunt was at Cane Hill, nearly one hundred miles from Springfield but only about thirty miles from Hindman. The opportunity was too great for the aggressive Hindman to pass up. He believed that if he moved quickly and with stealth, he could overwhelm Blunt's smaller force before Federal reinforcements could arrive from Springfield. The road to Missouri would then be open to him. The ever-cautious Holmes initially rejected the plan but relented when Hindman assured him that he would return to Fort Smith as soon as the operation was concluded.

Hindman sent a small cavalry detachment across the Boston Mountains as a diversion and on December 3 the main body of eleven thousand men and twenty-two cannon moved out and proceeded slowly northward. Hindman hoped to swing undetected around Blunt's left flank and strike him from the east. His army was composed largely of raw recruits and reluctant conscripts and was short of ammunition and rations, but it was still a potent force. The fact that there was any army at all was a tribute to Hindman's brilliance as an organizer, recruiter, and administrator. In these areas he had few peers on either side anywhere in the war.

Blunt was aware of his own vulnerable position, but retreat was not in his nature. Rather than fall back to the safety of Missouri, he took a strong defensive position at Cane Hill, and, on December 2, he telegraphed the two divisions at Springfield to march immediately to join him. On December 6, Hindman successfully slipped undetected to the east of Cane Hill only to learn that night that more Federal troops were moving toward him down the Telegraph Road from Springfield. The command of these two Federal divisions had passed to Francis J. Herron, who earlier had been wounded and captured while making a courageous stand against Rebel infantry at Pea Ridge (an action for which he won the Medal of Honor). In a truly incredible feat, about one-half of Herron's seven thousand troops covered the 110 miles from Springfield to Fayetteville in only three days, arriving on December 6 and clashing with advance elements of Hindman's cavalry.

Hindman realized that he was in a dangerous position, caught between two Federal forces whose combined strength roughly equaled his own. If he attacked Blunt as he had planned, he exposed his rear to an attack from Herron. If he turned and attacked

Herron, he suffered the same danger from Blunt. After weighing his options, he moved to high ground beyond the Illinois River about ten miles west of Fayetteville, established a defensive position near the Prairie Grove Presbyterian Church, and waited for the Yankees to make the next move. He did not have long to wait. See plate 32 following page 270.

Herron had less than half as many men as Hindman, and his troops were exhausted from their long march. Still he did not hesitate. The Federal soldiers crossed the Illinois River on the morning of December 7 and opened an artillery barrage on the Confederate position with twenty-four rifled cannon. As it had at Pea Ridge, the superiority of the Federal artillery would play an important role in the outcome of the battle. Around noon, Herron ordered a portion of his troops to assault the Confederate right, where his artillery had done its greatest damage and where it appeared the Rebels were retreating. The blue-clad soldiers charged forward and crested the hill but were met by a withering barrage of Rebel rifle fire that decimated their ranks and sent the survivors scurrying back down the slope. A Confederate counterattack was driven back by Federal artillery. See plate 33 following page 270.

The stalemate continued until the early afternoon when Hindman decided to take advantage of his numerical superiority and longer lines to sweep down the hill and envelop the Federal right. A decisive Confederate victory loomed when Blunt, alerted by the rumble of artillery, arrived from Cane Hill. His arrival extended the Federal line, equalized the odds, and continued the stalemate. Despite intense fighting that lasted until dark, neither side could dislodge the other or gain any significant advantage. Because they still held their position atop the hill when the fighting ended, the Battle of Prairie Grove was a tactical victory for the Confederates. But during the night of December 7–8, Hindman, his ammunition depleted, withdrew his hungry and exhausted soldiers from the field and began a long, slow retreat to Van Buren, and then on down the Arkansas River to Little Rock. A Federal officer later recalled, "For forces engaged, there was no more stubborn fight and no greater casualties in any battle of the war than at Prairie Grove, Arkansas." Each side suffered over 1,250 casualties, and Confederate losses were compounded by widespread desertions.

The sights and smells of the battlefield etched themselves indelibly in the minds of all who fought there. Wounded men, too weak to reach the safety of their own lines, crawled into bales of hay for warmth. When the firing ignited the bales, many were too weak to crawl out and burned to death. The day after the battle, hogs from area farms feasted on the carcasses of dead soldiers. Wounded Confederate soldiers were taken to Cane Hill, wounded Federals to Fayetteville. A prominent Fayetteville citizen, William Baxter, visited one of the town's makeshift hospital where, he reported,

> the entire floor was so thickly covered with mangled and bleeding men that it was difficult to thread my way among them; some were mortally wounded, the life fast escaping through a ghastly hole in the breast; the limbs of others were shattered and useless, the faces of others so disfigured as to seem scarcely human; the bloody bandages, hair clotted, and garments stained with blood, and all these with but little cov-

> ering, and no other couch than the straw, with which the floor was strewed, made up a scene more pitiable and horrible than I had ever conceived possible before.

Baxter noted that twenty other buildings offered similar scenes.

At the end of December Blunt led eight thousand men across the frigid Boston Mountains and raided Van Buren. The Federals seized and burned four steamboats, destroyed badly needed Confederate supplies, and looted local businesses before returning to their camps at Prairie Grove and Cane Hill. The Van Buren raid was a fitting end to a year of Confederate disaster and Union success in Arkansas. In two major battles and numerous smaller skirmishes, Federal forces had established a firm foothold in northwest Arkansas and seriously undermined the Confederate state government's control over the region of the state north of the Arkansas River. A Federal army had occupied Helena, and Union gunboats were now a common sight on the Mississippi River in eastern Arkansas. By the end of the year, Confederate forces in Arkansas, unable to match the Federals in men and supplies, turned increasingly to guerrilla warfare and cavalry raids.

The Federal invasion also disrupted the day-to-day operations of government and society. William Shea has noted, "Dozens of county and local governments ceased to function as judges, sheriffs, clerks, and other officeholders fled or failed to carry out their duties. Taxes went uncollected, lawsuits went unheard, and complaints went unanswered. With courts closed and jails open, the thin veneer of civilization quickly eroded. Incidents of murder, torture, rape, theft, and wanton destruction increased dramatically."

An incident near the site of the Prairie Grove battle confirms Shea's observation. After the two armies moved on, area residents were left at the mercy of guerrillas and bandits. A group of men professing to be Confederate partisans visited the William Morton home on the western edge of the battlefield. After gaining the family's confidence, they seized William Morton and tied him up. "Old man," one threatened, "it's not your politics I care for, it's your money, and we're going to have it." When Morton refused to reveal the location of the money, the men heated two shovels in the family fireplace and began burning the bottoms of his feet. Morton's daughter Nancy threw water on the shovels and on the fire, but another member of the gang pointed a pistol at her and beat her away. When Morton still refused to give up his money, the gang took him outside and threatened to hang him. Finally Morton gave in. The gang took all the money, ransacked the house, and departed. "We all then went to bed shivering with cold," Nancy Morton remembered, "afraid to make a fire."

Poor harvests in both 1861 and 1862 further exacerbated the hardships for those who remained at home. Anna Mitchell of Havana had seen both her husband and her older brother join the Confederate army, leaving no able-bodied male on the family farm. She remembered:

> We had a hard time to keep body and soul together. The women plowed the field and planted and cultivated the corn. Some women had to walk five miles to a mill to get meal for their sack of corn, and frequently there was no meal, nothing but

> bran, which they cooked and ate. . . . Mother and myself never knew one day what we have to eat or wear the next. Spinning and weaving constantly was one part of our work. When our homes began to look comfortable, the Federal raiders would come and take horses, food and clothing. We had then to begin things all over again.

To compound the family's problems, Anna's husband was killed at the Battle of Shiloh.

For the next two and a half years, the citizens of the state who lived north of the Arkansas River would experience the horrors of civil war to an extent matched by few other Americans. For many the struggle to preserve slavery and the southern way of life would quickly be overshadowed by a struggle merely to survive.

The Union Triumphant: The War in 1863

As the year 1863 began, the nature of the conflict was dramatically altered. Shortly after the Battle of Antietam (Maryland) in September 1862, President Lincoln issued his preliminary Emancipation Proclamation, which declared that slaves in those states still in rebellion on January 1, 1863, would be "then, thenceforward, and forever free." Neither Arkansas nor any other Confederate state took advantage of the president's three-month window to give up the rebellion and thus maintain the institution of slavery, but the proclamation transformed the Civil War into a crusade to end slavery as well as to preserve the Union, and it severely dimmed the prospect of European intervention on the side of the Confederacy.

The new year also found Arkansas Confederates in an increasingly desperate situation. Federal victories at Pea Ridge and Prairie Grove the previous year had helped secure Missouri for the Union and had established a Federal presence in northwest Arkansas. The seizure of Helena in July 1862 strengthened Federal control of the Mississippi River north of Vicksburg and was a constant thorn in the side of Arkansas Confederates. Van Dorn's precipitate withdrawal greatly impaired the ability of Arkansas Confederates to defend the state, and Hindman's draconian policies weakened the morale of Confederate sympathizers and alienated many who might otherwise have supported the southern cause.

In spite of all this, Union forces were still a long way from regaining control of Arkansas. Seizing certain areas of northwest Arkansas proved to be easier than holding on to them. As the second full year of the war began, the region remained a battleground, and attacks from Rebel soldiers and partisans made Federal control there tenuous at best. The same was true in the eastern part of the state where Federal control in the so-called District of Eastern Arkansas was largely limited to the town of Helena. Patrols and foraging parties that ventured beyond the limits of the town were subject to frequent and often-deadly encounters with Confederate cavalry and guerrillas.

In January 1863 Richmond appointed Edmund Kirby Smith to replace the much-maligned Theophilus Holmes as commander of the Department of the Trans-Mississippi but left Holmes in charge of Arkansas. At the demand of the entire Arkansas delegation to the Confederate congress, Jefferson Davis transferred Hindman east of the Mississippi River. Hindman's removal did not bring an end to the internal divisions within Arkansas society. Rather the discontent that had simmered during his dictatorial tenure bubbled to the surface in 1863 in the form of widespread resistance to Confederate authority. A strong Unionist tradition had always existed in the mountainous regions of northwest Arkansas, but by late 1862 signs of discontent were appearing in other parts of the state as well.

Historian Carl Moneyhon has demonstrated in a recent study that resistance to Confederate authority in late 1862 and 1863 was strongest in southwest Arkansas, especially in the region south and west of the Saline River. Unlike the mountainous northwest, the southwestern part of the state had a developing plantation agriculture and a significant slave population. Most of the counties in the region had given majorities to the pro-slavery candidate John C. Breckinridge in the presidential election of 1860 and had supported secession in both state conventions in 1861. After secession the region's young men rushed to enlist in the Confederate cause. Camden alone supplied thirteen companies (thirteen hundred men or about three-fourths of the town's adult white male population in 1860) by September 1861, and fifteen hundred Union County men enlisted in Confederate service.

By the war's second winter, however, the early enthusiasm had given way to a widespread disenchantment. Holmes had taken note of this, writing in a December 1862 letter to Confederate president Jefferson Davis of "the growing disaffection to the war among the people." He attributed this disaffection to a variety of factors including a food shortage brought on by a drought the previous summer, spiraling inflation, the failure to pay or adequately provision the soldiers, and discontent with the Confederacy's conscription laws, particularly the provision which exempted one white man on each plantation for every twenty slaves. Holmes informed the president that he could not control the situation without imposing martial law.

In Camden, John Brown noted in his diary, a "good deal of excitement" in opposition to conscription, "especially on account of the exemption law, which exempts slave holders having twenty slaves." He went on to note that "some are still opposed to the war in toto. Some are unwilling to leave their families unprovided as they are[,] some have been in the army and have been dissatisfied with their treatment and the conduct of their officers." All of these factors had combined, he wrote, to create "a sprinkle of disloyalty beyond what was expected."

In late January 1863 President Davis agreed to suspend the writ of *habeas corpus*, and Holmes declared martial law on February 9. He further authorized the raising of local partisan ranger units to round up deserters and enforce the conscription laws and sent some regular army units to assist in the task. Maj. James T. Elliott, a prominent Camden resident who had been president of the Mississippi, Ouachita, and Red River Railroad before the war, was named provost marshal for the second district of Arkansas and given command of both local and regular army units.

Resistance to Confederate authority took many forms, however, and proved difficult to suppress. In January between forty and fifty draftees walked out of a conscript camp in Magnolia. February brought rumors of the formation of a secret organization dedicated to resisting conscription and advocating an end to the war and a return to the Union. Branches of the Union League sprang up in Calhoun, Clark, and Pike counties.

That same month a force of 250 mounted Confederates set out after a band of eighty-three Unionists and deserters led by an Arkadelphia Unionist named Andy Brown. Brown's band had committed a series of thefts in the Ouachita Mountains northwest of Arkadelphia. On February 15 the Confederates caught up with Brown near McGrew's Mill on the Walnut Fork of the Ouachita River about halfway between Hot Springs and Mount Ida. In the battle that ensued the Confederates inflicted about thirty-five casualties, took twenty prisoners, and captured a substantial quantity of provisions and stolen items while suffering only one man killed and five wounded. About thirty of Brown's party fled north and crossed the swollen Ouachita River. The Confederates chose not to pursue them. Three weeks after the engagement at McGrew's Mill, Brown and twenty-seven survivors reported to Col. Marcus LaRue Harrison at Fayetteville, and some of them joined the First Arkansas Infantry (Union).

In Pike County another band of dissidents launched attacks on area settlements from its base at a mountain pass at the head of the Little Missouri River. A group of area residents attacked the band's stronghold, killing some outright and capturing and hanging two of the ringleaders. In Calhoun County authorities rounded up and hanged three members of the local Union League. Confederate military courts were also set up to prosecute dissidents. Since no records were kept of these proceedings, the extent of the actions taken by these courts is impossible to assess, though some Unionists later insisted that hundreds of deserters were tried and executed by the courts.

Despite these harsh actions, dissent and resistance to authority persisted. Confederate agents sent to the region in the fall of 1863 reported that anti-Confederate sentiment had actually increased. One noted that in Columbia County there was "undoubtedly a Union sentiment prevailing among a large class of citizens here." More draconian measures followed. John Brown noted, "The military have been sent out to bring them [the dissidents] in and in some cases, some have [been] arrested & been shot or hung & others have left the country to join the enemy." A Union officer returning from the region in 1864 reported, "Every conceivable means has been used to force [the dissidents] into the rebel service; they have been hung by scores; they have been hunted down with blood hounds by the slaveholding rebels of the Red river Valley; they have been robbed of their property, chained and imprisoned." Still the resistance continued.

One area newspaper described the disloyal elements as "deserters, disaffected persons, and turbulent characters," and Confederate authorities often portrayed them as little more than jayhawkers and bandits, which some undoubtedly were. But the available evidence also indicates that a strong element of Unionism fueled the resistance to Confederate authority in the state. Several contemporary observers noted that much of the opposition was class based. Judge John Brown of Camden recorded in his diary that many of the resisters were "poor men whose families are unprovided at home," and Clark County editor Samuel M. Scott wrote to Governor Flanagin that "the cry of poor men being obliged to fight for the rich may be heard on all sides." Carl Moneyhon has concluded that "from the beginning those who fought for the Confederacy came to see themselves as poor men who were having to fight a war to benefit rich men. Their own opportunities were being squandered in a conflict that had no goal other than the protection of slavery. Their fight was not only with conscription but also with the ruling class."

This internal dissent ate away at the state's morale and caused Confederate authorities to detach badly needed troops to deal with the situation. In the meantime, the military situation in the state was deteriorating. In January John Brown noted in his diary, "The enemy destroying with fire and sword as they go in the vicinity of the Mis[sissippi] river & the people moving their negroes & stock as fast as possible." He closed his entry by remarking sarcastically, "What a beautiful thing this peaceable secession is!!"

The Confederates' situation would have taxed the abilities of a much more competent officer than Theophilus Holmes. But for all his shortcomings (and they were many), Holmes understood the importance of defending the river approach up the Arkansas to Little Rock. In late 1862, he ordered the construction of an earthen fort approximately 120 miles downriver from the capital at Arkansas Post. The Post had played an important role in the state's history since its founding in 1686 by a party of French explorers under the command of La Salle's chief lieutenant, Henri de Tonty. In the intervening 176 years since its founding, the Post had occupied several different locations. In 1862 a Union officer described it as "a small village, the capital of Arkansas County . . . situated on elevated ground, above the reach of the floods . . . surrounded by a fruitful country, abounding in cattle, corn, and cotton."

The site selected for the Confederate fort was on high ground at the head of a horseshoe bend with a commanding view of the river for over a mile in either direction. By mid-November 1862, the earthen-walled structure, known as Fort Hindman, was nearing completion. It was diamond shaped, three hundred feet on each side, and armed with three heavy and eight smaller cannon. A line of rifle pits extended westward from the fort for about a mile to a stream called Post Bayou. The garrison of approximately five thousand troops from Texas, Arkansas, and Louisiana was commanded by Brig. Gen. Thomas Churchill, a Kentuckian and Mexican War veteran, whose marriage to Ambrose Sevier's daughter, Anne, had assured him a place in the state's political elite. See plate 34 following page 270.

Churchill determined to use the Post both to protect the river approaches to Little Rock and to serve as a base of operations for harassing Union communication and supply lines on the Mississippi River. In late December, Confederate forces operating out of the Post captured an unarmed Union supply ship on the Mississippi eight miles below Napoleon and towed it back to Fort Hindman. This Rebel triumph attracted the attention of Union forces downriver near Vicksburg. Unable to crack the defenses of that "Confederate Gibraltar," Union commanders decided to deal with the threat posed by the Post.

On January 8, 1863, Union major general John McClernand loaded 32,000 infantry,

1,000 cavalry, and 40 pieces of artillery on board 60 transports and started upriver from Vicksburg, escorted by a small flotilla of rams and gunboats under the command of Admr. David D. Porter. At 5 P.M. on January 9, the Federal troops began disembarking at Nortrebe's farm about three miles below Fort Hindman. Late the following day McClernand sent the gunboats upriver to engage the fort's guns, while he began moving his troops to a plateau north of the fort. After a fierce exchange, the gunboats succeeded in silencing most of the fort's artillery. Union troops continued moving into position during the frigid night of January 10–11.

Fort Hindman had not been designed to confront such overwhelming numbers. Yet that same night, Churchill received a telegraphic dispatch from Holmes in Little Rock ordering him to "hold out till help arrived or all dead." Against such odds and with the possibility of help remote, such an order was absurd. One Texas soldier remarked, "When it comes to our number holding out against such odds it is all bosh, and if 'Granny' Holmes was down here where he could smell a little gunpowder, he would get better of the 'hold on' fit which so recently seized him at Little Rock." Nonetheless, Churchill determined to do all he could to see the order carried out or at least to hold out until nightfall when his command might cut its way through the Union lines to safety.

At 1 P.M. on January 11, the Federal gunboats once again moved upriver, pounding the fort from close range and lobbing explosive shells over the walls. Shortly after the bombardment commenced, soldiers on the far right of the Union line under the command of William Tecumseh Sherman moved forward to attack the Rebel rifle pits. Soon the whole Union line was in motion. Heavy small-arms fire from the entrenched defenders staggered and halted the advancing blue line, but by 3 P.M., Federal troops on the Union right had reached to within one hundred yards of the rifle pits, while those on the left had reached the ditch that surrounded the fort.

As Federal troops prepared for a final assault, white flags of surrender appeared along part of the Confederate line. This astonished and outraged Churchill, who had not given the order to surrender, but Union troops quickly crowded into the area where the white flags had appeared, making any further resistance futile. Reluctantly, Churchill ordered the remainder of his command to lay down their arms. He had suffered 60 killed and 75–80 wounded. His remaining 4,793 men were taken prisoner. In addition, the Confederates lost vast quantities of sorely needed arms, ammunition, and supplies. The victory had not come cheaply for the Northern army. Over a thousand men were killed, wounded, or missing. McClernand ordered the destruction of Fort Hindman and steamed with his command back to Milliken's Bend near Vicksburg.

The loss of Arkansas Post was another devastating setback for Arkansas Confederates. A Little Rock editor wrote on January 17, "The present is a dark day in the history of our State. . . . The taking of the Post is an unexpected blow to our people, and one which will be felt throughout our length and breadth, as it is the removal of the only impediment offered in our river . . . to the approaches of the gunboats."

Despite the fact that their ability to defend the state was increasingly being called into question, some Confederate commanders in Arkansas continued to think in terms of the offensive and continued to view the conquest of Missouri as their main goal. On April 16, 1863, Brig. Gen. William Cabell, a thirty-six-year-old Virginian and West Point graduate, led nine hundred Confederate cavalry north from Ozark to attack the Federal garrison occupying Fayetteville. A Federal officer described the town as "a beautiful little hamlet nestling among the foothills of the Ozark range, . . . the chief education center of the state, the home of culture, refinement, and that inborn hospitality so characteristic of the South. . . . The Public Square . . . was surrounded by stores and shops, broken only . . . by an old-fashioned tavern."

Cabell's men reached the outskirts of the town before sunrise on Saturday, April 18. He placed his two pieces of artillery on a hillside east of town and opened fire. The Rebel cavalry charged "with wild and deafening shouts" up Dickson Street toward the Federal commander's headquarters. For four hours an intense firefight raged around the headquarters house.

The Battle of Fayetteville was a microcosm of the whole war, with the First Arkansas Cavalry (Confederate) battling the First Arkansas Cavalry (Union). Around 9 A.M. the Rebels launched a desperate charge against the Union right only to run into "a galling crossfire . . . piling rebel men and horses in heaps" in front of the Federals' ordnance office on College Avenue. Unable to advance any farther, the Confederates slowly withdrew, leaving approximately seventy-five men killed, wounded, or missing.

Two days after the battle, the Federal commander received orders to move his troops to Springfield, Missouri, and, shortly thereafter, Cabell's command returned to occupy peacefully the town they had failed to take by storm. The town changed hands several times during the course of the war, and perhaps no community in the state suffered more from the ravages of war. William Baxter noted how the war had disrupted the normal patterns of life. "Schools and institutions of learning all broken up, churches abandoned, the Sabbath unnoted, every thing around, indeed, denoting a rapid lapse into barbarism, all trade at an end, nearly all travel suspended, the comforts of life nearly all gone, the absolute necessities difficult to be obtained."

Everywhere were the constant reminders of the presence or recent departure of the opposing armies. Baxter wrote, "[T]he fences had nearly all disappeared, shrubbery and fruit-trees were ruined, houses were deserted, nearly all the domestic animals killed, dead cavalry-horses lay here and there; the farms, for miles around were laid waste, the fences having been used to keep up the hundreds of campfires which were seldom permitted to go out by night or day; stables were pulled down, outbuildings burnt, and the very spirit of destruction seemed to rule the hour."

At the same time that Cabell was leaving to attack Fayetteville, another Confederate commander was preparing to embark on a more ambitious raid. John Sappington Marmaduke, the twenty-nine-year-old son of a politically prominent Missouri family, had studied at Harvard and Yale before graduating from West Point in 1857. Beginning the war as a colonel in the Missouri militia, he had, by the beginning of 1863, risen to the rank of brigadier general. Marmaduke was in many ways the very embodiment of the southern cavalier, his unquestioned courage matched only by his inflated sense of personal honor. Both characteristics would strongly affect the course of his career in Arkansas during the war.

The son of a prominent Missouri family, John Sappington Marmaduke played a key role in the Civil War in Arkansas. *Courtesy of the State Historical Society of Missouri.*

In January he had raided Springfield, Missouri, and he was convinced that a strong Confederate show of strength in Missouri would rally southern supporters there. Holmes warned Marmaduke that Missouri Confederates would be hesitant to support him unless there was some guarantee of a permanent Rebel presence in the state, but Marmaduke was not dissuaded. He convinced Holmes that a Missouri raid would replenish Confederate stores and relieve the Federal pressure on Arkansas and, perhaps, Vicksburg as well. It was a far-fetched idea, but Marmaduke was a forceful and persuasive advocate, and Holmes eventually gave in and authorized the raid.

Marmaduke left from the Eleven Points River north of Batesville on April 17 with over five thousand men, but almost twelve hundred of these had no weapons, and nine hundred had no horses. The ever-optimistic Marmaduke hoped to equip them from captured Federal supplies. He planned to strike the Union force at Bloomfield, Missouri, but after several scattered skirmishes the Federals withdrew to the fortified Union supply base at Cape Girardeau on the Mississippi River. As Marmaduke waited outside the town, unwilling to risk an assault on this strong position, his status soon changed from the hunter to the hunted. Federal soldiers steamed down the Mississippi to reinforce the garrison at Cape Girardeau, and a second Union army moved quickly from the west to support them.

Marmaduke began a hasty retreat along the military road atop Crowley's Ridge, an elevated strip of land extending south from Cape Girardeau to Helena. As he did so, two Federal armies with a combined strength of eight thousand united to pursue him. He sent a construction party ahead to build a bridge across the St. Francis River, the dividing line between Arkansas and Missouri in the "bootheel" of southeast Missouri.

During the night of May 1–2, the raiders crossed single file over the bobbing, rickety bridge and ascended the heights along the Arkansas bank known as Chalk Bluff. The horses were too heavy for the makeshift structure and were forced to attempt to swim the fast-moving stream. Many of the exhausted animals could not make it. Area residents reported that a large number of dead horses floated downstream to an old mill drift. The Confederate rear guard crossed back into Arkansas near dawn on May 2, cut the bridge supports, and watched the bridge break in two and float downstream. The Federals showed no desire to follow the raiders back into Arkansas.

Marmaduke's raid failed to reverse the Rebels' sagging fortunes in Arkansas. As spring gave way to summer, it became increasingly clear that if the Confederacy in Arkansas were to survive, it would require more than bold, ambitious failures; it would require a decisive victory, and soon. In June, General Holmes met with Sterling Price to plan for what they hoped would be just such a victory.

The object of their discussion was Helena, the Mississippi River port city located at the point where Crowley's Ridge meets the river. In 1860 Helena was a busy agricultural and commercial center 70 miles downriver from Memphis and 230 miles above Vicksburg, with a population of 1,024 white citizens and 527 black slaves. After the Union occupation in July 1862, it had become a jumping-off point for Union forces operating against Vicksburg, and its population had exploded with the addition of twenty thousand Federal troops and additional thousands of former slaves who had followed the Union army to freedom. Health and sanitary conditions were so deplorable and disease so rampant that some Union soldiers had rechristened the town "Hell-in Arkansas." But while Helena was anathema to white Union soldiers, for some former slaves, it was the starting point on the road to freedom. In April 1863 three companies of black men were inducted into the Union army forming the First Arkansas Volunteer Infantry Regiment (African Descent). By June a second such regiment had been formed.

For Confederate leaders in Arkansas, Helena was seen as the key to retaking the initiative in the state. If the town could be recaptured, the disastrous course of the war in Arkansas might be reversed, and Federal troops might have to be diverted to Helena from the ever-tightening Federal siege of Vicksburg. Should Vicksburg fall, Helena could provide the Confederacy with a much-needed strategic position on the river. When scouts informed Holmes that the departure of large numbers of Union troops for Vicksburg had seriously depleted the Federal garrison at Helena, the Confederate commander decided to attack.

But Holmes had failed to carry out any serious reconnaissance of Helena's defenses. When his army arrived outside the town, he quickly surmised that, despite its reduced garrison (roughly four thousand effective men), Helena would not be an easy conquest. The Federal commander, Benjamin M. Prentiss, had utilized the steep hills and deeply thicketed ravines around the town to great advantage. He fortified the four large hills that formed a rough semicircle around the town with artillery protected by rifle pits. Closer to town stood Fort Curtis, an earthen bastion astride the major east-west road into Helena. Finally the gunboat *USS Tyler* lay offshore, ready to move quickly to support any threatened position.

Despite serious misgivings, Holmes decided to order the attack. At a council of war on the evening of July 3, he drew up a plan for a three-pronged, coordinated advance by over 6,000 men on the following morning. General Marmaduke with 1,750 men would attack from the northwest, Gen. James Fagan, a former Arkansas legislator, would strike from the southwest with 1,300 men, and Price would lead the main body of 3,000 men against the center of the Union defenses. Holmes told his commanders to begin the attack "at daylight." See plate 35 following page 270.

Coordinated attacks were difficult under the best of circumstances, and conditions on this Fourth of July were far from ideal. Marmaduke's attack was stalled by Federal fire coming from the levee to his left. On the Rebel right, a communications problem hindered the assault. Fagan had interpreted Holmes's order to attack "at daylight" to mean first light, and he sent his men in accordingly. But when he looked to his left, Price was nowhere to be seen. The Missourian had interpreted "at daylight" to mean sunrise, and thus the main Confederate assault did not begin for another hour. The failure to coordinate the attacks allowed the Federals to concentrate their fire against individual Rebel units.

Coordinated attack: A military tactic in which various elements of an attacking force launch their assaults at the same time so that the enemy cannot concentrate its forces against any one attack.

The Confederates fought with a desperate bravery, marching uphill one noted "amid the leaden rain and iron hail." Price's attack against the center of the Federal line temporarily captured one of the hilltop strong points, but confusion, the July heat, and a withering Federal fire that seemed to come from all directions compelled Holmes to order a retreat. Before noon, the Battle of Helena was over. The Rebels retreated, leaving hundreds of dead and wounded men littering the hills around the town. They had suffered over 1,600 casualties and gained nothing. Federal casualties totaled only 239. A Wisconsin soldier summed up the battle in a letter to his father: "The general opinion here is that the enemy fought desperately and with a bravery and determination worthy of a better cause."

The devastating Confederate defeat at Helena was compounded by the news that Confederate general Robert E. Lee had been repulsed at Gettysburg, Pennsylvania, on July 3 and was retreating with heavy casualties into Virginia. Even more ominous for Arkansas Confederates was the news that the South's Mississippi River stronghold at Vicksburg had surrendered to Gen. Ulysses Grant on July 4. A Rebel soldier from Cane Hill summed up the situation in a letter to his fiancée, noting, "This department is now fully cut off from the eastern portion of the government, and we must stand or fall alone. No helping hand can be extended across the Mississippi River to aid us. . . . The varying war cloud is now growing dense and dark, but hope looms beyond."

As the late summer of 1863 approached, however, hope was an increasingly scarce commodity in Confederate Arkansas. Federal victories in the Indian Territory forced the evacuation of Fort Smith in late August. By early September, Union forces had neutralized Rebel strongholds at both ends of the Arkansas River. Only the state capital at Little Rock remained in Confederate hands. Residents of the capital were well aware of the implications of the fall of Vicksburg for their city. A local editor wrote that "Any head, with a thimble full of brains, ought to know that should that city be captured ... the state of Arkansas falls an easy prey to the combined and various columns of the enemy." Before the month of July was out, those fears proved to be well founded.

Union major general Frederick Steele, a New Yorker and a West Point classmate of Grant, arrived in Helena to take command of all Federal forces in the state and quickly set about preparing to capture Little Rock. On August 10 and 11, 1863, Steele's infantry, some six thousand strong, left Helena and headed for Clarendon on the White River where they would link up with a like number of Federal cavalry moving south from Missouri.

In Little Rock, one of Theophilus Holmes's chronic illnesses gave Sterling Price another chance to command, although this particular command at this particular time was a dubious honor. There were only eight thousand men present for duty, and many Arkansans believed that Confederate authorities in the Trans-Mississippi had written off the further defense of Arkansas in favor of establishing a new defensive line along the Red River.

While Price was under no illusions about his ability to hold Little Rock against a strong enemy force, he tackled his new job with enthusiasm, ordering out cavalry units to scout and harass the Federals, constructing a strong defensive position on the north side of the Arkansas River, and issuing an appeal to the citizens of Little Rock to rally to the city's defense. The appeal drew little response. A Confederate surgeon in Little Rock noted, "[T]he dangers now menacing her [Little Rock] kindles no patriotic fire to blaze forth and consume the invader.... Her chivalry has long since gone from her shores."

At sunrise on August 25, advance elements of the Federal cavalry collided with Confederate cavalry at Brownsville (near present-day Lonoke). After a brisk exchange, the outnumbered Rebels withdrew. Two days later, the two sides clashed again at Reed's Bridge on Bayou Meto twelve miles northeast of Little Rock. Again the Rebels slowed the Federal advance, but again they withdrew, this time to the outskirts of the city. The main Federal force, reinforced to a strength of 14,500, followed in the cavalry's wake and reached the Arkansas River downstream from the capital at Ashley's Mill (near present-day Scott) on September 7.

As the Federal army prepared to cross the river, the Confederates suffered a self-inflicted wound. On September 6 two of Price's top generals, John Marmaduke and L. M. Walker, fought a duel that resulted in Walker's death. Enmity between the two men had been building since July when Marmaduke questioned Walker's competence and his courage at the Battle of Helena. Animosity had increased when Marmaduke was assigned to serve under Walker in the Little Rock campaign. The two men and their seconds met on the Godfrey Le Fevre plantation seven miles below Little Rock to settle the matter with pistols at ten paces. The encounter was one of the last recorded duels in Arkansas history, and it spread dissension through the Confederate ranks at a critical time. See plate 36 following page 270.

On the morning of September 10, Steele sent his cavalry across a pontoon bridge over the Arkansas River and began to move his infantry up the north bank of the river toward Little Rock. Price's worst fears had been realized. He had concentrated his defenses on the north bank in the hope that the Federal commander would attack him head on. But he knew that the Arkansas River was fordable at several points downstream from the capital, and once the Federals got across it and moved on the city from the south bank, his position was untenable. He began to withdraw his troops from their positions north of the river, crossing them back into Little Rock on a pontoon bridge and sending them southwest toward Arkadelphia.

South of the river, another group of Rebels made a brief stand at Fourche Bayou before they too fell back toward the city and joined the retreat. The last Confederate defender left Little Rock around 5 P.M. Federal cavalry entered the city shortly thereafter, and at 7 P.M. Little Rock's civil authorities formally surrendered the city. It had been one month since Steele set out from Helena, and now, at a cost of only 137 casualties, his forces had seized the state capital and recaptured the arsenal that Capt. James Totten had surrendered some two and a half years earlier. The Confederates also abandoned Pine Bluff, and on September 14, Steele sent a detachment of cavalry to the town.

The fall of the Little Rock had a particularly demoralizing effect on the Rebel soldiers. In a letter to his wife in Quitman, William Garner acknowledged that "I have never until the fall of Little Rock felt the sting of being an exile." As the main body of Price's army moved south toward Arkadelphia, desertions increased. Garner wrote to his wife on September 15, "Our company have nearly all deserted. . . . I will never, no never, desert. . . . I expect our property will be taken by January or before, but only hope that they may leave enough for you and the children to live on comfortably."

Garner's concern over family and property was well founded, for many central Arkansas residents now found themselves at the mercy of the Yankees. Like William Garner's wife and many other Arkansas women, Susan Fletcher was left alone on her Pulaski County plantation after her husband enlisted in the Confederate service. Following the fall of Little Rock, she recalled,

> After we were visited by the first half dozen squads of blue coats, we knew what civil war was when it was brought to your door. They first demanded water, then feed, after which they began to look around to see what could be carried away or destroyed. . . . they killed the cattle on one occasion. I saw my hillside pasture red with the blood of slain cattle. They tore photographs from the wall, took our combs and every vestige of food. We would have to send neighbors back to the woods for food, as not a crumb of anything would be left.

A Pine Bluff woman wrote that the Federals were "going around stealing horses . . . hunting up firearms, & taking everything they thought proper." Both women could sympathize with a captured Rebel soldier who told Mrs. Fletcher, "I hate blue so hard I never expect to allow anything blue on my farm, not even a blue hog."

However, many central Arkansas residents benefited from the Federal occupation, as Little Rock businesses experienced a revival. A local editor wrote that "the streets are filled with a restless, quick-motioned business people. . . . [E]very store and storehouse is full, drays and wagons crowd the streets; two theaters are in full blast and all is bustle and business."

In mid-September Steele noted that "a deputation of the most respectable citizens of Pine Bluff" had requested that he send more troops to protect the town and its cotton from Rebel raiders. He responded by sending additional cavalrymen to garrison the town, bringing the total Federal strength there to 550 men. The troops were commanded by Col. Powell Clayton, a Kansas officer who had fought at Wilson's Creek, Helena, and in the Little Rock campaign. Many Arkansas Confederates considered Clayton to be the best Union cavalry officer west of the Mississippi River, and even some Confederate sympathizers in Pine Bluff were impressed by him. "He is a very gentlemanly man," one local woman noted, "and by his humane and obliging manners has quite won the people." Many Pine Bluff citizens voluntarily took an oath of loyalty to the Union, causing one surprised citizen of the town to remark, "There are more union people here and in L. R. than anyone ever thought."

The most enthusiastic "union people" were African Americans. Though they have left few written records, the actions of black Arkansans left little doubt as to their sentiments. Wherever Union armies went, blacks deserted the plantations to follow them. A white female resident of Pine Bluff expressed concern with the large number of former slaves who poured into the town after the Union occupation, noting that "they came pouring in by the 100's—every ones servants ran off to P. Bluff, there is scarcely a house here that has a servant left. They came in such numbers that they [Federal authorities] did not know what to do with them." To handle this massive influx of former slaves, Clayton established large camps east and west of the city.

While Steele was consolidating his hold on Little Rock and Clayton was establishing a Federal presence in Pine Bluff, Sterling Price was withdrawing the bulk of the Confederate infantry to Camden on the Ouachita River. The ever-aggressive Marmaduke held the Rebel cavalry at Princeton (Dallas County), and despite the reverses of the previous nine months, he was determined to take the war to the enemy. Little Rock was too strongly defended, but the smaller Federal garrison at Pine Bluff seemed vulnerable, particularly if the Rebels had the element of surprise.

On Saturday, October 24, 1863, Marmaduke led over two thousand cavalry supported by twelve pieces of artillery across the Saline River and through the soggy bottomlands toward Pine Bluff, reaching a point just outside the town after daylight on Sunday morning. Here he divided his command into three columns to approach the town from the southeast, southwest, and northwest. A cannon shot from his artillery would signal the start of the attack.

Almost immediately things went badly for the Confederates. The element of surprise was lost around 8 A.M. when one of Marmaduke's advancing columns encountered a Federal patrol. Shots were exchanged, and a Federal courier raced back to town to warn Clayton of the impending attack. A second piece of bad luck awaited the Rebels. By attacking on a Sunday morning, Marmaduke had expected to catch the Federals off guard. Unbeknown to him, Sunday was the day that Clayton conducted his weekly review of the troops. As the alarmed courier dashed into the courthouse square, Federal troops were already turning out for their inspection.

Clayton wasted no time after he learned of the Rebel advance. He sent skirmishers out in all directions, placed cannon to command the main approaches to the square, and set his contraband force to work barricading the streets leading into the square with cotton bales from a nearby warehouse. The former slaves accomplished the task in less than half an hour.

The Confederate attack began around 9 A.M. Despite failing to catch the Federals totally by surprise, Marmaduke still enjoyed a manpower advantage of four to one, and the Rebels quickly drove the Federal skirmishers back into the courthouse square. Throughout the remainder of the morning and into the early afternoon, the Rebels blasted away at the barricaded Yankees with artillery and small-arms fire, trapping many Pine Bluff civilians in the middle of the fighting. One Union soldier recalled that "a scene of wildest confusion prevailed, as their broadsides came surging through the streets, menacing friend and foe. Many of them [the civilians] fled to the river and concealed themselves under the bank, while others remained in their dwellings, half frantic with fear throughout the day."

Throughout the encounter, Clayton remained in the saddle, calmly directing and encouraging his men as the Rebels' shells whistled around him. "Colonel Clayton rode master-spirit of the storm," one Federal soldier recalled, "his commanding figure and conspicuous uniform were seen wherever danger threatened. . . . [I]t is one of the strange anomalies of the war that he was not killed."

The Rebels set fire to over six hundred bales of cotton and inflicted heavy damage on the town, but they could not penetrate the Federals' inner defense ring. Around 2 P.M. Marmaduke ordered a retreat, taking some three hundred of the former slaves with him as prisoners, as well as some 250 horses and mules. "The Federals," he wrote in his official report, "fought like devils."

Clayton's leadership at Pine Bluff against superior odds added to his already considerable reputation. He praised the courage of his troops and particularly singled out the former slaves, noting, "The negroes did me excellent service . . . and deserve much therefore." A Federal soldier concurred, writing that the African Americans "worked patiently, and with an unselfish devotion to our cause that goes far to remove the jaundiced prejudice of color." Ironically, white cotton and black labor, so essential to the southern way of life, had saved the Union army on this Sunday morning.

As Marmaduke was withdrawing from his failed assault on Pine Bluff, fellow Rebel cavalryman Jo Shelby was returning from one of the most spectacular raids of the war. The Kentucky-born Shelby had moved to Missouri in the 1850s and had amassed considerable wealth as a hemp planter, rope manufacturer, and steamboat owner. He had recruited a proslavery cavalry unit to fight in "Bleeding Kansas" in the 1850s, and, when the Civil War began, had accepted a commission as a captain in the pro-Confederate Missouri State Guard. He later became a colonel, then a brigadier general in the Confederate army. Few soldiers on either side took part in more battles in Missouri and Arkansas than Shelby, and he soon gained a reputation from friend and foe alike as a tough, aggressive cavalry officer. One Union officer later referred to him as "the best cavalry general of the South."

In late September Shelby had a falling out with General Holmes, and after a fiery exchange of words, Shelby left Arkadelphia with eight hundred men. Moving north through Huntsville and the ruins of Bentonville, which had been burned by Federal troops, the raiders entered southwest Missouri. Even the battle-hardened Shelby, was alarmed by the desolate conditions in the southern and southwestern portions of his home state. "In many places for forty miles not a single habitation is to be found," he later wrote, "for on the road we met delicate females fleeing southward, driving ox teams, barefooted, ragged, and suffering even for bread." In early October they captured a Federal supply depot at Neosho and moved northeast toward the state capital at Jefferson City.

The raiders' rapid advance alarmed Federal authorities in Missouri who had considered the region safe at last from a large-scale Confederate raid. By the time the Rebels reached the vicinity of the capital, however, Federal troops from all over the state were rushing to intercept them. Shelby began a fighting retreat southward and crossed back into Arkansas with the Federals in hot pursuit.

He reached Clarksville on October 26 and crossed the Arkansas River. His "great raid" had covered over fifteen hundred miles, killed or captured over a thousand enemy soldiers, seized or destroyed almost two million dollars' worth of property and supplies, torn up railroads and bridges, captured six thousand horses and mules, and gained eight hundred recruits. But in the end, Missouri was no closer to being won for the Confederacy. The people of the state were, Shelby claimed, "as a mass, true to the South and her institutions, yet needing the strong presence of a Confederate army to make them volunteers." That was something which neither Shelby nor any other Confederate commander could provide.

Shelby's raid, like those that preceded it, did little to improve Confederate fortunes in Arkansas. At the year's end, the flag of the Union once again flew over a large portion of the state. Federal forces held the line of the Arkansas River and controlled the major towns of Helena, Fort Smith, Little Rock, and Pine Bluff. But actual Federal control outside the major towns was tenuous at best. Partisan bands operated behind the lines, harassing Federal patrols and threatening lines of communication and supply.

Confederate authority was largely confined to the southwest corner of the state. After the fall of Little Rock, the Confederate capital was moved to Washington in southwest Arkansas, and the Confederate military forces were encamped there and at Murfreesboro, Camden, and Springhill. As Michael Dougan has noted, "Only bad roads, burned out houses, and abandoned fields separated Confederate from Union Arkansas. In the vast no-man's land which constituted three fourths of the state, both armies foraged, and bushwhacker bands, with and without legal sanction, operated."

Confederate Resurgence and Collapse: The War in 1864 and 1865

If 1863 had been a disastrous year for Arkansas Confederates, 1864 began on an equally ominous note. In late December 1863, seventeen-year-old David Dodd was returning to Camden after attending to some family business in Little Rock when he was detained by a Union patrol along the Benton Road some twenty miles south of the capital. A search revealed that Dodd, who had previously served as a telegrapher for the Confederate army in Louisiana, carried a Morse-coded message detailing the disposition of part of the Federal defenses in Little Rock.

On January 5, 1864, a military commission in Little Rock found him guilty of spying and sentenced him to be hanged. Residents of the capital made several appeals to General Steele to spare Dodd's life, but the Federal commander refused to intervene. Dodd was hanged on January 8 on the grounds of St. John's Masonic School where he had once attended classes. Though Dodd was almost certainly guilty, his youth, his refusal to implicate others, and the calm dignity with which he faced his death earned him an enduring place in Arkansas history as "the boy martyr of the Confederacy."

The Dodd affair notwithstanding, Frederick Steele pursued a conciliatory policy toward Arkansas Confederates. In accord with President Lincoln's "Ten Percent Plan," (which permitted a state to form a loyal government and be recognized by the president whenever 10 percent of the state's voters took an oath affirming loyalty to the Union and support for emancipation), Steele had begun to administer the amnesty oath, and, in January 1864, he called for a constitutional convention and the election of a provisional Unionist governor.

In March while Unionist voters were going to the polls to approve the constitution and elect officials for the provisional government, Federal forces prepared to embark on an ambitious military venture. The Red River expedition, as it was styled, was a prelude to a grand Union design that would see Federal armies move simultaneously against Mobile, Richmond, and Atlanta, the object being to tie down Confederate defenders in all theaters, thereby preventing them from reinforcing one another. The Trans-Mississippi aspect of this grand strategy called for Steele to march southwest from Little Rock while another Federal army of 30,000 men under Nathaniel P. Banks would move up from New Orleans and ascend the Red River. The two armies would converge on and seize Shreveport, Louisiana, the Confederate headquarters in the Trans-Mississippi, and then move on to invade Texas. If successful, the operation would render the *coup de grâce* to Confederate forces in southern Arkansas and northern Louisiana, would lead to the reassertion of Federal authority in Texas, and would result in the seizure of millions of dollars' worth of Confederate cotton and other supplies.

Steele was to leave Little Rock with 8,500 men. At Arkadelphia, seventy miles to the southwest, he would be joined by the Brig. Gen. John M. Thayer's Frontier Division, which was moving southeast from Fort Smith. Both Steele and Banks had serious misgivings about the operation (as did their newly appointed overall commander, Ulysses Grant). Steele noted that his proposed route of march was over bad roads through a region almost destitute of provisions, and he feared increased guerrilla activity and a renewed threat to his supply lines if he left Little Rock. But his objections were overruled, and on March 23, 1864, he set out. A week later, the Federals reached Arkadelphia, having encountered neither the Rebels nor Thayer. As Steele pressed on toward Washington, however, Confederate cavalry began to snap at his column.

When the Federal columns reached the Little Missouri River at Elkins Ferry, Price, who was under orders to prevent Steele from linking up with Banks, led his Confederates out of Camden and moved to meet them. Price's force had been seriously weakened when two of his infantry divisions were ordered to Louisiana to oppose Banks. Nonetheless, the Confederates took up positions along Steele's line of march at Prairie D'Ane (near present-day Prescott). On April 9 Thayer's division finally caught up with Steele's main body a few miles south of the Little Missouri River, but the newcomers brought few supplies and thus served to further deplete Steele's already scarce provisions. Price was also reinforced by fifteen hundred men in two mounted brigades from the Indian Territory, one composed of Texans and another of Choctaw Indians.

By April 10, Steele's columns had moved to within a mile of the Confederate entrenchments at Prairie D'Ane, where they stopped and threw up earthworks. Neither army seemed eager to directly confront the other. On April 12, Price withdrew to near Washington. Steel realized that he could not reach Shreveport, and with his path to Camden now clear, the Federal commander turned his army to the east and made for the Ouachita River town some forty miles away. Price took up pursuit, and Rebel cavalry again slashed at the front and rear of the Federal column, but the Yankees reached the safety of Camden's fortifications on April 15.

Price established his headquarters a few miles outside town. Outnumbered two to one, he could not attack Camden, but he instructed his cavalry to watch the roads leading from the town for Federal patrols or foraging parties. Steele had ordered supplies to be rushed to Camden from Little Rock and Pine Bluff. When they did not arrive by April 17, he sent a large foraging party west from the town along the Washington-Camden Road. The party consisted of almost two hundred wagons escorted by over a thousand cavalry and infantry (including four hundred black soldiers from the First Kansas Volunteer Infantry) and four cannon. See plate 37 following page 270.

Alerted by their patrols, about 3,600 Confederate cavalry (composed of Marmaduke's Arkansans and the Texas and Choctaw brigades from the Indian Territory) backed by twelve cannon took a position between the returning supply train and Camden along high ground at Poison Spring fourteen miles west of the town. The Federals detected the presence of the Confederates in time to form a defensive position, but the Rebels soon overwhelmed them. The First Kansas bore the brunt of the attack. For many Rebel soldiers, the rules of warfare did not apply to black troops, whom they regarded as no more than runaway slaves. At Poison Spring, the Rebels shot wounded black soldiers as they lay helpless on the ground, gunned down others as they tried to surrender, and deliberately drove the captured wagons over the bodies of wounded blacks. The First Kansas lost 117 killed and 65 wounded out of a force of 400.

As the survivors of the Federal column staggered into Camden, the full extent of the defeat became apparent. Total Federal casualties at Poison Spring were 204 killed and 97 wounded. In addition, the Federals lost 170 wagons and over 1,200 mules. The Confederates suffered only 13 killed and fewer than 100 total casualties. The contents of the captured wagons only added to the Rebels' fury. They contained not only corn but "every kind of provision from the farm-yard, the pantry, the dairy, and the sideboard, . . . men's, women's and children's clothing, household furniture, gardening implements, the tools of the mechanic, and the poor contents of the negro hut."

For Steele, the debacle at Poison Spring was compounded by the news of Banks's defeat and subsequent retreat in Louisiana, which freed thousands of additional Confederates to concentrate against his embattled command at Camden. On April 20, a supply train reached Camden from Pine Bluff carrying ten days' worth of provisions. Two days later, Steele sent the 240-wagon train back to Pine Bluff for additional provisions, escorted by 1,400 troops and accompanied by a large number of civilians eager to leave the town and about three hundred former slaves. Three days out of Camden the train approached a series of gristmills owned by Hastings Marks. Four thousand Confederate cavalry waited along the road. At 8 A.M. when the Federal advance guard came into view, the Rebels attacked.

One division led by William Cabell struck the wagon train from the southeast. The Federal troops resisted fiercely, and a desperate struggle ensued for the next hour and a half. As this fighting raged, a second Rebel division led by Jo Shelby attacked along the Camden road from the northeast, striking the left flank and rear of the Federal line and driving the Yankees back. After five hours of intense fighting, the Federal commander surrendered. Remarkably he had suffered only about a hundred men killed, but the Rebels took thirteen hundred prisoners and seized all the wagons. Finding few supplies in the wagons, the Confederates robbed many of the prisoners, and reports surfaced that many of the unarmed freedmen had been shot down in cold blood. Total Confederate casualties were fewer than three hundred. A Federal soldier later acknowledged that the little-known Battle of Marks' Mill "was one of the most substantial successes gained by the western Confederates during the war."

For Steele, it was the final straw. With supplies rapidly dwindling and the Confederate forces outside Camden growing, he had no choice but to attempt to get back to Little Rock. The Federals quietly stole out of Camden before dawn on April 26 and headed toward the capital, two rivers and a hundred miles to the north. It was the chance the Confederates had been waiting for, but for once their cavalry patrols let them down. By the time the Rebels realized that the Federals were gone, Steele's forces were well on their way. Confederate cavalry units slashed at the retreating column as it moved slowly through the Ouachita and Saline bottomlands, and a sharp engagement occurred near Princeton.

On April 29 twenty-two miles north of Princeton, the Union army reached the Saline River crossing at Jenkins' Ferry (about twelve miles southwest of present-day Sheridan and a little over forty miles from Little Rock), and Steele's engineers quickly began construction of a pontoon bridge. As soon as the bridge was in place, Steele began crossing his men to the north bank. It was a slow process under the best of conditions, and a driving rain made it even more so. The riverbank soon became "a sea of mud." Wagons sank to their axles and mules lost their footing. "The rain came down in torrents, . . ." a Federal soldier noted, "the men became exhausted, and both they and the animals sank down in the mud and mire, wherever they were, to seek a few hours' repose."

At 8 A.M. on April 30, while the Federal wagon train still stretched back two miles down the road toward Princeton, the main body of the pursuing Confederate army reached the ferry and attacked the retreating Yankees. Steele had protected the crossing point with rifle pits and breastworks, and his soldiers gave ground grudgingly. The return of Price's two divisions from Louisiana increased Confederate strength to about four thousand men, but Federal forces benefited from the weather and the terrain of the battlefield. From the point where the attack began, the terrain sloped down to the riverbank funneling the attacking force into an area only about a quarter mile across. With a swamp to one side and a hill to the other, flanking movements were impossible, and the Confederates were unable to deploy their entire force at one time. Rain-softened ground slowed the attackers, and smoke and mist obscured much of the field. Time and again the Confederates charged, only to be driven back with heavy losses.

The Second Kansas Colored Infantry Regiment fought with particular ferocity at Jenkins' Ferry. The regiment was the companion unit to the First Kansas, and the memory of Poison Spring was fresh on their minds. Before leaving Camden, the officers of the regiment had agreed "that in the future the regiment would take no prisoners so long as the Rebels continued to murder our men." At Jenkins' Ferry, the Second Kansas put that philosophy into practice. The regiment overran a Confederate battery and bayoneted every Confederate gunner, including three who were attempting to surrender. Later in the day, as they were covering the retreat of the last elements of Steele's army, the Second Kansas searched the battlefield for wounded Union soldiers. While assisting their own wounded, however, they slit the throats and otherwise mutilated the bodies of wounded Rebels. For the duration of the conflict, the war between Confederates and black Union soldiers would be one of "no quarter."

Around 12:30 in the afternoon the exhausted Rebels called off the attack, and by 3 P.M. the entire Federal army was safely on the north bank of the river. Steele ordered the pontoon bridge destroyed to prevent further pursuit, and the bespattered Federal columns sloshed on toward Little Rock. They reached the capital on May 3, looking, one observer noted, "as if they had been rolled in the mud." The Camden Expedition (as the Arkansas part of the Red River campaign came to be called) was the greatest Federal disaster of the Civil War in Arkansas. Union forces lost over 2,500 men killed, wounded, or missing, hundreds of wagons, thousands of livestock, and gained not one inch of ground.

The failure of the Federals' Camden Expedition breathed new life into Arkansas Confederates. The threat of a Rebel invasion of north-central Arkansas, combined with a shortage of horses and food, forced Union forces to abandon Batesville and Jacksonport. Confederate guerrillas, encouraged by the Federal debacle, raided federally leased plantations around Helena and tore up stretches of railroad track between DeValls Bluff and Little Rock.

In Chicot County in late May and early June 1864, Rebel cavalry operating along the levee so disrupted Federal shipping on the Mississippi River that six thousand Federal troops, headed upriver to Memphis, were ordered to disembark briefly in southeast

Arkansas to disperse them. The Confederates took up positions behind a slow-moving stream called Ditch Bayou that flowed into nearby Lake Chicot. From midmorning until midafternoon on June 6, six hundred Confederates, protected from a direct assault by the bayou, held off three thousand Yankees, inflicting over 150 casualties while losing only four killed and thirty-three wounded. Finally, their artillery ammunition exhausted, the Rebels withdrew. The remainder of the Federal force—wet, weary, and angry—moved on to Lake Village where they burned several buildings before reembarking the following morning for Memphis. Daniel Sutherland has noted, "The brilliant but unheralded Confederate triumph at Ditch Bayou . . . , the last significant battle on Arkansas soil, was overshadowed by continued guerrilla action, which had long since come to characterize the war in Arkansas."

Like their fellow citizens in northwest Arkansas, the residents of the southeastern part of the state suffered greatly from the depredations of both armies and from outlaw gangs. In 1864 a Chicot County resident wrote to a friend, "We have been tossed and tumbled about considerably by the Feds and our own soldiers and then by bands of independent marauders calling themselves 'guerillas' and having authority from almost any or every general in the Confederacy or out of it." Citizens of the county were trapped, he noted, "between the Hawk & Buzzard."

The same statement could have been made by residents of other regions of the state. A soldier from Quitman in north-central Arkansas did not specify which side he was referring to when he wrote to his wife, "If you hear of an army about to pass, hide all your corn and bacon for they will steal what you have got." In northwest Arkansas guerrilla activity was such a problem in the summer of 1864 that the Federal commander at Fayetteville, Col. Marcus Larue Harrison, ordered the destruction of some of the very gristmills he had been ordered to protect. The three mills, one in Benton County and two in Washington County, were owned by Confederate sympathizers, and Harrison believed them to be gathering points and recruiting sites for Confederate guerrillas.

Nonetheless, the destruction of these three facilities in a region where numerous other mills had already been destroyed by bushwhackers and partisan bands cost the already economically strapped region forty-five thousand dollars in annual productivity and further contributed to the hardships experienced by civilians of all political persuasions. Thousands fled the region. By the end of the year, many of the counties along the Missouri line were virtually devoid of people. In an attempt to stem the exodus and boost agricultural production, Harrison began the creation of "post colonies," guarded agricultural communities made up of men capable of bearing arms who agreed to take an oath of loyalty to the Union and to settle their families on abandoned land within a ten-mile radius of small fortified positions garrisoned by home guard troops. Here they would help defend the community while farming individual parcels of land. Another such community went into operation near Prairie Grove, and below Pine Bluff, a "freedmen's home farm" was established.

Despite the limited success of these ventures, life was increasingly difficult for most Arkansans, black and white. "For the ordinary Arkansas civilian caught in the storm of war, legitimate economic activity had practically come to a standstill by the summer of 1864," Dan Sutherland notes. "Nearly all industry had ceased. Cotton and woolen factories, gristmills, sawmills, saltpeter works, and most craft shops had been closed or destroyed. Financial inflation had made any manufactured articles and most other product incredibly expensive." At Little Rock and the other few places firmly in Federal control, conditions were much better. But at isolated outposts, unreliable transportation and the activities of guerrillas and outlaws made everyday life both difficult and dangerous.

The task of supplying the Federal garrison at Fort Smith proved particularly vexing. Corn and other crops had been planted in the region in the spring, but rotted in the fields at harvest time for lack of labor. Supplies coming overland by wagon from Fort Scott on the Kansas-Missouri border had to pass through desolate, guerrilla-infested country, and it took approximately two hundred wagons to carry the same amount of supplies carried by one steamboat. Therefore the river route from Little Rock was much preferred. Moving supplies by river was a difficult enough task in peacetime given the ever-changing nature of the Arkansas River. When water levels were adequate, a boat could travel upriver from the capital to Fort Smith in four days. But for much of the winter of 1864 low water levels prevented navigation all the way to Fort Smith.

In addition Confederate Indian guerrillas led by Stand Watie were a constant thorn in the side of Union forces. Watie, the talented Cherokee leader, had risen to the rank of brigadier general in the Confederate army. Acting in conjunction with white guerrillas and Chickasaw and Choctaw cavalry units, Watie's forces disrupted supplies and harassed Federal forces at Fort Smith so severely throughout the summer and fall that government authorities in Washington, D.C., decided in early December 1864 to abandon the post altogether. The Federal garrison had actually started for Little Rock when Gen. Ulysses Grant ordered the evacuation halted and the fort maintained.

It seemed that the Confederate commanders in Arkansas had at last found a formula that might, at best, win back the state or, at worst, confine Federal influence to Little Rock and a handful of strongly garrisoned towns. But it was not to be. Price, another native son of the "Show Me" state, saw a chance to realize the dream of a triumphant return to Missouri that he had harbored ever since his ignominious retreat from that state in February 1862.

On September 19, 1864, he led twelve thousand men (four thousand of them without weapons and a thousand with no horses) across the Missouri line and headed for St. Louis. Over the course of the next four and a half weeks, he recruited new soldiers, lost others, burned some towns, tore up bridges and railroads, overran several smaller Federal garrisons, threatened (though he did not capture) both St. Louis and Jefferson City, criss-crossed the state from east to west all the way into Kansas, and generally caused such an uproar that Federal authorities dispatched over twenty thousand troops to deal with him. The two main armies clashed in and around Westport, Missouri, on October 22 and 23 in the largest Civil War battle (in terms of the number of men engaged) fought west of the Mississippi. The Confederates lost at least fifteen hundred men killed and wounded, and another two thousand were taken prisoner.

Price turned his defeated army southward, but ten days later Federal forces caught up with him at Mine Creek in Kansas and inflicted another 1,200 casualties. By the time he returned to Arkansas on October 30, Price had only 4,000 survivors. With this ragged remnant, he moved briefly into the Indian Territory and Texas, before returning to southwest Arkansas with 3,500 men, the majority of them unarmed. In a little over two months, Price had squandered the momentum that had been won the previous spring and in the process had destroyed the high esteem in which he had been held by many of his troops. "Men are greatly demoralized and we present a pitiable forlorn aspect," one Rebel veteran grumbled. "God damn Old Price."

In late 1864, events on the national political scene were also trending against the Confederacy. On Tuesday, November 8, voters in the North reelected Abraham Lincoln to a second term as president. Lincoln's election dashed any hope in the South for a negotiated peace. "From all accounts I suppose Lincoln is reelected," a delta resident noted, "and perhaps another 4 years [of] war."

While Lincoln celebrated his victory in Washington, D.C., the Confederate government at Washington, Arkansas, had all but ceased to function. Price's removal of so much of the Confederate military presence in south Arkansas had led to the further deterioration of law and order south of the Arkansas River. His Missouri raid did claim one major casualty among Arkansas Federals, however. Frederick Steele had conquered Little Rock, reasserted Federal authority, and established a new Unionist government in the state, but his conciliatory policy toward Arkansas Confederates had always been too conciliatory for some Arkansas Unionists. Blamed for the failure of the disastrous Camden expedition and for allowing Price to raid Missouri, he was replaced in December by Gen. Joseph J. Reynolds.

In 1864, while much of the Confederacy was coming apart, Arkansas Confederates had enjoyed their most successful year of the entire war. But, in the end, it availed them nothing. In aptly summarizing the tumultuous events of that year, Daniel Sutherland has written, "The Federals, through miscalculation, poor generalship, and lack of initiative, had nearly lost Arkansas in 1864; only at the last minute, and as a result of poor judgment by the Confederates, were they able to steal it back."

With the failure of Price's raid, Union forces in Arkansas once again gained the upper hand, but events east of the Mississippi soon robbed them of their advantage. Federal reinforcements were needed in Georgia and the Carolinas, where Sherman relentlessly pursued Confederate forces under Joseph Johnston, and along the gulf coast at Mobile.

By early 1865, the antagonists in Arkansas, prevented by lack of numbers from conducting major offensive operations, adopted defensive stances. The Federals strengthened their line of supply from Helena through DeValls Bluff to Little Rock and maintained a tenuous hold on Fort Smith and smaller towns upriver from the capital. Many of the Federal troops now garrisoning the state were themselves Arkansans, either prewar Unionists or former slaves. Confederate forces fell back behind the line of the Ouachita River in southwest Arkansas. If there were to be one final battle for control of the state, it would have to await developments east of the river.

A few Confederate sympathizers continued to find hope in rumors of European intervention (the chances of which had long since passed) or of decisive Rebel victories against Grant or Sherman (which did not occur). But for most Arkansas Confederates, the harsh reality of defeat was beginning to set in. "This is the darkest hour our infant nation ever saw," a Phillips County woman recorded in her diary. "Our armies have all been defeated and scattered, our resources nearly exhausted, our men dispirited and demoralized. My God! What is to become of us?"

The news of the surrender of Confederate generals Robert E. Lee on April 9 and Joseph Johnston on April 26 accelerated the collapse of Confederate Arkansas. Desertions multiplied, illicit trading with the enemy proliferated, famine threatened. In early May a Federal officer in southwest Missouri reported to his superior that "between Cassville [Missouri] and Fayetteville, several deaths from starvation have occurred of women and children the past month." A Federal spy in southwest Arkansas concurred. "Arkansas," he reported, "is starved out."

As the Confederate army dissolved, the last vestiges of law and social stability evaporated. In May a group of women stormed the Confederate commissary in Lewisville (Lafayette County), demanding and receiving food for the town's hungry civilians. Confederate officers stole army supplies only to be themselves robbed by their own men. "We are experiencing a state of perfect anarchy," Camden resident John Brown wrote in late May. "We have no Government, military or civil, a condition most to be dreaded of all others." The formal surrender of Confederate forces in the Trans-Mississippi did not take place until June 2, 1865, but by that time, the Confederacy in Arkansas had already ceased to exist.

The Civil War was the greatest disaster in Arkansas history. By some estimates, as many as ten thousand Arkansans lost their lives in the struggle. Each death represented a life cut short, a dream unfulfilled, a family deprived of a father, a son, or a brother. Countless other men who survived the war were scarred for life, both physically and emotionally. Property losses were staggering. For slave owners, the losses in slaves alone totaled over a hundred million dollars. Land values declined by almost thirty-four million dollars. The number of horses dropped by 50 percent, mules and cattle by almost as much.

The hardships and suffering these losses inflicted on the residents of the state are impossible to quantify, but are clearly revealed in the remembrances of those who lived through them. "We were without a dollar, our negroes were freed, our horses and mules had either been 'pressed' [impressed] or confiscated," a Camden woman remembered. "We had no hogs, no poultry except one old turkey hen that had stolen a nest in the woods and so escaped." Susan Fletcher, returning from Washington, Arkansas, to her home near Little Rock at the end of the war described the conditions she saw in Saline and Pulaski counties. "Desolation met our gaze," she wrote, "abandoned and burned homes; cultivated land, overgrown with bushes; half starved women and children; gaunt, ragged men, stumbling along the road, just mustered out of the army, trying to find their families and friends and wondering if they had a home left. We found our home burned to the ground, but went to the home of a relative until we could collect our thoughts and decide what was best to be done." Not surprisingly, the war left a legacy of bitterness that would take many years to assuage.

But for the former slaves, the war marked the coming of freedom and the "Year of Jubilo," so long hoped for. A Chicot County slave remembered the arrival of Federal troops on her plantation. "I heard them tell all the slaves they were free," she later told an interviewer. "A man . . . called for the three nearby plantations to meet at our place. Then he got up on a platform with another man beside him and declared peace and freedom. He p'inted to a colored man and yelled, 'You're as free as I am.' Old colored folks . . . that was on sticks, throwed them sticks away and shouted." After generations of bondage and hopelessness, African Americans in Arkansas had, in a very brief period, made the transition from slaves to contraband and then to freedmen and freedwomen. What that freedom would mean remained to be seen. As the fires of war subsided, Arkansans of all colors and political persuasions looked toward an uncertain future with a mixture of hope and apprehension.

Year of Jubilo: African American corruption of the biblical term "Year of Jubilee," it refers to the coming of freedom to the slaves. In the Book of Leviticus (Old Testament), the Year of Jubilee is said to occur once in every fifty years. In that year, all slaves are set free, all debts are forgiven, and the glories and mercy of God are particularly manifest.

CHAPTER TEN

"A Harnessed Revolution": Reconstruction in Arkansas, 1865–1880

The era of Reconstruction that followed the Civil War was one of the most tumultuous and controversial periods in the history of the state and the nation. The term "Reconstruction" actually applies to several distinct but related aspects of the immediate post–Civil War period. Political Reconstruction dealt with the process of determining how the seceded states would resume their place in a reunited nation and who would control the political fortunes of those states. Economic Reconstruction concerned the attempt by white southerners to recover economically from the devastation of the war, by black southerners to establish their economic viability in the free labor system, and by the Reconstruction governments to reshape the South in the economic image of the North. Social Reconstruction involved the process of determining how the former slaves and former masters would interact in the new social arrangements brought on by the war and emancipation. The overlapping and intertwining of these various aspects made Reconstruction a complex and confusing era.

Arkansas under Presidential Reconstruction

Though generally considered to have begun with the surrender of the Southern armies in 1865, Reconstruction actually began well before the war ended. The Presidential Reconstruction plan put forward by Abraham Lincoln in his annual message to Congress on December 8, 1863, was one of the most lenient policies ever applied by a victorious government to defeated insurrectionists. The president offered a "full pardon . . . with restoration of all rights of property, except as to slaves" to all rebels who would take an oath of future loyalty to the Constitution and agree to abide by acts of Congress and presidential proclamations regarding slavery. Only high-ranking Confederate leaders were excluded from this policy, and they could apply for pardons to the president on an individual basis. When the number of people taking the oath reached 10 percent of those who had voted in the election of 1860, those citizens could form a new state government, which the president would recognize. In the case of Arkansas, that meant that the process of forming a new state government could begin when only slightly over 5,400 persons took the oath. Shortly after Federal forces seized Little Rock in September 1863, Maj. Gen. Frederick Steele, the commander of Union forces in Arkansas and *de facto* military governor of the state, began the process of reestablishing a loyal state government.

Following the announcement of the president's plan in December, Arkansas Unionists began taking the required oath, and, by early January 1864, the 10 percent requirement had been met. That same month, Unionists from twenty-four of the state's fifty-seven counties assembled in Little Rock to draft a new constitution. The new document was similar to the state's first constitution of 1836, except for a provision abolishing slavery. The convention also chose a provisional slate of officers. The document and slate of officials were submitted to the voters in March of 1864.

The election was in no way a truly statewide or representative process. Confederate forces still controlled portions of southern and southwestern Arkansas, and much of the state outside of the major population centers was still a virtual no-man's land. With only slightly more than twelve thousand Arkansans casting ballots, the document was overwhelmingly approved, a slate of provisional state officials chosen, and a new state legislature elected. Fittingly, Isaac Murphy, the lone holdout against secession in the state convention of 1861 and a man whose devotion to the Union had not wavered during the trying months and years thereafter, was elected governor.

That new legislature chose Elisha Baxter and William Fishback to be the state's United States senators. Baxter had a record of service to the Union during the war, but Fishback had performed a series of political flip-flops between 1860 and 1864 that led many Arkansas Unionists and Radical Republicans in the national Congress to question his loyalty. Baxter and Fishback soon became part of the developing struggle between the president and Congress over control of Reconstruction. When the two men presented their credentials in Washington, the U.S. Senate, uncomfortable with Lincoln's lenient policies, refused to seat them.

This refusal confirmed the tenuous legal nature of the Murphy government, recognized by the president but not by Congress. The problems facing the new administration were staggering. As Murphy noted in his inaugural address, the loyal state government began "under very embarrassing surroundings; without money power, without military power."

The end of the war in April 1865 created additional problems. The assassination of President Lincoln removed the architect of the lenient plan of Reconstruction and destroyed the South's best hope for peaceful reunification. While his successor, Andrew Johnson of Tennessee, pursued a plan very similar to that proposed by the slain president—repudiation of secession and the Confederate debt, abolition of slavery, and ratification of the Thirteenth Amendment—he lacked Lincoln's stature and political skills and soon found himself at war with congressional Republicans.

The return of Confederate troops who had fought east of the Mississippi River threatened to add to the opposition that the Unionist state government faced. The previous year, in an attempt to head off this threat, the Unionist state legislature had passed a law requiring a second loyalty oath as a prerequisite for voting. To be eligible, a person had to swear that he had not supported the Confederacy since the establishment of the loyal state government in March 1864. With this provision in place, the Murphy government felt confident enough to call for congressional elections in October 1865.

With many former Confederates disqualified, fewer than seven thousand voters cast ballots. Still, the opposition party, composed largely of prewar Democrats and some former Whigs and styling itself as the Conservatives, made a surprisingly strong showing. The administration soon received an additional dose of bad news. First the national Congress, citing the low voter turnout, refused to seat the newly elected congressmen. Then, in the case of *Rison et al v. Farr*, the state supreme court struck down the state's loyalty oath as unconstitutional.

The lone holdout against secession at the convention of 1861, Isaac Murphy was elected governor of Arkansas in 1864. *Courtesy of J. N. Heiskell Collection/UALR Archives and Special Collections.*

Thus encouraged, Conservatives began to prepare an all-out effort for the next election in August 1866. Intimidation and violence against blacks and Unionists were commonplace. The results of this first postwar election conducted without restrictions on the former Confederates

Black Union soldiers are mustered out of service at Little Rock in 1866. The sketch was done by Alfred R. Waud for *Harper's Weekly. Courtesy UALR Archives and Special Collections.*

bore out the worst fears of Arkansas Unionists. Conservative candidates swept away almost the entire Unionist ticket elected in 1864. Only Governor Murphy and the secretary of state, both of whom had four-year terms and were not up for reelection, survived, and Conservatives seemed certain to recapture those two offices in 1868. Former Confederates were also returned to power in many counties.

Conservatives: Political faction composed of prewar Democrats and some former Whigs who opposed the Republican Party's plans for Reconstruction.

The new state legislature, which assembled in November, included many of the state's antebellum ruling elite, several of whom had served in the Confederate Congress or the Rebel army. The general assembly enacted laws (over Governor Murphy's veto) legitimizing Confederate debts and making only Confederate veterans eligible for state pensions, and even considered a resolution commending former Confederate president Jefferson Davis.

The new legislature passed no restrictive labor laws such as the infamous Mississippi "Black Codes," which severely restricted the economic rights of the freedpeople, but neither did it permit African Americans to vote, hold office, serve on juries, marry whites, or have access to public education. It did, however, choose two ex-Confederates, including former Confederate senator Augustus Garland, to represent the state in the U.S. Senate. That body refused to seat Garland or any other senator from the former Confederate states. That refusal notwithstanding, it seemed that, despite the devastation, death, and dislocation of the war, many of the same men who had dominated Arkansas politics in the antebellum years were rapidly returning to power.

Many members of that class were also engaged in trying to restore their prewar economic status. Arkansans of all classes had been hit hard by the war, and some of the state's wealthiest citizens had seen their fortunes wiped out and their antebellum lifestyle destroyed. But as Carl Moneyhon has noted in a recent study, wealthy individuals generally survived the war years and maintained control over their property better than their poorer neighbors. "The loss of their slaves had a major economic impact," he notes, "but they were still in a better position than others to reestablish their lives and fortunes. Poorer individuals and families did not have as much to lose, but their losses were more disastrous, often involving everything."

The ability to maintain control of the land was particularly important. Land was the major form of wealth in the state and the commodity on which economic, social, and political power were based. For planters in the southern and eastern parts of the state, the key to economic survival lay in maintaining control of the land and reasserting control over the labor force. For the freedmen, the challenge was to use their freedom to enhance their political, economic, and social independence from the planters. Many left the plantations to seek opportunities in the towns and cities. But such opportunities were few and far between. The majority remained on the land and sought to gain for themselves a share of the state's agricultural bounty to which their labor had for so long contributed.

These freedmen and women rightly concluded that ownership of land was critical to attaining their goals. Many hoped and expected that the federal government would redistribute land after the war (the oft-heard rumors of "forty acres and a mule"), and

Gen. E. O. C. Ord, head of the military district that included Arkansas, proposed using confiscated lands to provide homesteads for freedmen. But Congress and the president refused to support the idea, insisting that confiscated lands be returned to their previous owners once they received a presidential pardon.

By and large the planters managed to maintain ownership of their land and thus were in a strong bargaining position with the freedmen. Still, without a labor force, the land was of little value, and planters now had to negotiate with their former slaves for their services. In the months following the end of the war, labor relations were in flux, and a wide variety of arrangements between planters and laborers emerged. One Arkansas planter noted that "on twenty plantations around me, there are ten different styles of contracts."

Initially many planters employed a wage system similar to that used on northern farms. One account from 1866 noted that the price for labor was about $13 per month for males and $9 for females. Another from early 1867 reported that wages for field hands ranged from $15 to $30 per month, with first-class field hands getting $18 per month including rations, but it added, "Only a few who are the most intelligent of the blacks and who can act as 'heads of gangs' or overseers receive the maximum."

That report also revealed that many freedmen disliked the wage system because the use of gang labor and the close supervision by overseers too closely resembled slavery. The severe shortage of money in the region often made the wage system difficult for many planters as well. In a relatively short time, therefore, the notion of wage labor gave way to a variety of "share" arrangements. Initially, many contracts called for the planter to pay his laborers with a share of the crop at the end of the year rather than with cash wages. Many planters favored this "share wage" system because it forced the laborer to share the risks of the crop and still gave the planter a large measure of control over his labor force.

Over time, a third arrangement, share tenantry or sharecropping, gained increasing popularity. Under this system a landowner rented a plot of land to an individual family to farm independently and furnished them everything necessary to make a crop. The owner would then receive a share of the crop as rent. If the cropper provided his own tools and/or animals, he could retain a larger share of the crop. Freedmen preferred this system because it gave them more autonomy and held out the hope that, with good weather and good prices, a sharecropper could eventually save enough to purchase his own land and become an independent farmer.

Sharecropping: System in which a tenant farmer gives a portion of his crop to the landowner for the right to farm a parcel of land.

One share tenantry contract between Calhoun County planter J. C. Barrow and freedman James Blanset stipulated:

> the said James Blanset of the first part, agrees to rent a west portion of the bottom field, some twenty acres from the said Barrow on the said Barrow's farm, and agrees to pay him for the rent thereof, one third of the corn, and one fourth of the cotton, and one fourth of the Sweet potatoes raised during the year . . . and house the same at the usual time, then haul the seed cotton to some near gin, with Barrow's wagons

> and mules, have it ginned; and the said Barrow agrees to furnish the said Blanset the necessary supplies to make the said crop, and the said Blanset agrees to pay the said Barrow for them out of his portion of the crop and the said Barrow agrees to not seize upon the said crop unless the said Blanset attempts to deceive or defraud the said Barrow, and that we will consult each other before setting upon the subject of selling the same.

The task of supervising the contractual arrangements between planters and laborers fell to the Bureau of Refugees, Freedmen, and Abandoned Lands, more commonly known as the Freedmen's Bureau. Created by Congress in March 1865, the bureau was under the overall leadership of Maj. Gen. Oliver O. Howard and assistant commissioners in the various southern states. In Arkansas, three Union officers—Brevet Maj. Gen. John W. Sprague (March 1865–October 1866), Brevet Maj. Gen. E. O. C. Ord (October 1866–March 1867), and Brevet Maj. Gen. Charles H. Smith (March 1867–May 1869)—served as assistant commissioners, reporting directly to General Howard and supervising the work of seventy-nine local agents.

Freedmen's Bureau: Officially known as the Bureau of Refugees, Freedmen, and Abandoned Lands, this federal agency was charged by Congress with negotiating labor contracts, providing medical care, setting up schools, and adjudicating land disputes for the former slaves.

These agents (thirty-six civilians and forty-three army officers) were assigned to thirty-six locations centered primarily in thirty towns south, east, and west of Little Rock, the sites determined by the proximity of major rivers, large black populations, and cotton plantations. In addition to supervising labor contracts, the bureau's mission was to provide food, shelter, and medical care for the former slaves, to provide for their education, to help protect their legal rights, and to ease the transition from slavery to free labor.

The success or failure of the Freedmen's Bureau in Arkansas was determined largely by the mindset and actions of these local agents. For most Arkansans, black and white, the local agent *was* the Freedmen's Bureau. As historian Randy Finley has noted in his recent study of the bureau in Arkansas, "Agents' racial attitudes and ideologies—ranging from humanitarianism and paternalism to racism—critically shaped the workings of the bureau in Arkansas." Some agents worked diligently and often at great personal risk to secure rights for those freedmen and freedwomen under their supervision, while others acted as little more than labor agents for the planters.

With their ability to regain control of the state legislature, to retain their land, and to secure their labor, Arkansas's planter elite seemed on the verge of reclaiming their prewar status and of returning Arkansas society to something closely resembling its antebellum arrangement. But economic and political developments soon dramatically altered the direction of affairs in Arkansas.

Agricultural activity quickened with the end of the fighting. In 1865 returning Arkansas soldiers tended crops already sown, planted late crops of cotton and corn, and looked expectantly to 1866 as they prepared to resume and expand their operations in the first full year of peace. High cotton prices in the immediate postwar period encouraged many Arkansans to plant more cotton and less corn in the spring of 1866, risking self-sufficiency in an attempt to recoup wartime losses. The revival of agricultural activity spurred a corresponding growth in commercial activity in Arkansas towns and created a great demand for labor that boded well for the freedmen. It seemed that a good crop season in 1866 could lead to a rapid return to the prosperity that had characterized the late 1850s, and, in so doing, assuage the bitterness of the war and ease the transition from a slave-based to a free labor society. But heavy rains in the late spring of 1866 caused severe flooding along the state's major rivers. The floods were followed by a midsummer drought. In late summer, the heavy rains returned, accompanied in some areas by armyworms that stripped cotton plants bare. Fertile areas along the rivers were hardest hit, and the fall harvest was well below expectations.

Those freedmen, farmers, and planters who survived the debacle of 1866 looked to 1867 as a make-or-break year. Once again they were disappointed. The pattern of spring floods, midsummer drought, and insect infestation was depressingly reminiscent of the previous year. The result was another small harvest. In the fall, Arkansas farmers were dealt another blow when cotton prices collapsed, falling to about one-half of their 1866 level.

As with the war, those at the bottom of the economic scale were hit hardest by the crop failures. For the freedmen, hardships brought on by natural forces were compounded by human factors. Merchants charged them exorbitant prices and usurious interest, planters failed to fulfill contractual obligations, refused to let literate freedmen examine the books, and cheated those who could neither read nor add. Other planters waited until the harvest was completed, then drove freedmen from the land without settling their accounts. Freedmen's Bureau agents were inundated with complaints. One Bureau agent reported, "Many of the colored people are being swindled out of their year's work and the cold winter which is approaching will find them destitute of even the common necessities of life."

White yeomen farmers were also in trouble. Deeply in debt after two years of poor harvests, most found credit still available, but with a stipulation. Despite the short crops and the dramatic fall in prices, merchants and other creditors still looked to cotton as the best collateral. When cotton prices remained low, farmers found themselves in an ever-deepening cycle of debt that would continue well into the next century.

The planter class survived the economic downturn better than their poorer neighbors, but many were hard hit, and almost all soon came to realize that the golden years were over. Even before the disastrous season of 1867, the editor of the *Arkansas Gazette* had written, "The day of making sudden fortunes in agricultural pursuits has passed." Chicot County planter Elisha Worthington —who by 1864 had taken at least 167 of 543 slaves to Tarrant County, Texas, where he rented land and, presumably, produced cotton—had regained control of his four plantations and a sizable portion of his labor force after the war. But in 1866 he was forced to sell his prize plantation, Sunnyside, to pay off old debts. In 1870 he still owned five thousand acres, but only one thousand of those were improved, and one of his three remaining plantations was valued at only $100.

Lycurgus Johnson of neighboring Lakeport plantation survived somewhat better than did Worthington and many other planters. He managed to hold onto the majority of his 4,600 prewar acres and much of his labor force and accommodated himself better than most planters to the new system of free labor. A local Freedmen's Bureau agent reported that Johnson did his one hundred hands "the fullest justice" and referred to him as a "model man of Chicot County." Still the total value of Johnson's taxable property fell from $171,581 in 1860 to $18,556 in 1865. In 1860 Lakeport had produced 1,300 bales of cotton, which ranked Johnson fifth among Chicot County planters. In 1870, Lakeport's six hundred bales made Johnson the largest producer in the county. That Johnson was a postwar "success story" is a clear indication that even those cotton aristocrats who survived the twin scourges of war and poor harvests ruled over a greatly diminished realm.

The decision to concentrate on cotton in the immediate postwar period when prices were high was an understandable one, but Arkansans of all economic classes paid a severe penalty for that decision. As Carl Moneyhon has noted, "Nature and the price of cotton were critical factors in the state's postwar economic life, but the decision of Arkansans in 1866 to emphasize cotton helped tie their farms to a crop that languished for the next hundred years and left Arkansas a legacy of poverty."

As the antebellum elites struggled to maintain their economic viability, other events were threatening their political hegemony. In April 1866 Congress enacted, over the president's veto, a Civil Rights Act that defined all persons born in the United States as citizens and provided a federal guarantee for the "full and equal benefit of all laws and proceedings for the security of person and property" regardless of race. A short time later, Congress approved the Fourteenth Amendment, which voided all Confederate debts, prohibited states from violating the civil rights of any of its citizens, provided for a reduction in congressional representation for those states that denied the vote to any adult male, and prohibited any person from holding a state or federal office who had at any time taken an oath to support the Constitution and subsequently supported the rebellion.

Only one former Confederate state (Tennessee) ratified the amendment. Both houses of the Conservative-dominated Arkansas legislature overwhelmingly rejected the proposal, and they were supported in this action by President Johnson, who was now engaged in a fierce struggle with the Radical elements in Congress for control of the Reconstruction process. The actions of the Arkansas legislature were mirrored in numerous other state legislatures across the South. The failure to guarantee the political and civil rights of the freedmen, the insistence on returning to positions of power in both the state and national government those who had only recently taken up arms against the United States, and the violence directed against freedmen and Unionists combined with the president's combative intransigence to provoke an understandably sharp reaction among northern moderates and to tilt the political balance of power in the Radicals' favor. In so doing it doomed to failure the lenient plans of Presidential Reconstruction and the conciliatory policies of Governor Murphy.

Radicals: Republicans who favored a harsh Reconstruction policy toward the former Confederate states.

Three months after Conservative-Democratic elements regained control of the Arkansas legislature, Republicans easily gained over two-thirds of the seats in both the U.S. Senate and the House of Representatives, assuring them of the ability to override presidential vetoes. The views of the Radical element of the Republican Party, which had previously been in the minority, were now clearly the dominant sentiment. The fighting between the weakened president and an emboldened Congress continued throughout 1867.

In March 1868, the House brought charges of impeachment against the president. The charges were more political than substantive, and the Senate narrowly failed to convict Johnson, but what remained of his power and influence were effectively destroyed. Arkansas and the rest of the former Confederate states, having missed an opportunity to adopt a conciliatory approach and perhaps reenter the Union under the lenient plan of Presidential Reconstruction, now would have to contend with a much harsher plan.

Congressional Reconstruction and the "Gospel of Prosperity"

The plan for Congressional Reconstruction was embodied in the Military Reconstruction Act, passed, over the president's veto, in March 1867. The act divided the former Confederate states into five military districts, each under the control of a military officer authorized to keep order, to protect the rights of the freedmen, and to utilize military tribunals in place of civil courts where necessary. The act further specified that new state constitutions providing for universal male suffrage be drafted, approved by a majority of the state's voters, and accepted by Congress. In addition, state legislatures were required to ratify the Fourteenth Amendment. Only those persons who could swear an "ironclad oath" that they had not aided or abetted the Confederacy were permitted to participate in the process. A Second Reconstruction Act in late March specifically directed the military commanders to register all adult males who could take the oath. A Third Reconstruction Act followed in July empowering the military commanders to replace state or local officials.

Arkansas and Mississippi constituted the Fourth Military District under the command of Gen. E. O. C. Ord, a former assistant commissioner of the Freedmen's Bureau in Arkansas. Ord advised the state legislature, then in recess, not to reconvene and restricted the authority and jurisdiction of the state courts, especially as it pertained to relations between blacks and whites. Governor Murphy was allowed to remain in office and worked closely with Ord for the remainder of his term, albeit in a clearly subservient position. Under Ord's direction, registration began for the November election on whether to call for a constitutional convention. The Third Reconstruction Act placed great power in the hands of those officials who registered voters, enabling them to disqualify not only those who clearly fell under the prohibitions of the Fourteenth Amendment but many who were only suspected of disloyalty.

In the November election, 27,576 Arkansans voted for the convention, while 13,558 opposed. Seventy delegates chosen in that election assembled in the hall of the House of Representatives in Little Rock in early January 1868. Throughout the South, critics referred to these biracial, Republican-dominated assemblies as "Black and Tan" conventions, and the hostile *Arkansas Gazette* described the Arkansas convention as "a bastard collection whose putridity stinks in the nostrils of all decency." The delegates were a diverse group, but contrary to the *Gazette*'s description, the assembly contained some very capable members. Approximately two-thirds of the delegates were Radical Republicans, the remainder Conservatives or unaligned.

The Radicals fell into three categories—the first (and, in Arkansas, the most politically powerful) group was composed of northerners who had come to Arkansas during or after the war. Derided as "carpetbaggers" by conservative whites who saw them as political opportunists, most had actually come South to pursue economic gain and to help transform the region into a free labor economy like that of the North. Others were teachers, missionaries, or Freedmen's Bureau agents who had come south to assist the former slaves in the difficult transition to freedom. The second group consisted of southerners who had been Unionists before the war or had gone over to the Unionist side during or after the war. In Arkansas they included prewar Whigs, mountain Unionists, and converted Rebels. Many white southerners viewed these "scalawags" as traitors to their own people and despised them even more than the carpetbaggers.

Carpetbaggers: Derisive name given by southerners to northerners who came to the South after the war for economic or political gain.

Scalawags: Derisive name given by southerners to white southerners who collaborated with northern Republicans during Reconstruction.

African Americans composed the third element of the Radical coalition. Eight blacks were delegates to the constitutional convention. Delegate William H. Grey, a minister familiar with parliamentary procedure, was active in the debates and was considered to be one of the most eloquent orators at the convention. Delegate James Mason, the mulatto son of wealthy Chicot County planter Elisha Worthington and one of his slaves, had been educated at Oberlin College and at the French Military Academy. When Worthington fled to Texas during the war with many of the family slaves, he left Mason in charge of his Sunnyside plantation, one of the largest in the South. Considered one of the more independent-minded of the Radical delegates, Mason would later become the county judge and leading political power in Chicot County.

The constitution produced by the convention gave African Americans the right to vote, serve on juries, hold office, and serve in the militia. It provided for the first system of free public schools in Arkansas for citizens of both races and for the establishment of a state university. The new constitution also redrew legislative districts to give greater representation to the Delta and the southwestern regions of the state and strengthened the power of the executive, giving the governor a four-year term and vastly expanded powers, including wide-ranging appointive powers. It disfranchised anyone who had taken an oath of allegiance to the United States and then served or aided the Confederacy as well as anyone "who during the late rebellion violated the rules of civilized warfare."

Conservatives objected to many of the provisions but were helpless to change them. Even some of the independent-minded Radicals, like James Mason, were less than totally satisfied with the document but supported it because of its protection of black rights. The vote on ratification was scheduled for two weeks in mid-March 1868. To ensure the desired outcome, the convention placed the election machinery completely in the hands of the Radicals.

Before the war, William H. Grey, a free person of color, had worked for the governor of Virginia and was well versed in parliamentary procedure. He was among the most active and eloquent delegates to the constitutional convention of 1868. *Courtesy of the Arkansas History Commission.*

Black Arkansans were eager to begin actively participating in the political process, and many joined political societies or clubs. The most significant of these was the Union League. Originally a northern white, middle-class, patriotic organization during the Civil War years, the league became a political vehicle for the freedmen in the early postwar period. In Arkansas and throughout the South, the league's principal goal was to raise the political consciousness of African Americans and to encourage them to vote. Thanks in no small part to the efforts of the Union League, 22,000 black Arkansans registered to vote between May and November of 1868.

Union League: Originally a northern white, middle-class, patriotic organization during the Civil War years, the league became a political vehicle for the freedmen in the early postwar period. Its principal goal was to raise the consciousness of African Americans and to encourage them to vote.

Conservatives were divided on what strategy to pursue. Some refused to participate in the election campaign in any way, while others urged using any means to defeat ratification. The major issue in the campaign was the granting of full civil and political rights to black Arkansans. Many Conservative elements viewed this as an attempt not only to radically transform Arkansas society but also to ensure the political ascendancy of the Republican Party through black suffrage. The Conservative-Democratic coalition expressed its intent to maintain "a WHITE MAN'S government in a WHITE MAN'S COUNTRY."

The campaign was marred by irregularities on both sides. In a telling action, the military authorities controlling the state established separate voting places from those sanctioned by the Radical-dominated election commission. The latter conducted balloting for state and congressional offices as well as a referendum on the constitution.

They required all voters to swear that they were not barred from voting by any of the provisions in the proposed constitution, that they would support the Constitution and laws of the United States and the state of Arkansas, and that they accepted the civil and political equality of all men. Most Conservatives who chose to participate in the election opted for the military poll, which required no oath and recorded votes only for and against the new constitution. Not surprisingly, the state poll reported an overwhelming majority for ratification, while the results of the military poll showed only a narrow majority in favor. With virtually no opposition, Republican candidates swept to easy victories in the state and congressional races.

Conservatives charged that a "fair" election would have returned an overwhelming majority against ratification, and in this they were probably correct, though a "fair" election in this overheated context was out of the question. Gen. A. C. Gillem, who had succeeded General Ord as commander of the Fourth Military District, certified the results and the slate of officers elected at the same time, and the U.S. Congress accepted them, again over the president's veto. The new state legislature quickly ratified the Fourteenth Amendment, and having thus satisfied the conditions set down by the Reconstruction Acts, Arkansas reentered the Union on June 22, 1868.

The newly elected governor was a man already familiar to many Arkansans. Powell Clayton had established a wartime reputation among many Arkansas Confederates as the best Federal cavalry commander west of the Mississippi River and had distinguished himself at the Battle of Pine Bluff in 1863. Even before the war ended, Clayton purchased a cotton plantation near Pine Bluff where he settled after the war. In December 1865, he married Adaline McGraw of Helena, the daughter of a steamboat captain who had served as a major in the Confederate army. In April 1867 Clayton had been active in the creation of the Republican Party in Arkansas, which included most of the state's Unionists, and had received the new party's nomination for governor. While not a delegate to the constitutional convention, he had campaigned hard for ratification.

Clayton's election marked a dramatic departure in the history of Reconstruction in Arkansas. Both departing governor Murphy and the new governor had been born in Pennsylvania, and both had been staunch Unionists during the war, but there the similarities ended. Murphy had a long history in the state and was known for his conciliatory nature. Clayton was an outsider, a "carpetbagger" to his opponents, who was by nature confrontational. Murphy had tried, without much success, to bring together the disparate elements of Arkansas society and to heal the wounds of the war. Clayton tended to view Reconstruction as little more than a continuation of the war (which in many ways it was), and he employed many of the same aggressive tactics he had used in that conflict.

Clayton and the Republican-dominated legislature hoped to accomplish four major objectives—to put an end to the widespread violence in the state, to implement the Republican program of protection of the civil and political rights of black Arkansans, to rebuild and restructure the state's economy, and to build a viable and lasting Republican Party in Arkansas. The governor did not hesitate to use his vastly expanded powers to accomplish these ends. The new constitution empowered the governor to appoint county officials to serve until the next election, and Clayton quickly used this power to build a personal political base. In Conway County, for example, the governor's appointees for county judge, clerk, sheriff, treasurer, coroner, and assessor were all veterans of the Union army. Similar appointments were made in other counties.

Considered by many to be the best Union cavalry officer west of the Mississippi during the war, Powell Clayton became the first Republican governor of Arkansas after the war's end. *Courtesy of J. N. Heiskell Collection/UALR Archives and Special Collections.*

The governor also moved to address the question of economic development, modeled along the lines of what came to be called the "gospel of prosperity." Anticipating the New South movement of the late nineteenth century, Republican leaders sought to transform the South into a diversified economy along the lines of the free labor system of the North. As historian Eric Foner notes, "With the aid of the state, they believed, the backward South could be transformed into a society of booming factories, bustling towns, a diversified agriculture freed from the plantation's dominance, and abundant employment opportunities for black and white alike."

To pay for this economic development and for expanded government services, the legislature raised property tax rates and ordered the reassessment of real estate at market value. Historians have disagreed over the extent of the increase and the degree to which the new revenues helped the state. Thomas Staples, in his landmark 1923 work *Reconstruction in Arkansas, 1862–1874*, argued that the new taxes were "exceedingly heavy" and accomplished little in the way of improvements. Despite the expenditure by the state of over ten million dollars in the period between 1868 and 1874, Staples noted, one government report estimated public improvements at only $100,000.

More recent historians have challenged Staples conclusions. In a 1994 study entitled *The Impact of the Civil War and Reconstruction on Arkansas*, Carl Moneyhon contended, "The increases were not as outrageous as the Republicans' opponents charged, and most of the money went to actual improvements." Nevertheless, as Moneyhon notes, the new assessments, coming on the heels of two bad crop seasons and falling cotton prices, were particularly hard on large landowners and gave the Democrats a powerful political issue. Republican leaders hoped that in the long run their economic plan would draw support from a wide range of southerners—former Whigs, entrepreneurs, merchants, and working-class people of both races—thereby reshaping southern politics and establishing a solid base of Republican support.

Part of the plan was a push to dramatically increase immigration. In 1868 the legislature, at the governor's urging, established the Commission of Immigration and State Lands, with the hope of attracting northern capital and labor to the state. The commission printed fifteen thousand pamphlets (ten thousand in English and five thousand in German) extolling the state's fertile soil, cheap land, and ambitious railroad-building plan. But limited resources prevented the widespread dissemination of this information, and its effect on immigration was unclear. The effort was further hurt by a scandal involving the commissioner. Some immigrants did come, but most were small farmers (black and white) from other southern states.

Another element of the Republican economic plan was the building of levees. Frequent flooding had been a major problem for Arkansans living along the state's rivers, ruining crops and keeping fertile land out of production. The state issued three million dollars in levee bonds, resulting in the construction of fifty-three miles of levees. But critics charged that many of the levees were poorly constructed and that the state aid had mainly benefited a small group of Clayton supporters. In any event, the state's poor credit caused the bonds to rapidly depreciate in value, and by the early 1870s the plan was dropped.

As important as immigration and levee building were to the state's economic development, the central element was railroad construction. A letter from a group of Mississippi freedmen summed up the sentiment of many Arkansans as well, "The day we commens to work on a Rail Road . . . it would make this whole South flourish." Nowhere was the need more pressing than in Arkansas. Only about sixty-five miles of track were in operation in the state when the Civil War began, and none had been added in the intervening years.

Enthusiasm for railroads was not limited to Republicans. In 1867 the Conservative-Democrat-controlled state legislature had passed a railroad-building plan. Clayton and the Republican-dominated legislature took up where the Conservatives left off, putting forward a plan for government assistance to railroad companies that the voters overwhelmingly approved. The plan proposed to pay selected companies $10,000 per mile of track laid for railroads receiving federal land grants and $15,000 per mile for others. The large amounts of money involved made the prospect of railroad building extremely appealing to ambitious entrepreneurs and unscrupulous politicians, many of whom were prominent figures in the new companies' boards of directors.

Eventually eighty-six companies were chartered, though some smaller companies later consolidated. Only five railroads whose routes followed the state's main arteries of commerce received state credit in bonds. By the end of Reconstruction, an additional 662 miles of track had been laid at a cost to the state of about $90,000,000. One scholarly examination of railroad building in the state concluded that "the Arkansas case is one in which the mileage actually constructed under state aid approached very closely the mileage for which [state] assistance was intended."

Still, the railroad-building boom was far from an unqualified success. The Arkansas economy was not developed enough to support even a few railroads, much less eighty-six. All companies receiving state money eventually went bankrupt, many of them without ever laying any track. These defaults added to an already severe debt problem including over $3,000,000 remaining from the collapse of the State Bank and the Real Estate Bank that the Republicans had hoped to retire.

White Terror and Martial Law

An even more pressing problem for Clayton was the persistence of widespread violence in the state. Some Conservative elements, barred from participation in the political process by the Military Reconstruction Act, were determined to use any and all means to oppose the new government. One of those means was the Ku Klux Klan. Founded as a secretive social fraternity in Pulaski, Tennessee, in the spring of 1866, the Klan soon evolved into a vigilante organization dedicated to the preservation of white supremacy. By the spring of 1868, Klan chapters were reported to be in operation at Little Rock, Pine Bluff, Batesville, Fort Smith, Arkadelphia, Searcy, Camden, El Dorado, Monticello, and numerous other areas around the state. Often portrayed as undisciplined thugs, the Arkansas Klan, in many areas of the state, was a highly organized paramilitary force serving the aims of the Conservative-Democratic Party. Its membership, especially in high leadership positions, included many prominent and well-to-do citizens.

Ku Klux Klan: Secretive organization founded originally as a social fraternity by Confederate veterans in Pulaski, Tennessee, in 1866. The Klan became a terroristic organization that functioned as the paramilitary arm of the Conservative-Democratic Party during the Reconstruction era, attacking freedmen, government officials, and Republicans.

To be sure, there had been violence directed against freedmen and white Unionists prior to the spring of 1868. But the Klan's appearance on the scene coincided with the beginning of the intense and bitter struggle leading up to the 1868 fall elections, and it provided a vehicle for those who were determined to retake control of the state's fortunes by any means necessary. Because of its secretive nature, it is difficult to ascertain whether the organization pursued a specific agenda. Some contemporaries believed that the Klan was determined to influence the fall elections in 1868 by hindering voter registration and intimidating freedmen and other Republican voters. Others, including Gen. C. H. Smith, the federal commander in Arkansas, believed the goal was nothing less than the overthrow of the Republican-controlled state government.

It is equally difficult to determine whether there was any statewide organization to the Arkansas Klan. Gen. Robert Shaver from Jackson County claimed to be the leader of the statewide organization and later boasted that he could assemble fifteen thousand armed men on short notice. Shaver also claimed that he was, at one point, on the verge of leading as many as ten thousand mounted men on Little Rock to capture the legislature, the supreme court, and the entire state government. "I had my foot in the stirrup;

and in another moment I'd have been in the saddle and away," he later recalled, when a message postponing the operation arrived from the acknowledged Grand Wizard in Memphis, former Confederate general Nathan Bedford Forrest. No creditable evidence exists to support Shaver's claims. While state and regional leaders may have exerted some degree of influence, it seems clear that many Klan units were locally organized and controlled and that these units operated largely independently of one another.

But while there is little evidence of the command structure and specific goals of the Klan, evidence of Klan-conducted and Klan-inspired violence is extensive. Even allowing for the possibility of exaggeration and outright fabrication by Republican editors and officials, compelling evidence exists to indicate a massive campaign of terror and violence in all but the northern counties in the state in 1868. Historian Allen Trelease has estimated that over two hundred Arkansans were murdered on the eve of the 1868 presidential election. Reports from Bradley and Columbia counties in the southern part of the state indicated that bands of armed men roamed the countryside threatening Unionists of both races. In late August 1868 a state legislator from Columbia County informed the governor that ten black men had been murdered in a period of twenty days.

In October Klansmen seized a Monticello deputy sheriff from his home at night. They tied one end of a rope around his neck, tied the other end around the neck of a local black man, led the two men a short distance away from the house, and shot them both to death. They then entangled the two lifeless bodies in an embrace and placed them in the middle of the road where they remained for two days. The following month two black preachers who were also Republican leaders in the county were taken from their homes and whipped. White Republican leaders were also threatened with death, and blacks were warned that they would be killed if they attempted to vote in the coming election.

In southwest Arkansas the chairman of the Lafayette County voter registration board reported to the governor that he had been forced to flee for his life, and added that "there was an organization formed of from one to two hundred men, for the avowed object of killing Union men, of both colors, who would not join democratic clubs and vote their ticket. Some ten to fifteen colored men were shot down for this cause, and I had reliable information that if I attempted to register [any voters] I would be assassinated."

At Lewisville, the county seat, seven black and one white Unionist were killed in a single day. Between mid-July and late August twenty men were killed within a ten-mile radius of the town. The Freedmen's Bureau agent for the county reported that eight freedmen had been murdered by white men. Only one arrest had been made, and the arrested man had been released after a gang of twenty-five armed whites rode into town, filled the courthouse, and threatened bloodshed if the accused were not released. He further noted, "Mr. Hawkins who is building the school house here has been informed that it would be advisable for him to leave here immediately. There are a class of men who have arraid themselves against the law and swear that it shall not be executed." He warned that unless a detachment of soldiers was sent, "I shall have to take leave or do as our Circuit Judge and others do in Columbia County—take to the woods at night."

In those southwestern counties that bordered Texas, the violence was particularly intense. The region was home to a vicious desperado named Cullen Montgomery Baker. Described by his most recent biographers as a cold-blooded murderer and sociopath, Baker's story illustrates the complex and often tenuous relationship between the common outlaw element and the Ku Klux Klan. There is no evidence to indicate that Baker ever expressed any strong feelings about blacks before the war, and his dedication to the Confederacy during the conflict was lukewarm at best. He may have been part of a guerrilla band that operated out of the Sulphur River bottoms in northeast Texas and southwest Arkansas. If Baker's wartime experience did little to serve the Confederate cause, however, it did generate an intense hatred of blacks.

There is some evidence to suggest that after the war Baker attempted to settle down and lead a normal life, but the death of his second wife in March 1866 seems to have "unhinged" him. By the following year Baker had begun to direct his antisocial tendencies toward the freedmen and the federal government. In September Baker and an outlaw gang ambushed a federal detachment killing four soldiers and mortally wounding another. It was the beginning of a career that would make him a pariah to many respectable citizens of the region but a hero to others who saw him as a defender of the "Lost Cause." Baker also gained support from some planters who saw him as a regulator of the activities of the freedmen. At first Baker apparently murdered blacks indiscriminately but later directed his attention to those who attempted to utilize their newly gained citizenship rights. Planters in Miller County in extreme southwest Arkansas often used Baker to help regulate their labor force. Blacks who had labored to bring in the crop were often run off at settlement time, while those who attempted to flee the plantations were rounded up and brought back.

Baker's activities increased after the beginning of Congressional Reconstruction, but the link between Baker and the Ku Klux Klan, if any, is impossible to determine with any certainty. It is clear, however, that their combined activities created a true reign of terror in southwest Arkansas and northeast Texas. In late October Baker and his gang ambushed a party consisting of the sheriff of Little River County, an assistant United States assessor, the local Freedmen's Bureau agent, and a local freedman as they approached the community of Rocky Comfort (near present-day Foreman). The sheriff managed to escape, but the other three men were killed. Before the year 1868 was over Baker killed another Freedmen's Bureau agent, several federal soldiers, and an indeterminate number of freedmen and spread terror throughout the southwestern section of the state. His reign of terror ended on January 6, 1869, when a posse of local citizens shot and killed him near the community of Bright Star.

Despite its large black population eastern Arkansas was not immune to the threats, intimidation, and violence that occurred across much of the rest of the state. In May a Freedmen's Bureau agent from Osceola wrote to General Smith that a black church had been burned and that "the Freedmen have been warned that the so called Ku Klucks would make the Union Leaguer a visit and kill the leaders." In October U.S. representative James M. Hinds and fellow Republican Joseph Brooks were shot from ambush as they rode through Monroe County canvassing for the candidacy of Ulysses Grant in the upcoming presidential election. Hinds was killed and Brooks wounded. Hinds was the highest-ranking government official to be killed in any state during Reconstruction. The assailants, who may or may not have been Klansmen, were never caught.

Crittenden County, directly across the Mississippi River from Memphis, was described by one historian as "the most persistent center of Klan activity in Arkansas." The local Freedmen's Bureau agent, a Union army veteran named E. G. Barker, was shot through an open window of his office at Marion and seriously wounded. (It marked the second time that the agent had been the target of an assassination attempt.) His clerk, who assumed the agent's duties, reported that hundreds of local freedmen were fleeing to his plantation for protection, and he urgently requested troops. In Mississippi County, a gang of lawless men, who may or may not have been Klansmen, murdered a local doctor who was a member of the state legislature. The same gang later killed six freedmen.

Woodruff County was the scene of some of the most intense Klan activity in the state. But it was also home to one of the Klan's most implacable foes—D. P. Upham. Upham was a Massachusetts native and a Union veteran who had come to Arkansas in 1865 with Brig. Gen. Alexander Shaler's Seventh Army Corps and was stationed at DeValls Bluff. A carpetbagger's carpetbagger, Upham had arrived in the state with ten dollars in his pocket, but he skillfully used his connection with Shaler to bolster his economic position during the war.

Local commanders like Shaler had great power over the leasing of abandoned lands and the granting of licenses to engage in certain businesses. Upham used his influence with Shaler to secure the required licenses and leases in return for a share of the business. By these methods he soon became a part owner of a saloon, a cotton plantation, and a steamboat charter firm. Using the money gained in these endeavors, Upham was able to become the sole owner of a saloon in Jacksonport and a mercantile store in Augusta. In August 1865 he and his wife settled in Augusta, the county seat of Woodruff County. Using the profits from his various enterprises, Upham invested in land and soon became one of the biggest landowners and leading citizens of Woodruff County.

With the advent of Congressional Reconstruction Upham took an active role in the creation of the state Republican Party, and in March 1868 he was elected to the state legislature where he voted the straight Radical line. His ethical shortcomings notwithstanding, Upham was a staunch defender of the rights of the freedmen and a dedicated foe of the Klan. In letters to his brother he chronicled the rise of the organization in Woodruff County. An August 1868 letter noted, "The Rebel murderers have now a regular arrangement in every county to put out of the way leading Republicans." In September he wrote, "There is no longer any doubt but what the rebels are well-organized, and in secret too, probably in shape of 'Ku Klux.'"

In August the Klan twice attacked delegates to the district Republican convention, wounding one and killing another. In response to Klan activities Upham organized a county militia composed almost entirely of local black men, many of them former Union soldiers. When the governor ordered the organization of the state militia in late

August, Upham became actively involved in its recruitment. Democrats placed a bounty on Upham, repeatedly offering to pay young men, black and white, to kill him. On October 2 he and the county registrar were traveling in the north part of the county when they were ambushed by three men concealed in a thicket. Both were seriously wounded, but unfortunately for the Klan, both survived. Upham would soon make the Klan pay dearly for the assault.

Even former Confederate leaders fell victim to the atmosphere of violence. In September 1868, former congressman and Confederate general Thomas Hindman was murdered at his home in Helena. Hindman had spent the last months of the war in San Antonio after a serious eye injury forced him from active duty in the Confederate army. Indicted for treason by the United States Court for the Eastern District of Arkansas, Hindman, his wife, and the couple's four remaining children (his five-year-old daughter Sallie had died on the trip from Georgia to San Antonio) crossed the Rio Grande into Mexico in early June 1866, intending to establish a new life there. But less than two years later financial difficulties and the unstable nature of the Mexican government forced Hindman and many other Confederate expatriates to return to the United States. By April 1867 he and his family were back in Helena.

Denied a presidential pardon, Hindman nonetheless soon became involved in politics, urging Conservatives to accept the Reconstruction Acts, take the required oath, and work diligently to defeat the Republicans at the ballot box. Unlike many of his Conservative allies, he urged Democrats to reach out to the freedmen in order to form a biracial coalition against the Republicans. His oratorical skills apparently undiminished, Hindman soon threatened to once again become a major force in Arkansas politics. On the evening of September 27, 1868, he was relaxing with his family in the sitting room of the family home when an assailant fired a shot through an open window mortally wounding him. The identity of the killer was never discovered.

Despite numerous threats against his life, including what was in all probability an aborted assassination attempt in the fall of 1868, Governor Clayton acted decisively and with great personal courage to stem the violence. Along with moderate Conservative leader and former Confederate senator Augustus Garland, he personally intervened to try to end racial and political strife in Conway County, one of the state's most troubled regions in the postwar years. When violent disturbances threatened to disrupt voter registration in four counties during the fall elections of 1868, the governor rejected the voter registrations from those counties. In addition he employed a dozen undercover agents to infiltrate the Klan and report on its activities. One of the agents was murdered when his true identity was revealed.

The federal government, however, neither matched nor supported the governor's actions. An appeal for federal troops to supplement the small force remaining in Arkansas was rejected, as was a subsequent request to use the arms stored in the federal arsenal at Little Rock. Finally Clayton sent agents to purchase guns in the North. In October 1868, the guns were delivered to Memphis, but the steamer *Hesper*, chartered to deliver the weapons to Little Rock, was run aground by another vessel on the

Mississippi River below Memphis. Masked men boarded the vessel and seized its cargo, confiscating some and dumping the rest into the river.

The Election of 1868

Despite these setbacks Clayton managed to hold the state for the Republican ticket. Citing violence against voter registration officials that caused the registrars to resign their posts, he rejected the registration in Ashley, Bradley, Columbia, Craighead, Greene, Hot Spring, Lafayette, Mississippi, Randolph, Sevier, Sharp, and Woodruff counties, effectively excluding them from the election. In addition there was no registration in Lawrence County and no returns from Fulton County. Of these fourteen counties only two had recorded majorities for the constitution the previous April. The results from the November 3 balloting showed 22,112 votes for Republican presidential candidate Ulysses Grant to 19,078 for Democrat Horatio Seymour of New York. (Arkansas's five electoral votes contributed to Grant's 214 to 80 electoral vote majority.) The Republicans also retained all three of the state's congressional seats. Democrats charged that voters in the counties whose registrations had been rejected would have provided the margin of victory for their candidates, but it is impossible to determine whether the number of potential Democratic voters who were unable to cast ballots would have offset the number of Republican voters who were intimidated away from the polls by the Klan.

The day after the election Clayton declared martial law in Ashley, Bradley, Columbia, Lafayette, Mississippi, Woodruff, Craighead, Greene, Sevier, and Little River counties, proclaiming them to be "in a state of insurrection" with the civil authorities "utterly powerless to preserve order and to protect the lives of the citizens." He later extended it to include Conway, Crittenden, Drew, and Fulton counties. Since membership was limited to eligible voters, the militia was composed largely of blacks and white Unionists. The state was then divided into four military districts, although little attention was paid to the northwest part of the state where Klan support was minimal and Republican support was strongest. Three Unionist state legislators were placed in charge of the remaining three districts, and the various units of the state militia were ordered to rendezvous at designated points around the state.

> **Martial law:** The imposition of military government over a designated area, usually for a temporary period during an emergency situation when the civilian government is unable or unwilling to maintain order or provide essential services.

The declaration of martial law and the subsequent activities of the militia constitute one of the most controversial aspects of Reconstruction in Arkansas. Violent clashes between the militia and local residents were commonplace. In southwest Arkansas, residents in and around the town of Center Point (present-day Howard County) claimed to have been unaware of the governor's declaration of martial law when a large body of armed and mounted men without uniforms or any symbol of authority rode into town and demanded that a local merchant open his store so that they might search for hidden weapons. When the merchant refused, the armed men

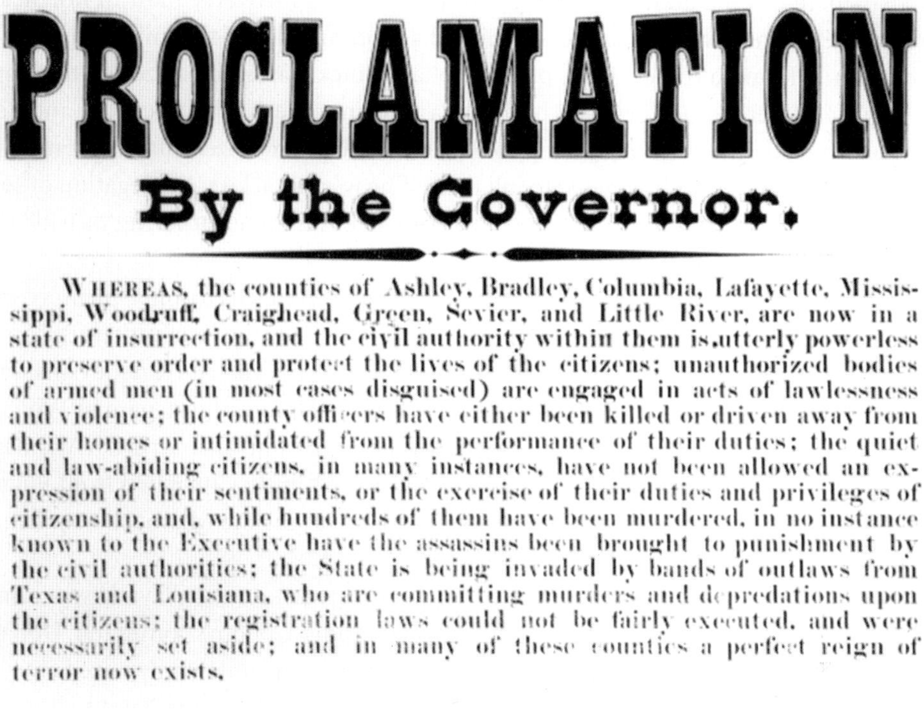

PROCLAMATION

By the Governor.

WHEREAS, the counties of Ashley, Bradley, Columbia, Lafayette, Mississippi, Woodruff, Craighead, Green, Sevier, and Little River, are now in a state of insurrection, and the civil authority within them is utterly powerless to preserve order and protect the lives of the citizens; unauthorized bodies of armed men (in most cases disguised) are engaged in acts of lawlessness and violence; the county officers have either been killed or driven away from their homes or intimidated from the performance of their duties; the quiet and law-abiding citizens, in many instances, have not been allowed an expression of their sentiments, or the exercise of their duties and privileges of citizenship, and, while hundreds of them have been murdered, in no instance known to the Executive have the assassins been brought to punishment by the civil authorities; the State is being invaded by bands of outlaws from Texas and Louisiana, who are committing murders and depredations upon the citizens; the registration laws could not be fairly executed, and were necessarily set aside; and in many of these counties a perfect reign of terror now exists.

Governor Clayton's proclamation of martial law. *Courtesy of the Arkansas History Commission.*

forcibly entered "and completely gutted the store, taking away bridles, saddles, and everything else they wanted." The following day a crowd of local citizens, estimated at between 150 and 400 in number, confronted four hundred militiamen, and shots were exchanged. Reports later indicated that one militiaman and eight local residents were killed. The militia took sixty prisoners and raided a local Ku Klux Klan den.

Near Paraclifta, twenty miles south of Center Point, a woman was raped by a black militiaman while four accomplices robbed her house. The militia commander had the perpetrators arrested and tried. The rapist was shot by firing squad and the others dismissed from the service, but reports of theft and brutality against the local population continued throughout southern and southwestern Arkansas.

At Monticello in southeast Arkansas, fourteen men suspected of being members of the Ku Klux Klan were alleged to have murdered a deputy sheriff and a local freedman. The militia, composed of three companies of black troops, arrested one of the perpetrators and held him for trial. In December 1868, a group of prominent Drew County citizens visited the governor in Little Rock and pledged that they would form a bipartisan "home guard" in the county to preserve law and order if the governor would restore civil authority. Clayton agreed, and three members of the home guard joined with three militia officers in unanimously convicting the alleged murderer, who was subsequently executed by firing squad. The remaining suspects reportedly fled the county.

Nowhere did the actions of the militia stir more controversy than in northeast Arkansas. The man whom Clayton appointed as commander of the militia in the district was the Klan's old foe, D. P. Upham. Upham quickly assembled 120 white troops at Augusta. When reports reached him that a force numbering between 300 and 400 men was outside the town preparing to attack him, Upham seized fifteen prominent citizens as hostages and threatened to kill them if he were attacked. A delegation of several influential townspeople intervened to convince the force gathering outside the town to call off the attack.

Meanwhile, a detachment of black militia moving from Helena to join Upham's command was besieged in the county courthouse at Marion. Only the timely intervention of a group of some six hundred Missouri troops rescued the militia. The Missourians were a band of irregulars under the command of a former Union officer named William Monks. Hardened veterans of guerrilla war in southern Missouri and northern Arkansas, Monks's band engaged the Klan in a series of skirmishes as they marched from Fulton County to Crittenden County. Local residents charged that the Missourians pillaged homesteads in their path as they advanced.

From the inception of the campaign in northeast Arkansas, Clayton was bombarded by complaints of abuse by the militia forces under Upham's command. Upham and one of his top subordinates admitted that the militia had unlawfully seized civilian property, had killed four prisoners when they "attempted to escape," and had raped two white women. The perpetrators of the latter outrage, four black militiamen, were arrested, tried, and executed by firing squad.

Clayton found the charges serious enough to appoint his adjutant general to investigate them, and he later personally investigated the charges in Crittenden County. Both investigations exonerated Upham, but a formal report by an assistant inspector general to the adjutant general of the Department of Louisiana conceded:

> It would be impossible anywhere to call into existence a force as this has been, for temporary purposes, and not have violations of order and military law. There was no other way to maintain the militia but to subsist it on the country—collecting supplies by a system of contributions levied on the people.... Subordinates at times doubtless exceeded their orders; also persons not of the forces, but representing themselves as belonging to them, in some instances plundered the people.

Civilian authority was restored in the southwest district in mid-January 1869, in the southeast district in early February, and in the remainder of the state in late March.

While it is clear that many of the charges lodged against the militia were exaggerated or, in some cases, totally fabricated, the evidence of depredations by the militia is so widespread and so pervasive that it cannot be discounted. It is equally clear that Clayton's declaration of martial law and deployment of the militia, combined with the desire of many law-abiding Arkansans of all political persuasions for a return to law and order, contributed to the rapid decline of the Arkansas Klan and the restoration of some semblance of civility. Eric Foner has noted, "Scores of suspected Klansmen were arrested; three were executed after trials by military courts, and numerous others fled the state. By early 1869, order had been restored and the Klan destroyed." While it is an overstatement to say that the Klan had been destroyed in the state, it is possible to argue, as Allen Trelease does, that Clayton "accomplished more than any other Southern governor in suppressing the Ku Klux conspiracy."

The exact nature or even the existence of such a conspiracy is still a matter of conjecture. Clayton's critics contended that the governor deliberately exaggerated the extent of the violence and the size and power of the Arkansas Klan in order to further his own political ends and those of the Republican Party. But while there is no hard evidence to suggest that there was a statewide plot to overthrow the Clayton regime, local Klan chapters clearly employed intimidation and violence to influence elections on the local and county level. In addition, as Clayton biographer William Burnside has noted, there was a concerted effort by members of the Klan and sympathetic newspaper editors to undermine the authority of the state government and obstruct its effectiveness.

But if Clayton's actions were effective in suppressing Klan violence, they also left a legacy of bitterness with many white Arkansans that severely undermined his attempts to build support for the Republican Party in Arkansas. Clayton had other political troubles as well. Martial law had scarcely ended when the governor faced a revolt from within his own party.

Republican Schism and Conservative Resurgence

In April 1869 Lt. Gov. James Johnson and a group of Republican state legislators met to organize opposition to the Clayton regime. The new faction, which styled itself the "Liberals," advocated an end to government corruption, greater economy in government, the curtailing of the governor's powers, and an immediate end to all restrictions on voting rights for former Confederates. Identified with the national Liberal Republican movement that opposed the administration of President Grant, the Liberal Party in Arkansas charged Clayton with extravagance, mismanagement, corruption, and abuse of his power, particularly as it related to his role as commander-in-chief of the militia.

These charges aside, much of the opposition was personal rather than ideological. Johnson, a Madison County resident who had served as an officer in the Union army during the war, and other native Arkansas Unionists had chafed at the dominance of the Republican Party and of state government by "outsiders" like Clayton and at the governor's domineering nature. Clayton clearly understood the importance of patronage in maintaining his political hold on the state government and of the Republican Party. The governor had used the vast patronage power that the new constitution had bestowed on him to appoint men who were loyal not only to the party but to him personally, and, William Burnside notes, "apparently did not see much difference between loyalty to the party and loyalty to Powell Clayton. . . . [He] sought to lead his party as he had commanded his regiment."

The breach widened in the summer of 1869 when Clayton went to New York to arrange for the American Exchange National Bank to act as the fiscal agent for financing the state debt. Perhaps fearing what actions Johnson might take in his absence, Clayton did not inform the lieutenant governor of his departure. But some of Johnson's supporters got word of the governor's absence and urged Johnson to leave his northwest Arkansas home and come to Little Rock to assume power. Johnson did come to Little Rock, though exactly what he intended to do when he arrived is unclear. It was a moot point because Clayton hastened back to the capital, arriving before Johnson. The lieutenant governor made a public speech condemning Clayton, before, in the governor's words "sneak[ing] back to his mountain home."

Johnson returned to Little Rock in October, however, to help formally organize the insurgent Republicans. Meanwhile, with an election year approaching and his administration under attack both from within and without the Republican Party, Clayton shifted tactics. In an unusually conciliatory address, the governor co-opted most of the Liberals platform, advocating lower taxes and the removal of voting disabilities from former Confederates and urged his listeners to "let bygones be bygones; help neighbors, avoid jealousy; let us as one man and one voice strike hands together to build up the fallen fortunes of Arkansas." Longtime observers might well have wondered what had come over the governor in his abbreviated trip to New York. Clayton spent the remaining months prior to the 1870 election attempting to mend fences within his own party and solidifying his control over county organizations, while the Conservative-Democrats vigorously pursued a voter registration campaign.

Liberal gains in the 1870 elections were held to a minimum, but despite disfranchisement, the governor's control of the election machinery, and widespread fraud, the Conservative-Democrats reemerged as a legitimate force in both houses of the state legislature. It was clear to Governor Clayton and other Republicans that the end of voting disabilities on former Confederates would place the Republican Party in Arkansas in dire straits. In the January session of the new legislature, Clayton pursued the U.S. Senate seat that was up for election. He was overwhelmingly elected, garnering not only the votes of his Republican supporters but also those of Conservative-Democrats who wanted him out of the state. But while Clayton was ready to assume the Senate seat, he was unwilling to turn the governor's office over to his greatest enemy in the party—Lieutenant Governor Johnson.

What followed was pure political farce. Pro-Clayton forces tried to have Johnson impeached. When this failed, a coalition of Democrats and Liberal Republicans succeeded in having the House pass articles of impeachment against Clayton. Arkansas law provided that the governor would be suspended when the House informed the Senate of its action. Pro-Clayton senators refused to enter the chamber thereby denying the House managers a quorum. Johnson formally demanded that Clayton surrender the office but was rebuffed. Rumors of violence swept the capital.

The end of the crisis came when Clayton persuaded the secretary of state to resign his office and offered the vacant position to the lieutenant governor. Amazingly, Johnson accepted the offer. With the lieutenant governor's position vacant, the line of succession passed to the president of the senate, Ozra Hadley, a devoted Clayton ally.

Hadley served out the remainder of the term in a caretaker capacity. Clayton took his seat in the U.S. Senate in March 1871. But while Clayton was gone, he saw to it that he was not forgotten. He remained a powerful figure in Arkansas and national Republican politics until his death in 1914.

As for Johnson, his reasons for accepting the secretary of state's position remain a mystery. Rumors were rampant that he had been paid off, but no conclusive evidence was ever produced to support such a claim. The rumors, however, were enough to end his career as a major player in state politics. With both Clayton and his main challenger within the party now out of the picture, a fierce new battle soon developed for political ascendancy in Arkansas.

The man who came to lead the insurgent wing of the Republican Party, Joseph Brooks, was a former Methodist minister from Iowa with a voice "like a brindle-tail bull." Brooks had been the dominant figure at the constitutional convention of 1868 and had supported Governor Clayton's employment of the militia in 1869 before later falling out with the governor. In 1871 Brooks announced his intention to seek the governorship in the 1872 election. He was a formidable candidate. His strong record on civil rights drew support from black Arkansans, and his platform of "Universal suffrage, universal amnesty, and honest men in office" combined with his opposition to Clayton gave him strong appeal to many Democrats and other Conservatives.

Without the services of their longtime leader and confronted by a candidate with wide appeal and great political skills, the Regular (Pro-Clayton) Republicans faced the greatest challenge in their brief history. Meeting in convention in August, they dumped the colorless Hadley and nominated in his place the Batesville merchant and lawyer Elisha Baxter. Baxter was a native of North Carolina who had moved to Batesville in 1852 and served two terms in the state legislature in the 1850s. His exact political position before the war is difficult to determine. Purported to be a Whig, he had supported Thomas Hindman in the elections of 1858 and 1860 but had opposed secession.

Though described by one historian as "timid," Baxter's wartime experiences were the stuff of adventure novels. When Federal forces occupied Batesville in 1862, he was offered a commission in the Union army but declined. When Confederate forces reoccupied the area, Baxter fled to Missouri where he took a job as a schoolteacher. In 1863 he was captured by a Confederate raiding party led by Col. Robert C. Newton and returned to Arkansas to stand trial for treason. Friends in Little Rock helped him to escape, and he began a long and dangerous flight to Union lines in Missouri, surviving on little more than corn and berries. Arriving in Springfield, he recruited a mounted infantry regiment and became its colonel.

After Little Rock fell to Union forces, Baxter served the Murphy government as a member of the state supreme court and was later elected by the Unionist legislature to the U.S. Senate, though the Radical-controlled body refused to seat him. Governor Clayton later appointed him as judge of the Third Judicial District. The platform of the Regular Republicans (often referred to as "Minstrels" after the previous occupation of one of their leaders) differed little from that of the Brooks "Brindletail" faction.

The nomination of Brooks and Baxter by the opposing factions within the

Ohio native Joseph Brooks was a Methodist preacher who served as a chaplain in the Union army during the war. He later became the leader of a faction in the state Republican Party that was opposed to Gov. Powell Clayton. *Courtesy of the Arkansas History Commission.*

Elisha Baxter came to Arkansas in 1852 while in his mid-twenties. A leader of the "Minstrel" faction of the state Republican Party, he was declared the winner of the disputed election of 1872. *Courtesy of J. N. Heiskell Collection/UALR Archives and Special Collections.*

Republican Party set the stage for the Brooks-Baxter War, one of the most confused and confusing episodes in all of Arkansas history. As Michael Dougan has noted, "That carpetbagger Brooks ran with Democratic and scalawag support against a scalawag nominated by a Party composed almost exclusively of carpetbaggers was enough to bewilder most voters as well as the modern student." Brooks's oratorical skills gave him a great advantage, but Baxter had an advantage of his own; namely, control of the election machinery. In the final analysis, it proved decisive.

The election in early November 1872 was marred by the now all-too-familiar pattern of fraud, intimidation, and stuffed ballot boxes. Returns from four counties were declared invalid and thrown out. "Official" returns revealed that Baxter had won by a vote of 41,681 to 38,415. Brooks's partisans fiercely contested the results but were frustrated in their attempts to have the election overturned. The legislature, dominated by Regular Republicans, failed to grant Brooks a hearing. Thus frustrated in the legislature, the Brooks forces turned to the courts. In June 1873 the state attorney general initiated a *quo warranto* proceeding against Baxter, requiring the governor to prove the validity of his claim to the office. The Brooks forces hoped for a favorable ruling from the state supreme court which was headed by Chief Justice John McClure, a former Clayton ally and appointee and a Brooks supporter. The court denied the writ over McClure's dissent.

That same month, Brooks filed a complaint against Baxter in Pulaski Circuit Court claiming that Baxter had usurped the governor's office without authority. In response,

Baxter filed a *demurrer* (a pleading that asserts that, even if the charges of the other party are true, they are insufficient to constitute a cause of action) and no further action was taken for a time. The Regular Republicans also retained control of the legislature, and Arkansas gave its eight electoral votes to President Grant, though the U.S. Congress threw out the state's electoral votes on a technicality.

In his brief inaugural, Baxter expressed the hope that his election would "mark the commencement of a new era of peace and good feeling in the history of Arkansas." Noting that "[t]he disfranchisement of certain classes for participation in the rebellion is a great impediment in the way of restoring fraternal feeling among the people.... [I]t is needless for me to say that I desire the immediate enfranchisement of those persons who are now denied a voice in the selection of their rulers." He moved quickly to make good that pledge. An amendment restoring the vote was put to the voters in March 1873 and passed overwhelmingly. Thus Arkansas became the last state to remove voting disabilities on former Confederates.

The new governor appointed Conservative-Democrats and Liberals as well as Regular Republicans to government positions. After the legislature adjourned in April, a combination of gubernatorial appointments and resignations resulted in almost forty legislative vacancies, necessitating a special election in November 1873. The results reflected the changes wrought by the recent passage of the new franchise amendment. Democrats were elected to fill practically all the legislative vacancies, giving them control of the state legislature for the first time since the advent of Congressional Reconstruction.

Baxter continued to broaden his appeal to all factions, but in so doing he began to alienate his own base. Particularly offensive to Republicans of all stripes was the appointment of former Confederate colonel Robert Newton to head the state militia (the same Robert Newton who had arrested Baxter for treason in 1863). But despite their disapproval of many of his actions, Clayton and fellow U.S. senator Stephen F. Dorsey continued to support Baxter.

The following year, however, a major schism occurred that severely threatened the future of the Baxter administration. Democratic success in the special election gave rise to a call for a special convention to draft a new constitution more in line with Conservative-Democratic principles. The prospect of a new charter that threatened to undo all that Republicans had worked for since 1868 sent shock waves through Republican ranks. When it became apparent that Baxter favored the calling of a convention, Senators Powell and Dorsey hastened to Little Rock to attempt to exert their influence on the governor.

That same month, Baxter announced that all the railroad bonds that had been issued by the Reconstruction government (including apparently $400,000 worth that had been issued by him personally) had been issued in violation of the constitution and indicated that he would not issue any more such bonds. One of the railroad companies affected by this order was closely associated with Senator Dorsey. Even more significantly, this action by the governor threatened to undermine the very foundation of the Republicans' plan for economic Reconstruction as well as the state's credit. For

Dorsey and Clayton, this was the last straw. Deserting Baxter, they allied themselves with Brooks and persuaded a friendly Pulaski County circuit judge to bring up the case of *Brooks v. Baxter* (filed ten months previously) and, on April 15, 1874, the judge declared Brooks the legal governor of Arkansas.

Brooks was sworn in by Chief Justice McClure, and shortly thereafter Brooks and over a dozen armed men marched to the statehouse and forced the startled Baxter to vacate the governor's office. Baxter and his supporters established themselves at the Anthony House, a local hotel located less than three blocks east of the capitol near the intersection of Markham and Scott streets. There they laid plans to retake the office. Main Street became the dividing line between the two opposing forces, and federal troops served as a peacekeeping force in attempting to keep the two sides apart. The surreal nature of the situation increased when both sides organized militias, each commanded by a former Confederate officer.

The schism in Republican ranks also divided other political constituencies in Arkansas. Some Democrats and other Conservatives had supported Brooks in the election as the best hope of unseating the hated Regular Republicans, and they welcomed his *coup d'état*. Others, including prominent Little Rock attorneys Augustus Garland and U. M. Rose, remembered Brooks's staunch radicalism in the early days of the Clayton regime and feared his ascension to the governor's chair. Garland, a prewar Whig and former Confederate senator, understood that the Conservative-Democratic element in the state could be a critical swing vote in the struggle between opposing factions in the Republican Party and that Baxter could be the instrument of the state's deliverance from Reconstruction. He and Baxter had become friends, and the embattled governor sought to bolster his position through Garland's standing in the community and his keen legal mind.

For Baxter, Garland was a major weapon in his struggle to retain his office, but for Garland, Baxter was only a means to an end. In a revealing letter to former Confederate governor Harris Flanagin, Garland candidly admitted, "It is small moment really who is Govr. of these two, but it is of great moment to settle these troubles and get a government by & from the people." These sentiments were shared by Robert Ward Johnson and Albert Pike, now residents of Washington, D.C., who supported Baxter's cause in the nation's capital.

African Americans were also divided over the issue. When the call for volunteers went out from the rival militias, black Arkansans rallied to both camps. On the last day of April, a predominantly black force of two hundred Baxter supporters led by a charismatic ex-Confederate soldier named Hercules King Cannon White steamed downriver from Pine Bluff to New Gascony, about twenty-five miles below the town, where they surprised and routed a black company of Brooks supporters, killing seven and wounding thirty. A week later two hundred Brooks men ambushed a steamboat carrying forty Baxter supporters near the point where Palarm Creek enters the Arkansas River upstream from Little Rock, killing or wounding half of them and disabling the boat.

Skirmishes between rival factions broke out throughout the state, but Little Rock

Reinforcements for Joseph Brooks head across the Arkansas River toward the state capitol during the Brooks-Baxter War in this 1874 sketch done for *Leslie's* by an unknown artist. *Courtesy of UALR Archives and Special Collections.*

remained the center of the controversy. Volunteers for both sides flooded into the city until the number of armed men reached about three thousand with each faction seeking desperately to secure weapons and ammunition. Scattered incidents of gunfire erupted resulting in a few casualties on both sides, and the potential for widespread bloodshed increased with each passing day.

Many Arkansans cared less about who occupied the governor's office than they did about the restoration of stability and order to state government. They joined the warring factions in appealing to President Grant to intervene. Finally on May 15, 1874, one month to the day after the crisis began, the president, convinced that serious violence was imminent, telegraphed his support for Baxter and ordered the Brooks forces to disband. He cushioned the blow by appointing Brooks to the position of postmaster at Little Rock.

The following month, voters went to the polls to decide whether to hold a convention to write a new constitution and to choose delegates to that convention. This first statewide election since the end of restrictions on former Confederates gave clear evidence of a new day in Arkansas politics. The convention was approved by a margin of almost ten to one (80,259 to 8,547), and Conservative-Democrats won over seventy of the ninety-one delegate positions. Thomas Staples has noted, "The Democratic members were elected and came together under the impression that they were to be the chief actors in a work of reform. That reform, as they understood it, was to be the undoing of the work of the Republican Party in Arkansas as far as the state constitution was concerned."

The convention assembled on July 14, 1874, and remained in session until early September. The document it produced provided for the civil and political rights of all citizens regardless of race (a necessary concession to prevent the possibility of federal intervention), but otherwise it undid many of the most significant measures the Republicans had written into the constitution of 1868. The governor's term was shortened to two years, his powers were dramatically reduced, and his salary, along with those of other state officials, kept very low. Gubernatorial vetoes could be overridden by a simple majority vote. Whereas the constitution of 1868 had given the governor the power to appoint many state officials, the new document made all major government offices subject to popular election.

In addition, the convention placed severe restraints on the taxing powers of both state and local governments by imposing low maximum rates. As a result, public education and other government services would be chronically underfunded. Many of the powers that had been assumed by the state during Reconstruction were returned to county and municipal governments, entities that were almost always dominated by local landed and business elites. In the final analysis, the constitution of 1874 largely succeeded in accomplishing most of the "reforms" that the Conservative-Democrats had sought, which is to say that it precluded the kind of strong executive leadership and activist government that Powell Clayton and the Republicans had pursued.

On October 13, 1874, the voters went to the polls to vote for or against ratification of the proposed constitution and to elect officials to serve under the new document if adopted. Arkansas Republicans, their hopes for maintaining their hold on power tied to the increasingly unlikely prospect of federal intervention, did not put forward candidates for state offices. In the largest voter turnout in Arkansas history to that time, the Conservative-Democrats not only won control of those offices but also returned overwhelming majorities in the state legislature (thirty-one Democrats to two Republicans in the Senate, eighty Democrats to ten Republicans in the House) and elected Augustus H. Garland governor.

A prominent Whig attorney in the antebellum period, Garland had supported John Bell of the Constitutional Union Party for president in 1860. Elected to represent Pulaski County in the secession convention of 1861, he had opposed secession until President Lincoln's call for troops. Through a combination of personal magnetism and ability, he had risen rapidly through the ranks of the Confederate government, serving first as representative and later as senator in the Confederate congress.

Disfranchised by the Fourteenth Amendment, he had, through the influence of powerful friends, obtained a pardon from President Johnson in July 1865, only seventeen days after submitting his request. Garland then returned to his law practice. Though he had been admitted to the bar of the U.S. Supreme Court in 1860, his inability to take the "ironclad oath" that he had never born arms against the United States nor held office in a government hostile to it prevented him from arguing cases before the Court. In the case of *Ex Parte Garland* (1866), he successfully challenged the prohibition as unconstitutional and regained the right to appear before the Court. When Governor Baxter declined the Democratic Party's nomination for governor in 1874, the convention turned to Garland, and he won easy nomination and election.

The new legislature that assembled in November 1874 wasted little time in completing the unraveling of the constitution of 1868 by placing the assessment of property in the hands of locally elected assessors rather than officials appointed by the governor. This measure made it possible for politically powerful propertied interests to control

A prominent Whig attorney before the Civil War, Augustus H. Garland served in the Confederate senate during the conflict. After the war he was elected governor of Arkansas and United States senator and later served as attorney general of the United States under Grover Cleveland, becoming the first Arkansan ever to serve in a cabinet position. *Courtesy of the Arkansas History Commission.*

the assessment process, and it ensured the continued economic hegemony of state's landed interests.

Only the long-anticipated report of a special committee of the U.S. House of Representatives charged with investigating the Brooks-Baxter controversy stood between the Conservative-Democrats and their goal of reclaiming control of the state government. The committee's majority report, submitted in early February 1875, concluded that the federal government should not interfere with the existing state government. The full House officially accepted the report on March 2. Three days later, Senator Clayton, who had labored diligently to overturn the Baxter government, conceded defeat, telling his followers, "The action of Congress on Arkansas affairs is conclusive. The validity of the new constitution and the government established thereunder ought no longer to be questioned. It is the duty of Republicans to accept the verdict, and render the same acquiescence which we would have demanded had the case been reversed." Reconstruction in Arkansas was over.

The Legacy of Reconstruction

The Republican Reconstruction governments could take credit for some significant accomplishments, including dramatically expanding the amount of railroad mileage in the state, providing for the first state-supported institutions for the blind and deaf, and establishing the state's first system of free public education. In addition, the legislature, in March 1871, established the first state university, the Arkansas Industrial University (now the University of Arkansas). Fayetteville, long considered a center of learning in the state, was chosen as the site for the school. The community donated the land and issued $100,000 in municipal bonds to help finance construction of the university buildings. Two years later, the state established a normal school for African Americans at Pine Bluff (now the University of Arkansas at Pine Bluff). In other areas, such as economic diversification, penal reform, and the development of a viable second party, Reconstruction fell far short of what its proponents had hoped.

For black Arkansans, Reconstruction proved a mixed blessing. The Freedmen's Bureau enjoyed notable success in establishing schools for the former slaves, but in other areas it was less successful. Many of the gains made by African Americans in this period were the results of their own efforts. As Randy Finley has noted, "Freedpersons tested their freedom in many ways—by assuming new names, searching for lost family members, moving to new residences, working to provide for their families, learning to read and write, forming and attending their own churches, creating their own histories and myths, struggling to obtain land, and establishing different nuances in race, gender, and class."

For almost a quarter century after the end of the war, relations between the races were more ambiguous, fluid, and flexible than they had been previously or would be after the full flowering of "Jim Crow" segregation in the 1890s. While racial hostility and discrimination still existed, African Americans exercised a degree of political, social, and economic autonomy that would have been unthinkable in 1860. Under Republican rule, blacks played prominent roles in state politics. African Americans served as delegates to the constitutional conventions of 1868 and 1874, were represented in every general assembly between 1868 and 1893, and, particularly in areas with heavy black populations, held numerous offices at the county and local level.

Even the return of the Conservative-Democrats to power in 1874 did not lead to an immediate deterioration of the status of black Arkansans. In his inaugural address, Governor Garland struck a conciliatory tone, noting that while the laws should be rigidly enforced, "no man living under them should be unjustly or illegally deprived of one iota of his rights; and let no man be put in fear or injured, or denied any right on account of race, color or previous condition of servitude." His successor, William Miller, continued this moderate approach, and throughout the remainder of the decade the Democratic Party openly courted the black vote.

In the aftermath of emancipation, Arkansas planters, desperate for laborers, actively recruited workers from surrounding states. The prospect of fertile land, relatively generous terms, and the prospect of a more tolerant environment than neighboring Mississippi and Louisiana drew thousands of black farmers to the state. While most African Americans continued to be employed in agriculture, others found new opportunities in the state's urban areas, particularly Little Rock and Pine Bluff. In these more heterogeneous settings, blacks served on city councils and school boards; owned and operated boardinghouses, barbershops, saloons, and restaurants; entered the professions as teachers, clergymen, lawyers, and doctors; and formed their own religious and fraternal organizations. In Pine Bluff, an ex-slave named Wiley Jones worked, at various times, as a porter, a teamster, a barber, and a saloonkeeper. Through hard work, careful management, and shrewd investments, he acquired property throughout the city, including a racetrack (complete with thousands of dollars' worth of trotting horses) and the town's streetcar system. By the 1890s his total assets were estimated at over a quarter of a million dollars.

Jones was, of course, an exception, but the state did acquire a reputation as a place where African Americans might enjoy a better life. "Arkansas is destined to be the great Negro state of the country," remarked Henry Turner, a bishop of the African Methodist Episcopal Church. "The meagre [*sic*] prejudice compared to some states, and opportunity to acquire wealth, all conspire to make it inviting to the colored man. The colored people now have a better start than in any other state in the Union. . . . This is the state for colored men who wish to live by their merits." The message resonated with many African Americans, and between 1870 and 1890 the black population of the state more than doubled.

In the end, however, the promise that Arkansas had held out for African Americans went largely unfulfilled. The failure of the federal government to provide them with land prevented most black Arkansans from obtaining true independence. Tenancy and declining crop prices kept them in a position of economic and social inferiority, and the advent of Jim Crow in the 1890s closed the brief window of political, social, and economic opportunity that many had enjoyed. At the turn of the century, most black Arkansans remained second-class citizens, condemned to a grinding cycle of poverty and political powerlessness whose effects are still being felt. Though the gains made during Reconstruction laid the foundation for the civil rights movement of the next century, it remained, in Eric Foner's words, an "unfinished revolution."

Some of the reasons for the failure of Reconstruction to achieve its goals were beyond the control of any faction within the state or the region. The bad weather conditions of 1866 and 1867, the steep decline in the price of cotton, and the economic depression of the 1870s all contributed to problems faced by Reconstruction governments. But if the actions of former Confederates in the months following the end of the war destroyed any hope of a lenient Reconstruction, the actions of Republicans in the years between 1867 and 1874 helped assure the failure of Radical Reconstruction. Part of the blame lay with the northern Republicans who, by the end of the Reconstruction era, had simply lost the will to carry through on their commitments to restructuring southern society and guaranteeing civil rights for African Americans. Arkansas Republicans must also take a large measure of responsibility. As was the case elsewhere in the South, the progressive, even noble goals they had espoused fell victim to corruption, high taxes, and a perversion of the democratic process.

By refusing to restore the franchise for over four years, Arkansas Republicans undermined the foundation on which representative government is built. Denied access to the franchise, many former Confederates refused to recognize the legitimacy of the Republican government and sought to oppose any and all of its programs by any available means, including the use of violence. Widespread corruption further eroded support for the Republican regime. While it is undoubtedly true that, as with the abuses of Clayton's militia, much of the alleged corruption was exaggerated by opposition politicians and newspapers, real extravagance and corruption were all too common. Radical legislators submitted grossly inflated requests for travel reimbursement, appropriated funds to provide every member with ten daily newspapers (a virtual subsidy for Radical newspapers which had very little other support), and staffed the legislature with an assortment of functionaries in a thinly disguised effort to provide jobs for their supporters at the public expense. Republican partisans who obtained the state penitentiary lease were accused of selling furniture in the penitentiary cells to the state for more than five times its original cost. Two of the lessees were alleged to have replaced the penitentiary roof needlessly at state expense while they used the old roof on their private homes. Corruption also tainted federal officials in the state. The federal judge for the Western District of Arkansas, William Story, resigned while under investigation on charges of bribery, and three United States Marshals were dismissed after being charged with submitting false accounts and defrauding the government.

Revisionists have argued that such practices have accompanied almost every political organization and have pointed out that corruption in this period was a national rather than a peculiarly southern problem. Neither argument is totally persuasive. As Eric Foner has pointed out, "Corruption may be ubiquitous in American history, but it thrived in the Reconstruction South because of the specific circumstances of Republican rule." The disfranchisement of many Arkansans meant that public officials were not responsible to the people they purported to represent. The expansion of government services, the larger state budgets, the unprecedented amounts of money available to government officials, the corporations (particularly railroads) competing for government assistance, and the tenuous political and economic circumstances of many Republican officeholders combined to create an atmosphere conducive to corruption on a large scale.

Tax increases further undermined support for the Reconstruction government. To be sure, taxes in the antebellum period had been exceedingly low and government services almost nonexistent. But for many Arkansans the higher taxes exacerbated an already tenuous economic condition, and the new revenues often failed to achieve the promised results. In some Arkansas counties the property tax assessments increased by sevenfold during Reconstruction, with little to show in return.

Despite the increase in taxes, the state debt soared. When Isaac Murphy turned over the reins of government to Powell Clayton in 1868, the state had a surplus of $122,587. Six years later, when the Conservative-Democrats reclaimed control of the government, the state was over ten million dollars in debt. Many counties were also deeply in debt. For all these reasons, Republicans were unable to gain sufficient support among white

Arkansans to maintain themselves as a legitimate and viable second party. All of these factors, combined with its inability to maintain a united political front, doomed the party's efforts to permanently alter the direction of southern society and allowed Conservative forces to reclaim control of the state government.

"Redeemers": White southern Democrats who worked to bring Reconstruction to an end and to retake control of state government from the Republicans.

Democrats and other Conservative forces liked to refer to themselves as "the Redeemers" and their return to power as "Redemption." Their triumph in the elections of 1874 marked the climax of a remarkable political resurgence by Arkansas's prewar elite that matched or exceeded their economic revival. Relegated to the political sidelines by the advent of Congressional Reconstruction, they had employed both fair and foul means to maintain their political viability and bided their time until the split in Republican ranks in 1872 and the subsequent restoration of voting rights to former Confederates enabled them to regain their political dominance. The planter class emerged from the struggles of the Reconstruction era weaker and poorer than before the war but with their dominant position in Arkansas society restored. Nowhere was this more apparent than in the election of Augustus Garland and the men who followed him to the governor's office in the next two decades. William Miller (1877–1881) had been the Confederate state auditor, Thomas Churchill (1881–1883) a major general in the Confederate army, James Berry (1883–1885) a second lieutenant, Simon Hughes (1885–1889) and James Eagle (1889–1893) lieutenant colonels.

Even had these men been disposed to assume an activist, progressive stance, the new constitution's reduction in the powers of the governor and the strict limits on the ability to raise taxes thwarted any serious attempt to promote the general welfare of the people through government action. Limited government and low property taxes would well serve the interests of the state's landed elite far into the next century. Change would come to Arkansas in the last quarter of the nineteenth century, but it would often come in spite of rather than because of the efforts of the state government.

The war, emancipation, and Reconstruction had been truly revolutionary experiences for the state and the region. But the return to power of the antebellum elite ensured that Reconstruction would remain, in the words of the Mississippi planter James Alcorn, a "harnessed revolution."

CHAPTER ELEVEN

Arkansas in the New South, 1880–1900

During the last two decades of the nineteenth century, Arkansas began to recover from the devastation of the Civil War and embraced the process of reintegration into the national economy and culture. It did so within a southern context, however, and even though sectional reconciliation accompanied this period of transition, certain repressive institutions and a virulent racism also coalesced and solidified. Many of the state's leaders adopted the New South ideal outlined by Georgia's Henry Grady, particularly its emphasis on attracting northern capital in order to rebuild Arkansas. However, they eventually eschewed his notion of moderate race relations in favor of segregation and disfranchisement and the relegation of blacks into a rigid caste structure. Even here they found kindred spirits in the North, as voters disfranchised and denigrated eastern European immigrations flocking to that region's cities. Conciliation between the sections failed to fully obscure continuing differences, but the eager and enthusiastic participation of two regiments of Arkansas soldiers in the Spanish American War symbolized the distance traveled between 1865 and 1898.

Railroads, the Timber Industry, and Mining

Although the "new" in the New South had its limitations, Arkansas experienced considerable growth and some industrial advancement in the last twenty years of the nineteenth century. Most of the industries that came to Arkansas during the so-called gilded age were extractive in nature and orchestrated by out-of-state investors who had limited interest in promoting local development. Some home-grown entrepreneurs, however, capitalized on the demand for Arkansas agricultural and lumber resources and made fortunes for themselves. Scott Bond (1852–1933), a former slave who began renting acreage and farming it after the Civil War, later opened a mercantile establishment and began purchasing land. He skillfully negotiated the hyper racism of the era and eventually amassed a 12,000-acre plantation in St. Francis County. Lee Wilson (1865–1933), the son of a former slave owner, capitalized on the demand for lumber and parlayed a 400-acre inheritance into a 50,000-acre plantation empire in Mississippi County. But Bond and Wilson were relatively rare, and few Arkansans were able to accumulate sufficient capital to allow them to participate meaningfully in the two principle new industries that fueled Arkansas's limited growth: lumber and mining.

The railroad played the dual role of bringing northern investors into Arkansas and

Railroad and engine cars, with men. Mountain Pine, Arkansas. *Picture Collection, no. 3775. Special Collections Division, University of Arkansas Libraries, Fayetteville.*

opening up the state to the larger market. As Carl Moneyhon observes, the railroad constituted "the single most important force for change in the nation and in Arkansas" in the late nineteenth century. This marked a dramatic departure for the state. Despite over two decades of effort and the expenditure of considerable sums of capital and credit, less than a hundred miles of railroad had been completed within Arkansas on the eve of the Civil War. The plans and schemes of both Democrats and Republicans alike in the years immediately following the war yielded a network of rail lines, but at a greater cost than the state could afford. During the 1880s and 1890s, eastern capitalists like Jay Gould, who had an eye on Arkansas's forests, appropriated or purchased various lines, infused the effort with considerable capital, and dramatically expanded the state's railroad infrastructure. Gould was best known in Arkansas for the St. Louis and Iron Mountain Railroad, known as the Iron Mountain. St. Louis financier and cotton broker James W. Paramore, meanwhile, built the St. Louis Southwestern Railroad (known as the Cotton Belt) into Arkansas because he had an eye on the rich cotton lands stretching through the state and into Texas. By the end of the century, more than two thousand miles of rail lines stretched into all four corners of the state.

While the railroad began to transform the landscape in significant ways, not merely by the creation of hundreds of new towns but also by the terracing of roadbeds that cut across the state, the lumber industry, which at times merely accompanied the railroad and at other times was its raison d'être, dramatically altered the landscape and provided tens of thousands of new jobs. Lumber workers flooded to towns in northeastern Arkansas, like Marked Tree and Paragould, the latter at the conjunction of two railroads owned by John W. Paramore and Jay Gould. Men hungry for work swarmed into Ouachita Mountain communities in southwest Arkansas like Plainview, Mauldin, and Graysonia. Other young men went south from Little Rock to Grant County and found jobs in Sheridan. Large lumber mills producing millions of board feet of lumber a day dominated the towns in which they were located, both in terms of the physical space they occupied and in terms of the number of townspeople they employed. Relatively inexpensive temporary or roving mills, often operated by small landowners taking advantage of the market for lumber or by entrepreneurs who would "cut and run" whether they owned the land or not, were located in previously isolated places. While the railroads were crucial to the industry, roughnecks rafting logs down the Buffalo River in northwest Arkansas or the St. Frances River in eastern Arkansas utilized a more traditional method of transportation. The larger concerns typically located along rivers to take advantage of those waterways.

The cutting of old-growth timber across the state created opportunities for both small and large concerns. Indeed, just as the railroads brought prosperity to older towns and created many new ones, the lumber industry flooded these towns with workers who spent, and sometimes squandered, their earnings in local establishments. Others, like Elisha "Kidd" and George Abbott, who worked the sawmills of northeastern Arkansas, sent money home to their mother in southern Illinois, who was struggling to keep the family farm afloat. The brothers worked interchangeably, as opportunities presented themselves, for either the railroad or the lumber industry and corresponded frequently with their mother, with each other, and with another brother, Lewis. They passed on information about prospects for jobs in Arkansas, Missouri, Illinois, Kentucky, Tennessee, and Mississippi, suggesting the permeability of the sectional divide. It was Arkansas, however, that attracted most young men like the Abbott brothers. Indeed, except for Texas and Florida, Arkansas's immigration rate in this period far exceeded those of other southern states. While most of these immigrants were of southern origin, northerners were made increasingly welcome and helped, eventually, to achieve reconciliation of North and South by the end of the century.

The Abbott brothers' correspondence reveals that, contrary to the conventional view, the railroad and lumber workers of the late nineteenth century were not altogether the wild and reckless young men that they were frequently thought to be. Young and single, to be sure, they were also in close contact with one another and with "home." They lived a hazardous existence in the backwoods areas of the rapidly developing region, where they suffered particularly from illnesses brought on by malarial conditions in the swampy regions where they worked. Their letters typically began with "I am well, Mother," words meant to reassure her, but frequently a letter would describe a recent illness. They also faced other dangers, including the very real possibility of serious injury on the job. Kidd eventually lost one leg and a foot while working for the railroad. Indeed, railroad injuries were at their highest levels in the late nineteenth century, an era when the industry took little responsibility for those injured or killed.

Log workers on a raft, circa 1912. *Abbott Family Photographs.*

Although the railroad and lumber industries stimulated the economy, the workers (regardless of origin) that accompanied their arrival were not always welcome. As Ken Smith suggests in his important book on lumbering in the Ouachitas, *Sawmill, t*he wild and reckless behavior of unattached young men caused leaders of some older towns, particularly those which were thriving commercial centers for agricultural producers, to refuse to allow lumber mills to be established within their limits. Towns that owed their existence to the lumber industry, such as Marked Tree in northeastern Arkansas, found it necessary to fashion laws to govern the behavior of railroad and timber workers. Born out of a railroad work camp established at the site in 1882, Marked Tree was situated at a juncture of the St. Francis River and the Little River, making it an ideal location for lumber mills which soon began operating. In 1897 the rough logging camp incorporated as Marked Tree and the first council members enacted twelve ordinances, nine of which were aimed at controlling the behavior of the rowdy young men who constituted over a third of the male population. According to the 1900 census, 181 (68 percent) of the 266 adults living in Marked Tree were male, 109 (60.2 percent) of them were unmarried, and over half of them worked the mills. The town achieved a reputation for saloons, bawdy houses, and lawlessness.

On the other side of the state, Fort Smith, which was founded earlier in the century as a military post, played out a similar scenario. Although more settled and longer lived, Fort Smith's population was dominated by sawmill, railroad, and mine workers, and

Log camp in the woods, circa 1912. *Abbott Family Photographs.*

noisy saloons and brothels were commonplace. Judge Isaac Parker presided over the federal court for the Western District of Arkansas located in Fort Smith, and he had his hands full. Appointed in 1875 by Pres. U. S. Grant, Parker served until his death in 1896. He had been a Union army officer and as a Grant appointee represented Reconstruction government. His federal prosecutor was William Clayton, another former Union army officer and, moreover, brother to the former Republican governor of Arkansas, Powell Clayton. While Parker presided over the court, William Clayton ably prosecuted the outlaws brought to Fort Smith from western Arkansas and, particularly, from Indian Territory where a host of notorious outlaws staged their nefarious operations. A group of sometimes suspect and often fearless deputy marshals were responsible for apprehending the criminals. Among them was Bass Reeves, a former slave born in Crawford County, Arkansas, who gained a reputation for honesty and efficiency. But Charles Portis's characterization of a deputy marshal in the form of Rooster Cogburn in *True Grit* captures almost perfectly the type of man typically attracted to the position of hunting down and bringing to justice criminals in the court's jurisdiction. Given the mortality among the deputies, they needed to be tough. More than sixty-five deputy marshals lost their lives in the attempt to bring outlaws to Judge Parker's court. In the judge's early years on the bench, most of the deputy marshals would have been former Union soldiers; by the 1880s Cogburn would have fit the description of the typical deputy: a former Confederate, somewhat disreputable in character and demeanor, but willing to ride into hostile territory to track down notorious criminals. Jeff Bridges's portrayal of Cogburn in the 2011 Coen Brothers film does justice to both Portis's book and the historical context.

Parker's tenure on the court ended in 1896, the same year that his bench lost jurisdiction over affairs in Indian Territory. By that time, Fort Smith's reputation for lawlessness was no longer entirely deserved, but respectable townspeople found it difficult to throw off the notoriety associated with the town's past. The location of the federal district court for western Arkansas there actually had done little to aid them in establishing a new identity for Fort Smith. Indeed, "hanging judge" Parker's rough justice drew attention to the worst elements of the western district's population. But even his reputation was exaggerated. Of the 168 men sentenced to death during his twenty-one-year tenure as judge, only 88 actually stepped up to the gallows.

Far more than the administration of justice in Parker's court was taking place in Fort Smith in the late nineteenth century. The railroad facilitated the development of the New South timber industry in the state and opened up the coal mines of western Arkansas to larger markets. These markets included those states located to the north (Missouri, Nebraska, Minnesota, Kansas, and Iowa), and acted as yet another mechanism for transcending the boundaries of section and promoting reintegration into the larger economy. Small-scale mining operations dated back to the 1840s, but full-scale exploitation of the area's coal deposits had to wait for the completion of the Little Rock to Fort Smith branch of the Cairo and Fulton Railroad in 1879. A mixed agriculture had dominated the region's economy until then. Corn, wheat, dairy, apples, strawberries, and even some cotton were the predominant crops. The arrival of the railroad and the large-scale coal-mining operations like the Missouri, Kansas, and Texas Coal Company contributed to a significant increase in the population. In Sebastian County alone the population rose from 19,560 in 1880 to 36,935 in 1900, and the foreign-born population more than doubled, from 613 in 1880 to 1,365 in 1900. The coal mines attracted most of the newcomers, transforming some small agricultural settlements, like Jenny Lind founded before the Civil War, into coal company towns. Other towns, like Excelsior, Midland, Huntington, and Bonanza, owed their existence to the arrival of the industry. Many of the immigrant miners hailed from the north and even from Italy, Ireland, and Germany. The coal companies were not immune to the labor strife that marked the end of the nineteenth century across the country. Miners in Huntington, Arkansas, went out on strike in support of their compatriots in Pennsylvania and West Virginia in 1894, for example, and the United Mine Workers attracted many members working the mines of western Arkansas and eastern Oklahoma.

Union members and rowdy mine workers were not the kind of immigrants that the Arkansas Bureau of Immigration, founded in 1888, had in mind. Working in concert with railroads that offered excursion fares into Arkansas and speaking the language of the "New South" of Henry Grady's imagination, the Bureau of Immigration was endorsed by Democrats and Republicans alike, signaling an important reconciliation

Bureau of Immigration: An organization established in 1888 to attract the "right kind" of immigrant to the state, immigrants who would promote economic development.

within Arkansas. Gov. Simon P. Hughes, a Confederate veteran who converted from the Whig to the Democratic Party during the Civil War, was the featured speaker at the grand opening of the Immigration Convention in early 1888. The convention selected Logan Roots, a Union veteran who settled in the state following the Civil War and founded the Little Rock Oil Company in 1875, as their first president. They designated H. L. Remmel, a leader in the Republican Party, as secretary. Initial backers included such diverse elements of the political structure as Little Rock banker and leading Democrat W. B. Worthen; the Republican boss of Arkansas, Powell Clayton; and a Democratic outsider who would later become governor, William Fishback. In conjunction with the land departments of railroads like the St. Louis, Iron Mountain, and Southern, the bureau sponsored an exhibit at the St. Louis Exposition in 1888, and again in the famous Chicago World's Fair (also known as the World's Columbian Exhibition) in 1892–93. There Arkansas created a pavilion meant to advertise its accomplishments and prospects. While the bureau declared that it wanted immigrants "without regard to politics, creed, birthplace or profession," some newspapers, like the *Walnut Ridge Telepleane* proclaimed that it dared not be so liberal: "We don't want any anarchists in politics, we don't want any Mormons in religion, and we don't want any tramps by profession."

Solving the State's Debt Problem

Governor Hughes and others understood that the state had to resolve its chronic debt problem in order to realize its goal of attracting the most desirable immigrants, particularly those with money to invest. But even more was at stake for the need for investment capital was paramount in order to rebuild Arkansas, and most of that would have to come from outside the South. The failure of the real estate and the state banks in the early 1840s had saddled Arkansas with a poor reputation among potential investors. Governor after governor had attempted to deal with the state's bad credit reputation, but to no avail. The debt accruing from the banking fiasco was compounded by debt incurred by Reconstruction legislators eager to expand the state's railroad infrastructure and to repair and expand the levees of eastern Arkansas. Many Confederate veterans and Democrats had supported both endeavors, particularly eastern Arkansas planters, but mismanagement, fraud, and the national depression that began in the early 1870s, doomed these efforts.

Other southern states faced a similar crisis arising out of damage to their states from the war and from ill-fated attempts to invest in infrastructure. Many turned to an unorthodox solution, particularly in the years after Reconstruction was overthrown. In addition to Arkansas, the states of Alabama, Florida, Georgia, Louisiana, Tennessee, Virginia, and both Carolinas struggled to distinguish the "honest debt" from the "unjust debt." They eventually repudiated, scaled down, or adjusted the latter. William Meade Fishback led the forces of "repudiation" in Arkansas and identified the unjust debt as either fraudulently incurred or unfairly imposed on the people of the state by Reconstruction legislators. This was unfair and disingenuous, of course, for Democrats had supported and, in some cases, led efforts to expand the railroad network during

Repudiation: A process used to "repudiate" the so-called unjust debt accrued during Reconstruction.

Reconstruction. Although unorthodox, repudiation was a maneuver designed to resolve a growing economic crisis and to saddle the Republicans with the blame for postwar programs many Democrats had embraced. Fishback first voiced the idea of repudiation of the unjust debt as a delegate to the 1874 constitutional convention, when he attempted to insert repudiation into the document hammered out by delegates. This effort failed, but he was elected to the Arkansas General Assembly in 1876 and again in 1878 and continued to press the issue vigorously.

In addition to railroad and levee bonds, Fishback included the so-called Holford Bonds as among the "unjust" debt. The Holford Bonds originated with the Real Estate Bank fiasco. James Holford, a London financier, had purchased some of the bonds from a New York bank, the North American Trust and Banking Company, which was holding the bonds as security for a loan the Arkansas bankers had negotiated in 1840. The Arkansas commissioners who had executed the arrangement had made a crucial mistake, however. They had physically transferred the bonds to the New York bank, which then sold them to Holford. Forty years later Fishback and his allies would justify repudiation of this portion of the Real Estate Bank debt because the transaction was illegal. Holford was unaware that the Arkansas bank was already defaulting on its obligations, and neither the state of Arkansas nor Holford were aware that the New York bank was about to declare bankruptcy itself. During the years following his purchase, Holford continually pressed the state to make good on the bonds, and the Reconstruction legislature had attempted to do so by issuing new bonds, combining the original principal and the accrued interest. The solution was the orthodox answer to the problem in that it honored the principle of accepting responsibility for the debt and renewed a pledge to pay it. The state was in no position, however, to assume such responsibility, given its need to recover from the damage done to the state during the Civil War. Had the state developed its railroad infrastructure and repaired and expanded its levees, it would have been better positioned to promote economic development and thus have been in a better position to pay off the bonds issued for those purposes. The depression of 1873 and another in the 1890s, however, undermined any such progress toward economic revival and certainly doomed the effort to redeem the Holford bonds through refunding them.

Conservative-Democrats like Gov. August Garland (1874–1877) regarded Fishback's repudiation scheme as fiscally irresponsible, however. Garland feared that repudiation would further ruin the state's credit standing and threaten chances of attracting out-of-state investors. Garland had wrangled with the debt problem during his own term as governor, when he faced a dire situation. By the time he came into office, the state owed over $17 million, approximately $13 million accrued during Reconstruction. By the time he left office, he had presided over a significant reduction of the debt, but as the state's revenues stagnated with the hard times of the late 1870s and early 1880s, repudiation became much more popular. Still, William Read Miller, elected governor in 1876, joined Garland and U. M. Rose, a prominent Little Rock attorney, in opposing a repudiation amendment Fishback presented to the legislature, which was narrowly defeated in 1880. Their success

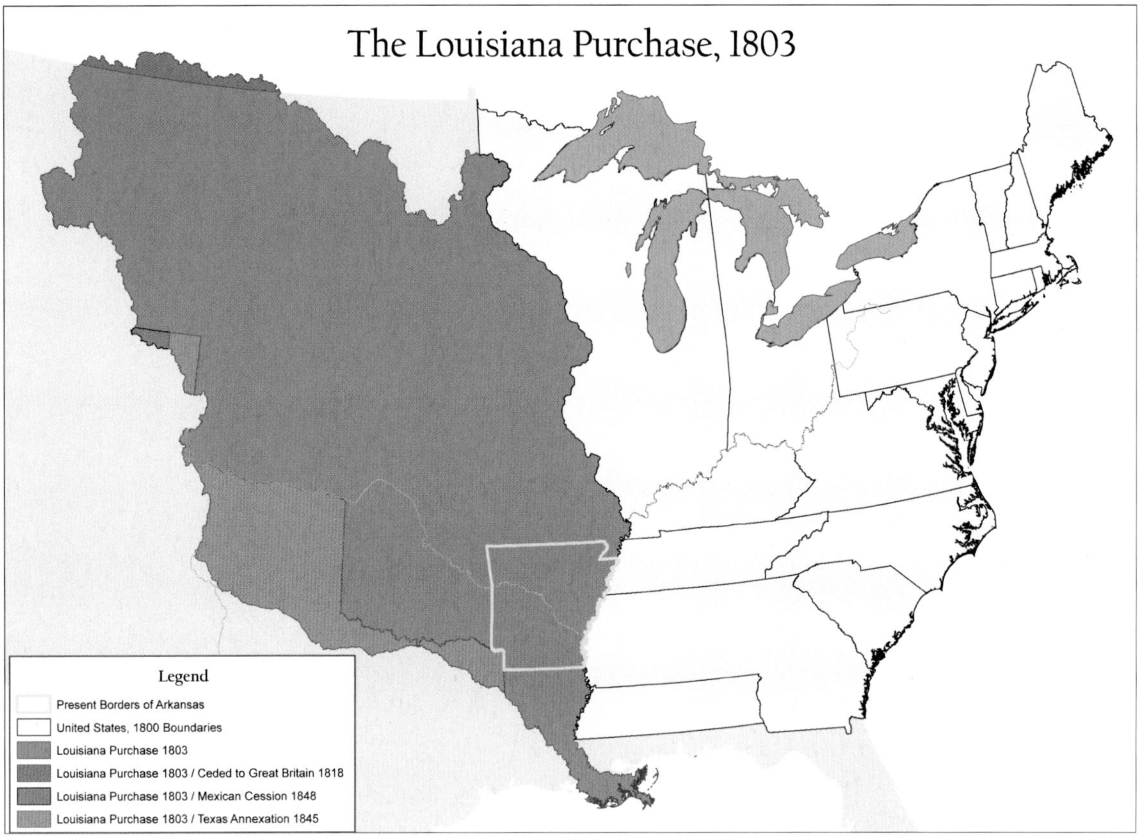

PLATE 19. Louisiana Purchase, 1803. *Courtesy of Joseph Swain.* (Source: National Atlas of the United States.)

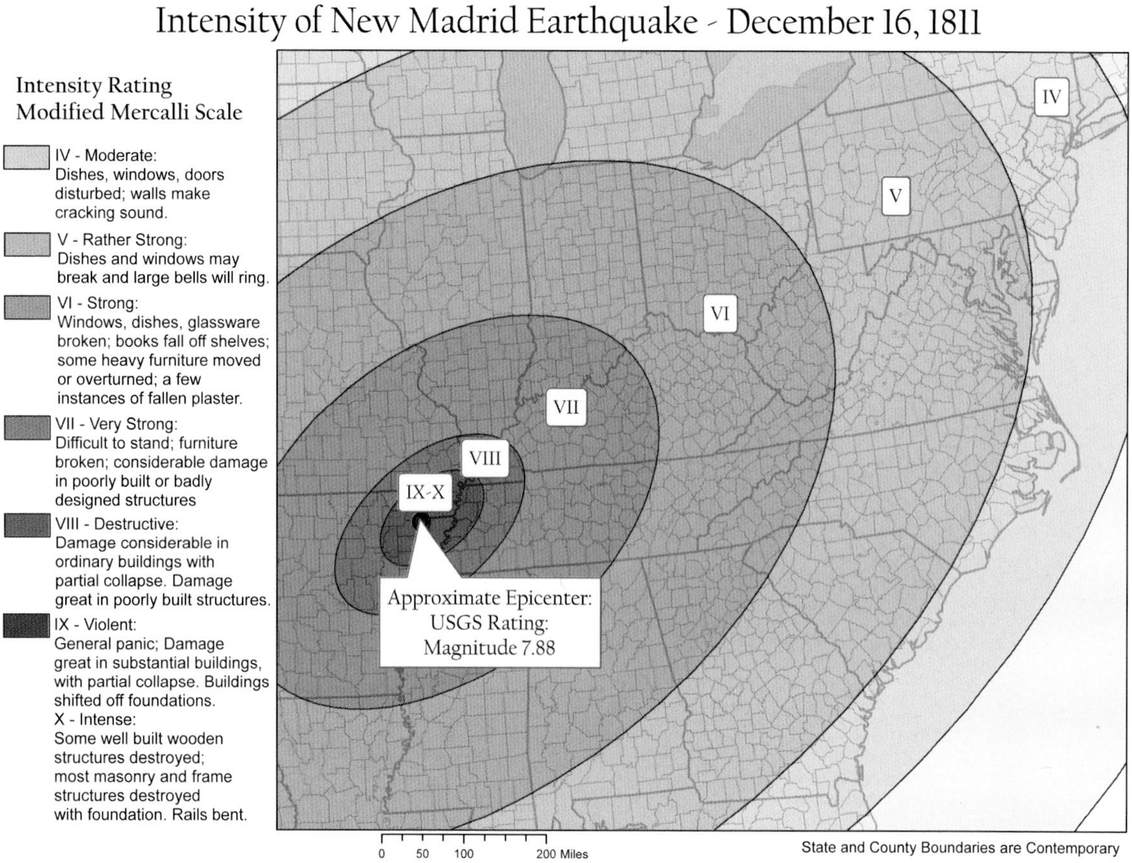
Intensity of New Madrid Earthquake - December 16, 1811
Intensity Rating
Modified Mercalli Scale
IV - Moderate:
Dishes, windows, doors disturbed; walls make cracking sound.
V - Rather Strong:
Dishes and windows may break and large bells will ring.
VI - Strong:
Windows, dishes, glassware broken; books fall off shelves; some heavy furniture moved or overturned; a few instances of fallen plaster.
VII - Very Strong:
Difficult to stand; furniture broken; considerable damage in poorly built or badly designed structures
VIII - Destructive:
Damage considerable in ordinary buildings with partial collapse. Damage great in poorly built structures.
IX - Violent:
General panic; Damage great in substantial buildings, with partial collapse. Buildings shifted off foundations.
X - Intense:
Some well built wooden structures destroyed; most masonry and frame structures destroyed with foundation. Rails bent.
IV
V
VI
VII
VIII
IX-X
Approximate Epicenter:
USGS Rating:
Magnitude 7.88
0
50
100
200 Miles
State and County Boundaries are Contemporary

PLATE 20. New Madrid Earthquake, December 16, 1811. *Courtesy of Joseph Swain.* (Sources: U.S. Geological Survey, Seismological Society of America, USGS: Earthquakes Hazards Program, National Atlas of the United States.)

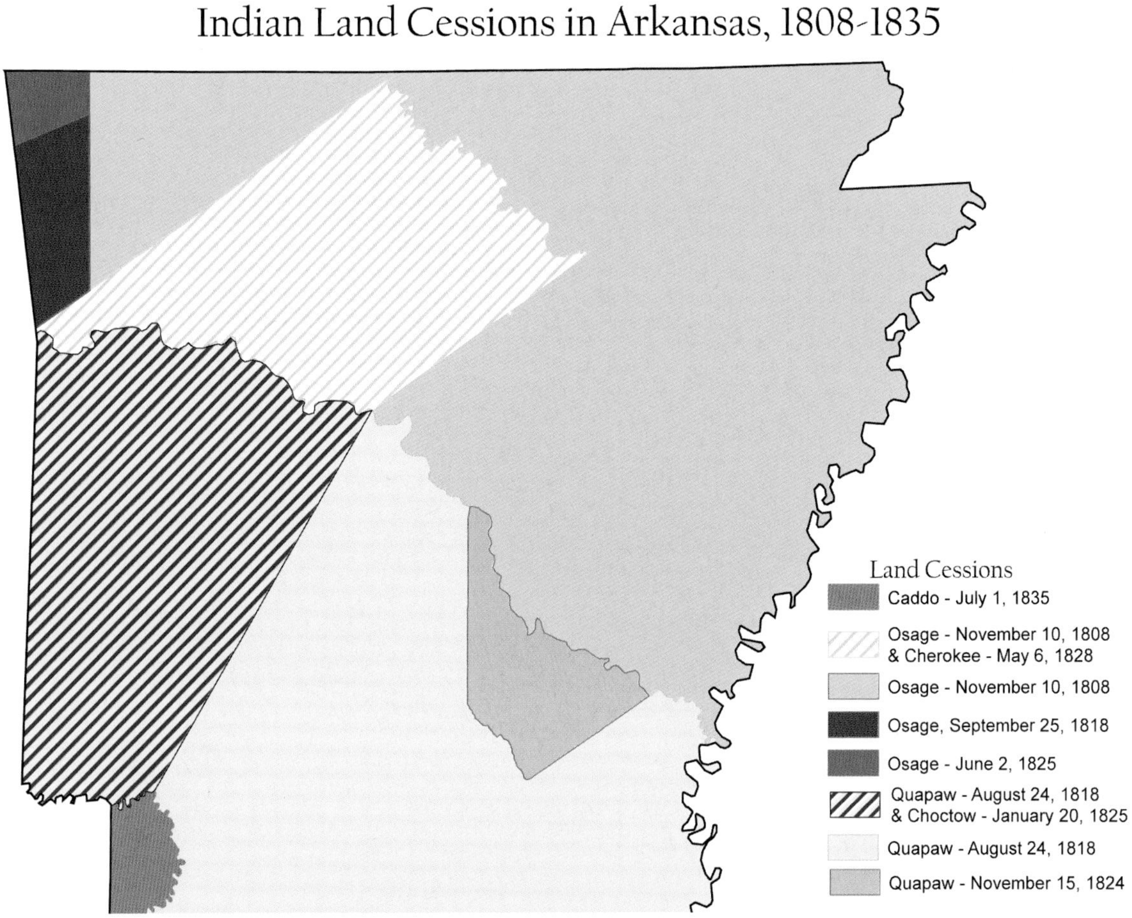

PLATE 21. Indian Land Cessions in Arkansas, 1808–1835. *Courtesy of Joseph Swain.* (Sources: Bureau of Indian Affairs, Minnesota Population Center, National Historical Geographic Information System, Smithsonian Institution, Government Printing Office, TnGenWeb Project, Inc.)

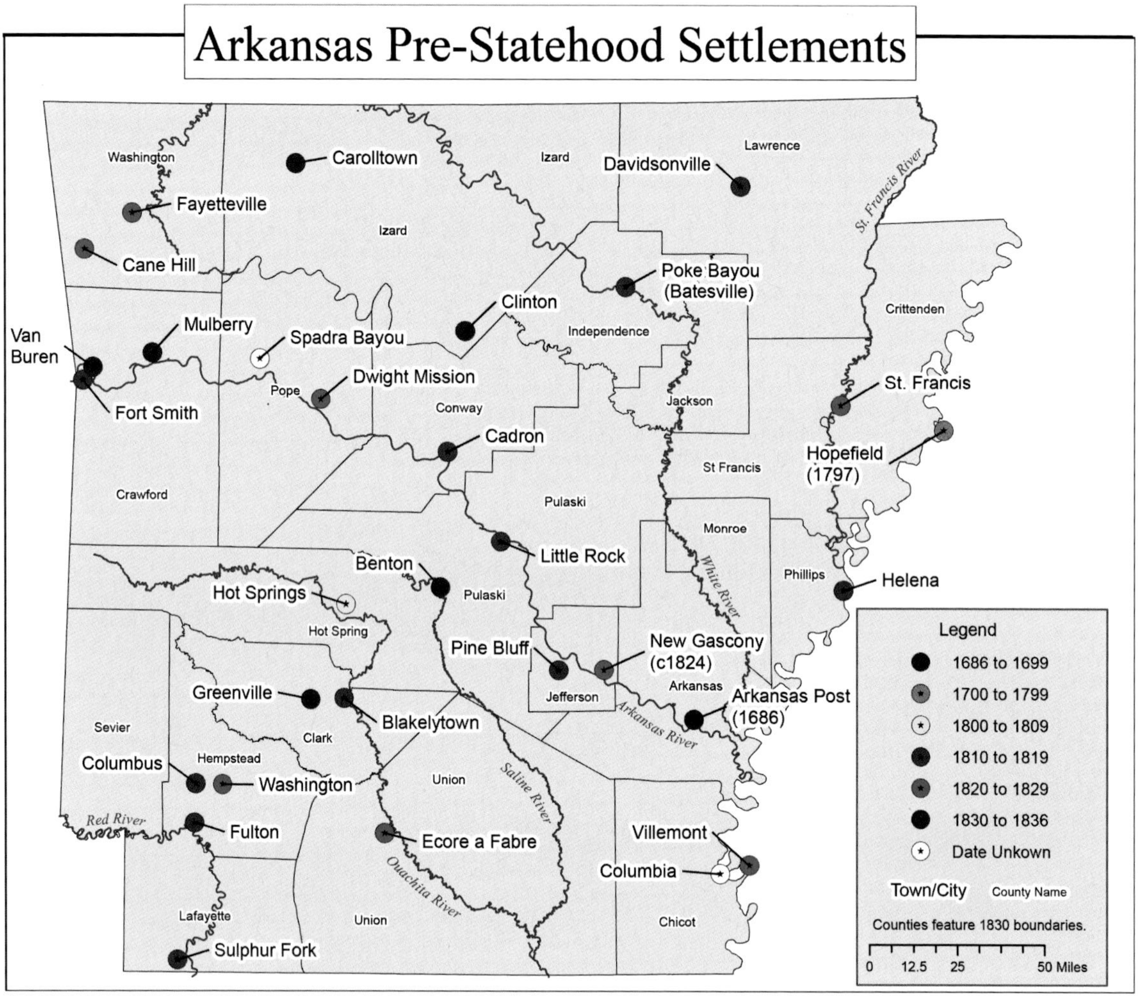

PLATE 22. Early Settlements. *Courtesy of Joseph Swain.* (Sources: Arkansas Gazetteer Online, *Historical Atlas of Arkansas, Encyclopedia of Arkansas Heritage & Culture,* Minnesota Population Center, National Historical Geographic Information System.)

PLATE 23. Arkansas's first state capitol as it appeared circa 1842, looking from Markham Street toward the Arkansas River, by artist Ken Oberste (1991). *Courtesy of the Old State House Museum.*

PLATE 24. A lithographic print of "The Arkansas Traveler" (1859), hand colored after an original painting by Edward Payson Washbourne. Leopold Grozilier, lithographer, J. H. Buford, printer. The original caption reads, "Designed by one of the natives and dedicated to Col. S. C. Faulkner." "The Arkansas Traveler" became nationally popular in the last half of the nineteenth century. It was reproduced by both J. H. Bufford and Currier and Ives. The dialogue provided many an entertainer with usable material, and the music is still played today. *Courtesy of the Historic Arkansas Museum, Little Rock.*

PLATE 25. Double-pen log cabins, similar to the one shown here, were common in antebellum Arkansas. This one was located in the Cane Hill area of northwest Arkansas. The inscription on this painting reads simply, "Log Cabin, L.J.C. 1882." *Courtesy of the Historic Arkansas Museum, Little Rock.*

PLATE 26. Eight Pointed Variable Star. Pieced quilt. Made and signed in corner by Juliana Steinkampf. Hempstead County, Arkansas, 1840–60. 72" x 91". *Courtesy of the Historic Arkansas Museum, Little Rock.*

PLATE 27. Lakeport plantation. Built in the late 1850s by Chicot County planter Lycurgus Johnson, the seventeen-room Lakeport plantation house was a showplace of the state's cotton aristocracy. By 1860 Johnson owned over four thousand acres of rich delta land and 155 slaves, and the plantation produced thirteen hundred bales of cotton and ten thousand bushels of corn. *Photo courtesy of Lakeport Plantation, Arkansas State University Heritage Site.*

PLATE 28. Major Civil War Battles in Arkansas. *Courtesy of Joseph Swain.* (Source: Encyclopedia of Arkansas History & Culture.)

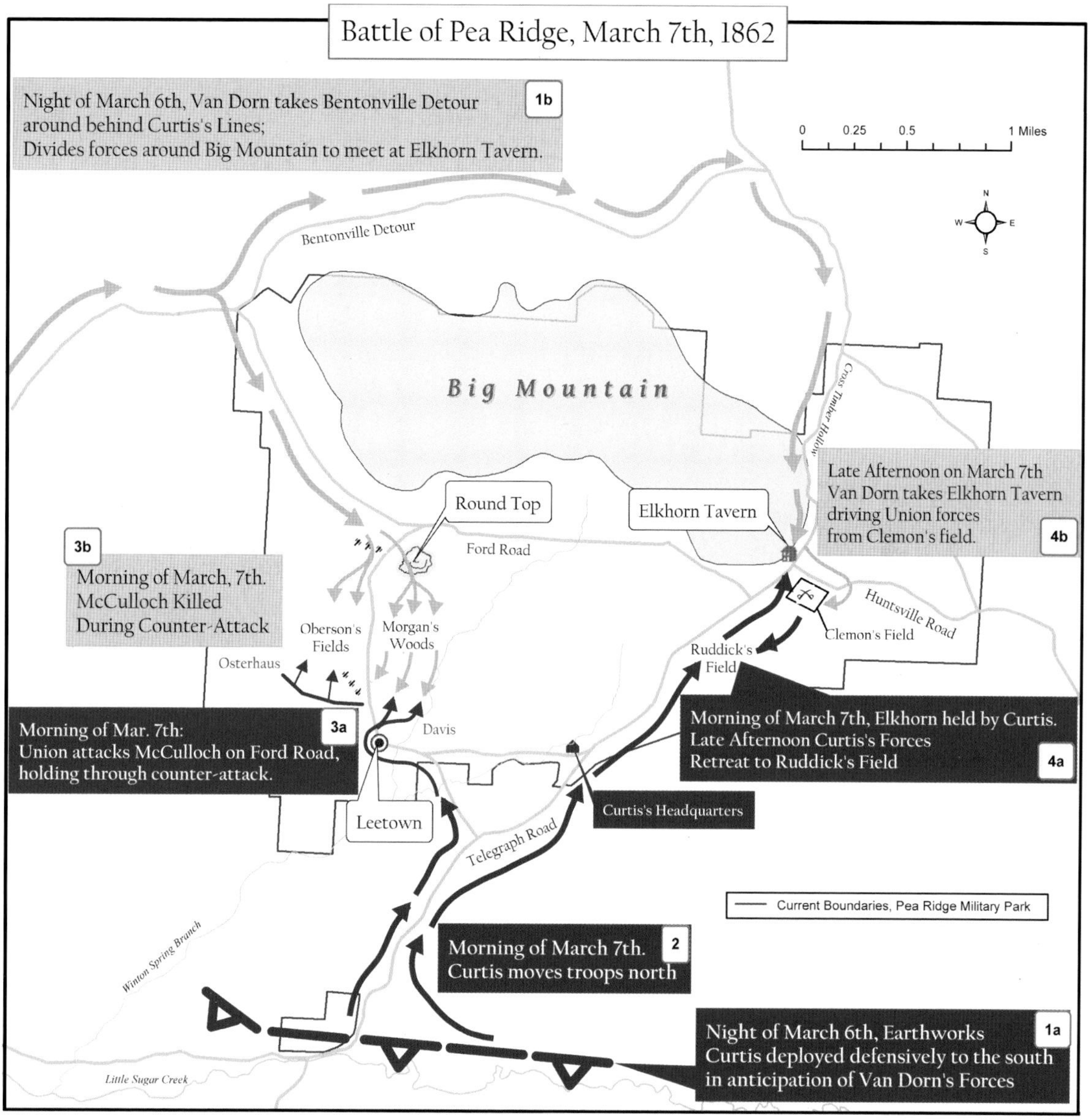
Battle of Pea Ridge, March 7th, 1862
Night of March 6th, Van Dorn takes Bentonville Detour around behind Curtis's Lines;
Divides forces around Big Mountain to meet at Elkhorn Tavern.
1b
0 0.25 0.5 1 Miles
N
W
E
S
Bentonville Detour
Big Mountain
Cross Timber Hollow
Late Afternoon on March 7th Van Dorn takes Elkhorn Tavern driving Union forces from Clemon's field.
4b
Round Top
Elkhorn Tavern
Ford Road
3b
Morning of March, 7th. McCulloch Killed During Counter-Attack
Oberson's Fields
Morgan's Woods
Huntsville Road
Clemon's Field
Ruddick's Field
Osterhaus
Morning of Mar. 7th: Union attacks McCulloch on Ford Road, holding through counter-attack.
3a
Davis
Morning of March 7th, Elkhorn held by Curtis. Late Afternoon Curtis's Forces Retreat to Ruddick's Field
4a
Leetown
Curtis's Headquarters
Telegraph Road
Current Boundaries, Pea Ridge Military Park
Winton Spring Branch
Morning of March 7th. Curtis moves troops north
2
Night of March 6th, Earthworks Curtis deployed defensively to the south in anticipation of Van Dorn's Forces
1a
Little Sugar Creek

PLATE 29. Battle of Pea Ridge, the first day, March 7, 1862. *Courtesy of Joseph Swain.* (Sources: Pea Ridge National Military Park, Arkansas Geographic Information Office.)

PLATE 30. "On the Battery." In this highly detailed painting by present-day artist Andy Thomas, Union and Confederate soldiers engage in fierce combat near Elkhorn Tavern in the late afternoon of the first day of the Battle of Pea Ridge, March 7, 1862. *Courtesy of Andy Thomas.*

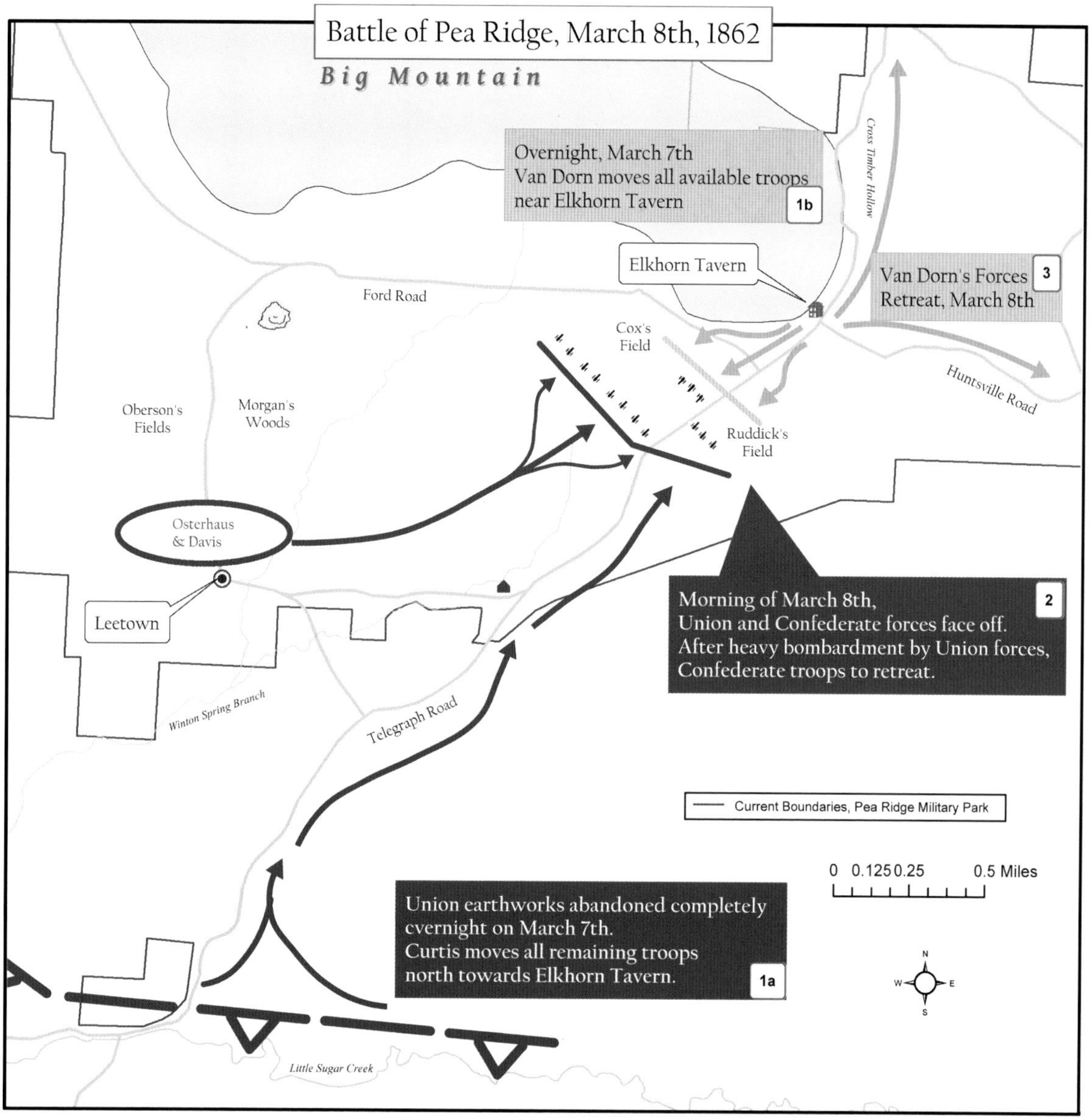

PLATE 31. Battle of Pea Ridge, March 8, 1862. *Courtesy of Joseph Swain.* (Sources: Pea Ridge National Military Park, Arkansas Geographic Information Office.)

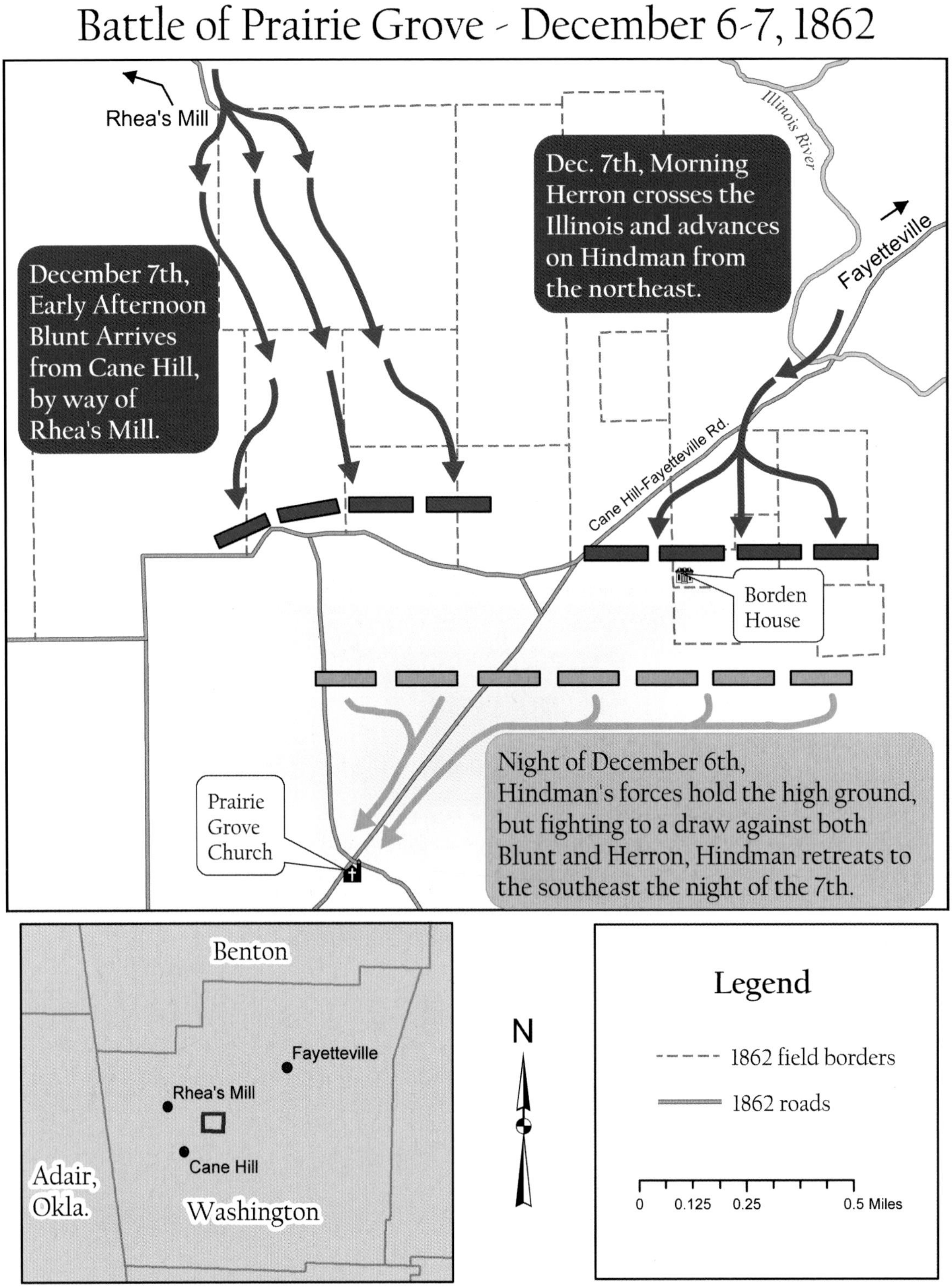

Battle of Prairie Grove - December 6-7, 1862
Rhea's Mill
Illinois River
Dec. 7th, Morning Herron crosses the Illinois and advances on Hindman from the northeast.
Fayetteville
December 7th, Early Afternoon Blunt Arrives from Cane Hill, by way of Rhea's Mill.
Cane Hill-Fayetteville Rd.
Borden House
Prairie Grove Church
Night of December 6th, Hindman's forces hold the high ground, but fighting to a draw against both Blunt and Herron, Hindman retreats to the southeast the night of the 7th.
Benton
Fayetteville
Rhea's Mill
Cane Hill
Adair, Okla.
Washington
N
Legend
1862 field borders
1862 roads
0
0.125
0.25
0.5 Miles

PLATE 32. Battle of Prairie Grove, December 6–7, 1862. *Courtesy of Joseph Swain.* (Sources: Center for Advanced Spatial Technologies: University of Arkansas, Arkansas Department of Parks and Tourism, Arkansas Geographic Information Office, National Atlas of the United States, *Encyclopedia of Arkansas Heritage & Culture.*)

PLATE 33. "The Bayonet or Retreat." In this painting by present-day artist Andy Thomas, Federal infantry are faced with the decision to continue the attack or withdraw after their second assault failed to dislodge Confederate troops from their position around the Borden house at the Battle of Prairie Grove, December 7, 1862. *Courtesy of Andy Thomas.*

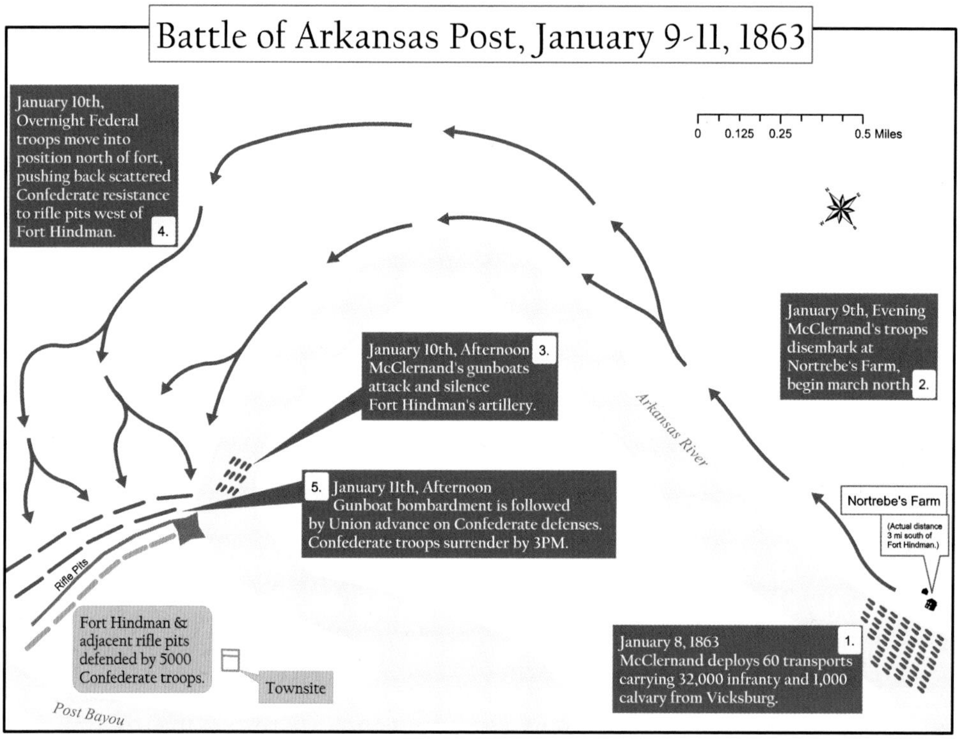

PLATE 34. Battle of Arkansas Post, January 9–11, 1863. *Courtesy of Joseph Swain.* (Sources: Arkansas Post National Memorial, Arkansas Geographic Information Office, University of Arkansas.)

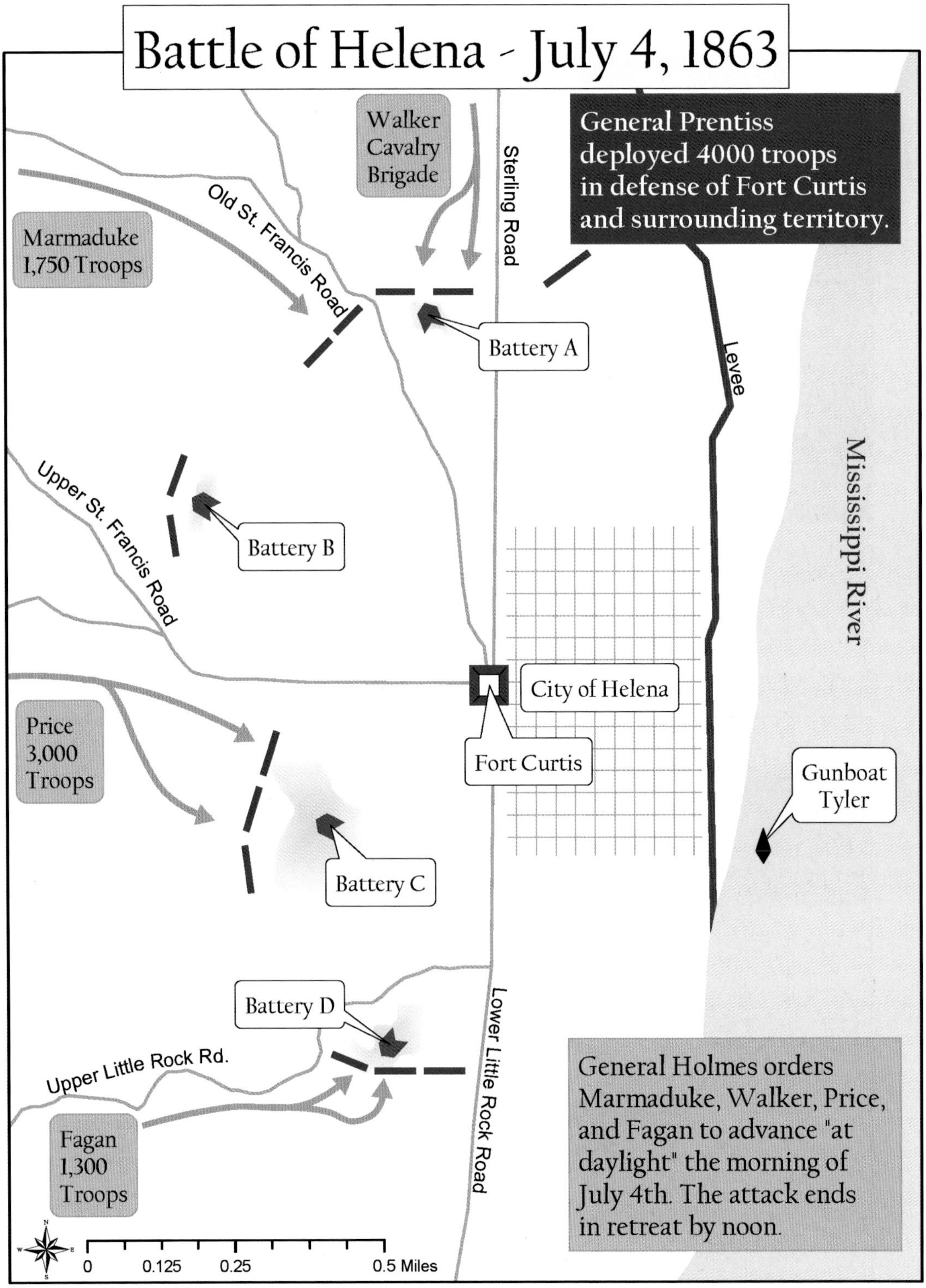

PLATE 35. Battle of Helena. *Courtesy of Joseph Swain.* (Sources: The Delta Cultural Center, *Encyclopedia of Arkansas History & Culture,* Arkansas Geographic Information Office, University of Arkansas.)

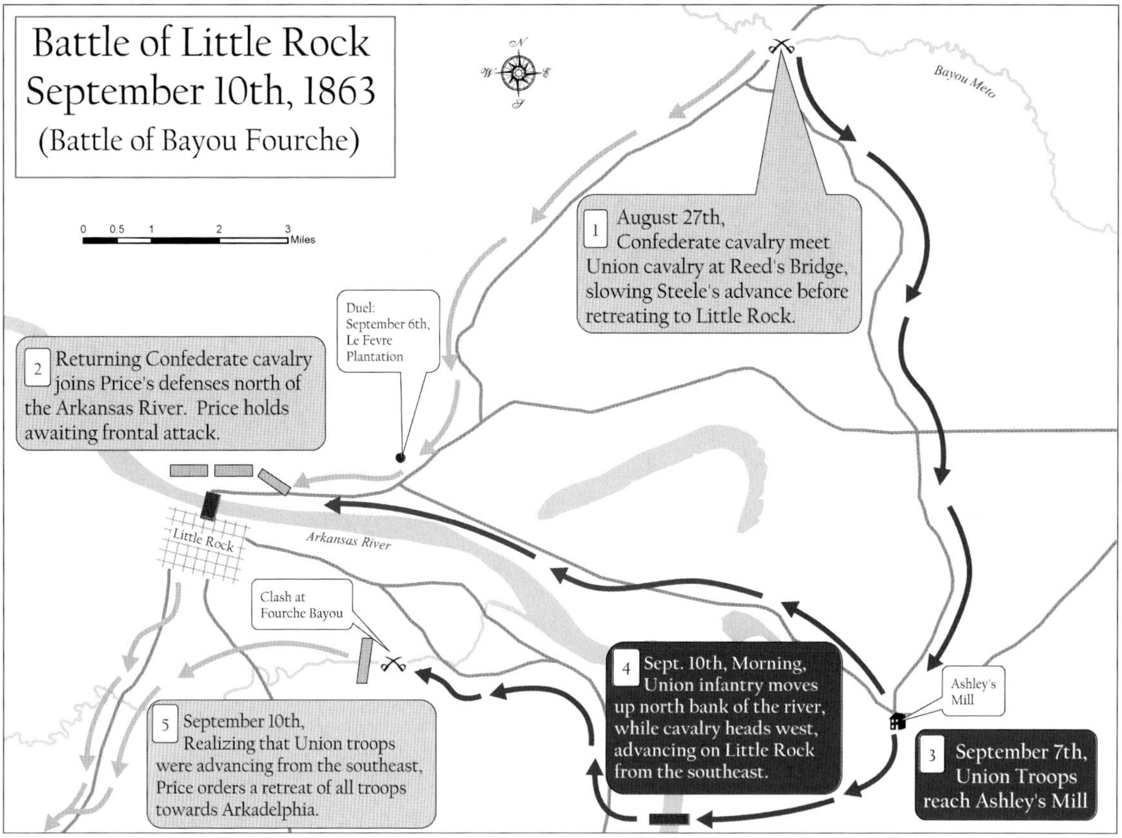

Battle of Little Rock
September 10th, 1863
(Battle of Bayou Fourche)
0 0.5 1 2 3 Miles
Bayou Meto
1 August 27th,
Confederate cavalry meet
Union cavalry at Reed's Bridge,
slowing Steele's advance before
retreating to Little Rock.
Duel:
September 6th,
Le Fevre
Plantation
2 Returning Confederate cavalry
joins Price's defenses north of
the Arkansas River. Price holds
awaiting frontal attack.
Little Rock
Arkansas River
Clash at
Fourche Bayou
4 Sept. 10th, Morning,
Union infantry moves
up north bank of the river,
while cavalry heads west,
advancing on Little Rock
from the southeast.
Ashley's
Mill
5 September 10th,
Realizing that Union troops
were advancing from the southeast,
Price orders a retreat of all troops
towards Arkadelphia.
3 September 7th,
Union Troops
reach Ashley's Mill

PLATE 36. Battle of Little Rock, September 10, 1863. *Courtesy of Joseph Swain.* (Sources: Arkansas Geographic Information Office, *Encyclopedia of Arkansas History & Culture.*)

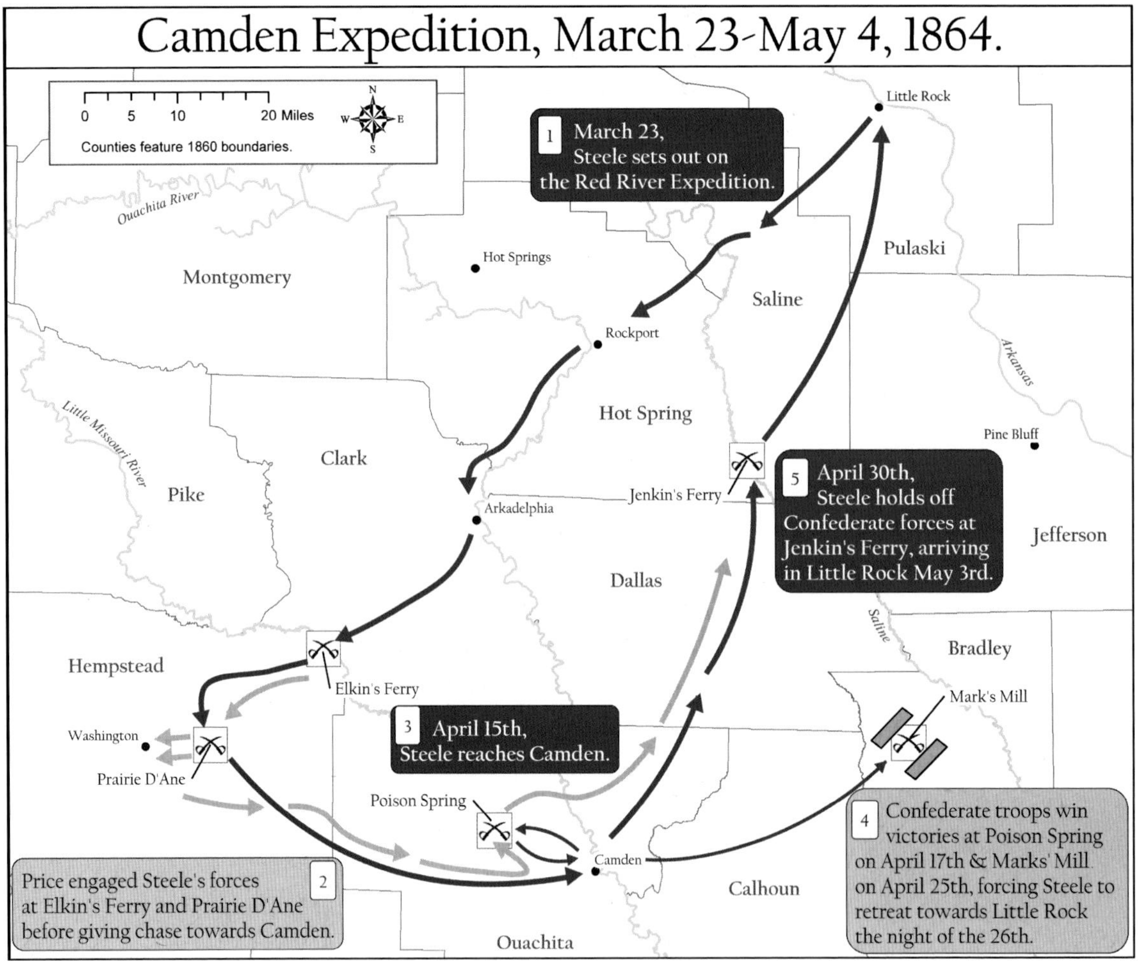

Camden Expedition, March 23-May 4, 1864.
0 5 10 20 Miles
Counties feature 1860 boundaries.
N
W
E
S
1 March 23, Steele sets out on the Red River Expedition.
Little Rock
Ouachita River
Montgomery
Hot Springs
Pulaski
Saline
Rockport
Arkansas
Hot Spring
Pine Bluff
Little Missouri River
Clark
Pike
Jenkin's Ferry
Arkadelphia
5 April 30th, Steele holds off Confederate forces at Jenkin's Ferry, arriving in Little Rock May 3rd.
Jefferson
Dallas
Saline
Bradley
Hempstead
Elkin's Ferry
Mark's Mill
Washington
3 April 15th, Steele reaches Camden.
Prairie D'Ane
Poison Spring
4 Confederate troops win victories at Poison Spring on April 17th & Marks' Mill on April 25th, forcing Steele to retreat towards Little Rock the night of the 26th.
Camden
Price engaged Steele's forces at Elkin's Ferry and Prairie D'Ane before giving chase towards Camden. 2
Calhoun
Ouachita

PLATE 37. Camden Expedition, March 23–May 4, 1864. *Courtesy of Joseph Swain.* (Sources: Arkansas Gazetteer Online, Arkansas Geographic Information Office, *Encyclopedia of Arkansas History & Culture.*)

in fighting off the Fishback amendment, which would forbid the use of state money to repay the "unjust" debt, was only temporary, however. During Thomas James Churchill's governorship (1881–1883), the legislature moved closer to repudiation by passing an act providing that the "unjust" debt go unreported in the biennial reports of the state auditor and the state treasurer. Although Churchill did not endorse it, he allowed the act to become law without his signature. The next governor, James Henderson Berry (1883–1885), capitulated completely to the forces of repudiation by urging submission of the Fishback amendment to voters. It was ratified in 1884.

Of course, repudiation may have relieved the state of the responsibility of repaying some its bondholders, but it hardly redeemed the state's reputation. Ironically, while shrugging off a good part of the debt, Berry and the legislature made greater efforts than their immediate predecessors to pay the so-called just indebtedness. During his administration most of the state's outstanding scrip was redeemed, some bonds were retired, and short-term loans were repaid. His successor in the governor's chair, Simon P. Hughes (1885–1889), went even further. A State Debt Board, composed of the governor, the auditor, the treasurer, and the attorney general, was created, and the just debt became their primary focus. They successfully reduced much of it and committed the state to paying down the remainder according to the board's recommendation.

Complicating the state's efforts to pay its debts and redeem its credit standing were certain generous favors bestowed upon railroad companies. In an effort to attract railroads and thus position Arkansas to expand economically, the state had made grants of land and provided tax incentives to railroad entrepreneurs. But controversy over railroad assessments and taxes, passenger and freight rates, and land grants soon arose and captured at least as much public attention as the debt repudiation issue. An unparalleled and unregulated expansion of railroads in the state led to perceived inequities, perhaps accentuated by the fact that most of the lines were owned by northern financiers like Jay Gould. Railroads had secured more than a million acres in land grants in Arkansas, and the low assessments and taxes they paid on that land generated much ill will. Added to that, the higher than average freight rates charged for lines outside the North excited considerable public outrage in Arkansas and elsewhere and, as historian C. Vann Woodward argues, was one reason industrialization was stymied in the South.

Railroad pools, which began to form in the 1870s and 1880s, were responsible for the disproportionate freight rates charged Arkansas and certain other states. These pools identified specific regions as warranting rate differentials on the basis of low population density and a number of other factors, including the low grade of the cargo, the existence of seasonal fluctuations in traffic, and a preponderance of one-way and local traffic. Population density in Arkansas had been increasing signicantly over the course of the century, but the state remained underpopulated and thus unattractive to railroad companies seeking to maximize their profits. Such companies identified a southern area composed of most of the states of the old Confederacy and a southwestern zone that included Arkansas, Texas, Louisiana, and part of New Mexico. See plate 38 following page 366.

State legislatures and governors throughout the South grappled with all three issues—the tax question, the land grants, and the rate differentials. Arkansas began to impose regulations on the lines operating within its boundaries in the early 1880s, but few of its citizens were satisfied by the state's efforts. Regulations were imposed on railroads of no more than fifty miles in length during Churchill's term, but this left the larger lines, such as those owned by Gould, untouched. Governor Berry convinced the legislature to create a railroad commission, composed of the governor, the auditor, and the secretary of state, but legislation mandating assessment of railroad property at the full value exempted certain classes of railroads so that the revenue raised was insignificant. In any case, the Railroad Commission had little clout and no teeth, and by the time Governor Eagle took office in 1889, it was defunct. Gov. James Clarke (1895–1897) attempted to reestablish the Railroad Commission in 1895 and engaged in a heated exchange with a number of legislators, some of whom may have been bribed by railroad officials to vote against such a commission. At one point the governor accosted legislator W. R. Jones with a gun and had to be restrained by bystanders. Ironically, it would be Daniel Webster Jones, governor between 1897 and 1901, who represented railroad interests in 1895 arguing against a Railroad Commission, who would finally convince the legislature to recreate the commission in March 1899.

That same year the Arkansas legislature ratified a compromise agreement with the United States Congress that settled a debt to the federal government arising out of the Real Estate Bank fiasco, a compromise involving railroad lands. The repudiation of the Holford bonds had addressed only part of the legacy of the failed bank. Of the two thousand bonds originally issued, Holford purchased only five hundred. Although some of the fifteen hundred remaining bonds had been retired, the United States Treasury held most of the rest. While governor in 1895, Clarke, together with Rep. Thomas McRae, negotiated with officials from the Treasury Department and worked out a compromise. It was agreed that the state owed the federal government $1,611,803.61. This amount was nearly offset, however, by the state's surrender of unsold swamplands to the federal government, swamplands originally donated to the state in 1850 by the federal government and valued at $1,451,231.61. This left the state owing only $273,000, and went a long way toward restoring Arkansas's credit and raised, if not entirely satisfied, hopes of positioning it to become more fully integrated into the national economy.

An amendment to the compromise agreement with the federal government over the debt, however, exacerbated longstanding animosities toward the railroads. Congress had allowed the amendment to the bill exempting certain lands claimed both by the state and by a railroad acquired by railroad magnate Jay Gould. The 1850 donation of swamplands to the state had been complicated in 1853 when the federal government inadvertently donated some of the same lands to railroads in an attempt to encourage expansion of rail lines across Arkansas. The state had always maintained that the grant to the railroad was void. Gould asserted his right to the land by virtue of having acquired the railroad that had been given the land, however mistakenly, in 1853. The situation went unresolved until the compromise bill negotiated in 1894–1895 brought it to the forefront. The amendment to the compromise bill, known as the Meiklejohn amendment, exempted lands claimed by Gould's Iron Mountain Railroad. The Arkansas legislature ratified the agreement in 1899, over Gov. Daniel Webster Jones's heated objection. Given the antipathy to railroads existing in Arkansas at the time, it was unpopular with the general population, and Atty. Gen. Jeff Davis would use the issue to good effect in his run for the governor's office in 1900.

Agricultural Reorganization and Crisis

Arkansans were initially optimistic about the prospects of recovery of the cotton economy in the years immediately following the Civil War, and they welcomed the arrival of the railroad as the herald of progress. It facilitated the spread of the cotton kingdom to areas in eastern and parts of southern Arkansas, which were being rapidly deforested, by providing a new and more efficient way of sending goods to market. However, significant dangers accompanied these new opportunities. Greater exposure to the marketplace meant increased vulnerability to market forces, and this was especially problematic because agricultural prices declined almost steadily during the fifty years following the Civil War. Thus some farmers who had engaged in only a nominal connection to the market prior to the coming of the railroad were being drawn into it at the worst possible time.

Even before the arrival of the railroad, however, farmers throughout Arkansas had been producing more cash crops. The Civil War brought such devastation to so many areas that farmers had to borrow to restore their farms to full operation, and many of them pledged to creditors to grow cash crops like cotton in order to secure advances. Cotton prices reached fifty cents a pound in the post–Civil War boom years of 1865 and 1866, which encouraged many farmers to expand cotton production at the expense of other crops, particularly corn. The percentage of those who owned their own farms declined steadily in the last two decades of the nineteenth century, especially in the areas dominated by cotton cultivation. More and more men were farming on acres owned by others, but the proliferation of small farms suggested to some reading the agricultural census that the plantation was disappearing. In fact, most of these small farming operations were operated by tenants and sharecroppers and signaled the concentration of landownership into fewer hands. The plantation model of development had survived the Civil War and adapted to the loss of slave labor. The tenancy and sharecropping system, in fact, perpetuated the plantation model of development that included an impoverished workforce and that inhibited modernization. Arkansas farmers, like those in the rest of the South, failed to adopt new farm technologies and remained wedded to its repressive labor system.

The sharecropping system had emerged in the years immediately following the Civil War after the contract labor system proved impractical. Contract labor had been employed during the war in order to keep the plantation system afloat and to provide a means of putting slaves back to work. In the postwar period, however, conflicts arose between the freedpeople and the planters. Freedmen wanted to own their own land but had no means to do so and plantation owners had too little cash income to pay wages. The emergence of sharecropping gave each something of what they wanted. Without capital, former slaves had little hope of landownership, but sharecropping allowed them to move out of the old slave quarters, finally, and onto twenty- to thirty-acre parcels that they operated semi-independently. Landowners "paid" them at the end of the year out of the proceeds of the crop rather than weekly or monthly as stipulated under the contract labor system. Sharecroppers typically received one-third of the cotton crop in return for a year's work. The system might have seemed a prudent arrangement, but it soon became corrupted by the commissary system. Sharecroppers required advances of supplies and foodstuffs in order to survive to the end of the year. Merchants in small towns often filled that need but eventually planters themselves opened commissaries and supplied their own sharecroppers. In order to maximize their profits, they charged exorbitant interest for credit purchases and soon sharecroppers became seriously indebted, so much so that the amount owed them at the end of the year for the crop they produced often fell short of the amount they were obligated to pay at the plantation commissary.

Even as freedpeople were becoming ensnared in the sharecropping system, many landless whites were gravitating to plantation jobs in the share-tenancy system. Some of these men had once owned farms and lost them to foreclosure. Many of them retained their tools and mules left over from a happier time and thus brought more to the bargaining table with planters. By this means they were able to secure one-half of the crop in return for their services. The law soon defined them as "owning the crop they produced" so they had standing in court should a dispute arise between the tenant and the landowner. It is doubtful, however, that many exercised that right. Planters achieved so much political power and social standing in local communities that any challenge to them from a relatively poor landless farmer would be in vain. And, meanwhile, tenants found it necessary to secure advances from merchants or from plantation commissaries and thus, like sharecroppers, became indebted. The divide between the sharecroppers and tenants was real, often marked by both class and race, but the differences were actually minimal. While most sharecroppers were black and most tenants were whites, they shared impoverishment and exploitation.

Regardless of status, all farmers endured the burden of a precipitous decline in cotton prices in the late nineteenth century. In 1867 cotton prices dropped from fifty cents a pound to seventeen or eighteen cents, and then ranged between twelve and eighteen cents until 1874 when prices dropped again, this time to eleven cents a pound. From that point until the 1890s farmers received no more than seven to eleven cents a pound, but worse was to come in the 1890s. In 1894 the price of cotton dropped below a nickel a pound. Added to this decline in prices was an increase in railroad rates. When farmers began to address their economic problems by forming the Agricultural Wheel in 1882, they identified high railroad rates as one of their chief complaints.

Agricultural Wheel: An organization founded in Prairie County in 1882 by farmers dissatisfied with the state's response to problems in the agricultural sector.

The Agricultural Wheel

On February 15, 1882, nine men who owned small farms met at a schoolhouse in Prairie County to discuss their common problems and agreed to form a farmers' organization. Initially the club was little more than an improvement association designed to disseminate information, but from the beginning the organizers expressed disillusionment with political leaders. All were themselves Democrats, but they were disgruntled and unhappy about the circumstances facing them and the apparent unwillingness of politicians to address their problems. Within a month of the first meeting, they named their organization the Agricultural Wheel, arguing that "no machinery can be run without a great drive wheel, and as that wheel moves and governs the entire machinery, however complex, so agriculture is the great wheel or power that controls the entire machinery of the world's industries." By this time the membership of the organization had tripled, and within a year the organization expanded to include five hundred members and had formed the State Agricultural Wheel, drawing members from throughout Arkansas. Three years later the Wheel had extended into several other states, and its name was changed to the National Agricultural Wheel.

Many farmers drawn to the Agricultural Wheel felt particular antipathy toward railroads because their owners were identified as among the "middlemen" who appropriated the profits farmers should have been receiving for their crops. Many resented the rate differentials that carriers charged farmers who lived in remote areas off the more heavily traveled lines. Other grievances against the railroad included favorable land grants and generous tax exemptions granted to them by a state government eager for railroad construction. The practice of extending free passes to legislators and other state government officials raised suspicions of collusion. But most of the complaints aired by the Wheelers only peripherally concerned the railroad. Indeed, their problems were far more complicated, and the solutions would prove to be elusive.

The difficulties faced by farmers in Arkansas were shared by farmers elsewhere, particularly those in the South and the Midwest. Overproduction in an age of declining farm prices, rising indebtedness, and an increasing rate of farm foreclosures plagued all farmers, but southern farmers also faced the infamous anaconda mortgage, whereby they were obliged to pledge their future crops in order to receive an advance. Many creditors demanded that specific crops, like cotton, be grown, and farmers were in no position to argue. While this had serious consequences for small landowning farmers, it had a particularly pernicious effect on the landless. Planters typically required their tenants and sharecroppers to sign crop lien mortgages and if the tenant owned mules and implements, they were also included in the document. Planters and local law enforcement officials believed that lien laws made it illegal for a tenant or sharecropper to leave a planter to whom he owed a debt, creating a situation known as debt peonage. Local law enforcement officials frequently arrested and returned absconding tenants and sharecroppers, essentially acting as the plantation owner's de facto police force.

Added to these structural problems were the perennial natural disasters that have

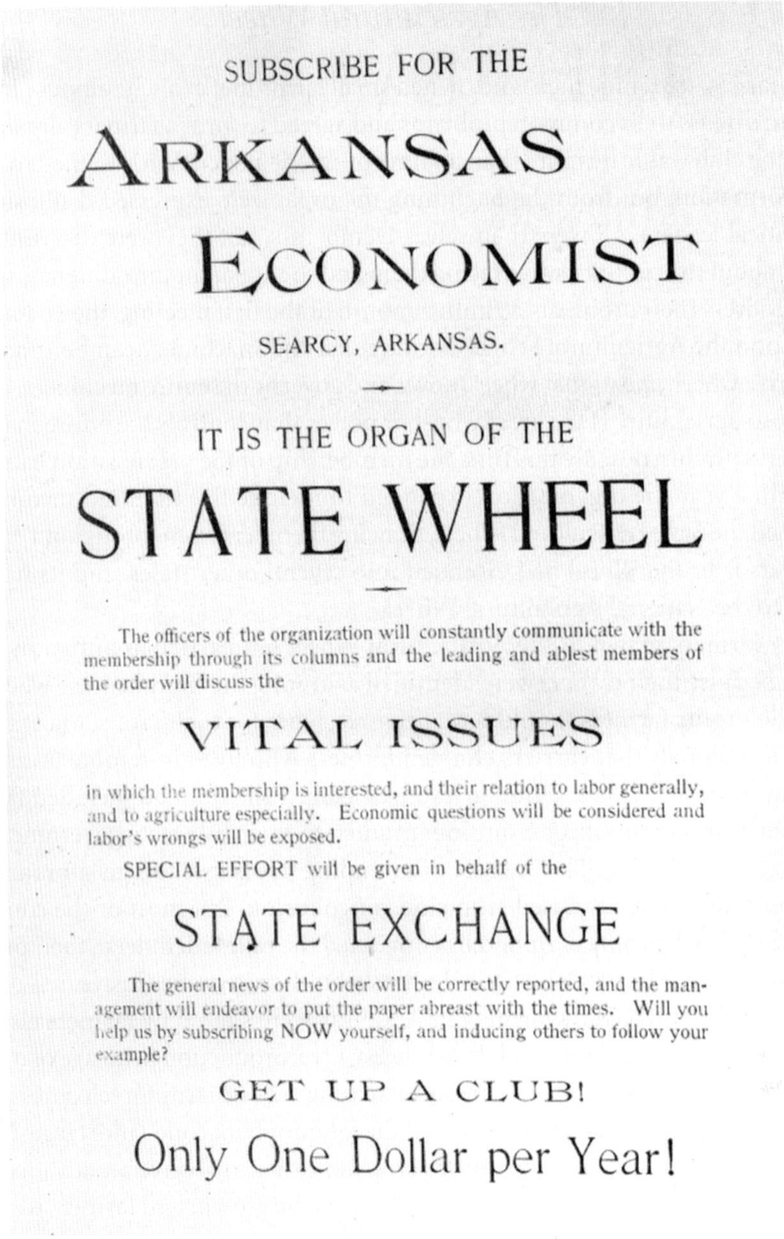

SUBSCRIBE FOR THE
ARKANSAS
ECONOMIST
SEARCY, ARKANSAS.
IT IS THE ORGAN OF THE
STATE WHEEL
The officers of the organization will constantly communicate with the membership through its columns and the leading and ablest members of the order will discuss the
VITAL ISSUES
in which the membership is interested, and their relation to labor generally, and to agriculture especially. Economic questions will be considered and labor's wrongs will be exposed.
SPECIAL EFFORT will be given in behalf of the
STATE EXCHANGE
The general news of the order will be correctly reported, and the management will endeavor to put the paper abreast with the times. Will you help us by subscribing NOW yourself, and inducing others to follow your example?
GET UP A CLUB!
Only One Dollar per Year!

Agricultural Wheel advertisement.

always afflicted farmers everywhere. The year before the founding of the Agricultural Wheel, Prairie County farmers suffered a severe drought which ruined the 1881 harvest. This was followed by a severe flood which threatened to interfere with spring 1882 planting. Farmers did not expect politicians to prevent natural disasters, but those who joined the Wheel believed that there were governmental remedies for some of their problems if only their political leaders would act. They wanted a reduction in taxes and, moreover, a suspension of tax payments until after the crisis passed. They wanted their homesteads exempted from farm foreclosures. They believed, moreover, that their own economic problems were exacerbated by the corruption of state and local officials and the greed of merchants, bankers, and other creditors. They resented the favorable treatment received by railroads, particularly given their own struggles. They viewed land speculators who purchased undeveloped land and held on to it, paying little or no taxes, as parasites.

Farmers elsewhere had expressed concerns similar to these and formed organizations to address their grievances. The Patrons of Husbandry, also known as the Grange, had been founded immediately after the Civil War and spread throughout the North, South, and West. By the mid-1870s there were approximately twenty thousand Grangers in Arkansas alone, and in 1875 John Thompson Jones, who was the Arkansas Grange's "Worthy Master," as its leader was called, was elected Worthy Master of the National Grange. By the late 1870s the Grange had been weakened in the South by the politics of Reconstruction, and, further, the organization was undermined because it admitted to membership men who were not farmers. The merchants, bankers, and brokers who had diluted the Grange were not admitted to membership in the Agricultural Wheel. Wheelers were determined to focus on the problems confronting those who actually farmed and went so far as to exclude from membership anyone who lived within the boundaries of a town or city.

The Agricultural Wheel was not the only organization of farmers to emerge in the wake of the Grange, and plenty of overlap existed among the various groups. Even before farmers in Prairie County met to form their association, farmers in Texas had created the Texas Farmers Alliance in 1878, and at the time the Agricultural Wheel was founded in 1882, the Farmers Alliance was beginning to spread into surrounding states, including Arkansas. In 1887 the Agricultural Wheel secured the support of the National Farmers Alliance, and for a time the local alliances were subordinate to the Wheel. This relationship strained to the breaking point when the Agricultural Wheel became politicized.

Leaders of the Arkansas Agricultural Wheel had come to understand that the remedies that farmers sought could only be gained if politicians supported reforms. They had attempted to work within the system by electing Democrats but had been disappointed in the results. In Arkansas and other southern states, the conservative Democrats had control over who secured the Democratic nominations for local, state, and federal offices, and these men rarely, no matter what they might say to farmers in stump speeches, broke with the party line once elected. Arkansas farmers soon came to believe that only through electing Wheel candidates could they be sure their interests would be served, and thus they began to field Wheelers and had some success at the local level. In 1886 their gubernatorial candidate, Charles E. Cunningham, ran a poor third behind the Democratic and Republican candidates, but a more formidable challenge was in the wind for 1888 despite internal dissension within the Wheel.

The Wheel had actually violated its constitution in 1886 when it ran its own gubernatorial candidate, and many members were resistant to doing so again. Most of them were lifelong Democrats and were vulnerable to the skillful manipulation of conservative

Democrats who could claim that defections from the party might lead to the restoration of Republican and black rule. While the Wheel struggled with this debate within its own ranks, another organization, the Union Labor Party, was gaining a following among both farmers and laborers. The Union Labor Party, which began in Wisconsin and was made up primarily of urban laborers, reshaped itself to match different constituencies as it moved south. In Arkansas it attracted disaffected farmers across the state and workers in the few industries that existed in Arkansas. Cunningham, the failed gubernatorial candidate in 1886, was both a Union Labor and a Wheel man. A member in the previous decade of the Greenback Party, which had advocated an inflationary policy supported by farmers, he embodied the perspective of many Arkansas farmers. By 1888, after the Union Labor Party had united agrarian and labor organizations behind its banner, Cunningham was designated as its vice presidential candidate.

Union Labor Party: A political party created by the Agricultural Wheel and the Knights of Labor, which ran candidates in 1886 and 1888, putting pressure on the Democratic Party of Arkansas.

Trouble was on the horizon, however. At the Union Labor Party convention in Arkansas in April 1888, Isaac McCracken, president of the Arkansas Wheel and the National Agricultural Wheel, served as chairman. McCracken presided over a convention that selected a former state senator, C. M. Norwood, as its gubernatorial candidate. When the Union Labor Party fashioned a platform clearly meant to attract Wheelers, the Democratic press suggested that the Republicans were behind the party, and the Republican Party's endorsement of the Union Labor candidate (in the interest of broadening the opposition to the Democrats) gave credence to this accusation. At the Wheel convention, which met in May, delegates shied away from endorsing Norwood and instead passed a resolution that simply thanked the Union Labor Party for a platform that addressed the Wheel's concerns. Some Wheelers left the convention unhappy that the organization had not fully repudiated the Union Labor Party and, by implication, the Republicans with whom they were supposedly in cahoots, and burned their membership cards ceremoniously. They renewed their fidelity to the Democratic Party and decried the "bolters" that would return the state to Republican/black rule.

The Democrats, at their own convention which met May 31 to June 5, rejected proposals supported by Wheelers and nominated a candidate for governor, James P. Eagle, who indicated in his acceptance speech that the state of Arkansas had never been more prosperous. Such remarks in the face of the continuing decline in agricultural prices, together with the failure of the Democrats to address Wheeler demands, made it impossible for many farmers to support the Democratic candidate, despite their concerns about the taint of Republican connivance with the Union Labor Party.

Election results attest to the fact that many farmers supported the Union Labor candidate against the Democrat. The election that took place on September 3, 1888, was marked by fraud and intimidation, but Norwood secured majorities in a number of delta counties with large numbers of black Republicans as well as predominantly white hill-country counties in south Arkansas and in the southwest. He came within 15,002 votes of winning. Eagle won 99,214 votes to Norwood's 84,213. Norwood challenged the vote and only backed down when the legislature demanded of him a $40,000 bond before opening an investigation. Historians generally agree that Norwood almost certainly won the election but was denied the governorship because of out-and-out fraud. In 1890 another Wheeler ran on the Union Labor Party ticket and was again backed by Republicans. Governor Eagle ran for reelection and defeated Napoleon B. Fizer 106,267 to 85,181. Neither the Wheel nor the Union Labor Party recovered from the 1888 election and many former Wheelers aligned with the newly politicized Populist Party. The Farmers Alliance had finally come to the conclusion that some Wheelers reached in 1886: fielding their own candidates was their only option. By this time, however, the Democratic Party was taking steps to shore up its dominant position in Arkansas—and in the South generally.

The key element in the survival of the conservative Democrats in Arkansas, as elsewhere in the South, was their ability to adapt and their willingness to take extreme measures in the interests of maintaining political control. For example, they were not above using extralegal means to wrest control of county governments from Republicans and African Americans. In the summer of 1888, black officeholders in Crittenden County were marched at gunpoint to the train station where they were forced to board a train bound for Memphis. Warned not to return, they made their way to Little Rock through a circuitous route and appealed directly to Gov. Simon Hughes. Hughes refrained from taking any action in the case on the basis that he could only do so if the chief law enforcement official in the county, the Crittenden County sheriff, requested his intervention. The county sheriff, however, had apparently masterminded the coup and could hardly be expected to lodge a protest. When elections were held a few months later, county government was returned to white control. Not a single black candidate was elected, despite the fact that the county was overwhelmingly black. This not only ended black officeholding in Crittenden County but also signaled the end of "fusion," a process whereby white Democrats and black Republicans tacitly agreed to apportion a certain number of elected offices to each other. Fusion had worked to mediate differences by allowing Democrats to secure black votes and to permit black officeholders to gain election without having to endure violence and intimidation. After the summer of 1888, however, fusion agreements were no longer sought or secured.

Local elections were not the only arena plagued by controversy in 1888. In the same election, a Wheel-backed candidate for United States Congress from the second district was narrowly defeated. John M. Clayton, another brother to Arkansas's Republican boss—Powell Clayton—lost the election to Democrat Clifton R. Breckenridge by a vote of 17,857 to 17,011. Clayton contested the outcome and while pursuing his own investigation was assassinated on the night of January 29, 1889, in Plumerville (Conway County). Congress subsequently ruled that Clayton had been elected, but the assassin or assassins were never brought to justice. Kenneth Barnes's chilling account of the murder and subsequent investigation highlights the measures Democrats were willing to take in order to reassert their control. Certainly the federal government's inability to do more to remedy the situation indicated Washington's willingness to all but look the other way. And worse was to follow.

Challenges to African Americans

Disfranchisement:
Disfranchisement consisted of measures to prevent certain persons, particularly African Americans, from voting in elections.

Because black farmers had joined with whites in voting for the Union Labor Party candidates in both the 1888 and 1890 elections, Democrats determined that the surest way to maintain their political control was to eliminate the threat from below. The movement for disfranchisement spread across the South beginning in 1889 in Mississippi. In 1891 the legislature passed an act, under the guise of election reform, which effectively disfranchised a large part of the black electorate and denied the ballot to a smaller percentage of the white electorate. According to historian J. Morgan Kousser, 21 percent of black voters and 7 percent of white voters in Arkansas ceased to cast ballots after the 1891 election law. It gave greater authority to local white election officials and provided that they alone could mark the ballots of illiterate voters. Prior to that time illiterates could secure the assistance of friends or bring premarked ballots to the polls with them. After passage of the new election law, not only would they face personal embarrassment and perhaps the ridicule of elections officials, they could not be sure whether those officials marked their ballots as instructed. With 56 percent of black and 13 percent of white voters illiterate, the results were predictable. The Democrats secured their largest margin of victory in the 1892 election since the beginning of the challenge from discontented farmers. The number of voters dropped from 191,458 in 1890 to 156,186 in 1892.

Ironically, it was in that year that the Farmers Alliance finally realized the futility of working within the existing party structure and created the Populist or People's Party. The organizers of the Arkansas Union Labor Party reconstituted themselves as Populists, as members of the People's Party came to be known, and fielded J. P. Carnahan as their gubernatorial candidate. This time, however, the state's Republicans failed to endorse the agrarian candidate and ran one of their own, William G. Whipple, who would later go on to have a career as a federal prosecutor in Arkansas. But in 1892 neither the Republican nor the Populist candidates for governor came close to unseating the Democrat. The vote was 90,115 for Fishback, 31,117 for Carnahan, and 33,644 for Whipple. The remaining votes went to a Prohibition Party candidate.

Another disfranchising measure followed the 1891 election law. The electorate, reduced in number because of the 1891 legislation affecting illiterates, approved a poll-tax amendment that required the payment of a fee prior to voting. Although 75,847 voters cast ballots in favor of the poll-tax amendment while 56,589 voted against it, controversy emerged after the election because the Arkansas constitution required that the majority of voters casting ballots in an election must approve a constitutional amendment, and in this case many voters had failed to mark their ballots on the poll-tax question. Only 132,436 of 156,186 persons voting in the election voted on that issue, so the 75,847 votes in favor fell short of being a majority. However, the speaker of the house certified the election results as valid, and the poll tax was implemented. As historian

John Graves has argued, the individuals most likely to vote against such a measure—the poorest of both races—had been effectively disfranchised by the 1891 election law. The poll tax served to further discourage other poor voters, and then the legislature again contributed to the decline in voter turnout by passing an enforcement measure in 1895 that required potential voters to pay their poll tax months before an election. Only the most committed voters, only those who were not already intimidated by the requirements concerning illiterate voters, would remain active participants in the election process. It particularly impacted poor farmers, such as the growing number of tenants and sharecroppers, some of whom moved from one plantation to another every year and rarely maintained records, thus making it difficult for them to fulfill residency requirements. J. Morgan Kousser's figures indicate that the poll tax deterred an additional 15 percent of black voters and another 9 to 12 percent of white voters from exercising the franchise.

The White Primary rule implemented by the Democratic Party was the last disfranchising measure passed in Arkansas. This was even more obviously connected to agrarian discontent as it was designed in part to appease discontented Democrats on the local level by preventing the black vote from being used against them by party rivals. Democratic Party primaries, whereby Democrats competed with one another for the Democratic slot on the fall general election ballot, dated back to the 1870s, but had not completely replaced the old method of having local candidates selected at state conventions. The primary process allowed party members at the local level much greater control over the selection of their own candidates. In 1898 the State Democratic Central Committee required that all counties begin holding primary elections, and in 1906 it excluded black voters from participation in those elections. Since Arkansas and the rest of the South was thoroughly Democratic by that time, the Democratic candidate was guaranteed of success in the fall election, thus the selection of the Democratic candidate in the primary was crucially important to voters who wanted alternatives. Exclusion from participation in the primary election therefore amounted to another form of disfranchisement. As political scientist Diane D. Blair has suggested, the black and white poor alike might reasonably be assumed to be acting prudently in deciding not to waste what little they had to pay poll taxes simply for the privilege of voting for a Democratic candidate who did not represent their interests or a Republican candidate who had no hope of winning the election.

The disfranchising measures adopted in Arkansas had the same intention as those being fashioned to exclude foreign immigrants in the North—except that there they included English-language requirements unnecessary in the South. But Arkansas statutes more particularly resembled such measures passed elsewhere in the South, as were its Jim Crow (segregation) statutes. Jim Crow emerged first and foremost in urban areas, swelled in the last decades of the nineteenth century by blacks looking for opportunities unavailable in rural areas. Arkansas's segregation statutes dated back to the same legislative session that passed the election reform law. In passing the "separate coach law" of 1891, the Arkansas legislature was acting in concert with other southern states that also witnessed an unprecedented degree of urbanization.

In fact, the disfranchising and segregation statutes were only the legal arm of a new assault against African Americans. Mob violence aimed at African Americans rose dramatically in the 1890s, with lynchings of blacks accused of various crimes reaching its peak in that decade. Whites generally justified the lynchings as necessary to protect white womanhood, claiming that most lynching victims were rapists, but historians have discovered that very few of the black men lynched had actually assaulted a white woman. Many were lynched for petty crimes or for attempting to defend themselves against white violence. Mob action went hand-in-glove with the new legal strictures, which limited black opportunity and challenged black civil rights. Some African Americans, so disillusioned with the deteriorating circumstances confronting them, participated in the "back to Africa" movement. One very prominent black Arkansan, John Gray Lucas, a state legislator who had denounced the 1891 legislation in passionate terms, departed for Chicago, where he became that city's first black millionaire.

Other prominent blacks held their ground and achieved a measure of success, even in the more hostile environment prevailing in Arkansas. Ninth Street in Little Rock became a commercial and social focal point and a haven of safety (for the most part) for the black community. William Grant Still, who lived in Little Rock as a child, reported fond memories of his years there. Still's family left the state, and he grew up to become a prominent composer and was recognized as one of the talented African Americans who fostered the Harlem Renaissance. See plate 39 following page 366.

In Little Rock, meanwhile, John E. Bush founded the Mosaic Templars and Scipio Jones practiced law. Indeed, Little Rock was home to a small but distinguished group of African American professionals and businessmen who made up what Willard Gatewood calls a "black aristocracy." Like elite blacks in other cities—both North and South—Little Rock's black aristocracy was made up of African Americans who had been privileged slaves or were the descendants of privileged slaves. Some of them had been fathered by white slave masters and had been educated at Oberlin or in Europe. Others had been free in the antebellum period or were the children of such free people of color. Whatever their origins, they accumulated property and achieved considerable status within the black community. Some of them became prominent Republicans and engaged in "fusion" with Democrats until the 1890s when Democrats decided to end that arrangement. Those who remained politically active after the end of fusion typically relied on appointments to federal offices when Republicans held the presidency. John E. Bush, for example, was receiver of the United States land office in Little Rock. Bush had founded the Mosaic Templars, a burial and insurance agency, in 1882. According to John Graves, by 1913 the Mosaic Templars also operated "a building and loan association, a hospital in Hot Springs, and owned a two-hundred-thousand-dollar headquarters building at Ninth and Broadway streets in Little Rock; there were eighty thousand dues-paying members in twenty-six states, Central and South America, the Canal Zone, and the West Indies."

Mosaic Templars: A burial and insurance agency for African Americans which, by the early twentieth century, included a hospital and building and loan association.

Bush was closely allied with Booker T. Washington, who considered Bush as among the most prominent southern blacks, and was founder of the Little Rock chapter of the National Negro Business League.

While blacks in Little Rock found safety in numbers, blacks in the Arkansas countryside remained relatively isolated and vulnerable. Although groups of blacks occasionally resisted whitecapping activities visited upon them, they found local law enforcement officials unsympathetic to their attempts to defend themselves. Whitecapping, which emerged in the 1890s, was a phenomenon connected to competition between whites and blacks for places on the area's expanding plantations. Some whites, determined to secure plantation jobs, took matters into their own hands and sought to drive out black labor by force. Planters preferred black to white labor, for black laborers were cheaper and, because of disfranchising and segregation measures, more vulnerable. Ironically, some planters emerged as defenders of black sharecroppers in the face of the nightriding activities of landless whites. Many watched in horror as black labor departed, disillusioned with the laws aimed at relegating them to a second-class status. Some went to Kansas, others to Africa, but no matter where they went, they left planters in desperate need of another source of cheap labor.

Sunnyside plantation: a plantation with origins in the antebellum period but that was acquired by eastern financer Austin Corbin, who imported Italian laborers to ease a labor shortage.

One absentee landowner in Chicot County, Austin Corbin, devised a scheme to import families from Italy in order to farm his Sunnyside plantation. Corbin was a New York financier and railroad entrepreneur who came into possession of Sunnyside after its previous owners, Patrick and John C. Calhoun, the grandsons of the famous South Carolina proslavery politician, suffered financial reverses they could not overcome. In its heyday, Sunnyside had been the centerpiece of a vast plantation empire owned by Elisha Worthington, the largest slave owner in Arkansas. It passed through several hands after the Civil War before Corbin came into possession of it, and through his acquaintance with an Italian diplomat and with the mayor of Rome, he was able to carry through with his plan to settle Italians from central and northern Italy at Sunnyside. His death just six months after the experiment began complicated matters, and many of the Italian farmers began to complain about conditions on the plantation. Water was piped in from the river and stagnant ponds bred mosquitoes from which the Italians had no protection since none of their homes had screens. Thus malarial fevers and typhoid were striking them down, and many found themselves indebted to the company after the first year on the plantation. Within another year, most of the Italians departed, some of them moving to northwest Arkansas where they founded Tontitown and prospered. Some stayed on, however, and when the plantation was purchased by Mississippi interests, including LeRoy Percy, a new experiment with Italian labor would gain notoriety in the early twentieth century.

The reign of terror against blacks together with the imposition of segregation and disfranchisement created problems for Arkansas planters, but by defeating the populist challenge and erecting a legal structure that effectively relegated blacks to an inferior position, the Democratic Party guaranteed its ability to hold on to power in Arkansas for another seventy-five years. Yet at least the last two governors of the nineteenth century, James Clarke and Daniel Jones, had embraced some of the populist platform, particularly that stressing the monetization of silver, so that they constituted a shift from the conservative Democrats to a new kind of Arkansas Democrat. In holding on to power, the conservative Democrats had departed from the party line and ultimately made room for a politician who spoke the language of populism. Jeff Davis, who became governor in 1901, was clearly a renegade Democrat who was able to secure election precisely because of the primary election process that democratized the selection of candidates. As an outsider identified with populism, he would never have won the Democratic nomination under the old system, dominated as it was by cronyism. He was able to build on the continuing ferment among Arkansas's discontented white farmers by striking out at the old clique of Democratic Party politicians and what he termed the "high collared roosters of Little Rock." He also engaged in a virulent racist rhetoric representative of the extreme view of certain whites toward African Americans, and he carried that point of view into the twentieth century, perpetuating it and elaborating upon it.

Religion

As historian Charles Reagan Wilson notes, the predominantly Methodist and Baptist denominations within the South worked hand-in-hand with the government to enforce conformity to the notion of white supremacy and to the dominant economic, political, societal, and religious orthodoxy. In Arkansas, this connection was embodied in Gov. James P. Eagle (1889–1893), himself a Baptist minister. He served as president of the Arkansas Baptist Convention from 1880 to 1904. In 1902 he was elected president of the Southern Baptist Convention and was subsequently twice reelected.

Baptists and Methodists far outnumbered other Protestant denominations, but Presbyterians and the Disciples of Christ (or one of its offshoots) worshiped in every county of the state by the end of the nineteenth century. Despite sometimes intense denominational disputes among the various churches, there was unanimity among southern Protestants concerning the literal interpretation of the Bible and the omnipresence of God in the affairs of men. Because they were profoundly conservative in orientation and dedicated to the preservation of the status quo, Protestant churches often avoided addressing the problems confronted by labor, blacks, or the poor. A given church might organize aid to its own poor, but rarely sought to aid the poor in general. Many believed that the poor had no one but themselves to blame for their poverty. They viewed labor agitation as a direct threat to the established order and thus a serious danger. They believed that maintaining racial subordination of African Americans was ordained by God.

While African Americans shared many of the same assumptions about God and religion as whites, they hardly accepted the notion of God having ordained their subordination. Like whites, blacks largely embraced the Baptist and Methodist faiths, although in the years following the Civil War, blacks removed themselves from white churches they had attended during slavery and established their own churches. In addition to the African Methodist Episcopal Church, they flocked to various Baptist churches, and in smaller numbers they attended the Church of Divine Christ, the Church of God in Christ, and the Disciples of Christ. Although theirs too was a "civil religion," in that they saw a connection between church and state, they embraced a notion of racial uplift and cast their charitable nets beyond their own congregations. Increasingly cut off from political participation and treated as second-class citizens by state and local government officials, blacks congregated in their own churches for political and economic reasons as well as for religious and social purposes.

Although religion supported and even celebrated the patriarchy, women—both white and black—found the church to be one arena of activity that was open to them. This was true in the antebellum period, too, when women were barred from participation in many community organizations and prevented from establishing their own associations. In this context, they found it possible to begin organizing themselves into groups within their respective churches. They formed sewing circles, ladies aid societies, benevolent associations for widows and orphans, and in the late nineteenth century, district and state women's missionary organizations. Besides raising funds for buildings, furnishings, ministers' salaries, and other church debts, most church women's groups provided charitable assistance to members and friends. For example, the Benevolent Society of United Sisters No. 1, organized about 1874 by the women of Wesley Chapel in Little Rock, assisted church members and their families when illness, death, or other trouble struck. Members took turns nursing the sick, and, when necessary, assessed themselves to raise money for death benefits.

While most Arkansans worshiped in Protestant denominations, individuals with other religious orientations also established churches and temples in Arkansas. Although by the end of the nineteenth century, the typical Jewish immigrant, like those elsewhere in the nation, was of eastern European origins, the first Jews to come to the state were of German extraction. Abraham Block, for example, had been born in Bohemia in 1780, emigrated to the United States when he was twelve, and became a prosperous businessman in Richmond, Virginia. He relocated to Arkansas in 1823 and settled in Washington (Hempstead County), choosing that location because it promised business opportunities, located as it was on the Southwest Trail. He established a business and prospered in Arkansas, but was only able to attend synagogue on trips to New Orleans, for no Jewish synagogue existed in any location in Arkansas at that time. The Mitchell brothers (Jacob, Hyman, and Levi) settled in Little Rock around 1830 and soon established solid reputations among the business community. By 1836, Jews were scattered throughout the state, but were still few in number.

German Jews continued to migrate to Arkansas even after the Civil War, and a small but prosperous Jewish community developed in Little Rock. Smaller communities existed in Pine Bluff and Fort Smith. Prominent among the post–Civil War Jewish families was that of young Jacob Trieber, who was a teenager at the time his family settled in Helena,

Arkansas, in 1868. As an adult he aligned with the Republican Party, became a prominent lawyer, and was appointed the federal judge for the eastern district of Arkansas by Pres. William McKinley in 1900. The first Jew in the nation to occupy a federal judgeship, he rendered some crucial decisions concerning rights for African Americans. He eventually took up residence in Little Rock and became active in that city's Jewish community. Still heavily German in ethnic identity, Little Rock's Jews established Congregation B'Nai Israel in 1870, and the fact that the local newspaper frequently printed the rabbi's sermons suggests that they enjoyed some level of acceptance within the dominant Christian culture. Certainly Jacob Trieber successfully negotiated Arkansas's political and social landscape. He became president of the Arkansas Bar Association and the Masonic Grand Master of Arkansas. He also became a member of Little Rock's exclusive XV Club, an all-male dinner and lecture club with no more than fifteen men who met fifteen times a year to discuss the political problems of the day and to dine sumptuously. The club drew members from different religious and political persuasions who had achieved a notable measure of success and respect within the city's community.

Those of the Catholic faith had a much longer history in the state, stretching back to June 25, 1541, when Hernando de Soto held a ceremony at the Indian village of Casqui near present-day Parkin and erected a cross. But the De Soto party was only passing through, made no actual converts, and left no priests to proselyte among the Indians. Subsequent French and Spanish "occupation" of the territory failed to convert the Indian population to Catholicism and established only a very small European Catholic community. With the Louisiana Purchase in 1803, the protestant Anglo-Americans almost completely overwhelmed the Catholic influence. Nevertheless, in the nineteenth century, monks and nuns established monasteries and convents—in Little Rock, Pine Bluff, and Fort Smith—and Catholic communities began to grow in size and influence. By the end of the nineteenth century, several prominent Catholic families practiced their faith in many of Arkansas's towns. Indeed, Carl Moneyhon points out that in Little Rock, the largest single "denomination in 1900 was not even Protestant, it was Roman Catholic" with "over 23 percent of the citizens who stated a religious preference" claiming to be Catholic. Of course, that means all the Protestant denominations put together made the Protestant persuasion clearly dominant.

Religion occupied a central place in the lives of most Arkansans, and politicians, who were almost always members of a Baptist or Methodist denomination, frequently seasoned their political speeches with religious references, evoking the gospel in order to win votes. Indeed, they were skilled in the language of religion and understood how to reach the Arkansas electorate. In the early years, it was not uncommon for church services to be held in the county courthouse or some other public building until funds could be secured to construct a proper church building. Every aspect of life involved the church—birth, marriage, and death. The birth of a child was cause for comment from the preacher and celebration among the congregants, a marriage was a religious and a social occasion, and a death brought a community of worshipers together to grieve and celebrate the passage of a soul to glory. Membership in a church, moreover, offered something beyond spiritual sustenance, especially in isolated rural areas where there were few opportunities for entertainment. Some rural women only left their homes to attend church on Sundays or Wednesday evenings. Others might attend the "preaching" (religious service) and participate in "Sunday school" (Bible study), in addition to joining in with other women to plan picnics that took place on the church grounds. Suppers prepared by the church women provided a safe atmosphere for young people to meet and mingle under the watchful eye of their elders. Indeed, marrying within the family's denomination was often mandatory, and many a child faced censure for choosing a mate from outside the fold. Arkansans were serious about their religion, and it ran deep in their consciousness.

Women's Activism

Historians have argued that women's involvement in church organizations led eventually to movement into associations not directly connected to the church, particularly those involving issues that spoke to the health of the family. Thus many women gravitated toward the temperance movement, recognizing that excessive alcohol consumption by husbands and fathers endangered the family. They found a particularly effective venue for their concerns about alcohol once the Women's Christian Temperance Union (WCTU) was founded in 1873 in Ohio. Arkansas women became active within it almost immediately, organizing their own state chapter in 1878. From the beginning WCTU activists in Arkansas supported the "local option" approach to controlling alcohol consumption. Local option allowed voters in communities and rural areas to vote on whether to permit the licensing of saloons. If the voters approved, citizens wishing to establish a saloon had to circulate a petition to be presented to the county judge. If the petition contained the signatures of a majority of the registered voters in a particular town or township, the judge had to honor it.

Women's Christian Temperance Union: An organization founded in Ohio in 1873 to encourage "temperance" in the consumption of alcohol.

Local option: An initiative placed on the ballot in order to provide local area residents with the option of voting against the licensing of saloons in their communities.

Most members of the WCTU were middle-class white women, although separate chapters were organized by middle-class black women. While most of the WCTU women were housewives, the movement provided public forums from which to speak, including the *Arkansas Ladies' Journal* and the *Woman's Chronicle*. The newsletter of the national organization, the *White Ribboner*, was widely subscribed to. Wearing the WCTU's trademark white ribbons and carrying the organization's banner, Arkansas women began to attend state and national meetings of the WCTU in the 1880s in order to map strategy. By the mid-1880s, however, a coalition of men's prohibition and temperance groups combined to create the Arkansas Prohibition Alliance and deliberately excluded the WCTU and women activists. That organization helped create the state's Prohibition Party, which ran a candidate for governor in 1892. The snub left a lasting legacy of distrust between the WCTU and another men's prohibition group founded in the 1890s, the Anti-Saloon League, and highlighted once again the second-class status of women in Arkansas.

Excluded from politics and from participation in organizations like the Arkansas Prohibition Alliance and the Anti-Saloon League, women found ways to work within the system to make their influence felt. They became actively involved in auxiliary associations connected to fraternal organizations, and they also formed their own patriotic organizations. A number of fraternal organizations existed throughout Arkansas, and, as elsewhere, men responded to anti-lodge sentiments from women and religious groups by authorizing the formation of women's auxiliaries. Through these auxiliaries, women gained controlled glimpses into the groups' precepts. The Grand Chapter Order of the Eastern Star of the State of Arkansas was organized October 2, 1876; other sister orders in Arkansas included Kings' Daughters, Ladies of the Maccabees, and Pythian Sisters. One black fraternal order that originated in Arkansas, the Mosaic Templars of America, chartered on May 24, 1883, included women but in separate "lady chambers . . . under the special watch-care and guardianship of the Grand Mosaic Master." State and local chapters of the Daughters of the American Revolution, United Daughters of the Confederacy, Southern Memorial Association, and other patriotic societies provided Arkansas women with avenues for establishing memorials, preserving battlefields, and marking burial sites of soldiers. These groups also undertook a wide range of civic improvements, including beautification of parks and roadways, health and safety campaigns, hospital assistance, relief to crippled and needy children, and contributions to libraries. They also sponsored history essay contests and raised funds for student loans.

Although initiated in the late nineteenth century, the ladies' auxiliaries and women's club movement found fullest expression in the next century. Similarly, the women's club movement, which had roots in the 1890s, actually took off in the first decade of the twentieth century. These clubs allowed women with moderate and nonmilitant inclinations to express themselves through literary and aesthetic clubs. The clubs served as vehicles for personal, domestic, and community improvement, but since they were oriented toward improvement and change, women in them were eventually drawn into the nationwide progressive-era reform movement of the twentieth century. The twentieth-century version of the club movement thus led women to activist agendas and more public roles than many of them initially envisioned for themselves. The General Federation of Women's Clubs organized on the national level in 1890, and in 1897 the Arkansas Federation of Women's Clubs joined the national federation.

Although refraining from espousing an activist agenda in the nineteenth century, the women's club movement schooled women in a variety of ways for the role they would soon embrace. Participation in a club offered opportunities to broaden their horizons by challenging women to refine critical thinking skills, to engage in debate and speaking exercises, and to become knowledgeable in a wide range of fields. Many clubs emphasized study, reading, and discussion, and some chose to limit their work to those areas. Members of two clubs founded in 1888, the Philomathic Club of Helena

above: Ladies Aid Society cleaning cemetery. *Walnut Grove Home Demonstration Club Photographs. Special Collections Division, University of Arkansas Libraries, Fayetteville.*

Charlotte Andrews Stephens, first black teacher in Little Rock, Arkansas. *Courtesy of the Arkansas History Commission.*

and the Fort Smith Fortnightly Club, devoted themselves solely to reading and reviewing books. Several literary clubs, however, focused not simply on reading and reviewing books, but on founding community libraries. The Woman's Book Club of Helena organized in 1900 to establish and operate a city public library, and other groups followed suit in the more activist twentieth century.

The practice of segregation barred black women from participation in clubs organized by white women so black women chartered their own organizations. In 1896 they founded the National Association of Colored Women's Clubs. The first NACW federated club in the state was established in Little Rock in 1897. Charlotte Andrews Stephens, the first black teacher hired in the city public schools, was a charter member. Black women founded literary clubs in Little Rock, Newport, Brinkley, and Searcy, among other places. While some clubs were strictly literary in nature—like the Lotus Club and the Bay View Reading Club in Little Rock—clubs founded by middle-class black women frequently had a charitable component, speaking perhaps to the plight of the impoverished black community within which they lived. Black women in Pine Bluff created the Mothers League in 1893, and black women in Fort Smith founded the Ladies Relief and Missionary Corps in 1898. Clubs in Little Rock, Hot Springs, and Fort Smith supported homes for elderly black women. Like the clubs created by white women, black women's clubs became more numerous and activist in orientation in the progressive era of the twentieth century.

Both black and white women's clubs supported public education, and some women, like Little Rock's Charlotte Stephens, found employment opportunities because of the proliferation of public schools after the Civil War. In 1869 white teachers in Arkansas organized the State Teachers Association, and Ida Jo Brooks, daughter of would-be Republican governor Joseph Brooks, became in 1877 the first woman to serve as its president, as well as the first woman to serve as president of any state teachers association in the United States. Black teachers organized the State Colored Teachers Association in 1898. Salaries were low for both black and white teachers, however, and many, particularly in rural areas, found it necessary to board in some household in the neighborhood.

Although some women worked as teachers, it was not an entirely female profession. The teachers associations were of enormous importance to women, however, for it was the only avenue through which they could hope to exercise influence over the direction education was taking in the state. Reconstruction governments made public education a priority and the number of schools in the state, though chronically underfunded, greatly expanded. The public school hierarchy was entirely male, and legislators and governors looked to those men to implement policy. Women were often on the receiving end only of policy changes, but in the 1890s one development in particular likely accrued to their benefit: teacher institutes. When Josiah H. Shinn became superintendent of public instruction in 1890, he launched a series of teacher institutes that reached into communities across the state. In the first year alone, 2,242 teachers attended the seventy-six institutes he organized for the purpose of improving the quality of the teachers and thus raising the level of instruction. Grants from the Peabody Fund together with appropriations from the Arkansas legislature ensured the continuation of these institutes even after Shinn left his position in 1894. In 1899, when the legislature ceased appropriating funds for them, the Peabody Fund subsidized sixty-five institutes for white teachers and fifty-two for black teachers in 1899–1900. Thereafter, funds for teacher institutes dried up completely. Education and teacher education would become a major issue for the progressive governors of the early twentieth century.

Aside from teaching, few other employment opportunities existed for women. Midwifery was a profession long associated with women, but with the spread of doctors in the state in the late nineteenth century, that opportunity was slowly eroding. A woman might work as a clerk in a store or assist her husband in running his business, but most white women were confined to the home, and the expansion of jobs considered appropriate to women occurred principally in the next century. Black women might find work as a teacher in the black school system, if they were fortunate, but most worked as household servants or washerwomen at the same time they often assisted their husbands in fieldwork.

The fact that most professions were closed to women inspired some Arkansas women to join the suffrage movement. Women's suffrage in Arkansas was actually launched in 1868 when women packed the legislative gallery to listen to and applaud a proposal to extend suffrage to women in the proposed new state constitution. Some legislators ridiculed the notion that women were intellectually equipped to vote and others suggested that they were too refined for the rough and tumble business of politics. The measure failed, but Arkansas women continued to press for suffrage. Two women's journals were founded in the 1880s, both espousing suffrage for women. In 1884 Little Rock's Mrs. Mary W. Loughborough launched the *Arkansas Ladies' Journal*, which, though not solely dedicated to that one issue, called for women's suffrage. In 1888 three other women—Catherine Campbell Cunningham, Mrs. Mary Burt Brooks, and Mrs. William Cahoon—began publishing the *Woman's Chronicle*, which went further than Mrs. Loughborough's *Arkansas Ladies' Journal* in promoting suffrage for women. In fact, it soon became the chief organ for the women's suffrage movement in the South. It ceased publication in 1889, however, because of Cunningham's ill health. Despite the episodic nature of their journals, Arkansas women continued to host suffrage society meetings and speak out on the issue throughout the 1890s. Small auxiliary societies periodically sprang up in towns all over the state, but most of them were short lived. Forrest City, Lonoke, Clarksville, Beebe, and Judsonia all had organizations for a while, and women from those cities as well as from Hot Springs, Fort Smith, Hazen, Hope, Malvern, Suttgart, Ozark, and Rogers attended suffrage conventions in Little Rock. Arkansas suffragists were affiliated with Susan B. Anthony's American Woman Suffrage Association, filed annual reports with that organization, and sent delegates to national meetings. The century would close out with this nascent women's suffrage movement growing in strength, laying the groundwork for a successful campaign in the next decade and a half.

American Woman Suffrage Association: An organization of women who advocated for woman's suffrage with which most Arkansas suffrage supporters preferred over the more radical National Woman Suffrage Association.

For all the things that worked to bring Arkansas back into the mainstream of American politics and culture, the state remained distinctly southern. The railroad, lumber, and mining industries represented opportunities to link with the national marketplace but at a time when the country faced a series of economic crises, and Arkansas's fragile economy had greater difficulty weathering those particular storms. Lumber, mining, and agriculture were the primary growth industries, but they were largely extractive in nature and much of the wealth of the state was exported elsewhere; that is, the raw products stripped from the forests reserves, dug from the coal mines, and harvested from the farms. Challenges to a Democratic Party unresponsive to the problems facing agriculturalists united, for a time, farmers across racial and sectional lines, but the Democratic Party responded with an aggressive campaign to eliminate the threat from below by disfranchising a segment of the population: blacks and poor whites. White women achieved some gains, fighting for the right to vote and joining the crusade for prohibition, but they also reasserted their devotion to the southern cause by erecting memorials to Confederate veterans and otherwise demonstrating adherence to racial segregation. Although southern partisanship influenced both men and women in Arkansas, reconciliation with the North was equally potent and symbolized by the Arkansas exhibition at the Columbian exposition in 1892–1893 and, most dramatically, by the state's eager participation in the Spanish American War in 1898. The solution to the state's debt problem worked through by Governor Clarke in 1898 seemed to position Arkansas to assume equal status with other states. Although it would face a series of unexpected challenges in the next century, Arkansas would also embrace many progressive reforms—including women's suffrage and prohibition—that swept the rest of the nation and thus continue the process of reintegration even as it held on to its southern distinctiveness.

CHAPTER TWELVE

A Light in the Darkness: Limits of Progressive Reform, 1900–1920

Although Arkansas embraced certain elements of the nation's progressive reform movement of the early twentieth century, it did so in a manner consistent with its southernness. Historian Jack Kirby's book, *Darkness at the Dawning*, emphasizes the rise of a virulent new racism during the progressive era, and certainly Arkansas's version of reform remained anchored in its repressive racial system, one largely enacted in the last decade of the nineteenth century. Another legacy of the previous century involved the state's tradition of minimal taxation and its fragile economy. Newly relieved of a burdensome indebtedness originating in the failure of the state's banks in the 1840s, Arkansas made an effort to assume the activist role inspired by the progressive impulse sweeping the nation. The need to create new regulatory agencies, expand and reform the state's educational system, and extend the transportation network all required an unprecedented expenditure of funds, and the need to finance these enterprises often collided with the state's inability and unwillingness to raise sufficient tax revenue. Arkansas's low population provided for an inadequate tax base, and a fierce opposition to raising taxes among Arkansas's citizenry and politicians further complicated matters. In order to move beyond the bottom tier of states in various economic and social indices, Arkansas had to fund reform at an unrealistically high level. While the state managed to make some progress in spite of these obstacles, it did so without challenging elite interests and, in fact, often served them. Despite all of the genuine progress made in the first two decades of the twentieth century, a substantial minority of the population enjoyed few of the benefits and actually experienced repression and violence. The imposition of the White Primary in 1906, the last of three measures used to disfranchise black voters, and a massacre of blacks in Philips County in 1919 demonstrated the state's continuing legacy of racism. Although women made some important advances, largely on their own initiative, white and black women did not unite in common cause but segregated themselves into separate entities, forming independent literary clubs and prohibition organizations. The women's suffrage movement, like that elsewhere, largely remained a bastion of white *female* superiority.

The Impulse for Progressive Reform

The progressive movement began just after the turn of the century and marked an attempt by various interests to come to terms with a society in the midst of a dramatic transformation. The industrial revolution, urbanization, and the emergence of giant corporations seemed to threaten order and stability, and people throughout the country reacted by attempting numerous reforms. Although the movement is regarded largely as an urban phenomenon, city progressives had their rural and small-town counterparts in southern states like Arkansas. Not surprisingly, the reforms generated by southerners were often peculiar to the South and the rural experience, although many mirrored reforms occurring in the cities. Voting qualifications for immigrants in northern cities, for example, were not so very different from disfranchisement mechanisms applied to blacks. Indeed, many of the reforms passed during this era were repressive; that is, they limited the opportunities or the behavior of certain groups in American society, and they failed to gain the support of all who might term themselves progressives.

African American leaders and their white allies were not unmindful of the new racist ideology and grew concerned enough to form the National Association for the Advancement of Colored People (NAACP) in 1909. Among the founders was black intellectual W. E. B. Du Bois. Within a decade after its founding, black membership in the NAACP expanded as chapters were chartered in states, counties, cities, and towns. The organization was slow to develop in the South, however, until after Booker T. Washington's death in 1915. Washington had been hostile to the NAACP, largely because its agenda and strategy was diametrically opposed to his own. Washington preached economic self-help, foreswore political involvement, and essentially espoused acceptance of a racial status quo that included the political and social subordination of the black population. The NAACP directly challenged both segregation and disfranchisement and became intimately involved in certain high-profile criminal cases involving poor and often illiterate African Americans.

While Washington was alive, relatively few blacks, south or north, were willing to risk involvement with the NAACP, but once he died, the southern black elite often became the leaders in establishing branches of the organization. Little Rock's black aristocracy was no exception. In November 1918, some of the leading black businessmen and professionals in the city founded a local chapter of the NAACP. The list of founding members reads like a who's who of the Little Rock black establishment: A. E. and C. E. Bush, sons of John E. Bush, the founder of the Mosaic Templars in Little Rock; G. W. Ish, a black physician from an elite Little Rock family; Joseph A. Booker, president of Arkansas Baptist College; Dr. John M. Robinson, a prominent Little Rock physician; and Isaac Gillam, a well-known black politician. Like some other local chapters, however, the Little Rock chapter served principally as a social club rather than as a black activist organization. The black elite there was an insular group existing within a small city that had hardly outgrown its "frontier" status. They had carved out a comfortable existence for themselves, lived in fine homes in integrated neighborhoods, and enjoyed privileges that most other blacks did not have access to. Many of them had imbibed enough of the Washington accommodationist message to preclude any very activist agenda, and while other individuals within the organization were more militant, most were loath to risk what they had secured for the sake of pursuing the NAACP's goals

Booker T. Washington with Arkansas black leaders. *Seated:* Booker T. Washington; *standing, left to right:* Joseph Booker, Emmett J. Scott, and John E. Bush. *Courtesy Alice Saville Bush.*

of achieving civil and political rights for the black population as a whole. Some among the African American elite in Little Rock, however, would grow weary of the passive role the city's NAACP chapter adopted and pursue a more activist agenda, but this would not occur until the 1920s.

Even as the African American elite struggled to find a place in a new and more hostile environment, poor African Americans and their poor white counterparts found employment in the expanding railroad and lumber industries. The ramifications of this expansion reverberated throughout the state. Ambitious men in the delta recognized that there, at least, certain profitable possibilities existed once the forests were cut. Expensive drainage districts made possible cultivation of cotton and the development of the plantation system, and the railroads provided a basic infrastructure for moving cotton to market. For twenty-first-century environmentalists, draining the wetlands was an environmental disaster, destroying natural wildlife sanctuaries, wiping out habitats, and altering the migration habits of certain waterfowl. Yet drainage also led to the expansion of the plantation system there, bringing wealth to those who came to own the land. It also brought repressive institutions and led to social upheaval and violence as whites and blacks vied for places on the plantations and as homesteaders fought with planters over title to some of the richest land remaining in America. Still, the progressive package included a new emphasis on conservation, and Arkansas was one state where that impulse was played out. Big Lake National Wildlife Refuge was created in 1915 to protect the last remaining sizable swamp in Mississippi County and thus provide an important point in the great North American flyway for ducks and birds heading south from Canada for the winter.

An even larger victory for conservationists occurred in 1907 and arose out of even more unlikely circumstances. The coming of the railroad and the lumber industry had not had the same result in all parts of Arkansas, and this was directly related to the type of land encountered in different regions of the state. The development of the land beneath the timber depended on its fertility. While in eastern Arkansas enterprising and sometimes unscrupulous individuals drained the land and made enormous profits out of either selling it or turning to plantation agriculture, in the Ouachita Mountains, where the land was hilly and much less fertile, there was little incentive to appropriate cutover land for agricultural purposes. In addition to the absence of this incentive for clear-cutting, the Ouachita forest was favored by the fact that the conservation movement antedated its full exploitation, and farseeing individuals managed to place much of it within the newly created Arkansas National Forest in 1907, the first national forest in the South. Had the land beneath those forests been more fertile, there would likely have been greater opposition to the creation of the Arkansas National Forest, and the fate of the Ouachitas might have been much different.

Pres. Theodore "Teddy" Roosevelt championed conservation, of course, and certain other names of national prominence are associated with a variety of issues on the reform agenda. Senator Robert "Battling Bob" La Follette of Wisconsin is perhaps among the most prominent, and though no one of that stature came out of Arkansas, the state had its share of individuals who claimed, and sometimes deserved, a place among them, at least on the state level. Some of the reforms they pursued resembled those adopted elsewhere: regulations on railroads and corporations. But proponents of progressivism in Arkansas differed from those in northern cities in certain key areas. For example, prohibition, heavily supported by southerners, was opposed by urban bosses. Arkansas's progressive governors were typical of southern progressives in supporting such measures as prohibition.

Jeff Davis, who became governor in 1901, was the first to stake out a claim as a progressive governor in Arkansas, launching his career in a successful run for the state general assembly in 1890 by calling for prohibition. An inveterate race-baiter and unparalleled rabble-rouser, he first portrayed himself as a populist, stumping the state for William Jennings Bryan and free silver in 1896, although he was from a solidly upper-middle-class background. He won the state attorney generalship in 1898 and soon began to wage war over two issues that would later dominate his three terms as governor. He challenged the legality of the Kimbell State House Act, which authorized the construction of a new state capitol on the grounds of the old penitentiary building in Little Rock, arguing that a two-thirds vote—rather than a simple majority vote—was necessary to appropriate the initial $50,000 expenditure. He crowed against the "high-colored rooters" of Little Rock, portraying the Kimbell Act as an elitest sham. More to the point, he also positioned himself as a progressive and a trustbuster, interpreting the Rector Antitrust Act, passed in 1899, as prohibiting any kind of trust from doing business in Arkansas without regard to where it had been organized. Suits he filed while attorney general of Arkansas against fire insurance companies operating in Arkansas in 1899 resulted in widespread controversy, with many of the companies threatening to cancel policies. The state supreme court overruled him, but Davis had established himself as a spokesperson for the common people, a man facing off against privilege, and the people loved him. The state Democratic machine, however, was far from enamored of him. Despite being ridiculed by the press and branded as a renegade by his opponents in his 1900 run for governor, he swept into office and promised to continue forcefully interpreting the Rector Antitrust Act and to fight the construction of the new capitol.

While both of these controversies dominated his governorship, other issues soon came to the fore as well: convict leasing and prohibition. He was sincerely horrified by the conditions in the state prisons and in the largely unregulated convict lease camps. On the prohibition issue, however, he shifted sides and allied with the anti- prohibition forces as a result of his battle with the state Democratic Party machine over the new capitol and other issues. They accused him of being a drunkard and had him expelled from membership in the Second Baptist Church in Little Rock. His association with the liquor interests came to cloud his credentials as a southern progressive and his long-standing battle against the state Democratic establishment made it impossible for him to secure support for elimination of the convict leasing system. Throughout all his travails, the public continued to vote for him in large numbers, and in his last run for the governorship in 1904, he carried pro-Davis legislators into office as well.

In the 1904 campaign, Davis exhibited a much more strident racial demagoguery, and though many middle-class townspeople eschewed Davis's antiblack vitriol, his racism was hardly inconsistent with the Progressive impulse in the South or, indeed, in the nation as a whole. Thomas Dixon's *The Clansman*, a racist and highly inflammatory interpretation of Reconstruction that romanticized the Ku Klux Klan, was popular nationwide. Published in 1905, the book attracted the attention of D. W. Griffith and become the infamous *Birth of a Nation*, a film that incited riots in some cities when it premiered in 1915 and raised racial tensions everywhere. The controversy over the film continued well into the twentieth century. As the film historian Melvin Stokes notes, it was showing in 1957 in Little Rock when the Central High crisis erupted. Whether it contributed to the venom hurled at the nine black children attempting to integrate the school is hard to know, but it served as a point of reference then and earlier for white supremacists.

In the first decade of the twentieth century, Arkansas, like many other southern states, implemented a statewide primary system restricted to whites and reaffirmed the poll tax. Davis also began to champion a segregation of school taxes, in which only tax revenues collected from black citizens would fund black education. Since most blacks were mired in poverty so complete that they did not have to pay even the minimum taxes, the measure would have doomed black education. But that seemed to be Davis's point. He declared that educating blacks merely spoiled good field hands. The pro-Davis legislators who swept into office on his coattails in 1904, however, were to disappoint him on this, and other, issues. He initiated and lobbied for the passage of the Burgess School tax segregation bill, but the 1905 session of the legislature failed to pass the measure.

Burgess School Tax Segregation Bill: A bill that would have segregated local property tax revenues by race and effectively further undermined funding to black schools in the state.

Davis's third term was consumed primarily by his run for the Senate. He won that race and left the state in the hands of his handpicked predecessor, John Sebastian Little. When Little succumbed to a serious illness after only one month in office, Davis's longstanding enemy, Xenophon Overton Pindall, who was the incoming president pro tempore of the senate, soon took over. Pindall served until the general election in 1909, when George W. Donaghey was elected. Meanwhile, Davis went on to a lackluster career in the U.S. Senate. Aside from John Sebastian Little, all the men who occupied the governor's office in the period between 1907 and 1920 could claim at least some progressive accomplishments. Pindall secured a pure food and drug law, but his tenure in office—one year and seven months—was as "acting" governor, providing him with an insufficient base from which to launch a movement, and there is small indication that he had much impulse to do so. Aside from the food and drug law, he imposed a franchise tax on "foreign" (out-of-state) corporations and encouraged the legislature to pass a measure to prevent price discrimination.

Given Jeff Davis's often suspect credentials, George Washington Donaghey, who took office in 1909, was the first governor of Arkansas who could indisputably be labeled a progressive. Yet he, too, was squarely within the southern progressive tradition. Although he renovated the tax structure to allow for more public spending, in keeping with the demands of the progressive spirit, he supported reforms that did not fundamentally challenge Arkansas elites. He also sponsored initiatives in education and public health, and because of Donaghey, Arkansas was the only southern state to pass both the initiative and referendum that provided citizens with the means of playing a more direct role in fashioning the state's laws. He even brought William Jennings Bryan, the famous populist, to the state to help campaign for these reforms. The initiative process allowed voters to circulate a petition to get a measure on the ballot so that citizens could "initiate" legislation. The referendum allowed voters to pass judgment on a measure already passed by the legislature. Using the petition process to place an act of the legislature on the ballot, the people could affirm or reject it. Thus, ironically, just as the state was finalizing its disfranchisement of African Americans, it was passing impressive political reforms that essentially democratized legislation. As "democratic" as these reforms were, they were used in a manner that reflected the conservatism of the state's progressive spirit. For example, one of the first major initiatives launched in Arkansas was that involving prohibition. The Anti-Saloon League secured enough signatures to place a prohibition statute on the ballot in 1912, and although it went down to defeat, voters later used the referendum to validate a legislative act passed in 1915 which prohibited alcohol: In 1917 citizens circulated a petition to call for a popular vote on the statute, and this time Arkansans voted in favor of prohibition.

Convict Leasing

Perhaps Donaghey's most celebrated accomplishment was in finishing one battle Jeff Davis had waged, that against convict leasing. Conditions were primitive, brutal, and often deadly in convict camps. Because the greatest majority of convicts were African American, the system gained a reputation for imposing "slavery by another name" but many whites were ensnared as well, and it is perhaps as appropriate to identify it as a system that victimized the poor of both races. Donaghey was not alone among southern governors in pursuing the end of the convict leasing system, but he was in a better position than most to be especially knowledgeable about the practice. Prior to his election as governor, he had spent the major part of his professional life as a builder and in charge of a number of large construction projects where convicts were worked. Donaghey, in fact, served as the construction foreman during the early phase of the building of the new state capitol building and used convicts to dismantle the old penitentiary and to lay the foundation of the new building. The convicts he used in this project, however, resided within the existing penitentiary and were under the supervision of the state. As much as one-third of the prison population in Arkansas was in convict camps scattered throughout Arkansas, and there was little control over how they were treated or provided for. Aside from an unacceptable level of escapes, too many died from malnutrition and overwork and several highly publicized exposés brought the plight of convicts to the public's attention. Some of these highlighted the fact that black and white prisoners were housed together and thus played to the racist sentiments in a state that had only newly imposed segregation statutes on its black population.

Concern about convict leasing had mounted in the last decades of the nineteenth century and prompted Gov. James H. Berry to express concern about it in his farewell address in 1885. He decried conditions in the convict work camps and actually threatened to cancel leases if conditions did not improve. Three years later, penitentiary commissioners revealed that horrifying conditions existed at a mining camp at Coal Hill and signed a report calling for the cancellation of that particular camp's contract. In 1890 Gov. James P. Eagle criticized the entire convict lease system, and by 1892, the platform of the state Democratic Party included a provision for its abolition. Reforms passed by the legislature in 1893, however, stopped short of ending convict leasing, principally because legislators understood the fiscal constraints the state was operating under. While convict leasing did not generate a large amount of revenue, it passed the cost of caring for much of the prison population on to the lessees. Thus the 1893 legislation included a provision that allowed convict leasing if the state could not provide "equally remunerative employment." This loophole permitted the system to continue, although until 1899 most of the terms were for short periods rather than for the longer-term contracts that had become notorious. The shorter terms allowed for review of conditions at their expiration and thus, theoretically, provided for some check on abuses.

A new chapter in the struggle over convict leasing was opened in 1899 when it was determined to dismantle the old penitentiary in Little Rock and construct a new state capitol building on the grounds. As many as a third of the prisoners then residing there would have to be leased. The largest number of them went to the highest bidder, W. W. Dickinson of the Arkansas Brick and Manufacturing Company. Dickinson negotiated a ten-year lease, returning the state to the long-term lease arrangement that had been repudiated after the Coal Hill scandal. As attorney general and a member of the penitentiary board, Davis signed this lease in 1899, but as soon as he became governor in 1901, he began to condemn convict leasing and called for the cancellation of the Dickinson lease. He also called for a major restructuring of the penitentiary board, which was composed of the governor, auditor, secretary of state, attorney general, and commissioner of mines, manufacturing, and agriculture. Davis argued that with so many other responsibilities required of them, these constitutional officers could not devote sufficient attention to the oversight of the penitentiary or the far-flung convict camps. But Davis failed to convince either the penitentiary board or the legislature to end convict leasing. The chief issue that caused both entities to balk was all too familiar: the costs associated with taking over responsibility for the care of the convicts.

Governors in other southern states were also confronting the horror of convict leasing, and one solution adopted by some of them was that of purchasing and running a state convict farm. It was believed that, by placing prisoners on a farm under the watchful care of state-sanctioned officials, abuses could be kept to a minimum if not eliminated altogether. Davis urged the purchase of a six-thousand-acre tract in Jefferson County and vetoed two measures put forward by the legislature, one of which would have investigated the purchase of the Sunnyside property in Chicot County, which Davis argued was too unhealthy an area of the state. Just as the penitentiary board had not supported him in canceling the Dickinson contract, they did not support him in the purchase of the Jefferson County acreage. In November 1902 the board voted to purchase the Cummings farm in Lincoln County for $140,000.

Acting governor Pindall took no action against convict leasing during his brief tenure, and Gov. George Donaghey, elected in 1908, was frustrated in his efforts to effect the two reforms espoused by Davis, that of changing the composition of the penitentiary board and of ending convict leasing. All candidates for governor in 1908 opposed the system, and the Democratic Party platform also came out strongly against it. The year 1909 began auspiciously when the penitentiary board ruled in January that the

Dickinson lease, at the end of its ten-year agreement, had expired. The board ordered all prisoners returned, and the legislature quickly confirmed the decision, over Dickinson's objections. Donaghey proposed that the legislature censure convict leasing, but the legislature balked. It did vote to allow state prisoners to be used by counties in constructing roads. This was viewed as a reform at the time because convicts would be under county supervision, but many abuses later came to light as county officials developed a tendency to arrest people, particularly African Americans, on trumped up charges in order to place them in work camps run by friends and associates or even on projects in which they had an interest. Meanwhile, the penitentiary board was still divided over the issue of convict leasing. Donaghey could convince only one other member of the board to condemn the system. The issue was a $100,000 penitentiary debt that the other commissioners hoped could be reduced by leasing convicts.

The Democratic Party platform in 1910 failed to condemn the system as harshly as it had in 1908. None of the candidates for governor condoned the system so it did not emerge as a major issue. Upon reelection, Donaghey again asked the legislature in 1911 to end convict leasing, arguing that more deaths and escapes occurred on the convict lease farms. When the legislature ended without acting on the issue, he immediately called for a special session. The abolition of the convict lease system was one of five items on his agenda. Again, he failed to secure passage of legislation that would have outlawed convict leasing. The house approved the measure, but the senate failed to take it up. Frustrated over and over again in his efforts to end convict leasing, Donaghey moved toward a radical solution. In early 1912, he began to talk about pardoning convicts in county camps if abuses did not stop. In December 1912, he attended a governors' conference and heard Gov. Cole Blease of South Carolina reveal that he had pardoned convicts there in order to dramatize the abuse of prisoners. Donaghey returned to the state, sent aides out to gather data on the prisoners (type of crime, length of term in prison, etc.) and then on December 17 pardoned 360 convicts, 44 in county farms and 316 of the 850 convicts in the penitentiary. Most of those pardoned were serving short sentences for relatively minor crimes and had served over half their sentences. This effectively ended convict leasing in the state because it made it impossible for the state to supply convicts to those who wished to lease them.

When newly elected governor Joseph T. Robinson attended his first meeting of the penitentiary board after taking the oath of office, he called for the abolition of convict leasing. It passed unanimously. On the same day, a bill was introduced in the legislature that both called for the appointment of a three-person board of penitentiary commissioners (to be appointed by the governor) and outlawed convict leasing. It easily passed both the house and the senate and was signed by Robinson on February 21, 1913. Abuses continued but convict leasing was over.

Political "In-fighting" within the Democratic Party

Joseph Robinson's election to the governor's office occurred within the context of a struggle for power within the Democratic Party. It is axiomatic among southern historians and political scientists that in the one-party South of that era, all important decisions were made at the Democratic primary, and that few important issues divided candidates. Although Robinson would align with some of the most reactionary forces in Arkansas to capture the governor's chair—the old Jeff Davis machine—he established a solid progressive record during his brief tenure in that office. He served as governor less than two months, but he played an active role in directing a legislative session that passed a corrupt practices act and created three state agencies: a state banking department, a bureau of labor and statistics, and a highway commission. All three agencies spoke to some progressive impulse. The state banking department was designed to ensure that the banks throughout the state operated on a sound financial basis; the Bureau of Labor and Statistics was supposed to help the unemployed find work, although it was too poorly financed to offer much assistance; and the highway commission was to oversee the expansion of the state highway system. Perhaps had he remained governor, Robinson's progressive legacy would have been greater, but he aspired to higher office, and the opportunity to capture the Senate seat upon Jeff Davis's untimely death was too tempting. Robinson would go on to have a distinguished career in the Senate, running as the vice presidential candidate with Al Smith in 1928, and becoming a crucial figure in the southern wing of Pres. Franklin Delano Roosevelt's New Deal coalition.

It had been a strange alliance with Davis that had probably helped Robinson capture the governor's race by the large margin he amassed, and it was, in part, the loyalty of the old Davis machine that soon propelled him into the Senate. In the governor's race, Donaghey was running for a third term against the advice of veteran Democrats and was vulnerable on a number of fronts. It can be argued, in fact, that Robinson helped Davis more than Davis helped Robinson. Davis himself was running for a second term in the Senate, but presented an easy target because of his less-than-stellar performance as a senator. His bombastic antics in the Senate upon first reaching the nation's capitol seemed out of place and buffoonish. He scorned the high-hat social scene and became more and more isolated. The expense of living in Washington and the neglect of his law practice in Little Rock ultimately led to long absences from the Senate as he returned to the state in an attempt to keep both his law practice and his economic ship afloat.

Meanwhile, Davis's credentials as the defender of the little man were called into question over a complicated legal dispute concerning title to tens of thousands of acres of land within the so-called sunk lands of northeastern Arkansas. The dispute had its origins in the failure of surveyors in the early 1850s to survey certain lands in Mississippi and Poinsett counties, lands that had been "sunk" by the New Madrid earthquakes of 1811–1812. Through the Swamp Land Act of 1849, Congress awarded states the right to claim federal swamplands within their borders provided they survey the land and present the surveys to the government. Those entrusted with that responsibility in Arkansas determined

Sunk lands: Land "sunk" by the New Madrid earthquakes of 1811 and 1812 that became the center of controversy in the early twentieth century over its ownership.

that certain submerged lands in Mississippi and Poinsett counties were not swamps but lakes and thus avoided having to survey them. When the St. Francis Levee District was created in 1894, the state awarded all the unsold swamplands within its eight-county jurisdiction (which included Mississippi and Poinsett counties) to the district. The district began to sell the land and use the funds to begin building levees to protect against floods and, incidentally, to drain much of the land. Meanwhile, the state passed an act in 1902 allowing landowners to form county drainage districts, sell bonds to fund construction, and then tax themselves to pay off the bonds. Both the St. Francis Levee District and the drainage districts thus created hundreds of thousands of acres of dry land. A dispute arose when some landowners claimed the drained land through the principle of riparian right. According to that principle, when a landowner drained a lake fronting on his property, he had the right to claim the new dried land up to halfway across the lake. If he owned all the land around the lake, he could claim all the land recovered in the drainage project. The federal government asserted a counterclaim to the drained land, arguing that the principle of riparian rights only applied to lakes—rather than swamps—and that, in any case, the sunk lands had never passed out of federal hands according to the 1849 swampland act because they were never surveyed. The federal government then compounded the controversy by announcing that it would open the area to homesteaders, and would-be settlers soon swarmed into the area to lay claim to the valuable acreage. Certain plantation owners, Lee Wilson in Mississippi County and Ernest Ritter in Poinsett County, were two of the riparian claimants and soon found themselves in federal litigation. The Ritter and Wilson cases went all the way to the Supreme Court in 1917 and 1918. Ritter and Wilson lost their cases, but in 1922 Congress provided that riparian claimants, like Wilson and Ritter, were entitled to preferential rights to purchase the lands they had made improvements upon.

Whatever the final outcome of the dispute over the sunk lands, in 1910, when the House Committee on Public Lands held hearings on the matter, it became clear that Jeff Davis had been hired by the St. Francis Levee District to represent them in the dispute. If the St. Francis Levee District prevailed in asserting the right to sell the land to a number of lumbermen, planters, and speculators, hundreds of homesteaders in the disputed area stood to lose. Davis, the supposed champion of the little man, wasted no time in criticizing the homesteaders as feckless, irresponsible, and even in cahoots with Wilson and Ritter in some kind of ill-defined scheme to outmaneuver the St. Francis Levee District. When it became known during the public hearings in the House that Davis represented the district and stood to gain if they prevailed, his credibility with the House committee and the average Arkansan back home, eroded considerably.

With his credibility so obviously shaken, Davis was struggling for his political life, and the anti-Davis Democrats determined to mount a challenge. The perfect candidate presented himself in the form of Stephen Brundidge, a popular ex-congressman. In his twelve years in Congress (1897–1909), he had established a record as a moderate progressive, and he was an excellent stump speaker, one calculated to give Davis his most difficult challenge ever. Davis barely defeated him in the Senate race. In fact, Brundidge had the

Elijah Abbot homestead, circa 1915. *Abbott Family Photographs.*

election stolen from him in Poinsett County when ballots were lost in the levee. The "swamp Democrats" had delivered, perhaps for the favors done during the sunk lands controversy. Brundidge then challenged George Hays, an old Davis crony, for the governor's seat vacated when Robinson went to the Senate. Again, the swamp Democrats delivered for their man, and Brundidge saw another victory slip through his fingers when Phillips County election officials simply held their returns back until the other precincts had reported and then reported enough ballots for Hays to secure election.

Hays took over the governor's office at a time when public sentiment favored reform, but he concerned himself more with building a political constituency than providing progressive leadership. Supported by the remnants of the old Davis machine and by the St. Francis Levee District, Hays made sure that the latter remained an appointive rather than elective body, despite the fact that he had called for that very change while campaigning for the governor's office. Once in office, he recognized the value in terms of patronage of the board remaining an appointive body. He also defeated a primary election reform measure that would have ended the kind of manipulation of the ballot box that had won him election to the governor's office. That election reform would have required the publication of the names of all registered voters prior to the election so that it would not be possible to juggle returns at the last minute as had happened in Phillips County.

Nevertheless, Hays acquiesced in the legislature's ambitious progressive reform agenda. The Alexander Road Improvement Act allowed counties to create road improvement districts with the power to issue bonds; state elections, which had been held in September, were moved to coincide with federal elections in November; and a law protecting investors from stock and bond fraud was passed. Finally, a measure designed as protection for working women, a nine-hour maximum day, six-day maximum week, was enacted. While some historians have suggested that this law actually discriminated against women by limiting their opportunities, others have argued that this was a first step to regulating the hours of all workers. It merely started with women because legislators could be convinced more easily by the rationale of protecting women.

Alexander Road Improvement Act: This act, passed in 1915, allowed counties to sell bonds to fund road construction, which led to an explosion of road construction but made it difficult for the state to manage.

Women's Activism—Suffrage and Prohibition

Women made other significant gains during the Hays's administration, although Hays can hardly be credited with responsibility for it. Since late in the nineteenth century, Arkansas women had been organizing in more public ways and agitating for various reforms. By the time that Hays was elected governor, there was sufficient support in the legislature to secure passage of legislation granting married women the right to enter into contracts and own property separate from that of their husbands. While Donaghey was governor, the Arkansas women's suffrage movement, which had been moribund since the late 1880s, was revived in 1911. A new Arkansas suffrage association was organized and began to lobby the legislature heavily to give women the right to vote in primary elections, which, by then, were limited to white participation. Arkansas suffragists were middle-class white women associated with the more conservative American Women's Suffrage Association rather than the National American Woman Suffrage Association founded by the more radical Alice Paul in 1913. The Arkansas association's conservative identity likely made it more acceptable to women like Anne Brough, whose husband would become governor in 1917. It was in that year that Mrs. Brough, along with her husband, appeared on the steps of the new state capitol at a suffrage rally, and it was in that year that the legislature voted to allow women to vote in Arkansas primary elections. Encouraged by this victory, Arkansas suffragists then began to work tirelessly for a suffrage amendment to the state constitution and were successful in placing such a measure on the 1920 ballot. However, before that election could take place, the United States Congress passed the federal women suffrage amendment in 1919. Arkansas suffragists greeted its passage with optimism, believing that it would have no difficulty being ratified. Under the leadership of Mrs. Florence B. Cotnam, the first woman to address the state general assembly and the president of the Arkansas Equal Suffrage League, and Mrs. O. F. Ellington, president of the Arkansas Women's Suffrage Association, women successfully lobbied the state legislature to make Arkansas the twelfth state in the union and the second in the South to ratify the Susan B. Anthony Amendment on July 20, 1919.

Women's suffrage delegation on the steps of the capitol with Governor Charles Hillman Brough, summer 1919, holding rally in support of the women's suffrage amendment to the constitution. Mrs. Brough appears on the far left (in dark jumper and hat with flower). *Courtesy of the Arkansas History Commission.*

Suffrage was not the only reform that attracted women, however. Another issue that involved women and captured even greater attention across the state was prohibition. Although women had found themselves largely excluded from the male-dominated Prohibition Party and from the Anti-Saloon League in the late nineteenth century, they continued to work through the Arkansas branch of the Women's Christian Temperance Union. The WCTU expanded rapidly in the first decade of the twentieth century with many Arkansas counties organizing branches, establishing firm foundations on the local level, and sending representatives to state and national meetings. The women knew and understood the communities they were working within better than did the Anti-Saloon League, which was also attempting to organize on the county level in this period. The Anti-Saloon League's cohorts were businessmen, churchmen, and manufacturers.

Organizations like the WCTU and the Anti-Saloon League were not alone in waging war against demon rum. As Ben F. Johnson III persuasively argues in his book, *John*

Barleycorn Must Die, the campaign to curtail alcohol consumption was a colorful and complex phenomenon. The prohibition drive brought together certain disparate groups with little in common beyond that one issue. For progressives, prohibition made perfect sense as a reform measure because they perceived the very real connection between alcohol abuse and both criminality and disease. Some religions forbade the consumption of alcohol as a matter of course, and other religious leaders merely believed that sober men made better Christians. Manufacturers desired a stable workforce of sober working men who were believed to be less likely than drinkers to break expensive equipment, to injure themselves or their coworkers, or to miss many hours or days of work due to drunkenness. Women, of course, supported the movement because they wished to bring stability to families struggling with husbands and fathers who wasted precious resources on alcohol and sometimes abused their wives and children. Other Arkansans saw a danger in the commingling of the races in saloons and honkytonks, and thus linked the issue of prohibition with an opportunity to remedy violations of segregation sensibilities.

By the end of the first decade of the twentieth century, the Anti-Saloon League, charging ahead without consulting the WCTU or other temperance advocates, launched a crusade for outright statewide prohibition. Since 1873 temperance advocates in Arkansas had, by contrast, supported local option. Communities across the state had successfully banned alcohol using the local option approach. When the community voted to adopt local option, they set in motion a specific set of procedures. If a majority of the voters within the area approved local option, someone wishing to open a saloon would have to secure signatures of a majority of registered voters, which he would then have to present to the county judge. Once this process was complete and the county judge gave his approval, the saloon could be opened for business. Anti-Saloon League activists, however, concluded that local option was not working to close enough saloons and used the newly passed initiative process to circulate their own petition, a petition to put a prohibition measure on the ballot in the 1912 election. WCTU leaders were skeptical about the likelihood of success and feared that the effort would backfire and result in a new resolve on the part of the liquor interests. They campaigned for its passage once it was on the ballot, but, as they suspected, voters decisively rejected it. Rather than strengthening the liquor interests, however, it generated a renewed interest on the part of the public in the issue, a renewed interest that the WCTU and the Anti-Saloon League were eager to capitalize on.

The next turn on the road to outright prohibition occurred within the legislature and revealed certain attitudes about race. Prohibition forces had studied the results of the 1912 election, observed that counties with a high percentage of black citizens had rejected the statute, and concluded that it would be useful to eliminate the black vote. Black voters had turned out in large numbers in 1912 because of the presence on the ballot of an amendment that would have required educational tests to qualify to vote. The measure included a grandfather clause exempting illiterate white voters from the tests. It stipulated that those whose grandfathers had voted would not be disfranchised by the act. In 1912, it would have been difficult to find an African American whose grandfather, likely a slave forty-five years earlier, had voted. Thus the statute was obviously directed specifically at limiting the black vote. But blacks would not tolerate yet another measure designed to limit their right to vote, and turned out to defeat it. Prohibitionists, meanwhile, misinterpreted the black vote in areas where prohibition failed. What went unobserved or unappreciated by those supporting prohibition was that middle-class black communities were as likely as middle-class white communities to support prohibition. The black voter need not be an obstacle. Many delta towns of any size included a black business district of barbers, dry goods merchants, doctors, and dentists. These businessmen and their wives, were similar to the middle-class white community in supporting prohibition reform. Few whites recognized class distinctions within the black community, however, and, in fact, few blacks could move into a middle-class station in life. Still, the black church exerted a strong influence on both town and rural African Americans and many preachers and their congregations supported prohibition. What the prohibitionists focused on in the 1912 election, however, were towns where the lumber and railroad industries existed, industries that occupied primarily single black and white men. Because of the nature of these enterprises, workers of both races were often separated from home and family. Free from its responsibilities and restraints, they were more likely to frequent saloons. In other words, it was not race alone that mattered when it came to prohibition.

Despite the obvious connection between marital status and drinking, regardless of race, prohibition forces made a connection between black men and liquor, and their understanding of this connection was made manifest by an amendment presented by an east Arkansas legislator, L. Clyde Going, of Harrisburg (Poinsett County). Representing the Twenty-ninth Senatorial District, Going proposed legislation that modified the local option petition process so that only white registered voters could sign a petition to open a saloon. The passage of the Going Amendment in 1913, however, did not further limit the number of saloons operating in Arkansas. For example, there were enough white voters willing to sign a petition to keep saloons open in Marked Tree, a town in Going's own Poinsett County. Marked Tree was a lumber mill town with only a small white middle class and was dominated by white and black male millworkers. That gender, class, and marital status more than the racial composition of a community would decide the issue should have been made apparent by the results there.

Prohibition forces finally turned to the legislature itself to achieve their goals. Having failed at the polls and finding the Going Amendment insufficient, they influenced the legislature to pass a "Bone Dry" law in February 1915, a law that was to take effect on January 1, 1916. It was in that year that Charles Hillman Brough, who strongly supported prohibition, was elected governor. Active in the Southern Sociological Congress, he believed that society had a responsibility to solve social problems. When yet another initiated measure appeared on the ballot in 1917, this one intended to overturn the Bone Dry law by resurrecting the local option approach, he campaigned against it, and this time voters went the way of prohibition, voting to maintain the statute. The last chapter in the controversy developed after the state supreme court ruled in 1917 that the law did not prohibit citizens from bringing liquor into the state for their own personal use. This actually contradicted a federal law, the Webb-Kenyon law passed by Congress in 1913, which prohibited the transportation of liquor into any area where it was illegal. The federal courts in the state began arresting and fining people for violations of the Webb-Kenyon bill, while pressure mounted in the Arkansas legislature to close the loophole. A year elapsed before the legislature acted, however, and in the intervening period federal district courts in the state fined and jailed violators. Brough influenced the Arkansas legislature to close the loophole in 1919 and explicitly prohibit the transportation of liquor into the state.

Ida Jo Brooks. *University of Arkansas for Medical Sciences Historical Research Center.*

Women, largely through the WCTU, played a major role in influencing the passage of the Bone Dry law, and they took an active interest in other reforms, such as those having to do with health and education. Women who sought to test certain occupational boundaries, however, found themselves thwarted and frustrated. Ida Jo Brooks, who had surmounted obstacles in the past—she was the first woman president of the Arkansas Teachers Association (1883–1887)—was stung by rejection in 1887 when she attempted to attend the University of Arkansas Medical School. She was prominent in the Little Rock social scene, having been a member of every elite women's club in Little Rock and active in the WCTU, but her determination to become a physician led her to leave the state to attend medical school in Boston after her own state's medical education establishment deemed her unworthy solely on the basis of her gender. After nine years practicing homeopathic medicine in the northeast, she returned to Little Rock in 1900 and specialized in the treatment of children's diseases. Growing concerned about mental illness among women, she returned to Massachusetts in 1903 to join the staff of Middleborough Mental Hospital where she specialized in psychiatry. By 1906 she was back in Little Rock practicing psychiatry, became assistant medical inspector for the Little Rock School District in 1907, and was appointed an associate professor at the Arkansas Medical School in 1914, thus finally entering a door that had previously been closed to her. She was to find, however, that rejection on the basis of gender would still frustrate her goals. In 1920 the Republican Party nominated her for state superintendent of public instruction, but the attorney general ruled that while women could vote, they could not hold office and thus her name was removed from the ballot. Other women would challenge this decision in the years to come and begin to hold various political offices, from the lowliest county-level position to the United States Senate.

Within a few years of Brooks's disappointment, women sought and secured election to office in Arkansas. Jefferson County voters sent Frances Mathews Jones Hunt to the state legislature in 1923 and elected Franke Van Valkenburg Land county treasurer. Voters in Winslow, Arkansas, elected Maud Duncan mayor in 1925 and voted in an all-female town council. Known as the "petticoat government," they performed in their positions well enough to win reelection. Pulaski County sent its first woman to the state assembly in 1927. Florence McRaven's ambitions led her to run for the state senate in 1930 but she lost. The same year McRaven gave up her seat in the legislature, however, Hattie Wyatt Caraway was appointed to fill her husband's seat in the United States Senate. Caraway became the first woman elected in her own right to the Senate in 1932. One of the hallmarks of her first campaign was making use of nurseries so that potential women voters could hear her campaign speeches without being distracted by their children. Caraway served until 1945, when she retired from the Senate and assumed a position in the federal government.

Petticoat government: Refers to the all-woman government of Winslow, Arkansas, which secured election in 1925.

Although the level of activism among women in Arkansas increased substantially in the early decades of the twentieth century, most Arkansas women focused their energies in activities associated with their churches and schools. In other words, they did not venture far from the venue that was regarded as more squarely within the women's sphere. Because of the overwhelmingly rural nature of the state, even the literary club movement was beyond the experience of the typical Arkansas woman. Literary clubs were located within towns and cities, and while the number of clubs vastly expanded in the twentieth century, they rarely included members who lived very far into the countryside. Much of the population was located in isolated rural areas, and without an adequate transportation network, rural families traveled within a small radius of their homes. Some families were so isolated that church and school attendance was sporadic, although rural churches and schools were the principle institutions that figured in their lives. Yet newspapers and magazines penetrated even the most remote areas and exposed women to the new ideas that were reshaping women's experience in towns and cities across the state. While many women remained enmeshed within the patriarchal family structure and were enjoined by their religious leaders to obey their husbands without question, many others were enjoying the benefits of the "companionate marriage"; that is, a marriage based on mutual respect, greater autonomy for women, and enhanced communication between husbands and wives. Historians typically identify the late nineteenth century as the period in which the

Companionate marriage: A marriage in which women enjoyed more autonomy, greater communication, and mutual respect with their husbands.

companionate marriage surfaced. They cite the lower birth rate as one piece of evidence for its existence. Given the fact that the only means of birth control aside from coitus interruptus was abstinence, greater communication between partners was a prerequisite. A greater number of women, moreover, were electing to seek divorces rather than endure unacceptable situations. The divorce rate across the nation rose in the late nineteenth century, and Arkansas, with rather liberal divorce laws, was no exception. This did not mean that these divorced women established female-headed households, however. Most of them returned to the homes of their mothers and fathers, and with few resources and limited occupational opportunities, many women remained in abusive relationships. Many others were fortunate enough to establish affectionate relationships with husbands who provided for them adequately, even if they continued to adhere to the patriarchal household model.

Reforms in Education, Health, and Roads

Prohibition, which attempted to curb excessive behavior that contributed to instability within the family and community, threatened to disrupt the workplace, and, indirectly at least, challenged the racial status quo, was essentially a "negative" progressive reform. It sought to prohibit undesirable behavior. Other progressive-era reforms, such as efforts to improve the educational system and enhance the health of the state's citizens, were "positive," in that they were not predicated on the notion of eliminating bad behavior but on improving existing conditions. Efforts to expand and develop the state's transportation network also fall into this category, and although economic development was the most important motivating factor for the creation of a more comprehensive road system in the state, better roads increased access to schools and health facilities as well as to social and trading activities in towns and cities.

Governor Brough, who served from 1917 to 1921, was a college professor at the University of Arkansas before becoming governor, and was keenly interested in promoting education and literacy. He created a state literacy commission that was charged with the responsibility of investigating the state's low rate of literacy and outlining a plan to address the problem. Meanwhile, he sponsored educational reforms, such as a compulsory attendance law and the creation of local and county boards of education. Yet the trend toward bettering the educational system in Arkansas actually began prior to his tenure in office. Those interested in improving education, however, faced a number of obstacles, not the least of which was an insufficient tax base and the undervaluation of what taxable property did exist within the state.

Little could be done about the state's inadequate tax base, at least not in the short run, and because so many citizens successfully underrepresented their taxable wealth, a relatively high tax rate had been imposed in Arkansas. At twenty-seven mills Arkansas had the highest tax rate of any southern state, but citizens paid taxes based on only 30 percent of their taxable wealth and resisted all attempts to raise that level or to institute a comprehensive system of assessment. The 1874 constitution provided that the responsibility for assessments belonged to county governments, and many county officials proved all too willing to acquiesce in under assessing the property of their constituents. Legislators understood that it could mean political suicide to attempt to reform the system. George Donaghey's defeat by Joe T. Robinson in 1912 was due in large measure to his support of the Turner-Jacobsen Revenue Bill, a bill which would have provided for statewide reassessments and stripped county governments of authority over assessments by giving that responsibility to the circuit courts and a state tax commission. Both Hays and Brough proposed major reassessment, but after what had happened to Donaghey, they avoided confronting either the legislature or the people of the state over the issue. Brough introduced economy measures and reined in a legislature that had since 1907 approved expenditures that outstripped revenues, but fundamental tax reform eluded him just as it had other governors of the early twentieth century.

Turner-Jacobsen Revenue Bill: A progressive measure that would have provided for statewide reassessments and effectively stripped county governments of the power of assessment by giving that authority over to circuit courts and a state tax commission.

Delta planters and hill-country farmers alike were intent upon keeping taxes at a minimum. Many of them were particularly resistant to school taxes, and each had their own reasons for eschewing the value of public education. Delta planters, much like Jeff Davis, believed that education only ruined good field hands, but, unlike Jeff Davis, they would have included poor whites as well as blacks in that category. Many small farmers, whether they resided within the plantation sector or in the mountain regions, had little use for education for it brought them almost nothing that could be used to benefit on the farm and often took their youngsters away when they could be put to more productive uses. Most farmers instinctively understood the threat that the progressive agenda on education posed to their way of life, and they sensed that embedded within the rhetoric of uplift was an unapologetic lack of respect for rural culture. In part because Arkansas had faced a peculiar set of problems dating back to the nineteenth century—the banking fiasco, secession, and reconstruction—which left most of its population unable to profit off the industrial revolution, its people were out of step with much of the rest of the nation. No matter how much city and town dwellers might wish to pull the farm folk of Arkansas into the industrial age, the overwhelmingly rural nature of the state and its dependence on agriculture acted as a substantial check on those efforts.

From the point of view of progressives, the educational system represented one of the most chaotically organized and undisciplined institutions in the state. At the beginning of the century, there was no state board of education, only a superintendent of instruction who merely reported statistics. Teachers were abysmally trained, with few of them having college degrees and many of them having only eighth-grade educations. With no compulsory attendance laws, fewer than half of school-age children attended and most of them for less than half the term. Of the nearly five thousand school districts, five hundred enrolled under twenty pupils, and some occupied buildings that were so badly in need of repair that they were simply abandoned during the winter months. This, perhaps, partly accounted for the fact that the state had the lowest average number of days of school in the region. Few high schools existed and of those that did exist, almost none outside of the larger towns and cities was accredited.

In 1902 the state superintendent of public instruction abruptly broke with the precedent of simply reporting statistics and began to criticize the disorganized nature of the educational system in the state. He suggested that the schools within each county be unified under the direction of a single county supervisor who would report to him. The Arkansas Teachers Association also began to press for reform and prompted the creation of the Arkansas Education Commission in 1908. Still, systematic organization of the school system eluded reformers. The commission's report in 1911 outlined a comprehensive plan for improving the state's schools and was instrumental in influencing the creation of a high school board that year, which provided some means of bringing order to secondary education. That board was given the authority to classify high schools and to determine curriculum. It was also given the authority to distribute funds for teacher education. It performed as the only administrative educational unit in the state until the formation of the State Board of Education later that year, which provided state aid for high schools. The Arkansas Supreme Court invalidated the aid plan in 1915, but the General Education Board of New York, a charitable body that had been extending funds to high schools in Arkansas, continued to operate in the state and the high school system continued to expand.

The high school board's authority to distribute aid for teacher education spoke to another pressing need in Arkansas. When the legislature ended expenditures for state normal schools in 1899, after almost a decade of extending such aid, the state became ineligible for matching funds from the Peabody Foundation. Teachers, who were notoriously underpaid, had to undertake teacher training courses at their own expense. In 1903 the legislature mandated more stringent examination and licensing procedures for teachers and in 1907 required teachers to attend summer normal institutes. The state superintendent of public instruction sponsored the institutes, and within a very few years fully 90 percent of the state's teachers were participating. Also in 1907, the State Teachers Association, together with the Farmers Union, convinced the state legislature to create a normal school at Conway, and by 1910 both that school and the University of Arkansas were offering summer terms for teachers.

Other persistent problems were also addressed in the progressive-era decades. At the beginning of the century, there was no graded course of study, but in 1903 one was instituted and improved upon in the years to come. There was also no supervision over the selection of textbooks for use in the schools. The 1899 legislature gave counties the authority to require uniformity in textbooks, and by 1917 a state commission began selecting textbooks for use in all public schools. Many children, however, could not afford to purchase textbooks. But a larger and more intractable problem required much greater attention. A high percentage of the state's children did not attend school or attended only sporadically. In 1899, 64.2 percent of children aged five to eighteen attended school, compared to 69.1 percent in Mississippi, 74.6 percent in Tennessee, and 70.1 percent in Missouri. Only Arkansas's neighbors to the south fared worse. In Texas the percentage was 52.2 percent, and in Louisiana it was 40.6 percent. In all of those neighbor states, however, the average duration of school days far surpassed that of the state of Arkansas. In Arkansas, children attended schools an average of 70 days; in Texas, 111.5 days; in Louisiana, 146.3 days; in Tennessee, 89 days; and in Mississippi, 101.6 days. A split term, allowing rural children to work around the needs of the farming enterprise existed, but many children failed to attend regularly in the months when the schools were open. The first compulsory attendance law was passed in 1909, but it was poorly enforced. In 1917 the legislature passed an act much more specific in its language, requiring that all children aged seven to fifteen attend school. It also mandated that they attend at least three-fourths of the session. Further legislation in 1927 authorized county boards of education to set minimum school terms of 120 days and just three years later the average school term had been lengthened to 148 days.

One problem that would defy solution until certain other developments took shape involved the existence of far too many small school districts, many of them with one teacher providing instruction on the whole range of subjects to all the students enrolled. This huge number of districts made for great variation both in the quality of instruction and the resources communities could bring to bear on education. Yet local communities and their legislators were determined to maintain these schools, and the road system, in any case, was so inadequate that little could be accomplished until it was significantly improved and extended. As the roads improved and the population began to shift in mid-century, particularly during World War II, the consolidation movement gained momentum. In 1900 there were 4,903 school districts. By 1920 that number had increased to 5,118, reflecting the emergence of new communities in certain parts of the state in the early twentieth century. Because of the concerted efforts on the part of educators and certain public figures, the number of districts began to decline in the 1920s. By 1930 the number of districts had declined to 3,478; by 1940 it had dropped to 2,920 districts; and in 1948, before the legislature passed a school consolidation bill eliminating those schools with under 350 students, there were 1,589 schools. The law reduced the number of districts to 424.

During this entire period of reform, black schools functioned at a level far below that of white schools, and most white reformers were content to allow that situation to remain unchanged. Black leaders took an interest in the schools within their towns and cities, but the majority of black youngsters resided in the rural areas of the Delta, and those schools proved beyond any doubt that the doctrine of "separate but equal" as established in the 1896 *Plessy v. Ferguson* decision bore no resemblance to reality. Facilities were inferior, schoolbooks were often ragged hand-me-downs from white schools, and black teachers were even more poorly trained and underpaid than whites. Black children were less likely than white children to attend school and more likely to be illiterate. The sentiments of Jeff Davis and other white leaders toward black education was shared by the vast majority of whites and acted as a significant obstacle to improvement. Yet the black educational system provided an important institutional arena for black teachers and citizens, principally in towns and cities, and played a significant role in the lives of the black adults and children. Becoming a teacher was a signal accomplishment for a black man or woman, and even though black teachers were less likely than white teachers to be college trained, they took pride in their occupations, cared deeply for their schools, and played an important role in the black community.

Efforts to improve the educational system in Arkansas coincided with a drive to improve the health of the state's citizens. Arkansas created a permanent State Board of Health in 1913 just in time to record information about an outbreak of spinal meningitis in northeastern Arkansas. It would be another year before the state created a Bureau of Vital Statistics, which began to keep records on births and deaths in 1914, and in 1917 it began to maintain records on marriages. The 1913 spinal meningitis epidemic apparently began in a lumber camp outside the town of Lepanto. The surgeon general's report, probably relying on figures provided to it by the state, reported only seventeen deaths, but local sources indicate a much higher fatality rate, a rate so high, in fact, that some bodies were said to have been buried in mass graves. Whether the State Board of Health was too inexperienced to accurately ascertain the correct figures or whether local sources misrepresented the figures, the outbreak was serious enough to warrant a quarantine of the area. Imposing quarantines was one power given to the new board, as was the creation of county and city boards of health. Newspapers in nearby Memphis, Tennessee, publicized the epidemic but did so in a manner calculated to reassure its readership. A number of yellow fever epidemics had occurred in that city, one in 1867 that took the life of the husband and four children of Mother Jones and one in 1878 so severe that over five thousand people died. Although understandably sensitive about the prospect of an epidemic virtually on their doorstep, the Memphis newspapers cautioned calm. One woman, Della Dick (later Della Dick Abbott), who lost a husband and two children to the epidemic, however, encountered hysterical officials at the Missouri border when she tried to return to her family in Illinois. They turned her away after burning all her possessions. Della had followed her husband, Robert Dick, to Arkansas after his half- brother, Elisha "Kidd" Abbott, had promised him work logging on his homestead. After being turned away at the Missouri border, Della returned to her brother-in-law's shack and soon married him. He had lost his own wife to the epidemic.

Although the State Board of Health initially had only minimal authority, its responsibilities expanded in the few years after its creation. Working in cooperation with private agencies such as the Rockefeller Sanitary Commission, the federal government and, sometimes, the Arkansas Federation of Women's Clubs, it carried out a variety of health initiatives. In addition to collecting vital statistics and supervising health inspections of public eating establishments, the board made recommendations for improvement in water and sewer systems across the state. When an embarrassingly large number of potential servicemen were denied enlistment during World War I because of a high incidence of venereal disease, the board laid plans to launch an extensive education campaign in 1919 to raise public awareness of the disease and its consequences.

Abbott family women and children, circa 1910. *Abbott Family Photographs.*

In the 1920s the board helped improve the health of infants and mothers by utilizing federal funds made available through the Sheppard-Towner Act. As a result, infant mortality rates dropped and life expectancy increased.

Largely because of the efforts of the state and private organizations, considerable progress was made in combating a number of diseases in the first two decades of the twentieth century. Blacks as well as whites were the beneficiaries of programs to eliminate hookworm, programs sponsored by the Rockefeller Sanitary Commission. Although the problem in Arkansas was not as severe as in most other southern states, the commission found that 25 percent of the state's schoolchildren suffered from hookworm, and in some isolated rural districts, the incidence of the disease reached 65 percent. Another initiative sponsored by that commission addressed the malaria problem in the delta, and a campaign to eradicate mosquitos in Crossett, Arkansas, in 1916, was so successful it was to serve as a model for other such efforts. Another agency, the American Red Cross, concentrated on a problem endemic in the Delta. The flood of 1912–1913 brought that agency to the state, and its relief workers identified pellagra, a dietary deficiency that could be deadly, as a major problem. While some success was had during the progressive years in educating the public about this serious illness, the Red Cross would again report a high incidence of pellagra when the flood of 1927 brought them back to the Arkansas Delta.

If hookworm and malaria were not entirely wiped out, they were greatly reduced. In a number of towns and cities, water supplies were purified and the incidence of typhoid fever dropped as a result. The State Board of Health instituted a policy in 1916 requiring that all schoolchildren, teachers, and school staff be inoculated against smallpox, thus ensuring a dramatic decline in that disease. A tuberculosis sanitarium was founded in Booneville in 1910, providing a safe and comfortable place for sufferers to live in quarantine until the disease ran its course. It served only white patients, however, and it was not until 1931 that a sanitarium for black patients was opened near Little Rock.

Initiatives in health and education resulted in some real progress for the state, just as another development in this era saw tangible results: road construction. Arkansans had embraced the age of the automobile with as much enthusiasm as other Americans but soon discovered that the narrow, unpaved, and often deeply rutted roads, barely maneuvered by horses and wagons, were simply impassable by automobile. Many who purchased automobiles did so for reasons unconnected to their livelihoods, but for traveling salesmen, delivery men, and, particularly, farmers who wanted a faster way to get their crops to market, the necessity of improving the state's roads had a special urgency to it. Thus a wide variety of citizens supported improvements to the road system, and as early as 1907, the state legislature passed an act allowing citizens to form local road improvement districts, sell bonds to fund construction, and tax themselves to pay off the bonds. In 1911 the legislature required drivers to purchase licenses. A state highway commission was established in 1913, but it had little control or oversight over the widely scattered road improvement districts. The Alexander Road Improvement Act, passed in 1915, allowed counties to float bonds to facilitate road construction but only further intensified the localized nature of road construction. However, the state was able to qualify for federal aid to roads in 1917.

World War I constituted a watershed in both the use of the automobile and the recognition of the value of good roads. Wartime Arkansans could easily understand the importance of an adequate transportation system, whereby troops could be moved rapidly wherever they were needed. Intensified interest in road building and wartime prosperity allowed a larger segment of the population to purchase automobiles. A legislature eager to promote roads and please their constituents passed hundreds of road improvement laws in 1919, laws that accelerated the construction of roads. Governor Brough had hoped to include a provision for greater supervision on the part of the state, but acquiesced in the passage of legislation that gave even greater autonomy to county officials administering the road improvement districts. By the end of his term, it became apparent that local control over the building of roads had created a host of problems, problems born of mismanagement, fraud, and incompetence. Finally, when the economy began to falter after the war, particularly in 1920, taxpayers found it difficult to pay their road improvement taxes, but the decentralized nature of the road improvement districts made it difficult for state legislators to remedy the situation. Thus, the road dilemma was analogous to the school situation. Not only were they expensive, they were extremely decentralized. The recognition of the importance of improving the schools and extending the road system led those who promoted these reforms to acquiesce to the insistence on local control, despite the fact that local control was essentially inefficient. It would be left to the governors of the 1920s to solve the problem.

The Great War and Its Aftermath: Reaction and Repression

World War I brought more than new energy to road construction to the state of Arkansas, and much of Governor Brough's first term was taken up with the war effort. He not only organized the state in support of the war, he also took to the road and delivered more than six hundred speeches. A veteran Chautauqua lecturer, his speeches helped raise funds for the Red Cross and the Liberty Loan campaigns, and although his language was more moderate than some promoters of the war, he equated support for the war with true patriotism and dissent against the war as the voice of the traitor. After several years of asking Americans to remain neutral with regard to the war in Europe, Pres. Woodrow Wilson, who had, in fact, always been pro-British, initiated an intemperate campaign to promote the war. Wilson created a Committee on Public Information (CPI), which was largely a propaganda agency, and the Council of National Defense, which was to coordinate the industries and resources of the country toward the purpose of supporting the war effort. The CPI launched a campaign that was so successful in promoting the war that any dissent was labeled treasonous. As a result, historians have catalogued massive violations of civil liberties during the war that spilled over into even more inexcusable infringements after the war as "one hundred percent Americanism" prevailed as the catch phrase of the immediate postwar period. In Arkansas these were manifested in two events: the Cleburne County draft war in 1918 and the Elaine Race Riot in Phillips County in 1919.

Governor Brough created the Arkansas State Council of Defense, which was designed to organize the state's industries and resources for the war effort, and also to promote the war, thus assuming the Committee on Public Information's role as propaganda agency. While German Americans in other parts of the country were encountering sometimes violent discrimination, in Arkansas it was draft evaders, known as slackers, that incurred the wrath of super patriots, or at least those acting under the guise of patriotism. In Cleburne County a small religious sect, the Russellites (Jehovah's Witnesses), opposed the war on religious grounds. Believing that the world was coming to an end as a result of the war and that all men participating in the conflict would be doomed to eternal hellfire, they refused to honor the draft. When local officials attempted to arrest Bliss Adkisson, an alleged draft evader at his home, gunfire broke out, a deputy was mortally wounded, and a standoff ensued. Eight Russellite men left their homes and retreated into the nearby woods. Rumors spread that their numbers were much larger and that they planned to attack Heber Springs. Posses from Heber Springs, Searcy, Pearson, and Quitman scoured the woods, the wives and children of reported Russellites were taken into custody and grilled for information. The entire encounter ended peacefully enough when the eight fugitive Russellites gave themselves up. A subsequent investigation suggested that local officials, whose attempt to arrest the draft violators had sparked the incident, were motivated by personal gain, hoping to find hoarded goods that they could claim as payment for rounding up draft evaders. Although the official army report also suggested that the episode might have been avoided altogether had local authorities been aware of the options open to genuine conscientious objectors and had the Russellites been informed of those options, in the climate created by Wilson's war propaganda machine, it was quite difficult for anyone to secure a release from the draft for conscientious objection.

The super patriotism inspired by the war spilled over into the postwar period, and likely played a role in slowing if not destroying the impulse for progressive reforms. One disappointment that Governor Brough endured was the failure of the Arkansas voter to approve a new constitution, one which was a progressive document compared to the 1874 Confederate constitution that continued to serve as the state's instrument of government. Brough had fought hard to convene the constitutional convention, but the document hammered out by that convention did not receive a sufficient number of popular votes to pass in 1918. The most telling blot upon Governor Brough's progressive credentials, however, involved the thorny issue of race. Prior to his governorship he had served as chairman of the University Commission on the Southern Race Question, and although he fully supported segregation and believed that African Americans were inherently inferior, he also acknowledged that they had certain basic rights. In short, he was a paternalistic racist, possessing more enlightened views than many whites of his generation. When the Elaine Race Riot erupted in Phillips County in the fall of 1919, Brough arranged with the secretary of war to dispatch federal troops to the area to restore order. While he later accepted the white version of events, he appointed a special commission made up of prominent whites and blacks to encourage more harmonious relations between the races.

The events in Elaine, near Helena, certainly indicated that harmony between the races was lacking, but they epitomized far more than simply racism. Black farmers in the area had founded the Farmers and Household Union of America and were planning to file suit against planters over settlement of the crop. Sharecroppers, who worked twenty- to forty-acre farmsteads for planters, marketed their crops through the planter and depended upon him to deduct the "furnish" (supplies extended during the crop year) and pay them the difference. Because of high interest rates in plantation commissaries and because some planters manipulated their books (leading many sharecroppers to believe that all planters manipulated books), there was rarely much left for the typical sharecropper after the crop was marketed and the furnish deducted. Increased demand and higher prices for cotton during World War I raised the expectations of Delta blacks in general and black sharecroppers in particular. The return of black veterans who had experienced conditions in the army far superior to anything they had enjoyed previously in the Delta, coupled with the demands of black sharecroppers there for a greater

Farmers and Household Union of America: a union of black sharecroppers formed in eastern Arkansas in order to secure better settlement with the planters for whom they labored.

share of the farm profits made during the war, created an explosive situation, especially given the precipitous drop in prices for agricultural commodities that followed the war.

The causes of the Elaine conflict were embedded deep within the social and economic structure of the area and signaled a clash between the planter class and black sharecroppers. Because of the large black population, race overshadowed economics in the minds of most who participated in or observed the crisis. Certainly racial violence had long prevailed in the Delta. Although lynchings had declined in the first two decades of the twentieth century, incidents of nightriding or "whitecapping" against African Americans had become more visible. These incidents were related to a vast expansion of the plantation system, due in part to extensive drainage enterprises, in eastern Arkansas and pitted black sharecroppers against white tenants. Both hoped to secure a tenancy on the new plantations, and organized bands of whitecappers sought to drive African Americans away. Some of the earliest reported incidents occurred in Phillips County, and in 1898 the local newspaper characterized the whitecappers as lawless and irresponsible.

Whitecapping: The term used to describe nightriders who concealed their identity and attacked blacks.

Indeed, planters saw the efforts of whitecappers as a threat to a cheap black labor supply, and when nightriding activities in Cross County reached epidemic proportions in 1903, the planters banded together to hire white detectives to apprehend the perpetrators. The whitecappers there had burned homes and barns, destroyed crops, and threatened not only black sharecroppers but also white planters and their families. These methods had succeeded in forcing an exodus of approximately two hundred African Americans from the area. In March 1903, when the chief detective hired by the planters to capture the whitecappers was murdered by them instead, the stage was set for a confrontation between law enforcement officials and a segment of the community that was sympathetic to the effort to discourage black sharecroppers from settling in the area. Twelve men suspected of having taken part in the detective's murder were sequestered in Wynne, the county seat, and crowds of people wandered the streets, some ready to storm the jail and free the alleged perpetrators, some in search of the remaining detectives whom they hoped to lynch. Federal officers soon claimed jurisdiction and charges were filed in federal district court in Helena against the twelve suspects. The charge was that the whitecappers had violated the "right to employment" of the African Americans, a right that was, it was argued, guaranteed by the Thirteenth Amendment.

Even as the twelve Cross County men awaited trial in federal court, another incident took place in neighboring Poinsett County, an incident that was to lead to the indictment of fifteen other men on identical charges. The Poinsett County situation arose when a new sawmill opened in the town of White Hall, located on Crowley's Ridge just south of the Harrisburg, the county seat. The sawmill owners determined to hire only black labor, because it was cheaper, and a group of armed white men converged on the mill late one night carrying torches and demanding that the black workers be replaced with white workers. Although apparently motivated by racism, this incident, too, had its economic component. Farmers, who were experiencing an unprecedented rate of farm foreclosure in this period, relied on off-farm jobs to pay their debts and feed their families. As the enraged farmers stood before the White Hall sawmill, the mill owners called the local constable but were disappointed to discover that his sentiments rested with the whitecappers. The mill owners closed down rather than concede, but the incident had captured the attention of federal officers who were likely on the alert because of events in Cross County.

When the two cases came up for trial in October 1904, the Cross County defendants were favored by the poor memories of dozens of witnesses who were unwilling to testify against them. The Poinsett County whitecappers were not so fortunate. Three of the fifteen alleged whitecappers were convicted of having violated the Thirteenth Amendment right to employment of the black sawmill workers. Judge Jacob Trieber, who was federal judge for the eastern district of Arkansas, fashioned the unique charge. William G. Whipple, the federal prosecutor, argued the case for the government. The defendants were represented by L. Clyde Going of Harrisburg, who would go on to become a state senator and sponsor the Going Amendment to the local option law in 1913. He appealed the decision to the Supreme Court, which overturned the convictions in *Hodges v. U.S.* in 1906, ruling that there was no right to employment guaranteed or anywhere in the Constitution. The Court reasoned that the Thirteenth Amendment had abolished slavery and beyond that, African Americans would have to take "their chances with other citizens in the states where they should make their homes." Because the Thirteenth Amendment restricted only the actions of states, not those of individuals, Congress was "not empowered . . . to make it an offense against the United States" for private citizens "to compel Negro citizens by intimidation and force, to desist from performing their contracts of employment." It was now open season on African Americans in the Arkansas Delta, and the *Hodges v. U.S.* decision would stand for sixty years. Congress implicitly overturned it in its 1964 Civil Rights Act, but the U.S. Supreme Court explicitly overturned it in a 1968 decision. In the interim, African Americans found little remedy in the face of violent intimidation in the workplace or in any other arena in Arkansas or in the South in general. Although the state passed a nightriding law in 1909, it was rarely called into use.

At the same time that some planters were hiring white detectives to track down whitecappers who were attempting to drive off black labor, other planters were engaging in isolated, one-on-one confrontations with their black sharecroppers over settlement of the crop. Many planters were simply keeping their sharecroppers indebted and unable to leave the plantation. If indebted sharecroppers left plantations, local law enforcement officials would track them down and return them to the planters to whom they were indebted. In fact, the practice of debt peonage had become so widespread in the South that the federal government launched an investigation in 1902, and at least two Arkansas planters were convicted of peonage in Ashley County in 1905. The

Debt peonage: The process whereby tenants and sharecroppers became inextricably indebted to the planters for whom they worked.

attorneys pressing the peonage cases were William Whipple, the federal prosecutor in the whitecapping cases, and U. S. Bratton, who would later gain fame as the attorney who initially represented the African Americans who formed the Progressive Farmers and Household Union of America in 1919.

Some blacks chose to leave the Arkansas Delta rather than endure the debt, the violence, and the intimidation they encountered there. The exodus of African Americans from the Delta actually began in the late nineteenth century. Most went to other parts of the United States but some headed "back to Africa," a phenomenon that Ken Barnes writes eloquently about. Although a massive black migration from the South would begin during World War I, many African Americans had as much attachment to the South as did white southerners and were loath to stray far from their birthplaces. The blacks who founded the Progressive Farmers and Household Union of America were among those who chose to attempt to remain in place and make the system work more equitably. At first blush it seems surprising that the Elaine Race Riot would occur in Phillips County, for a grand experiment in black education had been ongoing there for decades. In 1864 a group of northern Quakers came to Phillips County to open an orphanage for lost or abandoned black children. The venture matured and expanded over the next sixty years and became Southland College. It coexisted, sometimes uneasily, with the local white population, and the Quakers were careful to remain aloof from controversial matters. In the interest of protecting their students and their enterprise from censure, the dedicated educators at Southland College elected to remain silent over the Elaine riot and abstained from any involvement or comment.

As recent studies by Grif Stockley, Nan Woodruff, and Robert Whitaker have demonstrated, the Progressive Farmers and Household Union of America was taking on a formidable system. As blacks began to organize their union, word drifted back to planters who either honestly or deliberately misinterpreted their intentions. They believed that blacks were organizing an insurrection and were planning to seize their lands and murder them. In fact, the union leaders had hired U. S. Bratton, a prominent Little Rock attorney and former federal prosecutor, to represent them in suits they hoped to file for fair settlement of the crop, and they were attempting to keep their plans secret for fear that planters would devise a legal strategy against them. Planters learned that something was afoot, though, and tensions in both the white and black communities began to rise. When gunfire was exchanged outside a rural church near Hoop Spur, where a union meeting was underway, the white community sprang into action to put down what they characterized as a racial revolution. Planters joined forces with whites who would likely have constituted the ranks of whitecappers they had sought to subdue earlier. Planters found, however, that they could not control what had been unleashed. Armed whites hunted down and shot innocent blacks by the dozens, perhaps by the hundreds, and local authorities finally asked Governor Brough to arrange for federal troops to intervene when it appeared that incarcerated blacks and a white attorney representing them might be lynched. Planters later appealed to authorities to release many of the blacks who had been arrested for fear their cotton crop

Elaine Twelve. *Courtesy of the Arkansas History Commission.*

would not be harvested on schedule. Twelve blacks were subsequently condemned to death, largely on the basis of coerced testimony in trials that lasted only minutes. The NAACP launched an investigation and pursued a series of appeals that eventually resulted in their release. Scipio Jones, a prominent black attorney in Little Rock, played a major role in representing the "Elaine twelve" and many other black Arkansans contributed to the cost of the appeals.

The Elaine Race Riot dramatically illustrated that the vision of a New Arkansas did not include a substantial segment of the state's population. And while the progressive-era reforms and programs sought to bring the state into the twentieth century, they came at a cost, a cost the state could ill afford. The convict lease system had been dismantled, the educational system had been greatly expanded, a new statehouse constructed, and a variety of new agencies created to address health and educational needs of the state's citizens. While all of these accomplishments are laudable, between 1900 and 1920, state expenditures rose from $2.5 million to $15.5 million. The road system had been greatly expanded, but the problems inherent in the local improvement districts were about to show themselves, and the governors of the 1920s would have to deal with the consequences. Perhaps had the economic situation remained as healthy and robust as it was during World War I, Arkansas could have built on its accomplishments and enjoyed a new era of prosperity and progress. But economic catastrophe and two natural disasters—a flood in 1927 and a drought in 1931—faced the state and undermined the plans and dreams of those who saw a greater Arkansas on the horizon.

CHAPTER THIRTEEN

Darker Forces on the Horizon: Natural Disasters and Great Depression, 1920–1940

As Arkansas began to embrace new innovations in transportation and communication in the third and fourth decades of the twentieth century, it remained shackled to its rural past and hampered by unprecedented economic and environmental challenges. The dedication to local control interfered with the rational development of an efficient road and highway system; and the determination of certain entrenched individuals to control access to the electrical power market, particularly to the underdeveloped rural areas, slowed the state's adoption of modern devices and appliances. Far more problematic for Arkansas, however, was the agricultural depression that struck immediately after World War I, a depression that lifted only lightly and then settled in with a grim tenacity that predated the country's Great Depression. The economic situation undercut efforts to improve and expand the road system and the state's educational infrastructure. Meanwhile, the legacy of the Elaine Race Riot haunted the state, the KKK reemerged, and two highly publicized lynchings brought further notoriety. To add insult to injury, two horrific natural disasters hit the state. The flood of 1927 and the drought of 1930–1931 must have seemed like divine retribution. As the Great Depression fastened its grip on the nation, Arkansas stumbled into the New Deal with a governor who foreswore the activist state and with a president who prescribed a federal remedy for the country's ills. This would turn out to be an important contrast. As the state withdrew from its previous progressive commitment, its people turned toward the federal government to solve its problems.

Foundations of the Economic Disaster

Most sectors of the American economy recovered rather quickly from the economic collapse that followed World War I. The reduction in the production of war materials that led to layoffs and strikes in the industrial states in 1919 was more than adequately offset by the renewed production of automobiles, which stimulated the growth of the oil and gasoline industries. While these relatively new industries capitalized on the emerging consumer culture eager to partake of the phenomenon of installment purchasing of automobiles and a variety of labor-saving devices such as washing machines, certain older industries—agricultural, railroads, and mining—faced a continuing crisis from which they were unable to recover. And despite its New South rhetoric and attempts to attract industry, Arkansas remained overwhelmingly wedded to the depressed sector of agriculture. As the price for cotton declined precipitously in 1919, some farmers took matters into their own hands and posted notices on cotton gins warning them to close down until prices rose again. The agenda of the progressive governors and legislators did not include a remedy for this crisis facing the state's farmers, and, indeed, had the state attempted to fashion one, it is unlikely its independent-minded farmers would have appreciated the effort. It would take a full decade of calamity before that attitude would be modified, and it would be molded by hardship and fired in necessity.

Any attempt on the part of the state to address the difficulties facing its farmers would have been in vain, for the problem in the agricultural sector was a complex one which defied easy solutions. The state's farmers were divided between the plantation owners of the Delta, the rice farmers in the Grand Prairie region, and the smaller farmers from the hills. Their problems were similar in that they were overproducing their respective agricultural commodities but dissimilar in the nature of the markets they produced for. Plantation owners and rice farmers were engaged in production for a world market while the small farmers growing vegetables and fruits or raising livestock tended to produce for a regional or national market. The rice farmers were relatively well mechanized, relied on seasonal wage laborers, and sold to customers nationally and abroad. The hill-country small farmers looked to their own families to supply their labor needs with the occasional use of an extra farmhand or two. The planters differed in that they relied on mule power, an impoverished underclass, and a set of repressive institutions designed to keep that underclass dependent. However they were organized, whether they were internationally, nationally, or regionally oriented, whether they were large or small operators, Arkansas's farmers experienced steady erosion in the prices they received for the crops they raised, and they all began a slow conversion to reliance on federal solutions.

Those associated with the mining industry were to discover that they were not immune to the problems facing agriculture. While coal mining had been on the decline for some time by the 1920s, the bauxite industry had been expanding and seemed to offer much promise. Bauxite was a key ingredient in the making of aluminum, which was becoming increasingly necessary to the transportation, chemical, electrical, and building industries. A substantial source of bauxite was discovered in the late nineteenth century to exist near Benton, Arkansas, and there a fledgling bauxite mining industry developed slowly in the first decade of the twentieth century. By the outbreak of World War I, the industry was thriving and the town of Bauxite—a "company" town—had been founded. Smaller outlying communities housing workers of different ethnic identities sprang up: Mexico, Africa, Italy, and Alabama Town, among others. By the end of the 1920s, however, the industries that fed on bauxite were themselves faced with economic disaster, and the bauxite industry in Arkansas began to falter.

While agriculture and mining succumbed to market forces beyond their control, another industry that had seemed to offer great hope failed to deliver. Oil was discovered near El Dorado in south Arkansas in 1921 and launched a boom that played out all too soon. Many of those who sought to exploit the area's precious reserves of oil had little understanding of the careful process that had to be followed in order to extract the commodity. This led to both economic and environmental disaster. Many wildcatters (independent operators) did not fully comprehend that the water and natural gas trapped below the surface with the oil provided the necessary pressure to bring the oil to the surface. They allowed the natural gas to escape and set it afire; burning it off to get it out of the way so they could get to the oil. They understood that the natural gas itself was a potentially important commodity, but they also knew that oil was much more valuable. They then pumped the water, which was heavily salinated, to the surface and allowed it to gather in pools. The land so "salinated" was made worthless for years, and many creeks and streams were fouled. In the end, they succeeded in getting only a small portion of the oil out of the ground, and they wreaked environmental havoc on the land and streams in the area. Much of these oil reserves remain underground today, and while technology does exist to bring the oil to the surface, it is simply too expensive to be cost effective. Despite the mistakes they made, the oil boom did provide jobs and economic benefit to many families who worked the industry. Most of the wildcatters, however, exploited the boom and left the area. Some stayed and worked to build communities, but others, like H. L. Hunt, who got his start in the Arkansas oil boom, moved on to other opportunities elsewhere and never looked back.

Crisis in Agriculture

While the oil and bauxite industries declined in importance, agriculture remained central to the state's economy. It faced a crisis of unprecedented proportions. Not since the Civil War had it confronted such a irresolvable situation that seemed—and very nearly was—unending. This crisis was destined to lead to a fundamental reorganization of the plantation system as farmers began to look toward the federal government for solutions to their chronic problems. A crucial player in their growing orientation to Washington was the Agricultural Extension Service, headquartered in the state's university. Although not technically a federal agency, the extension service received federal funds and carried out policies that were at least partially promulgated by the Department of Agriculture. Its origins in Arkansas can be traced back to the founding of the University of Arkansas as a land-grant college responsible in part for agricultural education. In 1862 Congress passed the Morrill Act, which was intended to support agricultural education, and the Reconstruction government of Arkansas made sure that Arkansas qualified for Morrill funds when it created Arkansas Industrial University (later the University of Arkansas) in 1871. In 1887 the Hatch Act provided for the funding of experiment stations attached to agricultural

Morrill Act of 1862: An act passed by the United States Government in 1862 that provided for the creation of land-grant colleges in states to support agricultural education.

colleges, and Arkansas began to establish such stations in various locations around the state. The second Morrill Act, one passed in 1890, provided that funds be distributed directly to black institutions of higher education and essentially saved the Branch Normal School in Pine Bluff, Arkansas, from extinction. It had been created in 1873 as a branch of Arkansas Industrial University and was to serve the purpose of educating the state's black citizens. Had the second Morrill Act not been passed, it is likely the school would have closed. In 1914 the Smith-Lever Act greatly expanded the scope of agricultural education by creating the Agricultural Extension Service and providing federal funds to supply farm agents to agricultural counties throughout the country. Farm agents had been working on an experimental basis in several rural states for more than a decade at the time Smith-Lever was passed. Under the act the new extension service was to hire and supervise the agents, and the counties were to provide matching funds to pay their salaries. The system was slow to grow, however, with some counties dubious about the value of the program and many farmers suspicious of college-educated advisors who considered themselves more knowledgeable about farming than the farmers who had devoted their lives to the enterprise. The agricultural depression of the 1920s, however, provided an important turning point in the relationship between the state's farmers and the extension service's farm agents.

Morrill Act of 1890: Commonly referred to as the second Morrill Act, the 1890 act provided that funds were to be distributed directly to black institutions to support agricultural education.

Smith-Lever Act: Passed in 1914, the Smith-Lever Act created the Agricultural Extension Program, greatly expanding the scope of agricultural education that came out of land-grant institutions like the University of Arkansas.

Farm agents preached the gospel of diversification and advised farmers on crop rotation, fertilizers, seed selection, and livestock breeding practices. They held demonstrations on the use of fertilizer or certain new seed types. But, more important, in the midst of the agricultural depression facing farmers, the farm agents offered them practical solutions to the shortage of agricultural credit and helped them form marketing associations designed to secure higher prices for farm commodities. Neither of these efforts proved to have much lasting value, however. The agricultural credit associations, which were funded in part by the federal government's Agricultural Credit Act in 1923, were organized by farmers and businessmen on the county level, but they addressed only the short-term credit needs of farmers and did little to address the crisis in farm mortgages that led to record numbers of foreclosures. The credit associations only enabled farmers to secure crop loans, allowing them to continue producing in an era of steadily decreasing farm prices. Essentially, they merely put off the inevitable bankruptcy that awaited many of them. The agricultural marketing cooperatives operated without federal funds until the Agricultural Marketing Act of 1929. Even after 1929 they suffered, as did the credit associations, from a lack of sufficient funding. But the marketing cooperatives also suffered from the failure of those who joined them to live up to the promises they made to market their crops through the associations. It was easy enough to make the pledge when the association promoter was on hand to encourage cooperation and answer questions, but when faced with the necessity of meeting the demands of creditors at the end of the crop year, many farmers chose to honor their obligations.

While in the throes of this economic challenge, the ongoing struggle between planters and sharecroppers in the Arkansas Delta took on a greater urgency. The extension service's farm agents entered this arena with great trepidation and proved more eager to avoid challenging planters than they did to assist black sharecroppers. The white farm agents worked exclusively with white farmers, and the few black agents appointed in the Delta wisely refrained from policies that might have affronted planters. H. C. Ray, who was hired in 1915 to serve as the first African American farm agent in Arkansas, focused much of his effort on black farm owners. His superior, C. W. Watson, who directed the Arkansas Farm Demonstration program, reported the fears of planters that sharecroppers who diversified, paid off their debts, and had money in the bank were less likely to work within the tenant system. As the black agent system expanded under Ray's direction, black agents worked with sharecroppers only with the permission of planters and avoided any conflict that might have inhibited the expansion of the farm demonstration program. Despite the agricultural depression of the 1920s, he and his white superiors were able to convince many county quorum courts to contribute the funds necessary to maintain and expand the black agent system. They argued that rather than challenging the plantation system, the rural uplift program sponsored by the black agents could stem the tide of the black exodus, an exodus that had picked up after World War I. The program encouraged black farmers to grow their own food for home consumption but to continue to grow the cotton demanded by their planters, and some planters cooperated enthusiastically with the black agents. One planter, D. S. Farrar of Mississippi County, supplied garden plots for his black tenants and offered prizes to those who participated in demonstration programs.

White agents exhibited as much hesitancy to involve themselves in controversial matters as did black agents, for extension service policy was to avoid challenging the social system prevailing in the Delta. The agency understood that to do so would endanger their reception among planters and thus endanger expansion of their programs. As the agricultural depression deepened and the black exodus from the Arkansas Delta accelerated in the 1920s, the nature of the relationship between planters and sharecroppers became more exploitative and more explosive, and the extension service's farm agents were in no position to advise planters or to assist black sharecroppers.

Race Relations

With the agricultural crisis driving even prominent planters close to bankruptcy, the tendency was to wring what profits could be realized from the most vulnerable partner in the plantation enterprise: the black sharecropper. The emergence of a revitalized Ku Klux Klan during and immediately following the war gave institutionalized racism an added legitimacy, although, to be sure, the new KKK was not only racist but anti-Semitic, anti-Catholic, and anti-foreign. It also saw itself as the moral arbiter of the communities it functioned within, addressing the evils of illicit liquor distilling, prostitution, and wife beating. Regardless of its claims to serving as a necessary check to such abuses, the KKK functioned as the unofficial military arm of a planter class growing anxious about the exodus of agricultural labor and weary of a deepening crisis in the agricultural economy. Although some Klan groups were town-based organizations that appealed largely to the new business class, others had distinctly rural orientations. Klan groups even formed in the Ozark Mountains, although they tended to be oriented toward issues other than race. With only a small black population present, Ozark mountain residents focused their frustrations on activities that appeared to threaten the stability of their communities. Many of these devout Christians viewed with alarm the activities of moonshiners, for example, and took to the KKK as a means of restoring order and stability. Even those Klan groups that were identified with certain towns depended upon membership from the rural areas. Indeed, the thousands of Klan members who gathered at meetings on the outskirts of small towns in Arkansas were necessarily rural rather than town dwellers. For example, a Klan rally that took place on Crowley's Ridge near Harrisburg in Poinsett County attracted eighteen hundred men in 1922. The next year from thirty-five hundred to five thousand people attended another Klan rally in the same area. Given the fact that Harrisburg had a population of only 1,352 people in 1920, most of those who attended would have been rural rather than town dwellers. Many planters, moreover, lived within small Delta towns and had commercial interests that wedded them to the business class that is commonly associated with the new Klan.

Although the Klan was clearly active in the Arkansas Delta in the early 1920s, there is no evidence that it was responsible for a notorious lynching that occurred at Nodena Landing in early 1921. Henry Lowery had shot and killed both the planter for whom he worked, O. T. Craig, and the planter's married daughter. He also wounded Craig's sons. The confrontation was precipitated by a dispute over settlement of the crop proceeds and occurred on Christmas Day 1920, when Lowery went to Craig's home to demand payment. Lowery, though wounded, escaped but was later apprehended in El Paso, Texas, and extradited to Arkansas. The train carrying him back to Arkansas was intercepted by a group of men in Sardis, Mississippi, where it had made a routine stop. The men took Lowery back to Arkansas by automobile and burned him alive in front of a crowd of approximately six hundred people at Nodena Landing, not far from the crime scene. Memphis newspapers had widely publicized the train's route and announced the imminent lynching. Public officials in Arkansas decried the event, and at least one historian has argued that it contributed to a subsequent crackdown on lynching in the state.

The lynching of Henry Lowery occurred just seventy-two hours after the newly inaugurated governor declared "Law and Order Day." Gov. Thomas McRae had designated January 23, 1921, as a day dedicated to the principle of law and order, and while he was outraged by the Lowery lynching, he was only one of several prominent Arkansans who spoke out against it. McRae's own background provided him with impeccable credentials as a "southerner"—as a boy he had been a courier for Confederate forces in Washington,

Arkansas—and allowed him to speak out against extreme racism without fear of being labeled "soft" on the "negro" question. His long and distinguished service as a state legislator and as a U.S. congressman gave him additional stature and respectability. He was elected governor in 1920 at a time when the Republican Party itself was divided on the race question, fielding two candidates, a Lily White and a Black and Tan. The Lily Whites feared that black Republicans kept the Republican Party from recruiting white members, thus they shunned blacks. The Black and Tan Republicans, on the other hand, made some effort to attract blacks to the party, believing that they could be of more benefit than harm, that the ballots they cast for Republicans candidates would outnumber the white ballots their inclusion might discourage. In any case, McRae remained above the question of race during his campaign. In his bid for reelection in 1922, the Little Rock chapter of the KKK supported him, although he had not sought their endorsement, while the state chapter threw their support to his opponent. Still, McRae had no trouble winning reelection. While Brough might have been expected to act on behalf of racial moderation because of his connection to the Southern Sociological Conference, it was McRae who in 1925 released the last of the twelve black men sentenced to death in the Elaine Race Riot, although, to be sure, by that time the case against the men had become so hopeless that only token resistance to the pardoning arose. McRae's position on race remained that of a southern conservative Democrat, paternalistic and protective. He was no spokesman for equality, integration, or voting rights.

Lynchings of black men were in decline in the South in the twentieth century, having reached their peak in the 1890s. Governor McRae and other state and local officials in Arkansas were determined in the 1920s to end that kind of lawlessness altogether, but several highly publicized lynchings occurred despite their best efforts. Most white southerners who attempted to justify lynchings did so on the basis that they were the appropriate punishment for the sexual attacks of depraved black men on white women. The record, however, does not bear out that point of view. Few lynchings in Arkansas or elsewhere in the South were the outcome of sexual attacks on white women. Some, like the Henry Lowery lynching, were connected to disputes between planters and sharecroppers. Others were the result of battles between whites and blacks over "opportunities" to work the plantation. Some were in response to crimes like murder or arson. Whatever their real motivations, in the post–World War I era, they also reflected a population of whites that was itself apprehensive in the face of the turmoil caused by the economic recession following World War I, a turmoil which made the emergence of a revitalized KKK possible. In fact, a KKK initiation occurred in 1923, on the very site where Lowery was lynched, and the next year, a new school erected for African Americans in nearby Wilson was destroyed by fire in the early morning hours on the day it was to be dedicated.

One other outcome of the Lowery lynching was a purported plan to "crack down on" black fraternal organizations. Lowery had been aided in his escape by his brothers in the Odd Fellows Lodge, and several of them had been arrested for their trouble. No evidence surfaces that black lodges were raided though prudent African Americans may have curtailed their activities until the furor subsided. Indeed, it would have been difficult for the white community to successfully undertake such a campaign against black organizations. Lodges had become an integral part of the black community and were often associated with the black church, the most important of institutions for African Americans. In fact, a new organization, the Universal Negro Improvement Association (UNIA), began functioning in Arkansas in the early 1920s and there were approximately forty such organizations in Arkansas and at least half a dozen in Mississippi County by 1922, although none of them were located in south Mississippi County near the scene of the Lowery lynching. Inspired by Marcus Garvey, the UNIA promoted self-help and self-defense, and it particularly emphasized the protection of black women from the designs of white men. The organization appealed to the most successful of landless black farmers, and units were often connected to black churches. They openly paraded their membership in the clubs, and the white community apparently accepted them without controversy, perhaps because they also preached antimiscegenation.

United Negro Improvement Association: Inspired by Marcus Garvey and promoting self-help and self-defense, particularly in protecting black women from the unwanted advances of white men, the UNIA had at least forty branches in Arkansas in the 1920s.

Despite a concerted campaign on the part of leading lawmakers in the state to eliminate mob justice in the 1920s, a lynching occurred in May 1927 that revealed the deepest fears of the white community. John Carter, who was described in some reports as "simple minded," had attacked two white women, a mother and daughter, on a road south of Little Rock. The women fought him off, escaped, and alerted authorities. Carter was apprehended, and there the incident might have ended in a law-abiding fashion. But his attack on the white women had been preceded by the rape and murder of a white child at the hands of a black youth who, through the careful actions of the Little Rock chief of police, was spirited out of town and away from the clutches of an angry white crowd. In a sense, the mob that took Carter, riddled him with bullets, and then rioted for three hours in the heart of the black business district was avenging the child's death. But the crowd also attacked innocent blacks who happened to be on the street and ransacked black businesses, delivering a chilling message to the black community. Like most lynchings, it was a very public affair that served notice to blacks to stay within their inferior station in life and to refrain from challenging the white community.

The violence facing the black community stirred some African American leaders to action. Dr. John M. Robinson, one of the founders of Little Rock's chapter of the NAACP in 1918 who had grown weary of its timidity in addressing the political handicaps facing blacks, launched a campaign to end the White Primary in 1928. He was chagrined when the New York office of the NAACP refused his request to support his effort on the grounds that the black elite in Arkansas had not been supportive of the NAACP. He knew that Little Rock's black elites had contributed to the NAACP-led defense of the twelve black men sentenced to death for their involvement in the Elaine Race Riot in 1919. Indeed, a prominent black attorney representing the Elaine Twelve,

Scipio Jones, was part of the Little Rock black establishment. Given the contributions blacks in Little Rock had made to the defense of the Elaine Twelve, the NAACP's denial of funds on the grounds that Little Rock's blacks had not been forthcoming enough seems specious indeed. The fact is that in 1928 the NAACP was supporting similar cases challenging the white primary in Virginia, Florida, and Texas and likely wanted to avoid spreading resources too thin by including yet another case from yet another state. Still, the NAACP did make decisions about distribution of funds based on the amount of support it received from the various states.

Dr. Robinson was left to pursue his initiatives on his own. In the same year that Robinson sought support from the NAACP, he founded the Arkansas Negro Democratic Association (ANDA), and it was through this organization that he hoped to challenge the white primary. He pursued the suit even without NAACP support, but in 1930 the Arkansas Supreme Court upheld the white-only Democratic primary in *Robinson v. Holman*. Dr. Robinson's organization remained alive but became inactive during the difficult 1930s, and he left it to a later generation of African American leaders to launch the next phase of black activism in Arkansas.

Natural Disasters

The Carter lynching created apprehension among Arkansans that the negative publicity would inhibit national efforts to aid the state's flood sufferers. Although flooding along the Arkansas River was minor compared to that along the Mississippi River, it was severe enough to cause significant damage. In fact, the 1927 flood brought devastation to many parts of Arkansas, and the state was depending upon aid from the federal government and the Red Cross. The flood was the greatest natural disaster to hit the state since the New Madrid earthquakes of 1811–1812. It would have diverted any governor's attention from the normal course of business, but John E. Martineau's election to head the Tri-State Flood Commission, made up of the states of Arkansas, Mississippi, and Louisiana, required him to make several trips to Washington, D.C., to work closely with Herbert Hoover, who had been appointed by President Coolidge to head relief efforts. Martineau's appointment was a testament to the fact that of the eight states affected —Illinois, Missouri, Kentucky, Arkansas, Tennessee, Mississippi, Louisiana, and Oklahoma—Arkansas was the hardest hit. Over five million acres were flooded in the state, and over two million of those acres were normally devoted to agriculture. Louisiana and Mississippi were also seriously inundated with floodwaters, but Arkansas had almost as many agricultural acres flooded as Louisiana and Mississippi combined (Arkansas, 2,024,210; Louisiana, 1,167,522; and Mississippi, 976,905).

The flood began in the late spring and extended nearly one thousand miles from Cairo, Illinois, to the Gulf of Mexico. In Arkansas most of the damage occurred in counties along the Mississippi River, which suffered thirteen breaks in its levees, but some interior counties were also seriously affected. There were twenty-six breaks on the Arkansas River, sixty-seven on the White River, and twelve on the St. Francis. Hundreds

Nineteen twenty-seven flood in McGehee, Arkansas, May 1, 1927. *Joseph T. Robinson Papers, Box 431, photograph no. 4, Special Collections, University of Arkansas, Fayetteville.*

of thousands of acres were flooded along these and other interior waterways in Arkansas. Although the number of deaths was relatively low, over fifty-five thousand homes in Arkansas were inundated with floodwaters, and the American Red Cross extended emergency aid to over two hundred thousand Arkansans. Because the flood came after weeks of rain and the newspapers had repeatedly reported the increasing likelihood of disaster, many farmers had time to remove their livestock before the waters reached them. Still, it was projected to take twenty-five to thirty carloads of oil to burn the more than twenty-five thousand carcasses of horses, cows, mules, and hogs not moved to safety in time. As slow as the water was to move onto the Arkansas landscape, it was even slower in moving off. Hundreds of thousands of acres remained flooded well into the summer, beyond the time when crops might have been planted.

The first response of the Red Cross was to rescue flood refugees and place them in camps. For the first time in a natural disaster, the radio was used to coordinate rescue efforts and airplanes were used to locate refugees clinging to tree limbs or gathered on rooftops or levees. A variety of watercraft—rowboats, motorboats, barges, towboats, and flatboats—nearly two thousand of them—were then dispatched to rescue the victims in Arkansas. They were then transported, usually by train, to one of eighty camps in the state, ranging in size from a few hundred in camps like that located at Selma

Black extension staff in Arkansas (H. C. Ray sitting in middle on front row). University of Arkansas Cooperative Extension Service Records (MC1145), Box 10, photograph no. 18. *Special Collections Division, University of Arkansas Libraries, Fayetteville.*

(Drew County) to over fifteen thousand in Forrest City. The quick response on the part of the Red Cross and private citizens, who participated in the rescue effort, was one reason why so few deaths were reported in Arkansas.

Ironically, it was the flood of 1927 that offered black agent H. C. Ray the opportunity to demonstrate the value of the black farm agent system to the state and to Arkansas planters. Ray and the black agents under his direction were put in charge of organizing part of the relief effort, operating soup kitchens, building hospitals, and helping to run some of the camps. While in the camps, many black sharecroppers and tenants were given demonstrations on sanitation, hygiene, tool repair, better farming methods, and a variety of other rural uplift ideas. During the reconstruction effort after the flood, Ray helped supervise the rebuilding and whitewashing of hundreds of homes. Despite all his efforts, most tenants and sharecroppers returned to live in conditions of squalor and poverty. In the months following the flood, the Red Cross discovered health problems among the population of tenants and sharecroppers that were directly related to the practices of plantation agriculture.

The danger of disease was of great concern to the agency. As one medical doctor in Arkansas reported to the Red Cross after the worst of the flood was over, the most pressing matter to consider after rescuing people from tree limbs and rooftops was the spread of disease. The crowded conditions at the Red Cross camps, where displaced persons were housed, stimulated fears of epidemic. As the floodwaters subsided, stagnant pools of water, sometimes laden with the carcasses of dead animals, provided the perfect breeding ground for mosquitoes that could carry disease. The three major health concerns were typhoid, malaria, and dysentery, but the Red Cross also worried about smallpox and launched a massive effort to prevent an outbreak of epidemic diseases that frequently accompanied natural disaster.

But the greatest health problem came as something of a surprise to Red Cross officials, and for a short time they debated the appropriateness of any effort to combat it.

The debate within Red Cross circles revealed their reluctance to intervene in a situation having its origins more in local social and economic arrangements than in natural disaster. Pellagra, a dietary deficiency that could lead to death but was most frequently manifested in skin rashes and lethargy, became an acute problem in the months after the flood. Health officials had only recently become cognizant of the causes of the disease—a diet of fatback, molasses, and corn—but had discovered that a concentrated form of pure yeast, administered on a regular basis for up to six weeks, restored most patients to health. The critical issue was a lack of fresh vegetables, and planters typically forbade or discouraged their tenants and sharecroppers from devoting valuable agricultural acreage to the production of vegetables. The crucial question for Red Cross officials was whether the high incidence of the disease was a consequence of the flood or a preexisting condition. They were authorized to distribute aid to flood sufferers, not to address the human costs of the plantation system in eastern Arkansas. They understood that the disease was prevalent in the Mississippi Valley region, and particularly in eastern Arkansas, and that the diet was connected to the poor economic conditions of plantation laborers. Incidences of the disease rose and fell with the farm economy. Too often without kitchen gardens that provided vegetables and without cows that furnished milk, Delta residents experienced a high incidence of the disease, but when economic conditions were good, they could purchase fresh vegetables in the summer, and they could afford to keep a cow. Ultimately, the Red Cross determined that the flood had worsened the condition by destroying gardens that otherwise provided green vegetables to people on the verge of the disease. Thus, the Red Cross rationalized its effort to address the problem and began an impressive campaign to distribute yeast throughout the affected area.

Pellagra: A disease that stemmed from a dietary deficiency (lack of fresh vegetables) and led to a variety of debilitating symptoms such as skin rashes, lethargy and, in extreme cases, death.

The primitive state of public health in Arkansas made extending medical care to the flood sufferers distinctly problematic, however. Although a state health department existed, it was a poorly organized and underfunded affair with limited responsibility and expertise. Red Cross officials reviewing the incidences of typhoid, smallpox, and pellagra over the previous five years, in an effort to establish a base-line comparison, concluded that the morbidity reports produced by the state were worthless and provided no reliable information. Red Cross funds had to be dispersed to place public health nurses in various counties to dispense yeast to fight pellagra and quinine to address the symptoms of malaria. They also vaccinated people against smallpox and offered advice on screening homes to prevent malaria. Local doctors and pharmacists were called into service to assist the nurses but in some cases disputes arose, disputes that were sometimes the result of professional jealousy and sometimes reflected real differences of opinion about treatment. By July 30, 1927, however, twenty-three nurses had devoted 819 days of service to seventeen counties, and despite some problems, several counties requested the continuation of their services.

The problem between the public health nurses and some local medical care providers remained a largely internal problem that the state and the Red Cross worked out on an individual basis. But another controversy emerged in the months after the flood that gained national attention. Planters became concerned that black sharecroppers housed in the various Red Cross camps scattered over eastern Arkansas would not return to the plantations from which they had come and thus would not honor the debts they had incurred at the plantation commissaries prior to the flood. In addition, some planters still hoped to plant a crop, perhaps only a crop of corn or hay, but they needed agricultural labor in order to do so. In an era when blacks were moving from the South to the North, the prospect of a further reduction in this labor force caused great concern among planters. In order to avoid causing additional strain on the agricultural economy of the region, the Red Cross agreed to release black sharecroppers from its camps only after their respective planters called for them. The spectacle of hapless flood sufferers confined to camps made for poor publicity for the Red Cross and threatened to interrupt the flow of charitable dollars. Nevertheless, the agency continued in its policy, fearing the consequences of a massive shift in population that could cripple the plantation system and inhibit economic recovery after the flood.

The Red Cross effort to salvage the plantation system continued with the distribution of free seed and continued into the 1928 crop year with a massive loan program. These programs were oriented toward farm and plantation owners. At Herbert Hoover's suggestion, the Arkansas Farm Credit Corporation was organized and was authorized to sell stock of up to $1,000,000 in shares of $100 each. By mid-July of 1928, they had sold $676,815 in stock, and the list of stockholders was a veritable "who's who" of Arkansas: Senator Joe T. Robinson, prominent eastern Arkansas planter R. E. Lee Wilson, Arkansas Power and Light executive Harvey Couch, and several leading bankers in the state. The directors of the corporation were all conservative Arkansas bankers: Moorhead Wright, chairman of the board of directors of the Union Trust Company; William Niemeyer, who was an officer with the Bankers Trust Company; and W. A. Hicks, who was president of the American Southern Trust Company. Hicks was elected to serve as the new corporation's president. Altogether, Arkansas stockholders accounted for $158,635 of capital stock of the $676,815 invested. Herbert Hoover arranged for the Flood Credits Corporation of New York to subscribe to $250,000 in capital stock. Investors from several other states, particularly those close in proximity to Arkansas, accounted for the rest. As originally envisioned the program was designed to help all farmers, but its directors determined to deliver aid to the large planters first, arguing that the small farmers could be supplied through local credit. However, its policies probably helped to consolidate the power and guarantee the expansion of the larger plantation owners at the expense of the small farmers.

The Arkansas Farm Credit Corporation was hardly responsible for the conditions that made the small farmer increasingly vulnerable in the 1920s, and it is unlikely that a different policy on its part would have saved the small farm from the forces arrayed against it. In the economic environment prevailing in the 1920s, only the fortunate few could avoid collapse, and they tended to be those endowed with the most land and least indebtedness. In the decade between 1920 and 1930, the percentage of farms operated by owners decreased from 48.6 percent to 36.8 percent. Correspondingly, those operated by tenants increased from 51.4 percent to 63.2 percent. The percentage of black landowners dropped from 21.3 to 14.4, and in the Delta, where tenancy was concentrated, the situation for black farmers went from bad to worse. For example, in Mississippi County, white and black tenancy together increased from 82 to 90 percent in that one decade, and black landownership declined from a mere 4.4 to 3.4 percent. While small farmers of both races were being pushed into tenancy and their holdings absorbed by planters, black sharecroppers and tenants endured a harrowing decade of racism and abuse. Because of the reluctance of the farm extension agent and Red Cross workers to act on behalf of black sharecroppers in any way that might have interfered with the workings of the plantation system, African Americans in rural Arkansas, as elsewhere, were largely left to the mercy of the planters for whom they worked.

Indeed, perhaps the most lasting legacy of the Red Cross was the message planters received that interference from this outside agency did not disrupt its relations with tenants and sharecroppers. Together the farm agents and the Red Cross officials demonstrated that planters need not be afraid of outside forces working with their tenants and sharecroppers, that they did not pose a threat. The lessons learned during the flood of 1927 would have a chance to be tested again during the drought of 1930–1931.

The drought was a different kind of disaster, but it was equally devastating. When it struck in 1930, Arkansans had barely recovered from the flood of 1927 and were confronting a deepening crisis in its agricultural economy. As crops wilted in the fields and livestock weakened and died, the Red Cross was finally prevailed upon to recognize the drought as a disaster and stepped in to render aid, just as it had during the flood. No one had to be rescued from treetops, but many had to be fed and provided with replacement livestock, feed, and seed. This relief effort was also plagued by controversy, however.

The first controversy to emerge involved the failure of relief forms to be distributed in England, Arkansas, resulting in a delay of relief supplies to farmers in need. Although referred to as the "England food riot," it was little more than a gathering of angry farmers demanding that the proper forms be dispensed so they could apply for relief. It passed quickly enough when the necessity for the forms was waived and the relief dispensed. But another controversy passed more slowly. When it became known that some planters were requiring their tenants and sharecroppers to work in exchange for relief supplies, the national headquarters of the Red Cross issued an order condemning the practice. Planters complained bitterly, believing that relief given too freely threatened their labor supply.

The Arkansas Roads Scandal

By 1931, the state was facing a crisis of enormous proportions. The economic collapse that struck the country in 1929 was compounded in Arkansas by its two natural disasters and the fact that its farm economy had been in the throes of depression for most of the decade. Together these factors left the state's resources stretched beyond its ability to provide much relief to its citizenry. The progressive governors of the 1920s had promoted expensive programs, particularly the expansion of the road system, which the state could no longer afford. The problem of how to fund payment of highway bonds plagued all the governors of the 1930s, but this was not a new problem. When McRae took office in 1921, an "Arkansas Roads Scandal" was already on the horizon. The legislators who sponsored the Alexander Road Improvement Act in the previous decade had intended to facilitate the expansion of the road system in the state but secured support for the act by placing funding and administration in local hands. Passed while George Hays was governor, it was during Governor Brough's administration, and at his urging, that many road improvement districts were created and the state's road system expanded. While this approach had its advantages, most of which were political, it was an abysmal failure. Counties were allowed to issue bonds to fund construction of roads, bonds that were to be paid by taxing landowners. Those few counties that administered the improvement districts responsibly built roads that all but ended at the county line, where rough tracks trailed off into fields that turned into mud bogs during the rainy season. Many road improvement districts did little more than incur debts that taxpayers were responsible for discharging even though roads failed to materialize.

By 1921 the road system was in such disarray in Arkansas that the state's ability to take part in a federal program of road construction, whereby matching funds could be received, was in jeopardy. Defeated by the state senate in his initial efforts to address the problem, McRae managed to secure passage of a one-cent-per-gallon gasoline tax, part of which was to be credited to the state highway fund, and which reflected his opinion that those who used the roads should help pay for their construction. The governor also succeeded in increasing license and registration fees, all of which went to the state highway fund. These minor achievements hardly solved the road problem, which became even more acute when the federal government threatened to withhold highway funds unless the state centralized road construction in the state highway department. The governor and a forty-member commission appointed to study the roads scandal urged the legislature to abolish the road improvement districts and put the highway department in charge. When the legislature rejected his proposal, federal funds were withdrawn, and many of the road improvement districts faced bankruptcy. Only then did the legislature pass the Harrelson Road Act in October 1923. Even though the state highway commission secured supervisory control over construction and maintenance of the state's roads under this act, the legislation by no means solved the problem. The separate road districts continued to exist, and the supervisory role of the state highway commission was so modest that it did little to mitigate the abuses of the individual road districts.

Harrelson Road Act: An act passed in 1923 in order to provide a more rational management of the state highway system and secure federal funds.

By the time that John E. Martineau became governor in 1927, the county road districts were either bankrupt or very close to it. Martineau secured legislation that allowed the state to assume the debts and responsibilities of the road improvement districts and launched the Martineau road plan, an ambitious state highway construction program. Martineau's successor in office, Harvey Parnell, secured passage of legislation authorizing $18 million in bonds to continue the expansion of the Martineau road program and additional legislation permitting the sale of $7.5 million in bonds to finance a highway toll-bridge construction program. However, Parnell's ambitious plans for expansion of the highway system in Arkansas were largely undermined by the deteriorating economic situation and the drought of 1930–1931.

Progress and Disappointment in Educational Reforms

Governor Parnell's plan to improve the educational system was another casualty of the economic catastrophe facing the state. Attempts to expand and improve education in Arkansas received the enthusiastic support of most of the decade's governors, and much of the rhetoric focused on the connection between an educated population and the state's development. Despite some significant improvements in the decade after Donaghey's tenure, Arkansas faced a crisis in education by the time McRae took office in 1921. According to a report arising out of a federal survey conducted in 1921–1922, Arkansas's children received an education that would put them at a distinct disadvantage later in life, an education that did not prepare them for the modern world. The school system remained seriously underfunded, and although the figures for school attendance had improved, the average school term of six months was the shortest in the country. Few teachers, especially in the rural districts, had received college educations, and many had not completed high school. In fact, high school attendance was the second lowest in the country.

McRae was sincere in his efforts to improve the educational system in Arkansas, but he faced a reluctant legislature and his tenure in office corresponded with the beginnings of the economic crisis in the state. His only success in the area of education during his first term involved instituting a millage basis for continued funding of higher education. The millage system meant that higher education funding would no longer be dependent upon legislative appropriations but would be built into the tax structure in a more fundamental way. During his second term McRae's accomplishments were more substantial. In order to address the serious shortcomings in Arkansas's education system, Governor McRae understood that an even more aggressive funding strategy had to be adopted, and he believed that the tax structure needed revising. The legislature responded by passing a severance tax with all proceeds accruing to public education, but an income tax—and later a tobacco tax—also earmarked for education, were declared unconstitutional. Before he left office, however, McRae persuaded the legislature to restructure the tobacco tax in a way that passed muster with the Arkansas Supreme Court.

McRae was aided in his education campaign by an alliance of educators and urban progressives located in the state's largest towns. The alliance would last beyond McRae's term in office. In order to fund education in the poor rural districts where property taxes did not provide enough revenue to support schools, it was necessary to revise the tax structure to require businesses and corporations located in urban areas like Little Rock to share the burden. Gov. Harvey Parnell, who took office in 1928 after Martineau's surprise appointment to the federal judiciary, viewed establishing a more equitable system of taxation as crucial to achieving his goals in education and roads. He was able to secure passage of the Hall Net Income Tax Law in February 1929, which established a system of equitable taxation on incomes, a system of taxation that did not place most of the burden on rural Arkansans. It was also under his leadership that some rural schools were consolidated, a school bus system was inaugurated, and the school term was lengthened.

Harvey Parnell and the End of Reform

Although Parnell had begun his political career in the state legislature in 1919 as a spokesman for industrial expansion, as governor he found it necessary to appeal to a largely rural constituency interested primarily in solutions to problems in the agricultural economy. Much of Parnell's time and attention in 1928, his first year in office, was taken up with the presidential race, which required him to explain to that rural—and Protestant—constituency why they would vote for a Catholic New Yorker for president of the United States. Al Smith was running on the Democratic ticket, but a prominent Arkansan, Joseph T. Robinson, was running as his vice presidential candidate. Parnell stumped the state for the Smith-Robinson ticket and held Arkansas in the Democratic fold while many other southern states backed Herbert Hoover, the Republican candidate. Smith's Catholicism and his identification as a "wet" on the issue of prohibition rankled many Arkansans, but the majority voted for him, either out of loyalty to the party or affection for Joe Robinson. The vote reflected no ideological differences between Arkansas and its southern neighbors, however. In the same election, they also approved a measure banning the teaching of evolution in Arkansas schools.

However laudable Parnell's road construction and education initiatives were, by 1930 the state treasury was considerably depleted, and his opponent in the governor's race that year, Brooks Hays, declared that any further bond issues would bankrupt the state. But the expansion of the road system was popular with voters and Parnell won the election. In the next two years he would preside over a state stricken with economic collapse and facing yet another natural disaster, the drought of 1930–1931.

By the early 1930s, Governor Parnell's progressive agenda was facing extinction. His laudable but expensive road construction and educational programs had exhausted the state's coffers, particularly because many taxpayers had engaged in a silent but potent tax revolt. They had simply ceased paying their road, drainage, real estate, and personal property taxes. By 1930 millions of acres were subject to confiscation by the state, but officials preferred payment of taxes to confiscation—land values had dropped drastically and there were few buyers even in that market—and, while resorting to strong warnings, they provided for tax extensions, hoping to receive some revenues. With falling revenues and an agricultural economy reeling from another natural disaster in 1931, Parnell was moved to cut state expenditures, despite his belief that recovery was imminent.

Just as some Americans blamed President Hoover for the Great Depression, some Arkansans branded Parnell the architect of the disastrous economic situation facing the state, particularly those in agriculture. Departing drastically from his previous commitment to promoting agribusiness, Parnell began to trumpet the "back to the land movement," suggesting that farmers diversify and strive for self-sufficiency rather than produce crops for a market that was rapidly vanishing. Agricultural extension agents throughout the state had been calling for diversification for more than a decade and many, even in the cotton-dependent Delta, were beginning to urge the production of food crops so that farmers could at least feed their families in an era when the price they were receiving for cotton was below the cost of production. Parnell stopped short, however, of calling for any specific measures designed to force diversification. It was the legislature that passed an act calling for a reduction in cotton acreage, but it was too little, too late, and they had no enforcement mechanism in place.

By 1932 no segment of the state's economy could warrant optimism. Farm incomes had plummeted, and nearly 40 percent of the labor force was unemployed. Bank deposits dwindled, and a record number of banks closed across the state as anxious depositors rushed to try to withdraw what they could. Private charities had long been exhausted, and the needs of the state were so great that Arkansas was the recipient of more Reconstruction Finance Corporation (RFC) loans than any other single state. As the situation went from bad to worse, Parnell became the scapegoat. The legislature passed a resolution condemning him as having presided over the most corrupt administration since Reconstruction. They rescinded the resolution a few days later, but they had made their point. The perception was that the progressive-era governor had ruined the state's finances with profligate spending, particularly on the highway program (which was, in fact, riddled with corruption). Notwithstanding the fact that the legislature and the citizens of Arkansas had strongly supported, even demanded, the extension of the highway system, they blamed the governor for having launched a program that the state could ill afford in the face of a Great Depression of unprecedented proportions.

Junius Marion Futrell and the Conservative Resurgence

It was in this context that the state elected its most conservative governor in decades. Gov. Junius Marion Futrell, of the northeastern Arkansas Delta, came from a plantation background, and he brought to the governor's office considerable experience in state politics. He had served in both the general assembly and the state senate. As president pro tempore of the latter in 1913, he took over as acting governor after Joe Robinson went to the United States Senate in February of that year and served until George Hays was elected that summer. He later became a circuit judge in the Second Judicial District and then chancellor of the Twelfth District. The people of the state elected him as much for his fiscal conservatism, however, as they did for his experience.

At first blush it seems ironic that in the same year Arkansas citizens voted overwhelmingly for Franklin Delano Roosevelt as president, a man who would move the country to accept a much more activist federal government, they also selected a man to fill the governor's chair who repudiated an activist state government. In fact, the two men shared only one thing in common. They acknowledged the existence of a crisis and claimed to have a solution. That Roosevelt's solution would take the country in one direction while Futrell's would take the state in another could not have been foreseen by the average voter. While Roosevelt had not been very specific about his plans, Futrell had campaigned on a platform of retrenchment. He fulfilled his pledge to reduce state expenditures and return the state to a cash basis. Significantly, however, had the federal government not engaged in massive relief programs and launched a plan to rescue agriculture—both of which would pump massive amounts of money into the state—Futrell's severe retrenchment would have brought widespread hardship to the state's people.

By the time that Futrell assumed the governorship, the state's highway debt had reached the staggering sum of $146,000,000, and he identified paying off that debt as his first priority. But he also had in mind devising a new strategy for funding the highway system. He wanted to consolidate all the highway debts into one, a scheme that was not to the liking of many out-of-state bondholders, and the legislature first balked at the governor's plan. They did agree to his proposal to increase fees for truck and automobile licenses and for commercial vehicles as well as increased taxes on the sale of oil and gas. Futrell called a special session in 1934 and pushed his Highway Refunding Act through.

Rather than blame Governor Parnell for the fiscal crisis facing the state, Futrell believed that the highway debt problem was the result of profligate spending on the part of the legislature. He proposed two amendments to the state constitution that severely restricted the taxing and spending power of the legislature—and of the state in general—and marked a dramatic departure from the direction that progressive governors had been taking the state in the previous two decades. Brough's rationale for a state constitutional convention in 1918 had been in part to remake the constitution in such a way as to make it more flexible on the issue of state expenditures for progressive programs. Governor Parnell had considered a constitutional convention while he was governor but had realized that the state could not afford to attempt such a thing given the economic crisis facing the state during his tenure. Both, in any case, had quite a different constitution in mind than had Futrell, a fiscal conservative who believed fervently that the state should play a very small role in the affairs of its citizens. The state was merely to allow them to pursue life, liberty, and the pursuit of happiness, but otherwise stay out of their business. Thus, he proposed the Nineteenth Amendment, which limited legislative appropriations to a fixed amount and required a three-fourths vote in each house of the legislature, or approval of voters in a general election, before taxes could be increased. The Twentieth Amendment required voter approval before the state could issue new bonds. Voters approved both amendments in a subsequent election.

Convinced that poverty and unemployment resulted from a lack of individual initiative, Futrell was unsympathetic to direct relief programs. Believing that education beyond the primary grades was unnecessary, he reduced expenditures to high schools. Both of these attitudes reflected Futrell's northeastern Arkansas Delta background. He had been raised in a socioeconomic system that needed a large underclass of laborers who planters believed needed to be forced to work. They feared relief programs that might offer their tenants and sharecroppers an alternative. Planter manipulation of Red Cross relief is a case in point. This mass of impoverished workers, moreover, needed no education. In fact, education beyond the rudimentary level might encourage aspirations beyond what could be realized in the Delta and cause that labor force to depart, adding to the migration that was so much despised and feared by the planters. No friend to industrialization, which constituted yet another challenge to the plantation economy, Futrell represented a throwback to the period before the progressive governors of the early twentieth century and even the New South advocates of the late nineteenth century.

Futrell's attitudes toward direct relief and education led to a showdown between the state and the Federal Emergency Relief Administration (FERA) in 1934. The FERA, under the leadership of Harry Hopkins, devised a two-pronged program providing for both works projects and direct relief. The states were expected to share the costs of the programs. Given Futrell's attitude toward direct relief and toward education, he was content to divert a greater share of federal funds toward those programs than seemed appropriate to Hopkins. When the Arkansas Legislature's 1934 property tax relief package made it clear that the state would rely on the FERA dollars to fund education at an even higher level, Hopkins's patience with Futrell was exhausted. Hopkins notified the governor that all federal aid to Arkansas—including that extended through the agricultural programs—would cease as of March 1, 1935, unless Arkansas raised state funding for education and appropriated $1.5 million for public welfare.

Hopkins's threat to cease funding all federal programs in Arkansas captured the attention of Delta planters who began pressuring Futrell to resolve the situation before federal dollars were cut off from programs they needed. In response, Futrell began to fashion measures to meet the expense of providing matching funds for the FERA programs. The state's cost was projected to be $1,500,000. His solution was yet another example of his conservatism and yet another rejection of progressive-era reforms. He called for the repeal of prohibition so liquor sales could be taxed. He supported the legalization of gambling, providing for the opening of a dog track in West Memphis and a horse racing track in Hot Springs, both of which would be subject to taxation. He initially refused to endorse a tax on retail sales but eventually urged passage of it when it became clear that his endorsement was necessary to get the measure through the state senate. This package of legislation was not completed until after the March 1, 1935, deadline had come and gone and federal funds were lost. The loss of those funds encouraged the legislature to enact all three measures.

The Agricultural Adjustment Administration

Whatever his attitude about the FERA, Futrell supported federal programs designed to aid agriculture. Indeed, prominent planters in Arkansas and in the South heavily influenced the formation and management of the agency charged with revitalizing the farming sector, the Agricultural Adjustment Administration (AAA). By the time that Roosevelt was inaugurated and his advisors had successfully devised a program for the farming sector, farmers and planters had their crops in the ground and were looking forward to a banner production year, notwithstanding the low prices they were likely to receive. Arkansas senator Joseph Robinson and representative William Driver helped fashion legislation calling for a plow-up of up to 30 percent of those crops and laid the groundwork for an acreage restriction program that would take shape in the next year. Although many planters by the end of the decade would grow weary of the restrictions on raising certain crops, they embraced the AAA program in 1933 when they were teetering on the edge of bankruptcy. By that time farmers in Arkansas and elsewhere had endured more than a decade of collapsing farm prices. Cotton was selling for five cents per pound, and the cost of producing the crop was far more than the return farmers realized. Credit facilities had almost completely dried up, mortgage indebtedness was at an all-time high, and some of the most prominent planters in the state turned to the Reconstruction Finance Corporation (RFC), a creature of Pres. Herbert Hoover's administration, for relief. Although some farmers in the state refused to participate in the plow-up campaign, most were eager to secure federal funds for bankruptcy was often the only alternative.

Agricultural Adjustment Administration: An act of Congress designed to revitalize the country's agricultural sector by providing for a means of production control.

The Agricultural Extension Service's farm agent played a crucial role in helping to facilitate the acceptance of the program. Despite the advice of Brooks Hays, who conducted a tour of the state for the Federal Emergency Relief Administration in 1933 and who would later become a United States congressman from Arkansas, the farm agents were charged with the responsibility of organizing the AAA program in 1933. Hays had warned that the farm agents were the tools of the Delta planters and could not be trusted to address the interests of the sharecroppers and tenants who worked the plantations. Although this assertion accurately characterized the situation existing in many counties, it reflected the fact that farm agents depended upon the goodwill of the landowners in the counties within which they worked. If the farm agent did not satisfy their needs, the entire extension program in their counties would be placed in jeopardy. The implementation of the AAA programs through the offices of the farm agents confirmed the importance of the extension program and guaranteed its continuation in Arkansas.

The farm agents held meetings to introduce the AAA plow-up program, distributed the forms that farmers needed to utilize, appointed the county and township AAA committees to supervise the selection of acres to be plowed up, and handled the disbursements of the checks to farmers. In 1934 they introduced the AAA's crop reduction program and again played a major role in coordinating and supervising the program. It was in that year that the words of warning issued by Brooks Hays in 1933 would seem prophetic. Tenants and sharecroppers began to object to the way AAA was being implemented. The issue at hand was the distribution of payments connected to the 1933 plow-up program and the fear that the same might occur with the crop reduction payments for 1934. In

Joe T. Robinson touting the New Deal. *Joseph T. Robinson Papers (MC MS R563), Supplement I, Series 4, Box 18, file 20, item 71. Special Collections, University of Arkansas Libraries, Fayetteville.*

order to participate in both programs, planters had to withdraw up to 30 percent of their land from the cultivation of a particular crop, such as cotton. Those farmers agreeing to withdraw cotton acres from production engaged in a legal fiction with the AAA in that they were regarded as having "rented" those acres to the federal government. They received a rental payment, when, in fact, they retained full possession of those acres and could grow other crops on them as long as those crops were not among those identified as overproduced. In addition to the rental payment, farmers received an adjustment once the cotton crop was marketed if the price they received did not reach a certain minimum level. Many planters, encouraged by agricultural agents, put the rented land into soybean production, a soil-building crop, and since they no longer needed the labor required to produce cotton, thousands of tenants and sharecroppers were thrown out of work at a time when industrial recovery was not yet taking place.

The AAA program as implemented accelerated a migration of African Americans out of the rural South and into some areas of the urban South but particularly into northern, midwestern, and western cities. Donald Holley regards this as the "second great emancipation" whereby planters were freed of the need for labor and thus threw off the corrupt tenancy and sharecropping system in favor of machines and, eventually, a variety of chemicals, some of which also reduced labor needs. The displacement caused by the AAA compelled landless whites to abandon the agricultural way of life and seek opportunities elsewhere. As Jarod Roll in *Spirit of Rebellion* suggests, however, many clung to the farms and plantations they labored on. Drawing on a rich trove of resources on the boot heel of Missouri, Roll convincingly argues that they embraced a producerist ideology, celebrated the agricultural enterprise, and made every effort to fight displacement. Landless men in Alabama formed a Sharecroppers Union while those in northeastern Arkansas—not so very far from Roll's boot heel of Missouri—organized the Southern Tenant Farmers Union (STFU) to fight evictions and seek a share of the crop.

Southern Tenant Farmers Union: Founded in 1934 in Poinsett County by sharecroppers and tenants (both black and white) because planters were not only not sharing AAA crop subsidy payments with them, they were also often evicting them from plantations.

The Southern Tenant Farmers Union

Rumblings of discontent had been heard elsewhere in northeastern Arkansas even before Poinsett County tenants and sharecroppers formed the STFU. In adjacent Mississippi County, which bordered the boot heel, fifteen tenants and sharecroppers filed suit against Lee Wilson & Company in the fall of 1933, but the judge threw the case out of court arguing lack of jurisdiction. It was in July 1934 that tenants and sharecroppers banded together in Poinsett County and formed the STFU. Clay East, a local businessman and member of a well-respected farm family, together with H. L. Mitchell, another small businessman, influenced the founding of the organization. Mitchell had converted East to socialism, and they subsequently hosted a visit to Poinsett County by Norman Thomas, the leader of the Socialist Party of America and perennial candidate for president. The organization they founded was avowedly interracial, and its initial goals were to stop evictions from plantations in the area and to force planters to share the crop subsidy payments with those still on plantations. Later, they added securing higher wages for agricultural laborers, such as those picking or hoeing cotton, to their goals, and carried out some successful strikes. Some in the Agricultural Adjustment Administration in Washington, D.C., were sympathetic to their demands, but President Roosevelt, desperate to hang on to conservative southern Democrats in Congress, turned a deaf ear to the pleas of STFU representatives, and in 1935 those in charge of the AAA fired those within the agency who were sympathetic to the STFU. In Arkansas, Oklahoma, and Missouri, which together had about 35,000 STFU members, planters and local officials practiced a more traditional method of discouraging the union. Nightriders, commonly believed to be plantation thugs, routinely broke up union meetings. Constables and sheriff's deputies disrupted others, sometimes arresting the STFU members, particularly those leading the meetings. Shots were fired into the homes of suspected union members and even the attorney representing the union. Finally, enemies of the STFU played to the racism of the white members of the union with some success.

Norman Thomas speaking to a union meeting. *Southern Historical Collection, UNC–Chapel Hill.*

Although the integration within the STFU has been somewhat exaggerated, it is nevertheless true that interracial cooperation existed in many STFU locals and marked a dramatic departure from earlier attempts by farmers to organize. In the late nineteenth century, the Agricultural Wheel, made up of small farm owners and some few tenants, operated separate white and black Wheels. Although some blacks were allowed to attend a state meeting, white and black Wheelers had little contact. But even that distant relationship left the Wheel vulnerable to charges that it was the tool of blacks and Republicans and probably cost them dearly at the polls. The goals of the Wheel, meanwhile, were quite different from those of the STFU, and the membership of the two organizations best illustrates that point. Although some tenants belonged to the Wheel, it was principally made up of small farm owners who wanted mortgage debt relief, regulation of railroads, and a more flexible monetary system. Three decades later, the Farmers and Household Union of America (FHUA), an organization of black sharecroppers, banded together to hire attorneys to represent them in suits they planned to file against the planters for whom they worked. Their efforts were misinterpreted, either deliberately or innocently, and a major race riot occurred at Elaine. In any event, the FHUA's organizing efforts provided its enemies with a potent weapon against such unions: the use of violent racism.

Arkansas farmworkers at union meeting. *Courtesy Louise Boyle.*

In fact, one of the founding members of the STFU was Isaac Shaw, who had been a member of the ill-fated Farmers and Household Union of America. In July 1934, at the first meeting of the organization that would become the STFU, Shaw argued that blacks and whites should organize together. He drew explicitly upon his earlier experience, and the six other black men and the eleven whites gathered at that meeting agreed that since they shared similar problems and oppressors, they should organize as one union. Shrewdly, however, the STFU leadership determined that each STFU local should decide the issue of whether to be interracial or segregated on their own, and this policy probably greatly facilitated the expansion of the union. Elected officials in the national STFU office always included blacks and whites. Eventually, planters would play to the racism of a white president who would turn over the union's membership records to them. Although he later recanted, the damage had been done, and the union was seriously weakened. A brief flirtation with Commonwealth College, a socialist institution near Mena, Arkansas, which proved to have ties with the Communist Party, also discredited the union.

Yet the STFU could claim some measure of success. H. L. Mitchell and other union representatives created significant problems for one of the largest cotton planters in the South, Lee Wilson & Company, when it alleged to a *Washington Post* reporter that the three largest recipients of AAA payments in 1934 and 1935, Lee Wilson & Company of Mississippi County, Chapman and Dewey Land Company of Poinsett County, and Delta

Farmers coming back from Blytheville. *Courtesy of the Arkansas History Commission.*

Pine & Land Company located in the state of Mississippi, were refusing to share subsidies and evicting tenants and sharecroppers wholesale, throwing them onto relief rolls. While it investigated the matter the AAA suspended payments to Lee Wilson & Company in 1936, a suspension that continued into the early 1940s. In 1941, however, their payments, at least back to 1938, were restored. Perhaps more important to landless farmers in Arkansas, the publicity surrounding the violent attacks on union members, together with the agitation of the union's leadership in Washington, D.C., forced Governor Futrell to establish a state commission to study the situation. But among those appointed to the committee were two employees of Lee Wilson & Company and the company's attorney. Although it included STFU representation, it was loaded with those hostile to the union. Before its report could be issued, however, President Roosevelt appointed a Farm Tenancy Commission, and its report, unlike that eventually issued by the state commission, was unsparing in its criticisms of the farm tenancy system. Congress finally responded in 1937 by passing the Bankhead-Jones Farm Tenancy Act, which, among other things, established the Farm Security Administration (FSA), an agency designed to put displaced tenants on their own farms. The FSA absorbed what remained of the Resettlement Administration, which had established some resettlement communities in Arkansas.

Other New Deal Programs

The most famous resettlement community was one located in Mississippi County and named for the state FERA director, William R. Dyess. A native of Mississippi County, Dyess was from a plantation family and held many of Governor Futrell's reservations about direct relief. The Dyess Colony settlement was touted as a model, but the publicity photographs, which showed rows of whitewashed houses and smiling farmers and their wives working in the community canning facility, could not long disguise the fact that considerable unrest and dissatisfaction existed there. An STFU chapter was established there, for example. The community was run much like a plantation and the farmers, many of whom had been farm owners prior to the Depression, found themselves under the authority of the local FERA director and the farm extension agent. Planters had never been enthusiastic about the Resettlement Administration, but they had exercised some influence with it, particularly on the local level. They had little influence, however, with the FSA and that agency became unpopular with planters, who saw it competing with them for valuable agricultural acreage, and, in any case, actually helped few tenants and sharecroppers, since most of those placed on the camps were failed farm owners. The FSA communities were accused of being socialistic and were eventually abolished by a less friendly Congress in 1944. By that time, a massive transformation of southern agriculture was fully underway, a transformation which eventually eliminated the farm tenancy system altogether.

Another federal agency also led to significant changes and secured the cooperation of the state's most prominent citizens: the Works Progress Administration. The WPA was essentially a successor to the FERA's Civil Works Administration (CWA). The CWA had been charged with putting the able-bodied unemployed to work. Direct relief was administered only to the unemployable poor and women with dependent children. The CWA, and later the WPA, put people to work on building roads, digging drainage ditches, and erecting public buildings, among other things. One significant difference between the WPA and the CWA was the role that local communities played. Communities pledged 50 percent of the funds for road improvements, for example, and received grants from the WPA for the remainder. Together with the Civilian Conservation Corps (CCC), which employed single young men and engaged in conservation measures, the WPA gave thousands of men gainful employment and helped transform the state in significant ways. CCC workers terraced lands to prevent erosion and planted trees; the WPA significantly improved the state's transportation network through the construction of roads and left a lasting legacy in the way of public buildings, such as libraries, courthouses, and schools. Not only did CCC workers develop outdoor parks like those at Petit Jean in Conway County and at Devil's Den in Washington County, they built Mather Lodge at the former and several cabins at the latter. Many WPA workers engaged in "writers' projects" and created a valuable archive of county histories, church histories, and the famous slave narratives. Many women and some African Americans were employed in these endeavors.

Works Progress Administration: The Works Progress Administration put people to work in a variety of jobs but worked in concert with local communities to locate projects there.

While the AAA had its greatest impact in the Delta, the federal programs that first penetrated the Ozarks and the Ouachitas were the WPA and the CCC. Farmers in those areas were typically more self-reliant and less dependent upon marketing their crops outside their own communities. The collapse of the cotton market hardly mattered to them, for cotton was not a crop they grew. Accustomed to barter and to a cash-scarce economy, many hardly knew that a depression existed, and the CCC and WPA jobs provided some with the first cash wages they had ever known. Those wages opened a whole new world of goods and services to previously isolated communities, and together with WPA projects, which funded the construction of schools and libraries, generated a new appreciation of the world outside their isolated farmsteads.

Rural Electrification

Rural electrification: Founded in 1935, the Rural Electrification Administration provided federal funds to help create rural electric cooperatives.

Another important New Deal–era program that challenged the isolation of country people was rural electrification. The Rural Electrification Administration (REA), created in 1935, began to operate in Arkansas in 1937, making loans to rural electric cooperatives in order to expand electric service to rural areas. It was slow to grow in many parts of rural America, largely because of the hostility of existing power companies. Arkansas Power and Light (AP&L) was not enthusiastic about the expenditure of federal funds to subsidize competitors for the rural market, but like power companies in other states, AP&L had largely ignored that market and had focused instead on expanding services in towns and cities. Private power companies, like AP&L, were necessarily dedicated to securing returns for their stockholders, and they understood that exploiting the easiest to reach areas first guaranteed the quickest return on investment. Yet the rural market had potential, and Harvey Couch, founder and director of AP&L, devised an "Arkansas plan," which he submitted to the REA. The plan would have funneled REA loans through AP&L, which would then extend loans and supply the power to the rural cooperatives. It was clearly an attempt to make sure AP&L profited from the extension of power to rural populations, and the REA rejected the plan. Although AP&L remained hostile to the funding of competitors in the form of rural electric cooperatives, powerful countervailing forces operated to mediate that entity's hostility. Planters in eastern Arkansas, for example, supported the expansion of electrification and promoted some joint efforts between AP&L and local cooperatives in the extension of electrical service to rural areas. After a fitful start, electrification accelerated during and immediately after World War II.

The extension of electrical service to rural Arkansas transformed the lives of the state's farm families. Townspeople and city folk had been enjoying the benefits of the modern conveniences electricity made possible for two or three decades by the time the REA was created, but country people still worked or read by the kerosene lamp, hauled water from wells or creeks, and depended upon the woodstove to cook their meals and heat their homes. In other words, they lived much as their grandparents had lived in the nineteenth century. Whether wealthy Delta planter or poor sharecropper, whether prosperous hill-country farmer or simple backwoodsman, life without electricity meant a much harder and ruder existence. Of course, some people could afford to hire others to haul the water or carry the firewood, freeing themselves of the backbreaking routine of such chores. They could afford to purchase and fuel more than a solitary lamp, lighting all the rooms in their house so they could read or work and their children could do their lessons. They would have a woman come to do the wash or take the wash to a washerwoman who likely spent six to seven days a week doing other people's laundry. They could hire someone to cook the meals on the wood-burning stove and put another to the task of ironing the clothes, no small task given the weight of the irons. Thus women of means could escape the worst inconveniences but most country women lacked the resources to hire others to do these chores, and their days were filled with backbreaking work and their evenings were spent in darkness. Many rural families lived a relatively primitive existence in homes without electricity, but rural schools were no better and in many cases even worse. They were drafty, poorly lighted affairs, and many of them had inadequate facilities for heating in the winter months. Indeed, they were dangerous affairs as more than one schoolhouse burned down as a result of a poorly tended stove. Many of them had no toilet facilities, and male and female children used designated areas of the woods to take care of their bodily functions. With no way to wash up, they likely spread germs among themselves more readily than might otherwise have been the case. Some advocates of rural electrification suggested that the poor academic performance of rural children was directly related to the inadequate structures they were schooled in. In addition to providing better lighting, electricity made possible the use of a wider variety of teaching tools, including filmstrips and motion pictures. Instruction in foreign languages was greatly augmented by the use of phonograph records, but perhaps most attractive to many rural people was the development of skills that could be more readily put to use at home or on the farm. In the larger rural schools, girls were given instruction in home economics; for example, cooking on electric ranges or hot plates. Boys received training in metal and woodwork and in how to repair and operate modern farm machinery.

By allowing indoor plumbing and more reliable means of illumination, refrigeration, and climate control, electricity clearly improved the quality of life for farm families and made country schools safer and more comfortable. Electrical service also greatly augmented certain farming operations. Dairy farmers who had struggled for generations with the problem of milk going sour before reaching the dairy processing facility could now purchase storage tanks cooled by electrical power. Milking usually began at 3:30 or 4:00 A.M., and for the first hour or so (depending upon time of year) farmers had to milk their cows in relative darkness. The kerosene lamps used by most Arkansans provided only about twenty-five watts of light, and many farmers were fearful of using them in their barns in any case because one spark fallen on a bed of straw could send the whole edifice up in flames. Farmers could also invest in milking machines, which reduced their labor needs and increased the number of cows that could be milked. Those farmers who grew their own grain to feed their livestock could now use electric grinders, greatly reducing the amount of labor required. As Robert Caro describes the situation in Texas, without an electric grinder, the farmer would "get the corn kernels for his mules and horses by sticking ears of corn—hundreds of ears of corn—one by one into a corn sheller and cranking it for hours." For those who grew cotton, the use of the electric motor was essential. Without one, the farmer "had to unload cotton seed by hand, and then shovel it into the barn by hand; to saw wood by hand, by swinging an axe or riding one end of a ripsaw." For farmers who produced chickens, the availability of electricity made possible the use of cooling fans as well as electrically powered incubators, which worked a virtual revolution in the industry.

Most country people enthusiastically responded to the possibility of receiving electrical power, and the rural electric cooperatives (and eventually AP&L) worked to make it available to the widest possible number of consumers. Potential customers in rural areas were offered the opportunity to help defray the costs by cutting and laying the poles themselves in order to string the electrical line to their homes and barns. The REA provided blueprints giving detailed instructions in how to wire existing structures, and they worked with the Agricultural Extension Service to bring the information to the farmers and their families. It was not a problem-free transition, however. By 1947, the agricultural agent in south Mississippi County was reporting that "inadequate wiring systems and overloaded lines are the chief problems in rural electrification on farms that have available electricity." The problem was widespread. A 4-H team competing in a statewide contest in Fayetteville that year received considerable attention and won the blue ribbon for their demonstration on the cost of inadequate wiring. That demonstration was subsequently replicated at the county level throughout the state. Many farmers continued to be bothered by low voltage or by overloads, which burned out motors on a variety of electrical items. Improperly regulating electrical current accounted for the overloads, and the rapid extension of electric service beyond available capacity accounted for the low voltage many farm families had to endure. Many discovered they could run only one electrical appliance at a time or risk blowing a fuse. Occasionally, a home would burn down because of the way it had been wired, and this raised fears in the minds of many existing and potential consumers. Despite these problems, the number of rural customers served by electricity expanded rapidly in the 1940s and 1950s, rising from 67,689 in 1945 to 327,115 in 1960.

Just as the Agricultural Extension Service's farm agents worked with farm men to bring electricity to the countryside, its home demonstration agents worked with farm women to introduce them to indoor plumbing, electric light fixtures, and a variety of labor-saving devices for use in the home. These appliances helped transform the drudgery of the work of the typical farmwife, giving her more time to devote to the nutritional needs of her children and to the beautification projects inside her home and in her yard. Electricity not only meant dependable refrigeration for foodstuffs and better lighting, it also resulted in an expansion of phonographs and radios, both of which opened up a new world of sounds and sensations to farm families.

Social Activities

Radio and moving pictures provided new avenues of entertainment and captured a wide audience in the state, but many rural people lived in isolated areas and could not always avail themselves of these opportunities. Most rural people did not yet have electricity so radios were still beyond them, and many of them only rarely visited the larger towns where movie houses operated. The promise of a traveling carnival or the arrival

Claybrook Tigers, Crittenden County, circa 1935. The Tigers were a semiprofessional black baseball team that played competitively against Negro League baseball teams. *Courtesy John R. Haddock.*

of the circus might be enough to encourage them to navigate the rough roads and come to town. Air shows, which became increasingly popular after World War I, could inspire a large crowd.

In this context, traditional social activities continued to flourish. People gathered in rural communities and churches to attend picnics and barbeques, and the Fourth of July celebration was a major event in any community's social calendar. Prominent businessmen, farmers, and planters often sponsored these events as a way to seal their identities as public-spirited leaders. Speakers, whether they were political, religious, or secular in orientation, could always find a welcome at any gathering or might themselves inspire a crowd. Indeed, people flocked to hear almost anyone speak. When Norman Thomas, the famous socialist, was invited to address a group of disgruntled sharecroppers in Poinsett County in 1934, even planters and businessmen who hardly agreed with his socialist philosophy came to listen. While some historians have regarded this as evidence that these planters and businessmen were there to keep tabs on what the sharecroppers were up to, the fact is that socialist speakers had been traveling Arkansas since early in the century and had frequently attracted large crowds.

Baseball became enormously popular in the early twentieth century, and by the 1920s many small towns fielded teams. As the 1920s and 1930s wore on and the economic depression and natural disasters brought great hardship, baseball provided an avenue where individuals could demonstrate their prowess and fans could experience vicariously the accomplishment of the athlete and the vanquishing of foes. It was an empowering experience that helped them cope with the problems that confronted them. Whatever they meant to the individual on a personal level, they provided town spirit in a time when such was sadly lacking. With farmers and businessmen facing hard times, they badly needed the boost that their baseball teams gave them. Town rivalries, which might have their origins in very real economic and political competition, could be played out on the diamond. Businesses and banks sponsored the teams, and businessmen, professional men, white-collar workers, millworkers, and farmers filled out the rosters. Many teams had paid managers who took their responsibilities seriously and expected their teams to play to win. Although the towns were supposed to field players who were actually their own residents, some managers hired former professional players to give their teams the edge. It was frowned upon, but widely practiced. Shoeless Joe Jackson of the "Black Sox" scandal played for an Arkansas City team in 1920, hitting a bases-loaded home run to win the game. Many famous ballplayers got their start playing on such teams, including the Dean brothers (Jay "Dizzy" and Paul "Daffy") from Lucas, Arkansas, and Brooks Robinson, who was born in Little Rock and grew up playing on local teams in the 1950s.

While class boundaries were often ignored when recruiting baseball players, racial segregation was never challenged. African Americans had their own baseball teams and were sometimes allowed to use the white ballparks. A prominent black farmer and logger from Crittenden County, John C. Claybrook, sponsored the Claybrook Tigers, a semi-professional black baseball team, which played and often beat some of the best Negro League teams in the nation. The black community found that social gatherings of all sorts were closed to them, although they were sometimes allowed to attend special "negro" days at the county fair, the circus, or the carnival. Their own churches and schools provided them with their greatest opportunity to gather and enjoy social space away from the denigratory attitudes of whites. Many black leaders in towns across the state were often careful to invite white leaders to black events as a way to secure their approval and "protection." White newspaper editors frequently condescended to report on black social gatherings when white leaders were present, offering comments that suggested they were surprised at the level of performance the black community achieved.

While groups of people gathered in public spaces for a variety of entertainment and social occasions, exclusive clubs brought smaller groups of like-minded people together. Men gathered in Masonic lodges, and women in literary clubs. Hunting and fishing clubs became increasingly popular in the early twentieth century, much to the chagrin of many local residents who resented the fences that demarcated the boundaries of the hunting preserves. Many people resented the erection of fences that kept them out of areas they had traditionally hunted within, particularly when many of the hunters who enjoyed these preserves came from out of state. Whether hunting within a preserve or elsewhere, the sport enjoyed as much popularity in the 1920s and 1930s as it had earlier. Whether rich man or poor, whether well known or obscure, hunting and fishing brought groups of (largely) men together. These men often engaged in considerable carousing, drinking, and gambling while removed from the constraints of family and community. Tall tales about exploits while on hunting and fishing excursions became a kind of art form, and Senator Joseph T. Robinson was perhaps one of its supreme practitioners. While polling down the White River on a fishing expedition, he told a story designed to defend the size of fish in his own Prairie County:

> Up there the streams back up when it floods and when the water goes down again there'll be a pond out in cotton fields as big as a lake. And in these ponds there'll be fish. In one of these ponds last year there was something so big nobody could catch it. Broke their tackle and went away with their rods. So one day we took an anchor and baited it with a dead calf and tossed it in on the end of a two-inch rope tied to a grandpappy of all cottonwood trees in Prairie County. Pretty soon the cottonwood begins to buckle and we knew we had him. We hitched on six pair of oxen and we pulled him out. He was a catfish. And when we cut him open, what do you think we found? We found a pair of harnessed mules and wagon and seven acres of burnt ground.

As historian Kenneth Hubbell tells it, one of the other fishermen conceded the contest by remarking, "Hell, I ought to have known a senator would tell the biggest lie."

Political Infighting among Democrats

By the time that Governor Futrell left office in 1937, recovery in the farming sector was well underway, despite the disruption of the tenancy system. While he had initially obstructed some federal programs, such as the FERA, the threatened loss of federal funds forced him to cooperate. Had the federal programs not been implemented in Arkansas, Futrell's severe retrenchment program might have led to much greater hardship among at least some of the state's population. He had greatly reduced state services, laid off state workers and forced others to take salary cuts, and encouraged the passage of two amendments that seriously curtailed the funding of state government expenditures. When Futrell left office, the state was operating on a cash basis and actually enjoyed a treasury surplus. But because of the curtailment of state government services and because of the AAA, the FERA, the WPA, and the CCC, people were more oriented toward the federal government than ever before.

The great irony of Carl Edward Bailey's governorship (1937–1941) was that he was a great supporter of the New Deal, but he was at odds with many of the Arkansans who ran the New Deal agencies both inside and outside the state. A political outsider, he first won elective office in 1930 as state prosecuting attorney in the Sixth Judicial District (Pulaski and Perry counties) and, as fate would have it, prosecuted a case in 1930 that would earn him a formidable enemy, Senator Joseph T. Robinson. Robinson would later influence the selection of many who served in federal agencies, people who would have been the natural allies of Bailey but who owed their positions to Robinson. The trial that pitted Robinson against Bailey involved A. B. Banks, who presided over a banking empire that included the American Exchange Trust Company of Little Rock. When it collapsed in 1930, sixty-six other Arkansas banks, scattered throughout the state, also failed. Bailey charged Banks with accepting deposits in these banks despite the fact that he knew they were about to fail. Robinson represented Banks and believed that he was being made a scapegoat. Bailey secured a conviction, and although Banks was pardoned before beginning his prison sentence, Bailey was widely applauded for having pursued Banks. Despite the feelings of many citizens in Arkansas regarding the matter, Robinson and other prominent Old Guard Democrats were bitter in their contempt for Bailey, who had, essentially, attacked one of their own in his prosecution of Banks.

Rather than work to build a relationship with the Old Guard Democrats, Bailey formed an alliance with Brooks Hays, another political outsider who had gained a reputation as an opponent of the existing power structure. He supported Hays in his unsuccessful run for the Fifth Congressional District seat in 1933 against David D. Terry. Terry had the support of Senator Robinson, Governor Futrell, and Internal Revenue collector Homer Adkins. This marked the beginning of a political rivalry between Bailey and Adkins that would last for the next decade and a half, but, in the meantime, Bailey would stand against yet another Old Guard Democrat, Hal Norwood, in the race for attorney general in 1934. Riding on the publicity of the Banks trial, Bailey bested Norwood, who was the incumbent, in a narrow victory.

The differences between his humanitarian philosophy and that of Governor Futrell became evident very early in Bailey's tenure as attorney general. Bailey was unswerving in his dedication to New Deal programs that provided for direct relief to "unemployables"; in other words, women, children, the elderly, or the infirm. Futrell believed that the poor had no one but themselves to blame and that the state should not, in any case, assume the role of dispensing direct relief. Despite his sentiments in favor of such programs, Bailey revealed another aspect of his character once Futrell was forced into creating a Department of Public Welfare or risk losing federal funds. Bailey's own political ambitions led him to fear that the governor would use the creation of the agency as a way to bolster the political establishment. The governor who appreciated Bailey's ambitious streak, nevertheless attempted to prevent him from assuming any of the credit for the creation of the agency. Despite his misgivings about Bailey, Futrell found himself in the unenviable position of having to approve an action of Bailey's that gained his enemy much popular press. A New York gangster, Charles "Lucky" Luciano, had fled to Arkansas to escape prosecution and set up house in Hot Springs. When Bailey ordered his arrest and extradition, despite a $50,000 bribe offer from one of the gangster's friends, Futrell approved the order, but it was Bailey who received the lion's share of publicity over the affair. Much to the chagrin of the political establishment in Arkansas, Bailey was able to use the matter to catapult himself into the governor's office.

As governor, Bailey fashioned a state civil service system, arguing that appointments to crucial state positions should be on a merit basis rather than on a political basis. In fact, he was hoping to replace the old system by which Democratic Party stalwarts awarded positions for party loyalty. He understood that most people in office in the state owed allegiance to his political enemies. He came to appreciate, however, that in order to build his own political constituency, he needed to be able to appoint people in his own right rather than rely on a merit system. When the unpopular measure came up for reconsideration during his second term in office, he allowed a bill repealing it to become law without his signature.

One casualty of Bailey's battle with the Democratic Party machine and the federal officeholders was his efforts to refund the highway debt. During his first term he secured legislative approval to sell new highway bonds, but a depression in the bond market in 1937 scuttled the effort, and when he sponsored new measures in 1939, his political enemies, led chiefly by Homer Adkins, sabotaged the scheme. Understanding that his enemies had powerful friends in crucial positions in New Deal agencies, Bailey made a decision to replace some of them, and he probably believed that once Robinson died in 1937 that he would be able to do so with impunity. Before launching a battle to oust some of these officeholders, however, Bailey first attempted to secure Robinson's Senate seat by using his domination of the Democratic state committee to have himself nominated rather than hold a Democratic primary. This seemed out of keeping with his consistent attacks against such manipulations and his opponents made sure the public recognized that fact. He still had to win a special election in the fall, and the Old Guard, led by Homer Adkins, convinced John E. Miller to run as an independent in the special election and many New Deal officeholders, in fear of losing their own jobs if someone like Bailey were in such an important patronage position, campaigned for Miller. Miller defeated him easily.

Bailey was bitter and vulnerable in the 1938 reelection campaign for governor. He took nothing for granted, admitted having made mistakes and, with Adkins preoccupied with campaigning for Hattie Caraway's reelection against John McClellan, he was able to secure election to the customary second term. Realizing more than ever the obstacle that the federal officeholders in the state represented, Bailey began to remove some of them from office and attack others. He fired W. A. Rooksbery, director of unemployment compensation, but one of the most highly publicized contests was that between the governor and WPA director Floyd Sharp. Bailey accused Sharp of using WPA workers in a political battle against him, and the governor's friends in the legislature attempted to investigate the unrest at Dyess Colony, the FSA community in Mississippi County, as a way to embarrass and weaken Sharp. The old party machine was still very much alive, however, and closed ranks in the legislature.

A more obscure case involved the firing of C. C. Randall, the assistant director of the Arkansas Extension Agency in April 1939. It was the University of Arkansas Board of Trustees that actually fired Randall, but it had reportedly done so at the governor's request. Bailey justified Randall's dismissal on the basis that he had failed to cooperate with New Deal agencies in Washington, but representatives of those agencies wrote letters attesting to Randall's cooperation. The Farm Bureau claimed that Bailey's motivation was simply to put his own man in place and called to mind Bailey's removal of Rooksbery. The Farm Bureau had first been created in Arkansas in the early 1920s but

Mississippi County, resettled family, Dyess Colony. *Courtesy of the Arkansas History Commission.*

had dwindled in membership in that difficult decade and was not resuscitated until 1935. The leaders of the revival were planters, principally in eastern Arkansas. Ironically, this newly revitalized Farm Bureau became the chief defender of Randall, a man they had sometimes been uncomfortable with because of his criticisms of the tenancy system. It was an obscure incident in Crittenden County, together with Bailey's determination to put his own men in place, that may have immediately precipitated Randall's downfall. Small farmers there had complained that the farm agent assigned to the county was showing favoritism to planters. Randall, as assistant director of the agency, met with the county judge and the two decided to move the agent to another county. The agent agreed to the move but then planters in Crittenden County complained. Randall refused to back down and was subsequently fired. By this point in time, Bailey was successfully courting the eastern Arkansas planters, who had become less enchanted with some of the New Deal programs. Crittenden County was one of the more populous of the Delta counties, and, in any case, there was a certain convergence of interests. He could appeal to an important constituency and at the same time put a new man in place who would owe loyalty to him. Not only was Bailey able to replace Randall, he was also able to appoint a new dean of agriculture/director of agricultural extension at the university. Deane G. Carter had been designated as the new dean/director to replace Dan T. Gray, who was to retire in July. But when Carter objected to Randall's firing, he undermined his own position.

The sudden death of the president of the university, John C. Futrall, in an automobile accident in September 1939, gave Bailey another opportunity to appoint a man who would be loyal to him and to court an important political ally in northwest Arkansas. He had almost no constituency in that part of the state, and after his loss to Miller in the run for the Senate seat in 1938, he was determined to build a political organization there. He focused much of his efforts on securing the allegiance of the *Northwest Arkansas Times*, run by Roberta Fulbright, a formidable and noteworthy newspaperwoman. When Futrall died, Bailey recognized an opportunity to solidify this alliance and appointed James William Fulbright, Roberta's son, to the top administrative position at the university. This caused considerable consternation among the faculty, who assumed they had a role to play in the selection of their own president and who had doubts about Fulbright's qualifications. Although a Rhodes scholar and an attorney, he had no academic credentials of any substance, having published no articles or books and having been on the faculty—at the Law School—for only one year at the time of his appointment. Nevertheless, he proved to be an energetic spokesperson for the university and understood that the university played an important role in preparing the state's future political and economic leaders.

But Fulbright would have little time to demonstrate his mastery of the job at hand. His appointment became an issue during the gubernatorial election in 1940, and his fate was sealed by the outcome of that election. Despite Bailey's efforts to court the Delta vote and build a constituency in northwest Arkansas, he discovered when he ran for the almost unprecedented third term that he had failed to build a political following capable of sustaining him. Homer Adkins, on the contrary, had the backing of the federal officeholders in the state and the entire Arkansas congressional delegation. He put Bailey on the defensive on the third-term issue and on the failed highway refinancing plan. Adkins defeated Bailey and subsequently launched his own refinancing plan, but one of his first acts as governor was to fire Fulbright at his earliest opportunity, a meeting of the board of trustees on June 9, 1941—the first meeting after Adkins's inauguration—which happened to be commencement day.

Governor Adkins's attention would soon be consumed by the nation's entry into World War II, and, indeed, the state would find its resources stretched beyond its limits in the next few years. Arkansas had endured some wrenching changes in the previous two decades and was not positioned particularly well to capitalize on some of the opportunities presenting themselves in a nation gearing up for world war. It remained predominantly rural; it had a transportation network that was inferior; it had only a modest industrial sector; and its educational system had not prepared its population for the modern world. While the state government had largely withdrawn from its previous activist agenda and instituted constitutional amendments that severely restricted its taxing and spending powers, the federal government had assumed a much larger role in the lives of Arkansans. World War II would accelerate the trend toward a reliance on federal programs and play an instrumental role in a massive demographic shift that had its origins, in part, in New Deal programs. Those programs funneled cash into the hands of planters who began to experiment with mechanization, a phenomenon that would become more practical with the invention of a marketable mechanical cotton harvester in the mid-1940s. Tenants and sharecroppers dispossessed by AAA programs would flock to jobs in war industries, principally in other states, and many would never return. The next two and a half decades would witness a major transformation in the state, a transformation that could not have been foreseen or forestalled.

CHAPTER FOURTEEN

From World War to New Era, 1940–1954

"World War II rather than the Civil War is the crucial event of southern history," declared historian Morton Sosna in his presidential address before the Southern Historical Association meeting in 1982. Some in the rather partisan audience gasped in surprise. Scholars who had focused their studies on the devastation of the Civil War and the challenges that followed it might be characterized as appropriately skeptical if not downright outraged at the suggestion. Nevertheless, in narrowing his definition of "crucial" to mean whether significant change occurred, Sosna was on solid ground. By the time he made his provocative observation, scholars had already demonstrated that the antebellum elite survived the Civil War intact and in control, that the status of African Americans only briefly improved, and that the labor-intensive plantation economy survived the devastation of war and defeat. Not until World War II, Sosna argues, was the South truly made to change and then largely because of massive infusions of capital in the form of military spending. Perhaps a bit overeager to prove his point, Sosna dismisses too readily the importance of the black migration that began long before World War II; he also dismisses the impact of New Deal programs when, in fact, they caused a shift in crops and the stirrings of mechanization which began the process of radically altering labor systems in the South. History never happens in a vacuum. What came before is as important as what came after an event—or a war—and its measure has to be taken in context. Nevertheless, World War II marked a dramatic and important moment in southern history and in Arkansas history. The $300 million spent on military bases and war-related industries in Arkansas resulted in unprecedented prosperity, but a massive demographic shift led to enormous challenges during and after the war. A new militancy on the part of a younger generation of African American activists emerged and began to challenge the racial status quo. The absence of male figures in households and the movement of women and young people into the workforce disrupted the family structure. While the Civil War might occupy an important place in the imaginations of Arkansans today, World War II contributed to vast changes in the way Arkansans lived and worked. The region and the state would never be the same.

Arkansas on the Home Front

A surprise attack by the Japanese on Pearl Harbor on December 7, 1941, stunned America and brought the nation into the conflagration known as World War II.

Although some Arkansans were aware of the possibility of America's involvement in the war in Europe, like most Americans, they were surprised by the avenue through which the United States entered the conflict brewing abroad. The state's newspapers had been featuring stories on Hitler's rise to power and Germany's military expansion since the early 1930s. Germany's sudden invasion of Poland in 1939, which ended England's policy of appeasement and hurled Europe toward another devastating war, riveted the American population. As France collapsed and British, French, and Belgium soldiers were evacuated from Dunkirk in 1940, many Americans—Arkansans among them—began to abandon their isolationist sentiments and inch toward support for intervention or, at the very least, efforts to aid the British. While Japanese expansion in the Pacific captured some attention, most newspapers focused on the dramatic events taking shape in Europe. The day following the attack on Pearl Harbor, Pres. Franklin Roosevelt gave his famous "a day which will live in infamy" speech, asking Congress to declare war against Japan, a request almost all of them were eager to approve. Given Japan's Tri-partite pact with Germany and Italy, Roosevelt and Congress understood that it would be only a matter of days before both Germany and Italy entered the war against the United States. Arkansans responded much like other Americans. Men rushing to enlist overwhelmed recruiting offices, and local communities eagerly embraced every opportunity to demonstrate their support for the war effort.

Selective Service Act of 1940: The first peace-time draft in American history, the Selective Service Act of 1940, reflected the rising tensions in Europe and the Pacific and the growing likelihood of American involvement.

The Selective Service Act of 1940, the first peacetime draft in American history, had established a mechanism for mobilizing an army, but it was necessary over the months immediately following the outbreak of hostilities to refine the procedures. At first the people in the towns of Arkansas gathered at train and bus stations to send their draftees and enlistees off to Camp Robinson or Fort Chaffee with gifts from civic organizations. High school marching bands played in the background, and mayors and town councilmen made speeches about bravery and patriotism. Within weeks, however, as many as 50 percent of the young men returned, having failed their physical examinations, a dismal reminder of the absence of adequate health care and the nutritional deficiencies in the average Arkansas diet. A smaller percentage of Arkansans were initially rejected because of educational deficiencies, particularly illiteracy. The educational qualifications were quickly relaxed, however, and the military adjusted the rules so that potential soldiers reported first for their physical examination and, if accepted, were allowed to return home for a two-week furlough. More personal farewells replaced the public displays of support as crowds ceased gathering to send draftees off. But this is not to suggest any decreasing enthusiasm for the war or any diminishment of support for servicemen. Newspapers continued to remind its readers of the exploits of local soldiers, often featuring letters from the front and photographs of their young men in uniform. Detailed news of the progress of the war, sometimes accompanied by maps or photographs of prominent generals and admirals, routinely appeared on the front pages of newspapers.

In one way or another, everyone participated in the war effort, whether they themselves served in the military or stayed at home, whether they had a loved one on the front or no family member or friend in harm's way. At a minimum the war's impact was felt through rationing demands that severely limited certain goods. Sales of some products, such as canned meat and fish, were for a while entirely frozen while purchases of others, like sugar, important in rural communities to preserve fruits, were closely rationed. Typically the government issued coupon books that contained a limited number of certificates. One of the first coupon books, for example, contained twenty-eight certificates, and it took eight to accompany the purchase of a pound of sugar. By the end of the first full year of the war, coffee was added to the list, and in early 1943 sales of butter and fats were briefly halted until a rationing regimen could be established.

Rationing: The rationing of items (such as sugar, coffee, butter, and tires) during World War II.

While rationing food products altered the dietary habits of virtually every Arkansan, the rationing of tires and gasoline made it necessary to limit travel and to find alternative means of sending goods to market. County farm and home demonstration agents, who typically traveled extensively within their respective areas, had to alter their method of operation and seriously curtail outreach programs, just when farmers and their wives needed advice about how to incorporate the rationing of necessary items into their operations. Because farmers were expected to produce as much for the war effort as possible, the government selectively reduced rationing of gasoline for producing farmers, but many other individuals who depended upon travel to reach customers suffered loss of income, and most people found it necessary to curtail travel for purely social purposes. Thus the livelihoods of many were threatened and social patterns were altered.

Arkansans who stayed at home also actively supported the war effort in a number of ways. Communities met and exceeded quotas on the amount they were to raise for the Red Cross relief effort. So many Arkansans contributed to war loan and war bond drives that Arkansas ranked twelfth among all the states in money raised, despite its near bottom ranking in per capita income. While many Arkansans opened their pocketbooks, others donated their time by collecting scrap metal and rubber. Even as the first draftees/enlistees were leaving their homes, plans to launch scrap-metal campaigns were being laid. Farmers brought metal objects to town or piled them on the roadside for committee members to pick up and deliver to central locations. Women whose sons, husbands, brothers, or fathers were away at war contributed in this effort. They also often worked in the Red Cross surgical dressing rooms, rolling bandages to send to the front. So successful was this Red Cross endeavor that the quotas were frequently met and work suspended periodically, only to be suddenly resumed when a major offensive required a new supply of bandages. The reopening of the Red Cross dressing room served as a grim reminder of the tragic news that might come to any one of the women working there. As they rolled bandages for some unknown soldier or sailor, they must have wondered whether their own loved ones would need such a bandage, but by being active, they relieved their sense of helplessness.

Those responsible for organizing farm and industrial production for the war faced particularly serious challenges. In the years immediately preceding the war, a farm labor surplus had developed but with the outbreak of hostilities, the more customary labor shortage reemerged. Because it was connected to a national emergency, the government was willing to play a more active role in attempting to solve the problem. In fact, the Department of Agriculture had been anticipating a labor shortage since October 1939 when a report generated by the Bureau of Agricultural Economics began to circulate. The Army Industrial College had asked the bureau to project how excess farm labor might be transferred to industrial production in the event of war, and the report generated on October 12, 1939, created some anxiety. It revealed that if the industrial sector absorbed all the excess farm labor, a shortfall of 695,000 workers would remain. This report assumed that farm laborers, who had been experiencing a declining standard of living and a lack of protective legislation in the 1930s, would abandon the farms in great numbers, but the report also revealed what should have been obvious: While the transfer of farm labor would not fully satisfy the needs of the industrial sector, it would lead to a farm labor crisis of enormous proportions.

In the face of these staggering statistics, the Department of Agriculture was directed to take aggressive steps. Aside from fashioning some policies to ameliorate the condition of farm laborers to make remaining in the rural environment more attractive, the department understood that farmers and planters would need to resort to more unusual sources of labor. By early 1942 farm leaders throughout Arkansas and elsewhere began holding meetings to develop plans to deal with the situation, and by the fall of that year they publicized a "work, fight, or go to jail" campaign. County farm agents in the Delta coordinated with farmers to recruit labor from the hill counties and from towns. Retired and marginally handicapped people were recruited. They also looked beyond the border to Mexican nationals and to German and Italian prisoners of war. An agreement signed between the United States and the Mexican government in June 1942 outlined a set of provisions governing the importation of Mexican nationals, known as braceros, to various sections of the country. The prospective employers were made responsible for transportation costs and housing, and a minimum wage level was established. Over the next few years, thousands of braceros were placed in Arkansas, principally in the plantation areas.

German and Italian prisoners of war were also used to address the labor shortage in agriculture. Although the United States was initially reluctant to bring captured enemy soldiers to the United States, overcrowding in Britain and the recognition that the prisoners could play an important role in addressing the labor shortage, convinced policy makers to reconsider the security concerns they first entertained. Approximately twenty-three thousand prisoners of war (POW) were relocated to Arkansas by fall of 1943, many of them captured when the Axis forces surrendered after the success of the allies' North Africa campaign in May 1943. The vast majority of POWs placed in camps in Arkansas were German, and they assisted in virtually every aspect of the agricultural process, and some worked in

POW labor: German and Italian prisoners of war used in Arkansas to help with agricultural labor.

Arkansas County Development by Census Year, 1820-1920

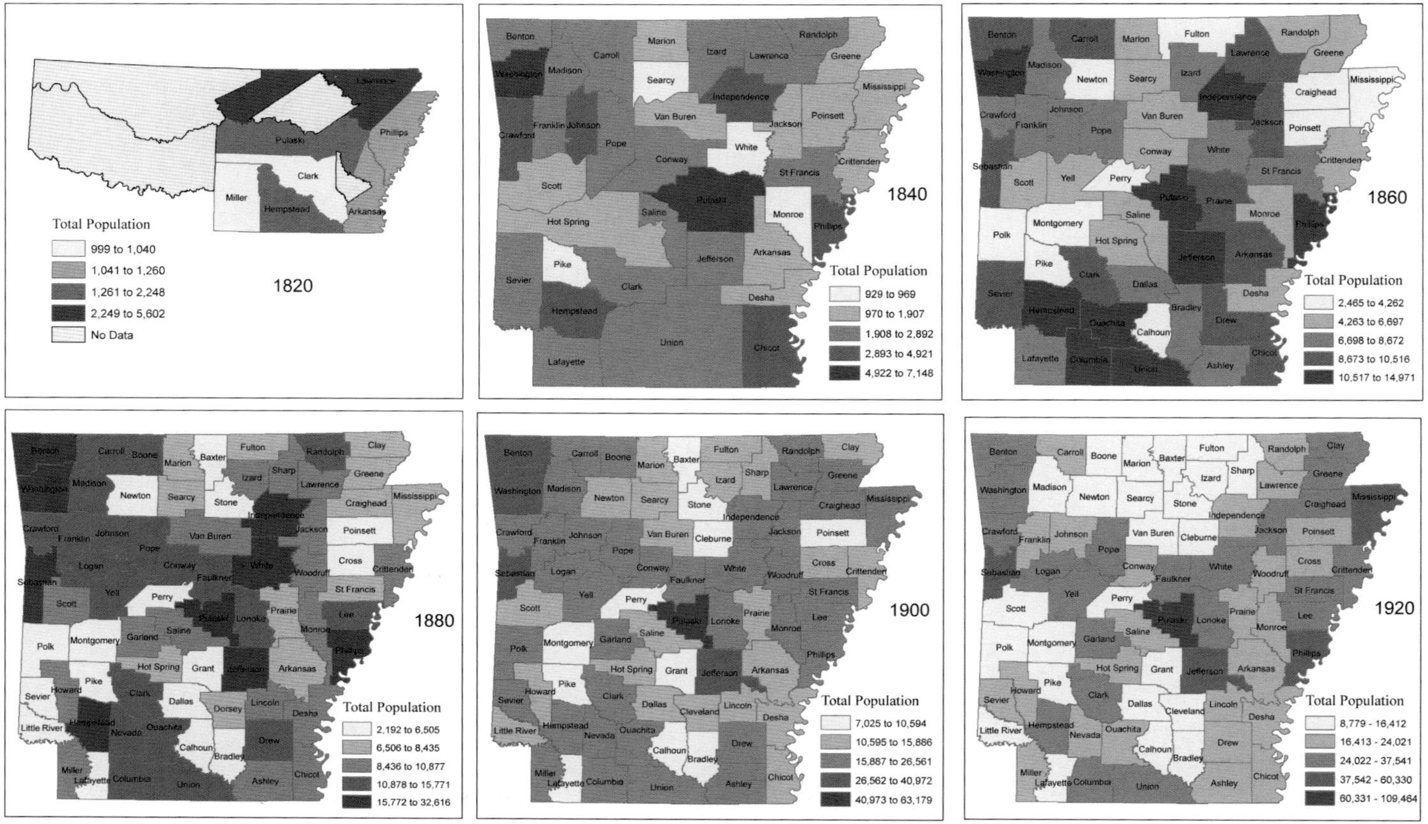

PLATE 38. Arkansas County Development by Census Year, 1820–1920. *Courtesy of Joseph Swain.* (Source: Minnesota Population Center, National Historical Geographic Information System.)

PLATE 39. Portrait of William Grant Still. *Courtesy of Special Collections, University of Arkansas Libraries, Fayetteville.*

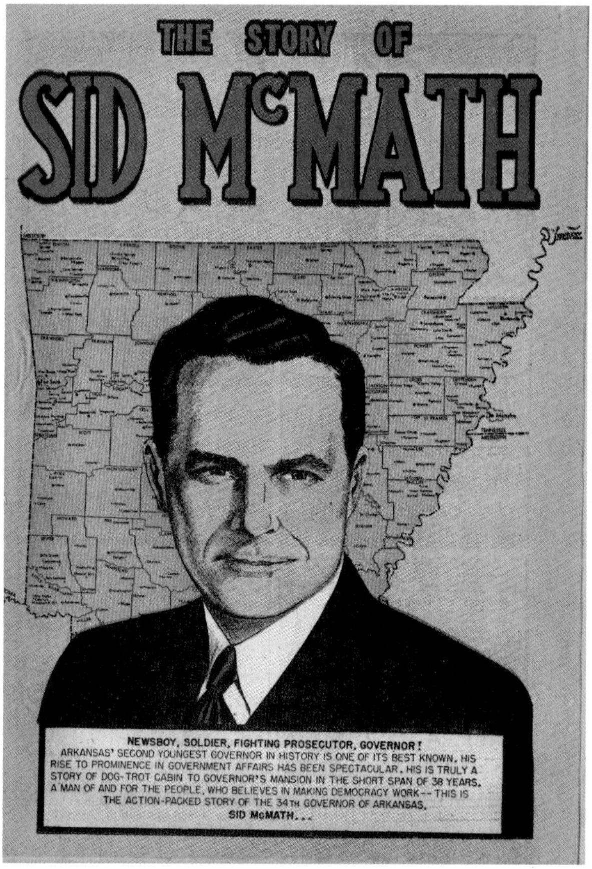

PLATE 40. Gov. Sidney McMath comic book. *Sidney S. McMath Papers (MC 899), Box 5, file 1. Special Collections, University of Arkansas Libraries, Fayetteville.*

PLATE 41. Orval Faubus. *Orval Faubus Addendum Papers (MC 922), Box 49, item 237. Special Collections, University of Arkansas Libraries, Fayetteville.*

above: PLATE 42. Women voters for Orval Faubus. *Orval Faubus Addendum Papers (MC 922), Box 49, item 225. Special Collections, University of Arkansas Libraries, Fayetteville.*

PLATE 43. J. William Fulbright by Louis Freund (1948). *Louis and Elsie Freund Papers (MC 1927). Special Collections, University of Arkansas Libraries, Fayetteville.*

PLATE 44. Vada Sheid. *Photograph. Vada Sheid Legislative Papers (MC 930), Box 27, item 29. Special Collections, University of Arkansas Libraries, Fayetteville.*

PLATE 45. Dale Bumpers with farmer. *Dale Bumpers Papers [Unprocessed], Box 2, item 1. Special Collections, University of Arkansas Libraries, Fayetteville.*

above: PLATE 46. Gov. David Pryor. Pryor before the Arkansas General Assembly, Gubernatorial Inauguration [1975]. *David Pryor Papers (MC 336), Box 598, item 192. Photograph.*

PLATE 47. Gov. William Jefferson Clinton. *Photograph. Vada Sheid Legislative Papers (MC 930), Box 27, item 15. Special Collections, University of Arkansas Libraries, Fayetteville.*

Earthquake Activity in Central Arkansas, 2011

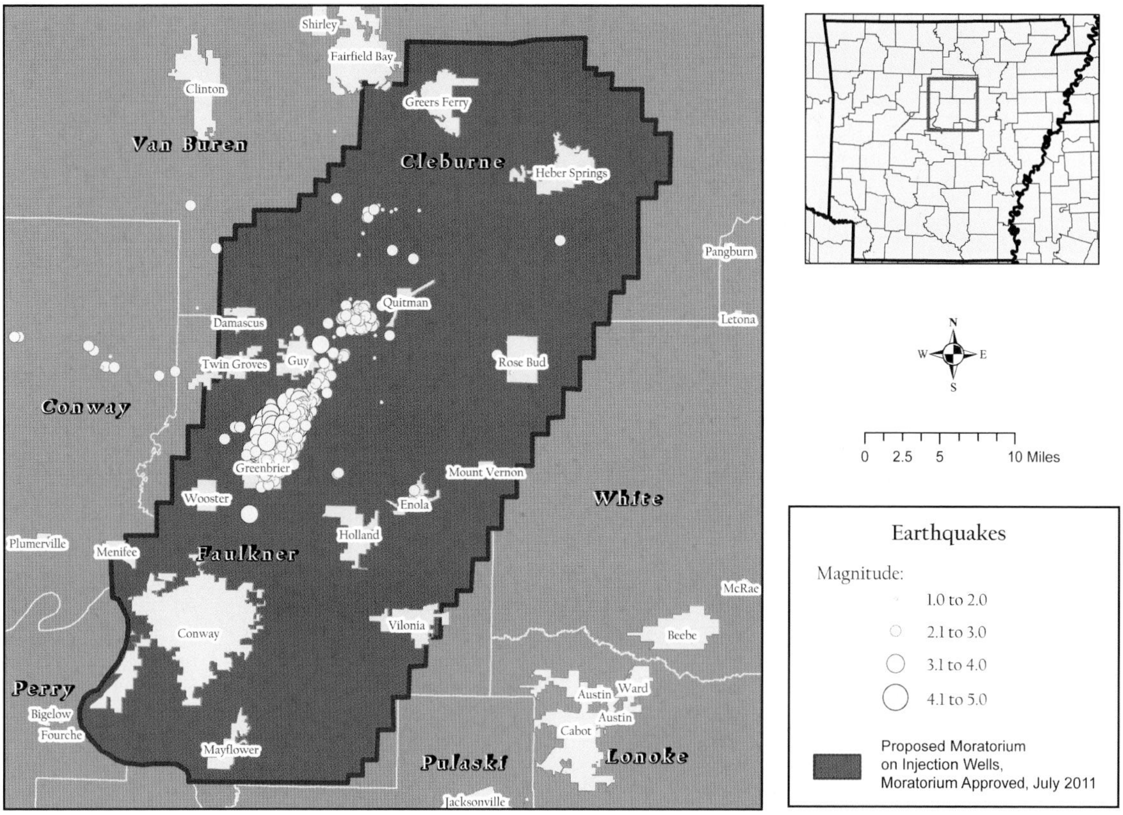

PLATE 48. Earthquake Activity in Central Arkansas, 2011. *Courtesy of Joseph Swain.* (Sources: Arkansas Geographic Information Office, Arkansas Oil and Gas Commission, U.S. Geological Survey, National Atlas of the United States.)

PLATE 49. Watering up the Rice at Bondsville, Mississippi County, Arkansas, Harvest, 2012. This image demonstrates the necessity of well water. *Photographer: Norwood Creeh.*

PLATE 50. Round Module Cotton Picker, Mississippi County, Arkansas, Harvest, 2011. This image demonstrates the new economies of scale at work in the cotton field. *Photographer: Norwood Creech.*

PLATE 51. Spraying Soybeans for Worms, Poinsett County, Arkansas, Harvest, 2012. *Photographer: Norwood Creech.*

PLATE 52. Watering up Beans with Poly-Pipe, Poinsett County, Arkansas, Spring 2012. *Photographer: Norwood Creech.*

PLATE 53. Jim Guy Tucker. *Courtesy UALR Center for Arkansas History and Culture.*

PLATE 54. Mike Huckabee. Photographer, Kirk Jordan. *Courtesy of the Arkansas Secretary of State's office.*

PLATE 55. Mike Beebe. *Courtesy of the Arkansas Governor's Office.*

PLATE 56. Thorncrown Chapel. Thorncrown Chapel is one of Jones's most famous architectural achievements and is clearly reflective of the influence of Frank Lloyd Wright. *Fay Jones Collection (MC 1373), Series VI, Subseries I, Box 10. Special Collections, University of Arkansas Libraries, Fayetteville.*

the timber industry. Three principle centers existed in the state: Camp Robinson in North Little Rock, Camp Chaffee in Fort Smith, and Camp Dermott in Dermott. A number of branch camps, particularly in the Delta, were erected in order to place the prisoners closer to the farmers needing labor. The local farm labor clerk, a person attached to the county farm agent's office after the war began, assisted farmers and planters in filling out the paperwork to apply for POW branch camps. The local farmers and the businessmen in agricultural communities identified appropriate local sites for these camps, hired construction crews to erect the barracks and guardhouses, and provided facilities for military personnel assigned to security. The army transported the prisoners to the branch camps and then it was the responsibility of the farm labor clerk to work with those in need of labor. Farmers would transport their allotment of prisoners to and from the camps, and despite the fact that they did so without a military guard, there were few escape attempts in Arkansas. The interior location of the state made flight more difficult and the good conditions within the camps dampened enthusiasm for escape.

Another response to the labor shortage was a renewed interest in mechanization. Farm agents established committees to encourage the purchase and sharing of farm equipment, and the number of tractors on Arkansas farms more than doubled, from 12,564 to 26,537 between 1940 and 1945. Meanwhile, farmers and planters in the delta became more intensely interested in experiments with mechanical cotton harvesters. As Don Holly has ably demonstrated, versions of a mechanical cotton harvester had been showcased by the Rust brothers as early as the mid-1930s. John D. Rust and his brother, Mack, lacked the funds to go into production of the machine, however, and given the existing labor surplus, planters and farmers needed more convincing to abandon their old methods. World War II proved to be the watershed. The labor shortage that accompanied the war played a major role in encouraging the mechanization of agriculture, a phenomenon that would have significant long-term ramifications for Arkansas, the South, and the nation.

A migration from the South to the North and the West, which had begun to take shape during and immediately following World War I and was given impetus by New Deal programs, accelerated during World War II. Aside from the labor crisis in agriculture, another serious consequence of the demographic shift was its impact on the educational infrastructure in the state. Teachers left for the military or to take significantly higher-paying jobs in industry, leading to a severe shortage. With close to 50 percent of the state's teachers abandoning their jobs in the educational system for other opportunities, many schools failed to open in the fall of 1942. The trend toward school consolidation, a phenomenon encouraged by the state but long resisted on the local level, accelerated as a result of the teacher shortage. Some federal aid was made available for schools near defense industries, but southern congressmen—often supported by southern governors like Arkansas's Homer Adkins—blocked wide-scale federal aid to schools, largely because the program under consideration would have allocated proportional funds to white and black schools, challenging the practice of southern states to apportion school funds unequally and thus implicitly challenging white supremacy.

Adkins squandered an opportunity to ease the crisis in education in order to maintain the principle of segregation, but he did not hesitate to pursue all opportunities open to him in order to promote industrial development. Despite the governor's efforts and those of Arkansas's congressional delegation, the state was not as successful as others in attracting war industries, largely because of Arkansas's poor infrastructure and undereducated population. Although some Arkansans found jobs in war-related industries within the state, most went elsewhere to pursue these opportunities. Nevertheless, six military ordnance plants were located in various locations: Camden, El Dorado, Hope, Jacksonville, Marche, and Pine Bluff. The twenty-five thousand workers—mostly women—produced explosive materials, detonators, fuses, and explosive primers at five of these six plants. The sixth facility, located at Hope, served as a proving ground for testing ordnance.

Because shorter winters made Arkansas a desirable location for the placement of military training bases, a number of them were established around the state and tended to have a largely positive impact on the local economy. They hired some civilians for a variety of purposes, and the trainees spent their money in nearby communities. North Little Rock saw the largest number of army recruits, where nearly three-quarters of a million trainees passed through Camp Robinson. The camp had been created in 1917 and was originally named Camp Pike after Gen. Zebulon Montgomery Pike. It was renamed after Senator Joseph T. Robinson in 1937 and vastly expanded during World War II, serving as a basic training camp and as a facility to prepare army medics. Although far fewer trainees passed through the army air bases established in Blytheville, Walnut Ridge, Newport, and Stuttgart, the presence of military personnel and the availability of a limited number of civilian positions impacted those towns as well. The state's insular location worked against the location of navy bases, but navy installations could be found in a number of locations, including an Army and Navy General Hospital in Hot Springs, a navy ordnance plant at Shumaker, and several administrative and recruiting offices in Little Rock and elsewhere.

Japanese internment camps: Camps established in western states and in Arkansas to house Japanese Americans removed from the West coast in 1942.

Perhaps the most controversial "war-related" facilities in the state were the Japanese internment camps in southeastern Arkansas. Arkansas officials initially resisted the relocation of Japanese Americans from the west coast to Arkansas, a resistance based largely on racism and suspicion. The forced relocation of Japanese Americans, most of them American born, reflected widespread sentiment that they were loyal to the emperor of Japan and posed a potential military threat. But racism also lay behind the arguments that led to presidential order 9102 on March 18, 1942, calling for the removal of approximately 120,000 people of Japanese descent from the west coast to ten camps in seven interior states, principally in the west. Two camps were placed in Arkansas, one at Jerome, near Dermott, where 8,497 Japanese American families were interned; and the other at Rohwer, near McGehee, where a larger number, approximately 16,000, were incarcerated. The tax-delinquent lands had been acquired by the Farm Security Administration through a trust agreement with the state in the late 1930s. The undeveloped and heavily wooded land was poorly drained, and the FSA had wisely refrained from establishing communities there. In 1942 the War Relocation Board acquired it for the purpose of placing the Japanese Americans on it. Unenthusiastic about the establishment of the camps in Arkansas in the first place, Governor Adkins refused to allow Japanese Americans to be used as farm laborers, despite the fact that planters in eastern Arkansas wished to recruit them. Adkins also denied Japanese American children admission to the state's schools, rationalizing that it would place too great a burden on an already overextended school system. Not to be outdone by the governor, the legislature barred Japanese Americans from purchasing property in the state. That measure was later declared unconstitutional.

The Japanese American families relocated to Arkansas endured a wrenching separation from the world they knew on the west coast. Forced from their homes with only a forty-eight-hour notice, many of them sold houses and businesses for only a fraction of their worth. They lined up at train and bus stations and were transported to hastily constructed barracks behind barbed-wire fences in isolated locations. Although family units were maintained, life within the camps proved especially damaging to the traditional patriarchal structure and thoroughly demoralizing, particularly for the adults. Since the state refused to open its educational facilities to the children, schools were established within the camps, often with white teachers from the region. The curriculum was designed to promote their basic educational needs but with a special emphasis on civics and patriotism. Given the loosening of parental authority, many children found the camps to be a liberating experience, an irony of no small note. Four-year-old George Takei, perhaps the most famous internee in Arkansas, holds fond memories of playing with other children at the Rohwer internment camp, but his family's story illustrates both the problems faced by internees and the strength of character his parents exhibited. His father, a real estate salesman in Los Angeles before being interned, upon arrival in Arkansas was elected to the Camp Community Council as a barrack's representative. However, when filling out the "Statement of United States Citizen of Japanese Ancestry" required of all internees, both his parents answered "no" to question 28. The question required them to foreswear allegiance to the emperor of Japan and swear loyalty to the United States. Like many others, the Takeis felt no loyalty to the emperor and interpreted the question to imply otherwise. So many answered question 28 in the negative that a camp in Arizona was established for them at Tula Lake and the Takei's were transferred there.

A number of young men from the camps (274 from Rohwer and 52 from Jerome) found another way to establish their loyalty. They joined the 442nd Regimental Combat Team, a unit made up almost entirely of men of Japanese descent, and many of them distinguished themselves in combat. Although Ted Takayuki Tanouye was never himself in one of the internee camps, having joined the army before the executive order requiring removal of the Japanese Americans, his family was interned at Jerome and then at Rohrer after the former closed in June 1944. He rose to the rank of technical sergeant, was deployed to Italy in July 1944, and was awarded the Distinguished Service Cross for leading his platoon under hostile fire on July 7, 1944. He recovered from wounds he suffered that day only to die on September 6, 1944, of injuries resulting from an exploding land mine near San Mauro, Italy. His family, meanwhile, remained behind barbed wire in Arkansas. In 2000, after a review of those of Japanese ancestry who had received the Distinguished Service Cross, he was awarded the Congressional Medal of Honor, which was accepted by surviving members of his family.

Forced relocation and internment undermined the patriarchal structure in Japanese American families. Although not nearly so dramatic by comparison, the absence of male authority figures in other households in Arkansas, black and white, posed a challenge to the family and to society. Men, who left their wives and children behind in Arkansas, whether they went into the military or departed to seek employment in war industries, inadvertently brought about a profound social disruption that reverberated for years. Even if they stayed in Arkansas and moved their families to the towns or cities to work in munitions plants, for example, they contributed to overcrowding, which stretched housing and educational resources to the breaking point. Married women, who moved to town to work in war industries, to rejoin husbands, or simply because the absence of the family's breadwinner made living in a rural setting untenable, found it necessary to reestablish support networks in unfamiliar and often alien-seeming circumstances.

Women took the brunt of the home front disruption, often laboring under contradictory demands placed upon them. If they remained within the household and eschewed employment, they were expected to grow victory gardens, work in Red Cross dressing rooms, and assume other various and sundry duties associated with winning the war. They assumed these new obligations at the same time that they shouldered sole responsibility for maintaining the household and oversight of their children. Few resources existed to aid them. Women who chose to work—or who were forced to work given economic exigencies—were doubly burdened. The hostility toward women in the workforce that peaked during the Great Depression, a hostility based upon the often mistaken notion that women were taking jobs that men might have otherwise occupied, eased considerably during World War II but was by no means altogether absent. Given that it was desirable for women to contribute in some tangible way toward the war effort, certain jobs previously closed to women became available. Still, most women labored in unskilled or traditional clerical positions, and married women particularly found themselves the object of criticism for the lack of supervision over their children.

Although nationwide figures show that between 1940 and 1945 most women who entered the labor force were young and single, the percentage of married women working increased from 13.9 to 22.5 percent. Given that Arkansas was not as successful in securing industry during the war, the figures are probably less for the state. Nevertheless, juvenile delinquency rates rose sharply in Arkansas and, as historian Calvin Smith has noted, social workers, the press, and even the state legislature recognized it as a crisis in the family and often blamed working mothers for it. In fact, juvenile delinquency rates always increase during wartime—in the United States and across the world—and the problems are much more complex than the failure of mothers to supervise their children. Blaming working mothers for the problem reflects the continuing prejudice against married women in the workforce, a hangover from the Great Depression.

Regardless of its causes, increasing cases of juvenile delinquency and a sharp rise in venereal disease rates among young women preoccupied social workers and policy makers during World War II. Most of the experienced and more qualified social workers had departed for war or higher-paying jobs elsewhere, however, and analysis of the problem was often shallow and based on prejudice. A few instances of married women who flagrantly evaded their responsibilities to their children were used as evidence of a widespread trend. In fact, the problem was systemic and reflected a number of factors that should have been obvious. The absence of male authority figures, whether fathers, older brothers, or male teachers, certainly played a role. The preoccupation of married women—whether they worked or not—with a new set of responsibilities was also a factor. But the move to towns and cities introduced teenagers to new temptations, some of which could be fulfilled because of the availability of a variety jobs for them. Although many of them dutifully surrendered their earnings to their mothers (and fathers if they were present), others indulged in a variety of new pastimes, some of which presented them with certain new temptations leading to encounters with the law.

Increasing rates of venereal disease, particularly among young women who lived near military installations, also became a major preoccupation of health officials and policy makers. In some respects, this problem reflected the same circumstances that led to increasing rates of juvenile delinquency. The teenage girls had been transported to new urban settings and were no longer moored to church and family in the way they were before the war. They had spending money from jobs and came into contact with young military men on their way to war and possible death. The romance and excitement of it all was more than many could resist. Although it was clear that the presence of so many young men in military installations was the main contributor to the problem of venereal disease, an issue that the military itself was concerned with for its own reasons, the state focused, perhaps appropriately, on its impact on the civilian female population.

The state of Arkansas responded by attempting to enact legislation meant to strengthen the family. The measures they pursued appear to be a rather round-about way of addressing some very immediate problems, but the state was not accustomed to being involved in legislating social behavior. It did, however, have authority over marriage and divorce laws, and that is where their attention focused. The first bills to appear involved an effort to eliminate the "90-day divorce" and to require waiting periods and physical examinations before issuing marriage licenses. The divorce law had been passed in 1931 providing for a ninety-day residency, possibly in an effort to capitalize on the market for the lucrative divorce business, something that Hot Springs subsequently became particularly notorious for. Although evidence suggested that a large percentage of the divorces were secured by temporary transplants, particularly from border states, lawmakers pursued, without success, measures to revoke it. A Little Rock legislator, meanwhile, introduced a bill requiring physical and mental examinations fifteen days prior to applications for marriage licenses. This measure also failed to pass. Closer to the issue of juvenile delinquency, perhaps, was an effort to raise the legal age of marriage, a measure meant to discourage premarital sex and, presumably, venereal disease. The only measure to pass was one meant to prevent "gin marriages" (those contracted while the parties were intoxicated) by imposing a three-day waiting period prior to issuance of a marriage license, but county court clerks were allowed to waive the requirement on an individual basis so its effectiveness was questionable.

In the final analysis, nothing the legislature considered—or possibly could have considered—truly addressed the issues facing the family structure during the war. Once the war was over, the public and lawmakers no longer concerned themselves with such matters. Women, whether married or not and whether they wanted to or not, were forced from the workplace and back into households; and children and teenagers were subjected to greater supervision by male authority figures whether at home or in school. Calvin Smith suggests, however, that the patriarchal structure was not fully restored and the postwar period would witness the further erosion of the traditional family. Certainly growing opportunities for women and teenagers in the workforce, a trend that actually began much earlier in the century in accordance with the demands of the growing consumer society, set in motion forces that could not be turned back by legislative edict.

Arkansas on the Battlefields

Arkansas men who fought in World War II expressed concerns for the hardships worked on their families back home, but they were frequently more preoccupied by their own issues. The 194,645 Arkansans who fought in the war served in every branch of the military and in virtually every theater of war. They held the ground in the Aleutian Islands in Alaska against an attempt by the Japanese to establish staging areas there which they might have used to launch attacks on the United States. Others from the state joined battle on the Pacific Islands like Okinawa and Iwo Jima as the American Navy led the drive toward the Japanese homeland. Still others landed in North Africa and on the beaches of Normandy, fighting and, too often, dying in the war against Italy and Germany. In the end, 3,519 Arkansans lost their lives. Many were highly decorated for courage under fire and for significant contributions to the war effort. Eight Arkansas men won the Congressional Medal of Honor (MOH), counting one who enlisted in Michigan after failing his physical exam in Arkansas. They included four graduates of the University of Arkansas: Maurice "Footsie" Britt, Nathan Green Gordon, Edgar Harold Loyd, and Seymour W. Terry. Two of the four would survive the war, return to the state, and become prominent in Arkansas society and politics. Nathan Green Gordon, a navy pilot, won his MOH for risking his life under enemy fire in a daring air-sea rescue in a harbor off Papua, New Guinea, on February 15, 1944. A native of Morrilton (Conway County), he entered politics after the war and became the longest-running lieutenant governor in the history of the state, serving from 1947 to 1967. His successor in that political position was none other than Footsie Britt, a fellow student at the university and also a winner of the Medal of Honor. While serving as an officer in the Third Infantry Division, Britt participated in the battle to take Rome and was awarded the MOH for his heroism on November 10, 1943. He saved his battalion from certain defeat by taking a small unit of men into an intense firefight and in a close combat situation repulsed a determined force of Germans. Britt returned to Fort Smith (Sebastian County) after the war and went on to have a distinguished career in business and politics, serving two terms as lieutenant governor.

Two other University of Arkansas graduates who won the Medal of Honor died in different theaters of the war, one in France fighting the Germans and the other in Okinawa fighting the Japanese. Second Lt. Edgar Harold Loyd, a Mississippi County native, was serving as a rifle platoon leader under Patton's Third Army and was scheduled to receive the medal for heroism he exhibited during a battle to expel the Germans from the Moselle River in France in September 1944. Before he could receive the award, however, he was killed by sniper fire near Limey, France, on November 16, 1944. The final university recipient of the medal, 1st Lt. Seymour W. Terry from Little Rock (Pulaski County), was cited for bravery for conducting an assault under heavy enemy fire during the battle to take Zebra Hill on Okinawa on March 6, 1944. He died two days later of his injuries and was subsequently promoted to captain and posthumously awarded the Medal of Honor.

The other winners of the military's highest award were more typical of the Arkansas demographic. Jack Williams of Harrison (Boone County), graduated high school and bypassed a college education to enlist in the navy. He became a pharmacist mate first class and was killed in action in the battle to take Iwo Jima on March 3, 1945. Under heavy fire, Williams had gone to the aid of a seriously injured man, shielding the soldier's body with his own as enemy fire rained down. Although Williams himself was shot, he paused only long enough to dress his own wounds, and then continued to doctor others hit by gunfire. He was returning to the rear to seek treatment of his injuries when he was killed by sniper fire. James R. Hendrix was the son of a sharecropper from Lepanto (Poinsett County), who was drafted into the army at age eighteen. He was serving with Patton's Third Army as a private in Assenois, Belgium, during the Battle of the Bulge when he displayed acts of heroism—capturing two German artillery gun crews, rescuing a comrade from a burning vehicle, and holding off enemy fire enabling others to pull other wounded Americans to safety—which won him the MOH. His unit was attempting to reach Bastogne, a besieged garrison under heavy attack, a garrison famous for having played a crucial role in stopping the German's last desperate offensive against the Allied advance toward Berlin. William H. Thomas of Wynne (Cross County), was working on his father's farm when the war broke out. He was initially rejected for service because of a heart defect, but he was determined to serve so went Ypsilanti, Michigan, where he enlisted in 1944. A private first class, he died of wounds suffered in a battle to retake the Philippines on April 22, 1945. Finally, William Watson, who apparently moved with his family to Arkansas from Alabama as a child, had only seven years of grade school and worked on his father's farm until he enlisted in the marines in 1942. He was shot seven times during a battle on Iwo Jima, February 26–27, 1945, died of his wounds, and was posthumously awarded the Medal of Honor.

Another Arkansan, Paul Page Douglas Jr. of Paragould (Greene County), was twice recommended for the Medal of Honor. A fighter pilot who helped develop tactical strategies connected to the Republic P-47 Thunderbolt fighter plane, Douglas won the Distinguished Service Cross for his heroism in destroying German V-1 rockets aimed at England during the fall 1944 blitz. Two other Arkansans were also recognized for their service to the country: Charles "Savvy" Cooke from Fort Smith and Corydon McAlmont Wassell from Little Rock. Cooke was a University of Arkansas and Naval Academy graduate (1910) who received the Distinguished Service Medal for developing the two-ocean naval strategy during the war. Corydon Wassell was one of the first Americans during World War II to receive hero status after he refused to leave his severely injured men upon the evacuation of Java in the Netherlands, East Indies (now Indonesia), in the spring of 1942. A physician, he managed to move his patients to safety by convincing a British army convoy to transport them 150 miles over jungle roads to the coast where he persuaded the captain of a Dutch ship to take them to Australia. He received the Navy Cross and was made famous in a 1944 movie—*The Story of Dr. Wassell*—starring Gary Cooper.

Winners of medals for heroism would be the first to say that many of their comrades-in-arms deserved recognition for their own heroism and sacrifice. Few who served in World War II became famous or received much attention for their valorous service. Among those who endured a particularly grueling war were the members of the 206th Coast Artillery of the Arkansas National Guard, units attached to Arkansas Tech University in Russellville. They had been federalized in August 1941, four months before the Japanese attack on Pearl Harbor, and by early January 1942 they were preparing to depart for training at Fort Bliss, Texas. Among the 104 young men were "twenty-five members of the football team . . . every basketball letter man but one" and "the entire track team." They also included "eleven of 14 student councilmen and the president of the study body." The president of the university hosted a farewell dinner, followed by a heavily attended dance at which the Choral Club sang "God Bless America" in their honor. Like many such young men, they expected to do battle against the nation's foes, but after a year's training in Texas, they were sent to Dutch Harbor on Amaknak Island in Alaska. Their duty was to hold the island against a Japanese advance. Aside from bombing raids by the Japanese in 1942, however, the worst aspect of service there for the Arkansans was the weather. The average annual temperature was 38 degrees (F) and even in summer could dip to a low of 30 degrees. The sky was almost always overcast, the fog omnipresent, the winter days short, and the nights long. It also rained constantly with an average of 250 rainy days per year, the most of any location in the United States. A freakish weather phenomenon called "williwaw" further complicated life there. According to Donald M. Goldstein and Katherine V. Dillon, authors of *The*

Williwaw War, the men of the 206th "fought blinding, waist deep snow; sleet that struck as from a sandblaster; fogs so thick and persistent that fliers claimed it was clear enough for takeoff if they could see their copilots; the williwaw, that incredible wind that seemed to blow from every direction at once, and that blew away anything not fastened down." Three members of the 206th died of exposure within days of their arrival. They endured a harsh existence in a cruel environment that nothing in their lives had prepared them for. Their Arkansas backgrounds hardly conditioned them for the climate, and their training in the National Guard and later at Fort Bliss had equipped them for battle, not for boredom and the bitter, bleak existence at Dutch Harbor.

Arkansas women who served in the armed services during the war endured neither the ordeal of the Aleutian Islands nor the danger of the battlefield. Like other female enlistees, they were banned from armed combat and were initially restricted to non-combat zones. They often faced the derision of some of the public and even, occasionally, the media, presumably because of their temerity in assuming a male prerogative. At first regular army enlistment was not open to women. Instead, military authorities, recognizing the need, consented to the creation of the Women's Auxiliary Army Corps (WAAC). There, women performed essential functions that allowed male military members to redeploy to combat zones. In July 1, 1943, however, the Women's Army Corps (WAC) was created as part of the regular army, and some of these women found themselves in harm's way. Among them was Lucille Babcock of Little Rock, who was deployed to Italy and the Middle East. She was injured while driving her ambulance, which was overturned when a German "screaming Mimi" landed close by. But most Arkansans became more familiar with the home-front activities of the Women's Auxiliary Army Corps, which eventually opened several recruitment facilities and performed duties at a variety of training camps around the state. They worked in the Pine Bluff Arsenal; they performed clerical tasks thus freeing men for overseas duty; and when the military, in desperate need of men, began accepting illiterates, the WAACs also became tutors to bring the men up to a minimal standard of literacy.

Women's Auxiliary Army Corps: An organization that allowed women to take on clerical and other tasks so that military men could be deployed overseas.

Whether male or female, whether on the front lines fighting the enemy or serving in some other important way, the men and women of the armed services were being exposed to different worlds and vastly varying experiences that altered their perspectives and, in many cases, transformed them into different people. Some young men came back from the war ready to challenge the political establishment. Many women enjoyed new freedoms during the war that they were loath to give up. And African Americans believed they had earned the right to full citizenship. White citizens, however, remained devoted to the idea of white supremacy, and both those in uniform and those on the home front believed that *they* had earned the right to a continuation of that particular status quo. This would lead to confrontations and challenges during and after the war.

Civil Rights Activism

Like blacks elsewhere in the United States, African Americans in Arkansas believed they were fighting two wars, one against fascism abroad and another against racism at home. They referred to it as the "Double V" campaign and believed that the sacrifices they made during the war would establish their rights to full citizenship. African Americans contributed heavily to the Red Cross and War Bond drives, and they participated in the campaign to collect scrap metal. Many joined the military or were drafted, particularly after A. Philips Randolph, a black activist on the national level, lobbied the president to make certain that blacks were drafted according to their percentage of the population. He had observed that white planters in the South were using their control over the local selective service offices to maintain a plentiful supply of black labor. Randolph understood this control over the draft as another means by which southern planters exercised their hegemony over African Americans, the most impoverished and vulnerable population of laborers in the South. The edict establishing a rubric that made certain that African Americans drafted at a representative rate provided an avenue of escape from a life of toil and servitude. In June 1941, President Roosevelt issued Executive Order 8802, which stipulated that there was to be no discrimination of employment in industries securing government contracts, provided another escape route for African Americans, one that beckoned them to war industries in southern, northern, and western cities.

Executive Order 8802: An order issued by Pres. Franklin Roosevelt in 1942 forbidding discrimination of employment by defense industries.

Even before the war began, a new generation of black leaders in Arkansas pressed for a more assertive campaign for black rights. Harold Flowers, an attorney in Pine Bluff, formed the Committee on Negro Organizations (CNO) in 1940 to bring black organizations in Arkansas together to challenge the white-only policy of the state's Democratic Party. He had grown particularly impatient with the failure of Dr. John Robinson's organization, the Arkansas Negro Democratic Association (ANDA), to rebound from its defeat in 1930 when the Arkansas Supreme Court ruled against Robinson in the case he had filed against the white primary in 1928. In 1942, ANDA renewed its efforts and appealed to U.S. attorney general Francis Biddle to intercede on their behalf and rule the white primary illegal. When Attorney General Biddle rebuffed ANDA's 1942 appeal, its members attempted to vote in that year's election. Though unsuccessful in that effort, they did not have long to wait for justice. Black Texans—with the help of NAACP attorneys—had taken their case to the Supreme Court, which ruled in *Smith v. Allwright* in 1944 that the white primary violated the Fifteenth Amendment. Governor Adkins, angered by the decision, charged that it usurped states' rights, and he encouraged other southern governors to challenge it. Democratic Party officials across the South implemented measures

Arkansas Negro Democratic Association: Founded in 1928 in an unsuccessful attempt to overturn the use of the White Primary, which kept blacks from voting in primary elections.

designed to continue limiting black voting and officeholding. For example, black voters were hampered by a new invention, the double primary. They were allowed to vote in a special primary election held to select federal officeholders but continued to be barred from that held for state offices.

Perhaps it was evidence of interest and activity in Arkansas that inspired the NAACP to come to the support of a lawsuit initiated in 1942, a lawsuit inspired by the efforts of black educators in Little Rock to equalize the salaries of black teachers with those of white teachers. The Little Rock Classroom Teachers Association (CTA), which was an affiliate of the Arkansas Teachers Association (ATA), a statewide black teachers' organization, had appealed to the white school board in the spring of 1942 requesting that they equalize salaries. When the board refused their request, black teachers and principals assembled and agreed unanimously to approach the NAACP to secure their support in bringing a lawsuit against the school board. The association sent Thurgood Marshall to Arkansas to assist in the case. Marshall was destined to play a crucial role in the 1954 *Brown v. Board of Education* decision and to become the first black on the United States Supreme Court, but in 1942 he was a relatively young attorney, eager to be of assistance but willing to allow black attorneys in Little Rock to take the lead: J. R. Booker, Myles Hibbler, and Scipio Jones, the attorney who had represented the Elaine Twelve in 1919. It was the last case the old warrior would take on. Jones died in 1943. Sue Morris (aka Sue Cowan Williams), who was chair of the English department at Dunbar High, served as the complainant in the suit. Unfortunately for the case and for Morris personally, the U.S. District Court ruled against the black teachers in the fall of 1942, and Sue Morris was fired from her position at the end of the 1942–1943 school year. John H. Lewis, the principal of Dunbar High School, who testified in court that the salaries were unfair, was asked to resign.

Little Rock Classroom Teachers Association: An organization of black schoolteachers that filed a lawsuit against the Little Rock School Board for equalization of black and white teacher salaries in 1942.

The CTA and the NAACP appealed the case to the U.S. Eighth Circuit Court of Appeals in the fall of 1943. In June 1945 the Eighth Circuit overturned the decision and ordered Little Rock to equalize the salaries of black teachers, but the school board merely established a complicated new formula for calculating raises for the city's teachers. Part of that formula involved an evaluation of the colleges the teachers had secured their degrees from. Under the rubric, no black college, regardless of reputation, was highly rated. Since African Americans were routinely barred from attending white colleges in the South, the rubric clearly discriminated against them. Meanwhile, John Lewis became president of Philander Smith College in Little Rock until 1944 when he moved to Wilberforce, Ohio, to become the dean of the School of Theology attached to Wilberforce University. He never returned to Arkansas. Sue Morris secured a job in the Pine Bluff Arsenal after she was fired and then had to turn to domestic work in the postwar period. She was reinstated in 1952, but only after she wrote a letter of apology for having filed the suit.

Among those who championed Sue Morris's suit was L. C. Bates, publisher of the *State Press*, a black newspaper in Little Rock. Trained as a journalist, L. C. Bates had worked for newspapers in California, Colorado, Missouri, and Tennessee before coming to Arkansas to sell insurance. He longed to return to the newspaper business, however, and understood that if he owned his own newspaper he would be able to advocate freely for equal opportunity for African Americans. In 1941 L. C. and Daisy Bates invested their savings and purchased the *Twin City Press*, a black newspaper in Little Rock, which they renamed the *Arkansas State Press,* and began immediately to write editorials covering a wide range of issues confronting blacks. He decried discrimination in employment, police brutality against blacks, and the white primary system; and he called for repeal of the poll tax.

Between 1942 and 1945, Bates ran stories on the suit against the Little Rock School Board as it made its way from the lower courts to the Eighth Circuit, and reported extensively on other matters of concern to Arkansas's black citizens. When a black serviceman was beaten to death by a white police officer on Ninth Street in Little Rock on March 22, 1942, L. C. Bates wrote strong editorials, calling for a federal investigation after the police officer was acquitted. A federal grand jury convened but failed to indict him. Still, Little Rock authorities were forced to address the situation and assigned eight black officers to Ninth Street. Although it was a meager victory given the gravity of the offense, it energized the young activists. Bates had also championed Harold Flowers's efforts and that of ANDA in restarting the long struggle over the White Primary. Indeed, Bates and his wife, Daisy, would become leaders in a new faction of black civil rights activists in Arkansas. Weary of the status quo and energized after the war by returning black veterans, these black activists would play a crucial role in the civil rights movement that was soon to emerge.

Postwar Civil Rights

Just as civil rights activism did not begin during World War II, it did not end there either. As in other matters, the war provided activists with a new energy and enthusiasm, partly because African Americans made significant contributions to the war effort and expected to be rewarded for it. Daisy Bates would become the most famous of Arkansas activists in the postwar period, though her husband had the larger profile during and immediately after the war years. In 1946, however, while her husband was away on a trip and she was in charge of the newspaper, she wrote a highly critical article after a black picket was killed during a strike called by his CIO Union at the Southern Cotton Oil Mill in Little Rock. The historian Grif Stockley summarized the circumstances as follows: "In typical southern fashion, after a [black] picket named Walter Campbell was killed by his replacement, three other [black] pickets were arrested and found guilty of violating Arkansas's Anti-Labor Violence Law passed in 1943 and sentenced to a year's imprisonment." L. C. reviewed the story Daisy wrote about the convictions after his return to Little Rock, and although he had misgiving about it, he endorsed its publi-

L. C. and Daisy Bates with Hugh Patterson, publisher, *Arkansas Gazette.* The Theta Sigma chapter of Sigma Gamma Rho Sorority was honoring L. C. Bates at the Camelot Inn in Little Rock on February 19, 1977. *Daisy Bates Collection, Photograph no. 21, Special Collections Division, University of Arkansas Libraries, Fayetteville.*

cation. The article focused on Judge Lawrence C. Auten's charge to the jury "that the pickets could be found guilty if they aided or assisted, or just stood idly by while violence occurred." The judge, who was unused to criticism of any sort, bristled at the temerity of the black press and had both L. C. and Daisy arrested. Initially allowed to post bond after being fingerprinted and photographed, they secured the services of the CIO union's attorneys and returned to court on April 29 when they were sentenced to a $100 fine and ten days in jail. When Judge Auten denied them bail, the union's attorneys took the case to the state supreme court the same day and secured their release. The Bateses then filed an appeal of their conviction and in November the state's highest court exonerated them, citing freedom of the press.

The charged atmosphere that prevailed during the war clearly continued into the postwar period. There were limits, however, to which the state's politicians and citizens were willing to go. Some returning veterans fueled a challenge to the status quo, both in politics and in civil rights, but others had a greater desire to a return to normalcy. With only one notable exception—Gov. Sidney Sanders McMath (1948–1952)—the men who occupied the governorship clung to white supremacy ideology. Gov. Homer Adkins played a major role in challenging the *Smith v. Allwright* decision regarding the White Primary and encouraged the Arkansas legislature to establish the double primary. His successor, Benjamin Travis Laney Jr., elected governor in 1945, played an even higher-profile role in the effort to shore up black disfranchisement. Although Laney recognized that blacks had been unfairly treated and personally believed that changes would come, he was convinced they should evolve slowly and from within the South. When Pres. Harry Truman, in response to a report by his Civil Rights Committee, declared his support for an end to the poll tax, Laney and other southern governors screamed "states' rights," a term that became synonymous with maintaining the white supremacy status quo in the South. They were equally opposed to a federal statute against lynching, which would have allowed federal officers and courts to prosecute such extralegal mob actions. Governor Laney professed to understand the dark side of racial subordination of blacks in the South and said he regretted it, but he was unwilling to support any federal measures designed to remedy the situation, and he became so prominent among states' rights southern Democrats that they named him the national chairman of the Dixiecrat Party (States Rights Democratic Party). Southern politicians who opposed Truman in the 1948 presidential election were the architects of the new party. Although Laney's loyalty to the Democratic Party ran deep enough to trouble him about bolting to a third party, he became the permanent chairman of the Dixiecrats.

Meanwhile, a young marine veteran in Hot Springs was positioning himself to challenge the state's Democratic machine. Sidney McMath, who led what has come to be known as the "GI Revolt" in Garland County in 1946, would defy Laney's political ascendancy and offer an alternative position on race. He began in Hot Springs by confronting the corrupt Leo McLaughlin political machine in local elections, winning the office of prosecuting attorney, and thus positioning himself for a run for the governor's office two years later. He became the Democratic Party's nominee for the governor's office in 1948, defeating Laney in an almost unprecedented run for a third term in the party primary. Even as Laney assumed the leadership of the Dixiecrat Party south wide, he would not be able to convince Arkansans to vote anything but a Democratic ticket. Indeed, McMath is credited with keeping the state safe for the Democrats while four other southern states—South Carolina, Mississippi, Alabama, and Louisiana—voted the Dixiecrat ticket. Although he was a racial progressive—according to the standards of the time—who was a strong supporter of Pres. Harry Truman's civil rights agenda, McMath stopped short of supporting a federal antilynching law. Bowing to the states' rights arguments against it, he advocated passage of a state antilynching law. Nevertheless, he broke with precedent and appointed blacks to positions on boards and commissions that had always been the preserve of whites alone. He championed the repeal of the poll tax, and he attempted to equalize school funding. See plate 40 following page 366.

While white politicians were engaged in a struggle for power that often only peripherally involved the issue of civil rights, African American activists seized opportunities to move forward in this period. Silas Hunt, a native of Ashdown, Arkansas, became a pioneer in the integration of higher education in the state in 1948. He had excelled as a student at Booker T. Washington High School in Texarkana, serving as president of the student council and graduating as class salutatorian. He attended Arkansas Agricultural and Normal College in Pine Bluff (now the University of Arkansas at Pine Bluff) until he was drafted in 1942. While serving with the construction engineers during the Battle of the Bulge, he suffered wounds that would shorten his life. But he survived the war, returned to Pine Bluff, and finished his degree in English in 1947. Coincidentally, he became acquainted, possibly before he left for the war, with a young woman graduate of the college destined to blaze a trail in Oklahoma civil rights history. Ada Sipuel had completed her education and in 1946 applied for admission to the University of Oklahoma School of Law. When they denied her admission, she took her case to the U.S. Supreme Court, winning an important concession in 1948 when the nation's highest court ordered the state to provide her with a legal education equal to that offered to white students. When the state of Oklahoma hastily created a separate law school, one that could not possibly offer the same level of education, she again took her case to the Supreme Court, finally winning admittance in 1949.

Even as Ada Sipuel was in the midst of her struggle with the state of Oklahoma, Silas Hunt was completing his studies at AM&N. While there he made the acquaintance of Wiley Branton, a fellow student who was also destined to become an important civil rights figure in Arkansas. His key introduction, however, was to Harold Flowers, who had already established himself as a force to be reckoned with. Upon approaching graduation, Hunt began the process of applying to law schools, including the University of Arkansas School of Law in Fayetteville. On February 2, 1948, Hunt, Flowers, Branton, and an AM&N photographer, Geleve Grice, drove from Pine Bluff to Fayetteville with a single purpose in mind. They had watched with interest as the Sipuel case was making its way through the court system, and they had read with enthusiasm the announcement made on January 30 that the University of Arkansas would admit qualified black applicants. University officials, particularly the law school's dean, Robert Leflar, had observed the Supreme Court decisions in cases involving other states—such as the Sipuel case in Oklahoma—and understood that segregation at the graduate and professional school level was being successfully challenged. Leflar believed that such segregation was indefensible and worked to convince the board of trustees, an effort that resulted in the stunning announcement on January 30, 1948. When Hunt and his cohort appeared at the law school, Leflar reviewed his application personally and admitted him immediately. Although Hunt's classes were held in a basement room separate from white students, three to five white students elected to attend classes in the basement with him. He was not allowed to eat in the all-white cafeteria and was assigned a special study area in the library. He endured some harassment while on campus and according to George Haley, who later graduated from the law school, an automobile driver attempted to run Hunt down on the edge of campus.

Tragically, Silas Hunt was unable to complete his studies because of illness. He developed tuberculosis and was hospitalized at the Veterans Hospital in Springfield, Missouri, where he died on April 22, 1949. It was widely believed that his illness was complicated by wounds he suffered at the Battle of the Bulge. Jackie L. Shropshire, a graduate of Little Rock's Dunbar High School, entered the university's law school in the fall of 1948 and became the first African American to graduate in 1951. George Haley, brother to *Roots* author Alex Haley, was soon to follow.

Another civil rights pioneer, Edith Mae Irby, also made her appearance in Arkansas in 1948 when she integrated the University of Arkansas Medical School. Irby arrived in Little Rock on the day she was scheduled to register with little more than the funds she thought sufficient to pay her tuition and registration. Perhaps this was unwise, the hubris of the young, but she was fired by the determination to study medicine, a goal that originated with the death of an older sister when both were children. Edith Mae had nursed her sister, who was suffering from typhoid fever, and it left a lasting impression. Her sister's sickness and death had painfully revealed to her that African Americans too often had insufficient medical care, and she wanted to remedy that situation. The experience also left her with an insatiable desire to understand disease, a desire she began to fulfill in her high school studies. However, further disruption intervened when her father died after being thrown from a horse—another reminder of the inadequate medical facilities available to African Americans. The planter for whom he worked evicted the family, and they moved to Hot Springs to live with her maternal grandmother where Edith was eventually able to earn a high school diploma. Her mother found employment as a domestic in the city's hotels, and though she helped as much as she was able, Edith had to work her way through college. She graduated Knoxville College (a black private college in Tennessee) in 1947, returned to her home in Hot Springs, and applied to twelve medical colleges, including Arkansas's medical school, knowing it would be difficult to gain admission but hoping to stay in Arkansas for her medical school education. In order to increase her chances of success, she enrolled in two classes at the University of Chicago that summer. It was there that she learned she had been accepted into Arkansas's medical college from a *Time* magazine reporter who wanted her reaction.

Irby and her family were excited about the opportunity, and the black community in Hot Springs raised funds to help pay her tuition. Housing had been lined up for her in Little Rock, and she intended to find a job to help defray her living expenses. When she reached Little Rock, however, she discovered she was just shy of the amount necessary to register. Having been told by friends that if she needed help she should contact Daisy Bates, Irby found her at the *State Press*, secured the necessary funds, and paid her registration fees just in time to meet the deadline. Bates, however, went even further. Ascertaining that Irby's financial situation was fragile, Bates collected funds from various NAACP chapters around the state to support Irby's education. There began Irby's association with that organization, one that was deepened when she married James B. Jones, a professor at the University of Arkansas Mechanical and Normal College in Pine Bluff, a dedicated member of the local chapter of the NAACP. Like Silas Hunt, Edith

Mae Irby initially endured semi-segregated conditions although not in the classroom but in the library and cafeteria where black staff members set her table elegantly and decorated it with flowers. She successfully completed her medical school education and returned to Hot Springs to open a practice in 1952.

African Americans had struggled for civil rights long before World War II, but their enlistment in the military, their employment in war industries, and their contribution to the war effort in a number of other ways inspired a new generation of activists. Many, like Harold Flowers and L. C. and Daisy Bates, were poised even before the war to take the campaign for an end to disfranchisement and segregation to the next level. The war provided a kind of incubator, one in which the status quo in the state was challenged on a variety of levels. African American activists marched into the postwar years ready to do battle, and those in Little Rock found a ready audience in the new transplants moving to the city because of the transformation of agriculture. The rise of scientific agriculture was accompanied by a depopulation of the countryside, and many thousands of African Americans flocked to the state's capital city.

Transformation in Agriculture

Scientific agriculture: A term used to describe the capital-intensive agricultural enterprise that uses machines and chemicals and that arose in the South in the post–World War II period.

Policy makers during World War II began to predict the rise of "scientific agriculture"; that is, the development of agricultural processes that would involve mechanization and the use of chemicals, processes that would result in a dramatic reduction in the need for farm labor. While they foresaw this major reorganization of agriculture in the postwar period, they failed to fully anticipate the social and economic implications. A Post War Planning Commission, operating out of Washington, D.C., during the war, established state and local postwar planning committees, which reported their opinions about the direction that agriculture would take after the war. Although there was some disagreement, they generally concurred that farms would increase in size and that mechanization and the use of new chemicals (fertilizers, pesticides, etc.) would play an important role in making agriculture a far more capital-intensive enterprise. They foresaw that the need for farm labor, particularly in southern states like Arkansas, would decline dramatically. They understood that there would be an inevitable demographic shift, but refrained from suggesting policies that might have addressed the social and economic consequences of that shift. Arkansas planters and farmers were well represented on the postwar planning committees and believed that such consequences should take their natural course and be dealt with as they presented themselves.

The herald of change came in the form of a cumbersome-looking machine. Although planters in eastern Arkansas had experimented with mechanical cotton harvesters in the 1930s, the labor surplus that resulted from the evictions of tenants and sharecroppers because of the AAA program served as a disincentive to an abandonment

Three 2-row mechanical cotton pickers in a field, from back cover of brochure, "Where Agriculture and Industry Mean Business." *Lee Wilson & company Archives (MC1289). Special Collections Division, University of Arkansas Libraries, Fayetteville.*

of their traditional means of harvesting the crop. Labor was still cheap and the mechanical pickers being marketed seemed an unnecessary expense. In addition, as historian James Street argues, the mechanization of the cotton crop awaited the mass production of a marketable machine and that did not occur until after World War II. Even though the first dozen mechanical cotton pickers rolled off International Harvester's assembly line in 1943, the transition occurred slowly. The trash the new pickers stripped from the cotton stalks gummed up the gin works and caused costly delays. The old gins simply could not do a satisfactory job of removing the additional debris that the mechanical cotton harvesters necessarily produced. Cotton gins had to be retooled or new ones constructed in order to more adequately process machine-picked cotton.

While the new cotton gins solved the problems of debris-laden machine-picked cotton, another problem had to be overcome before full mechanization could occur. The labor of picking the cotton—whether by machines or humans—was only one part of the process. Until chemicals could be developed to cut down on the growth of weeds, a two-stage process of "chopping" the cotton had to be employed. In the first stage, usually during May and June, teams of cotton choppers walked the rows with hoes in hand and thinned the cotton to promote the healthy growth of plants that would produce an ample number of cotton bolls. Later in the summer, usually in July, a second stage of chopping took place when weeds were removed. No matter how many mechanical cotton harvesters planters purchased, until the development of weed-killing chemicals, they would still have to recruit labor to chop the cotton.

Finally, in order to embrace scientific agriculture, planters had to overcome an institutional constraint. They had to abandon the use of mules and invest in tractors. The purchase of tractors had been growing in the South since the New Deal when AAA programs funneled cash into the hands of planters and introduced them to new crops, like soybeans, that required mechanical harvesters. Mule power was insufficient to pull these new-fangled harvesters but with a labor surplus developing because of the dispossession of tenants and sharecroppers, there was little incentive for a full-scale transition to tractors. Besides, the breeding and marketing of mules had a long tradition in Arkansas, and many planters had not only invested heavily in the animals but also in the barns and equipment that were essential to their care and use. For small landowners and those tenants who remained on the land, mules and implements served as collateral for loans that kept them in business, reflecting established networks of finance and commerce. There was also a cultural attachment to mules that, by modern standards, seems almost inexplicable. Songs and stories of the stubborn and cantankerous mule abounded in the folklore of the South. Given the cultural and other constraints involved in the transition to tractors and thus mechanized agriculture, it is no wonder that Arkansas planters and farmers would be slow to fully embrace scientific agriculture.

Perhaps the most revolutionary aspect of the transformation in agriculture was its impact on farm labor. The transition to capital-intensive agriculture put additional stress on the sharecropping and tenancy system. The tenancy system had been undergoing challenges since the mass evictions stimulated by New Deal programs, but it was World War II that sounded its death knell. As sharecroppers and tenants abandoned the plantations to work in war industries or enlist in the military, POWs and Mexican nationals took their places. At the war's end, many sharecroppers and tenants were neither inclined nor encouraged to return to the countryside. The promise of jobs in the industrial sector in the north and on the west coast provided them with economic opportunities undreamed of at home in Arkansas. Meanwhile, other young men who in another age might have been interested in purchasing their own farms were more attracted to different career paths, in part because the GI Bill offered them college educations that were not designed to prepare them for farmwork. And even had they been interested in farming as a livelihood, the price of land was rising in tandem with the cost of the expensive new machinery, and government loan programs were not sufficient to provide them with the opportunity to purchase land. With the Post War Planning Commission reporting that the small farm was not going to be cost effective in the future, they promulgated very tight loan policies that were designed to discourage applications from veterans.

America's entry into a conflict in Korean in 1950 provided an opportunity for planters and farmers to place their labor needs into the context of yet another national emergency. While most Arkansans were riveted by the news of war and worried because Arkansas National Guard units were being called up for service, planters were pleased when President Truman established a commission on migratory labor to address the needs of agriculturalists. The commission held hearings across the country and heard from no fewer than sixty-six farmworkers and labor representatives who urged a cessation of the Bracero program, arguing that a sufficient supply of domestic farm labor existed. George Stith, a former STFU member from Arkansas who became a vice president of the National Farm Labor Union, an affiliate of the American Federation of Labor, argued that the Bracero program, which had the effect of reducing the cost of labor, would ensure the continued unemployment and underemployment of native southerners. There is probably some truth to his claims, but he was preaching to the wrong choir. Reducing the cost of labor probably seemed a good idea to policy makers, and the Department of Agriculture persisted in its support of the Bracero program. One advantage of the presence of the Mexicans in small towns throughout the state was that it enabled many small merchants to remain in business, even as much of the long-established rural population departed the region. With their traditional customers gone, many business people hired bilingual clerks to handle the Saturday trade with the Mexicans.

Agricultural communities in Arkansas began to face the consequences of mechanization and scientific agriculture by the late 1940s and early 1950s. Small-town merchants were particularly hard hit as farm laborers—the most crucial element of their clientele—began to move away to other opportunities. Business leaders began to cast about for ways to maintain a population sufficient to keep their towns alive, but plantation owners, skittish about their unpredictable labor needs given the uneven transition to mechanized agriculture, were either ambivalent about or downright hostile to these plans. In any case, it proved to be somewhat difficult to convince manufacturers to take a risk on Arkansas. The owners of these operations needed not only a sufficient supply of labor but also good roads that would provide an adequate transportation network. Town leaders and Arkansas legislators championed the development of a better highway system, but this merely took many customers away from small towns to larger towns where a wider variety of stores provided a more diverse array of items. Later, the newly emerging "big box" stores offered cheaper goods that also drained customers away from small towns. To add insult to injury, many plants that settled in small towns remained only a short while and moved further south in search of cheaper labor within a decade. It was a complicated and intractable problem that defied easy solution, but small-town boosters placed their hopes on industrial development, and they elected men to office who promulgated policies meant to promote it.

Economic Changes in the Early Postwar Period

While the agricultural sector was undergoing a dramatic transformation, the state's governors were working their own small revolution in the reorganization of Arkansas's administrative apparatus and its orientation to business and finance. Governor Laney, characterized by historians as a throwback to the progressive-era business governors, such as McRae, inherited the office after a period of considerable upheaval and transformation in the state. The demographic shifts that accelerated during World War II necessitated changes in the way the state carried on its business, and Laney was determined to make government more efficient. Thus a measure he presented to the legislature in February 1945 was designed to create a single general fund and consolidate agencies with overlapping responsibilities. He planned to pay off the state's non-highway debt, and at the same time reduce taxes. Buried within his package was also a deficit-spending prohibition that became a permanent fixture in Arkansas government. The main features of the Revenue Stabilization Act remain intact today. Prior to the act, the state deposited funds into over one hundred separate accounts, making it all but impossible to shift money when necessary. With a single general fund, the state could carry on its routine business in a much more efficient manner. Another strategy for ensuring efficiency involved consolidation of a number of agencies into new boards or commissions having broader responsibilities. For example, the Corporation Commission and the Utilities Commission were consolidated into the Public Service Commission. Ten existing boards and commissions were reorganized under the new Fiscal Control Board.

Laney focused particular attention on encouraging industrial development. He combined several offices and created a new agency, the Arkansas Resources and Development Commission (ARDC), a precursor to the Industrial Development Commission created by Faubus a few years later. The ARDC served as the centerpiece to Laney's "Arkansas Plan," which was to promote coordination among science, business, government, and citizens to encourage development. To persuade industry to settle in the state by keeping wages low, he supported a "Right to Work" law, which discouraged collective bargaining by prohibiting the "closed" union shop, thus straining his relationship with organized labor in the state. Both this piece of legislation and the Anti-Labor Violence Law of 1943 originated as part of a campaign by the Christian American Association, an extreme rightwing organization operating out of Houston and funded by Texas oil money. The Anti-Labor Violence law was the measure that led, indirectly, to L. C. and Daisy Bates's confrontation with Judge Auten in 1946. Although their attention was focused on the ramifications of the law as it pertained to black workers, their reporting of the Southern Cotton Mill strike created a powerful narrative that allowed the story to be told in a way that garnered attention. The two Southern Cotton Oil Mill strikers convicted in 1943 never spent anytime in jail, however. Their case was appealed to the U.S. Surepme Court on two separate occasions. Governor Sidney McMath later pardoned them when their appeals ran out. Others did spend time in the penitentiary for violating the law. The first pair convicted—two Pine Bluff painters who in the course of a heated argument asked a non-union contractor if he wanted to step outside, which the court ruled constituted the threat of violence—spent a year at Tucker. Other southern states were passing similar laws. It would eventually become clear that low-wage industries resulted in limited economic growth and blunted interest in furthering the educational accomplishments of the state's citizens. At the time, however, the focus of

Arkansas Resources and Development Commission: Created by the legislature to promote economic and industrial development in the state; it was soon renamed the Arkansas Industrial Development Commission.

most southern politicians, including those in Arkansas, was on promoting industrial development at all costs.

Laney also sponsored a major tax revision that increased certain sales taxes and the state income tax but lowered inheritance taxes, and he eliminated the state ad valorem property tax, reasoning that it should be apportioned on the local level. These measures were squarely within the southern conservative position regarding low and regressive taxation, sparing the wealthy and placing the burden on the working and middle classes. He stopped short of advocating additional taxes on gasoline that might have been earmarked for improvements to the highway system, believing that voters would not support it, even though he knew that it would eventually be necessary to pass another highway bond issue. That was a sensitive issue, given the fact that the state had defaulted on its highway bonds during the difficult 1930s and had only refunded those bonds during the Adkins administration.

Gov. Sidney Sanders McMath, who took office in 1949, seized the opportunity to improve the road system in Arkansas. Under his leadership the legislature passed a special bond issue to revamp and expand the state's highway system. Voters later approved it by a four to one margin. More miles of highway were built and improved upon during his tenure in office than under any other governor in the state's history. Although no impropriety on McMath's part was ever established, political contributions from contractors cast suspicion on him, and the governor's enemies, which included the Arkansas Power and Light Company and big business, took advantage of the allegations of wrongdoing. His strong advocacy of rural electric cooperatives had angered AP&L's executives and earned him their undying enmity. His support for labor, including an increased minimum wage law and augmented industrial safety codes, had hardly endeared him to the conservative business community.

Francis Adams Cherry defeated McMath in 1952, largely because he secured the support of the conservative business community by running on a platform of business efficiency, and once in office, he restructured the Fiscal Control Board by centralizing budget control under one office. The new entity was renamed the Department of Finance and Administration. Prior to his governorship and in response to the scandal in the highway department, the legislature had already mandated a restructuring of the Highway Commission. Cherry promoted additional reforms, however, in an effort to insulate the commission from political pressures, but the highway situation remained controversial. A major issue was the power exercised by the commission, which many legislators sought to curtail. Cherry had successfully encouraged the passage of legislation that favored localities that awarded right of way without cost to the state. Many legislators had second thoughts about this and about the power of the commission, and these two questions would figure prominently in Cherry's run for reelection. Cherry was ultimately defeated in his effort to secure a second term, but the highway controversy was only one issue that plagued him. The biggest problem was that he had no political organization when he entered office and he failed to create one.

The *Brown v. Board of Education* decision, which called for an end to the dual education system, was announced while Francis Cherry was running for reelection, and although he believed that this was an issue that should be decided on the local level, he was also convinced that the Supreme Court had spoken and should be obeyed. His position in this regard, however, did not seem to play a role in his defeat in his bid in the Democratic primary for a second term. His opponent, a political unknown from Madison County, Orval Faubus, briefly attempted to identify desegregation as the main issue in the primary campaign, but backed off once editorials in the *Arkansas Gazette* criticized his attempt to pander to racial fears in his campaign. Faubus believed that desegregation was the province of local government but implied that it could be delayed until some unspecified time in the future. Faubus once again raised the desegregation matter in the fall election against his Republican opponent, and this should have served as a sign of his true sentiments on the subject. His election to the office of governor against a Republican opponent was assured; he need not have raised such a divisive issue.

Conclusion

Although Morton Sosna may have overstated the case when he argued that World War II was more transformative than the Civil War for Arkansas, it is clear that tremendous changes occurred during the period between 1940 and 1954. However, white Democrats continued to hold power and promulgate essentially conservative policies on race and economic development. Only one governor postulated policies on civil rights that departed from the traditional approach, but he proved to be an exception. The economic policies adopted by the state were in keeping with the southern perspective on industrialization, a perspective that would prove to offer limited economic opportunities for the state and its citizens. As veterans returned from the battlefields of Europe and the pacific, they resumed their lives, some of them rising to prominent positions in business and government but, for the most part, white veterans accepted and sometimes even championed the racial status quo. Others secured an education on the GI Bill but mostly for jobs that did not encourage the pursuit of an agricultural lifestyle. A transition away from labor-intensive to capital-intensive agriculture, which accelerated during and after the war, proved to have profound implications over the long term. While many landless African Americans moved off the plantations, other black activists within Arkansas took an increasingly assertive stance against segregation and disfranchisement and sought their full measure of citizenship. Even as the black struggle for civil rights continued into the next decade, African American activists faced increasingly strident opposition from die-hard segregationists determined to maintain white supremacy. The election of Orval Faubus, another World War II veteran, proved decisive, though few could have imagined the extremism that would come to characterize his long tenure in office.

CHAPTER FIFTEEN

Stumbling toward a New Arkansas, 1954–1970

So powerful and dramatic was the civil rights struggle in Arkansas in this period, it is easy to miss other fundamental changes also taking place, some of them connected to the emergence of the fight for integration and voting rights. Arkansas's plantation sector moved into a new phase in the 1950s, undergoing a transition from labor-intensive to capital-intensive agriculture, one that necessitated a depopulation of the countryside and supposedly liberated its labor force from certain pervasive social, economic, and political constraints. Powerful countervailing forces limited the extent to which either the transformation or the liberation occurred, however. Remnants of the plantation culture and economy persisted both in the old plantation areas and in the state's capital city. The civil rights movement struck a blow against the traditional white elite and though the state's conservative legislature and Gov. Orval Faubus reeled, they recovered their footing and remained in charge of the apparatus that oversaw the limited integration that occurred. While tens of thousands moved from rural sectors in Arkansas to Little Rock or left the state entirely, many remained and Arkansas continued to have some of the poorest counties in the country. Those who moved into Little Rock or other towns found little to employ them and, indeed, Arkansas, like much of the South, struggled to maintain a seriously underemployed population. The small towns that managed to survive the demographic catastrophe that depopulation represented, struggled to find small industries that would keep their storefronts from being shuttered, but the old plantation mentality died hard, and planters, who set on local economic development committees, were often distinctly cool to industrial development. What industry they attracted, or permitted, paid low wages, little or no taxes, and made such a small investment in Arkansas that they easily abandoned the state at the first promising opportunity, moving away in search of cheaper labor and a better deal elsewhere. The old rural elite would lose their economic edge in this period as new actors—such as Sam Walton and his retail enterprise and Don Tyson and his chicken empire—dislodged them, but these new economic powerbrokers adapted the low-wage, low-skill workforce to their needs. The plantation mentality remained alive and well in Arkansas, influencing the direction of economic development and undermining the process of integration at every turn.

Agricultural Transformation

The transition in agriculture that began during the New Deal and accelerated during World War II reached its inevitable outcome by the mid-1960s. This led to what Jack Kirby called the emergence of the "neo-plantation," signaling the concentration of landownership into larger units and fewer owners and, especially, a dependence on the use of chemicals and machinery. The tenant farming system crumbled so rapidly that by 1960, sharecropping was no longer listed as a separate category on the agricultural census, and tenant farmers had a relatively small presence in farming areas. Seasonal wage labor became the norm. The Bracero program continued to play an important role in solving the plantation's labor issues in the 1950s, but as cotton planters struggled to manage the transition from handpicked to machine-picked cotton and maintain a cheap supply of labor, another threat emerged. New synthetic fabrics that had been developed during World War II were capturing an ever-larger share of the clothing market. Cotton was falling out of favor with many consumers and thus the demand for it began to drop. Cotton planters launched campaigns to encourage people to continue purchasing cotton products, but they were waging a losing battle. When in 1957 the Arkansas Education Department instituted a program promoting the use of synthetic fibers, fourteen Farm Bureau leaders visited Gov. Orval Faubus to request that the department cease spending public tax money on promoting a product that threatened the economic well-being of cotton farmers. On another front, planters lobbied successfully for a textile labeling law requiring manufacturers to list the materials used in various garments, enabling the public to determine whether a garment was made from cotton or synthetics.

Neo-plantation:
The neo-plantation is a term used by historian Jack Kirby to describe the capital-intensive plantation that arose in the post–World War II period.

With demand for cotton declining, Delta farmers and planters began to devote more acreage to soybean production. County farm agents had been encouraging this development since the 1920s, but it was initially promoted principally as a soil-building crop, and its commercial value was uncertain. To planters and farmers accustomed to cotton production and, furthermore, with an economic infrastructure in place in which planters secured crop financing through advances from cotton factors, soybean production was slow to expand. No significant increase in acreage devoted to soybeans took place until New Deal programs imposed acreage restrictions on cotton production in the 1930s. In part because those same programs put cash in the hands of many planters, the crop financing system began to loosen up. With an accompanying breakdown of the tenancy system, all that remained to inhibit a transition to another crop was a landscape of cotton gins and a romantic attachment to King Cotton. The need to reconstruct gins to meet the needs of the mechanical harvester made many small gins no longer viable, and the romance with cotton faded as the economic demands of the 1950s required planters and farmers to make some hard choices. By the 1980s, the Memphis Cotton Carnival, an annual event that drew many Arkansans, changed its name to Carnival Memphis, signifying the extent to which cotton had fallen in favor.

Black man sitting on a tractor with mules and cotton in background at cotton gin, circa 1937. *Lee Wilson & company Archives (Mc 1289). Special Collections Division, University of Arkansas Libraries, Fayetteville.*

Soybean production, like the new method of cultivating and harvesting cotton, was a capital-intensive rather than labor-intensive endeavor, and thus it contributed to the depopulation of the countryside. Between 1940 and 1970, the population in the Delta declined by 14.2 percent. In this same period, the population in the southwest section of the state experienced a 20.9 percent decline. Indeed, a fundamental demographic shift within the state was underway. The most dramatic population growth occurred in Pulaski County, home to Arkansas's capital city. A less dramatic but important shift in population patterns was occurring in northern and western Arkansas, both of which lost population in the 1940s and 1950s, but reversed that trend in the 1960s. For the delta and the southwest, however, there would be no reversal of fortune. The consequences for many small-town merchants in those areas were catastrophic. The presence of Mexican nationals for a few months during the chopping and harvesting season hardly compensated for the profound demographic change taking place. By the early 1960s, the Bracero program was dropped, in part because their labor was no longer needed and in part because the Mexican government had negotiated increasingly costly requirements (better pay, housing, etc.) for their nationals. Even as the use of Braceros became less common, the native black and white population departed in increasing numbers. The expansion of the road system contributed to this. In an earlier era it had been a boon to planters and merchants in small-town Arkansas, but it worked a

Bracero Program: Involved the use of Mexican nationals in the chopping and harvesting of the cotton crop from World War II to the mid-1960s.

different result in the 1950s. It now took potential customers to more urbanized locations, and the growth of chain stores, which tended to be clustered in more densely populated towns and cities, only accentuated this trend.

A different kind of transformation in agriculture had long been underway in northwest Arkansas, but it was in this period that it reached a certain level of sophistication. Just as plantation agriculture was maturing into agri-business in the 1950s and 1960s, poultry farming was developing into an industry. John Tyson and his son, Don, were the most successful practitioners, but it all began inauspiciously enough as a result of the collapse of the fruit industry in northwest Arkansas in the late 1920s. Poultry farming began to take shape at that time, and John Tyson started hauling chickens, as well as other produce, to Kansas City, Missouri, and soon opened his own hatchery. By the eve of World War II, he was trucking poultry to Cincinnati, Cleveland, and Detroit. The rationing of beef during the war was accompanied by subsidies to chicken farmers, which significantly benefited those most positioned to take advantage of it. Greatly enriched by the expansion of demand during the war, Tyson survived the postwar period when difficulties with disease and fluctuations in prices drove others into bankruptcy. The company began to buy out other producers and by the mid-1950s built its first processing plant. They contracted with local growers who were characterized as independent contractors but who essentially served the company's interests and at the company's discretion. Ironically, some analysts have described the relationship as a form of sharecropping, even as that kind of arrangement was disappearing in the Delta. By the mid-1960s chicken farming had become big business in northwest Arkansas, and the Tyson enterprise would soon spread well beyond Arkansas and the Midwest.

While the transition in plantation agriculture was nearly complete by 1970, the hill-country farmers were still finding their way through the advent of the chicken industry. The sharecropping system had virtually vanished; and a new set of "renters," who farmed up to a thousand acres each, worked the land with wage laborers. Meanwhile, the small upcountry farmers were turning more and more toward poultry farming and forming business relationships with operations like Tyson Foods that did not always work to their advantage. Both the neo-plantations of the Delta and the poultry farms of the hill country would continue to develop along these lines for the rest of the century.

Industrial and Economic Development

Despite the rhetoric of Arkansas's New South advocates in the late nineteenth century and over fifty years of efforts to promote economic development and expand industrial production in the state since then, little industrial base of significance had been established. Although strides made during World War II provided a basis upon which to build, the war industries closed down and jobs melted away. Governors Laney, McMath, and Cherry made industrial development a priority but the dearth of dense population centers and an undereducated population placed Arkansas at a disadvantage. In part in response to newly elected governor Orval Faubus, the Arkansas legislature created the Arkansas

Industrial Development Commission in 1955. Soon renamed the Arkansas Economic Development Commission (AEDC), it was a successor organization to Governor Laney's Arkansas Resources and Development Commission, and it was designed to promote economic and industrial development in Arkansas. To direct the new agency, Faubus appointed Winthrop Rockefeller, a New Yorker who had settled in Arkansas in 1953. Rockefeller approached the job with enthusiasm. He served as chairman of the AEDC for nine years and oversaw an impressive expansion of the industrial sector. The kind of industrial plants that settled in Arkansas, however, were of a character that did not significantly challenge the dominance of agricultural interests. While more than six hundred new industrial plants were established in the state during Rockefeller's tenure on the AEDC, providing over ninety thousand new jobs, those factories paid low wages to largely unskilled workers. Indeed, factories tended to move from the unionized North to southern states like Arkansas precisely because of the antiunion laws and low wages. But paying low wages meant that workers had little taxable—and spendable—income, and many of the plants were attracted by the fact that they would not be required to pay much, if any, taxes themselves. Sometimes they were provided land on which to build their plants. In other words, they made a minimum investment and paid low wages, thus the communities received questionable dividends from their presence. To add insult to injury, by the mid-1960s it was clear that Arkansas was serving as a way station for those industries on a trek south in search of lower wages. Towns that secured factories in 1955 would likely be looking for replacement factories a decade later.

The willingness of small towns to provide tax breaks and other incentives to these factories reveals the enormity of the challenges confronting them. With the rural population departing in ever-increasing numbers, the old agricultural-centered towns seemed destined for decline, and small businessmen and merchants became increasingly desperate. The undereducated population and a legacy of impoverishment that made any wage seem acceptable provided a ready employment base for low-skill, low-wage factories. Rockefeller encouraged the development of town economic development commissions, but many of them were dominated or heavily influenced by farmers and planters, some of whom were ambivalent about industrial development. With the transition from labor-intensive to capital-intensive agriculture unfolding only slowly, they feared the competition that employment opportunities in industry might present, and they sometimes acted as a check to the work of the committees. But they need not have been overly concerned. Many of the industrial jobs were taken by women whose husbands worked as seasonal farm laborers. The wives provided the year-round income, while the husbands worked only sporadically, searching, often in vain, for other employment when none was available in the farming sector.

According to Charles Aiken, author of *The Cotton Plantation South since the Civil War*, the towns that were most effective at attracting and maintaining small factories, however limited they were in the types of employment they provided, were those that boasted the most farsighted leadership. They also tended to be the towns that best negotiated the civil rights movement and integrated their schools with a minimum of controversy. Nevertheless, as historian Ben F. Johnson has noted, the first new factories to respond to the opportunities in Arkansas in the 1950s were to locate in areas with few African American residents, and a number of scholars have suggested that the peaceful desegregation of schools in Charleston and Fayetteville owed much to racial demographics. Certainly the existence of turmoil within certain Delta towns discouraged companies from locating industrial plants there. Companies sought to place their factories in quiet, moderate communities that were relatively free from controversy and strife, whether racial or otherwise.

Another crucial factor in a company's decision to place a factory in a particular town was a sufficient supply of labor, and sometimes they were in need of something other than the wives of seasonal farmworkers. Ironically, it was often a town's ability to maintain a significant proportion of its black population that made a difference. Typically, those towns that had a substantial black middle class, some of whose members exerted leadership and partnered with white leaders, retained a significant black population. It required exceptional leadership, both from the white and the black communities, to make the adjustments necessary to survive in the decades after World War II. Towns like Blytheville, Osceola, Pine Bluff, and Forrest City, which also enjoyed better access to major highways, serve as examples. This is not to suggest that they did not have difficulties, both economically and with race relations, but they surmounted the most significant challenges and were positioned to move beyond the past and establish a new legacy. The next few decades, however, would reveal that even there the struggle to overcome the past would challenge the most heroic efforts.

While the AEDC was attempting to promote economic development and attract industry to Arkansas, two dynamic enterprises were emerging on their own, one in Little Rock and the other in Bentonville: W. R. Stephens Investment Company and Wal-Mart Stores, Inc. Both of these companies would become prominent players in state, national, and international business. Wilton Robert "Witt" Stephens, born in Prattsville in 1907, began trading municipal bonds in 1932. Two years later he founded W. R. Stephens, Inc., and built a thriving investment company on the basis of buying and selling Arkansas highway, road, school, levee, and improvement district bonds. He laid the foundation of his empire during the Great Depression when bonds were selling for ten cents on the dollar. Calculating that the Reconstruction Finance Corporation would make certain that government bonds were redeemed, he purchased them and made a fortune doing so. The ratification of an amendment raising the maximum millage on school taxes, which he lobbied for in 1948, permitted schools to market bonds to fund construction projects. Stephens became the largest underwriter of such bonds. He broadened his own holdings to include banks, railroads, and coal and gold mines, but the most important investment he made was in gas production and distribution, particularly the purchase of Arkansas Louisiana Gas Company (Arkla) in 1954. Within two years he turned an unprofitable business into a moneymaker. By that time he was widely regarded as a "king maker" in Arkansas economics and politics, and on a first-name basis with governors, congressmen, and senators.

Sam Walton, a World War II veteran, took another path to business innovation, one that not only transformed one corner of the state but reshaped the retail business worldwide. Born in Kingfisher, Oklahoma, in 1918, he earned a business degree at the University of Oklahoma in 1940 and went to work for J.C. Penney before being inducted into the army in 1942. After the war he purchased a Ben Franklin five-and-dime store in Newport, Arkansas, and built it into a highly successful enterprise. His landlord there was so impressed with his success that he refused to renew Walton's lease and turned the property over to his son. In 1950 Sam Walton opened Walton's 5 & 10, another Ben Franklin store, in Bentonville. He was the first in the state to feature self-service shopping. Soon he opened stores in other small towns in the area but broke with Ben Franklin when they refused to countenance his desire to engage in aggressive discount marketing. He opened his first Wal-Mart store in Rogers in 1962. Working now with his brother, Bud, the Waltons were destined over the next decades to shape Wal-Mart, Inc., into the most innovative and influential company in the world.

These two business entrepreneurs, together with poultry producer and distributor John Tyson, depended upon and championed the expansion of Arkansas's transportation network. Witt Stephens understood that there was money to be made by the proposition and positioned himself to market road bonds to accomplish the task. Sam Walton, who learned to fly an airplane so he could visit and oversee his various franchises, dealt with the inferior road system in an unusual way, but better roads were essential to the long-term interests of Wal-Mart, Inc. John Tyson was more intimately familiar with the inadequacies of the roads than either Stephens or Walton, and as his enterprise expanded, so did his support for improvements to roads and highways. By 1959, the Arkansas Highway Department oversaw 11,022.12 miles of state highways, but 2,415.25 miles of them were unpaved gravel roads. More than half the county roads in the state were unpaved and some of them little more than dirt paths. John Tyson, who by then was in partnership with his son Don, found accessing his poultry producers under these circumstances to be far from ideal.

While the Arkansas Highway Department worked toward improving the state's road system, the agency also aggressively pursued federal funds to participate in the expansion of the nation's interstate highway system, an expansion promoted heavily by Pres. Dwight D. Eisenhower upon taking office in 1955. As a young West Point graduate during World War I, Eisenhower had crossed over the nation's inadequate highways and later, as Supreme Allied Commander in Europe during World War II, he came to appreciate the impressive German autobahn system. From his perspective, roads and highways were essential to national defense and, indeed, the 1956 act was officially called the Dwight D. Eisenhower National System of Interstate and Defense Highways. The federal government had been sharing the cost of constructing its highways across the country since the early 1920s, but the 1956 act raised the level of contributions from 60/40, established in 1954, to 90/10, a rate calculated to more rapidly accomplish the task that Eisenhower deemed necessary.

According to the Arkansas Highway Department, the state's first interstate consisted of a stretch of bypass in West Memphis begun in 1952 under an older cost-sharing rubric of 50/50. In 1954, under the newly established 60/40 formula, the southbound lanes of I-30 between Little Rock and Benton were completed. But the passage of the 1956 act, with 90 percent of the funds coming from the federal government, energized the department and encouraged a more aggressive campaign to extend the state's interstate highway system. A plan prepared by the department and approved in 1958 called for 525 miles of interstate along three major corridors: I-30 from the Texas state line at Texarkana to Little Rock; I-40 from the Oklahoma state line near Fort Smith through Little Rock and thence to Memphis; and I-55 from Memphis through West Memphis and then north to the Missouri border near Blytheville. Two smaller corridors were also approved: I-540 around Fort Smith connecting to I-40; and an I-430 loop to the west of Little Rock, which included a new bridge over the Arkansas River. All but 9 percent of the routes were entirely new—in other words, not over existing roadways. Once constructed, 77 percent of the state's population would be within fifty miles of an interstate highway.

The improvements in the state's highway system and the construction of interstates across Arkansas worked together with industrial and economic development to bring substantial change to the state. Although efforts at convincing industrial plants to come to Arkansas met with limited results and the transformation of agriculture, both in the Delta and in the hills, included a certain new set of challenges, the roads and highways opened a new world of opportunities to the state's citizens. Some of them chose to leave the state for better prospects elsewhere, given the limited kinds of development that actually occurred in Arkansas. Thousands left in search of employment in the expanding industrial sector in other parts of the country; thousands of others secured college educations and found little to keep them in Arkansas. The labor and "brain" drain would soon come to preoccupy officials and policy makers.

Faces like Flint against the Law, Part I

By the time the United States Supreme Court issued the *Brown v. Board of Education* decision in May 1954, Arkansas's African American population had already achieved certain successes in promoting integration of higher education in the state. The *Brown* decision, however, raised the stakes considerably. Token integration in professional and graduate schools had hardly registered as a problem for white southerners, but desegregating the public school system proved to be far more controversial. In *Brown*, the Supeme Court essentially invalidated the "separate but equal" decision rendered in *Plessy v. Ferguson* in 1896. Like southerners elsewhere, segregationists in Arkansas resisted in a variety of ways over the decades that followed the *Brown* decision, and they enjoyed the support of local and state officials in orchestrating plans to thwart integration. Orval Faubus launched efforts to thwart integration, but even after his methods failed, only

> ***Brown v. Board of Education*:** A U.S. Supreme Court decision rendered in 1954, which ruled that the doctrine of "separate but equal" established under *Plessy v. Ferguson* in 1896 was unconstitutional.

token integration occurred in the 1960s, largely because of so-called integration plans that were actually meant to maintain segregation. Indeed, according to a ruling of the Eighth Circuit Court of Appeals rendered in 1985, "The Executive and Legislative Branches of [Arkansas] State government set their faces like flint against the law."

The first reaction of white Arkansans to the *Brown* decision, however, was surprise. Even Pres. Dwight Eisenhower, who had appointed Earl Warren as chief justice of the Supreme Court, was caught off guard by the decision and later declared privately that his selection of Warren to head the Court had been the "biggest damn fool mistake I ever made." Eisenhower was justified in being taken aback. Warren, as a former conservative governor of California, had the right credentials from the Republican Party's point of view for appointment to the Supreme Court. He had served as California's attorney general when Franklin Roosevelt issued his executive order to intern Japanese Americans in 1942 and had played the lead role in orchestrating it. He must have seemed an unlikely risk to conservatives attached to the status quo. Instead, believing fervently that the 1896 *Plessy v. Ferguson* decision was wrong, he carefully lobbied, cajoled, and persuaded the other justices to issue a unanimous decision overturning the "separate but equal" doctrine and thus promoting integration of the country's schools.

In the months immediately following the *Brown* decision, it appeared that integration would occur without causing great difficulty in Arkansas. Schools in Fayetteville and Charleston, which both had small black populations, integrated without controversy in the fall of 1954. But this proved to be the lull before the storm. To complicate things, African Americans in Arkansas were not united in the approach to be taken. The cooperation of certain black elites in Arkansas with the NAACP in the suit Sue Morris brought against the Little Rock School Board in 1942 obscured a struggle between the old black elites and the more activist agenda of younger African Americans. To some extent, this struggle reflected the influence of the old black aristocracy on the local chapter of the NAACP, an influence that discouraged an aggressive challenge of the white power structure. Therefore, when L. C. and Daisy Bates became actively involved in the attempt to bring desegregation to Little Rock, they did not have the full support of the city's black aristocracy. As Calvin Smith has observed, even L. C. Bates had voiced reservations about integration and was, instead, an advocate of equality of opportunity for blacks. When he became convinced by early 1952 that separate facilities would never be equalized, he began writing strongly worded editorials in support of the NAACP's challenge to segregation in public education. He was pleased with the *Brown* decision in 1954, but warned his readers that even though the state's officials had reacted mildly to the decision, "things are going to be serious." A calm, quiet, dignified man, he was a master of understatement.

Bates was not alone among those who worked for change but feared the worst. Harry Ashmore, who was in charge of the editorial page of the *Arkansas Gazette*, coauthored a report predicting that integration would be an explosive issue. Ashmore had been commissioned by the Ford Foundation in 1953 to study the implications of the effects of the dual education system. The report, issued the day before the *Brown* decision, found that black children were greatly disadvantaged by the underfunded black schools and that southern states could not afford to provide an adequate education to either race by maintaining the dual system. Ashmore understood the forces arrayed against integration and played a role in organizing the Arkansas Council on Human Relations (ACHR) in Little Rock in 1955. It was loosely affiliated with the Southern Regional Council in Atlanta, Georgia, from which it received some funds and a good deal of advice. An interracial organization, the ACHR worked to promote peaceful integration but, as the Ford Foundation report suggested, they would be fighting an uphill battle.

Arkansas Council on Human Relations: Loosely affiliated with the Southern Regional Council in Atlanta, Georgia, the Arkansas Council on Human Relations was organized in 1955 in Little Rock in order to promote peaceful integration.

Regardless of the cautionary note sounded in the report, the ACHR pursued efforts to foster cooperation and conciliation between the races. In March 1956 they sponsored a workshop at Camp Aldersgate near Little Rock and brought people from around the state together to participate in discussions about how the organization could promote peaceful integration on the local level. Two speakers from Fisk University served as the official consultants. Unknown to them, the state police set up surveillance outside the camp and recorded the license plate numbers of all those who reported for the meeting. Still, the ACHR stayed the course. By early 1957 they were laying plans to sponsor a "brotherhood" week, when black and white ministers would meet and work together to ease tensions and encourage observance of the law. They teamed a black with a white minister to speak on the topic "A Christian Looks at Race Relations Today" at a church or to a church group that extended them an invitation. Organizers of the ACHR were disappointed by the failure of some church leaders to participate. Fred Darragh, a white businessman in Little Rock, who served as the first executive director of the ACHR, was outspoken in his criticisms of the timidity of many white ministers who refused to participate for fear of offending their congregations. Darragh's criticisms revealed the depth of the struggle ACHR members faced in their efforts to organize and promote peaceful integration.

African American activists and the ACHR would find no support from the state's governor, Orval Faubus. In retrospect, the statements Faubus made during his first run for office in 1954 should have served as fair warning. He had suggested that desegregation might be delayed and even outlined a strategy that might be pursued to guarantee it. However, once in office Faubus appointed blacks to the State Democratic Committee, something that would have been unthinkable just a few years earlier. Because of this, many people throughout the state regarded Faubus as a racial progressive, but in this case appearances proved to be deceiving. Faubus attempted to steer a middle path on the desegregation issue when he could, such as his success in avoiding a role in the school desegregation controversy in Hoxie in 1955, a small town of only 1,855 people in east Arkansas.

The Hoxie desegregation controversy foreshadowed the 1956 election and a dramatic shift to the right on Faubus's part. Yet when the Hoxie School Board decided to integrate, they had little reason to fear controversy. After all, Fayetteville and Charleston had integrated without incident the year before, and Hoxie was similar to them in racial demographics: overwhelmingly white. The Hoxie school term began on July 11, in keeping with a "split term," common in some agricultural communities that permitted a break in the fall so that children could participate in the cotton harvest. No incidents occurred on that day and things seemed to be proceeding according to plan. Although some segregationists were beginning to raise objections, a controversy only broke open after *Life* magazine decided to do a pictorial feature demonstrating peaceful integration in the South. They chose Hoxie, Arkansas, as their prime example. When the issue appeared on the newsstands on July 25, images of black and white children arm-in-arm aroused a segment of the white population. White agitators, mostly from elsewhere, flooded into Hoxie to protest. A small group of the most ardent among them launched a challenge to the school board, but the board refused to back down. When Governor Faubus declined to intervene to protect them against the crowds of hostile whites, the board was left virtually defenseless. They took their case to the federal courts, arguing that the protestors were trespassing on school property and disrupting the otherwise successful integration effort. Federal judge Thomas C. Trimble issued a restraining order against the segregationists and the Eighth Circuit Court of Appeals later backed his decision. The Hoxie schools remained integrated.

Hoxie desegregation controversy: Originated in Hoxie, Arkansas, a town in northeastern Arkansas, when the school board voted to desegregate. Rabid segregationists raised a storm of protest, and though they were unsuccessful in their efforts to keep the Hoxie schools from becoming desegregated, a potent new organization emerged to fight desegregation.

Despite the success of the efforts to integrate Hoxie schools, a potent new organization was coalescing behind the scenes during the Hoxie crisis. The White Citizens Council, organized initially in the state of Mississippi in 1954 to fight the *Brown* decision, had sprouted roots in Arkansas. State legislator James D. Johnson, who had played a small role in the segregationists stand in Hoxie, was a prominent organizer. He began giving speeches around the state to rally anti-integrationists, and believing Faubus to be vulnerable on the issue, he mounted a challenge to him in the 1956 Democratic primary. Faubus found it necessary to shore up support among those most opposed to desegregation, especially east Arkansas planters, and was able to cast himself as a more reputable segregationist than his opponent. Although Johnson was unsuccessful in dislodging the governor, he forced Faubus to move to the right on the segregation issue.

Orval Faubus was not alone among Arkansas politicians in opposing integration. He found support not only in the state legislature but also with Arkansas's congressional delegation. Arkansas's entire congressional delegation signed on to the "Southern Manifesto," a document challenging the *Brown* decision. South Carolina's Strom Thurmond, the standard-bearer for the Dixiecrats in 1948, wrote the initial draft, and it was almost certainly intended to serve as a rallying point for segregationists. It declared the Supreme Court's actions to be an abuse of power, among other things, but its principle objective was to prevent or, at the very least, delay integration. Arkansas's J. William Fulbright contributed to a revision of the document, supposedly in order to tone down its rhetoric, but Richard Russell of Georgia actually authored the final draft. In any case, with the state's congressional delegation signing on to the document, Faubus must have believed he had not only the rationale but the backing of a significant lobby in Congress.

Meanwhile, black activists were developing plans to integrate Little Rock schools. Frustrated that no movement toward integration followed a 1955 decision of the Supreme Court to proceed with desegregation with "all deliberate speed," the NAACP lined up a group of thirty-three black students, working through their parents, to file a suit that became known as *Aaron v. Cooper* (Aaron the name of the first child listed on the suit; Cooper being William G. Cooper, president of the Little Rock School Board). Their efforts and their suit were undermined by the actions of Little Rock's white school superintendent Virgil Blossom and the Little Rock School Board, which presented an integration plan that was far different from what the black activists promoted. It provided for only modest integration of Central High School, a school in a working-class neighborhood. Yet Daisy Bates and a small group of African American activists decided to work with Blossom, and they carefully selected nine students—who became known as the "Little Rock Nine"—to make the move into Central High School in the fall of 1957: Minnijean Brown, Elizabeth Eckford, Ernest Green, Thelma Mothershed, Melba Pattillo, Gloria Ray, Terrance Roberts, Jefferson Thomas, and Carlotta Walls. "

Aaron v. Cooper: A suit filed by the parents of thirty-three black students in Little Rock after the Supreme Court issued its "all deliberate speed" decision in 1955, a follow-up to the *Brown* decision in 1954.

Little Rock Nine: The nine black students who integrated Central High School in Little Rock in 1957.

Even as Bates was preparing the children for entry into Central High, Faubus took another step away from racial progressivism and mortgaged his political future to the extreme segregationists in order to secure approval of an ambitious twenty-two-million-dollar legislative package. To gain the support of east Arkansas planters for a package that included increases in benefits to the elderly and higher teacher salaries, Faubus acquiesced to four bills designed to delay desegregation, something that was not so very far from measures he hinted might be necessary in his first run for the governor's office in the race against Cherry. These measures, if Faubus had attempted to enforce them, would have provided financial aid to schools attempting to resist integration, changed school attendance laws in a manner designed to make sure that certain whites did not have to attend school with blacks, required the NAACP to publish its membership lists, and established a state sovereignty commission with the express purpose of studying how to effectively block federal integration efforts. When Faubus failed to enforce the four measures, pressure from the extreme segregationists mounted.

In August 1957, as the fall term of school approached, two important developments

Students and soldiers at Central High School, Little Rock. *Larry Obstinik Photo Archives, Special Collections Division, University of Arkansas Libraries, Fayetteville.*

occurred. First, federal judge John E. Miller ruled against the plaintiffs in *Aaron v. Cooper*, arguing that the plan for integration outlined by the school board was on track to take place. Under those circumstances, there was no reason to issue a court order mandating integration. This had the effect, however, of giving the Blossom plan for desegregating Central High greater visibility and, in a larger sense, established that the state could not ignore its responsibility to enforce the *Brown* decision. The governor must have realized that he could no longer obfuscate on the issue. The second development came from another direction entirely and placed additional pressure on Faubus. With the integration of Central High looming, the segregationists prepared to draw a line in the sand. They invited Gov. Marvin Griffin of Georgia to speak to the Little Rock White Citizens Council; after the speech he met with Faubus and convinced the governor to intervene.

According to Faubus biographer Roy Reed, the governor had his own objections to the Blossom plan. He was offended by the fact that Little Rock's integration would begin in a working-class school. A new school, Hall High, had been opened for upper-middle-class white children. Faubus, who came from a hill-country family of very modest means, was an outsider to the Little Rock society and business elite, and he felt snubbed by them. Whatever his motivations, after failing to convince the FBI that violence would occur if the desegregation plan was implemented, he called out the National Guard and state troopers and ordered them to prevent the "Little Rock Nine" from integrating Central High. So successful had Faubus been in straddling the issue that a woman who had worked with the Arkansas Council on Human Relations in Fayetteville to prepare the state for peaceful integration, awoke that morning to scenes broadcast on television of uniformed men surrounding the school and believed that the governor had called the military out to protect the black children and ensure peaceful integration. She was shocked to discover the truth and she, like many others, felt betrayed. To segregationists, however, Faubus was a hero.

The most iconic image captured on television cameras that September 4 morning featured Elizabeth Eckford walking stalwartly toward the front door of Central High, a crowd of hostile young people surrounding her. One female student followed her, apparently screaming invective, but Eckford soldiered on. She walked alone because she had not received an important message that morning; instead of meeting at the school as was originally planned, she was meant to go to Daisy Bates's home where the Little Rock Nine were to gather. From there the students were to convoy together. Bates had decided upon this change of plan upon receiving word of the crowds gathered before the school. But Eckford, who had already taken the bus to Central High, could not be reached and thus she made her solitary walk in vain. Once turned away from the door by grim-faced National Guardsmen, she had no option other than to walk back through the hostile crowd and wait for a bus to take her to safety. The other eight students were later also turned away, and the school remained closed to the Little Rock Nine for nearly three weeks.

When federal district judge Ronald Davies ordered integration to proceed on September 20, the stage was set for yet another ugly confrontation. In response to the judge's order, Faubus removed the National Guard but this merely left the Little Rock Nine vulnerable to a large crowd of angry and unruly whites who stood ready to defy the court order. The nine students appeared on September 23 and were ushered in through a back door while some in the crowd pounced on four black newspapermen, beating them severely. On September 24, 1957, responding to a request by the mayor of Little Rock, President Eisenhower sent the 101st Airborne Division into Little Rock and nationalized the Arkansas National Guard in order to enforce integration. Meanwhile, Harry Ashmore's strongly worded editorials led the *Gazette* into a period of struggle with segregationist forces in Arkansas that garnered him a Pulitzer Prize in 1958. The paper itself also received a Pulitzer that year, for public service for reporting on the crisis and the confrontation with Faubus.

The Little Rock Nine had gained entry into Central High, but they endured a difficult school year (1957–1958), so difficult, in fact, that one of their number, Minnijean Brown, was suspended in February 1958 for calling a student "white trash" for having struck her. On February 20, the school board petitioned the federal court to delay and desist from integration. Judge Harold J. Lemley granted the postponement in April, a decision that was immediately appealed by the same parties that had initiated the *Aaron v. Cooper* suit. The Eighth Circuit reversed his decision in August. This left all sides of the issue on tenterhooks as the fall 1958 school year was upon them. The school board delayed the beginning of classes to await the outcome of the appeal to the U.S. Supreme Court. When that body ruled in *Cooper v. Aaron* that integration must precede on schedule, Orval Faubus took the unprecedented step of simply closing the schools. As historian Sondra Gordy has demonstrated, the "lost year" created hardships for Little Rock's high school students and teachers alike. Still under contract, teachers sat in empty classrooms and walked eerily vacated hallways; students either attended private schools, some of them hastily created, or left the city altogether to continue their education. The closing of the schools was, of course, most difficult for the poorest students, particularly black students who had fewer options available to them.

It was high tide for segregationists as Dale Alford, an ophthalmologist and an extremist race-baiter, successfully waged a write-in campaign against Congressman Brooks Hays in the fall 1958 congressional elections. Hays, a moderate, had attempted to mediate by bringing Governor Faubus and President Eisenhower together to end the crisis. Segregationists also launched an attack against Harry Ashmore and the ACHR, labeling them agents of communism. In 1958 the Arkansas attorney general's office launched an investigation of the council and used Ashmore's association with it as evidence of its subversive character. A hearing was held before a special education committee of the Arkansas Legislative Council in December 1958, with Atty. Gen. Bruce Bennett conducting the interrogation of various witnesses. Daisy Bates and the NAACP were alleged to be in league with communists and communist front organizations. The report, laced with innuendo, circumstantial evidence, and unsubstantiated accusations, concluded that communists and fellow travelers were responsible for the racial unrest in Arkansas. The report also implied that until the interference of the communists and their dupes, African Americans in Arkansas had been content with their segregated status. The report's authors were either unfamiliar with the half-century struggle mounted by blacks in Arkansas on various fronts or had simply chosen to ignore it.

The Bennett report was only one part of a war against the NAACP and integrationist forces. It was also in 1958 that the legislature passed Act 10, which required state employees to report all memberships to any organizations over the previous five years. Introduced as an anticommunist bill, it was actually designed to identify and intimidate members of the NAACP. The threat was made all the more potent with the passage of Act 115, which made it illegal for state employees to belong to the NAACP. Although both acts were eventually ruled unconstitutional, they created problems for professors in colleges and universities within the state. James B. Jones, Edith Mae Irby's husband, faced expulsion from his position at the University of Arkansas at Pine Bluff under these circumstances, but he avoided it when Irby elected to accept an internship in internal medicine in Houston and the family moved there. At the University of Arkansas, meanwhile, a group of professors defied the act on grounds of academic freedom and refused to report their associations. Prof. John McKenney was fired, and when the university failed to reinstate him upon appeal, the American Association of University Professors (AAUP) placed the university on its censure list, a censure that was not lifted until 1968.

Although concerned about the attack on civil liberties represented in Acts 10 and 115, it was the firing of forty-four teachers on May 5, 1959, that prompted some moderate whites to assert themselves. A small group of prominent white women, the Women's Emergency Committee (WEC), had been working behind the scenes from the first days of the crisis to peacefully end the Central High crisis in favor of integration and had created an impressive political organization, compiling lists of voters and working to encourage moderate businessmen and civic leaders to become involved in the struggle. Whether in response to the WEC or because Little Rock was beginning to feel the results of the controversy in terms of lost business and industrial opportunities, the Little Rock Chamber of Commerce voted in March 1959 to reopen the schools and integrate on a limited basis. The vote was overwhelming: 819 to 245. Their opinion, though important, had no influence on the governor or the legislature however. In any case, the chamber attempted to avoid the label of "integrationists" by speaking in support of a new private high school, which had been created solely to provide a segregated facility for white children.

Women's Emergency Committee: A small group of prominent white women who worked behind the scenes to peacefully integrate Central High School and end the integration crisis.

Urging only limited integration was as far as the businessmen and civic leaders would go until the segregationists finally overstepped themselves and fired the forty-four teachers and administrators on May 5. The board's actions "shamed" some of them into creating a new organization called Stop This Outrageous Purge (STOP). Officially, they kept their distance from the WEC, although that organization supplied woman power in the form of campaign workers in a "recall" of the segregationist school board members. Those who supported the segregationists on the school board formed their own organization, which they called the Committee to Retain Our Segregated Schools (CROSS). Despite the imagery of their acronym, which was obviously intended to appeal to the religious sensibilities of the Little Rock electorate, voters removed the segregationists on the board and replaced them with three moderates.

Stop This Outrageous Purge: An organization formed by white business and civic leaders in Little Rock after the segregationists successfully fired white school board members favorable to integration.

The tide had turned. The businessmen and civic leaders who formed STOP would no longer tolerate the notoriety that accompanied segregationist efforts to prevent integration. Once the United States Supreme Court declared the school-closing law unconstitutional on June 18, 1959, the stage was set for the next episode in the integration of Central High. The new school board subsequently laid plans to integrate both Central and Hall high schools. The integration of Hall High School, located in a wealthier section of Little Rock, was in response to accusations that working-class children attending

Central High were to bear the brunt of integration. In other words, as Faubus biographer and respected journalist Roy Reed has pointed out, it was simply a "nod to class antagonisms." Little Rock schools reopened in the fall of 1959, integrated, but it was truly only token integration. Only six black children were admitted to the two high schools, three to Central and three to Hall.

Little Rock authorities would develop new strategies to delay integration in the next decade. Ben F. Johnson III provides a particularly astute assessment of the desegregation crisis in the *Arkansas Historical Quarterly* that includes an analysis of what transpired in the 1960s to ensure that only token integration took place. Part of the segregationist strategy hinged on residential segregation practices dating back to the years immediately preceding the *Brown* decision. Placing it in the context of the demographic revolution accompanying and following World War II, Johnson argues that as whites and blacks from rural Arkansas moved into Little Rock, they crowded up against each other in contiguous neighborhoods with some mixed neighborhoods developing. The city went so far in 1952 as to raze a black lower- and middle-class neighborhood as part of an effort to move the city's black population to eastern districts of Little Rock where they built a public housing subdivision. They had used funds provided by the federal government to build the Joseph A. Booker subdivision near Granite Mountain in east Little Rock. The intent of the small group of liberal whites who promoted a bond issue to match the federal funds was to provide better housing for the city's poor black population and some, like Adolphine Terry, a founder of the WEC, were dismayed by how the funds were used to serve quite another purpose. A housing authority employee, B. Finley Vinson, testified many years later that the black subdivision was "a device to maintain segregation of races . . . There was no bones made about it." For African Americans in the lower- and middle-class neighborhoods destroyed in the process, it was a disaster.

Although residential segregation predated the *Brown* decision, the practice continued and played a crucial role in the 1960s in the effort to forestall integration. The city continued to use urban renewal funds to raze black neighborhoods. The Little Rock Housing Authority, real estate operators, and mortgage lenders conspired to make certain that blacks did not purchase homes in certain white neighborhoods. As Johnson points out, one broker admitted to federal authorities that the phrase "Anyone Can Buy" was a signal to black purchasers that their applications would be welcome. If no such phrase accompanied an advertisement promoting the sale of a house, African Americans understood that their offers would not be entertained. At one point, a black realtor was almost denied his real estate license for having sold a home to a black family in a sacrosanct white neighborhood. According to Ben F. Johnson III, he had violated a regulation of the Arkansas Real Estate Commission that "a realtor should never be instrumental in introducing into a neighborhood a character of property or occupancy, members of any race or nationality, or any individuals whose presence will clearly be detrimental to property values in that neighborhood."

The city's leadership was largely satisfied with the progress they were making in imposing further residential segregation and in maintaining certain schools in Little Rock as basically white enclaves. A key component of their efforts was a "pupil assignment" scheme adopted by the legislature in 1959. Modeled after an Alabama law, it gave the school board authority to decide pupil placement on a case-by-case basis. By this means, the board successfully discouraged black children from moving into white schools. Black families were far from sanguine about the situation. In September 1964 Roosevelt and Delores Clark filed suit in federal court when their four children were denied admittance to an all-white school and directed instead to a black school. Represented by black activist attorney John Walker, who was affiliated with the NAACP Legal Defense Fund, they intended to test the constitutionality of the pupil placement law. The court would eventually rule in favor of Walker's clients in *Clark v. Board of Education of the Little Rock School District*, but Little Rock authorities knew it was vulnerable on the issue of pupil placement and dropped its use. They substituted the "freedom of choice" scheme, another way that southern cities had slowed or stopped integration. This enabled the city to use a loaded term—freedom—to hide behind the idea that everyone was free to choose, ignoring the fact that the city's long-term efforts at imposing residential segregation made integration more difficult. In fact, residential segregation imposed very real and significant constraints on African Americans who might want to send their children to the better-funded white schools. Public transit was both uneven and insufficient, and schools did not provide adequate transportation for students across school lines.

In 1966, the composition of the Little Rock School Board changed in a way that made it more receptive to pressure from black activists like John Walker and from the state's Department of Health, Education and Welfare. Both Walker and the agency were concerned about the trend toward white flight and how that might make it difficult for the city to comply with desegregation orders. It was in that year that Thomas E. Patterson became the first black member of the board; it was also in 1966 that Winslow Drummond, a member of a progressive law firmed headed by former governor Sidney McMath and Judge Henry Woods, was elected to the board. The school board commissioned a group of experts to analyze the situation in Little Rock and make specific recommendations to enable it to comply with desegregation orders and develop long-range plans. The University of Oregon's Bureau of Educational Research received the contract to pursue the study and issued a report in 1967 that contained a number of suggestions. Known as the Oregon Report, it would become controversial and was eventually repudiated.

The Oregon Report's recommendation that the district abandon the neighborhood school concept and, instead, conceive of itself as a single educational park proved to become its Achilles' heel. It provided those opposed to segregation a popular cause around which to rally a wide spectrum of the white population. Some in the black community also feared a move that would undermine their neighborhoods, but it was white opposition organized around a group called the "Education First Committee" that raised a storm of protest, sometimes laden with subtle and not-so-subtle racist rhetoric. Although the recommendations of the Oregon Report had been thoroughly repudiated by the time of the school board elections in 1967, it became an issue around which the segregationists rallied. They were able to elect two outspoken opponents to replace two moderate members of the board. Even a more modest plan put forward by Superintendent Parson (known as the Parson Plan), which would have required only a slight increase in busing within the district, was labeled as a danger to neighborhood schools, and in 1968 two more moderate members of the board were replaced. As Gene Vinzant argues, "the change from 1966 to 1968 in the make-up of the Little Rock School Board and its attitude toward desegregation was dramatic." According to Vinzant, "The move toward conservatism in Little Rock reflected a national mood of stiffening white resistance to 'forced integration.' Frustrated by the willingness of the white majority to make even modest steps in the direction of integration, black activists felt they had no alternative but to turn once again to the federal courts."

In 1968 the Supreme Court's ruling in *Green v. County School Board* provided an opportunity for black activists and others who supported integration to fight back. The *Green* decision made school districts indisputably responsible for ensuring that integration took place. Although the case had not arisen in Arkansas but in eastern Virginia, its applicability to the Arkansas situation was unmistakable. Declaring the "freedom of choice" plan inadequate as a means of achieving integration, the Court indicated that school districts had to eliminate all vestiges of segregation, "root and branch," a far cry from the "all deliberate speed" associated with the *Brown* decision. School boards across the South had been operating under the assumption that they merely had to refrain from deliberately and openly preventing integration. Having imposed residential segregation, they had unwittingly set the stage for the next great drama, one that would unfold in the 1970s, involving the busing of children, a phenomenon that became politically loaded and expensive. The segregationist would lose no time, and probably little sleep, in manipulating the issue of busing to further their cause.

The controversy over busing would emerge only after another Supreme Court decision in 1971, a discussion to be taken up in the next chapter. Meanwhile, the events that transpired in Little Rock in the late 1950s resulted in the postponement of integration in other towns in Arkansas. School boards in towns like Hot Springs, which had integration plans in place at the time of the Central High crisis, decided to delay. Town leaders there were concerned as much by the threat of violence as they were by the prospect of integration. As a tourist town dependent upon a good reputation for its continued prosperity, businessmen were fearful of the violent scenes that had occurred in Little Rock. By 1962, however, town leaders determined to introduce gradual integration and quietly implemented a plan that brought them into compliance with the *Brown* decision. Compliance, however, meant merely that they had integrated on a token basis only. Most black children continued to attend the underfunded black schools.

While Hot Springs was approaching the process of integration slowly and quietly, encountering little opposition, other towns, particularly those with heavy black populations like Earle, Arkansas, in Crittenden County, delayed until 1970 and then approached desegregation so heavy handedly that ugly confrontations occurred. Anyone familiar with the town's history would not have been surprised that it was destined for such notoriety. During Reconstruction it had been a center of Ku Klux Klan activity and as late as the mid-1930s it became infamous for a particularly egregious case of peonage. Using a cotton picker's strike as justification, the town marshal, Paul Peacher, arrested thirteen black men on vagrancy charges and, in cahoots with the town's mayor, had them remanded to him to work off their fines. This blatant violation against peonage laws was brought to the attention of Justice Department officials, and Peacher was subsequently convicted on federal peonage charges. However, his two-year jail sentence was suspended and a $3,500 fine was paid by local landowners who saw nothing wrong with his actions.

By 1970, the Peacher case was long forgotten and, in any case, the white power structure had learned nothing from it. Local white authorities were determined to shape court-ordered desegregation to their liking. Nearly 80 percent of the population was African American, however, and years of black activism and their collective sense of new possibilities had energized them, particularly the young among them. In retrospect, the two sides were headed for a showdown. When the white school board closed the black schools and summarily fired or demoted most of the black teachers, they exhibited their traditional sense of power and authority. When they relegated the black students to separate classrooms, they violated the desegregation plan they had submitted to the Arkansas Department of Health, Education and Welfare, but that agency refused to intervene when the facts were reported to them. School authorities were revealing not only their arrogance but also their ignorance of the mood and ambitions of these black youth, setting in motion forces they could not control. According to historian Michael Honey, who was then covering the story for the *Southern Patriot*, "the board's desegregation plan had resulted in the ouster of all blacks in leadership positions in the schools, and the rooting out of all symbols of black pride or heritage." In reaction, black students staged a "walkout" on Labor Day (not a holiday in Arkansas then), and what followed was a lesson in civil disobedience on the one side, and on the other side, an example of a violent reaction reminiscent of Bull Conner's vicious tactics in Birmingham, Alabama, seven years earlier.

The day following the walkout, groups of helmeted men arrested thirty black students for "parading without a license." During a spontaneous prayer pilgrimage that evening, "about 150 people walked toward City Hall, but before they arrived they were confronted by 15 to 20 units of State Troopers, city and county police, and a mob of whites. Without warning, police opened fire on the crowd. Townspeople and police charged into the fleeing marchers with clubs and tire chains, beating men, women and children to the ground." White authorities targeted leaders of the black community in subsequent arrests, including the Reverend Ezra Greer, a founder of the Crittenden County Improvement Association. The Reverend Greer and his wife were both beaten and jailed by police. In the weeks that followed this encounter, black students who refused to return to the classroom were harassed and their parents fired from their jobs and evicted from plantations. White officials were determined to minimize their compliance with federal mandates and officials in Arkansas allowed them to carry on with business as usual.

The desegregation of schools in the state was only one front in the African American

Student Nonviolent Coordinating Committee: An organization founded by black students at Howard University in Washington, D.C., in 1960. In 1962, they sent organizers into Arkansas to promote integration of public facilities and, eventually, voting rights.

struggle in Arkansas. In 1962, the Student Nonviolent Coordinating Committee (SNCC) began organizing activities in the state, and their efforts extended well beyond integration of public education and focused instead on public facilities like eating establishments and hospitals. It also took issue with continuing impediments to black voting. SNCC, founded in 1960 by black and white college students at Howard University in Washington, D.C., soon identified four southern states as needing special attention. Arkansas was one of them. After some organizing forays into the state in 1962, SNCC formerly launched its "Arkansas Project" in early 1963, and black students at Philander Smith College in Little Rock and at AM&N in Pine Bluff became actively involved. The first state headquarters was located in Pine Bluff, and a great deal of activity was centered in Delta towns. Its initial programs focused on integrating public facilities such as restaurants. Philander Smith students, for example, wrote "An Appeal to the Negroes of Little Rock," calling on them to boycott stores on Main Street, such as Woolworths, which refused to serve African Americans at its lunch counter. The Little Rock chapter of the National Council of Negro Women declared support for the boycott and for a subsequent sit-in demonstration at Woolworths. In the Delta, the Arkansas Project set up field offices in three towns, Helena, Pine Bluff, and Forrest City, each town having responsibility for a three- or four-county area within its vicinity. SNCC workers in those towns opened "freedom centers," where local blacks could gather and discuss the specific problems that concerned them. They offered tutoring programs in black history, English, and math, but they also schooled African Americans in how to attempt to integrate a public facility or to register to vote. The white response was predictable. Local law-enforcement officers harassed and sometimes beat SNCC workers, often arresting them on trumped-up charges.

February 1965 was a particularly active month for SNCC workers in Pine Bluff, and their activities captured considerable attention. Comedian Dick Gregory, and William Hansen, a white SNCC field secretary who founded the Arkansas Project, were sentenced to six months in jail and fined five hundred dollars for attempting to integrate a segregated truck stop, a decision they later successfully appealed. Shots were fired at the Reverend Benjamin Grinnage, a black SNCC worker (who later became the director of the Arkansas Project), while he was demonstrating at a local eating establishment. Thirty-nine blacks were arrested during that demonstration. Crowds of whites described by newsmen as "professional segregationists" taunted black demonstrators at another eating establishment in Pine Bluff. Fifteen blacks were arrested and SNCC worker James Jones, who as a student at AM&N College had joined SNCC in 1963, was roughed up by a state trooper. Just two years later Jones would have another very personal confrontation. In December 1965 his wife went into labor and was denied admission to the white section of Jefferson County Hospital.

Although these incidents were connected to attempts to integrate public facilities, feelings ran just as high over black efforts to vote. For Faubus and other southern politicians, the voting rights issue was particularly problematic. The governor realized the potential power of the black vote, which likely accounted for his decision to begin distancing himself from the extreme segregationists. Yet Faubus was distinctly uncomfortable with SNCC's activities in the Delta, in part because his white constituents and their state legislators felt particularly threatened. Given the growing likelihood of blacks recapturing the right to vote and the demographics of the Delta, the loss of white political control on the local level there was inevitable.

But the black struggle to secure the vote was hard fought, and even Faubus, who began to court the black vote, continued to appeal to white segregationists. In 1965 he called William Hansen a "professional agitator" and had SNCC activities under the surveillance of the state police. SNCC workers were undaunted. From the earliest days of SNCC's Arkansas Project, voting rights were a major focus. In the fall of 1963, for example, black high school students in Pine Bluff served as SNCC volunteers and canvassed door to door, encouraging blacks to pay their poll taxes and register to vote. Operating from a "Freedom House," SNCC workers distributed poll-tax books to black bars, restaurants, barbershops, and private homes throughout Pine Bluff. They sent volunteers to the downtown section on Friday nights and Saturdays, which were times when they were typically crowded with shoppers, and secured scores of voters that way. Other blacks were offered an opportunity to pay their poll taxes at churches on Sunday morning. By election day they had registered 2,876 black voters.

The Civil Rights Act of 1964 and the Voting Rights Act of 1965 followed rather than preceded the early efforts of SNCC in Arkansas and elsewhere, and these acts by Congress have to be understood in that context. The work of SNCC personnel and community volunteers drove the civil rights movement within the state and in the South as a whole and helped put pressure on Congress to end segregation and disfranchisement. Still, white society in eastern Arkansas remained dedicated to racial subordination. Most Delta schools finally integrated only after threats of court orders, court orders made more potent by the Civil Rights Act of 1964, which called for the withdrawal of federal funds to schools defying integration. Some Delta schools refused to integrate until forced by court order and some of them only integrated in the early 1970s. Efforts to integrate public facilities, such as hospitals, were also augmented by the 1964 act, which made it illegal for businesses engaged in interstate trade to refuse to serve blacks and denied federal funds to hospitals that failed to integrate. James Jones, the SNCC worker whose wife had been denied treatment in the white section of Jefferson County Hospital, filed a complaint on that basis shortly after the incident.

By the time that the Civil Rights Act of 1965 was passed, Orval Faubus had made his peace with integration and formed alliances with some black leaders. When he decided not to run for reelection in 1966, the Democratic Party made the mistake of selecting rabid race-baiter Jim Johnson to run in his place. Winthrop Rockefeller, who had broken with Faubus and run unsuccessfully against him in 1964, elected to run again in 1966 on the Republican ticket. Arkansas voters proved that they were not willing to return to the racial extremism that marked the Central High crisis and elected

Rockefeller. Significant numbers of white Democrats crossed party lines to elect Arkansas's first Republican governor since Reconstruction. Rockefeller's governorship did not signal a new era in race relations, however. Segregationist sentiment continued to smolder and the state legislature and Little Rock officials continued to erect barriers to integration. It could be argued that the rabid racism revealed during the Central High crisis in 1957 had merely gone underground. Although Rockefeller would be spectacularly unsuccessful in some of the economic and education measures he promulgated, he fashioned a new progressive agenda that later Democratic governors adapted and developed.

Winthrop Rockefeller

Winthrop Rockefeller was the grandson of John D. Rockefeller, the New York millionaire who founded Standard Oil and left both a fortune and a philanthropic legacy to his heirs. Although known for his often-ruthless business practices, John Rockefeller also favored certain charities and his heirs followed this tradition. Winthrop was no exception. Before coming to Arkansas in 1953, he served in the army during World War II and it was, in fact, a fellow combatant, Frank Newel of Little Rock, who first introduced him to the state. He purchased land on Petit Jean Mountain near Morrilton, Arkansas, built a mansion, started raising Santa Gertrudis cattle, and began philanthropic activities locally. He was appointed director of the Arkansas Economic Development Commission by Orval Faubus in 1954, and as director, he engaged in an ambitious campaign to convince industries to open plants in Arkansas. But the relationship between Faubus and Rockefeller began to cool in 1957. The segregationist stance taken by Faubus over the Central High issue disturbed Rockefeller for two reasons. First, maintaining a tradition established by his family, Winthrop had long been interested in issues concerning African Americans. He was convinced that blacks in Arkansas had been treated unfairly in the past, and he had been encouraged by the trend toward racial moderation exhibited by McMath and, it seemed at first, by Faubus. Second, the negative publicity devolving upon the state as a result of the Little Rock crisis inhibited efforts to convince industry to locate in Arkansas.

Whether Rockefeller had it in mind to enter the political arena before the Little Rock crisis, he certainly moved in that direction afterward. He faced long odds, however. A Republican in a solidly Democratic state, he had to build a political organization and woo a constituency. No Republican had been elected to a statewide office in the twentieth century in Arkansas, and Rockefeller would find it difficult to enter the small private club that constituted the Republican leadership in the state. The party, like that in other southern states, was made up of "post office" Republicans; that is, politicians who were content with federal patronage and understood that they could mount no effective campaign against the entrenched Democratic Party. With unlimited funds at his disposal, Rockefeller set to work building an organization. He lost his bid for the governorship against Faubus in 1964, but when Faubus decided not to run in 1966, Rockefeller was ready for the challenge. See plates 41 and 42 following page 366.

Although Faubus continued to enjoy considerable popularity with the white electorate, particularly, his decision not to run for reelection set up the circumstances for the first Republican victory in Arkansas since Reconstruction. Two other factors worked together to bring victory to Rockefeller in 1966. First, the man who captured the Democratic nomination was Jim Johnson, the very man who had helped bring the White Citizens Council to Arkansas in the wake of the Hoxie crisis. He was an avowed racist who spoke the language of the demagogue, and the Arkansas electorate was not willing to return to the politics of race that had marred the state's image in the previous decade. Even Faubus had moved away from the extremist position by 1966. Second, Rockefeller was able to secure 90 percent of the black vote, a new and growing force in Arkansas politics, given the Voting Rights Act of 1965. Although Rockefeller soundly defeated Jim Johnson, capturing majorities in Little Rock and most of the towns across the state, he faced an overwhelmingly Democratic and hostile legislature. He believed that the educational system needed fundamental reforms in order to attract industry and to prepare the state's citizens for a modern society, but his inability to lobby effectively doomed his education initiatives and much of the social legislation he sponsored. He did enjoy some success, however. He secured passage of measures that tightened insurance regulation and that more effectively regulated state banks and securities trading. The most significant piece of legislation passed during his governorship was the Freedom of Information Act, allowing the public access to public records and to the deliberations of public officials.

In a dramatic campaign that garnered headlines and attracted television cameras, he ordered the state police to close down illegal gambling in Hot Springs. In a less dramatic fashion, he created a commission to study how to more efficiently run the state's business, and he reformed the state civil service system. The governor also set out to reform the state's notorious prison system, ranked as one of the worst in the country, and brought in a professional penologist, Tom Murton. Murton, unfortunately, clashed with legislators, and then the governor himself, and engaged in a publicity campaign designed to speed up reform but which backfired. Under the glare of television cameras, he had bodies exhumed at the state prison, bodies of allegedly murdered inmates. It later turned out that they were the bodies from the graves of unclaimed inmates and paupers. Rather than being a success, Murton proved an embarrassment and was fired. Lasting solutions to the prison problem in Arkansas remained elusive.

Rockefeller secured a second term in office largely because the Democrats could mount no candidate untainted by association with Orval Faubus. State representative Marion Crank, despite being a Faubus associate, proved to be the strongest competitor, but the governor ran a well-organized campaign made more effective by the use of computerized mailings. In the end, it was the heavy black vote that allowed the governor to secure election with 52 percent of the overall vote. Having won election to a second term, Rockefeller proposed a number of revenue-generating measures and tax reforms, but he faced an even more hostile legislature. And he had not perfected effective lobbying techniques. Not satisfied with simply rejecting most of the governor's recommendations, the legislature seized control of the drafting of the Revenue Stabilization Act, which determined how state revenues were allocated, thus weakening the governor's office.

Rockefeller's hold on the electorate evaporated once the Democrats were able to field an attractive candidate in 1970. Only black voters remained loyal to him. During his two terms in office, blacks made some significant gains, securing a great many more state positions, including jobs as state troopers. Rockefeller also appointed a state Civil Rights Commission. Yet blacks were restless in the face of Rockefeller's racial moderation. They wanted more, faster. Although Rockefeller was the only southern governor to join in public mourning over the assassination of Martin Luther King Jr., and Little Rock escaped the violence that gripped many southern cities in response to his death, violence visited Little Rock later after the death of a black youth in prison, and Rockefeller had to call out the National Guard.

By 1970 Rockefeller was unpopular with most white voters and had established that he had no ability to work effectively with the legislature for passage of his legislative initiatives. He lost his bid for a third term in office in 1970 to Dale Leon Bumpers, a Democrat from Charleston, Arkansas. Rockefeller had failed to build an organization capable of sustaining the Republicans. Indeed, his was a brand of Republicanism that was not native to the state, and he was unable to shape a following that would sustain his moderate Republican stance. With his repudiation, the Republican Party had no one groomed to take his place and faced a series of moderate Democrats who posed a formidable challenge to them.

Arkansas's Powerful Congressional Delegation

Although the Republican Party would continue to have difficulties mounting a sufficient challenge to the Democratic Party in Arkansas, the Democratic Party itself was undergoing significant changes that would transform the kind of politicians elected to office. The Voting Rights Act of 1965 brought tens of thousands of new voters into play, but for a while Democrats themselves adapted sufficiently to attract these new voters. Still, politics in the state would undergo some significant changes. No longer could Democrats assume reelection and no longer would so many of them rise to the positions of power they had once occupied. With both Senate and House chairmanships made with seniority in mind, Arkansas's congressional delegation would not again enjoy the unprecedented power and authority they had assumed by the early 1970s. In 1973, they were unquestionably the most powerful single congressional delegation in Congress. In the House, Oren Harris served as a chair of the Commerce Committee, Ezekiel Candler "Took" Gathings as chair of the Agriculture Committee, and, particularly important, Wilbur Mills chaired the influential Ways and Means Committee. In the Senate, two Arkansans chaired especially powerful committees: John Little McClellan chaired the Appropriations Committee and J. William Fulbright headed the Foreign Relations Committee.

Most noteworthy was the service of McClellan, Mills, and Fulbright. Any assessment of them, however, must take into account their stance on civil rights. They served in office at a time when only a very few southern politicians departed from the southern perspective on race relations. They were not among that rare few. McClellan, Mills, and Fulbright all signed the Southern Manifesto in 1956, a document that declared southern opposition to court-ordered desegregation. Fulbright reportedly played a crucial role in toning down the document and, according to his biographer, Randall Bennett Woods, he became deeply disturbed by the murder of four black girls in a Birmingham, Alabama, church bombing in 1963 and began to work behind the scenes advising Pres. John F. Kennedy—and later President Johnson—in fashioning civil rights legislation. After their departure from Congress, younger politicians would take their place and, for the most part, take a very different perspective on civil rights. However, McClellan, Mills, and Fulbright made important contributions to the state and to the nation during their long tenures in office.

During Senator John L. McClellan's thirty-five-year career (1943–1977) in the Senate, he served not only as chair of the Appropriations Committee and the Government Operations Committee, but also of the Permanent Committee on Investigations. J. William Fulbright served in the House from 1943 to 1944 and then in the Senate from 1945 to 1974, during which time he launched the internationally known Fulbright Exchange Program and chaired the Senate Committee on Foreign Relations for fifteen years (1959–1974). Congressman Wilbur Mills was elected to the House in 1939 and served there for twenty-eight years (1939–1977), during which time he became the longest-serving chair of the powerful Ways and Means Committee and played a crucial role in the passage of the Medicare Bill in 1965.

John McClellan served in the Senate longer than any other Arkansan, from 1942 to 1977, allowing him to rise to a position of considerable power and influence. He first came to prominence when he played a role in removing Senator Joseph McCarthy from his chairmanship of the Senate Permanent Committee on Investigations in 1954. The Wisconsin Republican had become an embarrassment to members of Congress and even the Republican administration because of his bullying and abuse of witnesses. By 1954 McClellan became part of a small group of Democratic senators weary of McCarthy's tactics and determined to put a stop to them. Two incidents made his battle with McCarthy public: he led a walk-out from televised committee hearings, and he criticized the treatment of a black woman, Annie Lee Moss, by McCarthy's chief counsel, Roy Cohn. During his questioning of Moss, Cohn had alluded to a "confidential source" who allegedly confirmed Moss's membership in the Communist Party. McClellan, an accomplished attorney familiar with legal formalities, challenged Cohn in the use of an anonymous source. When Cohn attempted to remove his remark from the record, McClellan again challenged him, saying it could not be stricken, particularly from the public mind. "That's . . . the evil of it. Convicting people by rumor and hearsay and innuendo." McClellan became chair of the committee the next year when Democrats gained control of the Senate, and he served in that capacity for eighteen years (1955–1973), conducting several high-profile probes. His investigation into Labor Union activity exposed Jimmy Hoffa and the Teamsters Union to scrutiny and his probe of organized crime catapulted the committee's chief counsel, Robert F. Kennedy, to prominence.

McClellan was also able to rise to the position of chair of the Committee on Appropriations. Responsible for discretionary spending, that committee typically gave its members, particularly its chair, opportunities to bestow special favors on their constituents. Of special significance to Arkansas—and to Oklahoma—were appropriations to fund what became known as the McClellan-Kerr Arkansas River Navigation System. Launched in the 1930s, the project was intended for two purposes: First, to better control flooding along the river, a concern that had long existed but became indisputably essential after the great flood of 1927; second, to make the Arkansas River navigable through to Oklahoma. Congress was reluctant to authorize much beyond the creation of the Southwestern Division of the Corps of Engineers in 1936 because of the Great Depression, but in the succeeding years the Corps implemented some flood-control measures and constructed a few crucial locks and dams. As a member of the committee, McClellan had forcefully promoted these improvements. Once McClellan became chair in 1955, he worked closely with Senator Robert S. Kerr of Oklahoma and pushed the project through to completion. According to the *Encyclopedia of Arkansas History & Culture,* the Arkansas River Navigation System "is responsible for $1 billion to $2 billion in trade transportation in Arkansas each year and from $100 million to $1 billion in trade transportation in Oklahoma." By the time he died—in office—in 1977, he could look back on a distinguished career, one that secured an economic boom to the state in perpetuity.

In 1957, just three years after John McClellan assumed leadership of the Committee on Appropriations, Wilbur Mills became chair of the House Ways and Means Committee, a position he would hold until 1975. He remains the longest-serving chair of that committee. As his biographer, Kay Goss, puts it, "when anyone in Washington DC spoke of 'Mr. Chairman,' everyone understood that the reference was to Mills." The House Ways and Means Committee is the oldest standing committee of the House of Representatives and has responsibility for a broad range of matters, including banking, the bonded indebtedness of the U.S. Government, reciprocal trade agreements, Social Security, social services, and Medicare.

In his capacity as chair of the committee, Mills played a major role in shaping some aspects of President Johnson's Great Society, a program meant to provide a social safety net for America's poor. Mills's interest in social services for the poor and health care for the elderly was of longstanding. While serving as county judge of White County in the mid-1930s, he managed to secure a $5,000 appropriation from the quorum court to assist the county's poor in paying for hospital care and prescription medicine. As "Mr. Chairman" in the 1960s, he oversaw the extension of Social Security benefits to farmworkers and to the dependents of deceased parents. Most significantly for America's elderly citizens, he shaped the final version of the Medicare bill. As a fiscal conservative who advocated a balanced budget and sufficient tax revenues to fund government expenses, however, he was initially unsure about the wisdom of supporting—much less shaping—the Medicare bill. He eventually devised a formula that would fund its cost, a formula that included lowering taxes on the poorest citizens and raising taxes on the wealthiest. He said after he left office that his "greatest regret" was that he had failed—by only one vote—to secure national universal health insurance for all Americans.

The beginning of the end of Mills's long tenure in Congress started in an unlikely place and involved an equally unlikely person. In the early morning hours of October 9, 1974, Park Service Police, who were patrolling the Tidal Basin, a large reservoir between the Potomac River and the Washington Channel, pulled over a car driven by a former Nixon staffer for failure to turn on its lights. Mills, who was inebriated, was riding in the back with an Argentine stripper named Fanny Foxe. Before the police reached the car, Foxe dashed from the vehicle and jumped into the Tidal Basin, an act some believe was intended to distract the police. The incident did not prevent Mills from winning reelection—by a large margin—in early November, but a few weeks later he appeared on stage with Foxe and her husband at a burlesque theater in Boston. He was once again under the influence of alcohol. He subsequently resigned his chairmanship and did not seek reelection to his House seat in 1976. He joined Alcoholics Anonymous and became affiliated with the powerful New York law firm of Shea and Gould, working out of their Washington office. He spent the last years of his life working for that firm and raising funds for alcohol treatment centers.

J. William Fulbright is the most famous of the powerful Arkansas congressional delegation, mostly because of his role in the creation of the Fulbright Exchange Program and his high-profile criticism of American's extended war in Vietnam. He served one term in the House (1943–1944) and then defeated Hattie Caraway and took her place in the Senate in 1945. He became a member of the Senate Foreign Relations Committee and rose to the position of chair in 1959, serving in that capacity until he met defeat for reelection in 1974. Given his preoccupation with his committee work there and with a natural orientation to international concerns, he made his greatest contributions in foreign affairs. A Rhodes scholar and graduate of Georgetown University's prestigious law school, he seemed an unlikely person to connect to the Arkansas electorate. Observers remarked that he sometimes looked distinctly uncomfortable campaigning in Arkansas in casual clothing, preferring the suit and tie and his Senate committee room to checkered shirts and rural courthouses. Yet when the opportunity presented itself, he forcefully represented the interests of his rural constituency. For example, after chicken production in the United States glutted the world market, forcing down prices dramatically in Europe and undermining producers there, France and West Germany imposed tariffs on U.S. chicken. During the ensuing controversy, sometimes referred to as the Chicken War (1961–1964), Fulbright protested these trade sanctions at a conference sponsored by NATO to discuss nuclear disarmament. In the end, the United States imposed a 25 percent tariff on imported brandy, potato starch, dextrin, and light trucks from Europe. Only the tariff on light trucks remains in place today. See plate 43 following page 366.

Fulbright is perhaps best known as a particularly effective critic of the war in Vietnam, a criticism that arose during Johnson's presidency and lasted through Nixon's term in office. Although Fulbright's opposition is sometimes attributed to bitterness he felt about President Johnson's deception in the Gulf of Tonkin Affair, Fulbright had long been critical of a certain Cold War perspective that argued the necessity of responding to perceived threats from the USSR supposedly emanating from Asia and elsewhere with military force. Fulbright tended to see these as native-born, nationalist movements rather than a grand Soviet conspiracy. He was convinced that Vietnam was not a crucial front in the Cold War and became disillusioned with Johnson after the president convinced him that the South Vietnamese, backed by the Russians, had fired on a U.S. vessel in the Gulf of

Tonkin. Although the circumstances of the incident in the gulf were initially unclear, by the time Johnson spoke to Fulbright about it, the president knew that the vessel had not been fired on. Nevertheless, he convinced Fulbright to steer a resolution through Congress that authorized him to use military force without the necessity of securing a declaration of war. Johnson—and later Nixon—would use the resolution to expand the war in Vietnam. Fulbright's opposition to the war hinged on two factors. First, he believed that it was not in America's strategic interests to pursue wars on the periphery, that not every nationalist revolution was a Soviet scheme that required an American response. Second, he objected to the use of the Tonkin Resolution to fight an undeclared war, one that was very costly for America economically and in terms of loss of life. Of the over 500,000 American soldiers who were deployed to Vietnam, 58,220 died there. Among them were 589 Arkansans. Although he became a hero to many in the antiwar movement in the United States, he was actually no radical. His opposition to the war reflected a different understanding of the strategic importance of certain peripheral areas to America's national interests and a concern about the growing power of the executive branch of government. In the end, Fulbright's high-profile opposition to American involvement there contributed to his defeat in 1974 once Arkansas presented Democratic voters a moderate alternative in former governor Dale Leon Bumpers.

McClellan, Mills, and Fulbright had distinguished careers in Congress, leaving a considerable legacy. Fulbright has the highest profile internationally, raising issues about America's foreign policy that are still debated; McClellan's support for the Arkansas River Navigation System brought billions of dollars of revenue to the states of Arkansas and Oklahoma, revenue that continues to redound to the benefit of the citizens of the two states; and Mills's sponsorship of Medicare has aided countless elderly Arkansans and Americans. The end of their terms of office occurred between 1974 and 1977, and though their departures cannot be connected to Arkansas's changing electorate but to the death of one, the disgrace of another, and the third's stance on the Vietnam War, no politician elected to succeed them could ignore the black electorate.

The period between 1954 and 1970 was one of considerable turmoil and change in Arkansas. The social, economic, and political winds that swept across the state gave it a different face and a new posture, but many of the state's citizens remained undereducated and often impoverished. The Central High crisis continued to taint the state's image, and more subtle strategies for maintaining segregation emerged. The legacy of ill-paid agricultural jobs lived on in the Delta in the form of low-wage, low-skill employment in factories, factories that proved all too likely to be moving south in the pursuit of even lower-wage workers. Not much would change in the Delta in the years ahead, but a burst of economic activity in the northwest section of the state augered well for that area. In fact, certain families and entities in northwest Arkansas would soon overshadow the planters of the Delta in terms of wealth. Meanwhile, Little Rock would itself experience an economic revival, and certain individuals and companies there began to enjoy wealth and success. In the end, however, economic development did not move deeply into the fabric of Arkansas, and the next decades would see more of the same.

CHAPTER SIXTEEN

Arkansas in the Sunbelt South, 1970–1992

For most of the twentieth century, Arkansas policy makers promoted industrial development, believing that it would foster economic growth and prosperity. They did so without much success until after World War II, and the decades of the 1960s and 1970s were particularly propitious. Ben F. Johnson points out that "while manufacturing production increased by nearly 50 percent in the United States between 1967 and 1980, it soared by over 300 percent in Arkansas." These manufacturing enterprises were attracted to Arkansas because of its nonunion stance and the opportunity to pay low wages. While these jobs provided much-needed income to many Arkansans, wages were so low that some of those who held full-time jobs in manufacturing plants found themselves eligible for food stamp assistance. Because many communities were so eager to secure these industries that they reduced or eliminated taxes they would be subject to, they did not significantly enhance revenues for Arkansas communities. American manufacturers were themselves facing a crisis, however, as they endured stiff competition from some of the country's own Cold War allies. Indeed, the United States had expended enormous sums to revive the Japanese and Germany economies, for example, and by 1970 they were posing a significant challenge to U.S. manufacturers. Meanwhile, the nation began to shift to a service economy—banking, finance, health services, and the like—and in the direction of high-tech, turning away from the old manufacturing economy. In other words, just as Arkansas was finally able to register a manufacturing sector, the country was going in a different direction. This coincided with a related development: the Sunbelt South, a phenomenon that witnessed the growth of high-tech and the service-sector businesses in warmer climates; that is, generally below the 33rd parallel. Unfortunately, Arkansas, with an undereducated population, was not well positioned to participate in this new economy. Although some significant service-sector companies would emerge in the state, particularly Wal-Mart Corporation, no appreciable high-tech industry developed, and Arkansas is generally regarded by those who study the Sunbelt South as developing relatively too late and too little. The agricultural sector continued to thrive, however, especially in the 1970s as escalating crop prices made the decade "the state's most prosperous in the twentieth century." The 1980s would witness a sharp reversal of this agricultural prosperity, and the development of Arkansas's service-sector

Sunbelt South: Refers to the region below the 33rd parallel where high-tech and service-sector industries developed in the post–World War II era.

economy would soon begin to eclipse the state's farmers. This complex mix of economic factors would have long-term consequences both politically and economically and permeate all aspects of Arkansas's development.

Underlying Political, Demographic, and Economic Trends

The Voting Rights Act of 1965 served as a catalyst for significant political changes in the decades that followed its passage. The Democrats of the late nineteenth century had consolidated their power by disfranchising black voters, but after 1965, Democrats began to speak to issues that represented the interests of African Americans. As southern Democrats adopted more moderate positions on race, they no longer represented a buffer between the more liberal national Democratic Party and the ultra-Christian conservatism of much of the rural South. In this context, rural Arkansans, like their counterparts in other southern states, were increasingly drawn to the new Republican ideology, dominated as it was by both fiscal and social conservatism. Many Arkansas citizens wanted a well-ordered world but one in which they were free to pursue their interests unfettered by governmental interference. Although such desires—order and freedom—are often in conflict, their negotiation within the rural South demonstrates that they can be compatible. Many rural southerners appreciate a world ordered by Old Testament principles, but they want to be free of government interference in their affairs, free to purchase and carry guns, for example.

Arkansas was late in reorienting itself to the Republican Party, however, and if historians of the Sunbelt era are accurate in their assessment of the reasons for the new affinity of southerners for the GOP, then Arkansas's exceptionalism is understandable. According to their analysis, a major factor in the rise of the Republican Party in the South was a wave of immigration connected to the rise of the service-sector and high-tech industries. While Arkansas was to participate in this new economy, its early response was relatively anemic. Some immigration occurred, however, particularly in northern and western Arkansas as midwesterners moved into retirement communities like Cherokee Village and Bella Vista, both creations of entrepreneur John A. Cooper. Traditionally wedded to the Republican Party, they eventually helped solidify the party in northwestern Arkansas. Another set of migrants landed in central Arkansas, particularly around Little Rock, and assumed positions with the new jobs opening up in the service-sector economy. Often upwardly mobile and conservative in political philosophy, they settled in the suburbs springing up in Pulaski County.

Meanwhile, Delta planters, as elsewhere in the country, found themselves at a crossroads. As their economic woes began to deepen in the 1980s, they began to turn away from the Democratic Party. Although they were dependent upon federal subsidy programs, they wanted as little regulation as possible and were receptive to politicians who espoused a states' rights position. Republicans on the national level began to preach this message, stealing the thunder of the southern states' rights tradition exemplified by the Dixiecrats. National Democrats continued to support federal regulations, such as environmental initiatives designed to address the groundwater pollution problems created by the extensive use of pesticides, and pesticides were something planters were as dependent upon as they were upon federal subsidies. Arkansas Democrats running for Senate and congressional seats understood the importance of farm subsidies to their constituents, but found it increasingly difficult to negotiate the contradiction between the states' rights position that appealed to their constituents and their need for continued federal farm subsidies. To complicate matters further, farmers and planters would soon find themselves pawns in the Cold War against the Soviet Union. In response to the Soviet Union's invasion of Afghanistan in 1979, Pres. Jimmy Carter imposed an embargo on the sale of American-produced wheat to the Soviets. Although wheat was not one of the most important crops produced in Arkansas, it was a significant secondary crop, and farmers, through the state's Farm Bureau Federation, protested against it. Pres. Ronald Reagan lifted the embargo in April 1981, but the damage had been done. The Soviet Union had turned to other wheat producers, and though they eventually began buying American wheat, other factors contributed to a devastating farm crisis that deepened in the 1980s. The problems confronting agriculturalists in this era are complex and varied, depending on location and farm commodity, but they can be summarized as follows: The high prices for agricultural products in the 1970s led to higher land values and, in the super optimism then operating, many farmers and planters overextended themselves. The tight money policies enforced by the Reagan administration in the 1980s, together with historically high interest rates, resulted in a crash in farm prices and an increase in farm foreclosures. Like farmers elsewhere, Arkansas's planters and farmers became even more dependent upon government subsidies and continued to send Democrats to Congress who could be counted on to support a generous farm program. Nevertheless, though it was the tight money policies of a Republican president that accounted in part for their difficulties, prosperous farmers began to support Republican presidential candidates.

A significant demographic shift constituted another major factor underlying the erosion of the southern wing of the Democratic Party. A century earlier, the Delta region was experiencing unprecedented growth as a result of the extension of the railroad network, the emergence of the lumber industry, and the expansion of the plantation system. Planters had always exercised considerable power and influence within the Arkansas political system, and their position was solidified as the plantation system expanded. By the late twentieth century, the ground had literally been cut from beneath them. Railroads were all but obsolete and the state and interstate highway systems had worked a different result on the towns of Arkansas. The arrival of railroads had created many new towns and encouraged the growth of the population, but the expansion of the highway system encouraged a depopulation of eastern and southern Arkansas. The demographic changes that accompanied the transformation of plantation agriculture in the 1950s slowed, but blacks particularly continued their almost-century-long exodus from Delta counties (see chart). The efforts to attract smokestack industries to save small Delta towns had only modest success, in part because some planters could not quite bring themselves to fully support industrial development. A few well-situated towns convinced manufacturers to locate factories there, but their prosperity was fragile. The reliance on low-skill enterprises revealed the profound inadequacies in an educational system that had prepared the citizenry for little else but agricultural labor, and those industries, which paid little or no taxes to local government and low wages to its workers, proved to be of dubious benefit to the areas within which they settled. What benefit they bestowed proved all too transitory as many of them moved southward in search of even lower-wage labor, and most small towns found themselves on a treadmill, ever in search of yet another low-wage, low-skill factory to employ the remnants of its population. Indeed, Arkansas's plantation area was facing an uncertain future, and four of its counties have the dubious distinction of being among the one hundred poorest in the nation: Chicot, Lee, Monroe, and Phillips counties.

POPULATION BY RACE

PLACE	1940 WHITE	1990 WHITE	1940 BLACK	1990 BLACK
North/NW	296,140	483,724	2,809	3,036
West Central	288,667	431,909	23,601	22,741
Southwest	252,636	244,781	125,162	80,551
Eastern	522,127	531,776	287,924	175,384
Little Rock Area	112,877	252,554	43,182	92,200

While the old plantation counties struggled to maintain their population and save their towns, the northwestern part of the state experienced an unprecedented boom. This was in large part the result of the vast expansion of the service-sector economy in that region of the state. The most important leader in that expansion was Wal-Mart, Inc. By 1970, Sam Walton had moved his operation to another level, and over the next several decades his enterprise, now incorporated, would expand phenomenally, becoming a world-class economic giant and changing the very nature of the retail enterprise. As historian Brent Riffel suggests, he had already "penetrated the rural market in the 1960s, opening retail stores in small towns, and often becoming a community's central retail outlet." In the 1970s Wal-Mart opened its first distribution center and was listed on the New York Stock Exchange. In 1972, its first year on the stock exchange, Wal-Mart's stock split twice, signaling its strength and desirability. In 1977 it moved well beyond Arkansas as Wal-Mart began acquiring stores in Illinois and Michigan. It also introduced different services within its stores—including a pharmacy, an automobile service center, and a jewelry division. By 1979, annual sales reached more than a billion dollars. The company continued to acquire other stores in the 1980s, and its stock continued to split as it became a highly desirable and reliable commodity on the stock

Service-sector economy: An economy marked by significant service-sector business operations; that is, businesses that provide goods and services to consumers.

exchange. In 1984 Wal-Mart hired a dynamic chief executive officer, David Glass, who led the company through a remarkable period of growth. Under Glass's leadership, Wal-Mart expanded both nationwide and internationally, and soon vendors were moving into northwest Arkansas, eager to supply what was rapidly becoming the world's largest retail operation.

While the rise of the chicken and trucking industries in northwest Arkansas seems to pale in comparison, this phenomenon was extremely important and accounted for much of the economic expansion of the region. As Brent Riffel observes, Tyson Foods, Inc., also marketed internationally and experienced a period of rapid expansion in the 1980s, purchasing a hog-producing facility in North Carolina in 1977 and making it onto the Fortune 500 list in 1982. Soon it was selling to such fast-food giants as McDonald's. When it purchased Holly Farms in 1989, it doubled its market share and stood poised to buy out other companies in the coming decade. Meanwhile, a flood of workers came to Arkansas (and wherever else Tyson operated) to find employment in processing and related plants. Although these industries largely employed low-wage, unskilled labor, Tyson also hired highly paid executives in their corporate offices. Together with executives who came to work for the billion-dollar Wal-Mart Corporation they helped generate booms in the trucking industry, particularly J. B. Hunt Transport Services, and in the construction of expensive homes that set the stage for a reassessment of property values.

J. B. Hunt Transport Services, Inc., founded by Johnnie Bryan (J. B.) Hunt, had been operating since the 1960s, producing poultry litter for sale to farmers. Hunt, who began driving a truck in 1953 before launching his poultry litter enterprise, began his own trucking operation in 1969. He expanded rapidly in the 1970s, but his company owed much of its phenomenal success to the deregulation of the trucking industry in 1980. Unlike most companies, which preferred to hire independent truckers who bore the transportation costs themselves, J. B. Hunt owned his own trucks and depended on a cadre of drivers willing to accept low wages in exchange for steady employment. In the 1980s Hunt was able to secure a contract to haul for Wal-Mart, an extremely lucrative contract that propelled Hunt into a new arena. By the 1990s the company was worth a billion dollars. Headquartered in Lowell in northwest Arkansas, J. B. Hunt eventually became the largest publicly held trucking company in the United States and employed fifteen thousand people.

As the unemployment rate hovered close to 2 percent in northwest Arkansas by the early 1990s, the industry demand for low-wage, low-skill labor grew to exceed the available workforce. The poultry industry in particular found a ready and willing labor pool in the Hispanic communities of Texas, other southwestern states, and Mexico. As Hispanic people stepped into the job market created by that industry, they also found employment opportunities in the burgeoning construction industry. For the first time in its history, northwest Arkansas was no longer an overwhelmingly white, Anglo-Saxon and Protestant enclave. The significant Hispanic population developed its own subculture, which included cultural, economic, and religious enterprises, but the emergence of a rabid anti-immigration movement, made up in part of the transplanted midwesterners, turned what should have been merely a cultural phenomenon into a political issue. The anti-immigration movement complained that the expansion of the Hispanic population placed new demands upon the larger community, particularly in relation to the need for bilingual educational, law enforcement, and legal, medical, and social services. Much of the white community responded positively to these circumstances; some church and other organizations extended assistance and services to needy families. All of this did not transpire, however, without creating antagonisms fueled by stereotypes and misunderstandings.

Even as the unemployment rate in northwest Arkansas fell below the national average and economic prosperity reigned, the population growth of Little Rock and a few smaller cities accelerated. Stimulating this growth was the development of new economic enterprises in banking and finance, information technology, communications, and medical technology. Although Arkansas would experience no Sunbelt phenomenon similar to that occurring in Florida, Texas, and California, several Arkansas entrepreneurs with a central Arkansas focus moved into the service sector—if not the high-tech economy—and signaled their ability to appreciate the prospects of the developing service economy. One individual, Witt Stephens, parlayed a job as a bond salesman into his own investment company, Stephens, Inc. and leveraged the new wealth he acquired into the creation of a number of financial and business interests that played key roles in the economic transformation of the state. These interests included some more traditional enterprises like utilities, agriculture, banking, and retail merchandising, but they also included trading in commodities. In fact, at one point Stephens, Inc., was the largest commodities trader operating outside of Wall Street.

Other companies moving into the new service sector in central Arkansas included Acxiom, Alltel Corporation, and Dillard's Department Stores. Acxiom, founded in 1969 by Charles D. Ward of Conway, was originally called Demographics. Specializing in data information, which it sold to a variety of companies to assist them in direct marketing their products, it established a headquarters in Little Rock and opened offices in several cities around the globe. Although Alltel began as a small firm in 1943 selling telephone poles and cables for television stations, it merged with Mid-Continent Telephone Company in 1983 and moved into wireless phone services. While it relocated its headquarters to Ohio, Alltel maintained a regional office in Little Rock and became a major player in central Arkansas's economy. Even after the company sold to Verizon Wireless in 2008, it maintained an important force in the state. Dillard's Inc., the brainchild of William Thomas Dillard, began modestly in Nashville, Arkansas, with one small store and eventually became one of the largest retailer clothing and home-furnishing operations in the country. Little Rock became its headquarters in the 1960s and the company expanded rapidly in the 1970s and 1980s. As Little Rock grew in relation to the successes of enterprises like these, its suburbs expanded rapidly, suburbs settled by upwardly mobile and prosperous white-collar workers who had little connection to the rural economy that had once dominated both economically and politically within the state.

Faces like Flint against the Law, Part II

The creation of suburbs in Little Rock dated back to the post–World War II era when the rural population moved to the city and overloaded the existing housing infrastructure. However, the shape the suburbs took as white-only enclaves reflected the determination of city and county officials to maintain segregation. Two inseparable ideas underlay policy making in suburb location in this context. First, white supremacy remained a potent force, and segregation was a mainstay of that ideology; second, realtors, business interests, and many white property owners believed that a black presence in a white neighborhood lowered property values. The passage of the *Brown* decision in 1954 mandating desegregation of public education accelerated a trend toward the development of white suburbs that were designed by business interests and fostered by city and state officials. In the period between 1970 and 1992, a new phase of obstruction to the *Brown* decision developed.

> ***Swan v. Mecklenburg Board of Education:*** A U.S. Supreme Court decision rendered in 1971 that sanctioned the use of busing to achieve integration.

The state's dedication to white supremacy proved to have remarkable staying power, and although challenged by court decisions at many turns, the situation remained unresolved and integration incomplete in 1970. In 1971 a crucial Supreme Court decision (*Swann v. Mecklenburg Board of Education*) sanctioned the use of "busing" to accomplish integration. Contrary to the Court's intention, the implementation of busing in Little Rock—and elsewhere—only led to the increased segregation of city schools. Two key developments accounted for this. First, state and county government continued to support the growth of suburbs for whites only. Given that many of these suburbs were outside the Little Rock School District's boundaries and the courts' decisions focused only on integration within specific school districts, the growth in white suburbs in Pulaski County rather than within Little Rock took on a new urgency for those who opposed integration. In the meantime, the Court's decision also led to significant outmigration to Cabot (Lonoke County), Bryant (Saline County), and Sheridan (Grant County). The second means of subverting the *Swann* decision, the creation of private schools, was particularly effective. Because such schools were not funded by the state, they were not subject to federal rulings. The first school created in Little Rock in the aftermath of the *Swann* decision, Pulaski Academy (1971), was located in west Little Rock. Although one of the principal founders, William F. Rector, announced that children of all races would be welcome to apply, he used a coded reference signaling that black children would find a less-than-welcoming atmosphere. Ben F. Johnson quotes him as saying, "I even hope we'll be allowed to play 'Dixie' if we want to without having a riot about it." By that point in time, the playing of "Dixie" had been embraced by white supremacists and become a symbol of their cause. Black students understood what the song was meant to acknowledge, and its use in schools was intended to remind both black and white children of white supremacy ideology. Historian Gene Vinzant cites some telling figures: of the 878 students in Pulaski Academy in 1979, only 1 was black; and 97 percent of those in all the private academies combined were white. "When busing began in 1971, the 13,222 white students in the Little Rock School District had greatly outnumbered the estimated 5,400 whites in the county's private schools. By 1984, however, the number of white students in the county's private schools (8,436) significantly exceeded the number of white students in the Little Rock School District (5,265)." The statistics for the city's public schools are also telling. In 1971, the Little Rock School District was 74 percent white. By 1984, whites constituted only 30 percent of the population. Meanwhile, 78 percent of the students in the Pulaski County Special School District were white.

Racism was not the only reason—and for some whites not the reason at all—for the creation of private academies and white flight to the suburbs. As critics have pointed out, busing eroded neighborhood cohesion in both black and white communities and placed an added burden on children by moving them to unfamiliar locations. The time needed to travel also limited the ability of children, particularly low-income children, to participate in extracurricular activities. The burden was especially heavy on black children who were much more likely to be bused and placed in predominantly white schools. The problem was heightened by the anger of the white community over the busing issue and the reminders, like the playing of "Dixie" and the use of other Confederate symbols, of the ideology of white supremacy. Discipline problems arose in the heavily black schools, in part because white teachers and principals transferred to those schools were not accustomed to dealing with black students who, according to Gene Vinzant, had a different orientation to authority figures. Black teachers were shocked by the laxity with which white teachers approached discipline, particularly in the junior high schools. Under these circumstances, many white parents did not want their children to be among the few white students in a classroom. Many black parents, for different reasons, felt the same way and some of them—who could afford it—moved their children into private schools, too.

White flight had other implications, probably only dimly—if at all—foreseen by those who promoted them. Not only had the Little Rock School District (LRSD) become overwhelmingly black by 1980, black voters in the city became a powerful voting bloc. Together with white voters committed to integration, they elected a school board that was ready to address the re-segregation of the city's schools. In 1982, the LRSD board filed a suit against the Pulaski County Special School District (PCSSD) and the North Little Rock School District (NLRSD) reciting a litany of obstructive techniques, particularly the creation of white suburbs sanctioned by county and state officials, meant to thwart integration. LRSD sought consolidation of the three school districts in Pulaski County (LRSD, PCSSD, and NLRSD), and federal district judge Henry Woods rendered a decision in 1984 so ordering. Although the Eighth Circuit Court of Appeals would overrule him on the issue of consolidation in 1985, arguing that it was too drastic a remedy, the court agreed with Judge Woods's substantive findings and accepted the arguments of the plaintiffs (LRSD) regarding the obstructionist tactics employed to impede integration. The court was not retreating from the principle of integration, in other words, but instead of consolidation, it called for inter-district (across the three districts—LRSD, PCSSD, and NLRSD) integration plans to be drawn up and for the state to bear the cost of executing those plans.

Judge Gerald W. Heaney, of the U.S. Court of Appeals for the Eighth Circuit, wrote a lengthy decision in which he reviewed the implementation of residential segregation as a deliberate policy of city, county, and state governments designed to segregate the black population in certain neighborhoods. Behind the scenes of this decision had been considerable negotiation among the Eighth Circuit's distinguished jurists. Judge Richard Arnold played the most important role in convincing his fellow judges to reject the consolidation of the three school districts and instead settle on an inter-district remedy. Still, Judge Arnold would find it necessary to write a concurring and dissenting opinion in which he raised two objections to the majority opinion. As his biographer, Polly Price, suggests, Arnold believed the Eighth Circuit should have remanded the case "back to the district court to craft a new remedy." He also objected to the assignment of "historical guilt" as a factor in ordering the state to fund the remedy.

Regardless of Arnold's reservations, Judge Heaney detailed the history of the three school districts, particularly the methods employed by them to limit school desegregation and the litigation that had resulted from those efforts. He focused much of his attention on residential segregation. Even before Faubus blocked integration in 1957 and then closed schools rather than surrender segregation in 1958, the state and county government had engaged in policies that made integration structurally difficult to accomplish. After 1959, Little Rock continued to support residential segregation and pursued integration plans that, in fact, were intended to delay integration: pupil placement and "freedom of choice." By the late 1960s both of these had been repudiated by court decisions, but these adverse decisions only gave rise to new means of obstruction.

One other important finding in Judge Woods's 1984 decision that Judge Heaney and the majority on the Eighth Circuit found convincing involved a strategy employed by both North Little Rock and Pulaski County to force black students within their boundaries into the Little Rock School District, particularly above the junior high school level. In so doing, they were making Little Rock responsible for the education of black students at the high school level. This was a key finding in that it gave the appeals court the added leverage in reasoning that an inter-district remedy was warranted and that the state should foot the bill. The Eighth Circuit recited a history of collusion between the Pulaski County Special School District and the county and state government. The state had created the Pulaski County Special School District in 1927, apparently in order to facilitate the consolidation of rural school districts in the county. However, the new district provided only meager facilities for black children at the elementary school level and no black high schools. Black children wishing to attend high school were transported by the school district to the black high schools in Little Rock. In the early 1950s, according to the Appeals Court, the Pulaski County District had gone so far as to cooperate "with LRSD and the state in substantial inter district segregative acts by permitting the annexation of lands for the construction of a black residential housing project, the Granite Mountain project, thus insuring that the black students in the project would attend school in LRSD rather than PCSSD, and enhancing LRSD's position as the school district with the responsibility of educating black children."

The Pulaski County Special School District's segregative acts intensified after the *Green* decision in 1968 repudiated the so-called freedom of choice plan. The county devised a new means of supporting white flight to the suburbs. Until that time, whenever the city expanded its boundaries, the LRSD took over annexed areas. After the *Green* decision, newly annexed areas remained within the Pulaski County Special School District, thus enabling them to avoid having to comply with desegregation orders aimed at the Little Rock School District. To make matters worse for black children in the county, "after 1973, the PCSSD continued to close schools in black neighborhoods and to build new schools in distant suburbs that were the developing areas of white population." Given residential segregation policies that made it difficult for blacks to purchase houses in these new white neighborhoods, practices sanctioned by officials at all levels, these new schools were destined to be white-only over the long term. The new schools meant to service white students included Cato Elementary (1973), North Pulaski (1977), Northwood Junior High School (1980), and Robinson Middle School (1981). Meanwhile, black children suffered by comparison. The appeals court accepted the testimony of expert witness Dr. Robert Dentler that "the county took pains not to site new schools where they would be accessible to blacks, and others they dusted off dilapidated plants and arranged to have them as walk-in schools for black students well out of reach of possible transportation by white students." In other words, the county failed to build new schools "in or near the central part of the county, or to the east or southeast, where blacks live." Having pursued the policy of building new schools for white children while saddling black children with old and inferior facilities, the PCSSD and the state had a day of reckoning coming to them.

The North Little Rock School District also had a role to play in the drama unfolding over integration. It had been under court order since 1968 to integrate (*Davis v. Board of Education of the North Little Rock, Arkansas School District*), but residential segregation presented the city with some special problems of its own making. The petitioners in the case leading to the 1968 decision returned to court in 1977 raising a number of issues. Particularly relevant was the existence of the Dixie Addition within North Little Rock, a predominantly black residential area. The complaint alleged that the black students in the peculiarly named housing addition—who could miss the significance—were required to travel some distance to attend North East High School and two factors made that difficult and even dangerous. First, the school district was providing inadequate transportation for the students in the Dixie Addition; second, the students had to cross a busy interstate highway in order to reach the high school, located in the northeast section of the city. The court ordered the district to provide transportation.

> ***Davis v. Board of Education of the North Little Rock, Arkansas School District:*** A federal court order mandating that the North Little Rock School District integrate its schools.

While the provision that North Little Rock provide transportation potentially solved the problem for the children in the Dixie Addition, North Little Rock devised a new strategy for forcing its black children into the Little Rock schools, a strategy designed to keep its own schools white. According to the decision rendered by the Eighth Circuit Court of Appeals in 1985, the city had been engaged in "grossly over classifying its black pupils into special education and educable mentally retarded (EMR) categories." It did so at a rate over three and a half times that of Little Rock. The rates for black children compared to white children so characterized defied a national average by "two and one-half times as many black students as whites." Given these disparities, the Eighth Circuit found it impossible to accept North Little Rock's argument that the classification was justified because of social and economic factors: "These factors may explain why there may be more black than white EMR students, but do not explain why the NLRSD experience should be so different from that in the nation, in Arkansas, or in LRSD." Under the circumstances, many black children, unwilling to accept deprecating labels, either dropped out of school altogether or transferred to Little Rock, making Little Rock the school district responsible for black education.

In 1986 the Eighth Circuit outlined how inter-district integration might be achieved by the use of a strategy referred to as "majority to minority" transfers (M to M); the next year the court introduced the magnet school concept. Magnet schools were usually well funded and set up with a specialized curriculum designed to make them desirable options, attracting rather than compelling attendance. Both the magnet school concept and the M to M transfer system had been adopted elsewhere in the Eighth Circuit's jurisdiction and seemed promising. Recognizing that the courts had spoken and unwilling to pursue further litigation, the county's three school districts negotiated a compromise in 1989 meant to address the issue of inter-district desegregation. The Settlement Agreement resolved numerous funding issues related to the inter-district remedy, specifically how to fund the magnet schools and the M to M transfer program, and it incorporated by reference inter-district desegregation plans. The agreement, however, had to be approved by the legislature, and many legislators opposed it. Wealthier families, who inhabited the white enclaves in exclusive neighborhoods, were strongly opposed to ratification of the Settlement Agreement, and many in the legislature listened to them. Other legislators representing school districts outside of Little Rock and Pulaski County opposed it because it funneled a disproportionate percentage of the state's education dollars to the three Pulaski County school districts. The state was going to have to assume the burden of funding the remedy, a heavy expense but one which the Eighth Circuit believed the state should assume because of its complicity in creating the problem in the first place. Nevertheless, the legislature approved it on March 17, 1989, and then, when the state supreme court ruled all acts passed by the legislature that session as null and void because they had failed to pass a general appropriations bill, it secured passage again in late summer.

Settlement Agreement: Refers to a compromise between the Little Rock School District, the North Little Rock School District, and the Pulaski County Special School District that outlined how to fund court-mandated integration.

The Settlement Agreement was a compromise between the different parties and, as such, it required each to give up something. When Special Master Aubrey McCutcheon issued a sixty-page report blasting the agreement for surrendering too much and thus perpetuating rather than alleviating segregation, the stage was set for yet another confrontation. Shortly after McCutcheon's report was issued, Judge Henry Woods, who agreed with the special master on certain issues, ordered modifications that included providing a metropolitan supervisor, a man he would appoint, to oversee the desegregation of the three districts. He chose a well-respected administrator who was credited with having guided the Buffalo, New York, school district through successful desegregation, Eugene Reville. However, on July 2, 1990, a three-judge panel of the Eighth Circuit Court of Appeals overruled Woods on his modifications to the Settlement Agreement, essentially arguing that the parties to the agreement should be allowed to settle their own affairs without intervention of federal authorities—as long as they adhered to the spirit of the desegregation order. But that was just the problem. According to Judge Woods and Special Magistrate McCutcheon, the Settlement Agreement would only perpetuate segregation. In protest, Judge Woods recused himself from the case and McCutcheon resigned his position.

Upon Woods's recusal, federal judge Susan Weber Wright inherited the case. She was a conservative Republican appointed to the bench by Pres. George H. W. Bush in 1989, and she would keep the pressure on the schools to make certain they adhered to the plans as they stood under the Settlement Agreement and in keeping with the Eighth Circuit Court's position. However, the state would take steps over the next two decades to undermine various aspects of the agreement. Anyone familiar with Arkansas's record on the desegregation issue could hardly have been surprised.

The New Arkansas Women

An examination of the failure of the Equal Rights Amendment in the state reveals the profound conservatism of much of the population. By the early 1970s a challenge to women's liberation was being mounted by those who saw it as endangering the family. A century earlier, the drive for women's suffrage had been a major preoccupation of women activists, but women had been voting since 1920, and despite the rhetoric of those who fought for women's right to vote, they cast their ballots much like men. The notion that enfranchised women, with their special "female" sensibilities and instincts, would transform politics was not borne out. By the end of the century, the "exceptionality" of female voters had little currency, although it was clear that electing women to office did in some cases make a difference where women's issues were concerned. Yet there were relatively few women elected to high office—elsewhere or in Arkansas—despite the fact that women continued to be active politically through Democratic and Republican women's organizations and through the League of Women Voters. Vada Sheid, who was first elected to the General Assembly in 1966, also became the first woman elected to the Arkansas Senate in 1976. See plate 44 following page 366.

By the early 1970s, the National Organization of Women (NOW), which had a more activist agenda than the League of Women Voters, was attracting members in Arkansas. The moment of truth came in 1972, however, when Congress acted on two fronts. It passed Title IX, a federal regulation prohibiting sex discrimination in any school receiving federal funds, and it referred an Equal Rights Amendment to the states.

Title IX was inspired by the recognition that over the course of the twentieth century women had become a permanent fixture in the workplace and that great disparities in occupational status and in income existed between male and female workers. By 1974, almost 50 percent of all women between the ages of eighteen and sixty-four were employed outside the home, and almost one-sixth of America's families were headed by women. Most of them were working because they were single, widowed, divorced, separated, or deserted, or married to men who earned less than five thousand dollars a year. Of those who headed their own households, the majority of them were living at poverty or subpoverty levels. Title IX was predicated on the assumption that the problem had to be addressed at the level at which women were educated. To implement Title IX, Pres. Gerald Ford created a Commission on the Status of Women, and soon governors throughout the country appointed similar state women's commissions. Like his counterparts elsewhere, Gov. Dale Bumpers created such a state commission, and commission members took upon themselves the task of ascertaining to what extent sex discrimination existed in the state's public schools and colleges. They discovered disparities in varsity sports and sex-stereotyped curriculum offerings and requirements (such as home economics for girls and shop for boys). They attributed the fact that most school administrators were male while most public schoolteachers were female to the point of view that males should be awarded administrative positions because they had families to support, ignoring the fact that many women headed their own households or that their income was as essential to the family economy as was the husbands.

A 1978 study by the Scientific Manpower Commission, a private, nonprofit organization formed by major scientific societies to investigate employment trends and problems common to the sciences, confirmed what many commission members were coming to understand. The problem of disparities in income was not determined solely by the kind of employment that women undertook. Regardless of occupational category, women earned less than their male counterparts. In fact, males without high school diplomas made more money than women with college degrees, suggesting that eliminating obstacles to higher education for women was not enough. The study concluded that although a greater number of women were entering typically male professions (becoming engineers, doctors, dentists, etc.), "women's salaries [were] lower than those of men with comparable training and experience at every age, every degree level, in every field and with every type of employer." Already by 1978, however, signs of change were on the horizon. Beginning women engineers and chemists were securing higher salaries than male counterparts at the same level precisely because there were so few women in those fields, and companies and government agencies were eager to avoid violating affirmative action guidelines.

Meanwhile, the Women's Commissions broadened their agenda to include support for the Equal Rights Amendment. Originally written by Alice Paul in 1923 to guarantee equal rights for women, it was revived and passed by Congress in 1972 but ultimately failed to secure ratification. Within three years of its passage, thirty-five states quickly ratified the amendment, just three short of the necessary three-fourths to make it a part of the Constitution. Of the fifteen states that had not ratified it, ten were southern states: Alabama, Florida, Georgia, Louisiana, Mississippi, Missouri, North Carolina, South Carolina, Virginia, and Arkansas. Even as Women's Commission members made ratification a major part of their agenda, the opposition began to organize against it, and they operated on two fronts. First, they worked to convince legislators in states where the measure had barely passed to "rescind" their approval, something that involved those states and Congress in a bitter debate. Second, conservatives worked furiously to convince legislators in states that had not yet voted on ratification to reject it. By 1976, Arkansas was a battleground state, and Phyllis Schlafly, a conservative radio commentator and author, came to Arkansas to debate the issue with Diane Kincaid (later Diane Blair), a political scientist at the University of Arkansas and chair of the first Governor's Commission on the Status of Women. The commission was created in 1971 by then-governor Dale Bumpers to study the status of women in Arkansas. The highly publicized debate took place in the Capitol Building on Valentine's Day. The galleries were so crowded that nearly two hundred spectators, most of them women, sat on the floor or in chairs on the second-floor rotunda. Women who opposed the amendment waved banners against it while the women who supported it wore pro-ERA buttons.

Equal Rights Amendment: An amendment meant to ensure that women had equal rights with men that was passed by Congress in 1972 but that ultimately failed to secure ratification by the states.

Governor's Commission on the Status of Women: A commission created to evaluate the status of women in Arkansas.

The arguments made by both Schlafly and Kincaid were familiar to most of those who attended the event. Opponents to the ERA believed that many of the problems in modern society were due to the erosion of the traditional family structure, and they blamed the emancipation of women for the rising divorce rate, the increase in juvenile delinquency, and a decline in patriotism as reflected by anti–Vietnam War protests. Some believed that the Bible sanctioned the subordination of women to their husbands and that the decline in church membership was owing to feminism. Other opponents argued that a constitutional amendment was unnecessary, that the Fourteenth Amendment was protection enough, and that additional existing laws explicitly protected women against sex discrimination in employment and other areas. Some raised fears that the ERA amendment would eliminate some protections for married women and suggested that women would be forced into the workplace whether they wished to work or not. A heated debate arose over whether women would be required to register for the draft and fight alongside men in the trenches in case of war.

Proponents of the ERA rejected the argument that the emancipation of women was responsible for an erosion of the traditional family structure. They argued that the

Diane Kincaid (Blair) debating Phyllis Schlafly. *From* Arkansas Gazette, *February 15, 1975.*

economy of the late twentieth century required married women to contribute to the family income and those women deserved to receive "equal pay for equal work." They suggested that the Fourteenth Amendment did not provide enough protection for women and that since existing laws explicitly protecting the rights of women were statutory, they were subject to revision or elimination, and thus provided no permanent guarantee, at least not in the way that a constitutional amendment would. As to eliminating certain protections that women enjoyed, proponents of ERA argued that laws that conferred a specific benefit to women would be extended to men and those laws that no longer benefited women were the only ones that would be dispensed with. They denied that women would be required to work, and while they admitted that women would probably have to register for the draft, they asserted that women would not qualify physically for combat (the latter was something later feminists would reject).

Schlafly and Kincaid covered most of these arguments in their debate, and those who heard them claimed that both made eloquent speeches, but legislators would not allow the issue to be reported out of committee. However, the conservatives were not satisfied with the apparent victory. In 1977 a national conservative group, the Eagle Forum, created an Arkansas adjunct named FLAG (family, life, America, God) to fight ratification of the ERA by the state legislature. In 1979, as the amendment was being considered in the House State Agencies Committee, Gov. Bill Clinton called for the legislature to bring the amendment to a vote. Reminiscent of Governor Brough standing with his wife on the suffrage issue sixty years earlier, Clinton "met briefly with many of the ERA opponents in the governor's conference room and defended his support for the amendment. With his wife, Hillary Rodham, standing next to him, he said he regretted that the issue had become so divisive and resented the 'labeling' of ERA supporters as being against family life and religious values." Hillary Rodham Clinton, who by then had adopted her husband's surname, had served with Diane Kincaid on the first Women's Commission. The House State Agencies Committee subsequently voted 14 to 4 against bringing the measure to the floor of the legislature. Ultimately, an insufficient number of states approved the measure and the ERA amendment died on the vine.

The success of the opponents of the ERA amendment in linking it with a decline in family values and a growing lack of respect for God and country largely accounted for its failure in Arkansas and in most other southern states. Arkansas legislators had been able to see beyond arguments made against the extension of suffrage to women sixty years earlier, but the opposition to ERA was much better organized in the 1970s. The feminism of the 1970s was connected in the minds of many to the compendium of "causes" that emerged in the 1960s: agitation against the Vietnam War, the emergence of a more militant civil rights movement, and the excesses of the hippie movement. Added to that was the emergence of militant feminists who were associated with lesbianism or at least with anti-male bias. Although few of the feminists in Arkansas had any connection to the causes of the 1960s, and most of them had little tolerance for radical feminism, their opponents were able to capitalize on the perception that they and the amendment they fought for were a part of the disorder that seemed to threaten home and family.

New Political Economy

Although the ERA debate reflected the conservatism of the Arkansas electorate, the voters continued to elect Democrats to office far longer than voters in other southern states where a viable Republican Party began to emerge. This was delayed in Arkansas until the 1990s, largely because of two factors. One factor was economic and structural.

Upwardly mobile, middle-class whites constituted one segment of the voting population attracted to the fiscally conservative Republican philosophy, and they tended to mass in suburban areas located on the fringes of the larger cities. Southern cities had been on a growth pattern since World War II, and as the civil rights movement took shape, affluent whites flocked to suburbs. Although they might differ from their rural counterparts in terms of their educational and economic advantages, they, too, were attracted to the Republican message, particularly the conservative economic policies that Republican politicians espoused. Little Rock was the only city in Arkansas with a significant growth of suburbs, and voters in these suburbs would eventually become a reliable base of support for Republican candidates. A complimentary population trend was that occurring in northwest Arkansas, an area that had always been unusually hospitable to the Republican Party. The population explosion there, particularly given the kinds of people moving into the area (relatively prosperous retirees from the traditionally Republican Midwest and executives working for Wal-Mart and Tyson), would make northwest Arkansas an important component in the development of a more robust Arkansas Republican Party by the last decade of the twentieth century.

The second factor involved in delaying the development of the two-party system in Arkansas was the presence of moderate Democrats capable of negotiating a continuance of the fragile alliance between the Democratic Party and the essentially conservative Arkansas electorate. Ultimately, however, rural Arkansas would come to find the Republican social agenda more persuasive than that of the state's Democratic Party, a party growing more sympathetic to women's issues and transformed by the presence of a large number of newly enfranchised black voters. As outspoken opposition to abortion rights took shape in the rest of the nation, for example, it also became a factor in the disenchantment of the rural electorate with the Democratic Party in Arkansas. Although few state legislators of either party would venture a pro-choice opinion, the polarization of the two national parties on that issue made it easier for Republican candidates for Congress, for governor and, ultimately, for senator, to score points on the issue and capture a significant number of Arkansas voters. Meanwhile, black voters first showed their power by helping elect Republican Winthrop Rockefeller in 1966, but they proved loyal only to the man, not his party. Once Rockefeller was out of the picture and moderate Democrats arrived on the scene, blacks turned to them and, incidentally, helped transform the Democratic Party into something that many of the state's white rural voters found increasingly unattractive.

As political scientists Diane Blair and Jay Barth have argued, three successive Democratic governors helped maintain the Democratic Party in Arkansas. Characterizing them as the "big three," Blair and Barth see them as moderate and progressive rather than truly liberal in orientation, and this helped make them palatable to both the increasingly Republican-leaning suburban voters and the socially conservative rural electorate. At the same time that they called for improvements in education and health services, these governors also practiced fiscal restraint and promoted policies designed to maximize efficiency and economy. Given the troubling economy nationwide during this period, voters

Orval Faubus and Winthrop Rockefeller at "The House," Huntsville, Arkansas, 1967. *Orval Faubus Papers, Box 869, folder 4. Special Collections Division, University of Arkansas Libraries.*

showed their appreciation for their attention to both the needs of the state's citizens and the necessity of closely managing the state's finances. Although the "big three" concept has considerable merit, certain historical forces also shaped the programs and policies outlined by Dale Bumpers, David Pryor, and Bill Clinton. Arkansas's place in the national economy as a second-tier "Sunbelt" South state, limited the degree of economic growth in the state in the 1970s and 1980s. Yet its integration into the national economy made it more vulnerable to larger economic forces over which the state had little control. If, as historians of the Sunbelt South argue, the conservatism of these areas was tied to the growth of suburbs peopled by upwardly mobile young professionals or by Republican leaning retirees, Arkansas was underachieving. The three Democratic governors steered a course through a number of conflicting demands and opportunities, and while there were important similarities, there were some equally crucial differences between them, particularly concerning the last of the three.

Dale Leon Bumpers

Dale Leon Bumpers, a native of Charleston, Arkansas, had been raised during the Great Depression, and although he was a fiscal conservative, he was a social moderate who had a sincere desire to make Arkansas a better place for the greatest number of citizens. Some historians consider him the last of the state's governors to embrace New Deal liberalism, but the new political economy taking shape in the last thirty years of the twentieth century would witness the end of that political philosophy. Bumpers credited his father, who had served a term in the Arkansas legislature, for endowing him with a public service orientation. After a stint in the marines during World War II, Bumpers finished his BA degree at the University of Arkansas, and secured a law degree at Northwestern University. He returned to Charleston and began practicing law and running the family's hardware store. After the *Brown v. Board of Education* decision in 1954, he advised the local school board to accept the Court's decree and desegregate immediately. The board followed his advice and admitted eleven black students to the Charleston school. Fayetteville also admitted black students in the fall of 1954, and thus together these two towns ensured that Arkansas became the first of the eleven states of the former Confederacy to integrate. Bumpers ran for his first elective office in 1962—seeking his father's old seat in the state legislature—but lost. However, he defeated Orval Faubus in a run-off election for the democratic nomination for governor in 1970 and then defeated Winthrop Rockefeller in the fall general election. See plate 45 following page 366.

Bumpers enjoyed enormous success in the governor's office, largely because of his personal integrity, charisma, and sheer administrative ability. He was also both fortunate and unfortunate in that he assumed the governor's office at a particularly challenging time for the nation and the state. On the one hand, although the Nixon presidency underwent some convulsions during Bumpers's tenure in the governor's office (including the Watergate scandal and the president's resignation), parts of his domestic agenda worked to the advantage of Arkansas's poorest citizens. The expansion of welfare, particularly the Aid to Families with Dependent Children (AFDC) program, funneled much-needed funds to citizens nationwide, and since Arkansas had an unusually high percentage of impoverished people, it reached a number of the state's neediest families. Although a conservative backlash was even then beginning to take shape, Bumpers was able to move the state forward on a number of other fronts, in part because he introduced measures that had become palatable by virtue of being debated publicly prior to his election. While his predecessor in office, Winthrop Rockefeller, had been unable to secure their passage, he gave them currency, and Bumpers was able to push them through. Bumpers's success at where Rockefeller failed was partly due to the fact that he was dealing with a considerably different legislature, as many of the old Faubus cronies were gone, and the people of Arkansas were ready for at least some of the changes that Rockefeller had once championed.

On the other hand, Bumpers became governor at an enormously challenging time; that is, during a historic national and international crisis, one that would leave a lasting imprint on both the American and the international economy. The Vietnam War left the country saddled with unprecedented debt and high inflation, and Pres. Richard Nixon presided over a restructuring of economic policy meant to address the situation. But he made the dollar much more vulnerable to international currency markets by taking the country off the gold standard, and his wage and price controls merely contributed to the creation of more inflation and the most serious recession since the Great Depression (up to that point in time). Nixon's forceful support of Israel after that country was attacked by Egypt in 1973 led to an Arab oil embargo that contributed to further inflation and recession and resulted in long-term changes in energy policy. Ordinary citizens experienced the recession and oil crisis in varying ways, depending on their location. Those who lived in states with increasing populations, such as California and Florida, were the hardest hit. There the oil shortage led to long lines at service stations, a rare occurrence in Arkansas.

The state's citizens were not immune from the effects of the oil shortage. Independent truckers (that is, men who owned their own trucks but contracted with companies to haul freight), most of them working class and from rural backgrounds, were among the most outspoken. By December 1973, after the speed limit on the nation's interstates and highways had been reduced to 55 miles per hour, independent truckers, who were paid according to the mile, began a two-day, nationwide wildcat strike. Arkansas truckers hauled a variety of products but were especially active in transporting agriculture output, which remained the single largest commodity produced in the state. Farmers and planters themselves were dependent on cheap transportation, which, indeed, guaranteed lower food costs for urban dwellers, but the truckers bore the brunt of the hike in gas prices, which, together with the reduced speed limit, left them unable to break even. In some states striking truckers fired weapons at strikebreakers, and Arkansas was not without its share of violence. On December 15 the cab of a truck parked at Andy Jones Truck Stop in Widener (St. Francis County), Arkansas, was destroyed by a bomb planted beneath the floorboard. Located just off of Interstate 40, one of the most important freight conduits in the country, Widener might have seemed an unlikely place for such an event. The truck was owned by a small firm in Widener, M. E. (Gene) Johnson, Inc., who reported $15,000 worth of damage to the vehicle. No violence was reported in the many strike actions conducted at other locations across Arkansas. A hundred and fifty trucks blockaded a truck stop on Interstate 40 in North Little Rock; and twenty to thirty trucks blocked a Texaco Truck Center on Interstate 30 west of Little Rock. A Crystal Hill operation experiencing a blockage actually suspended the sale of diesel fuel, and an official there said of the truckers, "I agree with them, so I'll just go along with them." The two-day strike ended without further incident in Arkansas and though the 55-mile per hour speed limit remained in place, President Nixon released additional diesel fuel to alleviate the shortage.

Given the economic climate across the country, the progress made during Bumpers's administration is all the more remarkable. Convinced that Arkansas could only climb out of the bottom tier of states by developing a better-educated population, he made that a priority and achieved impressive results in terms of the passage of key pieces of legislation he promoted. Bumpers secured significant increases in teacher salaries and benefits, extended state support to include a kindergarten program, and successfully promoted a plan to provide free textbooks for high school students. State colleges benefited by an extensive construction program, and the dedication of more funds to community colleges encouraged the expansion of the two-year college system. This greatly increased access to education beyond the high school level, something that many small-town and rural Arkansans benefited from. By the end of the century, Arkansas ranked eleventh in the nation in terms of geographic accessibility to an institution of higher learning. Although this accomplishment enabled many to extend their educations beyond the high school level, it did little to improve the state's overall reputation in higher education circles. Gifted students who desired a quality higher education tended to leave Arkansas, and once gone, they remained elsewhere, spending their talent and income in other states. If the state was going to participate in the newly emerging high-tech and service economy, it was going to have to do better.

Another important area of progress achieved under Bumpers involved improvements in public health, a concern that was receiving much attention on the national level. When Senator Edward Kennedy proposed a universal national health care program, Nixon responded with a plan of his own, one that would have provided health insurance for low-income families and required that companies make health insurance available to all their employees. Neither plan passed, but the issue of health care in an era when expenditures in that area were rising phenomenally, earned a permanent place on the national agenda. Bumpers, meanwhile, secured passage of legislation designed to provide a wider range of services to the elderly and the handicapped. The governor's wife, Betty Bumpers, crusaded for immunization against childhood diseases and was able to create an awareness of its importance, thus influencing public policy in that direction.

Although the fragility of the national economy would have dictated a conservative path in fiscal matters, Bumpers was a dedicated fiscal conservative anyway and promoted measures that increased the efficiency of state government. Since Homer Adkins's governorship (1940–1944), the state's leaders had been attempting to create a more efficient administrative system, but Bumpers went further in streamlining the state's administration than all of his predecessors combined. Sixty agencies were consolidated into thirteen departments whose directors constituted the governor's cabinet. Other efficiency measures included the creation of a central personnel agency for hiring of state employees and the introduction of more modern budgeting and management techniques within state agencies.

In 1974 Bumpers departed the governor's office, having successfully challenged J. William Fulbright for the Senate seat he had occupied for thirty years. Fulbright, who had risen to the position of chair of the Senate Foreign Relations Committee, had alienated many Democrats and made an enemy of Republican president Richard Nixon because of his criticism of American involvement in Vietnam. Nixon identified Fulbright as a target for defeat, poured money into the Democratic primary campaign against him, and enabled Bumpers to secure election to the Senate. Had the Republican Party in Arkansas been in a position to mount an attractive Republican candidate that year, Arkansas might have gone the way of several other southern states. Not only did they fail to field a Republican capable of challenging Fulbright's Senate seat, the Republicans were unable to field a candidate capable of prevailing over the popular` David Hampton Pryor in the gubernatorial contest.

David Hampton Pryor

David Hampton Pryor is not generally characterized as a New Deal liberal. He stood on the cusp between moderates like Dale Bumpers and the newly emerging Democratic politicians of the South like William Jefferson Clinton who grasped the importance of the transformation of the national and international economy. Like Dale Bumpers, however, David Pryor came from a politically active family, but he began his own political career at a much younger age than did Dale Bumpers. He was heavily involved in student government during his years at the University of Arkansas, and after completing a degree in political science in 1957, he returned to his home in Camden and began running the family newspaper, the *Ouachita Citizen.* He was elected to the state legislature in 1960 when only twenty-six years old, and as one of the youthful legislators known as the "young Turks," he stood in opposition to Orval Faubus. See plate 46 following page 366.

While serving in the legislature, Pryor took classes at the School of Law at the University of Arkansas, graduating in 1964. In 1966, he secured election to the U.S. House of Representatives, representing the Fourth Congressional District, where he established a solid record as a political moderate from 1966 to 1972. As a member of the Credentials Committee at the 1968 National Democratic Convention, he voted against seating the infamous all-white delegation from Mississippi. Although he might have continued to enjoy an enviable career in the House, having secured a coveted seat on the powerful Appropriations Committee and having attracted wide attention by exposing abuses in nursing homes (after posing as an orderly on weekends), in 1972 Pryor challenged John McClellan for the Senate seat he had occupied since 1942. The youthful and enthusiastic Pryor contrasted sharply with the elderly and staid McClellan, but their differences were more significant than merely age and style. Pryor had already established himself as more progressive on the race issue. However, it was not his racial progressivism that proved to be his Achilles' heel. The political scientist Jay Barth, who characterizes Pryor as the most popular politician Arkansas ever produced, argues that "the turning point in the campaign came in a rare (for the day) televised debate, when an aggressive McClellan strongly attacked Pryor for his ties to organized labor." McClellan, who had led the attack against the Teamsters Union in 1959 as chair of the permanent subcommittee on investigations in the Senate, had considerable credibility on the question of labor unions and a deep animus toward them. "McClellan won the nomination with fifty-two percent of the two-candidate vote; it would be Pryor's last political defeat."

After his defeat, Pryor returned to Little Rock and practiced law, but he did not neglect his considerable following. Pryor's style had been highly personal, and he took great pains to attend numerous functions, shaking hands and talking one-on-one with individuals he had come to know over the years. In 1974 he mounted a successful campaign for governor, defeating his old nemesis, former governor Orval Faubus, who was trying to regain the office he forsook in 1966. Pryor easily defeated the Republican candidate in the general election with 66 percent of the vote. One thing working in Pryor's favor was the black vote. African Americans recognized in Pryor a man likely to better represent their interests. Indeed, the black electorate in Arkansas was already demonstrating its ability to influence elections. As John Kirk argues, by 1972, "Arkansas had ninety-nine black elected officials, the second highest number of any Southern state.

The same year, Little Rock optometrist Dr. Jerry Jewel became the first black member of the Arkansas Senate in the twentieth century." Three African Americans were elected to the Arkansas House of Representatives. "Throughout the state, African Americans won elective offices as aldermen, justices of the peace, school board members, city councilors, city recorders, and city clerks. These gains further stimulated black voter registration. By 1976, ninety-four percent of Arkansas's voting-age African Americans were registered, the highest proportion of any state in the South."

Unfortunately for Pryor, he became governor just as the national recession deepened. Although OPEC (Organization of Petroleum Exporting Countries) was beginning to recognize the folly of imposing an oil embargo as a tool to punish the United States for its support of Israel, gasoline shortages continued and stagflation developed. Stagflation is a phenomenon where the economic growth rate slows to a crawl at the same time that the inflation rate rises. The problem for policy makers is that solutions usually associated with curtailing the inflation rate stand to worsen the economic growth rate. Economists argue over both causes and solutions but, in the meantime, it led to the coinage of a new term—the misery index—which influenced the presidential elections of 1976 and 1980.

Given the prevailing national economic situation, the state's enduring conservatism reasserted itself. In his first term Pryor failed in his attempt to reform the state's retrograde 1874 constitution, and in his second term he was unable to secure passage of his "Arkansas Plan," which would have shifted power from the state to the local governments and reduced the state income tax by 25 percent. The opponents of the Arkansas Plan had a vested interest in maintaining the status quo, largely because they feared their own programs would suffer in the hands of local politicians. Many opposed it for entirely different reasons, however. They feared the reactionary forces in place in local government. But Governor Pryor had his successes. While practicing fiscal restraint, he created a number of new government units, including a Housing Development Agency designed to address the needs of moderate-income families by making home loans available to them and, in the face of the global oil crisis, he created an Energy Conservation and Policy Office charged with the responsibility of implementing a statewide energy-conservation plan. He also made some significant gubernatorial appointments of blacks and women. He appointed the first African American and the first woman to the state supreme court, and he made the first appointment of women to serve on the Highway Commission and the Industrial Development Commission.

Governor Pryor also demonstrated his affinity for preserving the state's history and culture. He consolidated six previously separate agencies to establish the Department of Natural and Cultural Heritage in 1975, and in 1976 he appointed a woman, Anne Bartley (Winthrop Rockefeller's stepdaughter), to head the agency. That was a cabinet-level post so Bartley became the first woman to serve in an Arkansas governor's cabinet. The creation of a cultural heritage department at the cabinet level coincided with the U.S. bicentennial celebration. Governor Pryor appointed a special bicentennial committee, a number of events were scheduled around the state to celebrate the event, and a replica of the liberty bell was installed in Little Rock. This began a cultural and historical renaissance in Arkansas that intensified in the 1980s and 1990s under future governors and at the behest of a number of dedicated individuals who were determined to recognize and celebrate the importance of Arkansas history and culture.

One particularly important cultural phenomenon that preoccupied certain state agencies and universities was reflected in the passage of federal laws while Pryor was in the governor's office. In January 1975, Pres. Gerald Ford signed into law the Indian Self Determination and Educational Assistance Acts, which acknowledged the right of Native Americans to self-determination and provided assistance for education. In 1978 the Indian Religious Freedom Act put an official end to the suppression of Native American religious practices. These acts did not directly impact many Native Americans in the state because most of Arkansas's Native American population had been removed in the antebellum period and were living in Oklahoma long before these acts were passed. However, subsequent legislation affected the way that Arkansas agencies and institutions dealt with artifacts recovered from archeological sites, particularly the Native American Graves Protection and Repatriation Act of 1990 (NAGPRA). As historian John Kirk observes, the act "permitted Indian tribes to reclaim artifacts and skeletal remains from museums and other federally funded Institutions." But as Jerome C. Rose, Thomas J. Green, and Victoria D. Green point out, other results of the legislation included an increase in the inventory and analysis of skeletal remains curated in museums and other institutions, as well as improvements in the handling and storage of all human remains in those institutions. Perhaps most important, the act led to a great increase in collaboration among Indians, archeologists, and biological anthropologists concerning the excavation, study, and repatriation of not only skeletal remains but of all archeological materials. This collaboration has been especially fruitful in Arkansas. Virtually all archeological investigations include consultation, and often more extensive collaboration, between Indians and archeologists. Caddos, Osages, Quapaws, and Tunicas have repatriated many ancestral remains from state institutions. In some cases, skeletal remains and associated funerary goods have been reburied at specifically designated cemeteries in Arkansas; in other cases, repatriated artifacts that cannot be associated with skeletal remains have found new educational uses in tribal museums and cultural centers, or are available for scholarly research at Arkansas institutions that continue to curate these materials but now on behalf of the descendant communities.

Native American Graves Protection and Repatriation Act: An act that allowed Native American groups to reclaim the remains of their ancestors and artifacts buried with them from museums.

After two terms as governor, Pryor decided to run again for the Senate in 1978, this time at McClellan's death in 1977. Pryor won the closely contested race against two strong contenders, Ray Thornton and Jim Guy Tucker, and returned to the nation's capital, this time as a senator. His popular and dynamic young attorney general, William Jefferson Clinton, a foe of utilities and champion of the ratepayer and consumer, ran a strong campaign to capture the governorship.

William Jefferson Clinton

By the time that William Jefferson Clinton took office in 1979, it was clear that changes in the national and international economic order signaled the end of the American "golden age" when the supremacy of the United States economy was unquestioned. The American manufacturing sector was no longer going to dominate the world market as powerful competitors in Europe and Asia began to out-produce the United States. In fact, Clinton recognized that a significant shift in the U.S. economy toward the service sector was taking shape, and he was the first Arkansas governor to heavily promote the service-sector and technology-based industries within the state. Traditional industrial development remained a focus but Clinton, only thirty-two years old when he took office in 1979, was a Phi Beta Kappa graduate of Georgetown, a Rhodes scholar, and a Yale Law graduate, and he recognized the importance of knowledge-based industries, such as the high-tech and service-sector businesses that characterized the Sunbelt phenomenon. He possessed the intellect and insight necessary to grasp the complexities of the transition that was then becoming obvious to only the most astute observers. Born in 1946 as William Jefferson Blythe III, in Hope, Arkansas, he began life in relatively unpromising circumstances. He lost his father at a young age and endured a precarious economic home life. As an adolescent, he took the name of his stepfather and in high school he decided to pursue a political career. See plate 47 following page 366.

Knowledge-based industry: An industry that relies on a highly skilled workforce to master the complexities of the science-based and technology-based world evolving in the late twentieth century.

Clinton's first foray into politics occurred in 1974 when he waged a campaign against Congressman John Paul Hammerschmidt, a Republican who represented the Third District. Although he failed to unseat Hammerschmidt, Clinton captured a surprising 48.5 percent of the popular vote and established himself as a potential political force. The publicity he received in that race helped him secure the office of state attorney general in 1975. As attorney general, he pursued a consumer-friendly policy, establishing himself as the foe of utilities, opposing the twenty-five-cent phone call, supporting victim compensation legislation, and chairing a national panel on the rights of the elderly. He easily won election to the governor's office in 1978, the second youngest governor in the state's history (after John Roane). In keeping with his understanding of the new economy, he proceeded to introduce an impressive array of proposals designed to promote education, conservation, health care, economic development, and highway construction and repair. His first legislative session was one of the most active in the state's history, and the new governor pursued his agenda with energy and enthusiasm. His education measures provided access to challenging programs for those who were gifted and talented. Health care, like education, was an area in which Arkansas suffered in comparison to other states, and Clinton's proposals there were designed to address these shortcomings. To confront the high infant mortality rate, he proposed funding a state prenatal intensive-care nursery; to face the aging population, a major demographic factor in the state, he proposed an expansion of in-home services for the elderly; and to contend with the abysmal shortcomings in rural health care, he sponsored the establishment of a Rural Health Development Office.

Clinton's programs in health and education elaborated upon the efforts of the governors who preceded him, but he departed from his immediate predecessors in other measures he sponsored. Rather than championing a growth of low-wage industries, he advocated an emphasis on small business development and international marketing. This emphasis was more feasible for Arkansas's cities than it was for the small towns experiencing decline, and the governor had little to recommend for them beyond continuing the effort to attract the traditional smokestack industries. Whether deliberately or not, he avoided confronting Delta agriculturalists when fashioning his conservation policy. Those agriculturalists were dependent upon pesticides, yet facing a groundwater pollution problem. His conservation program focused on establishing an Energy Department, creating a National and Scenic Rivers Commission, and a State Land Bank. The governor was deeply concerned about the difficulties confronting the state's African American population, particularly in the Arkansas Delta, and would later head a task force dedicated to finding solutions to the structural problems that prevailed in such regions across the South. Despite considerable efforts on the part of the Delta Commission and a number of philanthropic agencies, these problems have proven to be difficult to solve and remain a focus of much current attention.

Like most twentieth-century governors of the state, Clinton confronted another seemingly intractable problem, the state's road and highway system, and, like some of his predecessors, he was to learn that in sponsoring measures to finance road building and repair, he would incur serious political liability. With the support of the trucking industry and the Highway Commission, who lobbied intensively for his program, he convinced the legislature to enact a series of fee increases, principally in title transfer and vehicle registration fees, which significantly raised revenue for highway construction and repair. Clinton would discover in 1980 when running for reelection just how much the fee increases angered Arkansas voters.

The anger of the electorate over the increase in license tags was only a part of the problem confronting Clinton in the 1980 election. A serious economic recession continued to plague the nation and the state, a series of natural disasters darkened the mood further, and certain vested interests in Arkansas—utilities, timber, trucking, poultry, construction, and medicine—were tiring of the attitude of the brash young Clinton aides, who either failed to consult with them or brushed aside their concerns and suggestions. Clinton had a tendency to listen to a small circle of advisors who themselves were not necessarily in touch with the Arkansas electorate. He seemed too supremely confident of his own proposals and indifferent to the advice of those who understood the Arkansas electorate better than he. And then there was the Cuban refugee fiasco. When Pres. Jimmy Carter ordered some of the Cuban refugees sent to Fort Chaffee near Fort Smith, he failed to send sufficient security to accompany the refugees. Clinton's request for additional security was in vain. Some Arkansas pundits suggested that the close relationship between Carter and Clinton was responsible for situating the refugees in Arkansas, and when some of the refugees rioted in late May 1980, the governor's leadership was questioned. In fact, the relationship between Clinton and Carter had cooled, but that factor was not fully appreciated by most Arkansas voters. In any case, his Republican opponent in the fall 1980 elections used the refrain "car tags and Cubans" to defeat Clinton.

Frank White, who had been director of the AIDC under Gov. David Pryor, surprised everyone when he announced he would run against Clinton, but when he launched a campaign dominated by the issues of "Car Tags and Cubans," he quickly revealed Clinton's vulnerability. Pryor and other prominent Democrats were as surprised by Clinton's apparent weakness as they were that White elected to run as a Republican. White was a conservative, fundamentalist Christian, however, who claimed to feel more comfortable within the Republican Party, although he was unknown to that party's political functionaries. He had a solidly pro-business background, having worked as an account executive with Merrill-Lynch before going into management with Commercial National Bank. He had served on the board of directors of Arkansas Missouri Power Company, an association that would influence his thinking on utility regulation and figure prominently in his administration.

The Frank White Interlude

The election of the second Republican of the twentieth century to the governor's office coincided with Ronald Reagan's election to the presidency, and Frank White happened to have much more in common with Reagan than he did with Arkansas's previous Republican governor, Winthrop Rockefeller. Reagan, particularly, owed his election to the emergence of a coalition of old and new conservatives. As Eric Foner suggests, this coalition consisted of "Sunbelt surbanites and working class ethnics; anti-government crusaders and advocates of a more aggressive foreign policy; libertarians who believed in freeing the individual from restraint and the Christian Right, which sought to restore what they considered traditional moral values." Although Reagan proved much more adept at appealing to this diverse constituency than did Frank White, White embraced Reagan's "trickle down" economic theory. The promotion of the interests of the nation's—and Arkansas's—wealthiest citizens translated into tax cuts, assuming that the benefits would trickle down to the masses. Although it turns out that the nation's wealthiest citizens and corporations failed to deliver on this promise, using their new-found wealth to purchase luxuries and generating few new jobs, the idea of low taxes, always popular in Arkansas, had resonance country wide and became firmly planted in the nation's political economy.

Frank White's tenure in the governor's office coincided with another severe economic recession, one influenced by Reagan's embrace of supply-side (trickle-down) economics but also by yet another international incident, this time a U.S.-imposed embargo on the sale of wheat to the Soviet Union after it invaded Afghanistan. However, this recession was much shorter-lived and was quickly followed by a long period of

Frank White "Banana" cartoon, George Fisher, *Comic Relief.* This photograph originally appeared in the *Arkansas Gazette,* May 3, 1981.

economic expansion, an expansion accompanied by a relaxation of governmental regulations that had some significant consequences. "By the 1990s the richest 1 percent of Americans owned 40 percent of the nation's wealth, twice their share twenty years earlier."

The two issues that generated the greatest controversy during Frank White's administration were creation science and utility regulation. The issue over creation science emerged when certain legislators introduced a bill, which became Act 590, to require the teaching of creation science along with evolution in the state's schools. Although he did not originate it, White promised to sign it if it passed, and when he did so, a firestorm of criticism was leveled against him. The controversy ended after the law was overturned by the federal district court and the state declined to appeal the decision. Frank White's long association with the utility companies was clearly a factor in the second controversy to rock his administration. He wasted no time pursuing the interests of the utility industry, firing three leaders of the Arkansas Energy Department on inauguration day. He later abolished the Energy Department, combining it with the Arkansas Industrial Development Commission, thus potentially crippling utility regulation. He also allowed Arkansas Power and Light (AP&L) executives to meet with potential appointees to the Public Service Commission, which made it appear he was giving them a veto power over such appointments. When AP&L instituted a staggering $104 million rate increase, many believed that the governor had permitted it. The controversies accompanying White's administration greatly weakened him, but perhaps more fundamental to his defeat in 1982 was his failure to build a coalition capable of maintaining his political life. His support of a small group of powerful entities in the state could not long sustain him in elective office.

The New William Jefferson Clinton

While controversies buffeted during Frank White's governorship, Bill Clinton was reshaping himself and preparing to recapture the office he had forfeited in 1980. He solicited advice from politicians more in touch with the Arkansas electorate, and he brought Betsy Wright, a politically astute Texan, to the state to serve as an advisor. He also began to utilize his considerable personal skills to better advantage. Clinton, like Pryor, excelled in the personal style that characterized the most successful Arkansas politicians. He attended even the smallest of county fairs and countless civic club events, shaking hands and talking with anyone who wished to approach him. Nevertheless, he faced stiff competition in the Democratic primary in 1982, and the public reacted variously to two television commercials where he apologized to the citizens of Arkansas, particularly for the car tag increases. He secured 42 percent of the vote in the Democratic primary against four other candidates, which forced him into a runoff election, which he subsequently also won. He won the general election in the fall of 1983 with 55 percent of the vote. When he assumed the mantle of governor in 1983, Clinton pursued a different strategy and presented an altered image. Gone were the denims and his wife's use of her maiden name. Gone were many of the young Turks who had shaped his first governorship. This much more restrained Clinton consulted more seasoned Arkansas politicians and presented a much less ambitious package of proposals to the legislature.

The major issue confronting the governor in 1983 arose from an Arkansas Supreme Court ruling (*Dupree v. Alma*), which found the state's education funding formula unconstitutional. Inequity was built into the system in two ways. First, a significant part of a given county's school funding depended on local property taxes, and this was complicated by the fact that poor districts collected less revenue because their property values were low to begin with and their millage rates were inadequate. If the value of the property is low and the millage rate is low, the amount collected is low. The second problem arose from the manner in which state funding was allocated. In 1983, the state based its allocation to schools on a per child basis without reckoning with the fact that some schools were decreasing significantly in population while others were increasing. Since millage rates were the province of local government, and low property values reflected endemic economic problems not easily resolved by government, Clinton focused his attention on the amount the state allocated to education, and here the governor faced an unenviable dilemma. In order to provide equal funding to cover the state's portion of education costs, he could either raise taxes or reallocate resources away from schools experiencing a decrease in students and toward the growing districts. He chose the former, calling a special session of the legislature in November 1983 and succeeding in convincing the legislature to raise the state's sales tax from three to four cents. While this seemed to resolve the state's contribution to the problem, it left the issue of underfunding from the local property tax situation unaddressed, a situation that would lead to another Supreme Court decision nearly a decade later.

The 1984 election signaled Clinton's return to unquestioned political authority. He won 64 percent of the vote against three other Democrats in the primary election and 63 percent against the Republican in the general election. The first matter taken up after his reelection was the issue of the education reforms enacted in 1983. Recognizing the importance of the emerging service economy, realizing that Arkansas was poorly positioned to participate in the Sunbelt's high-tech revolution, Clinton was determined to promote improvements to education. Buoyed by the strong show of public support evidenced by his overwhelming reelection, which was seen as a referendum on the education standards, Clinton and the legislature resisted efforts to weaken them and to cancel teacher testing. When the Supreme Court again ruled the school funding formula unconstitutional in May 1983, Hillary Clinton spent the summer conducting statewide hearings. Out of these hearings came new education standards that included smaller class sizes and longer school day and year. But they also included mandatory testing of all teachers, an issue that angered the Arkansas Education Association and the state's teachers. The new education standards were introduced during a special legislative session in the fall of 1983. The principal focus of the 1984 legislative session was economic development. The governor's package was essentially conservative, however, and generated little opposition. The only significant controversy was the "Grand Gulf Affair," whereby the state was required by the federal government to pay to support a Mississippi power plant even though Arkansas would receive none of the power generated by the plant. This became an issue in his reelection campaign in 1984, but he won 61 percent of the vote in the primary and 64 percent in the general election, and this time he was winning a four-year term, something approved by voters in the previous election.

In was during his third term in office that Clinton presided over a cultural renaissance in Arkansas, one inspired largely by the sesquicentennial celebration in 1986. Although launched in 1982 by Tom Dillard, who was then director of the Department of Arkansas Natural and Cultural Heritage (now the Department of Arkansas Heritage), the sesquicentennial was given new life in 1986 when the legislature provided a $400,000 grant. Many communities around the state participated by taking part in town and county celebrations, and the *Arkansas Democrat* published sketches of 150 prominent Arkansans after the sesquicentennial commission created a "Project Pride" initiative. Arkansas Power and Light Company commissioned a song, "Arkansas You Run Deep in Me," and even the United States Postal Service contributed by authorizing a commemorative stamp featuring the Old State House in Little Rock. While the publications of books on Arkansas history, culture, geography, and natural history had been greatly augmented by the creation of the University of Arkansas Press in 1982 by Miller Williams and Willard Gatewood, the sesquicentennial commission inspired the county and local societies to create and publish their own histories. The renewed interest in Arkansas history led to the creation of the Arkansas History Education Coalition dedicated to reviving the teaching of the state's history in the Arkansas school system.

Cultural renaissance in Arkansas: Refers to a resurgence of interest in the state's history and culture.

While Clinton embraced the sesquicentennial celebration, the issues he pursued with greatest energy in his fourth term in office were tax reform and the regulation of lobbyists. Clinton appointed a blue-ribbon Tax Reform Commission whose charge was to recommend reform of the state's constitution, which required that all tax measures, with the exception of sales tax, secure a three-fourths majority in the legislature. Requiring a three-fourths majority made it possible for a small minority to derail legislation supported by the majority of the legislature. The commission ultimately suggested a constitutional amendment that would have required only a 60 percent majority. The measure was placed on the ballot in 1988, but despite the governor's energetic campaign in favor of it, it went down to defeat. Clinton was more successful in the initiative to regulate lobbyists. The state of Arkansas had the least regulation of lobbyists in the country. Clinton appointed a Code of Ethics Commission in June 1987 after a legislative session that witnessed a strongly obstructionist performance on the part of lobbyists. Although the legislature failed to enact the recommendations of the commission, voters approved the measures in 1988.

The 1989 legislative session was marred by a deteriorating relationship between the legislature and Clinton. The legislature resented the creation of the Code of Ethics Commission, but an old problem also resurfaced. Some of Clinton's aides and certain powerful senators were engaged in acrimonious disputes. When the legislature refused to approve of a $119 million settlement with the federal government over the longstanding Little Rock school desegregation suit, the governor, who understood that the price would be much higher if they delayed further, had to press through four votes in the house to secure its approval. It was subsequently challenged in court and a special session had to be called to approve it again.

One major issue in the 1990 election was Clinton's presidential aspirations. Clinton promised to serve out his four-year term if reelected governor and won by 54 percent of the vote in the primary and 57 percent in the general election, constituting his narrowest victory since 1982. Despite this diminution in support as reflected in the election figures, Clinton presented an ambitious set of initiatives to the legislature in 1991 and secured passage of much of his legislative program. In addition to new educational initiatives, which included a sizable increase in teacher salaries and thousands of new scholarships for college-bound students, the governor sponsored a program of new health services, including an expansion of school-based health clinics and an income tax withholding plan for children's health-care coverage. Extensive tax-reform measures were proposed and passed. Included among them was a corporate income tax with all funds generated from it dedicated to upgrading technical education. An Education Trust Fund was established through a one-half-cent increase in sales tax. The only truly new initiative sponsored by Clinton in this legislative session, however, was that of confronting environmental problems. He introduced measures to restructure the Pollution Control and Ecology Commission and to prohibit the approval of permits to companies moving in from out of state that had bad environmental records.

Despite his promise to serve out his four-year term, Clinton ultimately decided to run for president in 1992. This decision deeply antagonized many of Clinton's political foes, with results that reverberated to the highest levels. For example, Sheffield Nelson, who had lost a gubernatorial contest against Clinton in 1990, resented the fact that the press had failed to publicize allegations concerning Clinton's personal behavior. During the presidential campaign, Nelson allegedly fed such stories to the national media, which ultimately led to the so-called Whitewater investigation of supposed shady land deals. Nevertheless, Clinton, who was able to capitalize on yet another recession that began in 1991, defeated Republican president George Bush in the fall 1992 elections, thus paving the way for Lt. Gov. Jim Guy Tucker's assumption of the governor's office. Ironically, Tucker would soon become "collateral damage" in the Whitewater investigation aimed at Pres. Bill Clinton. Tucker would feel compelled to resign office in 1996 and another lieutenant governor, Mike Huckabee, the third Republican governor of Arkansas in the twentieth century, would assume the governorship.

The period between 1970 and 1992 was marked by a remarkable degree of change in Arkansas. By the early 1990s, in fact, the state was much more integrated into the national and international economy and thus subject to the vagaries of forces it was in no position to control. Although companies like Wal-Mart placed Arkansas in the forefront of business innovation, and other enterprises in the state achieved success in the new service-oriented economy, Arkansas did not emerge as one of the Sunbelt states, but that proved to be a blessing in disguise. The next two decades would witness a number of significant challenges accompanying the globalization of the American economy, challenges that brought near ruin to many of the Sunbelt states. Arkansas's more diverse economy and conservative fiscal policy shielded it from some of the worst effects of the recession that struck in the early twenty-first century. The state also benefited by the discovery of natural gas reserves, but problems would soon emerge in connection with the "Fayetteville Shale," and state officials would find themselves facing some tough decisions involving how to balance the environmental and economic implications.

CHAPTER SEVENTEEN

The Burden of Arkansas History, 1992–2012

Six years after the U.S. Supreme Court delivered the *Brown v. Board of Education* decision in 1954, C. Vann Woodward, an eminent southern historian and native-born Arkansan, published *The Burden of Southern History*, a book of essays that examined a number of vexing issues confronting the South. Echoing an argument he made in his *The Strange Career of Jim Crow,* published in 1955, he ruminated over the implications of the South's segregated system. According to Woodward, segregation was a "state way" rather than a "folk way," originating after the Civil War when ex-Confederates sought to maintain the Democratic Party's power at the expense of African Americans and poor whites. By using the term *state way,* Woodward was arguing that southern states had imposed the Jim Crow system, that it did not emerge as a natural system from among the folk, which would have implied a folk way. Convinced that the marriage of white supremacy and the Democratic Party hamstrung both the southern Democratic Party and many of its citizens, Woodward believed that with legal barriers eliminated, the South would transform into an integrated society. His hopes and expectations faltered, however, as a violent struggle over integration erupted not only in the South but also in the North, and it became apparent that while many whites across the country clung tenaciously to the old status quo in race relations, many blacks embraced separatism in place of integration. This was as true in the North as it was in the South, an irony that hardly escaped Woodward's notice. Irony, in fact, was another theme that preoccupied Woodward in *The Burden of Southern History* and irony, as it turns out, had a special place in the history of Arkansas.

State way: Refers to a system of customs sanctioned or created by statute.

Folk way: Refers to the customs and practices of folk.

In later editions of *Burden,* Woodward made clear his disappointment with the failure of the *Brown* decision to bring about a fully integrated society. In Arkansas, like elsewhere in the South, state-based obstacles to integration remained in place—and new ones were erected—but a day of reckoning was approaching. After a decision by the Eighth Circuit Court of Appeals in 1985 citing the state's complicity in the continuation of segregation and after a Settlement Agreement reached by contending parties in 1989, Arkansas began to attempt to unravel the damage it had done. From the mid-1990s on, the state expended

$50–70 million annually in this effort. Ironically, the cost of this remedy outweighed the expense of the dual education system in place before the *Brown* decision.

By the early twenty-first century, while the state and its citizens grappled with its civil rights legacy, it also struggled with the vestiges of its colonial economy, another issue confronting the South that preoccupied Woodward. To some extent, the state's historic reliance on cheap farm labor, together with extractive industries that sent the profits of Arkansas-based enterprises to out-of-state entities, depended upon the impoverishment of African Americans and poor whites. This reflected the strength of the planter class, largely located along the eastern border fronting the Mississippi River. Bankers and merchants in Little Rock and other towns, who furnished and catered to these planters, played their role in perpetuating this system, but beginning in the New South era of the late nineteenth century, new generations of entrepreneurs and politicians began to speak a different language and focus on other forms of economic development. Remaining wedded to the principle of cheap labor and fully capitalist in their orientation, they hoped to industrialize Arkansas, but they realized few tangible results until after World War II when the plantation system itself began to mechanize and underwent a scientific revolution. Still, efforts to attract industry to Arkansas achieved only marginal success, largely because the state's poor infrastructure and poorly educated population failed to attract a large response from out-of-state manufacturers. The reliance on cheap labor, which involved the continuing impoverishment of a significant segment of the population, included a poorly educated population, which, in turn, undermined efforts to industrialize and, later, to attract knowledge-based industries. As the rest of the South began to embrace the new Sunbelt industries, Arkansas, still hamstrung by its infrastructure and educational inadequacies, failed to participate significantly. By the early twenty-first century, however, a reversal of fortunes seemed to be on the horizon for Arkansas. Ironically, Arkansas, peculiarly insulated by its historic nemesis—the colonial (extractive) nature of its economy—was shielded from the worst of the economic recession facing the country, as knowledge-based industries took the brunt of the economic collapse. In this context, Arkansas positioned itself to step into the void left by failed enterprises elsewhere in the South and embrace the leaner and chastened knowledge-based economy.

Confronting the Education Dilemma

The civil rights movement remains an unfinished revolution in Arkansas as elsewhere. In central Arkansas, the focus of much of the state's attention, white flight to the suburbs and high enrollments of white students in a growing number of private schools undermined the state's efforts to accomplish the goals outlined by its 1989 Settlement Agreement. There were some successes, however. The creation of magnet schools had, according to Gene Vinzant, "apparently brought white flight almost to a standstill, especially at the elementary level. The magnet schools were particularly successful in keeping the enrollment near the target of 50 percent white and 50 percent black." The incentive schools, however, were overwhelmingly black, and the achievement gap between black and white students had not appreciably narrowed. The school district was still busing 14,000 students a day in 1997, but by 2007, as John Kirk puts it, the Little Rock School District went from "being a twenty-five-percent black minority district in 1957 . . . [to] . . . a twenty-four-percent white minority district in 2007. In effect there were no white students left to integrate." Although a number of schools in the district had become overwhelmingly black, the state, the school district, and many black officials favored "unitary status" as it relieved them from the burdensome requirements imposed by the court, requirements that most had come to believe were unworkable. This fact led federal judge Bill Wilson to rule in 2007 that the Little Rock School District was "unitary" (that is, no longer segregated and having unitary status), a ruling later ratified by the Eighth Circuit Court of Appeals.

Unitary status: A term applied to a ruling in the Little Rock desegregation case that characterized Little Rock School district as desegregated.

While the state expended from 50–70 million dollars per year for well over a decade to comply with the desegregation orders in Little Rock, other school districts in Arkansas suffered from funding shortfalls. Some perceived a connection between the two but others took a different lesson. They recognized that the state only expended such enormous sums because it was forced to do so by the federal courts, and they likely understood that the money spent on attempting to achieve integration in Little Rock would not necessarily have been spread out across the state to improve education generally without a court order to do so. At issue was the state's school funding formula. Schools were typically funded in Arkansas by a combination of local, state, and federal dollars. Although the federal contribution was important, more significant—and more within Arkansas's control—was that contributed on the state and local level. On the local level, citizens voted a certain number of tax mills to be allocated for support of public education. On the state level, the contribution to each school district was predicated on the amount provided to those districts the previous year. But demographic changes within Arkansas had resulted in a built-in problem. The state was allocating to each school district the same amount it had disbursed the year before, regardless of whether the number of children in each district had changed. There was no mechanism in place to correct for changes in enrollment and some growing districts objected to the funds allocated to shrinking districts. The catchphrase became "phantom students" and it had a powerful resonance with the public and, it turns out, with the courts.

In 1981 an important court case resulted when the Alma School District, along with ten others, filed suit against the State Department of Education alleging that Arkansas was not complying with the state constitution's guarantee of equal protection and "its requirement that the state provide a general, suitable, and efficient system of education." They cited the "phantom student" phenomenon and won at the lower court level (*Alma v. Dupree*) in 1981. The Arkansas Supreme Court upheld this decision in (*Dupree v. Alma*) in 1983. Governor Bill Clinton, who had recently been reelected to the governorship, was faced with the unenviable task of devising a plan to honor the court's ruling. He was either going to have to deprive some school districts of funds they desperately needed—the school districts shrinking the most were often already the poorest districts—or raise taxes to provide equal funds to all schools. He successfully pressed the state legislature to raise taxes in order to provide increased state funding to schools throughout Arkansas.

Dupree v. Alma: A case arising out of Alma, Arkansas, where the Arkansas Supreme Court ruled that the state's funding formula for public education was unconstitutional.

Although the increased funding appeared to address the issue of the funds allocated by the state, it was only a beginning. But a more fundamental problem existed. Given that schools were funded partially by local property taxes, considerable disparity continued to exist. In districts where property values were low, the amount collected might contribute only $1,000 to $2,000 per student. Meanwhile, districts with higher property values could generate $5,000 or more. To complicate matters, property taxes for schools were figured according to the millage rate assigned for the purpose. For example, local communities voted on the millage to be devoted to schools, but voters in some areas approved far less than 25 mills, a figure that came to be understood as the minimum amount necessary to generate sufficient funds from local resources. New litigants from Lake View in Phillips County filed suit in 1992, alleging that the funding formula remained unconstitutional, and two years later, chancery court judge Annabelle Imber, agreed with them. The state legislature, according to her ruling, had two years to remedy the situation.

Lake View suit: A suit arising out of Phillips County alleging that the state's funding formula for public education remained unconstitutional.

The first attempt to solve the problem involved two steps. First, the legislature passed three acts in 1995—Acts 916, 917, and 1194—which, taken together, addressed the local contribution to schools and revised the state funding formula, raising the state's contribution to public schools. Act 916 authorized a 10 percent surcharge to school districts that failed to raise their base millage available to support schools to a minimum of 25 mills. Act 916 required that all school districts raise their base millage available to education to 25 and also authorized a study that would analyze education standards and explore the question of what actually constituted an adequate education. Act 1194 provided for grants for new programs to begin to address the question of adequacy. Since local property taxes were the province of local taxpayers and governments, some critics claimed that Acts 916 and 917 violated the constitution, but members of the legislature anticipated such a charge and voted to place a constitutional amendment before the voters that would establish 25 mills as the minimum. On November 5, 1996, voters passed Amendment 74, effectively validating Acts 916 and 917.

The battle over school funding was far from over, however. Lake View litigants returned to court, dissatisfied with the failure of the legislature to fully equalize funding. In April 1997, the legislature passed Acts 1307 and 1361. The first essentially repealed the existing school funding formula and outlined how other millages (presumably passed for other purposes and underutilized) could be employed to raise the minimum number of mills allotted to support public education to the minimum 25 mills. Finally, it provided grants and various forms of financial aid to schools and outlined "what a general, suitable, and efficient system of education should include." Still, the Lake View litigants were dissatisfied. The state had not provided for a comprehensive funding system that remedied the basic inequity created by the great disparities in property values across the state. From May 1997 through 2005, the litigants and the state sparred, filing amended complaints and responses over the constitutionality of the 1994 and 1997 acts (as well as over attorney's fees). In 2002 the Arkansas Supreme Court again ruled that the state had failed to provide an adequate and equitable system of education. Arkansas officials made efforts to comply but in 2005 the court again held that they had failed. After further remedies were implemented, the court finally ruled in 2007 that the legislature "had taken the required and necessary legislative steps to assure that the school children of this state are provided an adequate education and a substantially equal education opportunity."

At the heart of this struggle over equity and adequacy was the desire to improve education in Arkansas. Enter the charter school movement, a movement dating back to 1988 when a professor at the University of Massachusetts first gave expression to the charter school idea. The concept was to focus narrowly on student outcomes rather than on issues like teacher salaries and certification, but as it developed, it increasingly became apparent that many of those in favor of charter schools were essentially repudiating the public education system. They believed that public education was a dismal failure and could not be redeemed. From their point of view, parents who wished to provide their children with a high-quality public education had the right to demand better, and the charter schools offered the best opportunity to do so. Speaking the language of "choice" and the "freedom to choose," they emphasized the role of the parents. Not all charter school advocates were motivated by hostility to public education, however, but focused on addressing the educational deficiencies of the state's poorest children.

Charter school movement: semiprivate schools that receive some public funding, and that focus on student outcomes rather than issues like teacher salaries, etc.

Regardless of motivation, by the early 1990s, Minnesota and California soon opened charter schools, allocating some public funds for their operation, and the movement soon expanded to include a total of forty-one states and the District of Columbia. By the early twenty-first century, charter schools became a part of the education debate in Arkansas, and considerable controversy attended this issue: Some argued that charter schools did not simply augment public education but, in fact, undermined it. State funds were allocated to charter schools—though at a lower amount than for public schools—and smaller districts faced a serious potential risk: consolidation. The state had established that in order for a school district to be viable—and avoid consolidation—it had to enroll a minimum of 350 students. If a school fell below that number for two years in a row, it became subject to consolidation. If the state approved the establishment of a charter school in a small district and that district was forced into consolidation, the state could be subject to a lawsuit, something advocates of public education had demonstrated a willingness to pursue. The proponents of charter schools believed they were offering a viable alternative to parents who wanted to afford their children the best possible education. But what about the children of parents either indifferent to their children's education or unable to devote more time to it because they were so heavily engaged in the struggle to make a living? For those children the best hope remained with the public school system.

Another troubling issue involving the charter schools was the allegation that they contributed to the problem of resegregation. It is an allegation that has arisen elsewhere across the country and that has pitted the Little Rock School District against the charter school movement. The fact that the state partially funds the charter schools may become an issue if it can be established that those schools promote resegregation. While there may be no constitutional right to attend integrated schools, actions by the state that contribute to segregated schools are another matter. The Eighth Circuit's 1985 ruling chronicled the state's role in perpetuating segregated schools, establishing a precedent that the state would ignore at its peril.

Education Week's Quality Counts Report: A report issued by *Education Week* in 2012, which lauded the state for its efforts to improve education but continued to find problems in certain areas.

Despite the many legitimate criticisms aimed at the state's public education system, Arkansas's efforts to improve its system of public education received high marks in *Education Week*'s 2012 Quality Counts Report, reflecting improvements that apparently have little to do with the existence of charter schools. Arkansas ranked number five, moving up from number six in the 2011 report. While the nation as a whole received a "C" grade, Arkansas earned a B-, bested only by Maryland, New York, Massachusetts, and Virginia. The state ranked first in the country for the linkages it established from its kindergarten through twelfth grade programs and second in terms of its efforts to improve its core of teachers. All of these items speak to Arkansas's dedication to the principle of providing a high-quality public education, but a telling difference exists between the rankings for improvement and those for performance. That student performance lags behind improvements in standards, assessment, and accountability is perhaps no surprise. In a range of performance-related indices, from student achievement to graduation rates, Arkansas earns only a D and ranks at thirty-fourth in the nation. Other negative marks reflect longstanding deficiencies that recent improvements can hardly be expected to overcome. For example, in the "chance for success" ratio, Arkansas ranked forty-fourth, but this measure included the educational levels of parents and family income. In terms of the number of adults with at least a two-year college degree, Arkansas ranks at fifty. This latter measure is particularly disappointing because Arkansas, based on proximity to institutions that offer at least a two-year degree, ranks highly in terms of access to higher education. The apparent success of the Arkansas lottery, launched in 2009, in sending a greater number of Arkansas high school graduates to college bodes well for the future, but it is too soon to forecast the long-term implications. By the fall of 2011, more Arkansas high school graduates than ever before were entering college, but nearly 50 percent of them required remedial courses in math, reading, and English. The lottery scholarships expose the continuing problems in the state's educational system and puts further pressure on Arkansas officials to remedy the situation. Just as urgent is the need to generate opportunities within Arkansas for this new college-educated population. The scholarships may relieve many families of the burden of educating their children—or see them remain without college educations—but opportunities must exist within the state if those new college graduates are to be expected to remain in the state.

From Colonial to Global Political Economy

The debate over public education in Arkansas is intimately connected to the state's economic future but that future depends on moving beyond some aspects of the state's past. Yet again, C. Vann Woodward has something instructive to contribute. In *Origins of the New South*, published in 1951, he focused attention on the "colonial" nature of the southern economy, one that relied on extractive industries that worked more to the benefit of the extractors—planters, lumber companies, and railroad barons—and to northern industrialists who sometimes extracted and almost always processed the raw materials. This failure to control the profits from its own resources plagued the state for most of its history, and its inability to participate in the southern Sunbelt phenomenon in the 1970s and 1980s seemed yet another example of Arkansas's failure to promote meaningful economic growth. The key feature of this new economy was knowledge-based industries, particularly in service areas and technology. Arkansas's undereducated population and inferior infrastructure inhibited its membership in the Sunbelt fraternity. Instead, its agricultural economy, despite some setbacks, thrived in the 1970s and 1980s, and its manufacturing sector grew, largely by attracting industries to its nonunion, low-wage opportunities. An astute observer, however, might have noticed that it was also in the 1970s and 1980s that certain Arkansas-born giants of capitalism—Wal-Mart, Stephens, Inc., Tyson Foods, J. B. Hunt, and Murphy Oil—were laying the groundwork for growth and development. In the early years of the twenty-first century, with the national economy faltering and the Sunbelt South crashing with it, Arkansas began to position itself to modernize its economy and become the new Sunbelt phenomenon.

Even as Arkansas began to embrace the new global economy, vestiges of the old colonial economic model remained and, indeed, emerged in new forms. An essay in C. Vann Woodward's *Burden of Southern History* focused on the many ironies that run through the South's history, and one of the most potent ironies of the early twenty-first century involved the ability of Arkansas and three western states, those which maintained a greater semblance of the colonial economy, to better withstand the economic crisis that virtually crippled the nation and the world. In the classic colonial economy, the "colony," or in this case Arkansas and the South, engages in the development of extractive industries that produce goods that are shipped elsewhere for manufacturing and development. In such situations, the greatest profits are delivered to parties outside the state and region and result in little economic development. Woodward focused his analysis on the South's colonial economy but had he turned his glance westward, he might have recognized a similar phenomenon there. Although Arkansas, North Dakota, Montana, and Wyoming suffered during the historic economic calamity of the early twenty-first century, they managed to endure precisely because they had failed to participate fully in the overheated economic expansion. They shared conservative fiscal policies and largely colonial (extractive) economies, but some of the particulars of their situations differed. In two states, Arkansas and North Dakota, new discoveries of natural gas and oil respectively—exceptionally lucrative extractive industries—shored up their economies. In Arkansas the Fayetteville Shale, a natural gas field, allowed the state to better withstand the shortfall in regular tax collections. Still, the state provided tax breaks to encourage exploitation of the Fayetteville Shale, limiting the revenue stream.

However much the exploitation of this resource benefited the state, this extractive industry, much like those of the past, entailed a certain environmental cost. Some concerns were raised about the "coincidence" of earthquakes in the Fayetteville Shale area of central Arkansas, perhaps connected to "fracking," the method used to extract the deposits of natural gas. In fracking, large quantities of water mixed with chemicals are injected into the earth's crust to produce small fractures. Workers then pump the water back out and extract the gas that is made accessible in the process. Not only have observers raised questions about the seismological abnormalities that sometimes develop in areas where fracking takes place, environmentalists have been concerned about the chemicals in the wastewater entering the groundwater system. While companies have been reticent to divulge the kind of chemicals and their quantities used in the process, many others have denied a connection between fracking and increased seismic activity. Concerns of residents and officials, however, have led some states to impose regulations and some countries have banned fracking altogether. In Arkansas the state's Oil and Gas Commission voted in July 2011 to close one well operation in central Arkansas using the fracking technology and imposed a moratorium on new drilling operations employing the method. The decision came in the wake of two days of testimony from residents of the region alarmed by increased seismic activity, including a 4.7-magnitude earthquake in February 2011. See plate 48 following page 366.

Fracking: A process of injecting water mixed with chemicals into the earth in order to extract trapped deposits of oil or natural gas.

While the discovery of lucrative natural gas deposits in Arkansas resulted in some new revenue for the state, its extraction represented yet another colonial model that provided little new revenue. In the early twenty-first century, the rise in the value of agricultural land attracted investors looking for a safe haven in an era when the value of home and commercial property plummeted. Investment companies seeking to diversify the portfolios of jittery clients purchased millions of acres of agricultural land across the country. The profits generated by the sale of agricultural commodities produced on land held by out-of-state investors do not accrue to the benefit of many Arkansans and does not greatly enhance tax revenues of local and state government. Indeed, southern agriculture—and perhaps agriculture in general across the country—had shifted into a new phase. The neo-plantations had given way to what one might characterize as portfolio plantations. Their advent was made possible by the greater use of chemicals and the greater economies of scale represented by the new round module cotton picker. See plate 49, 50, 51, and 52 following page 366.

The purchase of lands by investment companies introduces a potential instability in the value of such land. Agricultural land values are subject to the price of the commodities produced on them, and agricultural prices have historically fluctuated for a variety of reasons. Changes in government support policies or new competitors from abroad can send the prices for agricultural commodities and thus land values on a downward spiral. If short-term investors, made nervous by declining dividends, begin to dispose of their shares of agricultural lands, an economic collapse of unpredictable proportions may occur in the agricultural sector. Whether they sell their shares when the going gets rough or hold on to them, these portfolio planters are likely to have little interest in supporting the schools and roads in local communities and no impulse to concern themselves with the environmental consequences of the use of chemicals in the farming enterprise.

Throughout this period of economic adjustment, Arkansas maintained, for the most part, an attachment to moderate political candidates who espoused a largely conservative economic agenda. These politicians recognized the importance of the agricultural sector and other extractive industries to Arkansas at the same time they attempted to move the state into manufacturing and even further, toward the new knowledge-based industries that would make Arkansas into a new Sunbelt phenomenon. This was true of all three governors who served between 1992 to the present, beginning with Jim Guy Tucker who took over the office when Bill Clinton assumed the presidency. See plate 53 following page 366.

Jim Guy Tucker came to the governorship with substantial experience in public service and a particular interest in knowledge-based industries. An attorney, he began his political career in 1970 when he won the office of prosecuting attorney for the Sixth Judicial District. He moved quickly into the state's attorney generalship in 1972, where he served two terms. He won election to the U.S. Congress, representing the Second Congressional District in 1976. A failed attempt to win the Senate seat being vacated by John McClellan, which he lost to David Pryor, seemed to derail Tucker's political career in 1978, and he returned to the practice of law. This was an important and formative detour for Tucker. He began to engage in a number of business enterprises, including a cable company he founded with his wife—clearly a knowledge-based industry. His business interests, moreover, included an international component that placed him squarely in concert with the new global economy. However, Tucker never lost his taste for political office. He won the lieutenant governorship in 1990, just in time to step into the governor's office vacated when Clinton won the presidency. While in office he presided over a restructuring of the juvenile justice system, an interest of his connected to his days as a prosecuting attorney. He faced challenges arising out of the Lake View suit, which required additional funds to be allocated to education, and rather than raise taxes, he cut the budgets of a number of state agencies. He failed in an attempt to convince the voters to pass a 3.5-billion-dollar bond issue to support the maintenance and expansion of the state's highway system. Ironically, Tucker's governorship was cut short when he was convicted of a white-collar crime connected to an attempt to expand his cable business. He became ensnared in an investigation by Whitewater investigators looking into allegations made against Bill and Hillary Clinton regarding a failed real estate venture in Arkansas. In a completely unconnected matter, Tucker had apparently conspired to purchase a Texas cable company that Whitewater prosecutors alleged had fraudulently been declared bankrupt in order to avoid the payment of corporate income taxes. Tucker resigned on May 29, 1996, the day after his conviction, leaving the office to his lieutenant governor, Republican Mike Huckabee.

Although a Republican who presented himself as a social conservative, Huckabee proved to be fairly moderate, and, significantly, he promoted economic development that helped position Arkansas to embrace the new knowledge-based industries. He proved capable of securing the governor's office in his own right when he won reelection in 1998. Huckabee's brand of Republicanism, moreover, closely resembled that espoused by Frank White. Like White, he was both fiscally and socially conservative. The first Baptist minister to occupy the office since James P. Eagle (1889–1893), Huckabee, like Eagle, had also served as president of the Southern Baptist Convention. A fundamentalist Christian, he appealed to like-minded voters but also took positions on certain issues that made him acceptable to the suburban middle class and the traditional Republican voter in the northwest part of the state: fiscal conservatism. He created a commission to investigate the size of the state government, and after that commission made its report, he called for a dramatic reduction in the number of state agencies. Presenting a moderate persona while espousing socially conservative positions, he began to successfully negotiate the political arena in Arkansas. See plate 54 following page 366.

One of his first acts as governor was to launch a campaign to convince voters to endorse a bond issue to improve the state's deteriorating highway system, something his predecessor in office, Jim Guy Tucker, had attempted but failed to accomplish. The repair and expansion of the highway system was important to ordinary citizens as well as a number of well-connected business interests. J. B. Hunt Trucking, Tyson Inc., Dillard's Department Stores, and Wal-Mart, for example, stood to gain from the expansion of the highway system and, indeed, one key component of the state's effort to participate in the Sunbelt economic phenomenon involved the modernization of such infrastructure. In pursuing support for the bond issue, Huckabee exemplified the personal style and charisma that had made certain Democrats so successful in the past. He toured the state by bus and successfully convinced the Arkansas electorate to support the issue. Exuding what some of his counterparts referred to as "compassionate conservatism," he went to the airwaves to successfully pitch his ARKids First program, which expanded health care to 200,000 children in the state. He used funds from the Tobacco Settlement (1998) to fund the program. In the area of education he also struck a moderately progressive note and promoted policies crucial to moving Arkansas forward economically. With an unprecedented teacher shortage predicted in the early twenty-first century, he promised a dramatic raise in teacher salaries. With neighboring states paying higher salaries, the drain on the best and brightest teachers had begun to worry state officials.

In his third and final term in office, Huckabee faced a challenge that had plagued his predecessors in office and shadowed his governorship: education funding. When the court ruled in *Lake View v. Huckabee* in 2002 that the state's funding formula was inadequate, Huckabee was faced with the problem of how to raise sufficient funds in order to satisfy the court order. He raised the issue of the consolidation of small school districts into larger ones, thereby eliminating administrative and building costs and saving, potentially, millions of dollars. But he faced a serious backlash from small communities and many legislators who represented them. Although the legislature refused to force consolidation on the scale that Huckabee recommended, they did devise a formula that established the minimum number of students a school district had to have in order to remain viable economically: 350.

Despite the controversy that arose over the consolidation issue, Mike Huckabee was a popular governor. However, Arkansas voters, like voters elsewhere, had passed term-limit amendments in 1992 and 1998, the first aimed at legislators and the second at executive offices, including that of the governor. When his second full term expired in 2006, Huckabee stepped aside, leaving the governor's office open to challenge from an experienced and well-liked Democratic legislator, Mike Beebe. Beebe, like his predecessors, emphasized the development of knowledge-based industries and sponsored measures designed to improve the educational system in order to facilitate that development.

Mike Beebe had first been elected to the legislature in 1982—the same year he was designated the state's most outstanding trial lawyer—and immediately became involved in negotiations in the debate over public education arising out of the Alma suit over school funding. He later helped fashion legislation aimed at remedying the flaws identified by the federal court in the Little Rock desegregation cases. A term as attorney general (2002–2006) provided him with the opportunity to address these issues in an executive position. Both in the legislature and the attorney general's office, he earned a reputation as a hard-working and practical politician, focused on achieving results but not at the expense of his principles. Raised by a single parent, Beebe grew up under trying economic circumstances and developed a deeply felt empathy for those in similar circumstances. Though a fiscal conservative in many respects, he advocated the elimination of the sales tax on groceries, a burden that fell heavily on the working poor. Similarly, he supported a minimum wage, obviously directed at those at the bottom rung of the economic ladder. Finally, a fervent believer in the value of education and in the importance of early childhood development, he supported a progressive pre-kindergarten program that would benefit all children but particularly those at the lowest end of the economic spectrum. See plate 55 following page 366.

Skills Beebe developed during his two decades in the general assembly gave him the ability to work closely with the legislature in achieving his goals as governor, particularly in regards to reducing the tax on groceries and establishing an impressive pre-kindergarten program. At the same time, he came into office just as the worst economic crisis since the Great Depression hit the state and the nation. He trimmed the state budget, called a moratorium on raises for state employees, and instituted other cost-saving and fiscally conservative measures without sacrificing the pre-kindergarten program or the reduction in sales taxes on groceries. In other words, he maintained a fidelity to his campaign goals, goals that were far from mere rhetoric, at the same time he guided the state through a severe recession. He also recognized an opportunity to step into the void left by other states that were more devastated by the economic collapse. His strategic economic goals involved a multifaceted approach to economic development. Realizing that most of the state's population was too undereducated to step immediately into knowledge-based industries, he emphasized a continuation of efforts to promote traditional manufacturing in the state at the same time he endorsed the growth of high-tech and service-sector-related enterprises. From the time of taking office to 2012, Governor Beebe enjoyed enviable approval ratings, largely on the basis of his success in steering the state through the recession and the fact that he delivered on his campaign promise to lower grocery taxes. His style of leadership compared favorably to that of Dale Bumpers and David Pryor in that he exuded a moderate demeanor while championing progressive measures and conservative fiscal policies. It differed from that of his immediate predecessors, particularly Bill Clinton and Mike Huckabee, in that he preferred to keep a relatively low profile and work behind the scenes to accomplish his goals.

A factor of no little importance enabled Beebe to achieve remarkable success in securing his goals. He was able to capitalize on the power accruing to the governor's office in the face of term limits upon legislators. Term limits were designed to limit the number of terms officials could be elected and usually applied to "consecutive" terms. Three factors contributed to the increasing power of the governor in this context. First, although governor's terms were also limited, the governor's office, unlike that of legislators, is a full-time position. Second, to complicate matters, legislative sessions are characteristically short, providing newly elected legislators with only a limited opportunity to master the processes at work in the general assembly. The legislature meets in regular session in one 60-day period in odd number years, although sessions can be extended when two-thirds of the body votes to extend the session. Governors have frequently called special sessions in even numbered years but the sessions are typically focused narrowly on designated issues. Third, given that legislators are paid a very small salary, they must maintain their regular livelihoods, and thus they are part-time legislators and, given the brevity of legislative sessions, they have little opportunity to master the intricacies of the legislative process. Before term limits, experienced legislators acquired greater power and authority within the general assembly and provided continuity across time, allowing new legislators to gain a mastery of the processes.

The term-limits phenomenon is a national one and scholarly studies have revealed a number of interesting consequences. First, the accrual of power to the governor's office is an obvious result. Second, term limits require lobbyists to expend more time educating legislators, thus potentially limiting the influence of special interests. Third, the Republican Party in Arkansas has enjoyed significant success, particularly in the 2010 and 2012 elections. Before the 2010 election, Arkansas had a higher proportion of Democrats in its general assembly than any other state with the exception Massachusetts, Rhode Island, and Hawaii. Democrats held seventy-two of one hundred seats in the Arkansas house and twenty-seven of thirty-five seats in the state senate. In 2010, capitalizing on a poor economy nationwide and Tea Party appeal, the Republicans made significant inroads into Democratic political dominance, claiming forty-five of one hundred seats in the house and fifteen of thirty-five seats in the senate. In 2012, Republicans captured control of the general assembly. Some promises of term limits have not been fulfilled, however. Although promoted as a method of securing citizen-legislators, term limits have tended to result in the election of men and women who have had political experience at the local level as mayors, county judges, or as city councilmen/women. And it appears that imposition of term limits did not result in a significant increase in women and minorities in the legislature.

Arkansas's 1992 amendment imposing term limits on legislators included one aimed at the men and women sent to the U.S. house and senate. It was later ruled unconstitutional. Though states have established the authority to impose term limits on state offices, their efforts to limit the number of terms of its congressional delegates failed a constitutional test when the Supreme Court ruled in 1995 that states lacked the authority to impose limits on federal offices. In fact, even without term limits, Arkansas has had unusual turnover in its congressional delegation over the last twenty years, turnover that reflects a significant demographic shift in the state.

The rise of northwest Arkansas, the growth of Little Rock, and the decline of the Delta have had enormous implications for the state both economically and politically. By the year 2000 the Walton family, situated in northwest Arkansas and operating the phenomenally successful Wal-Mart retail chain, was estimated to be worth $108 billion, making them among the wealthiest in the world. The Stephens family, owner of Stephens, Inc., based in Little Rock, an investment banking establishment, had wealth estimated at $3.8 billion. Both appeared at the top of a list of the one hundred wealthiest families in Arkansas. At the same time, only two Delta planters appeared on the list, and their wealth ranked at seventy-fourth and eighty-fourth, respectively. Had a similar list been published one hundred years earlier, it would have been dominated by Delta planters.

Strikingly, while most of the wealthiest Arkansans have achieved this distinction outside of agricultural enterprises (the Tyson Corporation is the only "agricultural" entity at the top of the list), nearly three-quarters of the gross state product is farm generated, and over 40 percent of the value of the state's manufacturing output is derived from the processing of agricultural products. One hundred years ago the poorest Arkansans often worked for the wealthiest; today, those who continue to work the land for a living have little to do with the "new" economy's top movers and shakers. The paternalism that, however imperfectly, operated to make the circumstances of the poor of immediate relevance to the wealthy, has little direct counterpart in today's Arkansas, although some parallels remain. For example, Wal-Mart, Tyson, and other successful corporations employ large numbers of people in low-skill, low-wage jobs. Since the tremendous profits generated by these corporations are absorbed primarily by upper-echelon, managerial, and skilled personnel, the result is a tendency toward bipolarization into a two-class society separated by ever-increasing disparities in earnings as well as small prospects for advancement. This trend, which the nation as a whole has experienced, represents a second challenge to Arkansans hoping to build a future in which such disparities will be reduced.

The business orientation of the state's economic dynamos might augur a renewed interest in promoting roads and education, but the natural conservatism of business groups, particularly where taxes are concerned, leaves open the question of how to finance such improvements. And while the wealthiest Arkansans have enjoyed a decade of unparalleled prosperity, the middle class in Arkansas, as elsewhere, has not kept pace. The state's poor gained ground in the 1990s, relative to the poor in other areas of the country, but much of the rural population remains mired in a pervasive poverty and Arkansas's per capita income is well below the national average. Moreover, what seems indisputable is that the fastest-growing sectors of the American economy in the twenty-first century demand a more highly educated workforce than the state's educational infrastructure has so far proved capable of providing. This raises the question of whether Arkansas can build upon what progress it has recently made in generating high-tech employment opportunities. The major challenge facing Arkansas in the twenty-first century, therefore, will be finding solutions to the problems that have so far prevented the state from developing a truly first-rate educational system.

Arkansas's Cultural Heritage

Although C. Vann Woodward has contributed much to the understanding of southern (and Arkansas) history, there was one area in which he was deafeningly silent. He had little to say about the South's cultural legacy. He was virtually mute about the intellectuals, writers, and artists of the South, a disappointing omission. If the South—and Arkansas—had something unique to offer the nation, it certainly manifested itself in that arena. While Woodward focused his attention on the economic and political sphere, a vibrant cultural legacy was left unsung. His omission was shared by news outlets that focused attention on crises like the Little Rock fiasco in 1957. Television cameras captured the violence and insults aimed at defenseless black children and broadcast these images to the world, making the state notorious. Despite this unfortunate—and not entirely undeserved—portrayal, others in Arkansas were contributing something far more positive to American life and, indeed, to world culture. Few outside the state appreciated the role that Arkansas musicians played in the evolution of American popular music and even fewer understood the cross fertilization that occurred between black and white, between Delta and mountain musicians. Perhaps because Arkansas was situated between the South and the West—indeed, some refer to Arkansas as a part of the Southwest rather than the South—the state has served as an entrepôt for the blending of different sounds. Here was an area in which black and white Arkansans crossed racial lines freely in the interest of pursuing an authentic American art form.

The sounds emanating from the Delta and the sounds coming out of the mountains of Arkansas were never truly isolated from each other, but they initially developed more or less separately. Each had their origins in musical traditions from outside the state and, initially, outside the nation. The ballads sung by Arkansas's mountain musicians were carried over from Appalachia and had a distinct connection to the British Isles, although by the early twentieth century a unique American flavor could be discerned. Elements of minstrelsy and even blues forms had crept into some mountain music, and whites used instruments that had African origins. The Delta blues had African origins, of course, reflected in its use of percussive guitar accompaniments and falsetto vocal stylings. The slave experience in America also left a profound imprint on black music. Finding themselves in "another kind of slavery," as some historians refer to the post-emancipation sharecropping arrangement, black musicians carried African/slave music into another evolutionary stage. The blues is a sound that dates back to the late nineteenth and early twentieth century, and both the music and the lyrics speak to the sense of desperation that accompanied the black experience in an era of racial segregation and legal disfranchisement. While many blues singers sang songs about poverty and imprisonment, many others favored party music and devoted little time to songs that contained elements of social commentary whether implicit or explicit. Like white mountain musicians, many black bluesmen and blueswomen sang simple ballads about lost love, something common to the experience of all humans, black or white, American or otherwise.

Another important influence on both mountain and blues music was the gospel sound. Although the white and black communities of Arkansas shared a deep religiosity and a Protestant orientation, they were very different in the way they experienced church services and expressed themselves musically. Harkening back to African traditions, blacks engaged in the "call and response" pattern during the preacher's sermon. Similarly, the cadence and emotionalism of their music owed much to Africa but had been greatly influenced by their years of bondage. The work songs sung by slaves established a rhythm and beat calculated to create a pace that made the work seem to go more quickly and certainly more tolerably. Most whites, like most blacks in Arkansas, were of the Methodist or Baptist denominations, but there were differences between black and white church services and singing styles, differences that may have been more the result of differences in class rather than differences in race. Upper-class white Baptists and Methodists were typically less enthusiastic and more restrained. Some whites belonged to Pentecostal denominations that elicited emotional responses from their members but had no tradition of "call and response," and their gospel songs had no connection to either Africa or the slave experience. Some few, in fact, foreswore musical instruments entirely and allowed singing from approved hymnals only. Others embraced instrumentation and did not require their congregants to sing only hymns sanctioned by some church authority. However blacks and whites expressed their religion, their music was important and, indeed, the first music many young southerners of either race ever heard or sung was religious music. It ran deep in them and greatly influenced their secular music. John Handcock, a black Southern Tenant Farmers Union troubadour who penned union lyrics in the mid-1930s, understood the importance of religion in rural Arkansas, so he sang his songs to religious tunes precisely because they were familiar to, and reverberated psychologically with, both black and white sharecroppers and tenants.

The best-known black gospel singer of Arkansas origins is Sister Rosetta Tharpe, who was born in Cotton Plant in 1921, into a gospel singing family. Rosetta was touring professionally when she was six years old, performing both gospel and secular music. As folklorist Robert Cochran has observed, "Few artists covered such a range of styles—Tharpe performed with blues musicians (Muddy Waters), jazz artists (Cab Calloway and Lucky Millinder), and other gospel groups (The Caravans, the Dixie Hummingbirds, the James Cleveland Singers)." The number and character of the musical venues she performed in were as wide as her repertoire. While she appeared at the Newport Folk Festival, the Apollo Theater, the Cotton Club, and Carnegie Hall, she also performed in churches and a variety of nightclubs, small and large. Johnny Cash recalled that she was playing at an out-of-the-way nightclub in Chicago when he was there to perform at Soldier Field. She sang a rendition of "This Train" that reduced him to tears, but her performance was likely a mix of blues and gospel tunes, something she was famous for. One music critic credited her with having created pop gospel.

Rosetta's journey to national prominence began in Arkansas in an era when much of the state was relatively isolated and rural. But a singular new invention would pull them into a new world of music. Beginning in the 1920s, people could hear both secular and religious music on battery-operated radios and phonographs. After electrical power was extended into rural areas, radios were among the first items purchased, and indeed, the medium played an important role in the evolution of American popular music in the 1950s. Until then, families gathered around fireplaces, in their living rooms, or on their front porches—often with neighbors in attendance—and sang their songs with or without instrumentation. In the days before electricity, even those with battery-operated radios (which had a short life and were not always reliable) entertained themselves by family sing-alongs. Levon Helm, who was raised near Elaine, Arkansas, in Phillips County, remarked that "we were a musical family." Helm would grow up to play professionally with Ronnie Hawkins and the Hawks before becoming drummer for The Band, which gained fame first playing backup for Bob Dylan. Helm remembered that his mother "sang in a clear alto voice," and he said of his father, "All of us kids remember sitting on his lap in the evenings while he relaxed in his chair. He'd sing to us . . . [and] knew so many songs he was like a fountain of music." If not singing themselves, the Helm family listened to the radio. "We'd have to buy a battery two and a half feet long and maybe eight inches thick . . . I remember my dad pulling our tractor right up to the window of the house one night when the battery was down, and he plugged the radio into the tractor battery so we wouldn't lose the Grand Ole Opry, The Shadow, the Creaking Door, Amos 'n' Andy—those were the shows you couldn't miss."

Live religious music might be heard at home or in churches, but townspeople likely got their live secular music in music halls, or, depending on the sensibilities of the individuals involved, in honkytonks and juke joints. Country folk who did not travel to town often relied on country honkytonks, tucked into deep woods or down isolated roads. They might also enjoy traveling shows. Helm reported that "going to music shows was high-level entertainment for our family. They'd set up tents at the edge of Marvell and have a stage, folding chairs, and refreshments." Sometimes the Helm family heard the F. S. Walcott Rabbit's Foot Minstrels from Mississippi, who would "set up with the back of a big truck as their stage." Later, Helm's Canadian bandmates, seeking vicariously to immerse themselves in the culture Helm grew up with, would perform a song called "W. S. Walcott Medicine Show." The show that made the most lasting impression on Helm, however, was the "first show I remember . . . Bill Monroe and his Blue Grass Boys on a summer evening in 1946, when I was six years old. Boy, this really tattooed my brain. I've never forgotten it: Bill had a real good five-piece band." The Helm family had heard Monroe on the "Grand Ole Opry" and were thrilled to see him in person. "Here he was in the flesh," said Helm. While Helm himself would grow up to be a rock musician, this earliest influence was something very different. "They took that old hillbilly music, sped it up, and basically invented what is now known as bluegrass music."

Although Helm remembered his first hearing of Bill Monroe as a formative experience, he would be more heavily influenced by various African American musics, such as the blues programming emanating from nearby Helena. The pure blues sound of Helena became known to the world in the 1940s, principally because of the "King Biscuit Time" show at radio station KFFA, which featured the blues harmonica of Sonny Boy Williamson. It also served as a showcase for local talent all over the Delta—of Arkansas, Mississippi, Louisiana. Young and old blues singers alike would be allowed to sing live on the radio for fifteen to thirty minutes, receiving no pay for their services. Instead they would be allowed to plug an upcoming performance. (This phenomenon was not peculiar to the Delta or to blues, however, as white country musicians like Frankie Kelley were making the same kinds of arrangements with radio stations in Fayetteville and elsewhere.) Some of the most famous bluesmen of the 1930s and 1940s called Helena home and helped create a unique Arkansas blues sound: Williamson, Howlin' Wolf, Little Walter, and Robert Nighthawk. KFFA was heard as far away as Chicago, and the ongoing migration of blacks out of the Delta, which began in the post–World War I era, brought even more Delta blues north to Chicago and Detroit. There the Arkansas bluesmen put their electric guitars to work in a louder and more muscular fashion and contributed to the direction that Chicago blues was taking. William "Big Bill" Broonzy, who was born in 1893 in Mississippi but raised on a farm near Pine Bluff, is one of the best known of the Chicago transplants. He had an innovative guitar style that made him a favorite of Chicago audiences. He would go on to tour Europe, England, Africa, South America, and Australia.

Some Arkansas blues people stayed closer to home, however, like Robert Junior Lockwood, who would heavily influence the evolving Memphis blues. Lockwood was the stepson of blues great Robert Johnson, who passed on his Mississippi blues sound to the youth. Thus Arkansas Delta bluesmen influenced bluesmen in Louisiana, Mississippi, and Tennessee—not to mention those of Chicago and Harlem—and, in turn, were influenced by them. While roughhewn blues may have been black Arkansans most important musical export, smoother sounds would also emerge—such as the "jump" of Louis Jordan, who learned to play clarinet from his father in Brinkley, and, later, the urbane soul of Al Green, a native of Forrest City.

Although the radio was one place where segregation was hard to maintain, some radio stations were reluctant at first to play "race records"; that is, music recorded by blacks. Record companies actually had white singers record black songs, which were then deemed suitable for white radio audiences. There were a few black radio stations in various locations around the country, including WDIA in Memphis, which Arkansas Delta people could easily hear. Some white radio stations were eager to broadcast the black sound, and many businesses, particularly those catering to a black trade, were more than willing to advertise shows like "King Biscuit Time." By the end of the 1950s, rhythm-and-blues singers—principally black artists who had mixed blues with rock-and-roll—were readily played on white radio stations, although country blues was a sound that never achieved a wide audience there. Some whites did have an opportunity to hear Delta blues over their radio stations, and the minstrel shows that traveled the South included black musicians, but Levon Helm recalled that the audiences were segregated in the Walcott Rabbit's Foot Minstrel shows. "The audience was split down the middle by an aisle. On the left were the black to light-skinned folks, while the light-skinned to people with red hair sat on the right."

Whether the rest of America was ready for Delta blues, many young white musicians found inspiration in the sounds coming out of Helena, West Memphis, and North Little Rock. Those from sharecropping backgrounds had already had considerable exposure to black music from their personal association with black musicians. Billy Lee Riley grew up in various communities in northeastern Arkansas where his father worked as a painter or at any other job he could secure. While a small child living near Osceola, two black friends took him "around to the black section of town, [where we would] sit around for hours and listen to that music coming out of the juke joints and maybe watch guitar players sitting on the side of the street." Riley would later become one of Sun Studio's rockabilly players—rockabilly was a blend of fast blues and country, an early form of rock-and-roll. He learned to play the guitar from a white boy and two black friends but "the one I remember above them all was an old fella called Lightning Leon, who would play a harmonica and sing." Riley even cut a blues album using the name Lightening Leon as his own. Arkansas bluesmen also inspired young whites living worlds away from the Delta. Sonny Boy Williamson, for instance, became a favorite of a number of the stars of the "British Invasion," which in the mid-1960s introduced many American teenagers to their own nation's rich musical heritage.

Not all white musicians who were influenced by black musicians went the way of rock-and-roll or rock. Early in his career it was almost impossible to identify the style of music played by Charlie Rich. Rich, who was born in Colt, Arkansas, in 1932 and raised in Benton, Arkansas, credited a black blues-singing sharecropper named C. J. as having a major influence on his musical style. He was also attracted to jazz music from an early age, but he grew up listening to the "Grand Ole Opry" and his first big hit was "Lonely Weekends," a pure country music sound. When two songs he recorded went to the top of the country chart and then to the top of the pop chart in the early 1970s, he became a solid fixture in the music world. Although they were crossover hits, "Behind Closed Doors" and "Most Beautiful Girl in the World" made him a country music giant.

Like Billy Lee Riley, Rich was initially under contract at Sun Studios in Memphis, Tennessee. Sam Phillips, who ran Sun Records, discovered and recorded artists like Elvis Presley, Carl Perkins, Jerry Lee Lewis, and other rockabilly/rock-and-roll singers. Coming out of that mix of white country, black blues, and bluegrass, the musicians who passed through Sun Studios often took their styles in different directions. Another Sun Studio recording artist from Arkansas, Johnny Cash, would, like Charlie Rich, become a country music star. Cash was born in Kingsland, Arkansas, in 1932, but moved as a small child when his family secured a place at Dyess Colony, the ill-fated FSA community in Mississippi County. It was a hardscrabble existence, and he had a lot of opportunity to hear local blues. Osceola and the clubs that Billy Lee Riley remembers were very close at hand. West Memphis, Arkansas, in nearby Crittenden County, was a Mecca for bluesmen, and young whites like Cash from the surrounding area were drawn to the exotic sounds and scenes of roadhouses, bars, and brothels there. But Cash grew up listening to the "Grand Ole Opry" and to radio stations broadcasting from the Mexican border, which were airing hymns and ballads sung by the Carter Family. Cash himself showed musical talent early, singing gospel in church. However, his first hit recordings were blues-inspired songs like "Folsom Prison Blues" and "Rock Island Line." The latter was a prison song made famous by Huddie Ledbetter (Leadbelly) recordings but first discovered by the musicologist John Lomax when he was doing field recordings at Arkansas prisons in 1934. His driver at the time was Huddie Leadbelly, who heard the song and later recorded it. Cash's most famous songs, however, became country music standards, songs like "I Walk the Line" and "A Boy Named Sue."

Many of the young blues and country singers of Arkansas got their start with cheap guitars sold by Sears and Roebuck, but not all of them passed through Sun Studios on their way to fame and glory. Glen Campbell, born in Delight, Arkansas, in 1938, was given a cheap guitar by his father when he was only four years old, and by the time he was fourteen, he had dropped out of school, moved to New Mexico, and was playing professionally with his uncle Dick Bill's band. He was destined to have a string of hit records and became a popular music star. His sound was a blending of country and pop, but he never forgot his Arkansas roots, calling one of his thirty-seven Capitol albums, Arkansas.

For every Arkansas musician who gained fame and fortune, there were dozens who remained obscure, sometimes quite contentedly so. Many young men and women held down ordinary jobs during the day and played their music in the evenings and on weekends, with or without an audience. Others, like Emma Dusenberry, endured a sparse obscurity living in poverty. She was born in Georgia in 1862 but came to Arkansas when she was ten years old. She lived in a variety of locations in both the Delta and mountains and sang Anglo-American ballads. Folk archivists discovered her in the 1930s. Folk music collectors Alan Lomax from Texas and Vance Randolph from Fayetteville paid her visits and made field recordings of her songs. One hundred and sixteen of her songs are on deposit in the National Folk Music Archives and copies of all the field recordings are at the University of Arkansas Special Collections Division. She had a brief moment of fame in 1936 when she was taken to Little Rock to sing at the Arkansas centennial of statehood but then returned to Mena to live in the poverty to which she was accustomed.

The music tradition in Arkansas remains very much alive at the beginning of the twenty-first century, and towns like Helena and Mountain View have dedicated themselves to preserving the rich musical heritage of the state. Mountain View celebrates and seeks to preserve white mountain music, holding festivals and entertaining tourists from around the country and the world. Visitors are treated to special shows that feature local artists, but many of them appreciate the opportunity to hear ordinary pickers and singers sitting around the square playing for tips—or just playing. Helena sponsors the King Biscuit Festival every fall, attracting blues musicians from around the world. The harmonica, Sonny Boy Williamson's signature instrument, is especially featured. A host of young new songwriters, singers, and musicians have emerged in the last few decades and seem destined to perpetuate the tradition.

While C. Vann Woodward barely observed the contribution of musicians, artists, and writers in southern—or Arkansas—culture, they left an enduring legacy that continues to resonate into the twenty-first century. Arkansas certainly contributed a number of luminaries to southern culture. The poetry of John Gould Fletcher and Miller Williams has graced the pages of literary magazines and gained them international reputations. Maya Angelou, a poet and literary figure, has written one of the most riveting accounts of growing up in the South—in her case in Stamps, Arkansas—in modern southern literature. Architects Edward Durrell Stone and E. Fay Jones have gained reknown for now iconic structures like the latter's Thorncrown Chapel. Artists like Edward Washburn and Larry Alexander have portrayed Arkansas in very different ways but captured the imagination and the complexity of the state. Arkansas has also produced writers of great reknown, like Charles Portis of *True Grit* fame and Donald Harrington, who created the imaginary and compelling world of Stay More, Arkansas. While the Stay More oath—"I do solemnly swear that the country life is not only more peaceful than city life but more likely to last into contented old age"—may not resonate with the New South image, it has resonance for many twenty-first century Arkansans, something we share, almost certainly, with many Americans. See plate 56 following page 366.

Conclusion

Does C. Vann Woodward's *Burden of Southern History* continue to have relevance in today's Arkansas? Given the changes that have occurred—and have not occurred—since the book's publication in 1960, the answer is not obvious. Woodward's expectations concerning the emergence of a truly integrated society after *Brown v. Board of Education* foundered on the realities of a South and a nation more riven by racism than he imagined, a fact he began to reckon with in later editions of the book. However, as anyone who lived through the era would attest, considerable change has occurred, and as students of history might suggest, one should not expect centuries of racism and discrimination to disappear in a few short decades. Yet nothing good can come of the failure to complete the unfinished revolution begun by the *Brown* decision. Meanwhile, Arkansas's uneven integration into the global economy worked to its advantage during the early twenty-first century. Ironically, the continuation of vestiges of the colonial economy shielded the state from the worst aspects of a global economic meltdown. In any case, with a population only partly prepared to step into the new knowledge-based global economy, the best path toward economic expansion seems to be a continuation of a mixed economy: agriculture, manufacturing, and knowledge-based industries. Given the recent international economic collapse, the best choice seems to be the only choice for Arkansas.

SUGGESTED READINGS

Chapter One: A Land "Inferior to None"

The best source on the geography, geology, and climate of Arkansas is Thomas L. Foti and Gerald Hanson's *Arkansas and the Land* (University of Arkansas Press, 1992). See also Foti's *Arkansas, Its Land and People* (Arkansas Department of Education, 1976). A good brief account is Foti's entry "Geography and Geology" in the *Encyclopedia of Arkansas History & Culture* (online at http://encyclopediaofarkansas.net).

Chapter Two: Native American Prehistory

A good place to begin reading about Arkansas prehistory is the Arkansas Archeological Survey's Indians of Arkansas Web site, which can be accessed at http://arkarcheology.uark.edu/indiansofarkansas/index.html. Authoritative summaries of American Indian prehistory and ethnology in Arkansas and the mid-South are provided in several chapters of *The Handbook of North American Indians*, Volume 13 (Plains) and Volume 14 (Southeast), edited by William C. Sturtevant (Smithsonian Institution Press, 2001 and 2004). The prehistory of the eastern part of the state is given detailed coverage in Dan F. and Phyllis A. Morse's *Archaeology of the Central Mississippi Valley* (Academic Press, 1983). A collection of articles in *Arkansas Archaeology: Essays in Honor of Dan and Phyllis Morse*, edited by Robert C. Mainfort Jr. and Marvin D. Jeter (University of Arkansas Press, 1999), provides examples of recent research on prehistoric and historic archeology across the state.

The Domebo site excavations are reported in *Domebo: A Paleo-indian Mammoth Kill Site in the Prairie Plains*, by Frank C. Leonhardy (Contributions of the Museum of the Great Plains No. 1, Lawton, 1966). Information on Kimmswick can be found in "Kimmswick: A Clovis-Mastodon Association in Eastern Missouri" by Russell W. Graham, C. Vance Haynes, Donald Lee Johnson, and Marvin Kay in *Science* 213 (4512): 1115–17. The Cooper site excavations are summarized in *Bison Hunting at Cooper Site: Where Lightning Bolts Drew Thundering Herds*, by Leland C. Bement (University of Oklahoma Press, 1999). A detailed analysis of the Dalton-era Sloan site in eastern Arkansas, perhaps the oldest cemetery in the western hemisphere, is found in Dan F. Morse's *Sloan: A Paleoindian Dalton Cemetery in Arkansas* (Smithsonian Institution Press, 1997). A report on Middle Archaic foodways at the Jones Mill site appears in "Reconstructing Ancient Foodways at the Jones Mill Site (3HS28): Hot Spring County, Arkansas," by Mary Beth Trubitt, Kathryn Parker, and Lucretia Kelly in the *Caddo Archeology Journal* 21:43–70. Good summaries of the origins of agriculture in the mid-South are provided in Gayle Fritz's essay, "Native Farming Systems and Ecosystems in the Mississippi River Valley," in *Imperfect Balance: Landscape Transformations in the*

Precolumbian Americas, edited by David L. Lentz (Columbia University Press, 2000), and in several contributions found in Bruce Smith's edited volume, *Rivers of Change: Essays on Early Agriculture in Eastern North America* (Smithsonian Institution Press, 1992). Radiocarbon assays confirming the age of early mound building in southeastern Arkansas are reported by Marvin Jeter in "ARF-Funded AMS Date Confirms Age of 'The Oldest Little Mound in Arkansas,'" in *Field Notes: Newsletter of the Arkansas Archeological Society* 354:3–5. The most accessible work on the Poverty Point site is Jon L. Gibson's *The Ancient Mounds of Poverty Point: Place of Rings* (University Press of Florida, 2000). Tristram R. Kidder's work on the impacts of global climate changes on the Poverty Point culture is reported in "Climate Change and the Archaic to Woodland Transition (3000–2500 Cal B.P.) in the Mississippi River Basin," *American Antiquity* 71(2): 195–231. The Dirst site excavations along the Buffalo River are presented by George Sabo III and Randall L. Guendling in *Archeological Investigations at 3MR80-Area D in the Rush Development Area, Buffalo National River, Arkansas, Vol. I and II* (Southwest Cultural Resources Center Professional Papers No. 38 and 50. Santa Fe, 1990, 1992). James Ford's excavations at the Helena Mounds are reported in *Hopewell Culture Burial Mounds Near Helena, Arkansas* (Anthropological Papers of the American Museum of Natural History, Vol. 50, Part 1. New York, 1963). Martha Rolingson's long-term research of the Toltec Mounds site and the Plum Bayou culture is summarized in *Toltec Mounds: Archeology of the Mound-and-Plaza Complex* (Arkansas Archeological Survey Research Series, #65, Fayetteville, 2012). Additional information on the Woodland Period in Arkansas and the mid-South is provided in various chapters of *The Woodland Southeast*, edited by David G. Anderson and Robert C. Mainfort Jr. (The University of Alabama Press, 2002). A handsomely illustrated volume on Mississippian pottery from eastern Arkansas is *Gifts of the Great River: Arkansas Effigy Pottery from the Edwin Curtiss Collection*, by John H. House (Peabody Museum Press, 2003). Ann Early's study of Caddo salt making is reported in *Caddoan Saltmakers in the Ouachita Valley: The Hardman Site* (Arkansas Archeological Survey Research Series No. 43. Fayetteville, 1993). Studies of the Parkin and Nodena communities in northeast Arkansas include *Parkin: The 1978–1979 Archeological Investigations of a Cross County, Arkansas Site* by Phyllis A. Morse (Arkansas Archeological Survey Research Series No. 13. Fayetteville, 1981); *Nodena: An Account of 90 Years of Archeological Investigation in Southeast Mississippi County, Arkansas*, edited by Dan F. Morse (Arkansas Archeological Survey Research Series No. 30. Fayetteville, rev. 2008), and *Archeological Investigations at Upper Nodena: 1973 Field Season*, edited by Robert C. Mainfort Jr. (Arkansas Archeological Survey Research Series No. 64. Fayetteville, 2010). Studies of Parkin and Nodena mortuary practices are provided in Thomas Gannon's *A Mortuary Analysis of the Vernon Paul Site (3CS25): Sociopolitical Organization at a Late Mississippian Site in Cross County, Arkansas* (Arkansas Archeological Survey Research Report No. 30. Fayetteville, 2002) and Rita Fisher-Carroll's *Mortuary Behavior at Upper Nodena* (Arkansas Archeological Survey Research Series No. 59. Fayetteville, 2001). The current research program at Parkin is detailed by Jeffrey M. Mitchem in "Mississippian Research at Parkin Archeological State Park," in *Proceedings of the 14th Mid-South Archaeological Conference*, edited by Richard Walling, Camille Wharey, and

Camille Stanley (Special Publications No. 1, Panamerican Consultants, Memphis). Information on Caddo settlement patterns is provided in *Contributions to the Archeology of the Great Bend Region of the Red River Valley*, edited by Frank F. Schambach and Frank Rackerby (Arkansas Archeological Survey Research Series No. 22. Fayetteville, 1982) and *Two Caddoan Farmsteads in the Red River Valley: The Archeology of the McLelland and Joe Clark Sites*, edited by David B. Kelley (Arkansas Archeological Survey Research Series No. 51. Fayetteville, 1997). A recent issue of the journal *Southeastern Archaeology* (vol. 29, no. 2 [Winter 2010]) also contains a series of articles on Caddo settlement patterns incorporating the results of recent geophysical investigations at sites in the Caddo area. Studies of Mississippian mortuary practices, including James A. Brown's interpretation of the Great Mortuary at Spiro, are found in *Mississippian Mortuary Practices: Beyond Hierarchy and the Representationist Perspective*, edited by Lynne P. Sullivan and Robert C. Mainfort Jr. (University Press of Florida, 2010). Several interesting articles on the Southeastern Ceremonial Complex and its art are provided in the lavishly illustrated volume *Hero, Hawk, and Open Hand: American Indian Art of the Ancient Midwest and South*, edited by Richard F. Townsend (The Art Institute of Chicago and Yale University Press, 2004), and additional information from the most recent studies is found in *Ancient Objects and Sacred Realms: Interpretations of Mississippian Iconography*, edited by F. Kent Reilly III and James F. Garber (University of Texas Press, 2007), and *Visualizing the Sacred: Cosmic Visions, Regionalism, and the Art of the Mississippian World*, edited by George E. Lankford, F. Kent Reilly III, and James F. Garber (University of Texas Press, 2011). Marvin Kay and George Sabo's investigations on Mississippian mound sites in the western Ozarks are outlined in "Mortuary Ritual and Winter Solstice Imagery of the Harlan-Style Charnel House," by Marvin Kay and George Sabo III, *Southeastern Archaeology* 25(1): 29–47. Tree-ring evidence for drought conditions in prehistoric Arkansas and the mid-South are presented in "A 450-Year Drought Reconstruction for Arkansas, United States," by David W. Stahle, Malcolm K. Cleaveland, and John G. Hehr in *Nature* 316:530–32 and "Tree-ring Reconstructed Megadroughts over North America since AD 1300," by David W. Stahle, Falco F. Fye, and E. R. Cook in *Climate Change* 83:133–49.

Online resources include the Race & Ethnicity/Native American section of the *Encyclopedia of Arkansas History & Culture* (http://encyclopediaofarkansas.net/) and the Indians of Arkansas Web site hosted by the Arkansas Archeological Survey (http://arkarcheology.uark.edu/indiansofarkansas/index.html). The Hampson Museum, part of the Arkansas State Park system, in collaboration with the Center for Advanced Spatial Technology at the University of Arkansas, also has an online Virtual Hampson Museum that provides 3D artifact images and a village reconstruction of the Nodena Site (http://hampson.cast.uark.edu).

Chapter Three: Spanish and French Explorations in the Mississippi Valley

An excellent and very readable book on the sixteenth-century explorations of Hernando de Soto across the Southeast is Charles Hudson's *Knights of Spain, Warriors of the Sun*

(University of Georgia Press, 1997). A series of papers focusing on the expedition as it approached and crossed the Mississippi River into present-day Arkansas is provided in *The Expedition of Hernando de Soto West of the Mississippi, 1541–1543*, edited by Gloria A. Young and Michael P. Hoffman (University of Arkansas Press, 1993). The four extant accounts of the De Soto expedition are available in modern English translations in *The De Soto Chronicles: The Expedition of Hernando de Soto to North America in 1539–1543*, 2 vols., edited by Lawrence A. Clayton, Vernon James Knight Jr., and Edward C. Moore (The University of Alabama Press, 1993). An important series of essays providing critical evaluation of the De Soto accounts is found in *The Hernando de Soto Expedition: History, Historiography, and "Discovery" in the Southeast*, edited by Patricia Galloway (University of Nebraska Press, 1997). Disruptions affecting Southeastern Indians during the protohistoric and early historic period are given thorough consideration in *Mapping the Mississippian Shatter Zone: The Colonial Indian Salve Trade and Regional Instability in the American South*, edited by Robbie Ethridge and Sheri M. Shuck-Hall (University of Nebraska Press, 2009).

The most comprehensive history of French exploration and colonization in the American South is provided by Marcel Giraud in his five-volume *A History of French Louisiana*; volumes 1, 2, and 5 are available in English translation from the Louisiana State University Press. Additional essays and some primary source materials on early French explorations in the Mississippi Valley are found in *Frenchmen and French Ways in the Mississippi Valley*, edited by John F. McDermott (University of Illinois Press, 1969); *La Salle and His Legacy: Frenchmen and Indians in the Lower Mississippi Valley*, edited by Patricia K. Galloway (University Press of Mississippi, 1982); and *La Salle, the Mississippi, and the Gulf Coast*, edited by Robert S. Weddle (Texas A&M University Press, 1987). The interactions of French explorers and settlers with Quapaw Indians in Arkansas are given detailed consideration in *The Rumble of a Distant Drum: The Quapaws and Old World Newcomers, 1673–1804*, by Morris S. Arnold (University of Arkansas Press, 2000). Spanish colonial activities in the region are treated in *The Spanish in the Mississippi Valley, 1762–1804*, edited by John F. McDermott (University of Illinois Press, 1974), and *The Spanish Frontier in North America*, by David J. Weber (Yale University Press, 1992). Two important collections of essays on Native Americans and Europeans during Arkansas's colonial era are *Arkansas before the Americans*, edited by Hester A. Davis (Arkansas Archeological Survey Research Series No. 40, 1991), and *Cultural Encounters in the Early South: Indians and Europeans in Arkansas*, compiled by Jeannie M. Whayne (University of Arkansas Press, 1995). Kathleen DuVal's *The Native Ground: Indians and Colonists in the Heart of the Continent* (University of Pennsylvania Press, 2006) traces events from the early exploration era through the subsequent era of colonial settlement.

Chapter Four: New Traditions for a New World: Seventeenth- and Eighteenth-Century Native Americans in Arkansas

An introduction to the historic Indians of Arkansas that includes a brief review of their encounters with early Spanish and French explorers is provided in *Paths of Our Children: The Historic Indians of Arkansas,* by George Sabo III (Arkansas Archeological Survey Popular Series No. 3, revised 2001). A recently published collection that includes several essays on Arkansas Indians is *Indians of the Greater Southeast: Historical Archaeology and Ethnohistory,* edited by Bonnie G. McEwan (University Press of Florida, 2000).

The standard reference on the Quapaws is W. David Baird's *The Quapaws: A History of the Downstream People* (University of Oklahoma Press, 1980). A shorter treatment aimed at general audiences is found in Baird's *The Quapaws* (Chelsea House, 1989). Comprehensive histories and ethnographies of the Osages, written by prominent members of the tribe, include John Joseph Mathews's *The Osages: Children of the Middle Waters* (University of Oklahoma Press, 1961) and *A History of the Osage People* by Louis F. Burns (The University of Alabama Press, 2004). Other valuable sources on the Osages include *The Imperial Osages: Spanish-Indian Diplomacy in the Mississippi Valley,* by Gilbert C. Din and Abraham P. Nasatir (University of Oklahoma Press, 1983); *The Osage: An Ethnohistorical Study of Hegemony on the Prairie-Plains,* by Willard H. Rollings (University of Missouri Press, 1992); and *The Osage and the Invisible World: From the Works of Francis La Flesche,* edited by Garrick A. Bailey (University of Oklahoma Press, 1995). A useful introduction for general audiences is found in Terry P. Wilson's *The Osage* (Chelsea House, 1988). The impact of European contact on Caddo Indians is examined in *"The Caddo Nation": Archaeological and Historical Perspectives,* by Timothy K. Perttula. Reconstructions of Caddo culture based on early European accounts are available in Herbert Eugene Bolton's *The Hasinais: Southern Caddoans as Seen by the Earliest Europeans* (University of Oklahoma Press, 1986) and in the newly reissued version of John R. Swanton's classic *Source Material on the History and Ethnology of the Caddo Indians* (University of Oklahoma Press, 1996). Caddo histories penned by prominent tribal members include *Hasinai: A Traditional History of the Caddo Confederacy,* by Vynola Beaver Newkumet and Howard L. Meredith (Texas A&M University Press, 1988), and *Caddo Indians: Where We Come From,* by Cecile Elkins Carter (University of Oklahoma Press, 1995). Important new additions to the historical literature on Caddo Indians are represented by F. Todd Smith's *The Caddo Indians: Tribes at the Convergence of Empires, 1542–1854* (Texas A&M University Press, 1995) and *The Caddos, the Wichitas, and the United States, 1846–1901* (Texas A&M University Press, 1996), and *The Caddo Chiefdoms: Caddo Economics and Politics, 700–1835,* by David LaVere (University of Nebraska Press, 1998). A general review of the culture and history of the Tunica-Biloxi people is available in Jeffrey P. Brain's *The Tunica-Biloxi* (Chelsea House, 1990), and Tristram R. Kidder provides a review of the Koroas in "The Koroa Indians of the Mississippi Valley," *Mississippi Archaeologist* 23(2): 1–42. Modern efforts to preserve ancient traditions among groups tracing their ancestry back to Arkansas and surrounding states are treated in *Dancing on Common Ground: Tribal Cultures and Alliances on the Southern Plains,* by Howard L. Meredith (University Press of Kansas, 1995).

Chapter Five: Indians and Colonists in the Arkansas Country, 1686–1803

Three books by Morris S. Arnold provide an essential introduction to Arkansas colonial history. *Unequal Laws Unto a Savage Race: European Legal Traditions in Arkansas, 1686–1836* (University of Arkansas Press, 1985) provides a treatment of the French and Spanish legal systems in colonial Arkansas and also includes a great deal of social history along with an extended discussion of the various locations of Arkansas Post in the seventeenth and eighteenth centuries. Arnold's *Colonial Arkansas, 1686–1804: A Social and Cultural History* (University of Arkansas Press, 1991) furnishes a discussion of various aspects of the social and cultural history of seventeenth- and eighteenth-century Arkansas, including the sites of colonial European settlements, architecture, the social structure of the European population, the state of science and religion, the military, and the legal system. There is some attention given to European and Indian relations as well. Finally, the *Rumble of a Distant Drum: The Quapaws and Old World Newcomers, 1673–1804* (University of Arkansas Press, 2000) examines a wide range of relations between Quapaws and Europeans in colonial Arkansas, including intermarriage, trade, and military alliances. There is also a discussion of attempts by French and Spanish officials to apply European law to the Indians of the region and to convert them to Christianity.

Several new studies of different aspects of Arkansas's colonial history have been published over the last decade and offer some additional insights. Kathleen DuVal, *The Native Ground: Indians and Colonists in the Heart of the Continent* (University of Pennsylvania Press, 2006) is an essential treatment of colonial efforts in mid-America, including Arkansas. Wendy St. John, "The Chickasaw-Quapaw Alliance in the Revolutionary Era," *Arkansas Historical Quarterly* 68 (Autumn 2009): 272–82. Sonia Toudji, "The Happiest Consequences: Sexual Unions and Frontier Survival at Arkansas Post" (*Arkansas Historical Quarterly* 70 [Spring 2011]: 45–56) argues that marriages and other conjugal arrangements between Frenchmen and Quapaws were common in colonial Arkansas. Also useful are Kathleen DuVal, "Indian Intermarriage and Métissage in Colonial Louisiana" (*William and Mary Quarterly*, 3d Series) 65 [April 2008]: 207–304; John H. House, "Wallace Bottom: A Colonial-Era Archaeological Site in the Menard Locality, Eastern Arkansas" (*Southeastern Archaeology* 21 [Winter 2002]: 257–68); and George E. Lankford, "Town Making in the Southeastern Ozarks" (*Independence County Chronicle* 31 [October 1989–January 1990]: 1–19). Joseph Patrick Key, "The Calumet and the Cross: Religious Encounters in the Lower Mississippi Valley," *Arkansas Historical Quarterly* 61 (Summer 2002): 152–68.

Earlier treatments of the colonial era, somewhat dated but still useful if used with caution, can be found in two articles by Stanley Faye: "The Arkansas Post of Louisiana: French Domination" (*Louisiana Historical Quarterly* 16 [July 1943]: 633–721) and "The Arkansas Post of Louisiana: Spanish Domination" (*Louisiana Historical Quarterly* 17 [July 1944]: 629–716). Faye's main virtue is that he was the first to exploit in a professional way the various European archival materials that bear on colonial Arkansas history. Gilbert C. Din's "Arkansas Post in the American Revolution" (*Arkansas Historical Quarterly* 40 [Spring 1981]: 3–30) provides an important description of the battle fought at Arkansas Post in the American Revolution and the events that led up to and followed it.

Colonial European contact with Arkansas's native peoples is treated in several useful sources. Samuel Dorris Dickinson's "Quapaw Indian Dances" (*Pulaski County Historical Review* 32 [Fall 1984]: 42–50) furnishes a revealing description and discussion of Quapaw dances that draws on various early sources. Din's "Between a Rock and a Hard Place: The Indian Trade in Spanish Arkansas" in *Cultural Encounters in the Early South: Indians and Europeans in Arkansas*, edited by Jeannie M. Whayne (University of Arkansas Press, 1995) discusses the Indian trade at and around Arkansas Post in the Spanish colonial period. Din and Abraham P. Nasatir's *The Imperial Osages: Spanish-Indian Diplomacy in the Mississippi Valley* (University of Oklahoma Press, 1983) examines relations between the Osage tribe and the Spanish government during Louisiana's colonial period, including a great deal of important information about Arkansas Post. George Sabo's "Inconsistent Kin: French-Quapaw Relations at Arkansas Post" in *Arkansas Before the Americans*, edited by Hester A. Davis (Arkansas Archeological Survey Research Series No. 40, 1991) provides an important discussion, from an anthropological perspective, of various events involving Europeans and Quapaws that occurred in Arkansas Post during the French period. Sabo's "Rituals of Encounters: Interpreting Native American Views of European Explorers" in *Cultural Encounters in the Early South: Indians and Europeans in Arkansas*, edited by Jeannie M. Whayne (University of Arkansas Press, 1995), is an excellent article that reconstructs Indian ideas about European newcomers and how the Europeans were incorporated into the Quapaws' world and worldview.

Chapter Six: The Turbulent Path to Statehood: Arkansas Territory, 1803–1836

Although the historical literature on the territorial period in Arkansas is not abundant, there are a number of sources that provide a basic framework and a foundation for understanding the era. S. Charles Bolton's two books, *Territorial Ambition: Land and Society in Arkansas, 1800–1840* (University of Arkansas Press, 1993) and *Arkansas, 1800–1860: Remote and Restless* (University of Arkansas Press, 1998) should be a starting point for historians, students, and general readers. A vast scholarship on the history of slavery exists, but very few historians have included much analysis of the Arkansas experience in their broader general studies. One exception is Ira Berlin, *Many Thousands Gone: The First Two Centuries of Slavery in North America* (Belknap Press of Harvard University Press, 1998). Orville W. Taylor's *Negro Slavery in Arkansas* (1958, Reprint, University of Arkansas Press, 2000) remains the standard work on slavery in Arkansas. Donald P. McNeilly's *The Old South Frontier: Cotton Plantations and the Formation of Arkansas Society, 1819–1861* (University of Arkansas Press, 2000) provides an impressive overview of the development of plantations and the evolution of Arkansas society. For an account that focuses on kinship and gender issues, see Carolyn Earle Billingsley, *Communities of Kinship: Antebellum Families and the Settlement of the Cotton Frontier* (University of Georgia Press, 2004). For an unusually perceptive look at free black settlers in Arkansas in the antebellum period, see Billy D. Higgins, *A Stranger and a Sojourner: Peter Caulder, Free Black Frontiersman in Antebellum Arkansas* (University of Arkansas Press, 2004).

While Morris S. Arnold's work focuses on the colonial era, two of his three books provide essential background for understanding how conditions existing prior to the Louisiana Purchase set the stage for what was to follow: *Colonial Arkansas, 1686–1804: A Social and Cultural History* (University of Arkansas Press, 1991) and *Rumble of a Distant Drum: The Quapaws and Old World Newcomers, 1673–1804* (University of Arkansas Press, 2000). Arnold's *Unequal Laws Unto a Savage Race: European Legal Traditions in Arkansas, 1686–1836* actually extends beyond the colonial into the territorial era and demonstrates just how European legal traditions evolved. Lonnie J. White's *Politics on the Southwestern Frontier: Arkansas Territory, 1819–1838* (Memphis State University Press, 1964) is also an essential source.

While Bolton and Arnold give considerable and often subtle treatment to Native American history within Arkansas, other important works have focused on Native American history exclusively. Daniel Usner, in a broader study on Native Americans in the lower Mississippi River Valley, devoted some attention specifically to Arkansas in *American Indians in the Lower Mississippi Valley: Social and Economic Histories* (University of Nebraska Press, 1998). Kathleen DuVal's *The Native Ground: Indians and Colonists in the Heart of the Continent* (University of Pennsylvania Press, 2007) provides a thought-provoking analysis of Native Americans, particularly the Quapaw. W. David Baird's *The Quapaw Indians: A History of the Downstream People* (University of Oklahoma Press, 1980) is the basic book on the history of the Quapaws. Two important books on the Osages take different approaches to understanding them: Gilbert Din's *The Imperial Osages: Spanish-Indian Diplomacy in the Mississippi Valley* (University of Oklahoma Press, 1983) and Willard H. Rollings's *The Osage: An Ethnohistorical Study of Hegemony on the Prairie-Plains* (University of Missouri Press, 1992). For a more recent study by Rollings, see his *Unaffected by the Gospel: Osage Resistance to the Christian Invasion, 1673–1906: A Cultural Victory* (University of New Mexico Press, 2004). For another view on the Osages, consult John Joseph Mathews, *The Osages: Children of the Middle Waters* (University of Oklahoma Press, 1961). Two basic texts on the Caddo experience are Herbert Eugene Bolton's *The Hasinais: Southern Caddoans as Seen by the Earliest Europeans* (University of Oklahoma Press, 1987) and E. Todd Smith's *The Caddo Indians: Tribes at the Convergence of Empires, 1542–1854*. While there are many important works on the Cherokee experience, the most useful for the Arkansas experience is Stanley Hoig's *The Cherokees and Their Chiefs: In the Wake of Empire* (University of Arkansas Press, 1998). Finally, a volume that combines articles on Europeans and Native Americans is that edited by Jeannie M. Whayne, *Cultural Encounters in the Early South: Indians and Europeans in Arkansas* (University of Arkansas Press, 1995). George Sabo's book on the historic Indians of Arkansas is foundational reading: George Sabo III, *Paths of Our Children: Historic Indians of Arkansas*, rev. ed. (Arkansas Archeological Survey, 2001).

The drama of the New Madrid earthquakes has encouraged considerable study, including books by Jay Feldman, *When the River Ran Backwards: Empire, Intrigue, Murder, and the New Madrid Earthquakes* (Free Press, 2005), and Norma Hayes Bagnall's *On Shaky Ground: The New Madrid Earthquakes of 1811–1812* (University of Missouri

Press, 1996). A new book by Conevery Bolton Valencius is in the making and promises to add much needed rethinking of the cultural and environmental implications of the earthquakes. For earlier works on the earthquakes, see James Lal Penick Jr.'s *The New Madrid Earthquakes* (University of Missouri Press, 1981, revised edition). For the Geological Survey's point of view, see *The New Madrid Earthquakes: An Engineering-Geologic Interpretation of Relict Liquefaction Features*, written by Stephen F. Obermeier and edited by David P. Russ and Anthony J. Crone (Department of Interior, 1989).

The implications of the Louisiana Purchase have received a great deal of attention in the scholarly literature, and among the newest and most relevant works for Arkansas is Stephen Aron's *American Confluence: The Missouri Frontier from Borderland to Border States* (Indiana University Press, 2006). Another important work is Peter J. Kastor's *The Nation's Crucible: The Louisiana Purchase and the Creation of America* (Yale University Press, 2004). For the movement of planters from the older South to Arkansas after the purchase, see James David Miller's *South by Southwest: Planter Immigration and Identity in the Slave South* (University of Virginia Press, 2002). Most important is a book of essays edited by Patrick Williams, S. Charles Bolton, and Jeannie M. Whayne, *A Whole Country in Commotion: The Louisiana Purchase and the American South* (University of Arkansas Press, 2005).

The expedition of William Dunbar and George Hunter has yet to produce a book-length study, but their journals have been reproduced and are a valuable source of information. For Dunbar, *Forgotten Expedition: The Louisiana Purchase Journals of Dunbar and Hunter*, Trey Berry, Pam Beasley and Jeanne Clements, eds. (Louisiana State University Press, 2006), and *Life, Letters and Papers of William Dunbar, 1749–1810*, Mrs. Dunbar Rowland, ed. (Press of the Mississippi Historical Society, 1930). For Hunter, see *The Western Journals of Dr. George Hunter, 1796–1805* (American Philosophical Society, 1963), edited by John Francis McDermott. For a fascinating account of views of Arkansas by travelers, see Brooks Blevins, *Arkansas/Arkansaw* (University of Arkansas Press, 2009). Other accounts of early visitors to Arkansas territory can be found in Savoie Lottinville, ed., *A Journal of Travels into the Arkansas Territory during the Year 1819 by Thomas Nuttall* (University of Arkansas Press, 1999) and, for a later view, see George Featherstonhaugh's *1835 Geological Report of the Examination made in 1834 of the Elevated Country Between the Missouri and Red Rivers* (U.S. Army Corps of Engineers, 1835) and Featherstonhaugh's *Excursion Through the Slave States, from Washington on the Potomac, to the Frontier of Mexico; with Sketches of Popular Manners and Geological Notices* (Harper and Brothers, 1844). For an interesting biography of Featherstonhaugh, see Edmund Berkeley and Dorothy Smith Berkeley, *George William Featherstonhaugh: The First U.S. Government Geologist* (The University of Alabama Press, 1988). Henry R. Schoolcraft's journal, which is an account of his tour of Missouri and Arkansas in 1818 and 1819, has been edited by Hugh Park and published as *Schoolcraft in the Ozarks* (Press-Argus Printers, 1955). Schoolcraft's account was also reedited and published as *Rude Pursuits and Rugged Peaks: Schoolcraft's Ozark Journal, 1818–1819* with an introduction by Milton D. Rafferty (University of Arkansas Press,

1996). *Arkansas, Arkansas: Writers and Writings from the Delta to the Ozarks, 1541–1960* (University of Arkansas Press, 1999) by John Caldwell Guilds, provides insightful commentary on the early traveler accounts. For letters and correspondence between officials during the territorial era, consult the *Territorial Papers of the United States* published by the Government Printing Office. For a particularly astute account of life in Arkansas and Missouri in the antebellum period, see Conevery Bolton Valencius, *The Health of the Country: How American Settlers Understood Themselves and Their Land* (Basic Books, 2002). Valencius will soon publish a book on the New Madrid earthquakes in the region.

Chapter Seven: "The Rights and Rank to Which We Are Entitled": Arkansas in the Early Statehood Period, 1836–1850

A good general survey of the state's history is Michael Dougan's *Arkansas Odyssey: The Saga of Arkansas from Prehistoric Times to the Present* (Rose Publishing, 1994). Another interesting account is Bob Lancaster's *The Jungles of Arkansas: A Personal History of the Wonder State* (University of Arkansas Press, 1989). A good overview of the territorial and early statehood periods is S. Charles Bolton's *Territorial Ambition: Land and Society in Arkansas, 1800–1840* (University of Arkansas Press, 1993). Bolton's more recent *Arkansas, 1800–1860: Remote and Restless* (University of Arkansas Press, 1998) expands on the previous volume and covers the period up to the Civil War. Lonnie J. White's *Politics on the Southwestern Frontier: Arkansas Territory, 1819–1836* (Memphis State University Press, 1964) is an excellent source for examining the political developments of the territorial period. D. A. Stokes's "The First State Elections in 1836" in the *Arkansas Historical Quarterly*, Vol. 20 (Summer 1961) is also helpful.

The state's early history as chronicled in its leading newspaper can be found in Margaret Ross's *Arkansas Gazette: The Early Years, 1819–1866* (Arkansas Gazette Foundation, 1969). A good collection of primary sources can be found in *A Documentary History of Arkansas*, C. Fred Williams, S. Charles Bolton, Carl Moneyhon, and LeRoy Williams, eds. (University of Arkansas Press, 1984). On the men who led the state during this period, see *The Governors of Arkansas: Essays in Political Biography*, 2nd edition, edited by Timothy P. Donovan, Willard B. Gatewood, and Jeannie M. Whayne (University of Arkansas Press, 1995). Inaugural addresses of the state's chief executives can be found in *Dreams of Power and the Power of Dreams: The Inaugural Addresses of the Governors of Arkansas*, edited by Marvin DeBoer (University of Arkansas Press, 1988).

For brief sketches of governors and other major figures in the state's history, see Nancy A. Williams, ed., *Arkansas Biography: A Collection of Notable Lives* (University of Arkansas Press, 2000). Walter L. Brown's definitive biography, *A Life of Albert Pike* (University of Arkansas Press, 1997), not only sheds light on one of the major figures of antebellum Arkansas but also provides a good overview of the state's early history, including the early political parties and the Mexican War. Another major figure in antebellum Arkansas is examined in William W. Hughes's *Archibald Yell* (University of

Arkansas Press, 1988). U. M. Rose's "Chester Ashley" in *Publications of the Arkansas Historical Association,* Vol. 3 (1911), is a good brief account of a powerful political leader in the territorial and early statehood period.

Ted Worley's "The Control of the Real Estate Bank of Arkansas," in the *Mississippi Valley Historical Review*, Vol. 37 (December 1950) helps unravel the banking fiasco. William Oates Ragdale's *They Sought a Land: A Settlement in the Arkansas River Valley, 1840–1870* (University of Arkansas Press, 1997) is also useful. A revealing diary of an Arkansas woman in the early statehood period is "The Private Journal of Mary Ann Owen Sims," edited by Clifford Dale Whitman, in the *Arkansas Historical Quarterly*, Vol. 35 (Summer and Fall 1976).

On the two major religious denominations in the antebellum period, see E. Glenn Hinson's *A History of Baptists in Arkansas, 1818–1978,* Walter N. Vernon's *Methodism in Arkansas, 1816–1976* (Joint Committee for the History of Arkansas Methodism, 1976), and, more recently, Nancy Britton's *Two Centuries of Methodism in Arkansas, 1800–2000* (August House, 2000).

On various aspects of Arkansas society and culture in the antebellum period, see Walter Moffatt's "Arkansas Schools, 1819–1840" in the *Arkansas Historical Quarterly*, Vol. 12 (Spring 1953) and "Transportation in Arkansas, 1819–1840" in the *Arkansas Historical Quarterly*, Vol. 15 (Fall 1956). An excellent recent study is Carolyn Billingsley's *Communities of Kinship: Antebellum Families and the Settlement of the Cotton Frontier* (University of Georgia Press, 2004). Robert B. Walz's "Migration into Arkansas, 1820–1880: Incentives and Means of Travel" in the *Arkansas Historical Quarterly*, Vol. 17 (Winter 1958) is also a good source. On the development of Arkansas's image, see Brooks Blevins's *Arkansas/ Arkansaw: How Bear Hunters, Hillbillies, & Good Ol' Boys Defined a State* (University of Arkansas Press, 2009).

Priscilla McArthur's *Arkansas in the Gold Rush* (August House, 1986) is a good account of this exciting period in the state's history. On the Mountain Meadows massacre, the standard account is Juanita Brooks, *The Mountain Meadows Massacre* (University of Oklahoma Press, 1991). A more recent interpretation can be found in Will Bagley's *Blood of the Prophets: Brigham Young and the Massacre at Mountain Meadows* (University of Oklahoma Press, 2004).

Chapter Eight: Prosperity and Peril: Arkansas in the Late Antebellum Period, 1850–1861

Ted Worley's "Pope County One Hundred Years Ago" in the *Arkansas Historical Quarterly,* Vol. 13 (Summer 1954) provides a good examination of an Arkansas county that was, in many ways, typical of the state as a whole. A good description of the early history of Mississippi County can be found in the first chapter of Jeannie M. Whayne's *Delta Empire: Lee Wilson and the Transformation of Agriculture in the New South* (Louisiana State University Press, 2011). On the history of some of the state's most famous structures, see *Sentinels of History: Reflections on Arkansas Properties on the National Register of Historic*

Places, Mark Christ and Cathryn Slater, eds. (University of Arkansas Press, 2000). Swannee Bennett and William B. Worthen's *Arkansas Made: A Survey of the Decorative, Mechanical, and Fine Arts Produced in Arkansas, 1819–1970*, 2 vols. (University of Arkansas Press, 1991) provides a unique perspective.

On river travel, see Mattie Brown's "River Transportation in Arkansas, 1819–1890" in the *Arkansas Historical Quarterly*, Vol. 1 (December 1942). On steamboats three good sources are Carl D. Lane's *American Paddle Steamboats* (Coward-McCann, 1943), Louis C. Hunter's, *Steamboats on the Western Rivers: An Economic and Technological History* (Dover, 1977; originally published by Harvard University Press, 1949), and Herbert Quick and Edward Quick's *Mississippi Steamboatin': A History of Steamboating on the Mississippi and Its Tributaries* (Henry Holt and Company, 1926). See also Edith McCall's *Henry Miller Shreve and the Navigation of America's Inland Waterways* (Louisiana State University Press, 1984). A good Arkansas perspective is Duane Huddleston, Sammie Rose, and Pat Wood's *Steamboats and Ferries on White River: A Heritage Revisited* (University of Central Arkansas Press, 1995).

A good description of a cotton-growing operation in the antebellum era can be found in U. B. Phillips's *American Negro Slavery: A Survey of the Supply, Employment and Control of Negro Labor As Determined by the Plantation Regime* (Louisiana State University Press, 1966). Eugene Genovese's *Roll: The World the Slaves Made* (Random House, 1974; Vintage Books, 1976) remains one of the best books on American slavery. On slave religion, Albert Raboteau's *Slave Religion: The "Invisible Institution" in the Antebellum South, 1740–1870* (Oxford University Press, 1978) is an excellent source. The standard account of the institution in Arkansas is Orville Taylor's *Negro Slavery in Arkansas* (Duke University Press, 1958; recently reissued in paperback by the University of Arkansas Press). Several excellent recent interpretations of slavery in Arkansas can be found in the spring 1999 issue of the *Arkansas Historical Quarterly*, which is completely devoted to the topic. Of special interest are Carl Moneyhon's "The Slave Family in Arkansas" and Gary Battershell's "The Socioeconomic Role of Slavery in the Arkansas Upcountry." George E. Lankford, ed., *Bearing Witness: Memories of Arkansas Slavery* (University of Arkansas Press, 2003) concentrates on the Arkansas slave narratives.

On the events leading up to secession, see James Woods's *Rebellion and Realignment: Arkansas's Road to Secession* (University of Arkansas Press, 1987). Also valuable is Jack Scroggs, "Arkansas in the Secession Crisis," in the *Arkansas Historical Quarterly*, Vol. 12 (Autumn 1953). On the politics of the 1850s, see Elsie M. Lewis's unpublished doctoral dissertation, "From Nationalism to Disunion: A Short Study of the Secession Movement in Arkansas, 1850–1861" (University of Chicago, 1947), and also her article "Robert Ward Johnson: Militant Spokesman for the Old South-West" in the *Arkansas Historical Quarterly*, Vol. 13 (Spring 1954). See also Michael B. Dougan's "A Look at the 'Family' in Arkansas Politics, 1858–1865" in the *Arkansas Historical Quarterly*, Vol. 29 (Summer 1970). The diary of a prominent Camden Whig, John Brown, in the collections of the Arkansas History Commission, is an interesting and insightful contemporary account of the period. An excellent overview of a plantation in southeast Arkansas is Willard B.

Gatewood's "Sunnyside: The Evolution of an Arkansas Plantation, 1840–1945," pp. 3–36, in *Shadows Over Sunnyside: An Arkansas Plantation in Transition,* 1830–1945, Jeannie Whayne, ed. (Fayetteville: University of Arkansas Press, 1993). Gatewood's essay provides rich detail on the largest slave owner in Arkansas, Elisha Worthington. The authors would like to acknowledge the contribution of Kelly Jones and Debbie M. Liles for documentation on Worthington's Texas venture during the Civil War.

Chapter Nine: "Between the Hawk & Buzzard": The Civil War in Arkansas, 1861–1865

On the Civil War era, an early twentieth-century account with a decidedly pro-Confederate, anti-Republican slant is David Y. Thomas's *Arkansas in the Civil War and Reconstruction, 1861–1874* (United Daughters of the Confederacy, 1926). On the war itself, there is John L. Ferguson's *Arkansas and the Civil War* (Pioneer Press, 1965). The best military overview is Mark Christ, ed., *Rugged and Sublime: The Civil War in Arkansas* (University of Arkansas Press, 1994). Another good source is *Civil War Arkansas: Beyond Battles and Leaders,* edited by Anne Bailey and Daniel Sutherland (University of Arkansas Press, 2000).

On Arkansas Unionism and resistance to Confederate authority, see Ted Worley's "The Arkansas Peace Society of 1861: A Study in Mountain Unionism," in the *Journal of Southern History*, Vol. 24 (November 1958) and Carl Moneyhon's "Disloyalty and Class Consciousness in Southwestern Arkansas, 1862–1865," in Bailey and Sutherland, *Civil War Arkansas: Beyond Battles and Leaders.* See also Frank Arey, "The Skirmish at McGrew's Mill," in the *Clark County Historical Journal* (2000). The hard choices the war posed for American Indians are examined in Laurence M. Hauptman's *Between Two Fires: American Indians in the Civil War* (Free Press, 1995). The controversial Battle of Poison Spring and the wider issue of the Confederate reaction to black Union soldiers in Arkansas are explored in Gregory J. W. Urwin's chapter, "'We Cannot Treat Negroes . . . as Prisoners of War': Racial Atrocities and Reprisals in Civil War Arkansas," in *Black Flag Over Dixie: Racial Atrocities and Reprisals in the Civil War,* edited by Gregory J. W. Urwin (Southern Illinois University Press, 2005).

On the economics of the Civil War and Reconstruction periods, see Carl Moneyhon, *The Impact of the Civil War and Reconstruction on Arkansas: Persistence in the Midst of Ruin* (Louisiana State University Press, 1994). On the political aspects of the war and its effect on Arkansas society, see Michael B. Dougan's *Confederate Arkansas: The People and Politics of a Frontier State in Wartime* (The University of Alabama Press, 1976). Robert R. Mackey's "Bushwhackers, Provosts, and Tories: The Guerrilla War in Arkansas," in *Guerrillas, Unionists, and Violence on the Confederate Home Front* (University of Arkansas Press, 1999), edited by Daniel Sutherland, provides a good account of that aspect of the war as does Sutherland's "Guerrillas: The Real War in Arkansas," in the aforementioned *Civil War Arkansas: Beyond Battles and Leaders.* See also Sutherland's recent work,

A Savage Conflict: The Decisive Role of Guerrillas in the American Civil War (Universtiy of North Carolina Press, 2009). Arkansas also figures prominently in Robert L. Kerby's *Kirby Smith's Confederacy: The Trans-Mississippi South, 1863–1865* (Columbia University Press, 1972).

A first-rate account of the biggest and most important battle in Arkansas is William L. Shea and Earl J. Hess's *Pea Ridge: Civil War Campaign in the West* (University of North Carolina Press, 1992). For a concise treatment of the battles of Pea Ridge and Prairie Grove, see Shea's *War in the West: Pea Ridge and Prairie Grove* (McWhiney Foundation Press, 1998). A fuller discussion of the Prairie Grove campaign is Shea's excellent recent study, *Fields of Blood: The Prairie Grove Campaign* (University of North Carolina Press, 2009). A good first-person account of the effects of the Civil War on northwest Arkansas is William Baxter's *Pea Ridge and Prairie Grove* (originally published in Cincinnati by Poe and Hitchcock in 1864; republished in paperback by the University of Arkansas Press in 2000). A good local history of the fighting in White County is Scott H. Akridge and Emmett E. Powers, *A Severe and Bloody Fight: The Battle of Whitney's Lane and Military Occupation of White County, Arkansas, May and June, 1862* (White County Historical Museum, 1996). On the decisive year of 1863, see Mark K. Christ's *Civil War Arkansas, 1863: The Battle for a State* (University of Oklahoma Press, 2010). The photographic legacy of the war in Arkansas is found in Bobby Roberts and Carl Moneyhon's *Portraits of Conflict: A Photographic History of Arkansas in the Civil War* (University of Arkansas Press, 1987). *The War of the Rebellion: A Compilation of the Official Records of the Union and Confederate Armies* (Government Printing Office, 1880–1901), a multivolume series, is an invaluable source, now available online.

There are numerous biographies of the war's major figures, including Diane Neal and Thomas W. Kremm's *The Lion of the South: General Thomas C. Hindman* (Mercer University Press, 1993). On the same topic, see Bobby L. Roberts, "Thomas C. Hindman, Jr.: Secessionist and Confederate General" (Master's thesis, University of Arkansas, 1972). One of the state's most accomplished commanders is chronicled in Craig L. Symonds's *Stonewall of the West: Patrick Cleburne and the Civil War* (University Press of Kansas, 1997). A more controversial figure is the subject of Arthur B. Carter's *The Tarnished Cavalier: Major General Earl Van Dorn, C.S.A.* (University of Tennessee Press, 1999). Another pivotal figure in the Trans-Mississippi is the subject of Albert Castel's *General Sterling Price and the Civil War in the West* (Louisiana State University Press, 1968). William H. Burnside's *The Honorable Powell Clayton* (University of Central Arkansas Press, 1991) examines the career of a major Union leader in the war and postwar eras. The story of Arkansas soldiers who fought west of the Appalachian Mountains is found in James Willis's massive *Arkansas Confederates in the Western Theater* (Morningside Press, 1998). The Spence Family Collection at the Old State House Museum provides a fascinating glimpse into the lives of two Arkansas soldiers. The family's Civil War letters are available in edited form in *Getting Used to Being Shot At: The Spence Family Civil War Letters*, Mark K. Christ, ed. (University of Arkansas Press, 2002). A good contemporary account of the war in central Arkansas by a female observer is "An Arkansas Lady in the Civil War: Reminiscences of Susan Fletcher," edited by Mary P. Fletcher in the *Arkansas Historical Quarterly*, Vol. 2 (December 1943). The "Diary of Susan Cook," in the *Phillips County Historical Quarterly*, Vols. 4–6 (December 1965–March 1968) provides an extensive look at a Delta woman's view of the conflict.

Chapter Ten: "A Harnessed Revolution": Reconstruction in Arkansas, 1865–1880

The best recent overview of Reconstruction on the national level is Eric Foner's *Reconstruction: America's Unfinished Revolution, 1863–1877* (Harper and Row, 1988). See also Richard N. Current's *Those Terrible Carpetbaggers* (Oxford University Press, 1988). On Reconstruction in Arkansas, the standard Dunning school interpretation is Thomas Staples, *Reconstruction in Arkansas, 1862–1874* (Longmans, Green & Company, 1923). Another perspective is George H. Thompson's *Arkansas and Reconstruction: The Influence of Geography, Economics, and Personality* (National University Publications, 1976). A good overview is Martha A. Ellenburg's unpublished doctoral dissertation, "Reconstruction in Arkansas" (University of Missouri, 1967). See also Orval Driggs's "The Issues of the Powell Clayton Regime, 1868–1871" in the *Arkansas Historical Quarterly*, Vol. 8 (Spring 1949). A more recent examination of the Civil War and Reconstruction eras in Arkansas is Thomas A. DeBlack's *With Fire and Sword: Arkansas, 1861–1874* (University of Arkansas Press, 2003).

An excellent account of the activities of the Freedmen's Bureau in the state is Randy Finley's *From Slavery to Uncertain Freedom: The Freedmen's Bureau in Arkansas, 1865–1869* (University of Arkansas Press, 1996). On the constitutional convention of 1868, two good sources are "The Arkansas Constitutional Convention of 1868: A Case Study in the Politics of Reconstruction," by Richard L. Hume in the *Journal of Southern History*, 39 (May 1973), and "The Negro Delegates in the Arkansas Constitutional Convention of 1868: A Group Profile," by Joseph M. St. Hilaire in the *Arkansas Historical Quarterly*, Vol. 33 (Spring 1974). A good examination of the controversial election of 1868 is Michael P. Kelley's "Partisan or Protector: Powell Clayton and the 1868 Presidential Election" in the *Ozark Historical Quarterly*, Vol. 3 (Spring 1974).

The Ku Klux Klan and the militia wars are covered in Allen W. Trelease's *White Terror: The Ku Klux Klan Conspiracy and Southern Reconstruction* (Louisiana State University Press, 1971). Another good source is Otis Singletary's *Negro Militia and Reconstruction* (University of Texas Press, 1957). The D. P. Upham letters in the Special Collections Department of the University of Arkansas at Little Rock library provide a valuable first-hand account of this turbulent era from a "carpetbagger's" perspective. See also Charles Rector's "D. P. Upham, Woodruff County Carpetbagger" in the *Arkansas Historical Quarterly*, Vol. 59 (Spring 2000). The life of an infamous Reconstruction outlaw is chronicled in Barry Crouch and Donaly Bryce's *Cullen Montgomery Baker, Reconstruction Desperado* (Louisiana State University Press, 1997).

A valuable primary source from one of the era's major figures is Powell Clayton's own account, *The Aftermath of the Civil War in Arkansas* (Neal Publishing Company, 1915). A contemporary account of Reconstruction in the state and the Brooks-Baxter War in particular is John M. Harrell's *The Brooks and Baxter War: A History of the Reconstruction Period in Arkansas* (Slawson Printing Company, 1893). See also Earl F. Woodward's "The Brooks and Baxter War in Arkansas, 1872–1874" in the Ark*ansas Historical Quarterly*, Vol. 30 (Winter 1971). An interesting account of corruption in the Federal District Court for the Western District of Arkansas is Frances Mitchell Ross's "'Getting Up Business' in the Western District of Arkansas, 1871–1874: What Style Leadership?" (unpublished manuscript). A fascinating local study is Kenneth C. Barnes's *Who Killed John Clayton? Political Violence and the Emergence of the New South, 1861–1893* (Duke University Press, 1998).

Chapters Eleven through Seventeen: General References

There are a number of standard works that provide essential background information for most of the time period covered in chapters 11 through 17. They include *The Governors of Arkansas: Essays in Political Biography*, 2nd edition (University of Arkansas Press, 1995), edited by Timothy P. Donovan, Willard B. Gatewood Jr., and Jeannie M. Whayne, which is an essential source for material on the state's governors. Diane D. Blair's *Arkansas Politics and Government: Do the People Rule?* (University of Nebraska Press, 1988) is the best single source on Arkansas politics generally. A new edition, published after Blair's death, is Diane D. Blair and Jay Barth, *Arkansas Politics and Government*, 2nd edition (University of Nebraska Press, 2005). *The Arkansas Delta: Land of Paradox*, edited by Jeannie M. Whayne and Willard B. Gatewood Jr., is an important source that ranges across social, economic, military, and political history (University of Arkansas Press, 1995). Carl Moneyhon's book, *Arkansas and the New South, 1874–1929* (University of Arkansas Press, 1997), which focuses on the period between 1874 and 1929, provides valuable insight into the evolution of Arkansas society in that time frame. John Gould Fletcher's *Arkansas* (University of North Carolina Press, 1947) remains a standard work in the field. The two volumes under one title edited by David Y. Thomas, *Arkansas and Its People: A History, 1541–1930*, provide a crucial source of information (American Historical Society, 1930). Michael B. Dougan's *Arkansas Odyssey: The Saga of Arkansas from Prehistoric Times to the Present* (Rose Publishing, 1994) is an excellent single-source volume for the state's history. Dougan's *Arkansas History: An Annotated Bibliography*, which he compiled with Tom W. Dillard and Timothy G. Nutt (Greenwood Press, 1995), is an excellent source book. A book edited by Janine Parry and Richard P. Want, *Readings in Arkansas Politics and Government* (University of Arkansas Press, 2009) is a very useful source, particularly on Arkansas political history. Ben F. Johnson III's excellent monograph, *Arkansas in Modern America: 1930–1999* (University of Arkansas Press, 2000), is the basic text covering the period between 1930 and 1999.

Three books by journalists, Harry S. Ashmore's *Arkansas: A Bicentennial History*

(Norton, 1978), Bob Lancaster's *The Jungles of Arkansas: A Personal History of the Wonder State* (University of Arkansas Press, 1989), and Leland Duval's *Arkansas: Colony and State* (Rose Publishing Company, 1973), contain a good deal of very useful information. C. J. Brown's *Cattle on a Thousand Hills: A History of the Cattle Industry in Arkansas* is an essential source for reading on that industry (University of Arkansas Press, 1996). Two works that stand as excellent sources of information about specific individuals or about the state's historic landmarks are as follows: *Arkansas Biography: A Collection of Notable Lives*, Nancy A. Williams, editor, and Jeannie M. Whayne, associate editor (University of Arkansas Press, 2000); and *Sentinels of History: Reflections on the National Register of Historic Places*, edited by Mark K. Christ and Cathryn H. Slater (University of Arkansas Press, 2000). For a particularly moving account of growing up in the Arkansas Delta, see Margaret Bolsterli, *Born in the Delta: Reflections on the Making of a Southern White Sensibility* (University of Tennessee Press, 1991), and for a history of her family's farm, see *During the Wind and Rain: The Jones Family Farm in the Arkansas Delta, 1848–2006* (University of Arkansas Press, 2008). For particularly illuminating oral history, see Bolsterli's *Things You Need to Hear: Collected Memories of Growing Up in Arkansas, 1890-1980* (University of Arkansas Press, 2012). Whayne's book, *A New Plantation South: Land, Labor, and Federal Favor in Twentieth-Century Arkansas* (University Press of Virginia, 1996), provides a scholarly overview of the evolution of a plantation system in northeastern Arkansas and her *Delta Empire: Lee Wilson and the Transformation of Agriculture in the New South* (Louisiana State University Press, 2011) uses the story of the 50,000-acre Lee Wilson plantation to examine the transition from slavery in the antebellum period to tenancy in the post–Civil War era to neo-plantations in the post–World War II period and to portfolio-plantations of the early twenty-first century. A crucial book by Brooks Blevins, *Hill Folks: A History of Arkansas Ozarkers and Their Image*, is essential reading on that little-studied region. For an intriguing analysis of a murder in the Ozarks, see Blevins's *Ghost of the Ozarks: Murder and Memory in the Upland South* (University of Arkansas Press, 2011). For an important study of the judiciary in the late nineteenth and early twentieth century that includes an analysis of Arkansas jurist Jacob Trieber, see Brent J. Aucoin, *A Rift in the Clouds: Race and the Southern Federal Judiciary, 1900–1910* (University of Arkansas Press, 2007).

The study of religion in Arkansas has resulted in a number of monographs. For Methodist history, see Rev. James A. Anderson, *Centennial History of Arkansas Methodism . . . A History of the Methodist Episcopal Church, South, in the State of Arkansas, 1815–1935* (L. B. White Printing Company, 1935) and Nancy Britton's two volumes, the first on the Methodist Church in Batesville and the second on the church in the entire state: *The First 100 Years of the First Methodist Church in Batesville* (August House, 1968) and *Two Centuries of Methodism in Arkansas, 1800–2000* (August House, 2000). For the Baptist Church, see Glenn E. Hinson, *A History of Baptists in Arkansas, 1818–1978* (Arkansas State Convention, 1979). For the Christian Church and the Disciples of Christ, see Lester G. McAllister, *Arkansas Disciples: A History of the Christian Church (Disciples of Christ) in Arkansas* (n.p. 1984), and David Edwin Harrell's *A Social*

History of the Disciples of Christ (Disciples of Christ Historical Society, 1966–1973). For an important new book on the formation and evolution of the Church of God in Christ, see Calvin White Jr., *Race, Religion, and Respectability: The Church of God in Christ and Its Rise to Respectability* (University of Arkansas Press, 2012). For Presbyterian history, see Thomas H. Campbell, *Cumberland Presbyterians* (1812–1884): *A People of Faith* (Arkansas Synod of Cumberland Presbyterian Church, 1985), and C. B. Moore et al., *The History of Presbyterianism in Arkansas, 1828–1902* (Press of the Arkansas Democrat Co., 1902). For the Episcopal Church, see Margaret S. White, *Already to Harvest: The Episcopal Church in Arkansas, 1838–1971* (Episcopal Diocese of Arkansas at the University Press of Sewanee, 1957). For Roman Catholics, see James M. Woods, *Mission and Memory, A History of the Catholic Church in Arkansas* (Diocese of Little Rock, 1993). For the Jewish experience in Arkansas, see Carolyn Gray LeMaster, *A Corner of the Tapestry: A History of the Jewish Experience in Arkansas, 1820s–1990s* (University of Arkansas Press, 1994). An important study of African Americans and religion that focuses on the delta generally but includes analysis of Arkansas, see John M. Giggie, *After Redemption: Jim Crow and the Transformation of African American Religion in the Delta, 1875–1915* (Oxford University Press, 2008).

For the development of agriculture and the lumber industry in the state, see Stephen Strausberg, *A Century of Research: Centennial History of the Arkansas Agricultural Experiment Station, 1888–1988* (University of Arkansas Press, 1989); Gary Zellar and Nancy Wyatt, *History of the Bumpers College: Evolution of Education in the Agricultural, Food and Life Sciences in Arkansas* (Arkansas Experiment Station Special Report 194, 1999); George W. Balogh, *Entrepreneurs in the Lumber Industry: Arkansas, 1881–1963* (Garland Publishing, 1995); and Kenneth L. Smith, *Sawmill: The Story of Cutting the Last Great Virgin Forest East of the Rockies* (University of Arkansas Press, 1986).

For books on education and on the development of colleges in Arkansas, see the following: Brooks Blevins, *Lyon College, 1872–2002: The Perseverance and Promise of an Arkansas College* (University of Arkansas Press, 2003); Richard Ostrander, *Head, Heart, and Hand: John Brown University and Modern Evangelical Higher Education* (University of Arkansas Press, 2003); C. Calvin Smith and Linda Walls Joshua, *Educating the Masses: The Unfolding History of Black School Administrators in Arkansas, 1900–2000* (University of Arkansas Press, 2003); and James F. Willis, *Southern Arkansas University: The Mulerider School's Centennial History, 1909–2009* (Southern Arkansas University Foundation, 2009). For a different look at education, see Thomas C. Kennedy, *A History of Southland College: The Society of Friends and Black Education in Arkansas* (University of Arkansas Press, 2009).

Although studies of the slave interviews conducted by the Works Progress Administration in the late 1930s might seem more appropriate for a different section of "suggested readings," in fact, they provide much useful information about those telling the stories and their lives after slavery, particularly in the 1930s. This is one of the many virtues of *Bearing Witness: Memories of Arkansas Slavery, Narratives from the*

1930s WPA Collections, edited by George Lankford (University of Arkansas Press, 2003).

For a provocative study of gay and lesbian history in Arkansas, see Brock Thompson, *The Un-Natural State: Arkansas and the Queer South* (University of Arkansas Press, 2010).

For a richly entertaining account of a variety of Arkansas stories and people, see Tom Dillard, *Statesmen, Scoundrels, and Eccentrics: A Gallery of Amazing Arkansans* (University of Arkansas Press, 2010).

Archeological publications provide much insight into the nature of the landscape and native populations. *The Lower Mississippi Valley Expeditions of Clarence Bloomfield Moore*, edited by Dan F. Morse and Phyllis A. Morse (The University of Alabama Press, 1998), includes Moore's venture into eastern Arkansas. See also *Arkansas Archeology: Essays in Honor of Dan and Phyllis Morse*, Robert C. Mainfort Jr. and Marvin D. Jeter (University of Arkansas Press, 2000). Leslie Stewart-Abernathy's *Ghost Boats on the Mississippi: Discovering Our Working Past* (Arkansas Archeological Survey, 2002) provides considerable insight into river traffic along the Mississippi River.

Chapter Eleven: Arkansas in the New South, 1880–1900

Only a few works have focused specifically on the period between 1880 and 1900, and they include a diary edited by Margaret Bolsterli, *Vinegar Pie and Chicken Bread: A Woman's Diary of Life in the Rural South* (University of Arkansas Press, 1981), an excellent source for women's history. Waddy William Moore's *Arkansas in the Gilded Age: 1874–1900* (Rose Publishing Company, 1976) provides a fine overview of the state in this era, while John William Graves, *Town and Country: Race Relations in an Urban-Rural Context, Arkansas, 1865–1905* (University of Arkansas Press, 1990), offers a superb treatment of the issue of race. Fon Louise Gordon's book, *Caste and Class: The Black Experience in Arkansas, 1880–1920* (University of Georgia Press, 1995), provides an interesting analysis that is as relevant for the next chapter as it is for this one. A particularly entertaining account of life in the Ozarks is *Life in the Leatherwoods: John Quincy Wolf*, edited by Gene Hyde and Brooks Blevins (University of Arkansas Press, 2000).

Judge Isaac Parker has been the subject of numerous treatments. Two recent studies provide new insights: Roger Tuller's insightful *"Let No Guilty Man Escape": A Judicial Biography of "Hanging Judge" Isaac C. Parker* (University of Oklahoma Press, 2001) and Michael J. Brodhead, *Isaac C. Parker: Federal Justice on the Frontier* (University of Oklahoma Press, 2003).

Kenneth Barnes has published two important and thought-provoking books on Arkansas topics: *Who Killed John Clayton? Political Violence and the Emergence of the New South, 1861–1893* (Duke University Press, 1998) and *Journey of Hope: The Back-to-Africa Movement in Arkansas in the Late 1800s* (University of North Carolina Press, 2004).

Chapter Twelve: A Light in the Darkness: Limits of Progressive Reform, 1900–1920

The Progressive era has received far more attention than has the gilded age in Arkansas. Several important studies of governors have appeared, beginning with Raymond Arsenault's *Wild Ass of the Ozarks: Jeff Davis and the Social Bases of Southern Politics* (University of Tennessee Press, 1984). The two most important progressive governors have had books published on them. Calvin R. Ledbetter Jr. in *Carpenter from Conway: George Washington Donaghey as Governor of Arkansas, 1909–1913* (University of Arkansas Press, 1993) details the history and administration of Governor Donaghey, arguably the most progressive governor of the period. Foy Lisenby's book on *Charles Hillman Brough: A Biography* (University of Arkansas Press, 1996) gives that progressive governor equal time. For a study of one of the state's most notable senators, see Cecil Edward Weller Jr., *Joe T. Robinson: Always a Loyal Democrat* (University of Arkansas Press, 1998). Richard L. Niswonger, *Arkansas Democratic Politics, 1896–1920* (University of Arkansas Press, 1990), provides an excellent overview of the state's political history in this era. To understand labor issues, see James R. Green, *Grass Roots Socialism: Radical Movements in the Southwest, 1895–1943* (Louisiana State University Press, 1978). *History of the Organization and Operations of the Board of Directors, St. Francis Levee District of Arkansas, 1893–1945* (St. Francis Levee District, n.d.), provides a wealth of information on that entity.

For books that cover one of the darkest episodes in Arkansas history, see Grif Stockley, *Blood in Their Eyes: The Elaine Race Massacres of 1919* (University of Arkansas Press, 2001), and Robert Whitaker, *On the Laps of Gods: The Red Summer of 1919 and the Struggle for Justice That Remade a Nation* (Random House, 2008). For a larger study of the history of the Mississippi Delta with a special emphasis on the Arkansas story, see Nan Woodruff, *American Congo: The African American Freedom Struggle in the Delta* (Harvard University Press, 2003).

Ben F. Johnson has contributed much to the understanding of Arkansas history, but his book on prohibition is a foundational book on that particular topic: Ben F. Johnson, *John Barleycorn Must Die: The War against Drink in Arkansas* (University of Arkansas Press, 2005).

Among the many virtues of Steven Hahn's Pulitzer-prize-winning book on the black struggle from slavery to 1920 is attention to the subject in Arkansas: Steven Hahn, *A Nation Under Our Feet: Black Political Struggles in the Rural South from Slavery to the Great Migration* (Belknap Press of Harvard University Press, 2003). Mary Rolinson's study of the University Negro Improvement Association also includes attention to the Arkansas story: Mary G. Rolinson, *Grassroots Garvism: The Universal Negro Improvement Association in the Rural South, 1920–1927* (University of North Carolina Press, 2007). An excellent addition to the history of black schools in the South, which includes references to Arkansas, is Mary Hoffschwelle's *The Rosenwald Schools of the American South: New Perspectives on the History of the South* (University Press of Florida, 2006).

Chapter Thirteen: Darker Forces on the Horizon: Natural Disasters and Great Depression, 1920–1940

The period covering the Great Depression has received even more attention than the Progressive era. Several publications transcend the time period, but have most relevance within it. Dorothy Stuck and Nan Snow's *Roberta: A Most Remarkable Fulbright* (University of Arkansas Press, 1997) is not only good women's history, it provides a keen analysis of social and political forces at work in Arkansas. Ben F. Johnson III's *Fierce Solitude: A Life of John Gould Fletcher* (University of Arkansas Press, 1994) provides far more than a biography of a literary and historical figure.

The two major natural disasters that hit the state in this period have received ample attention. The 1927 flood has been covered by Pete Daniel in *Deep'n as It Come: The 1927 Mississippi River Flood* (University of Arkansas Press, reprint, 1996; original edition published by Oxford University Press, 1977) and by John Barry, *Rising Tide: The Great Mississippi Flood of 1927 and How it Changed America* (Simon and Schuster, 1997). For the impact of the drought of 1930–1931 on Arkansas, see Nan Elizabeth Woodruff's *As Rare as Rain: Federal Relief in the Great Southern Draught of 1930–31* (University of Illinois Press, 1985). A new book on the 1937 flood by David Welky provides an excellent addition to the literature: *The Thousand-Year Flood: The Ohio-Mississippi Disaster of 1937* (University of Chicago Press, 2011).

A number of important books have been published on the Great Depression's impact on farmers. H. L. Mitchell's autobiography, *Mean Things Happening in This Land: The Life and Times of H. L. Mitchell, Cofounder of the Southern Tenant Farmers Union* (Allanheld, Osmun, 1979), provides crucial information about the founding of the Southern Tenant Farmers Union, and no fewer than four books focus on the STFU: David Eugene Conrad, *The Forgotten Farmer: The Story of Sharecroppers in the New Deal* (University of Illinois Press, 1965); Paul E. Mertz, *New Deal Policy and Southern Rural Poverty* (Louisiana State University Press, 1978); Donald H. Grubbs, *Cry from the Cotton: The Southern Tenant Farmers' Union and the New Deal* (University of Arkansas Press, 2000, reprint; originally published by University of North Carolina Press, 1971); and Howard Kester's *Revolt among the Sharecroppers* (University of Tennessee Press, reprint, 1997; originally published by Covici, Friede, 1936). For an examination of a radical college in Arkansas that had ties to the STFU, see William H. Cobb, *Radical Education in the Rural South: Commonwealth College, 1922–1940* (Wayne State University Press, 2000). Some failed tenants and sharecroppers found their way to Resettlement or Farm Security Administration communities, but as Donald Holley explains, most who found places in such communities were failed farm owners rather than tenants. See Holley's *Uncle Sam's Farmers: The New Deal Communities in the Lower Mississippi Valley* (University of Illinois Press, 1975). Holley's more recent book, *The Second Great Emancipation: The Mechanical Cotton Picker, Black Migration, and How They Shaped the Modern South* (University of Arkansas Press, 2000), extends beyond the period covered in this chapter but introduces the experiments with the mechanical cotton harvester that intensified in the 1930s. Two excellent books placing cotton cultivation into larger context are Charles S. Aiken's *The Cotton Plantation South since the Civil War* (Johns Hopkins University Press, 1998) and Gene Dattel's *Cotton and Race in the Making of America: The Human Cost of Economic Power* (Ivan R. Dee, 2009). Although Jarod Roll's book focuses on the Missouri Bootheel, it is instructive for those interested in the struggle of tenants and sharecroppers in this era: Jarod Roll, *Spirit of Rebellion: Labor and Religion in the New Cotton South* (University of Illinois Press, 2010).

For a look at the Ozarks in this period, see Brooks Blevins, *Hill Folk: A History of the Arkansas Ozarkers and Their Image* (University of North Carolina Press, 2002); Milton R. Rafferty, *The Ozarks: Land and Life* (University of Arkansas Press, 2001); and Lynn Morrow and Linda Myers-Phinney, *Shepherd of the Hills: Tourism Transforms the Ozarks, 1880s-1930s* (University of Arkansas Press, 1999). For an examination of south Arkansas, see John G. Ragsdale, *As We Were in South Arkansas* (August House, 1995).

David Malone's *Hattie and Huey: An Arkansas Tour* (University of Arkansas Press, 1989) provides an interesting treatment of Hattie Caraway and Huey Long. Stephen Wilson's *Harvey Couch: An Entrepreneur Brings Electricity to Arkansas* (August House, 1986) focuses on that important political and economic force in the state. For an interesting treatment of two Arkansans who became famous radio personalities, see Randal L. Hall, *Lum and Abner: Rural America and the Golden Age of Radio* (University Press of Kentucky, 2007). For the development of the Arkansas State Police, see Michael Lindsey, *The Big Hat Law: Arkansas and Its State Police, 1935–2000* (Butler Center Books, 2008).

Chapter Fourteen: From World War to New Era, 1940–1954

Several books about Arkansas's experience in World War II have been published, including C. Calvin Smith's *War and Wartime Changes* (University of Arkansas Press, 1986), which offers a valuable overview and analysis. For a look at those who served in the war, see *Unsung Valor: A GI's Story of World War II* by A. Cleveland Harrison (University Press of Mississippi, 2000). For an account of the experience of Arkansans in the Aleutians, see Donald M. Goldstein and Katherine V. Dillon, authors *The Williwaw War: The Arkansas National Guard in the Aleutians during World War II* (University of Arkansas Press, 1992). A particularly poignant account of the experience of Arkansans in World War II can be found in Nan Snow, *Letters Home* (Phoenix International, 2001). For an autobiography of an Arkansas's World War II veteran who became governor of the state, see Sidney S. McMath, *Promises Kept: A Memoir* (University of Arkansas Press, 2003).

No book-length study of the Japanese internment camps in Arkansas exists, but a fine recent study that includes analysis of the Arkansas camps can be found in Brian Masaru Hayashi, *Democratizing the Enemy: The Japanese American Internment* (Princeton University Press, 2004). Books by Grif Stockley and John Kirk focusing on civil rights and race relations (noted below) have some very useful information covering the World War II and immediate postwar period.

Chapter Fifteen: Stumbling toward a New Arkansas, 1954–1970

Most of the books published on this period focus on the Central High crisis or on figures connected to it in one way or another. A notable exception is the excellent book on J. William Fulbright by Randall S. Woods, *Fulbright: A Biography* (Cambridge University Press, 1995). Of the books that focus on Central High, some important recent books have contributed significantly to a fuller understanding of that experience and its long-term implications. Elizabeth Jacoway and C. Fred Williams, *Understanding the Little Rock Crisis: An Exercise in Remembrance and Reconciliation* (University of Arkansas Press, 1999). Elizabeth Jacoway's memoir, *Turn Away Thy Son: Little Rock, the Crisis That Shocked the World* (Free Press, 2007), provides a particularly interesting look at the Little Rock white elite during the crisis. For an important biography of Daisy Bates, see Grif Stockley, *Daisy Bates: Civil Rights Crusader from Arkansas* (University Press of Mississippi, 2005). Pete Daniel's award-winning account of the South in the 1950s includes a close analysis of the Central High crisis, *Lost Revolutions: The South in the 1950s* (University of North Carolina Press, 2000). For a study of an important Arkansas African American civil rights leader, see Judith L. Kilpatrick, *There When We Needed Him: Wiley Austin Branton, Civil Rights Warrior* (University of Arkansas Press, 2007). Will Counts, ed., *A Life Is More Than a Moment: The Desegregation of Little Rock's Central High* (Indiana University Press, 1999), includes some riveting essays by Arkansas journalists Ernest Dumas and Robert McCord. For an insightful study by a sociologist, see Johnny F. Williams, *African American Religion and the Civil Rights Movement in Arkansas* (University Press of Mississippi, 2003). Beth Roy, *Bitters in the Honey: Tales of Hope and Disappointment across Divides of Race and Time* (University of Arkansas Press, 1999), draws on oral history to focus on the experience of white students during the Central High crisis.

For accounts from among the Little Rock nine, see Melba Patillo Beals, *Warriors Don't Cry: A Searing Memoir of the Battle to Integrate Little Rock's Central High* (Pocket Books, 1994); Terrence Roberts, *Lessons from Little Rock* (Butler Center Books, 2009); and Carlotta Walls LaNier with Lisa Frazier Page, *A Mighty Long Way: My Journey to Justice at Little Rock Central High School* (One World/Ballantine Books, 2009).

For an important overview of race relations in Arkansas, see Grif Stockley, *Ruled by Race: Black/White Relations in Arkansas from Slavery to the Present* (University of Arkansas Press, 2008). John Kirk has contributed several important books to the subject of civil rights in Arkansas: *Race, Community, and Crisis: Little Rock, Arkansas, and the Civil Rights Struggle, 1940–1970* (University Press of Florida, 2002); *Redefining the Color Line: Black Activism in Little Rock, Arkansas, 1940–1970 Crisis* (University of Arkansas Press, 2007); *Beyond Little Rock: The Origins and Legacies of the Central High Crisis* (University of Arkansas Press, 2007); and an edited volume, *An Epitaph for Little Rock: A Fiftieth Anniversary Retrospective on the Central High Crisis* (University of Arkansas Press, 2008). His most recent contribution includes essays coedited with Jennifer Wallach: *Arsnick: The Student Nonviolent Coordinating Committee in Arkansas*, a very important contribution to the literature on civil rights in the state.

Jeff Woods's larger study of civil rights and anticommunism includes an insightful analysis of the activities of Arkansas's segregationists. See Jeff Woods, *Black Struggle, Red Scare: Segregation and Anti-Communism in the South, 1948–1968* (Louisiana State University Press, 2004). For a different look at African American life in this period, see Robert Cochran, *A Photographer of Note: Arkansas Artist Geleve Grice* (University of Arkansas Press, 2003).

Anyone interested in the history of the Central High crisis should begin with the accounts by those on the inside. Daisy Bates's *The Long Shadow of Little Rock* (University of Arkansas Press, 1986) tells the story from the African American perspective. Elizabeth Huckaby's *Crisis at Central High, Little Rock, 1957–58* (Louisiana State University Press, 1980) provides a sympathetic teacher's perspective. The account by Sara Alderman Murphy, edited by her son, Patrick C. Murphy III, *Breaking the Silence: Little Rock's Women's Emergency Committee to Open Our Schools, 1958–1963* (University of Arkansas Press, 1997), provides a glimpse into the workings of the Women's Emergency Committee. See Roy Reed's *Faubus: The Life and Times of an American Prodigal* (University of Arkansas Press, 1997) for a keen analysis of Faubus's contribution to the crisis. See also Reed's insightful memoir, *Beware of Limbo Dancers: A Correspondent's Adventures with the New York Times* (University of Arkansas Press, 2012). For a book that focuses on the "lost year," see Sondra Gordy, *Finding the Lost Year: What Happened When Little Rock Closed Its Public Schools* (University of Arkansas Press, 2009). Two books illuminate Brooks Hays's perspective: *James T. Baker, Brooks Hays* (Mercer University Press, 1989) and Hays's own *Politics Is My Parish* (Louisiana State University Press, 1981). David Chappell's *Inside Agitators: White Southerners in the Civil Rights Movement* (Johns Hopkins University Press, 1994) provides a comparative perspective. For a fresh look at the legal history of the Little Rock crisis, see Tony A. Freyer, *Little Rock on Trial: Cooper v. Aaron and School Desegregation* (University Press of Kansas, 2007). For an examination of the role of the interposition, see Frances Lisa Baer, *Resistance to Public School Desegregation: Little Rock, Arkansas, and Beyond* (LFB Scholarly Publishing, 2008). For an important new book on the crisis, see Karen Anderson, *Little Rock: Race and Resistance at Central High School* (Princeton University Press, 2010).

Political history has received some noteworthy attention from scholars. See especially Cathy Kunzinger Urwin's *Agenda for Reform: Winthrop Rockefeller as Governor of Arkansas, 1967–71* (University of Arkansas Press, 1991), John L. Ward's *The Arkansas Rockefeller* (Louisiana State University Press, 1978), and Ward's *Winthrop Rockefeller, Philanthropist: A Life of Change* (University of Arkansas Press, 2004). Diane D. Blair's *Arkansas Politics and Government: Do the People Rule?* (University of Nebraska Press, 1988) is essential reading, and a revision published after Blair's untimely death is equally useful: Diane D. Blair and Jay Barth, *Arkansas Politics and Government*, 2nd edition (University of Nebraska Press, 2005). A few "business histories" have been published which provide essential background information on some of the most important corporations in the state. They include *Wal-Mart: A History of Sam Walton's Retail Phenomenon* (Twayne, 1994), as well as Walton's autobiography, *Made in America*

(Doubleday, 1992). Marvin Schwartz's *Tyson: From Farm to Market* (University of Arkansas Press, 1992) provides useful information. A study by Lu Ann Jones on the role of women in farming includes a treatment of the poultry industry, providing insight into their experience in supplying poultry to Tysons: Lu Ann Jones, *Mama Learned Us to Work: Farm Women in the New South* (University of North Carolina Press, 2002). Brent Riffel's dissertation provides insight into the workings of the Tyson enterprise: Brenton Edward Riffel, "The Feathered Kingdom: Tyson Foods and the Transformation of American Land, Labor, and Law, 1930–2005" (University of Arkansas, 2008). For a particularly perceptive and penetrating analysis, see Steve Striffler, *Chicken: The Dangerous Transformation of America's Favorite Food* (Yale University Press, 2005). For the trucking industry, see Marvin Schwartz's *J. B. Hunt: The Long Haul to Success* (University of Arkansas Press, 1992). Leon J. Rosenberg's *Dillard's: The First Fifty Years* (University of Arkansas Press, 1988) is also useful. William H. Bowen, *The Boy from Altheimer: From the Depression to the Boardroom* (University of Arkansas Press, 2006), is an autobiography of a highly successful Little Rock attorney with many important business and professional connections.

Another less well known topic, conservation, has received little attention, but Neil Compton's *The Battle for the Buffalo River: A Twentieth-Century Conservation Crisis in the Ozarks* (University of Arkansas Press, 1992) provides an interesting treatment of the saga leading to the establishment of the Buffalo River as a national river. Another book-length study of the conservation issue is S. Charles Bolton's *Twenty-five Years Later: A History of the McClellan-Kerr Arkansas River Navigation System in Arkansas* (U.S. Army Corps of Engineers, 1995).

While no scholarly books on industrialization have been published, several books on the South's experience with industrialization provide considerable insight and have resonance with the Arkansas story. James C. Cobb's foundational work on the topic includes *Industrialization and Southern Society, 1877–1984* (University Press of Kentucky, 1984; reprint Dorsey Press, 1988) Philip Scranton, ed., *The Second Wave: Southern Industrialization from the 1940s to the 1970s* (University of Georgia Press, 2001).

Chapter Sixteen: Arkansas in the Sunbelt South, 1970–1992

Most of the best work done on Arkansas history in this period has focused on the state's political and economic giants. See Bethany Morton, *To Serve God and Wal-Mart: The Making of Christian Free Enterprise* (Harvard University Press, 2009), and Shane Hamilton, *Trucking Country: The Road to America's Wal-Mart Economy* (Princeton University Press, 2008). A book that focuses on the 1970 gubernatorial elections in four southern states includes special focus on Arkansas; Randy Sanders, *Mighty Peculiar Election: The New South Gubernatorial Campaigns of 1970 and the Changing Politics of Race* (University Press of Florida, 2002). A couple of insightful political autobiographies include Dale Bumpers, *The Best Lawyer in a One Lawyer Town* (Random House, 2003), and David Pryor and Don Harrell, *A Pryor Commitment: The Autobiography of David*

Pryor (Butler Center Books, 2008). For a study of the last days of the *Arkansas Gazette*, see Roy Reed, ed., *Looking Back at the Arkansas Gazette: An Oral History* (University of Arkansas Press, 2009). For a study of an important jurist from Arkansas who practiced in this period, see Polly J. Price, *Judge Richard S. Arnold: A Legacy of Justice on the Federal Bench* (Prometheus Books, 2009). Much of the information on the Little Rock desegregation case and the Alma and Lake View education funding cases came from primary documents, especially from two interviews conducted by the author with Gov. Mike Beebe. Another important source for the desegregation case was Gene Vinzant's doctoral dissertation, "Little Rock's Long Crisis: Schools and Race in Little Rock, Arkansas, 1863–2009" (University of Arkansas, 2009).

Chapter Seventeen: The Burden of Arkansas History, 1992–2012

For three classic studies of southern history, see Woodward's *Origins of the New South, 1877-1913* (LSU Press, 1951), *The Burden of Southern History* (LSU Press, 1960), and *The Strange Career of Jim Crow* (Oxford University Press, 1955). See also *The Ongoing Burden of Southern History: Politics and Identity in the Twenty-First Century South* (LSU Press, 2012), edited by Angie Maxwell, Todd Shields, and Jeannie Whayne.

While there are a number of books on folk music and blues, see Robert Cochran's excellent *Our Own Sweet Sounds: A Celebration of Popular Music in Arkansas* (University of Arkansas Press, 1996) for an overview of the Arkansas experience. See also his *Singing in Zion: Music and Song in the Life of an Arkansas Family* (University of Arkansas Press, 1999). Levon Helm's *This Wheel's on Fire: Levon Helm and the Story of the Band* (W. Morrow, 1993) and Johnny Cash's *The Autobiography* (Harper, 1997) are very good sources. For a book that includes interviews with Arkansas bluesmen, see *Goin' Back to Sweet Memphis: Conversations with the Blues,* Fred J. Hay, ed. (University of Georgia Press, 2001). For a book focusing on Rosetta Tharpe, see Gayle F. Ward, *Shout, Sister, Shout! The Untold Story of Rock-and-Roll Trailblazer Sister Rosetta Tharpe* (Beacon Press, 2007).

For information on globalization and the modern economy, I have relied on a variety of primary sources. One important scholarly study on globalization in the South provided some crucial context: *Globalization and the American South,* James C. Cobb and William Stueck, eds. (University of Georgia Press, 2005).

CONTRIBUTORS

JEANNIE M. WHAYNE is university professor of history at the University of Arkansas. She is the author of *A New Plantation South: Land, Labor, and Federal Favor in Twentieth-Century Arkansas* and *Delta Empire: Lee Wilson and the Transformation of Agriculture in the New South.*

THOMAS A. DEBLACK is professor of history at Arkansas Tech University. He is the author of *With Fire and Sword: Arkansas, 1861–1874.*

GEORGE SABO III is professor of anthropology at the University of Arkansas and archeologist with the Arkansas Archeological Survey. His publications include *Rock Art in Arkansas* and *Paths of Our Children: Historic Indians of Arkansas.*

MORRIS S. ARNOLD is a judge of the United States Court of Appeals for the Eighth Circuit and author of *Rumble of a Distant Drum: The Quapaws and the Old World Newcomers, 1673–1804.*

JOSEPH SWAIN is assistant professor of geography at Arkansas Tech University.

BEN F. JOHNSON III is professor of history at Southern Arkansas University and the author *Arkansas in Modern America.*

INDEX